Internet and the Law

Technology, Society, and Compromises

Internet and the Law

Technology, Society, and Compromises

Aaron Schwabach

A B C · C L I O

Santa Barbara, California
Denver, Colorado
Oxford, England

Library of Congress Cataloging-in-Publication Data

Schwabach, Aaron.
   Internet and the law : technology, society, and compromises / Aaron
Schwabach.
     p.   cm.
   Includes bibliographical references and index.
   ISBN 1-85109-731-7 (hardcover : alk. paper) — ISBN 1-85109-
736-8 (ebook)
   1. Internet—Law and legislation—United States—Encyclopedias.
2. Computer networks—Law and legislation—United States—
Encyclopedias.   3. Copyright and electronic data processing—United
States—Encyclopedias.   4. Copyright—Computer programs—United
States—Encyclopedias.   I. Title.

KF390.5.C6S39   2006
343.7309'944—dc22

                                                            2005025378

09 08 07 06   10 9 8 7 6 5 4 3 2 1

This book is also available on the World Wide Web as an e-Book. Visit
abc-clio.com for details.

ABC-CLIO, Inc.
130 Cremona Drive, P.O. Box 1911
Santa Barbara, California 93116-1911

This book is printed on acid-free paper.
Manufactured in the United States of America

To Veronica, Jessica and Qienyuan

_____

❖ CONTENTS ❖

Internet and the Law

The roots of the Internet and the current revolution in individual access to information go back many decades, even centuries, but the Internet as a widespread social phenomenon is just concluding its first decade. Few people had personal computers before the 1980s; few had access to the Internet, or any of its precursors, before the 1990s. The universal acceptance of the Internet happened nearly instantaneously, not only in the United States, but also around the world. Today the Internet is no longer a novelty but a part of daily life in most developed countries, and in many developing ones. Checking e-mail messages is as ordinary, and undeserving of comment, as checking phone messages; ordering products from a Web page is as unremarkable as ordering products from a catalog. As is true of many technologies that form part of the substrate of our way of life, relatively few people understand how the Internet actually works, but far more are willing to use it without understanding or questioning the technology involved.

A great many books have been written about the hardware infrastructure, the communications protocols, the software, and the people that make the Internet possible. This book is not one of them. It addresses a different problem: How does society's system of normative expectations—law, in other words—cope with this sudden change in the ground rules? Systems developed over centuries find themselves threatened by sudden change: The U.S. legal system spent two centuries working out a method of coping with the problem of access to pornography by juveniles; almost overnight, the Internet has rendered that system irrelevant. The legal systems of the world spent four and a half centuries—a period twice as long as the history of the United States as an independent nation—working out a system of copyright protection, carefully balancing the interests of creators, publishers, and consumers of copyrighted works. Now anyone can publish a work, or create a million copies of someone else's work, in seconds. Existing copyright law

has found itself unable to cope with the threat posed by the Internet, especially by the battle over file-sharing that dominates much of the discussion of Internet law and has created an unprecedented level of animosity between consumers and some sectors of the content industry. Unauthorized copying of intellectual property is nothing new, but on the whole the history of copyright law over the past four and a half centuries would probably appear, to anyone other than a copyright lawyer, to be a tale of unmitigated dullness.

Until now. New battles are fought daily in the three-sided conflict among content owners, consumers, and equipment manufacturers—the latter group sharing interests with both consumers and content owners; there are also signs that the copyright interests of content creators, especially in the music industry, are diverging from those of the content owners. The legal battles in this conflict are fought in Congress and other national legislatures, in the courts, and in international organizations such as the World Intellectual Property Organization and the World Trade Organization. At the same time there is an ongoing arms race, as content owners create ever more sophisticated means of copy protection and users find ever more sophisticated means of copying.

Many other areas of law are nearly as unsettled. The Internet poses grave threats to privacy, for example. Phone calls and letters are not recorded unless someone takes the trouble to record them, but everything that happens online is, or at least can be, recorded as a matter of course. At the same time, however, the Internet offers the potential for unprecedented privacy, through the use of sophisticated encryption. The balance struck long ago between the individual's desire for privacy and the legitimate crime-detection and national security interests of the government must somehow be adapted to take into account both universal recording of messages and the availability of encryption software.

No book could possibly cover everything that is going on in the world of Internet law; this book attempts, instead, to provide an overview of certain issues in which the degree of social change has been particularly great. The Internet is a tool for transmitting information; the Web and other information exchange services supported on the Internet are composed of information. As a result, the areas of law most affected have been those areas of law that deal with information. All areas of intellectual property law have been deeply affected by the Internet, because intellectual property rights are rights in information. Laws relating to freedom of expression are just as deeply affected; the global soapbox that once belonged only to the owners of large media companies now belongs to everyone. Laws relating to jurisdiction, choice of law, and recognition of foreign judgments are also affected; the global nature of the Internet greatly increases the number of ways in which legal systems may come into conflict with each other. The congressional struggle to control Internet pornography has highlighted one aspect of this problem: the inability of Congress to control access by U.S. citizens to content originating in other countries. Even if such a thing were possible, it might not be permissible or desirable. The French Yahoo! case has highlighted another aspect: the problem of determining the extent to which Internet users are responsible for complying not only with the laws of their own country, but the laws of other countries in which their message might be received—which is to say, all of the countries of the world.

Just as one book cannot address everything that happens on the Internet, one book cannot address the reaction of all of the world's legal systems to the Internet. This book focuses on one particular legal system—that of the United States. International law—the law governing interactions among nations rather than the law of specific foreign countries—is also addressed in detail where relevant, especially with regard to copyright and other intellectual property rights. Foreign law is addressed only in passing, however, when relevant to a particular case or question. And perhaps fortunately, both intellectual property rights and freedom of expression are governed in the United States mostly (although not entirely) by federal law. Even in areas where state law would ordinarily control, Congress has often preempted state law where the Internet is involved; thus, most of the time this book can focus on a single body of federal law rather than, as is the case in some other areas of law, a bewildering collection of the laws of fifty different states.

In this front portion of the book you will find, in addition to the table of contents and this preface, a historical overview of the development of Internet law focusing on relatively recent developments and a chronology covering a longer time frame in somewhat less detail. You will also find information on how to use this volume and on how to understand the various U.S. and international legal materials that are presented and discussed. Finally, before the entries begin, there is a table of abbreviations used in the text. These abbreviations are also explained in the articles in which they appear.

The entries are organized alphabetically. Each entry includes, in addition to the text, a list of legal sources, a list of cross-references, and a list of books, articles, and other sources either referred to in the text or suggested for further information on the topic. The entries are followed by additional general information. Law and the Internet each have their own languages, and one of the purposes of this book is to demystify those languages; thus, the first item to follow the topic entries is a glossary of legal and Internet terms used in the book. Another purpose of this book is to serve as a springboard for further discussion and research; the glossary is followed by a documents supplement, containing excerpts from some important treaties, statutes, cases, and other legal materials. There is also a topic finder to assist in locating the material in this book, a selected bibliography with annotations, a table of authorities listing all of the primary sources of law (treaties, statutes, cases, and the like) discussed in the book, and an index.

This book would not have been possible without the assistance of a large number of people. I'd particularly like to thank my research assistant, Krista Schelhaas; my editors, Anna Kaltenbach, Alicia Merritt and Peter Westwick;

Professors Art Cockfield of Queen's University (Ontario), John Glick of the University of San Diego, and Kevin Greene, Marybeth Herald, Steve Semeraro, Bryan Wildenthal, Richard Winchester, and Claire Wright of Thomas Jefferson School of Law, for advice and feedback; Thomas Jefferson School of Law, for giving me the time to work on this project; and my family, for their patience in putting up with me while I did. I hope that you enjoy reading this book as much as I did writing it, and that it will serve as a starting point for further research on and discussion of Internet and information technology law.

Although our national legal system is flexible and capable of making quick changes, it has often been baffled, at least temporarily, by the social and legal consequences of the rapid adoption of new technology. In the 1960s, for example, as computer programming began to take off, the United States Patent and Trademark Office (USPTO) dug in its collective heels and refused to issue any patents for computer programs. At that time computers themselves were new; the USPTO felt overwhelmed by the number of computer hardware patent applications it had received and the difficulty of understanding them, and apparently decided that enough was enough. During the administration of Lyndon Johnson, a presidential commission on software patents was persuaded to the USPTO's point of view; the commission report in turn influenced the Supreme Court's 1972 decision in a case called *Gottschalk v. Benson.* The Supreme Court's opinion in this case was widely understood (including, probably, by the justices themselves) as stating that computer software could not be patented. The USPTO, no doubt with a sigh of relief, suspended all pending applications for patents on computer software. The opinion in *Gottschalk,* which can most charitably be described as ill-advised or perhaps misunderstood, influenced legal developments in other countries; presumably these countries assumed that the United States, as the leader in computer technology at the time, knew what it was doing when it made computer programs unpatentable. Thus the countries of Europe, for example, formed the European Patent Treaty, which to this day excludes computer programs from its definition of patentable material.

In this manner one error, made by nonelected bureaucrats, has perpetuated itself throughout the world for decades and has distorted the development of software law. The Supreme Court eventually realized its error; in 1981 it backtracked a bit, and the USPTO re-

luctantly began to accept software patent applications. It was not until 1994 that the USPTO actually issued rules for software patent applications, after an opinion of the Federal Circuit (the federal appellate court that deals with patent cases) pointed out that to say that software was unpatentable was just plain wrong.

Because computer programs were, or were believed to be, unpatentable, some other form of intellectual property right had to be pressed into service to protect them. This turned out to be copyright; computer programs, patented or not, are protected by copyright law. The fit between copyright and computer programs is not perfect, however, and has required some legislative tinkering. Unlike other forms of copyrightable content—books, plays, songs, movies—computer programs are not valued for their content, but for their function. The number of people who read code for the pure pleasure of doing so is rather small. Programs are not "works" in the sense that the term had previously been used in copyright law; they are tools that happen to be made of information rather than of steel or wood. At times, when something new has come along that hasn't quite fit, Congress has carved out new forms of intellectual property protection; for example, the mask work used to create computer chips is given protection that is somewhat like patent but a bit more like copyright. Given a clear directive from the presidential commission or the Supreme Court, Congress might have done something similar for computer programs, which are more numerous and more economically and socially significant than semiconductor chip mask works.

No such category was created, however, and the entire history of intellectual property rights in computer programs has been altered as a result. Whether that alteration is a good or bad thing depends on one's perspective; the point is not so much that computer programs should or should not have been the subject of patent, copyright, or some third form of protection, but that things fell out the way they did more or less by accident. The justices of the Supreme Court in 1972 did not understand computers or computer programs; hardly anyone understood these things in 1972. Of those who understood, not one in a thousand anticipated the growth of something like the Internet beyond a select group of technical users, or that there might be sixth graders in Boise, Brussels, Belgrade, and Beijing writing code for class assignments. The law was made without any real awareness of what its consequences might be, for good or for ill; but ever since, the computer-programming world has had to work within the confines formed by that initial decision and subsequent attempts to modify it. In contrast, and perhaps as a result, the history of law and the Internet has been one of reaction.

Government created the Internet, but for the most part it has managed to avoid regulating it until after a problem has appeared. Although the Internet has no clear starting point, most histories trace its ancestry to the linking of four computers to form ARPANET in 1969. ARPANET, a project funded and conducted under the auspices of the U.S. Department of Defense, grew rapidly, but by 1981 it was still tiny: a network of 200 host systems.

ARPANET was a network for programmers, scientists, and other specialists using mainframes and sometimes minicomputers. In the mid-1970s, however, a new social phenomenon began: home computing. Computers that by today's standards are insanely overpriced toys nonetheless fulfilled most of the needs that their owners had for them: word processing, accounting, data storage and sorting, and games. And, with the addition of a device called a modem, they could communicate with other computers. At the time, few foresaw that this would be the single most popular use for home computing.

Purchasers of primitive early computers could use their 300 baud (no, not 300K; 300 baud—300 bits per second, more or less) modems to communicate with other users, one at a time, over a telephone line. For the most part, though, there wasn't much reason to do so. More useful were the bulletin board systems (BBSs) that began to spring up around the country. A BBS

allowed multiple users to communicate with each other and to view information stored on the BBS server at the same time. BBS users quickly began to use the services to do all of the things that human beings use other media of communication to do: socializing, expounding political theories, conducting business, dating, enjoying or providing entertainment. Proprietary networks—at first just glorified bulletin boards—came into being: CompuServe, Prodigy, America Online. Throughout the 1980s the various networks became increasingly interconnected; by 1990, when ARPANET officially ceased to exist, its demise was unnoticeable to most users. But the nascent Internet remained technically challenging: Because of the slow speed of the connections and the limited capacity of many computers, most communication was text-only. And a certain amount of technical proficiency was still required.

All of this changed between 1992 and 1994. In 1992 the World Wide Web, created by researchers at the European Center for Nuclear Research in Switzerland, became accessible to the world. And in 1994 the easy-to-use Netscape Web browser became available. Suddenly everyone with access to a computer could view any content on the Web—and, perhaps even more importantly, could create content and place it on the Web for others to view. The Web grew exponentially, in the literal sense of the word: For a while, the number of Web servers increased by an order of magnitude each year.

And the legal system was taken by surprise. While the Internet was used by a relatively small number of people, government had been content to ignore it. Suddenly everyone was using it, and some of those users were very unhappy with the ways in which others were using it. Among the first to demand that Congress do something were opponents of pornography, who were concerned both with the amount of pornographic content available on the Web and the fact that the content was available to minors. In 1996 Congress undertook its first, and unsuccessful, attempt to regulate Web content—the first step in a struggle that is not yet finished.

A year earlier the MP3 file format had been created; the music content industry seems not to have fully awakened to the danger it faced until 1997, however, with the launch of MP3.com. The content industry then joined the ranks of those demanding that the government Do Something, in this case to protect copyrighted content. This led to the sweeping reforms of copyright law in the Digital Millennium Copyright Act (DMCA) of 1998. Although the DMCA greatly tilted the legal balance of interests in favor of content owners, apparently the congressional thumb on the scale was insufficient to overcome the advantage given to users by technology. The content industry succeeded in crushing MP3 and later Napster, but file-sharing continues to grow, and the content industry continues to lobby for additional protection.

At this point the law of the Internet is still in flux; the ten years since the introduction of Netscape Navigator have been too short a time for any legal system to adapt to widespread social change. And we cannot predict the way the technology will develop in the future; we have little more idea of the ultimate effects of today's lawmaking on future social and technological development than the Supreme Court had in 1972 when it decided *Gottschalk*. But although this might suggest that the wise course would be to do nothing and await further developments, there are too many people making loud and contradicting demands for immediate action; Congress and the courts will have to choose as wisely as possible and hope for the best.

868

Chinese translation of the *Diamond Sutra*, the world's oldest surviving block-printed work (the first mass-produced work of literature), is published. The *Sutra*, now in the collection of the British Library, bears what is arguably a precursor to today's open-source licenses: "Reverently made for universal free distribution by Wang Jie on behalf of his two parents on the 13th day of the 4th moon of the 9th year of Xiantong."

1041

Chinese inventor Bi Sheng creates what is probably the world's first printing machine to use movable type.

1234

Yi Gyu-bo publishes the *New Code of Etiquette* in Korea; today it is the world's oldest surviving work printed with movable type.

c. 1430–1450

Printing presses are built by Johann Gutenberg and Laurens Coster in Europe.

1455–1468

Johann Gutenberg loses control of his printing business after becoming involved in several lawsuits.

1499

Johannes Trithemius publishes *Steganographia*, in which he sets forth the principles of steganography, or concealed content, later to become important in digital rights management technology. *Steganographia* is an *incunabulum*—a term including all books printed using either block printing or movable type in Europe before 1500. Incunabula are, not surprisingly, rare. Because there was rarely a commercial justification for reprinting them, their content was inaccessible to most of the world's population until the advent of the World Wide Web; today *Steganographia*, like Wang Jie's *Diamond Sutra*, is available to anyone with Web access. Paradoxically, it is the more recent out-of-print works that are most inaccessible, because although difficult to find in hard copy, they are still protected by copyright.

1557

The English government grants a monopoly on book publishing within England to the Stationer's Company. This is English law's first serious attempt to cope with the problem of copying printed works, a problem that arose soon after the invention of the printing press.

1661–1663 The *Eliot Indian Bible,* a translation of the Bible into Algonquin, is published in Cambridge, Massachusetts, becoming the first book printed in the English North American colonies.

1695 After 138 years, the Stationer's Company's monopoly on book printing comes to an end.

1695–1710 Multiple printing companies vie for market share in England; all works are deemed fair game, regardless of who first published them.

1710 The British (Scotland and England having been unified by the Act of Union in 1707) Parliament enacts the Statute of Anne, the first modern copyright law. The statute sets a copyright term of fourteen years for new works, renewable once.

1774 Britain's House of Lords decides *Donaldson v. Beckett,* establishing that copyright terms are of finite duration, even for works published by the Stationer's Company before the Statute of Anne.

1789 United States Constitution comes into effect. Article I, Section 8, Clause 8 (the Patent and Copyright Clause) declares that Congress shall have the power "To promote the Progress of Science and useful Arts, by securing for limited Times to Authors and Inventors the exclusive Right to their respective Writings and Discoveries."

1790 First U.S. Copyright Act provides for the same term of copyright protection as that provided by the Statute of Anne: fourteen years, renewable once.

1791 Bill of Rights (Amendments 1 through 10 to the U.S. Constitution) adopted. The first of the ten amendments declares in part that "Congress shall make no law . . . abridging the freedom of speech, or of the press; or the right of the people peaceably to assemble[.]"

1844 The world's first long-distance electronic communications system, a telegraph line between Washington and Boston, becomes operational.

1847 French composer Ernest Bourget wins a lawsuit against Ambassadeurs, a Paris café that played his music for the entertainment

The telegraph network was the world's first electronic information network. Did it present the legal system of the time with new challenges? What might some of those challenges have been? Were there lessons the legal system could draw from previous, nonelectronic information networks? Did the later advent of the telephone network present new challenges not presented by the telegraph network?

For comparison, think of some of the challenges faced by today's legal system in dealing with the Internet. Did the telephone and telegraph networks present new challenges for copyright law? For censorship? For law enforcement? For determining territorial jurisdiction?

of patrons—without his
permission.

1851 World's first successful
undersea cable connects
British and French telegraph
networks.

1858 Transatlantic telegraph cable
connects the United States
and Britain for three weeks
before ceasing to function.

1866 Two transatlantic cables are
laid, connecting Britain to
Canada and the United
States. Within the next few
years over 100,000 miles of
undersea cable are laid, in
addition to hundreds of
thousands of miles of surface
lines, connecting much of
the world to the telegraph
network.

1876 Telephone patented.

1877 Phonograph invented.

1878 World's first commercial
telephone exchange opens in
New Haven, Connecticut.

Association Littéraire et
Artistique Internationale
(International Artistic and
Literary Association)
founded by Victor Hugo
and others to seek an
international copyright
protection system.

1886 Berne Convention adopted.

1887 Motion pictures invented.

1909 U.S. Copyright Act of 1909
fails to conform to Berne
Convention standards, but
prohibits "unauthorized

mechanical reproduction of
musical compositions." The
act doubles the copyright
term, providing for a
twenty-eight-year term,
renewable once.

1955 Universal Copyright
Convention comes into
force for the United States.

1969 ARPANET launched; links
four computers.

1971 ARPANET now links two
dozen computers.

1972 First e-mail program
created.

U.S. Supreme Court decides
Gottschalk v. Benson, holding
that a mathematical
algorithm used in a
computer program is not
patentable. U.S. Patent and
Trademark Office suspends
all pending computer
program patent applications.

1976 Copyright Act of 1976
radically revises U.S.
copyright law. The act
preempts state laws, making
copyright entirely a federal
matter, and provides for a
copyright term of the
lifetime of the author plus
fifty years for individually,
non-pseudonymously and
non-anonymously authored
works, and a term of
seventy-five years from
publication or one hundred
years from creation for most
other works. (These terms
are later extended by the
Sonny Bono Copyright
Term Extension Act to
lifetime plus seventy, ninety-

five, and one hundred twenty years, respectively.) Nonetheless, U.S. copyright law still fails to conform to Berne Convention norms.

1981 U.S. Supreme Court holds that some computer programs are patentable; U.S. Patent and Trademark Office begins to accept applications for software patents.

1983 ARPANET switches to TCP/IP protocol.

1984 William Gibson publishes *Neuromancer,* creating a mystique for a network that does not yet exist.

Congress enacts the Computer Fraud and Abuse Act, an antihacking law.

Supreme Court decides *Sony Corporation of America v. Universal City Studios,* holding that the fact that a VCR can be used for copyright infringement does not make the device unlawful, nor does it make Sony liable for infringement by purchasers of VCRs; the VCR is capable of substantial noninfringing uses and is thus a "staple article of commerce."

1986 NSFNet launched; links five supercomputers.

1988 Internet worm attack infects 10 percent of Internet host systems.

Congress enacts Berne Convention Implementation Act, bringing U.S. copyright law into conformity with Berne Convention and enabling the United States to join the Berne Convention.

1990 **Using a** NeXT workstation Tim Berners-Lee creates the world's first Web page.

NSFNet replaces ARPANET.

1991 Berners-Lee's first Web page becomes available online, as do many other Web pages, including the first in the United States (at the Stanford Linear Accelerator Center).

Phil Zimmermann releases Pretty Good Privacy (PGP), a powerful encryption program. When PGP becomes available over the Internet, Zimmermann is investigated for violation of U.S. arms export control regulations.

1992 Internet Underground Music Archive offers downloads of copyrighted music to technically savvy (and very patient) users.

Congress enacts Audio Home Recording Act.

1993 National Center for Supercomputing Applications at the University of Illinois releases the Mosaic Web browser.

1994 Netscape Navigator released.

Yahoo! founded.

Agreement on Trade-Related Aspects of Intellectual Property Rights (TRIPS) adopted as part of the Marrakesh Agreement Establishing the World Trade Organization; creates a comprehensive legal regime governing all internationally acknowledged forms of intellectual property.

U.S. Court of Appeals for the Federal Circuit holds that a wide range of computer programs are patentable; U.S. Patent and Trademark Office publishes guidelines for software patent applications.

Federal district court in Massachusetts dismisses warez-trading case against David LaMacchia.

1995   MP3 file format patented.

Microsoft Internet Explorer released.

1996   Congress enacts Communications Decency Act and Child Pornography Prevention Act.

John Perry Barlow writes the Declaration of the Independence of Cyberspace.

1997   MP3.com founded.

Congress enacts the No Electronic Theft Act to control warez trading.

Supreme Court declares censorship provisions of Communications Decency Act unconstitutional.

1998   Netscape programmers launch Mozilla.org, open-sourcing Netscape's source code.

The Internet Corporation for Assigned Names and Numbers is formed by agreement between the Internet Assigned Numbers Authority and the U.S. Department of Commerce.

The Recording Industry Association of America (RIAA) launches the Secure Digital Music Initiative.

Diamond Multimedia begins marketing the first commercially available portable MP3 player, and is sued by the RIAA.

Congress enacts the Digital Millennium Copyright Act, the Sonny Bono Copyright Term Extension Act, the Child Online Protection Act, and the Children's Online Privacy Protection Act.

1999   Jon Lech Johansen, a fifteen-year-old Norwegian citizen, makes a program called DeCSS available over the Internet. CSS is the copy protection program used to prevent unauthorized copying on nearly all commercially produced DVDs; CSS-encrypted DVDs cannot be played on Linux systems. DeCSS can be used to play CSS-encrypted DVDs on

Linux systems. It can also be used to make unauthorized copies of CSS-encrypted DVDs. Johansen is prosecuted in Norway; persons who distribute DeCSS in the United States are sued by motion picture content companies.

Napster file-sharing service begins operating; Napster is immediately sued by RIAA and others for contributory and vicarious copyright infringement.

Congress enacts Anti-cybersquatting Consumer Protection Act.

The Ninth Circuit Court of Appeals holds that Diamond Multimedia may lawfully make and distribute its portable MP3 player, and that doing so does not make Diamond liable for copyright infringement.

2000

KaZaA begins operating. MP3.com is purchased by Vivendi; Bertelsmann Music Group invests in Napster.

MP3.com offers MyMP3.com, a service allowing users to download and play music if they can demonstrate a legal right to do so. It is sued by Universal Music Group and others, and subsequently ordered to pay $250 million in damages.

The Children's Internet Protection Act becomes law.

A federal district court holds that the Digital Millennium

2001

Copyright Act can constitutionally prohibit the distribution of DeCSS, and that in fact it does so.

Napster is ordered to block sharing of copyrighted files.

Dmitri Sklyarov, a Russian programmer, is arrested while attending a conference in Las Vegas. Sklyarov had written a program enabling users to break the copy protection used by Adobe's Acrobat E-Book Reader. Five months later the government drops its case against Sklyarov, but not against his employer, Elcom.

In response to the September 11 terrorist attacks, Congress enacts the USA PATRIOT Act, which among other things gives the government enhanced powers of surveillance over electronic communications.

The Second Circuit agrees that there is no constitutional bar to the Digital Millennium Copyright Act's ban on the distribution of programs such as DeCSS.

2002

End of Napster, at least in its original form.

WIPO Copyright and Performances and Phonograms treaties come into force.

The Supreme Court's decision in *Eldred v. Ashcroft* upholds the constitutionality of the Sonny Bono Copyright Term Extension Act.

A federal district court in California decides *United States v. Elcom* (Elcom is Dmitri Sklyarov's employer). The court holds, like the courts in the DeCSS case, that there is no constitutional bar to the Digital Millennium Copyright Act's ban on the distribution of software for the circumvention of copy protection measures.

Aimster, a file-sharing network, is found liable for copyright infringement.

2003 Apple launches iTunes, sells twenty-five million songs in first year.

Verizon Internet Services refuses to release the name of an individual Verizon subscriber to the RIAA; the RIAA sues, and a federal district court orders Verizon to disclose the information. The Court of Appeals for the D.C. Circuit reverses, holding that Verizon does not have to disclose the subscriber's name.

Hershey's Foods and Mrs. Field's Cookies agree to a settlement with the Federal Trade Commission for collecting information from children in violation of the Children's Online Privacy Protection Act.

RIAA sues individual users for file-sharing; among the first defendants to reach a settlement with the RIAA is Brianna LaHara, a twelve-year-old honor student who lives with her mother in public housing in New York City.

Supreme Court upholds constitutionality of Children's Internet Protection Act.

Federal district court in California holds that Grokster and other supernode-based, decentralized peer-to-peer file-sharing networks are not liable for contributory or vicarious copyright infringement.

In Norway, Jon Lech Johansen is acquitted of charges arising from the distribution of DeCSS; the acquittal is upheld on appeal.

2004 Mozilla Foundation releases Firefox, the first browser in many years to seriously challenge Internet Explorer.

RIAA files more suits against individual users.

Ninth Circuit Court of Appeals affirms district court's decisions that Grokster and others are not liable for contributory or vicarious copyright infringement.

In Norway, the government's Economic Crimes Unit drops its case against Jon Lech Johansen.

Supreme Court holds that censorship provisions of Child Online Protection Act may be unconstitutional and remands for trial on further factual issues.

2005

Supreme Court reverses Ninth Circuit's decision in the *Grokster* case.

❖ HOW TO USE THIS ENCYCLOPEDIA ❖

All professions are a conspiracy against the laity.
—George Bernard Shaw

Two mysterious professional cabals—lawyers and information technology professionals—have conspired to shroud Internet and law in jargon incomprehensible to anyone outside the two professions. This encyclopedia attempts to demystify Internet law; this section takes on the "law" side of Internet law, explaining how the various pieces of the U.S. and international legal systems fit together, as well as how to locate and use the various sources of law.

Overview of the U.S. Legal System

The United States has a federal system of government, meaning that its territorial subdivisions, the states, are not mere administrative divisions, but have a certain degree of sovereignty in their own right. They can, and often do, enact laws that are in conflict with each other. This makes the legal system of the United States extraordinarily complex; it is in fact more than fifty different legal systems (the systems of the states, the District of Columbia, the self-governing territories, and to a certain extent the Native American tribes), all of them subordinate in some, but not all, areas to the federal system.

Fortunately for our purposes, most of the law that governs the Internet in the United States is federal law. The Constitution gives the federal government authority over patents and copyrights and over interstate and foreign commerce. The First Amendment sets a baseline level of free speech protection below which the states may not go, although they may provide a higher level of protection if they wish. The Copyright Act of 1976, by its terms, specifically preempts state law. The Internet Corporation for Assigned Names and Numbers, though independent, was created by the U.S. Department of Commerce. The National Security Agency, which governs encryption technology, is a federal agency.

Even in the areas where state law governs, as in the case of most commercial law, the laws are often uniform: The states have agreed to adopt the same body of contracts law in order to simplify business transactions. This makes things simpler than they would be if, for example, we were attempting to study the law of marriage and divorce in all fifty states—an area of law in which there is a considerable difference from one state to the next.

The government of the United States, and for that matter of each of the individual states, has three branches: the legislative, the executive, and the judicial. The legislative branch—Congress—enacts statutes subject to the limits imposed by the Constitution. The executive branch carries out these laws; this may involve the making of regulations, if authorized by the statute. The president may also issue proclamations and executive orders that have the substantive effect of statutes, and the executive branch and the Senate have special duties with regard to international law. The judiciary branch can review statutes to determine whether they conflict with or exceed the authority granted by the Constitution and can review administrative regulations to determine whether they conflict with or exceed the authority granted by the authorizing statute. More often, however, the courts, especially at the trial level, are simply resolving disputes or determining how existing law should be applied.

The Legislative Branch

In addition to Congress itself, the legislative branch includes a handful of congressional agencies; these report to Congress itself rather than to the executive branch. An agency with particular relevance to the Internet is the Library of Congress; founded in 1800 by the donation of the books of Thomas Jefferson, the library now has well over 100 million volumes. It also includes the United States Copyright Office.

The Executive Branch

The executive branch of the federal government includes the president and his (or perhaps, someday, her) Executive Office, and various Cabinet-level departments, other departments, and independent executive agencies. Several of these are particularly important to Internet law. The Department of Justice, which includes the Federal Bureau of Investigation, has a wide range of investigative and enforcement duties under various statutes. The Department of Commerce includes the U.S. Patent and Trademark Office, and also created and maintains a link to the Internet Corporation for Assigned Names and Numbers. The Department of Defense not only created ARPANET, which in turn gave rise to the Internet, but also includes the National Security Agency, which oversees encryption. The eventual role of the Department of Homeland Security is not yet clear, but in addition to its other powers under the USA PATRIOT Act the department includes the Secret Service, which shares with the FBI the responsibility for the enforcement of the Computer Fraud and Abuse Act. In addition to these departments, two independent agencies play a large role in Internet law: the Federal Communications Commission, which regulates communication networks; and the Federal Trade Commission, which protects consumers from identity theft, phishing, scams, spam, and a host of other Internet hazards.

The Judicial Branch

The federal and state court systems in the United States have a three-tiered appellate structure. In the bottom tier are the trial courts; in the federal court system most of these courts are called "district" courts and are assigned responsibility for federal (but not state) cases arising within a particular district, which might be all or part of a state or territory. A few trial courts have specialized jurisdiction defined by subject matter instead of by territory and have names reflecting their specialty, such as the Court of International Trade.

Almost all federal lawsuits are initially brought in one of these federal trial courts. After the court reaches a decision on a particular matter, the losing party (with one exception)

is entitled to appeal the decision. The decision from which the losing party appeals need not be a final decision on the merits of the case, although appeals at earlier stages are subject to certain limits; an appeal from some decision prior to that final decision is called an interlocutory appeal. The one exception applies to criminal cases: The prosecution cannot appeal a final decision acquitting a defendant.

Decisions that are appealed go before an appellate court; cases might also come before these courts by various other procedural mechanisms. The appellate court will ordinarily review only questions of law, not findings of fact; that is, it will take the facts as found by the trial court and determine whether the trial court correctly applied the law in reaching its result.

Most of the appellate courts, like most of the trial courts, have jurisdiction defined by territory rather than by subject matter. Thus, for example, the Ninth Circuit Court of Appeals has jurisdiction over appeals from federal district courts in the states and territories bordering the Pacific, as well as Arizona, Idaho, Montana, and Nevada.

Reported decisions of appellate courts become part of the body of common law. They are binding precedent in future cases involving the same questions of law; trial courts within the appellate court's jurisdiction must follow the rules set down in the appellate court's decisions. The non-prevailing party on appeal is not entitled to further appellate review; however, he or she may nonetheless seek such review from a high court. In the federal and nearly every state court system (with the significant exceptions of New York and Maryland) these high courts are called supreme courts. (In New York and Maryland the highest courts are called the Court of Appeals, and in New York trial courts are called Supreme Courts, to the great confusion of persons from outside those states.) Each state high court is the ultimate arbiter (decider) of questions of state law; the United States Supreme Court is the ultimate arbiter of questions of U.S. constitutional law.

Although every non-prevailing party (except the state in a criminal case) may obtain review before a court of appeals, few decisions of those courts are reviewed at the high court level. The decision to review the case belongs to the court, not to the litigants. High courts are swamped with far more appeals, petitions for certiorari, and other requests for review than they can possibly accommodate; the court of appeals is thus the last stop for most litigants.

International and Foreign Law

International law, or more specifically public international law, is the body of law that governs interactions among nations. The study of the law of foreign countries is not international law but comparative law. The international nature of the Internet makes both international law and comparative law important; however, only international law has force within the U.S. legal system.

International law is either conventional (law made by treaties and other international agreements) or customary (normative expectations based on state practice undertaken out of a sense of legal obligation). In the United States, treaties are ratified by the president upon receipt of the advice and consent of the Senate (but not the House of Representatives). The treaties then become, at least in theory, part of U.S. federal law under Article VI, clause 2 of the Constitution. U.S. law makes a distinction, however, between treaties that are self-executing (and thus require no additional action by Congress in order to take effect in domestic law) and treaties that are not self-executing. Whether self-executing or not, all ratified treaties create obligations on the part of the United States with regard to other nations; however, only a self-executing treaty creates obligations enforceable by individuals in U.S. courts.

Treaties supersede any inconsistent prior federal legislation, but may in turn be superseded by subsequent federal legislation. Because Article VI, clause 2 provides that treaties "shall be the supreme Law of the Land; and the judges in every State shall be bound thereby, any Thing in the Constitution or Laws of any State to the Contrary notwithstanding[,]" treaties supersede inconsistent state law even if the state law is later in time than the treaty.

Customary international law has a hazier status; the nature and even the existence of rules of customary international law is often disputed, and even when a rule is undisputed, pinning an exact date to something that arises from state practice rather than from a document is often an impossible task. The Supreme Court's 1900 decision in *The Paquete Habana,* 175 U.S. 677, is often cited for the principle that customary international law is "part of our law, and must be ascertained and administered by the courts of justice of appropriate jurisdiction, as often as questions of right depending upon it are duly presented for their determination." However, the situation the Court addressed in *The Paquete Habana* was an unusual one: Two Cuban fishing vessels were seized by U.S. blockading ships during the Spanish-American War; in the absence of any international convention addressing such an act, the Court had to decide what law to apply "where there is no treaty, and no controlling executive or legislative act or judicial decision." It is quite a bit less clear what the outcome would be were a rule of customary international law to conflict with a federal statute.

While all sovereign nations share a body of international law, the domestic legal system of each country has its own unique characteristics. Roughly speaking, the legal systems of the world can be divided into four broad groups—Hindu law, Islamic law, common law, and civil law—with a few countries not fitting neatly into any of the groups and many more countries exhibiting characteristics of more than one group. Because the common law system is found in nearly all of the countries of the English-speaking world, there is a tendency on the part of English speakers to think of it as typical. However, it is actually quite atypical; it differs from the other systems most markedly in the importance assigned to judicial opinions. In most of the United States, England, most other English-speaking countries, and a few other countries law is made not only by legislatures but also by judges; this body of judge-made law is known as common law. The legal systems of these countries are often identified as common-law systems (or systems within the common-law tradition) in contrast to the world's other legal traditions, particularly the civil law tradition. The majority of the world's countries, on the other hand, follow legal traditions in some way derived from the Roman law; the legal systems of these countries are often spoken of collectively as belonging to the civil law tradition. (In the United States civil law systems are found in Louisiana and Puerto Rico, although these have inevitably been influenced by the common-law tradition of the remainder of the country.)

How to Find the Law

Finding federal legislative and administrative materials is fairly straightforward; finding federal cases is a bit more complex. International law materials are easy to find if the United States is a party, but somewhat more difficult if not. These materials—statutes, regulations, cases, and treaties—contain text that has legal effect and are called primary sources; other materials, such as treatises (not to be confused with treaties) and articles in professional journals contain someone else's opinion about the law and are called secondary sources.

This is an encyclopedia of Internet law (a secondary source), and all of the primary sources referred to in this volume are available online. Many of the secondary sources are, too: most of the articles, and a few of the books. Unlike most of the primary sources, however, they are protected by copyright, and some of them may not be available for free.

Statutes enacted by Congress and by state legislatures are collected in compilations, organized by subject matter, for ease of use. Federal statutes are compiled in the United States Code (U.S.C.). The U.S.C. is available online from a variety of sources; lawyers and law students generally use the annotated versions provided by Westlaw or Lexis, but these are proprietary services and charge a fee. One of the many excellent services offering the United States Code online for free is the Legal Information Institute at Cornell University: http://assembler.law.cornell.edu/uscode/; an official Web site is http://www.gpoaccess.gov/uscode/. Bound versions of the U.S.C. are also available from all law libraries and many other libraries. Commercial publishers issue annotated versions of the compiled federal statutes under the titles United States Code Annotated and United States Code Service, abbreviated

Although most sources of law are available on the Web, some, especially secondary sources, will require a trip to a law library and the assistance of a law librarian. Locating the law library nearest to you can be a challenge. Libraries maintained by law firms are likely to be inaccessible to the public, but law schools and bar associations generally allow at least limited public access to their collections. Some public library systems maintain law libraries, as well. A good place to start searching for the nearest law library is the Google directory (http://directory.google.com/Top/Society/Law/Law_Libraries/), which lists law libraries in the United States, Australia, Canada, Japan, and the United Kingdom. Many U.S. states also offer detailed lists of law libraries; the California court system maintains such a list at http://www.publiclawlibrary.com/find.html.

"U.S.C.A." and "U.S.C.S.," respectively; the annotations include references to cases interpreting each statute and to secondary sources discussing it, if any.

Federal administrative materials are published in the Federal Register, a daily publication. Regulations then appear in the Code of Federal Regulations (CFR), available online at http://www.gpoaccess.gov/cfr/index.html; other administrative publications of Internet law interest include the Federal Communications Commission Record and the Federal Trade Commission Decisions.

Cases are reported, if at all, in case reporters. These reporters include the opinion of the judge deciding the case, as well as information about the case. Important reporters of federal cases include the United States Reports, the Supreme Court Reporter, and the United States Reports (Lawyer's Edition), each of which contains decisions of the United States Supreme Court; the Federal Reporter, which includes decisions of the federal Courts of Appeals; and the Federal Supplement, which includes decisions of the federal district courts. Recent editions of the United States Reports are available in PDF format from the Supreme

Court's Web site at http://www.supremecourt-us.gov/opinions/opinions.html.

The easiest way to find a case online is simply to type the case name and cite into the Google search bar. Be careful, however; many cases have given rise to more than one published opinion, so check the cite information and date to be sure you have found the right opinion. Lexis and Westlaw also offer comprehensive case databases for all U.S. and many foreign jurisdictions, for a fee. The Legal Information Institute offers federal and New York cases at http://assembler.law.cornell.edu/, and most courts' Web sites offer their own cases.

As with cases, the easiest way to find treaties is by using Google. Most of the intellectual property treaties discussed in this volume are available from the World Intellectual Property Organization Web site at http://www.wipo.int/treaties/en/; TRIPS is available from the World Trade Organization Web site at http://www.wto.org/english/tratop_e/trips_e/trips_e.htm.

Secondary sources often must be located in hard copy. The professional and academic journal articles cited in this volume are available through Lexis, Westlaw, and HeinOnline, for a fee. Some may also be available for free on the Web sites of the journals or authors; a Google search for the title will reveal this. Only a few of the books cited are available online; I have indicated this by providing a Web address. Most will have to be located in hard copy, though, at libraries or booksellers.

Further Reading on Legal Research
- Robert C. Berring et al., *Finding the Law: An Abridged Edition of How to Find the Law,* 11th ed. (St. Paul, MN: West, 1999).
- Morris L. Cohen et al., *How to Find the Law,* 9th ed. (St. Paul, MN: West, 1989).
- Stephen Elias and Susan Levinkind, *Legal Research: How to Find and Understand the Law,* 11th ed. (Berkeley, CA: Nolo Press, 1992).
- Kent C. Olson and Morris L. Cohen, *Legal Research in a Nutshell,* 8th ed. (St. Paul, MN: West, 2003).

- Bruce D. Sales et al., *Doing Legal Research: A Guide for Social Scientists and Mental Health Professionals* (Thousand Oaks, CA: Sage Publications, 1997).

How to Read the Law

Understanding what a statute, regulation, case, or treaty means is not always straightforward. Lawyers spend three years as graduate students learning to understand the law, and often emerge realizing how little they actually do understand. If you are not a lawyer, and perhaps even if you are, you should never rely on your interpretation of the law when anything significant is at stake. The same goes for this book: It's intended as a general guide and a starting point for further legal research. It's a good source for a research paper, but don't set up an Internet company, enter into a contract, or sue somebody based on what you read here. Consult a lawyer instead: The law might have changed, or the information in the book might be insufficiently detailed.

There are two problems in understanding the law: understanding the language of the law, and understanding how all the pieces fit together. The first problem is baffling enough for nonlawyers; the second often baffles lawyers, and even judges, as well.

In the previous section you read about the sources of law. Statutes are often so verbose that they are difficult to understand, but their place in the scheme of things is fairly simple: Later statutes control over earlier statutes, and compiled codes such as the U.S.C. make things simple by deleting the parts that have been superseded and adding the new words. When you look at a compiled statute, you are looking at the law as it stood on the date the compiled statute was last revised. (If you are looking at the statute online, be careful not to mistake the date the Web page was revised for the date the statute was revised.) The statute will also be controlling over a prior case. Compiled regulations are similarly straightforward: The Code of Federal Regulations is published anew each year, and each volume contains the regulations in force as of the publication date.

Note that all of this only applies to authority from a single jurisdiction. A federal statute does not ordinarily control over a prior California statute or case on a question of California law; a California statute never controls over a New York statute or case on a question of New York law.

With cases, however, the situation is complex. Cases are added to reporters more or less chronologically, but each case refers to other cases. Sometimes it cites other cases approvingly; sometimes it reverses or overturns the decisions on other cases. There's no easy way to find out whether a particular case is still good law—that is, whether it still accurately states a rule of law—using case reporters alone; a citator service must also be used. A citator service employs attorneys to read all of the decisions from a particular jurisdiction, look at the cases cited in each opinion, and come up with a code describing the treatment given to each case.

Two national citator services are available: KeyCite, from Westlaw, and Shepard's Citations, available on Lexis and in hard copy. Understanding the information presented by these services requires specialized training. Although it is relatively easy to spot cases that have been overturned or reversed (marked with a red flag in KeyCite and a stop sign in the online version of Shepard's), even this information can easily be misinterpreted; it would be best to ask a law librarian or lawyer for help interpreting any information provided by citator services.

A large number of books have been written to help laypersons, law students, and lawyers navigate these complexities; many are cited in the "Sources and further reading" notes after each entry in this book. The books from Nolo Press are written for nonlawyers; the "Nutshells" and "Understanding" series are written primarily for law students. All three, though, are frequently relied on by lawyers as well. Books aimed at practicing attorneys and law professors tend to be somewhat inaccessible— Shaw's conspiracy against the laity. A few are included here, though, especially *McCarthy's Desk Encyclopedia of Intellectual Property,* an invaluable reference work.

How to Read the Cites Used in This Volume

The cites in this volume are based on the Harvard Bluebook (*A Uniform System of Citation,*

17th ed.). This is the format most often used by lawyers; it's been modified a bit here for easier understanding, mostly by eliminating some of the more arcane abbreviations and by including publisher information for all, not just some, books. The samples that follow cover the most frequently cited types of material:

Statute: Children's Internet Protection Act, 47 U.S.C. § 254(h)

"Children's Internet Protection Act" is the popular name of the statute. "U.S.C." indicates that the statute is federal, compiled in the United States Code. The U.S.C. is divided into fifty titles, each assigned to a particular subject matter; Title 47 deals with telecommunications. The symbol "§" means "section"; each title of the U.S.C. is further divided into sections. "254(h)" indicates that the statute is codified at section 254, subsection h of Title 47. (A true Bluebook cite would also include the date of publication of the U.S.C. bound volume, which is omitted here because it is confusing and not particularly useful: It is often mistaken for the date of enactment of the statute.)

Case: *Yahoo!, Inc. v. La Ligue Contre le Racisme et L'Antisemitisme,* 169 F.Supp.2d 1181 (N.D. Cal. 2001), reversed, 379 F.3d 1120 (9th Cir. 2004)

Case cites, like cases themselves, are the hardest to make sense of. If all you want to do is find the two opinions referred to by this cite, just type the cite into Google or take it to any law librarian. But the cite tells a story, too: This case was brought by Yahoo! and perhaps others (only the first named plaintiff is listed in the case name) against La Ligue Contre le Racisme et L'Antisémitisme (LICRA) and, again, perhaps others. The case was brought in federal trial court in the Northern District (N.D.) of California (Cal.): F.Supp. reports only decisions of federal trial courts, and all federal district courts are trial courts. It was decided in 2001, although it might have been brought in an earlier year. The party who lost in the Northern District of California appealed the decision to the Ninth Circuit Court of Appeals (9th Cir.); three years later, in 2004, the Ninth Circuit reversed the district court's decision. The first (district court) decision can be found in volume 169 of the Federal Supplement, Second Series, beginning on page 1181 (169 F.Supp.2d 1181); the

Ninth Circuit's decision can be found in volume 379 of the Federal Reporter, Third Series, beginning on page 1120 (379 F.3d 1120).

Treaty: **WIPO Copyright Treaty, Dec. 20, 1996, 36 I.L.M. 65 (1997)**

The WIPO Copyright Treaty was signed, or opened for signature, or adopted, or something of the sort on December 20, 1996; note that this is *not* the date on which the treaty entered into force. A copy of the treaty can be found in volume 36 of International Legal Materials, a publication of the American Society of International Law, beginning on page 65 (36 I.L.M. 65). Volume 36 was published in 1997.

Book: **Lawrence Lessig, *Code and Other Laws of Cyberspace* (New York: Basic Books 1999)**

The format used here for books differs from some other formats chiefly in the way the author's name is presented: first name, last name. The cite tells the name of the author, the title of the book, the city in which the book was published, the name of the publisher, and the year of publication. A true Bluebook cite would omit the city and publisher for this particular work.

Article (1): Hershey, Mrs. Fields Fined for Violating Children's Online Privacy, **ConsumerAffairs.com, Feb. 27, 2003, http://www.consumeraffairs.com/news03/candy_fines.html (visited November 18, 2004)**

This article is dated, but has no named author. If there were a named author, the name would appear before the title, as in the book cite above. This article appeared on the Web site ConsumerAffairs.com; because this is an online source, the Web address and date last visited are also given.

Article (2): **Eric Goldman, "A Road to No Warez: The No Electronic Theft Act and Criminal Copyright Infringement," 82 Oregon Law Review 369 (2003)**

Scholarly legal journals are consecutively paginated throughout the volume year. If the first issue in a volume year ends on page 200, the second issue will begin on page 201, not on page 1. Thus, each volume can be treated as a single volume, like a book; there is no need to cite the month or season in which the issue was printed. The cite format follows that used for case reporters and other primary sources: Eric Goldman's article on warez trading appears in volume 82 of the Oregon Law Review, beginning on page 369, and was published in 2003. (A true Bluebook cite would abbreviate the name of the journal, somewhat obscurely, as Or. L. Rev.)

How to Find Out More about Computer Terms

Law is not the only profession to conspire against the laity; the jargon of information technology professionals is, if anything, even more incomprehensible. Terms used in this volume are defined in the Glossary; for any terms not defined, however, or others that you might encounter in your research, a good source for definitions is Whatis.com: http://whatis.techtarget.com/.

❖ TABLE OF ABBREVIATIONS ❖

The abbreviations listed below appear in this volume. Most are also explained in the text, so there's no need to commit this list to memory. The use of the notes referring to legal sources is explained in the section "How to Read the Cites Used in This volume." Abbreviations that form company names are mostly omitted, where the company is known primarily by its abbreviation; few people, after all, think of IBM as "International Business Machines." Some abbreviations have become words, such as DVD (once "digital video disk," now the hokey-sounding "digital versatile disk"); they are not always explained in the text, but are included here for the curious.

§: Section
AACS: Advanced Access Content System
ACLU: American Civil Liberties Union
ACPA: Anticybersquatting Consumer Protection Act
ADP: Alliance for Digital Progress
AECA: Arms Export Control Act
AHRA: Audio Home Recording Act
ALA: American Library Association
ALAI: Association Littéraire et Artistique Internationale (International Artistic and Literary Association)
AOL: America Online
ARPANET: Advanced Research Projects Administration Network
Art.: Article
ASCAP: American Society of Composers, Authors and Publishers
ASCII: American Standard Code for Information Interchange

BBS: Bulletin Board System
BIRPI: Bureaux Internationaux Réunis pour la Protection de la Propriété Intellectuelle (United International Bureau for the Protection of Intellectual Property)

CALEA: Communications Assistance for Law Enforcement Act

CAN-SPAM Act: Controlling the Assault of Non-solicited Pornography and Marketing Act
CAPPS II: Computer Assisted Passenger Prescreening System
CARU: Children's Advertising Review of the Better Business Bureau
CD: Compact disk
CDA: Communications Decency Act
CDR: Campaign for Digital Rights
CD-ROM: Compact disk—read only memory
CERN: l'Organisation Européenne pour la Recherche Nucléaire (European Organization for Nuclear Research; originally Conseil Européene pour la Recherche Nucléaire)
CFAA: Computer Fraud and Abuse Act
CFR: Code of Federal Regulations
Cir.: Circuit Court of Appeals
CIPA: Children's Internet Protection Act
cl.: Clause
COPA: Child Online Protection Act
COPPA: Children's Online Privacy Protection Act
CSS: Content Scramble System

D.: Federal District Court
DAI: Digital Access Index
DAT: Digital audiotape
DDoS: Distributed denial of service [attack]
DeCSS: A program for decrypting CSS-encrypted DVDs
DMCA: Digital Millennium Copyright Act
DMCRA: Digital Media Consumers' Rights Act
DOJ: Department of Justice
DOS: (1) Disk operating system; (2) Denial-of-service
DPRSA: Digital Performance Right in Sound Recordings Act
DRM: Digital rights management
DSL: Digital Subscriber Line
DSP: Digital Speech Project
DVD: Digital versatile disk (originally digital video disk)

DVDCCA: DVD Copy Control Association

EDRi: European Digital Rights
EEA: Economic Espionage Act
EFF: Electronic Frontier Foundation
EU: European Union
EULA: End-user license agreement

F.: Federal Reporter
F.2d: Federal Reporter, Second Series
F.3d: Federal Reporter, Third Series
FBI: Federal Bureau of Investigation
FCC: Federal Communications Commission
F.C.C.R.: Federal Communications
    Commission Record
Fed.: Federal
FIDA: First Inventor Defense Act
FSF: Free Software Foundation
F.Supp.: Federal Supplement
F.Supp.2d: Federal Supplement, Second
    Series
FTC: Federal Trade Commission
FTP: File Transfer Protocol

GNU: Gnu's Not Unix (a recursive acronym)
GPL: General Public License
GPS: Global Positioning System
GUI: Graphical user interface

H.: House
H.R.: House of Representatives
HTML: Hypertext Markup Language
HTTP: Hypertext Transfer Protocol

IANA: Internet Assigned Numbers Authority
ICANN: Internet Corporation for Assigned
    Names and Numbers
IFRRO: International Federation of
    Reproduction Rights Organizations
I.L.M.: International Legal Materials
INDUCE Act: Inducing Infringement of
    Copyrights Act (originally Inducement
    Devolves into Unlawful Child
    Exploitation Act)
IP: (1) Internet protocol; (2) Internet
    provider; (3) intellectual property
IRC: Internet Relay Chat
ISP: Internet Service Provider
ITAR: International Traffic in Arms
    Regulation

KDD: Knowledge discovery in databases

LICRA: Ligue Contre le Racisme et
    L'Antisémitisme (League against Racism
    and Antisemitism)
L.N.T.S.: League of Nations Treaty Series

MIT: Massachusetts Institute of Technology
MP3: MPEG-1/2 Audio Layer 3
MPAA: Motion Picture Association of
    America
MPEG: Moving Pictures Experts Group

n.: Note
NCCUSL: National Conference of
    Commissioners on Uniform State Laws
NCIPA: Neighborhood Children's Internet
    Protection Act
NCSA: National Center for Supercomputing
    Applications
n.d.: No date
NET Act: No Electronic Theft Act
NSA: National Security Agency
NSFNet: National Science Foundation
    Network
NTIA: National Telecommunications and
    Information Administration

O.J.: Official Journal of the European
    Community
OSI: Open Society Institute
OSP: Online service provider

P2P: Peer-to-peer
PC: Personal computer
PCT: Patent Cooperation Treaty
PDEA: Public Domain Enhancement Act
PDF: [Adobe] Portable Document Format
PGP: Pretty Good Privacy encryption
    software
PIRATE Act: Protecting Intellectual Rights
    against Theft and Expropriation Act
PKC: Public key cryptography

RAM: Random access memory
Rep.: Report(s)
RIAA: Recording Industry Association of
    America
ROM: Read Only Memory
Rptr.: Reporter

RRO: Reproduction rights organization

RSA: Rivest-Shamir-Adleman encryption method

S.: Senate

SAFE Act: Security and Freedom through Encryption Act

SAFE ID Act: Secure Authentication Feature and Enhanced Identification Defense Act

SCMS: Serial Copy Management System

S. Ct.: Supreme Court Reporter

Sess.: Session

SF: Speculative fiction; also, less accurately, science fiction

SPY ACT: Securely Protect Yourself against Cyber Trespass Act

SPY BLOCK Act: Software Principles Yielding Better Levels of Consumer Knowledge Act

SSL: Secure Socket Layer

TCP/IP: Transmission Control Protocol/Internet Protocol

TLT: Trademark Law Treaty

TRIPS: Agreement on Trade-Related Aspects of Intellectual Property Rights

UCC: Uniform Commercial Code

U.C.C.: Universal Copyright Convention

UCITA: Uniform Computer Information Transactions Act

UCLA: University of California at Los Angeles

UETA: Uniform Electronic Transactions Act

UFMJRA: Uniform Foreign Money-Judgments Recognition Act

UK: United Kingdom

UN: United Nations

U.N.T.S.: United Nations Treaty Series

URL: Uniform Resource Locator

U.S.: (1) United States; (2) when used in case cites, United States Reports

USA PATRIOT Act: Uniting and Strengthening America by Providing Appropriate Tools Required to Intercept and Obstruct Terrorism Act

U.S.C.: United States Code

USCCAN: United States Code Congressional and Administrative News

USPTO: United States Patent and Trademark Office (also abbreviated PTO)

U.S.T.: United States Treaties and Other International Agreements

VARA: Visual Artists' Rights Act

VCR: Videocassette recorder

VHS: Video Home System (originally Vertical Helical Scan)

VOIP: Voice Over Internet Protocol

VPN: Virtual Private Network

WIPO: World Intellectual Property Organization

WL: Westlaw

WTO: World Trade Organization

WWW: World Wide Web

xCP: Extensible Content Protections

A

❖ AACC ❖

See Advanced Access Content System

❖ ABANDONWARE ❖

Abandonware is software that is no longer being sold or supported by its author, copyright owner, or licensed distributor. Software that is still being sold, but no longer supported, is sometimes also referred to as abandonware. Software becomes abandonware for various reasons. A software publisher might abandon a program because of declining sales, or because it was written for a hardware platform or operating system that is no longer being sold, such as the Apple II, Atari 800, or Commodore Amiga. Or the publisher might cease to exist as a corporate entity, for example, through bankruptcy or merger.

Because personal computers have not been around for long enough for the copyright on any programs written for them to expire, all abandonware that was once copyrighted is still copyrighted. Software that has been abandoned because its original publisher no longer exists is not automatically in the public domain, although in a few cases many rights may have been released under an open-source license. Some distributors and sharers of abandonware argue that the ethical objections to sharing copyrighted material do not apply to abandonware; the copyright owner is no longer selling the program, and thus is not being deprived of further sales (Goldman 2003, 405). Although there is some logic to this position, it is legally incorrect. When a corporate publisher ceases to exist through bankruptcy or merger with an-other publisher, its property, including its copyrights, are assigned to some new person. Copyrights held by an individual remain the property of that individual until she transfers them to someone else or dies; in the latter case they become a part of her estate.

Some corporate publishers do not undergo any formal dissolution process, however; they simply close their doors, without formally transferring their copyrights to anyone. In such a case it can be difficult to locate anyone with the legal right to authorize the making of copies. As a practical matter, such copyrights—and abandonware copyrights generally—are rarely enforced, although that could change in the future.

Old spreadsheets, word processing programs, and the like are of interest only to a limited number of enthusiasts. Abandoned games, however, are very popular. There has been a renewed interest in older game copyrights, because some games are adapted for use on mobile telephones, and those copyrights could be vigorously enforced in the future. The content industry generally takes the view that all unlicensed distribution of abandonware is harmful, because the abandoned programs might become valuable again at some point during the life of their copyright term. Balanced against this copyright interest is the valuable function abandonware sites play in preserving programs, especially games, that would otherwise be lost (Costikyan 2000).

See also: Copyright Infringement; File-Sharing; No Electronic Theft Act; Public Domain; Warez

Sources and further reading:
Greg Costikyan, "New Front in the Copyright
    Wars: Out-of-Print Computer Games," *N.Y.*

Times, May 18, 2000, available at http://www.
nytimes.com/library/tech/00/05/circuits/
articles/18aban.html (visited October 4, 2004).

Dan's 20th Century Abandonware,
http://home.pmt.org/~drose/aw.html (visited
November 9, 2004).

Eric Goldman, "A Road to No Warez: The No
Electronic Theft Act and Criminal Copyright
Infringement," 82 Oregon Law Review 369
(2003).

❖ ACTIVISM AND ADVOCACY GROUPS ❖

Advances in and increased use of computers and
information technology raise a wide variety of
political and legal issues. New activist and industry advocacy groups have sprung up to address these issues, and older groups have added
new issues to their traditional concerns. Three
areas that have given rise to a great deal of litigation and political activism are freedom of expression, privacy, and copyright. Many activist
and advocacy groups address a wide range of issues, while others have a single-issue focus.

Freedom of expression is a concern of the
American Civil Liberties Union (ACLU), and
the ACLU has been a plaintiff in actions brought
to determine the constitutionality of federal legislation attempting to regulate or restrict access
to Internet content. The action brought by the
ACLU challenging the first such congressional
attempt, the Communications Decency Act
(CDA), resulted in a United States Supreme
Court decision holding the content-restricting
portions of the CDA unconstitutional (*Reno v.
ACLU,* 521 U.S. 824). After the decision striking down the CDA, Congress enacted the Child
Online Protection Act (COPA), a second attempt to regulate Internet content, which was
also challenged in court by the ACLU. The
Supreme Court also expressed doubts about the
constitutionality of COPA, and remanded the
case to a lower court for trial on the issue of
whether blocking and filtering software could
provide a less restrictive alternative (*Ashcroft v.
ACLU,* 124 S. Ct. 2783). The ACLU has also,
although ultimately unsuccessfully, challenged
the Children's Internet Protection Act (*U.S. v.
American Library Association,* 539 U.S. 194).

On copyright issues, groups can be loosely
classified as either users' rights or content owners' rights groups. The division bears no relation to more general left-right political divisions; in fact, the most outspoken users' rights
advocate in Congress and the most outspoken
content owners' rights advocate are both Dem-
ocrats. The division is complicated further by
the ambivalent position of equipment and software manufacturers. Equipment manufacturers
are naturally inclined toward the users' rights
side of the dispute; enhanced copyright controls make equipment more complicated to
manufacture and thus either more expensive or
less profitable, and also decrease consumer demand because of compatibility issues and because many users want to use the equipment
they purchase to make copies, whether within
the fair use exception or outside it. But many
equipment manufacturers (Sony, for example)
are also content owners; there is thus an internal conflict.

Software companies suffer a similar conflict,
but although the balance for most equipment
makers tilts toward the users' rights side, for
software makers it tilts toward content owners'
rights. Software that allows duplication of copyrighted material will be easier to sell, but software itself is copyrighted content, and software
makers have an interest in its protection.

The Alliance for Digital Progress (ADP) is an
industry group founded to oppose govern-
ment-designed or mandated copyright protection technology. According to ADP's mission
statement, the organization "strongly opposes
efforts to make the government design and
mandate copy-protection technologies" ("ADP
Mission Statement"). Such government intervention, the ADP believes, can only interfere
with the smooth functioning of market mechanisms: "the best ways to meet consumer expectations and fight piracy include market-driven
efforts to educate consumers, create digital distribution strategies, develop innovative technology, and enforce existing laws" ("ADP Mission
Statement"). The ADP's members include
technology-industry giants such as Apple,
Cisco, Dell, Hewlett-Packard, IBM, Intel, Microsoft, and Motorola; they do not include the
Recording Industry Association of America

(RIAA) or the Motion Picture Association of America (MPAA). Although some of the ADP's members seem at times to lean toward the content owners' rights side, the ADP as a whole tends to find common cause with users' rights groups in opposing proposed legislation mandating top-down copyright controls. For example, the ADP successfully opposed the Consumer Broadband and Digital Television Promotion Act, a content-industry initiative.

The ADP is a single-issue group; the Electronic Frontier Foundation (EFF) is perhaps the best known of several advocacy groups addressing a wider array of computer and Internet law issues. Like the ADP, the EFF is alarmed by congressional efforts to mandate copyright control mechanisms. On copyright and other intellectual property issues the EFF is a users' rights group. Intellectual property is not the EFF's only concern, however; its "list of issues" includes, among other topics, anonymity, biometrics, censorship, intellectual property, privacy, public records, spam, and the USA PATRIOT Act. On all of these issues the EFF takes a consistent individual rights stance. According to the EFF's Web site, "governments and corporate interests worldwide are trying to prevent us from communicating freely through new technologies. . . . The Electronic Frontier Foundation (EFF) was created to defend our rights to think, speak, and share our ideas, thoughts, and needs using new technologies, such as the Internet and the World Wide Web" ("About EFF"). The EFF's activities in pursuit of these freedoms include providing support for lawsuits, education, and reporting on proposed legislation and administrative regulations.

The Free Software Foundation (FSF) is perhaps the most prominent of several ideologically motivated groups of software designers. Rather than focusing on legal and political solutions to the problem of corporate and government control of users' online autonomy, the FSF and others like it focus on the technological aspect. The core of the problem—that is, the aspect of computers and the Internet that allows them to lend themselves so readily to an architecture of control—is, in the FSF's opinion, the dominance of proprietary operating systems ("Philosophy of the GNU Project"

2004). Open-source operating systems such as GNU/Linux, a Linux-based operating system distributed by the FSF-sponsored GNU project, are designed by and in the interest of individual users rather than governments or large corporations. The FSF states that its mission is "to preserve, protect and promote the freedom to use, study, copy, modify, and redistribute computer software, and to defend the rights of Free Software users" ("GNU Operating System" 2004). Despite its anticorporate rhetoric the FSF enjoys support from a number of corporate sponsors, including Cisco, IBM, Novell, Sun, IBM, and TiVo. Many of these might either feel some antagonism toward the dominant maker of operating systems for personal computers—Microsoft—or feel threatened by content-industry attempts to tighten copyright controls.

In addition to the GNU Project, the FSF's activities include no-cost software development services for other free software developers, copyright licensing and compliance advice, and the Digital Speech Project (DSP). The DSP is concerned with changes in copyright law that would expand the rights of content owners and restrict the rights of users; it reports on and encourages opposition to proposed legislation of this sort.

Public Knowledge is another users' rights organization concerned with intellectual property law, especially copyright law. According to the organization's mission statement, Public Knowledge has four broad goals:

(1) Ensuring that U.S. intellectual property law [provides] an incentive to creators and innovators while benefiting the public through the free flow of information and ideas.
(2) Preserving an Internet that is built upon open standards and protocols and "end-to-end" architecture, thereby fostering innovation and user control.
(3) Protecting consumers of digital technology from market practices designed to erode competition, choice and fairness.
(4) Ensuring that international intellectual property policies are adopted through democratic processes and with public interest participation (*Public Knowledge Mission Statement*).

Like the DSP, Public Knowledge carries out its work through advocacy and reporting on legislation potentially affecting users' rights. It also carries out two special projects: Empowering Creators in the Digital Age, which attempts to determine a workable balance between the need of content creators (rather than distributors) for content protection and the need of those same content creators to be able to make use of prior copyrighted works; and the Open Access Project, the goal of which is the "free and unrestricted world-wide electronic distribution of peer-reviewed journal literature coupled with free and unrestricted access to that literature by scientists, scholars, teachers, students and others" ("Open Access Project").

Anti-DMCA is a similar users' rights group focusing on copyright issues in the United States. Similar groups outside the United States include the United Kingdom's Campaign for Digital Rights (CDR). Like the EFF, the CDR is concerned with freedom of expression as well as users' rights to fair use of copyrighted material. European Digital Rights (EDRi) focuses on copyright issues in the European Union. Users' rights advocacy groups in Europe include:

- Association Electronique Libre (Belgium)
- Associazione per la Liberta' nella Comunicazione Elettronica Interattiva (Italy)
- Bits of Freedom (the Netherlands)
- Chaos Computer Club (Germany)
- Cyber-Rights & Cyber-Liberties (United Kingdom)
- Digital Rights (Denmark)
- Electronic Frontier Finland
- Electronic Frontier Ireland
- Elektronisk Forpost Norge (Norway)
- Förderverein Informationstechnik und Gesellschaft (Germany)
- Forum InformatikerInnen für Frieden und gesellschaftliche Verantwortung (Germany)
- Foundation for Information Policy Research (United Kingdom)
- Fronteras Electronicas España (Spain)
- Imaginons un Réseau Internet Solidaire (IRIS)(France)

- Internet Society Bulgaria
- Netzwerk Neue Medien (Germany)
- Privacy International (United Kingdom)
- quintessenz (Austria)
- Swiss Internet User Group
- Verein für Internet-Benutzer Österreichs (Austria)

Other groups include Electronic Frontiers [*sic*] Australia and Electronic Frontier Canada.

Because there are many more users than there are content owners, users' rights groups tend to be more numerous and attract a broader base of support than content owners' rights groups. But because content is often worth money, the content owners' rights groups tend to be much better funded. Two groups that have been particularly prominent both legislatively (proposing and lobbying for legislation to enhance copyright protection) and judicially (bringing lawsuits to enforce content owners' rights) are the MPAA and the RIAA.

As the names imply, the MPAA is concerned with movies and the RIAA with music. Although the interests of the two groups are similar, they are not identical. The MPAA's members might currently be experiencing some lost profits due to piracy, but the threat to their business model is largely prospective. The RIAA members' business model—distribution of bundled music recordings on CDs or other media through retail outlets—is not only threatened but is technologically obsolete; a new business model is needed, and finding it has not been easy.

The MPAA's concern is that the spread of broadband and DVD recorders will make video piracy as easy as music piracy is now. Both the RIAA and the MPAA seek to protect content owners' rights through drafting and supporting proposed legislation to enhance copyright protections, through lawsuits against copyright infringers, and through the pursuit of technological solutions such as the "trusted computing" initiative.

Statutes Targeted by Activist Groups
- Child Online Protection Act, 47 U.S.C. § 231

- Children's Internet Protection Act, 47 U.S.C. § 254(h)
- Communications Decency Act, Pub. L. No. 104-104, § 502, 1996 U.S.S.C.A.N. (110 Stat.) 56,133 (later codified at 47 U.S.C. § 223)
- Copyright Act of 1976, 17 U.S.C. § 101
- Digital Millennium Copyright Act, Title I, Pub. L. No. 105-304, codified at 17 U.S.C. §§ 1201–05

Some Cases Involving Activist Groups
Supreme Court
- *Ashcroft v. American Civil Liberties Union,* 124 S. Ct. 2783 (2004)
- *Reno v. American Civil Liberties Union,* 521 U.S. 824 (1997)
- *United States v. American Library Association, Inc.,* 539 U.S. 194 (2003)

Federal Appellate Courts
- *Bernstein v. United States,* 176 F.3d 1132 (9th Cir. 1999); rehearing granted, opinion withdrawn, 192 F.3d 1308 (9th Cir. 1999)
- *Steve Jackson Games v. United States Secret Service,* 36 F.3d 457 (5th Cir. 1994)

See also: Budapest Open Access Initiative; Censorship; Child Online Protection Act; Children's Internet Protection Act; Communications Decency Act; Constitutional Law; Content Industry; Copyright; Declaration of the Independence of Cyberspace; Digital Millennium Copyright Act; Digital Millennium Copyright Act, Title I; File-Sharing; First Amendment; Open-Source; Privacy; Recording Industry Association of America

Sources and further reading:
Alliance for Digital Progress, "Alliance for Digital Progress Members," n.d., http://www.alliancefordigitalprogress.org/content/?p=CoalitionMembers (visited November 18, 2004).
"Alliance for Digital Progress Mission Statement," http://www.alliancefordigitalprogress.org/content/?p=MissionStatement/Principles (visited November 18, 2004).
Electronic Frontier Foundation, "About EFF: General Information about the Electronic Frontier Foundation," n.d., http://www.eff.org/about/ (visited November 18, 2004).
Free Software Foundation, "GNU Operating System," 2004, http://www.gnu.org/.
Mike Godwin, *Cyber Rights: Defending Free Speech in the Digital Age* (Cambridge, MA: MIT Press, 2003).
Tim Jordan, *Cyberpower: The Culture and Politics of Cyberspace and the Internet* (New York: Routledge, 1999).
Lawrence Lessig, *Free Culture: How Big Media Uses Technology and the Law to Lock Down Culture and Control Creativity* (New York: Penguin, 2004) (also available as a free download).
"Philosophy of the GNU Project," 2004, http://www.gnu.org/philosophy/ (visited November 18, 2004).
Public Knowledge, "The Open Access Project," n.d., available at http://www.publicknowledge.org/about/what/projects/open-access.html/view?searchterm=open%20access%20project (visited November 18, 2004).
"Public Knowledge Mission Statement," n.d., available at http://www.publicknowledge.org/about/what/mission (visited November 18, 2004).
Leslie David Simon et al., *Democracy and the Internet: Allies or Adversaries?* (Washington, DC: Woodrow Wilson Center Press, 2002).
Cass R. Sunstein, *Republic.Com* (Princeton, NJ: Princeton University Press, 2002).
Siva Vaidhyanathan, *The Anarchist in the Library: How the Clash between Freedom and Control Is Hacking the Real World and Crashing the System* (New York: Basic Books, 2004).

❖ ADVANCED ACCESS CONTENT SYSTEM ❖

Advanced Access Content System (AACS) is the name for a motion picture recording digital rights management technology still under development. When and if the technology is ready for the marketplace, it will allow consumers to transfer movies purchased on DVD to other devices, such as a computer or diskless portable player, but at the same time will make it more difficult to make and distribute large numbers of unauthorized copies. AACS will thus avoid many of the problems with Content Scramble System (CSS), the system now in use. CSS frustrates consumers because CSS-protected disks can only be played back on CSS-equipped DVD players—the recordings cannot be transferred to other media or devices. And CSS has proved easy to circumvent through the use of programs such as DeCSS; once a CSS key has been leaked or reverse-engineered, there is nothing the content industry can do to recapture it. AACS, on the other hand, will be designed so that individual keys can be retired without interfering with the functioning of the system as a whole; any keys that enter the public domain can be retired, enabling the content industry to minimize the damage without inconveniencing consumers (Borland 2004).

In order to defend its copyrights, the content industry has been forced to wage a battle on two fronts. One front is legal: The industry fights to increase the scope of copyright protection and penalties for infringement and sues infringers. The other front is technological: The industry seeks ways to make copyrighted recordings more difficult to copy. To do this effectively requires the cooperation of equipment manufacturers; a recording that cannot be played back on most people's media players, or that freezes, jitters, or stutters on playback, will be difficult to sell.

Historically equipment manufacturers have been dubious of copyright protection schemes initiated by the content industry. Incorporating copy protection and digital rights management technology makes equipment more expensive to manufacture and increases compatibility problems; at the same time, consumers would prefer not to have it. It is not in the interests of equipment manufacturers to benefit the content industry at their own and their customers' expense. In order to be workable, AACS will have to take the interests of equipment manufacturers (and their customers) into account. That the proposal seems to do so is evident from the number of manufacturers that have joined the AACS Licensing Authority, including IBM, Intel, Panasonic, Sony, and Toshiba; other members include AOL Time Warner, Disney, and Microsoft (Merritt 2004).

Another problem is compatibility with other digital rights management systems. Content delivery is in danger of becoming fragmented: Content recorded with a particular digital rights management technology can only be played back with players (whether hardware or software) equipped with that technology. Few consumers want to keep half a dozen different media players around; most are seeking a single player that can play all of the recordings they own. AACS seeks to resolve this problem as well; the Licensing Authority is working to ensure compatibility with digital rights management systems developed independently by the various members, including Microsoft's Windows Media, IBM's extensible content protection (xCP), and Digital Transmission Content Protection, developed by the 5C consortium (Hitachi, Intel, Matsushita, Sony, and Toshiba) and previously endorsed by AOL Time Warner (Borland 2004).

See also: DeCSS; Digital Rights Management; Piracy

Sources and further reading:
John Borland, Tech, "Studio Giants Team on New DVD Locks," *C/Net News.com,* July 14, 2004, available at http://news.com.com/Tech,+studio+giants+team+on+new+DVD+locks/2100-1025_3-5269286.html (visited October 6, 2004).

Rick Merritt, *Copyright Scheme Could Fuel Transition to High-Definition Systems, EE Times,* July 15, 2004, available at http://www.eetimes.com/showArticle.jhtml?articleID=23900919 (visited October 6, 2004).

❖ ADVERTISING ❖

Advertising is an essential component of the modern Internet. Revenues from advertising support many Web sites; without it, content on the Internet would be less plentiful and less varied. Some Internet advertisers, however, make their messages so intrusive that users and Web site operators feel that the advertisement is interfering with their enjoyment of the Internet; in these cases, legal action and demands for regulation may ensue. This unwelcome advertising can raise First Amendment and privacy issues. Internet advertising, welcome or not, can also raise trademark and jurisdictional issues. Adware placed on a user's computer without the user's knowledge or consent can raise an issue of trespass.

There are various types of Internet advertising; among the most common are banner ads, pop-ups, and e-mail advertisements. Banner ads show up as part of a Web page; they may be still or animated images, and clicking on them generally links the user to a Web site from which the advertised goods or services may be purchased. In format and visual effect they resemble advertisements in a printed magazine or newspaper. Pop-ups and pop-unders are advertisements that open as a separate browser page either above or under the page being viewed at the time. They are almost universally disliked by Web surfers and are used by a smaller number of advertisers than are banner ads. E-mail advertising can be roughly divided into two categories. In the first category are advertisements that the recipient has asked or consented to receive, such as notification of the publication of a new book by a favorite author or of a clearance sale from a clothing company from which the recipient has purchased clothes in the past. In the second category is unsolicited mass e-mail advertising, or spam.

Banner ads generally create relatively little resentment unless they contain indecent words or images; otherwise, users may read them or ignore them as they choose. Ads containing indecent content are generally confined to pornographic Web sites and other Web sites that a user might reasonably expect to contain such advertisements; Web site owners are unlikely to accept such advertising otherwise. A problem might occur, though, when unscrupulous advertisers hijack a Web site or an ad-placement system, replacing paid advertisers' content with their own. This hijacking is a crime (theft of services), and the hacking required to do it is also illegal.

Banner ads can be targeted to the viewer. Some banner ads are placed on a page in response to the nature of the content being viewed. For example, a news story about a baseball game might contain ads for baseball mem-

orabilia. Sometimes the ads are unintentionally absurd: An article about a public school district's ties to religious groups is accompanied by advertisements for men's neckwear decorated with Christian motifs—"religious ties" of a very different sort. Sometimes the ads are tasteless: An article about the crash of a hot-air balloon is accompanied by ads for balloon rides.

More worrisome to privacy advocates is the possibility of ads being targeted based on individual Web surfing habits. An Internet user who visits a news site each day and reads all of the stories about sailing may soon find that, whatever he views, he sees banner ads for sailboats and sailing supplies.

Another category of advertising includes sites that consist entirely of advertisements; these generally cause few legal problems. Users expect a site called www.toyota.com to contain information about Toyota automobiles, and are neither surprised nor offended to learn that it does. Similarly, they expect a retail Web site such as www.amazon.com to advertise goods for sale; they go there expecting, and indeed hoping, to encounter such advertising. Privacy issues arise, though, from the site's collection of information about viewers. Sites may generally use information collected from viewers as they wish to target future advertising and develop marketing strategies, subject to the terms of a privacy policy written by the company itself and displayed somewhere on the site. The use of information obtained from children is much more restricted, however. Under the Children's Online Privacy Protection Act (COPPA) commercial Web sites collecting information from children less than thirteen years of age must provide a privacy notice explaining what information is collected, how it is used, and under what circumstances and to whom it may be disclosed. In addition, no personal information—defined as information that might identify or permit communication with the child, such as a first or last name, address, e-mail address, telephone number, or social security number—may be obtained from a child without the verifiable consent of the child's parents. The Web site operator must provide the parents with a reasonable means to review the information; the parents must also have the opportunity to refuse to permit the Web site operator to use or maintain the information.

Considerable attention and concern has been focused on Internet "advertainment" and "advergames" aimed at children, such as the Neopets site. Under COPPA, a Web site operator may not condition a child's participation in a game, promotional sweepstakes, contest, or other activity upon the collection of any information not reasonably necessary to enable the child to participate in the activity. Some consumers' groups feel that in the case of advergames COPPA does not go far enough; Neopets' "immersive advertising" strategy, in which children are not exposed to banners or pop-ups but are instead exposed to product placement within the game itself, strikes some consumers' groups as insidious and dangerous (*The Guardian* 2002).

The targeting of pop-up and pop-under ads raises the same issues as the targeting of banner ads. In addition, pop-ups can act as parasites on sites to which they have not paid an advertising fee, appearing on the computers of users visiting those sites. And some sites are pop-up bait sites, existing primarily to trap unsuspecting visitors in a blizzard of pop-ups. These include typosquatting sites with names likely to be entered by someone misspelling the name of a popular Web site; predictably, they also include pornographic sites; rather oddly, they also include many sites offering the lyrics to popular songs. Visitors to one of these sites may be mousetrapped, with new pop-ups appearing faster than they can be closed; inexperienced Web surfers may have to shut down their computers in order to escape.

Sometimes advertising is generated by adware placed on the user's computer. Many inexperienced users consent to install this software, under the belief that they are gaining something else: a security program or a new cursor design, for example. Children are especially vulnerable to adware of this sort.

Many users and Internet service providers (ISPs) turn to self-help to avoid unwelcome advertising. Users can block pop-ups and some banner ads by using the Windows "hosts" file or a pop-up blocker. ISPs weed out enormous quantities of spam each day, preventing it from reaching their subscribers' computers. These self-help activities have in turn met with challenges from advertisers. Spammers, for instance, have sued America Online (AOL), claiming that its actions violate their First Amendment right to freedom of expression. The courts have rejected this argument; America Online is a private party, not a state actor, and the First Amendment does not require it to deliver e-mail (*America Online*, 948 F. Supp. 456).

Unwelcome advertising, especially spam, has also brought demands for government regulation. COPPA, discussed previously, is one result. The CAN-SPAM Act, a 2003 law designed to curb spammers, is another. And laws designed for off-line advertising also apply to Internet advertising: Commercial speech may be prohibited if it is untruthful, misleading, or deceptive or if its subject matter or presentation is illegal. It may also be subject to reasonable time, place, and manner restrictions.

Regulating advertising, on the Internet and in many other media, is the job of the Federal Trade Commission (FTC), and more specifically (although not exclusively) of the Division of Advertising Practices of the FTC's Bureau of Consumer Protection.

The FTC may take regulatory or administrative action or litigate against unfair, misleading, or false advertising. The FTC may regulate against, or issue a cease and desist order to prevent, advertising acts or practices that are unfair if two additional conditions are met. First, the act or practice must cause or be "likely to cause substantial injury to consumers, . . . not reasonably avoidable by consumers themselves." Second, the injury must not be "outweighed by countervailing benefits to consumers or to competition." In determining whether an act or practice is unfair, the FTC may consider public policy, but may not make public policy the primary basis for its action (15 U.S.C. § 45(n)).

An injury to consumers is substantial if a relatively small harm is inflicted upon a large number of consumers or if a greater harm is inflicted on even a small number of consumers; however, the harm must be more than merely trivial or speculative (Greenspan 1999).

The FTC may also take action against deceptive acts and practices: material misrepresentations, omissions, or practices that are "likely to mislead a consumer acting reasonably under the circumstances" (Greenspan 1999). This reasonable person standard can be adapted to match the target audience. A communication to an audience of children, for example, would be judged by whether it was likely to mislead a reasonable child.

The FTC has authority to regulate false advertising only if the advertising is for food, drugs, cosmetics, or medical devices, a category that includes a great deal of spam. Advertising for these products is false if it is materially misleading (Greenspan 1999).

The FTC has brought actions against scammers and spammers; it has imposed penalties on Web site operators for violations of their own privacy policies. It has declined, however, to create a federal "do not spam" registry as authorized by the CAN-SPAM Act of 2003, on the grounds that such a registry would be futile, in contrast to the popular "do not call" registry. It is far easier and cheaper to send spam from outside the United States than it is to move a telemarketing operation outside the United States. Without some form of global control, the FTC's registry would be useless. The FTC has issued a regulation requiring adult-oriented spam to be identified as such in the message header; however, misidentified adult-oriented spam persists.

A few specialized categories of advertising may also be regulated or prohibited. Advertising by attorneys, doctors, and other professionals may be regulated by professional associations, subject to limits imposed by the First Amendment. The status of tobacco advertising is still unclear; Congress can explicitly prohibit tobacco advertising over the Internet, and the European Union has already imposed such a prohibition, to take full effect in July 2005. As with spam, however, little can be done about advertising originating beyond a nation's borders. A similar problem applies to advertising for gambling.

Statutes
- Controlling the Assault of Non-solicited Pornography and Marketing (CAN-SPAM) Act of 2003, 15 U.S.C. §§ 7701–7713

- Unfair Methods of Competition, 15 U.S.C. § 45

European Union Directive
- Directive on the approximation of the laws, regulations, and administrative provisions of the Member States relating to the advertising and sponsorship of tobacco products, 2003 O.J. (L 152) 16

Case
- *America Online v. Cyber Promotions,* 948 F.Supp. 456 (E.D. Pa. 1996)

See also: Adware and Spyware; Censorship; Children's Online Privacy Protection Act; Cookies; Data Mining; DoubleClick; First Amendment; Gambling; Privacy; Spam

Sources and further reading:
Erik Anderson, "Protection of Trademarks from Use in Internet Advertising Banner Triggers: *Playboy v. Netscape,*" 40 *Jurimetrics Journal* 469 (2000).

Lori Irish Bauman, "Personal Jurisdiction and Internet Advertising," 14 *Computer Lawyer* 1 (1997).

Alan N. Greenspan, *Internet Advertising Laws and Regulations,* Practising Law Institute, 19th Annual Institute on Computer Law, February-March, 1999.

Jason Krause, "The National Pulse: Google Targeted in Trademark Disputes—Rulings Should Help Define What Is Protected in Internet Advertising," *ABA Journal E-Report* May 28, 2004.

Paul Lansing and Mark D. Halter, "Internet Advertising and Right to Privacy Issues," 80 *University of Detroit Mercy Law Review* 181 (2003).

"Pet Hates: The Gaming Site Neopets Is a Welcome Relief, Says Martin Headon," *The Guardian,* Oct. 31, 2002, available at http://www.guardian.co.uk/computergames/story/0,11500,822595,00.html (visited October 6, 2004).

"Policy Online Privacy/Data Sharing Internet Advertising Trade Group Issues Guidelines on Use of Web Bugs," *Cybercrime Law Report,* Dec. 16, 2002.

Christopher J. Schulte, "*Abracadabra International Ltd. v. Abracadabra Creations Inc.*—Internet Advertising Just Federalized the Nation's Service

Mark Law," 22 *Hamline Law Review* 563 (1999).

Sue Zeidler, "Livewire: Back to School Means Back to Advergames," *Reuters,* Sept. 15, 2004, available at http://www.reuters.com/ newsArticle.jhtml?type=technologyNews& storyID=6246387 (visited October 6, 2004).

❖ ADWARE AND SPYWARE ❖

Adware is software installed on a user's computer that causes advertisements to be displayed, often as pop-ups. These pop-ups generally appear while the user is surfing the Web, but can also appear at other times; they are neither authorized by nor related to the Web site that the user is viewing at the time. Adware that collects information about the user and passes that information to some other person is spyware. Adware is generally regarded as an annoyance, while spyware raises privacy and security issues and is considered by many users to be unethical rather than merely annoying.

Some adware is installed as part of commercially distributed programs and is directly related to that program. Antivirus programs, for example, prompt users when their subscriptions are about to expire. This prompt may appear as a pop-up whenever the user turns on the computer. A program that was installed as part of the antivirus program generates the pop-up, and this program could be considered adware. The level of annoyance it produces in the user is likely to be slight, however.

Users might also accept adware as the price of using popular free file-sharing, browser, and e-mail programs. Some users of these programs might be unaware that, by installing the programs, they have consented to the installation of adware. The information is contained in the clickwrap agreements, but few users actually read the agreements.

The Google toolbar includes a "page rank" feature that lets Google know where toolbar users are surfing; some consider this spyware, although the feature can be disabled with a single click. The Google toolbar also includes a pop-up blocker ("Identifying Spyware" n.d.). But the adware and spyware that arouses the greatest user rage—second only to spam as an unpopular advertising technique—is that installed on a user's computer by stealth or subterfuge.

Visitors to Web sites are often confronted with pop-up dialog boxes asking them to consent to the installation of a program such as WhenU, Gator (now Claria), or the now-defunct Xupiter. These programs are adware, but many users—especially children—may click "yes" to install the program, rather than "no" or "X" to close the dialog box, and thus install the adware. These programs, at least, give users the opportunity to refuse installation. More worrisome are drive-by downloads: programs that install themselves without presenting the user with the option of refusal, and without the user's knowledge (Urbach and Kibel 2004).

Adware and spyware can do more than serve pop-up advertising. It can turn a user's computer into a zombie, allowing it to be used in spamming or denial-of-service attacks. Home page hijackers change the user's browser home page. Spyware can be used not only for annoying advertisements but also for malicious hacking; it can provide hackers with access to and control over the computer on which it is installed. Keystroke loggers, screen capture programs, and similar programs can track and record all activity on a computer, enabling anyone who looks at the log to discover passwords, account numbers, and other vital security information. And all of these activities, sinister or not, take up disk space, memory, and processor resources; adware and spyware slow down the operation of the computer on which they are installed, sometimes seriously degrading performance.

Malicious uses of spyware are obviously illegal; however, adware installed with the consent of the user—even when the user does not understand what she is consenting to—may not be. Adware has given rise to a great many civil suits for damages and equitable relief. Most of these suits are brought by aggrieved Web site owners and trademark holders. U-Haul, for example, has sued over the unauthorized use of its trademarks in pop-ups generated by WhenU. com, Inc. WhenU.com has been sued frequently. Wells Fargo and Quicken Loans have sued because WhenU's software causes ads for other mortgage lenders to appear when users visit Wells Fargo or Quicken Loans Web sites. These suits have not been successful; although the ad software uses U-Haul's, Wells Fargo's and Quicken's trademarks to assign particular ads to users visiting the trademark holder's pages, that alone does not meet the elements of trademark infringement. A similar suit against WhenU by 1-800-Contacts resulted in an injunction against WhenU and is currently before the Second Circuit Court of Appeals. Meanwhile, multiple suits against Claria Corporation have been consolidated for trial before a federal court in Georgia; the outcomes of the Claria case and the 1-800-Contacts appeal could bring about changes in the law regarding adware. The federal government has also filed its first suit against a drive-by spyware installer (Sullivan 2004).

Opponents of adware and spyware have also pursued legislative change. Antispyware bills introduced in Congress include the Safeguard against Privacy Invasions Act and the Software Principles Yielding Better Levels of Consumer Knowledge ("SPY BLOCK") Act, introduced in the House of Representatives and in the Senate, respectively, in 2003. The Safeguard against Privacy Invasions Act, renamed the Securely Protect Yourself against Cyber Trespass Act ("SPY ACT"), passed the House of Representatives by a vote of 399 in favor to one against on October 5, 2004, and reported to the Senate on the following day.

Many states are considering similar legislation; in March 2004 Utah passed the nation's first state antispyware law, the Spyware Control Act. On September 28, 2004, California followed, when Governor Schwarzenegger approved the Consumer Protection against Computer Software Act. Adware distributors have brought suits to enjoin enforcement of the state statutes.

For most users the main issue that arises from adware and spyware is not its legality, but how to get rid of it. Laws restricting spyware might offer a long-term solution but will be ineffective against malicious hackers (whose activities are already illegal) and against parties outside the United States. The best way to fight

software is with software; many antiadware and antispyware programs are available. As with spam and viruses, there is an ongoing arms race between adware and antiadware software; complete protection requires the use of two or three programs. Popular and effective antiadware and antispyware programs include Ad-Aware, Hi-Jack This, PestPatrol, Spybot Search & Destroy, and Spy Sweeper. Many of these are available as free downloads for individual users, and others are inexpensive. Antivirus programs will also detect and remove some malicious spyware. A firewall program can prevent adware from sending information out of the user's computer; this will not solve the problem, but will at least address the privacy issues. A firewall's log may also be useful in identifying spyware.

Statutes and Proposed Legislation
Federal
- Safeguard against Privacy Invasions Act, H.R. 2929, 108th Cong., 1st Sess. (2003), reported to and passed by House of Representatives as Securely Protect Yourself against Cyber Trespass Act ("SPY ACT")
- Software Principles Yielding Better Levels of Consumer Knowledge ("SPY BLOCK") Act, S. 2145, 108th Cong., 2d Sess. (2003)

State
- Consumer Protection against Computer Software Act, S.B. 1436 (California 2004)
- Spyware Control Act, H.B. 323 (Utah 2004)

Cases
- *1-800-Contacts v. WhenU.com, Inc.*, 309 F.Supp.2d 467 (S.D. N.Y. 2003)
- *U-Haul International, Inc. v. WhenU.com, Inc.*, 2003 WL 21673722 (E.D. Va. 2003)
- *Wells Fargo & Co. v. WhenU.com, Inc.*, 293 F.Supp.2d 734 (E.D. Mich. 2003)

See also: Advertising; Cookies; Denial-of-Service Attack; Hacking; Malware; Privacy; Spam; Trademark; Trojan; Zombie

Sources and further reading:

"2d Cir. to Decide Legality of Injunction against Adware *1-800-Contacts Inc. v. WhenU.com Inc.,*" *Andrews Software Law Bulletin,* Apr. 1, 2004, at 12.

Kevin P. Cronin and Ronald N. Weikers, *Data Security and Privacy Law: Combating Cyberthreats § 8:44* (St. Paul, MN: West, 2004).

"Identifying Spyware: Malicious, Annoying or Misunderstood?" *Intranet Journal,* http://www.intranetjournal.com/spyware/identifypr.html (no date).

Andy Sullivan, "First Suit Filed against Internet 'Spyware,'" *Yahoo News,* Oct. 8, 2004, available at http://news.yahoo.com/news?tmpl=story&cid=1896&u=/nm/20041008/tc_nm/tech_spyware_dc_3&printer=1 (visited October 12, 2004).

Ronald R. Urbach and Gary A. Kibel, "Adware/Spyware: An Update Regarding Pending Litigation and Legislation," *Journal of Proprietary Rights,* July 2004, at 12.

❖ ANALOG HOLE ❖

See Analog Recording

❖ ANALOG RECORDING ❖

Digital rights management technology, including copy protection and copyright management information, can be relatively effective in protecting a digitally recorded work, such as a movie, from digital copying. In order to be played, however, the digital recording must ordinarily be converted to analog form; most households, for instance, have analog television displays. Media players, such as CD and DVD players, are therefore equipped with analog output ports; these can be connected to an analog display device—or to an analog recorder. The analog recording thus made can then be digitized, effectively washing it clean of any copy protection or copyright management information. This digital copy will be somewhat lower in quality than the original, but can be copied freely by anyone, without special knowledge, software, or equipment. This vulnerability to analog copying is referred to as the "analog hole" (see Woodford 2004, 275).

The analog hole represents a threat to copyright interests in movies and music. In the content industry's dream world, all communications between playback devices and displays would be digital, and encrypted. This would close the analog hole, and would also make it possible for equipment manufacturers to ensure that, for example, their DVD players could only be used with their TV displays and speakers. Consumers would no longer be able to choose which device to use to play a recording; recordings could only be played back on players and displays equipped with the appropriate decryption keys.

Because cracking copy protection is still fairly easy, the analog hole is probably exploited relatively rarely (Woodford 2004, 276). However, the legal status of analog copying is quite different from that of digital cracking-plus-copying. The anticircumvention provisions of the Digital Millennium Copyright Act (DMCA) specifically prohibit the latter (17 U.S.C. § 1201). The making of an analog copy of a digital work, however, may be protected by the fair use exception to copyright infringement. Copying for purposes of space-shifting—that is, for the consumer to play on another type of player, perhaps at another location, such as in a car—is fair use (*Diamond,* 180 F.3d 1072).

Content industry efforts to seal the analog hole include the trusted computing initiative and attempts to create robust watermarking that can survive digital-to-analog conversion, coupled with proposed legislation requiring all analog-to-digital recorders to be equipped with devices capable of recognizing the watermark and refusing to record the watermarked content (Crawford 2003, 619). Such attempts are likely to encounter opposition from users' rights advocates and perhaps equipment makers as well, whose production costs will be increased by adding technology that the consumer would prefer not to have. One relatively successful content industry initiative has been the use of Macrovision Corporation's copy-protection technology, which exploits the automatic gain control on most videocassette recorders (VCRs) to prevent the VCRs from making viewable copies of protected videotapes and

DVDs (Macrovision 2003, 2). The content industry has succeeded in making automatic gain control mandatory on new VCRs sold in or imported to the United States, making those VCRs unable to copy Macrovision-protected videos (17 U.S.C. § 1201(k)).

Statute
- Digital Millennium Copyright Act, 17 U.S.C. § 1201

Case
- *Recording Industry Association of America v. Diamond Multimedia Systems, Inc.,* 180 F.3d 1072 (9th Cir. 1999)

See also: Copyright; Copyright Infringement; DeCSS; Digital Millennium Copyright Act, Title I; Digital Rights Management; Fair Use (Copyright); Macrovision; Steganography

Sources and further reading:
Susan P. Crawford, "The Biology of the Broadcast Flag," 25 *Hastings Communications and Entertainment Law Journal* 603 (2003).
Macrovision Corporation, *Preserving an Effective DVD Copy Protection System,* Mar. 3, 2003, available at http://www.macrovision.com/pdfs/Preserving-an-effective-DVD-Copying-System_0303.pdf (visited October 21, 2004).
Chad Woodford, "Trusted Computing or Big Brother? Putting the Rights Back in Digital Rights Management," 75 *University of Colorado Law Review* 253 (2004).

❖ ANONYMITY ❖

Most Internet users are concerned to some extent about privacy; they do not want all of the information they send or receive over the Internet to be connected to them by name. Paradoxically, the Internet makes anonymity both easier and more difficult. In one sense, all Internet communication, except perhaps live videoconferencing, is anonymous: There is no way to verify with absolute certainty the identity of any other user. A user can post product reviews on Amazon, send e-mails to the *Wall Street Journal,* create a Geocities page, and participate in a chat group—all under a fictitious name, or several fictitious names. (Technically, these communications are generally pseudonymous rather than anonymous, because some name is usually used, and used consistently.)

In another sense, however, anonymity on the Internet is impossible. Every Internet communication is recorded. Some, such as the Amazon review, can be matched with the user's actual name, or with the credit card to which the user's Amazon purchases have been billed. Others can be matched to the IP address of the computer from which the user sent the communication. Companies like Doubleclick, Inc. track users' Web surfing habits and add the information to their databases; sophisticated data-mining techniques are then used to match and collate this information. As databases grow and data-mining techniques improve, it might eventually become possible for data miners to see, complete with summaries, a report on everything about a particular user that has ever been transmitted over the Internet—every Web site that user has ever visited, every link that user has ever clicked, and every piece of information that user has ever uploaded or downloaded, or at least every visit, click, upload, and download that has involved that user's computer.

Most people find the implications of this loss of privacy alarming; as a result, there is widespread support for laws to protect privacy on the Internet, especially in highly sensitive areas such as medical and financial data. The protection of anonymity, however, gathers less support. Most users would probably prefer not to be identified to every Web site they visit; however, anonymity has also been abused, especially by spammers. Legislative attempts to limit anonymity, such as a Georgia statute requiring all users to correctly identify themselves when sending e-mail (O.C.G.A. § 16-9-93.1), have been aimed at spammers. But anonymous communication is protected by the First Amendment, so long as it is not used for fraud or other unlawful purposes; the Georgia statute was declared unconstitutional by a federal court (*Miller,* 977 F.Supp. 1228).

Although spammers are a nuisance, other abusers of anonymity are more sinister. Terrorists and child pornographers can use anonymity to conceal their identities and encryption to conceal their communications. Online file-sharers can avoid prosecution and lawsuits by concealing their identities—although not everyone finds this sinister. As a result, there has been pressure to enact laws targeting certain uses of anonymity. This has been linked to the pressure to regulate encryption, first through the failed Clipper Chip initiative and later through controls on the export of encryption technology and statutes, such as the Communications Assistance for Law Enforcement Act, which requires telecommunication providers to assist the government in conducting surveillance. Some people are willing to accept this and the enhanced powers granted by the USA PATRIOT Act to pierce Internet anonymity in order to combat terrorist threats. They might be alarmed, though, at the prospect of using legal and technological tools designed to control terrorism against twelve-year-old file-swappers. Businesses are not happy at the prospect of being forced to reveal their customers' identities, either; telecommunications companies have continued to protect users' anonymity against private, rather than governmental, interests, and the courts have agreed: In a December 2003 file-sharing case a federal appellate court held that Verizon Internet Services did not have to turn over the name of a subscriber to the Recording Industry Association of America, even though the subscriber had allegedly shared copyrighted music files (*Verizon,* 351 F.3d 1229).

As in many areas of Internet law, technology marches ahead of legislation. Advances in encryption technology make it easier for truly determined users to remain anonymous, and services like the popular Anonymizer.com make anonymity available to the less technically sophisticated.

Statutes
Federal
- Communications Assistance for Law Enforcement Act (CALEA) of 1994, Pub. L. No. 103-414, 108 Stat. 4279
- Uniting and Strengthening America by Providing Appropriate Tools Required to Intercept and Obstruct Terrorism Act (USA PATRIOT Act) of 2001, Pub. L. No. 107-56, 115 Stat. 272

State
- Official Code of Georgia Annotated § 16-9-93.1

Cases
Federal Appellate Court
- *Recording Industry Ass'n of America, Inc. v. Verizon Internet Services,* 351 F.3d 1229 (D.C. Cir. 2003)

Federal Trial Court
- *American Civil Liberties Union of Georgia v. Miller,* 977 F.Supp. 1228 (N.D. Ga. 1997)

See also: Cookies; Data Mining; DoubleClick; Encryption; Privacy

Sources and further reading:
Orin S. Kerr, "Internet Surveillance Law after the USA Patriot Act: The Big Brother that Isn't," 97 *Northwestern University Law Review* 607 (2003).
Tal Z. Zarsky, "Thinking outside the Box: Considering Transparency, Anonymity, and Pseudonymity as Overall Solutions to the Problems of Information Privacy in the Internet Society," 58 *University of Miami Law Review* 991 (2004).

❖ ANTICIRCUMVENTION PROVISIONS ❖

See Digital Millennium Copyright Act

❖ ANTICYBERSQUATTING CONSUMER PROTECTION ACT ❖

See Cybersquatting

❖ ANTITRUST ❖

See Microsoft Antitrust Litigation

❖ AUDIO HOME RECORDING ACT ❖

In the mid-1980s the music content industry, having battled unsuccessfully against analog cassette recorders, found itself facing a far greater threat: home digital recorders, which could make unlimited numbers of copies with no degradation in quality. The industry lobbied successfully for protective legislation; perhaps too successfully, because the Audio Home Recording Act (AHRA) that resulted may have killed off the relatively harmless recording format at which it was aimed and made possible the growth of other formats. Of course, market factors and technological progress might have brought about the same result even in the absence of the AHRA.

The Audio Home Recording Act was originally aimed at the digital audiotape (DAT) recorders then on the market and may have been instrumental in killing the DAT format; today DAT is used almost exclusively by music professionals and engineers. The AHRA attempts to control recording in two ways: through copy-control technology and through a royalty on recorders and tapes. The copy-control technology required by the AHRA for DAT recorders is a primitive form of electronic rights management: the serial copy management system (SCMS). SCMS-equipped recorders place an inaudible identifying code on copies they make and will not make copies from originals bearing that code. In other words, second-generation copying is impossible; copies can only be made from the master.

The AHRA provides that "No person shall import, manufacture, or distribute any digital audio recording device or digital audio interface device" that does not incorporate SCMS or an equivalent electronic rights management technology (17 U.S.C. § 1002(a)). This provision, unlike the royalty provisions, is by its terms portable to other recording devices and could be the reason that stand-alone CD recorders and the like have never caught on: The statute defines a "digital audio recording device" as one "designed or marketed for the primary purpose of, and that is capable of, making a digital audio copied recording for private use" (17 U.S.C. § 1001(3)). Computers are capable of making such recordings, but that is not the primary purpose for which they are marketed and designed; thus the statute does not cover computers, and the home computer has become the music-copying device most frequently used by consumers (see, e.g., *RIAA v. Diamond Multimedia*, 180 F.3d at 1078; *RIAA v. Napster,* 239 F.3d at 1024).

The royalty provisions of the AHRA may have done more than any other provision to kill the DAT format. The AHRA imposes a royalty—from the consumer's point of view, a tax—on digital audio recording equipment and media (17 U.S.C. § 1003). Digital audio recorders are taxed at 2 percent, with a maximum royalty of eight dollars and a minimum of one dollar; digital recording media are taxed at 3 percent (17 U.S.C. § 1004). The taxes, or royalties, are collected by the Copyright Office and distributed to existing music industry copyright owners. A "digital audio recording medium," according to the AHRA, "is any material object in a form commonly distributed for use by individuals, that is primarily marketed or most commonly used by consumers for the purpose of making digital audio copied recordings by use of a digital audio recording device" (17 U.S.C. § 1001(4)(A)). This definition would seem to exclude most recordable CDs and DVDs, and the statute further provides that the definition of digital recording media specifically excludes any medium "that is primarily marketed and most commonly used by consumers either for the purpose of making copies of motion pictures or other audiovisual works or for the purpose of making copies of nonmusical literary works, including computer programs or data bases" (17 U.S.C. § 1001(4)(B)(ii)).

The royalty provisions have been criticized both as a presumption of guilt and as a tax on aspiring musicians for the benefit of established ones (Smith 2001). The apparent presumption is that all persons who buy digital audio recorders and media are going to use them to pirate music, although in fact most will not; the innocent thus subsidize the guilty. And the tax is imposed on legitimate copiers, as well, including those who are making copies of their own music, to which they own the copyright.

Although the statute exempts "professional model products"—recorders that are "designed, manufactured, marketed, and intended for use by recording professionals in the ordinary course of a lawful business" (17 U.S.C. § 1001(10)), that exemption is more likely to protect the established, successful professional than the garage band. Professionals with steady incomes can afford professional equipment; teenagers trying to start a band have to make do with what they can afford with their more limited means, or more often with what's already around the house.

As music copying has moved from the old-fashioned stereo system to the computer, and from there to the Internet, the royalty and SCMS provisions of the AHRA have become increasingly irrelevant. The AHRA has had one lasting effect, though, that in contrast to the remainder of the statute is actually beneficial to the consumer. It provides that "No action may be brought under this title alleging infringement of copyright . . . based on the noncommercial use by a consumer of such a device or medium for making digital musical recordings or analog musical recordings" (17 U.S.C. § 1008). The right of consumers to make such recordings had previously been unclear; the AHRA provides an unequivocal immunity for private, noncommercial recordings, including recordings of broadcast music.

Statutes

- Audio Home Recording Act, 17 U.S.C. §§ 1001–1003, 1008
- Digital Performance Right in Sound Recordings Act, 17 U.S.C. 106(6)

Cases

- *A&M Records, Inc. v. Napster, Inc.,* 239 F.3d 1004 (9th Cir. 2001)
- *Recording Industry Association of America v. Diamond Multimedia Systems, Inc.,* 180 F.3d 1072 (9th Cir. 1999)

See also: Content Industry; Copyright; Digital Audio Works; Digital Performance Right in Sound Recordings Act; Digital Rights Management; File-Sharing

Sources and further reading:
Rachel Gader-Shafran, "Confessions of a Serial Infringer: Can the Audio Home Recording Act of 1992 Protect the Consumer from Copy-Protected CDs?" *Intellectual Property Law Newsletter,* Winter 2003, at 10.
Aaron L. Melville, "The Future of the Audio Home Recording Act of 1992: Has It Survived the Millennium Bug?" 7 *Boston University Journal of Science and Technology Law* 372 (2001).
Eric Smith, "The DAT Tax," 2001, available at http://www.brouhaha.com/~eric/bad_laws/dat_tax.html (visited October 19, 2004).

B

❖

❖ BACKUP COPIES ❖

It is not clear whether or to what extent consumers of a copyrighted work have the right to make at least one backup or archival copy of the work, so that they will still have access to the work if the original is damaged or destroyed. One view is that such a right was acknowledged by the decision in *Recording Industry Association of America v. Diamond Multimedia Systems,* which recognized the permissibility of copying for space-shifting purposes. On the other hand, "there is as yet no generally recognized right to make a copy of a protected work, regardless of its format, for personal noncommercial use" (*United States v. Elcom* 203 F.Supp.2d at 1135).

If such a general right exists, it would be an exception to the exclusive right to make or authorize copies granted to the copyright holder by 17 U.S.C. § 106(1). Any right to make backup copies is itself limited by other statutes. The anticircumvention provisions of the Digital Millennium Copyright Act effectively outlaw the making of backup copies of copy-protected works, especially DVDs. However, analog backup copies may still be made, although they will be inferior in quality to the original. Attempts by content-industry lobbyists to obtain legislation requiring all analog video recorders to be equipped with devices capable of recognizing, and perhaps refusing to copy, protected digital works might cut off this option in the future, though.

The right to make backup copies of computer programs is more definite. Such copies may be made provided "that such new copy or adaptation is for archival purposes only and that all archival copies are destroyed in the event

that continued possession of the computer program should cease to be rightful" (17 U.S.C. § 117(a)(2)). This right, too, has limits; although a consumer may be permitted to make backup copies of programs, the sale of devices capable of making such copies—but more likely to be used for copyright infringement—may be prohibited as contributory infringement (*Atari,* 747 F.2d 1422).

Title I of the Digital Millennium Copyright Act directed the National Telecommunications and Information Administration of the Department of Commerce (NTIA) to undertake a study of Section 117 and the making of backup copies of computer programs. The NTIA reported that the DMCA's protection of technological protective measures from circumvention might interfere with the making of archival copies authorized by section 117. A greater worry was that section 117 was out of date; it bore no relation to current practice. Most system administrators and many home users backed up their systems periodically by making a copy of everything on the system. This took time and storage media space, but required little human effort; the backup could be set to take place automatically at a time when no one needed to use the system. This process involved copying copyrighted material other than computer programs and was thus not authorized by section 117. However, it would be costly, time consuming, and inefficient to go through each file on a system and identify it as a program or nonprogram file before backing up the system. It would be even more costly, time consuming, and inefficient to go through each file on each tape backup and delete any program files for which a license might have expired. The report observed that "There is a fundamental mismatch between accepted, prudent practices among most system administrators and other users, on the one hand, and section 117 on the other. As a consequence, few adhere to the law" (NTIA Report 2001). While the NTIA found no harm as a result of this noncompliance, it was concerned about the mismatch between law and reality, and recommended that the law be amended to "create a new archival exemption that provides expressly that backup copies may not be distributed" (NTIA Report 2001). No such legislative action has yet been taken, however, and the mismatch persists.

Statutes
- Copyright Act of 1976, 17 U.S.C. §§ 106, 117
- Digital Millennium Copyright Act, 17 U.S.C. § 1201

Cases
Federal Appellate Courts
- *Atari v. JS & A*, 747 F.2d 1422 (Fed. Cir. 1984)
- *Recording Industry Association of America v. Diamond Multimedia Systems, Inc.*, 180 F.3d 1072 (9th Cir. 1999)

Federal Trial Courts
- *United States v. Elcom, Ltd.*, 203 F.Supp.2d 1111 (N.D. Cal. 2002)

Reports
- United States Copyright Office, DMCA Section 104 Report: A Report of the Register of Copyrights Pursuant to §104 of the Digital Millennium Copyright Act, August 2001
- United States Department of Commerce, National Telecommunications and Information Administration, DMCA Sections 109 and 117 Report, 2001, available at http://www.ntia.doc.gov/ntiahome/occ/dmca2001/104gdmca.htm (visited June 2, 2005).

See also: Analog Recording; Copyright; Copyright Infringement; Digital Millennium Copyright Act, Title I; Digital Rights Management; Fair Use (Copyright); First Sale

❖ BERNE CONVENTION ❖

The Berne Convention for the Protection of Literary and Artistic Works, an international copyright treaty, was adopted in 1886. Copyrights, like all intellectual property rights, are territorial in nature; they provide the holder of the right with a monopoly for a limited time and within the territory of the sovereign granting the right. In the days before the Berne Convention, states were under no general obligation to recognize within their own territories copyrights granted by other sovereigns. This meant that a book copyrighted in France or the United Kingdom could be, and often was, reproduced without permission and without payment of royalties in other countries, such as the United States. Writers and publishers of the nineteenth century found the situation unacceptable; colonialism had spread European languages around the world, so that the works of British, French, and Spanish authors found a ready market abroad, but those authors received few or no royalties from those overseas sales. To address this situation European writers under the leadership of Victor Hugo, the author of *The Hunchback of Notre Dame* and *Les Misérables,* founded the Association Littéraire et Artistique Internationale (ALAI) in 1878. A central purpose of the ALAI was the adoption of an international copyright convention; this purpose was achieved eight years later with the adoption of the Berne Convention (ALAI *History*).

Since its initial adoption, the Berne Convention has been modified, adjusted, revised, or otherwise revisited several times: in 1896, 1908, 1914, 1928, 1948, 1967, 1971, and 1979. The convention is nearly universal: 155 countries are parties. This universality was not achieved overnight, however; several major countries have become parties only recently, notably the United States in 1988, China in 1992, and Russia in 1995. (Neither the Soviet

The Berne Convention and other international treaties are sources of public international law; they create rights and obligations between nations rather than between individuals. They confer rights on national governments to have their citizens' copyrights respected by other national governments and obligations to enact or otherwise adopt—and subsequently enforce—copyright laws in conformity with the treaty. The extent to which governments have actually carried out these obligations varies considerably. For a look at the copyright laws of individual countries, a good place to start is the UNESCO Collection of National Copyright Laws, available online at http://portal.unesco.org/culture/en/ev.php-URL_ID=14076&URL_DO=DO_TOPIC&URL_SECTION=201.html. A look at the UNESCO Collection reveals that Mongolia, for example, has a copyright law that in some respects conforms more to the Universal Copyright Convention (UCC), to which it is not a party, than to the Berne Convention, to which it became a party in 1998. Laos, on the other hand, has reported to UNESCO that it has no copyright legislation at all, although it is a party to the 1955 UCC. Cambodia, another non-Berne party, has an apparently Berne-compliant copyright law dating from 2003, with exceptions to address issues of national concern, such as a compulsory license for "the translation of works from Khmer language into the languages of the ethnic minorities or vice versa." Anyone who finds it intriguing to learn that the copyright law of Qatar, for example, specifically provides for copyright protection in architectural works can find hours of entertainment in the UNESCO Collection.

Union nor the government of Taiwan, formerly recognized by the United States and many other countries as the government of China, had been parties to the convention.) New parties continue to be added: Syria became a party on June 11, 2004.

For more than a century after the adoption of the Berne Convention the United States was not a party, largely because U.S. copyright law diverged significantly from the Berne Convention norm. The growth of the (mostly preelectronic) global information economy during this time, however, made it increasingly desirable for the United States to secure foreign protection of its copyrights and to protect the copyrights of foreign authors within its territory. To this end, the United States entered into multiple bilateral copyright agreements and two major multilateral agreements, the Buenos Aires Convention in 1911 and the Universal Copyright Convention (U.C.C.) in 1955.

The Buenos Aires Convention governed copyright relations between the United States and most of the countries of Latin America until the early 1960s, at which point most of its members had become parties to the U.C.C., although Colombia only become a party in 1976, Bolivia in 1989, and Uruguay in 1993. Honduras never became a party to the U.C.C., but became a party to the Berne Convention in 1990. The Buenos Aires Convention, although still technically in force, is insignificant today, as all of its parties are now parties to the U.C.C., the Berne Convention, or both. It is chiefly of interest as the source of a historical oddity: It is the reason for the words *all rights reserved* almost invariably, and unnecessarily, included on copyrighted works published in the United States (including this one). These words were necessary to claim certain rights under the Buenos Aires Convention, but are unnecessary under either the U.C.C. or the Berne Convention.

The U.C.C. came into existence largely as a result of congressional failure to reform the Copyright Act of 1909. Inconsistencies between the 1909 act and the Berne Convention made it impossible for the United States to become a party to the Berne Convention; the U.C.C. was developed as an alternative. Because many of the states with which the United States wished to enter into agreement were already parties to the Berne Convention, the U.C.C. includes a Berne Safeguard Clause (U.C.C. 1971, art. XVII(1)). This clause provides that no country that is a party to the Berne Convention may denounce that convention and choose instead to rely on the U.C.C. in copyright matters relating to other parties to the Berne Convention.

Although ninety-eight states are now parties to the U.C.C., the United States and most other U.C.C. parties are also parties to the Berne Convention, so the U.C.C. is nearly as unimportant in modern practice as the Buenos Aires Convention. The U.C.C. does, however, continue to govern such copyright matters as exist between the United States and the countries that are parties to the U.C.C. but not to the Berne Convention: Cambodia and Laos. And like the Buenos Aires Convention before it, the U.C.C. has left its mark on copyright notices: The familiar "©" symbol on copyright notices is sufficient to satisfy U.C.C. registration requirements for works published outside the territory of the contracting state (U.C.C. 1971, art. III(1)).

Even as the Berne Convention achieves universality, it in turn is being either supplemented or supplanted by the World Intellectual Property Organization (WIPO) Copyright Treaty and the agreement on Trade-Related Aspects of Intellectual Property Rights (TRIPS). Forty-seven countries are parties to the WIPO Copyright Treaty, a special agreement within the meaning of Article 20 of the Berne Convention; the WIPO Copyright Treaty may be viewed as supplementing the Berne Convention. And all of the 147 members of the World Trade Organization (WTO) are parties to TRIPS, although for some developing countries its provisions have not yet fully come into effect. TRIPS may be viewed as an alternative approach, outside the WIPO framework, but this analysis is weakened by the near-universality of both treaties. About two dozen countries are parties to TRIPS but not to the Berne Convention; five countries are parties to Berne but not to TRIPS. Thirteen countries are parties to neither; many of these countries are very small (Nauru, Palau, San Marino), experiencing difficulties (Afghanistan, Somalia), recently emerged (East Timor), or subject to a combination of these factors.

The leisurely evolution of international copyright law for more than a century has been replaced by a sense of urgency. Content owners believe that a truly universal copyright regime is necessary to protect their rights. In the age of the Internet, countries once deemed unimportant because of their small size, linguistic or geographical isolation, or limited publishing industry now have the same potential to be sources of copyright violation as much larger countries. These previously ignored countries now have the potential to become havens for copyright infringement, and infringing material posted on servers in those countries can be accessed by users anywhere in the world.

The Berne Convention remains the world's most comprehensive copyright agreement. The central obligation it imposes on its parties is to provide national treatment: Each state that is a party to the convention will accord the same recognition of copyright in works authored by nationals of other parties that it would accord to works by its own nationals. Under the Berne Convention, copyright in any qualifying work is automatic; neither registration nor notice on the face of the document are required. The "©" symbol is not required, nor are the words *copyright* or *all rights reserved*.

Despite the alterations made to U.S. copyright law in order to allow the United States to join the Berne Convention, some differences persist. Article 2, for example, defines "literary and artistic works" covered under the convention as including

> every production in the literary, scientific and artistic domain, whatever may be the mode or form of its expression, such as books, pamphlets and other writings; lectures, addresses, sermons and other works of the same nature; dramatic or dramatico-musical works; choreographic works and entertainments in dumb show; musical compositions with or without words; cinematographic works to which are assimilated works expressed by a process analogous to cinematography; works of drawing, painting, architecture, sculpture, engraving and lithography; photographic works to which are assimilated works expressed by a process analogous to photography; works of applied art; illustrations, maps, plans, sketches and three-dimensional works relative to geography, topography, architecture or science. (Berne Convention, art. 2(1))

This definition is both less concise and possibly less comprehensive than the U.S. Copyright

Act's "original works of authorship fixed in any tangible medium of expression." The Copyright Act also includes a list of copyrightable subject matter that, again, is not coextensive with the Berne list. Works of authorship under the Copyright Act include:

(1) literary works;
(2) musical works, including any accompanying words;
(3) dramatic works, including any accompanying music;
(4) pantomimes and choreographic works;
(5) pictorial, graphic, and sculptural works;
(6) motion pictures and other audiovisual works;
(7) sound recordings; and
(8) architectural works. (17 U.S.C. § 102(a))

The Copyright Act's definition is open-ended. (Computer programs are specifically made copyrightable by section 117 of the act.) And unlike the convention, the Copyright Act requires fixation in a tangible medium. The Berne Convention, however, takes into account that among its parties, which include nearly all of the countries in the world, there may be differences; Article 2(2) provides that "countries of the Union [may] prescribe that works in general or any specified categories of works shall not be protected unless they have been fixed in some material form."

Article 3 of the convention provides that the convention protects not only nationals of the countries that are parties, but nationals of other countries that are not parties, if the works of those nationals are published in the territory of a party either prior to or simultaneously with publication outside the Union established by the Berne Convention, consisting of all the countries that are parties. This, during the time before the United States was not a party to the convention, gave rise to another oddity: simultaneous publication in Canada. There might, of course, be sound business reasons for publishing a book or other work simultaneously in the United States and Canada, rather than simply shipping copies of the book printed in the United States to Canada (or, in the case of Canadian books, vice versa). But in the six decades between 1928, when Canada became a party, and 1988, when the United States did, U.S. publishers who could afford to do so published simultaneously in the territory of a Berne Convention party, usually Canada, in order to secure international rights under the Berne Convention.

The point of greatest continuing divergence between the Berne Convention and U.S. law is in the area of moral rights, however. Moral rights, in copyright law, are the right not to have one's work mutilated or distorted, the right to be acknowledged as the author of the work, and the right to determine when and in what fashion the work shall be presented to the public. These rights are called, respectively, the rights of integrity, paternity, and disclosure.

U.S. law has historically been unreceptive to moral rights, both because copyright is viewed as a purely economic right and because of the potential for conflict with the First Amendment. In contrast, Article 6*bis* of the Berne Convention provides that "[i]ndependently of the author's economic rights, and even after the transfer of the said rights, the author shall have the right to claim authorship of the work and to object to any distortion, mutilation or other modification of, or other derogatory action in relation to, the said work, which would be prejudicial to his honor or reputation." The United States has enacted a moral rights statute, the Visual Artists Rights Act (VARA), but its coverage is less broad than the international norm (17 U.S.C. § 106A). Some states have also enacted moral rights statutes, some of them broader than VARA, but these may be preempted by VARA and the Copyright Act.

A major obstacle to U.S. adoption of the Berne Convention was the term of copyright protection. Article 7 of the convention provides minimum terms for various types of works; for most works by individual authors the minimum term is the lifetime of the author plus fifty years. The Copyright Act of 1976 brought U.S. law into compliance with this standard.

Article 8 gives authors the exclusive right to authorize and make translations. Article 9 gives them the core right of the bundle of rights described by the term *copyright:* the exclusive right to make or authorize reproductions of copyrighted work, subject to narrowly defined exceptions. This right is detailed in the following articles, and Article 10 describes one of the exceptions: "utilization . . . compatible with fair practice," or fair use.

The duration of copyright had been perhaps the biggest stumbling block to U.S. adoption of the Berne Convention, but other obstacles had to be removed, including U.S. notice and registration requirements. Article 15 of the convention provides that the only formality necessary for copyright protection is that the author's name or clearly identifiable pseudonym "appear on the work in the usual manner." If the pseudonym does not clearly identify the author, "the publisher whose name appears on the work shall, in the absence of proof to the contrary, be deemed to represent the author." And party states may, by domestic law, designate a competent authority to represent the rights of unknown authors (Berne Convention art. 15).

Article 16 of the convention provides for seizure of infringing copies of protected works. Article 20 permits the parties to "enter into special agreements among themselves" granting rights more extensive than those granted by the Berne Convention; the WIPO Copyright Treaty is one such agreement. In the early 1990s the countries of the European Union agreed to a longer term of copyright protection, and the United States followed suit, albeit without any formal agreement, with the Sonny Bono Copyright Term Extension Act in 1998.

Since 1967, the Berne Convention has been administered by WIPO. It is also linked to TRIPS: Members of the World Trade Organization are required by TRIPS to accept almost all of the conditions of the Berne Convention even if they are not already Berne Convention parties (TRIPS art. 9). Through TRIPS, the WTO's dispute resolution procedure may also provide a forum for actions to enforce portions of the Berne Convention. The United States found itself defending an action in this forum in 2000, albeit an action based on Berne Convention terms incorporated directly into TRIPS. The European Union claimed that the United States had violated Article 13 of TRIPS, which incorporates the Berne Convention's constraints on exceptions to exclusive rights under national law: "Members shall confine limitations and exceptions to exclusive rights to certain special cases which do not conflict with a normal exploitation of the work and do not unreasonably prejudice the legitimate interests of the rights holder." The WTO's dispute resolution body agreed with the European Union that U.S. law failed to provide adequate protection for copyright holders with regard to performance or display of nondramatic musical works. In other words, despite the continuing trend toward greater copyright protection and the shrinking of the fair use and other exceptions, U.S. law still provided less copyright protection in this area than the international standard.

Treaties
- Agreement on Trade-Related Aspects of Intellectual Property Rights (TRIPS), Marrakesh Agreement Establishing the World Trade Organization, Annex 1C, Apr. 15, 1994, 33 I.L.M. 81 (1994)
- Buenos Aires Convention, Aug. 20, 1910, 38 Stat. 1785, 155 L.N.T.S. 179
- Convention Concerning the Creation of an International Union for the Protection of Literary and Artistic Works (Berne Convention), Sept. 9, 1886, as last revised at Paris, July 24, 1971 (amended 1979), 25 U.S.T. 1341, 828 U.N.T.S. 221
- Universal Copyright Convention, Sept. 6, 1952, 6 U.S.T. 2731, revised at Paris July 24, 1971, 25 U.S.T. 1341
- WIPO Copyright Treaty, Dec. 20, 1996, 36 I.L.M. 65 (1997)
- WIPO Performance and Phonograms Treaty, Dec. 20, 1996, 36 I.L.M. 76 (1997)

European Union Directive
- Council Directive 93/98/EEC of 29 October 1993 Harmonizing the Term of Protection of Copyright and Certain Related Rights, 1993 O.J. (L 290) 9

WTO Case
- Report of the WTO Panel, United States: Section 110(5) of the U.S. Copyright Act, WT/DS160/R, June 15, 2000

Statutes

- Copyright Act of 1976, 17 U.S.C. §§ 101-1332
- Sonny Bono Copyright Term Extension Act, Pub. L. 105-298, 112 Stat. 2827 (1998)
- Visual Artists Rights Act, 17 U.S.C. § 106A

See also: Copyright; Copyright Infringement; Digital Millennium Copyright Act, Title I; International Copyright Protection; Moral Rights; Public Domain; Sonny Bono Copyright Term Extension Act; TRIPS (Copyright); Universal Copyright Convention; WIPO; WIPO Copyright Treaty; WIPO Performances and Phonograms Treaty

Sources and further reading:

Association Littéraire et Artistique Internationale, *History,* n.d., http://www.alai.org/index-a. php?ch=pubAcc-historique-a&sm=1 (visited November 18, 2004).

Anthony D'Amato and Doris Estelle Long, eds., *International Intellectual Property Anthology* (Cincinnati, OH: Anderson Publishing, 1996).

Paul Goldstein, *International Copyright: Principles, Law, and Practice* (Oxford: Oxford University Press, 2000).

Makeen Fouad Makeen, *Copyright in a Global Information Society: The Scope of Copyright Protection under International, US, UK, and French Law* (New York: Aspen, 2001).

Sam Ricketson, *The Berne Convention for the Protection of Literary and Artistic Works: 1886–1986* (London: Centre for Commercial Law Studies, Queen Mary College, 1987).

Susan K. Sell, *Private Power, Public Law: The Globalization of Intellectual Property Rights* (Cambridge, UK: Cambridge University Press, 2003).

Martin Senftleben, *Copyright, Limitations and the Three-Step Test: An Analysis of the Three-Step Test in International and EC Copyright Law* (New York: Aspen, 2004).

❖ BLOCKING AND FILTERING SOFTWARE ❖

See Children's Internet Protection Act

❖ BROADBAND ❖

Broadband Internet access is Internet access at a higher speed than the maximum speed available through a dial-up connection, 56,000 bits per second. In general the term *broadband* is reserved for access at a speed of 512,000 bits per second or higher. Broadband access is available through dedicated Internet lines, as well as through existing telephone and cable lines. Existing telephone lines can be used to provide digital subscriber line (DSL) broadband access; existing cable television lines can be used for Internet access via a cable modem. From the point of view of most consumers, DSL and cable modem broadband access, the two most popular forms of broadband access, are roughly equivalent. The Federal Communications Commission (FCC), however, treats cable and telephone lines differently; consequently, the two forms of broadband access also receive different regulatory treatment. Wireless broadband is also growing in popularity. In 2003 the tiny island territory of Niue became the first self-governing territory to offer free, universal wireless broadband access. (Niue is internally self-governing, but New Zealand is responsible for its foreign affairs and defense [Turner, 1214–1215].) Several U.S. cities are also considering plans to provide city-wide wireless broadband (Wireless Philadelphia, n.d.).

The disparate regulatory treatment of cable and DSL broadband services has given rise to controversy; the greater popularity and availability of cable modem services has been blamed on regulatory obstacles placed in the path of DSL operators, and the FCC has been criticized for encouraging the unnecessary development of parallel infrastructure rather than guaranteeing competitive access to that infrastructure (Hundt 2004, 239). The FCC regulatory framework provides for different treatment of three categories of information transmission services: information services, cable services, and telecommunications services. In 2000 the Court of Appeals for the Ninth Circuit had held, in *AT&T Corp. v. City of Portland,* that cable broadband service is not a "cable service" within the meaning of the Communications Act; this prevented local governments from regulating

Broadband over Power Lines (BPL) sounds almost too good to be true. It promises high bandwidth Internet access without the disadvantages of cable or DSL: The speed of access will not decrease with the number of users or the distance from a telephone exchange, and uploads will be faster than downloads. The potential bandwidth is higher, making high-quality Internet video possible. And best of all, the infrastructure is already in place: Power lines already run to nearly every room in nearly every building in the developed world, and much of the developing world as well.

BPL providers could also give cable-Internet providers the much-needed competition that DSL has for the most part failed to provide. To encourage this competition, the Federal Communications Commission (FCC) has ruled that power utility companies may operate as unlicensed entities, free of most FCC telecommunications rules other than those regarding radio interference.

As with cable and DSL, the problem area for BPL is the last mile: Data cannot be transmitted through the step-down transformer between the power grid and the consumer's home. The transformer must be bypassed, either with a wireless transmitter or a physical bypass device. The wireless solution is cheaper and simpler but, like all wireless connections, raises security concerns. It has been successfully tested in North America and Europe, however; in Cincinatti, Ohio, 15,000 users already have BPL Internet connections.

Source

"Plugging in, at Last," *The Economist Technology Quarterly*, Dec. 4, 2004, at 3.

4819). The FCC's ruling resulted in challenges raised by at least seven petitions in federal courts. The challenges raised several objections, not so much to the classification of cable modem services alone, but to the disparate treatment of cable and DSL services. The various petitions urged that cable modem service should have received a dual classification as either an information service and a cable service or as an information service and a telecommunications service, or that DSL service should also have been classified as an information service (345 F.3d at 1127). The various petitions were brought together before the Ninth Circuit Court of Appeals in *Brand X Internet Services v. FCC*, in which the Ninth Circuit upheld the FCC's ruling classifying cable modem services as information services, but vacated the portion of the ruling stating that cable modem services were not also telecommunication services (345 F.3d at 1132). In June 2005 the Supreme Court reversed the Ninth Circuit's decision and remanded the case for further proceedings (125 S.Ct. 2688).

The regulatory climate in which broadband services operate is still uncertain. *Brand X* does not seem to be a final resolution of the issue; the battle for equal regulatory treatment of cable modem and DSL services and for competitive access to those company's lines—the "last mile" to the consumer's home or office—has not yet ended.

Statute

- Telecommunications Act of 1996, 47 U.S.C. § 151 et seq.

Cases

- *AT&T Corp. v. City of Portland*, 216 F.3d 871 (9th Cir. 2000)
- *Brand X Internet Services v. FCC*, 345 F.3d 1120 (9th Cir. 2003), reversed sub nom. *National Cable and Telecommunications Association v. Brand X Internet Services*, 125 S.Ct. 2688 (2005)

Agency Decision

- *In re Inquiry Concerning High-Speed Access to the Internet over Cable and*

cable modem services through their franchising authority (216 F.3d at 871), greatly liberalizing the market for cable modem services and contributing to the growth of the industry. In 2002 the FCC ruled that cable modem services were information services, not cable services or telecommunications services (17 F.C.C.R. at

Other Facilities, 17 F.C.C.R. 4798, 2002 WL 407567 (2002)

See also: Cable; Federal Communications Commission; Federal Trade Commission

Sources and further reading:
Christian R. Eriksen, "Cable Broadband: Did the Ninth Circuit Beat the FCC to the Punch in Last Mile Regulation?" 6 *Tulane Journal of Technology and Intellectual Property* 283 (2004).

Reed Hundt, "The Ineluctable Modality of Broadband," 21 *Yale Journal on Regulation* 239 (2004).

Mark A. Lemley and Lawrence Lessig, "The End of End-to-End: Preserving the Architecture of the Internet in the Broadband Era," 48 *UCLA Law Review* 925 (2001).

Kim Maxwell, *Residential Broadband: An Insider's Guide to the Battle for the Last Mile* (New York: John Wiley and Sons, 1998).

"Polynesians Get Free Wireless Web," BBC News, June 26, 2003, available at http://news.bbc.co.uk/1/hi/technology/3020158.stm.

Roderick W. Smith, *Broadband Internet Connections: A User's Guide to DSL and Cable* (Boston: Addison-Wesley Publishing Company, 2002).

James B. Speta, "Handicapping the Race for the Last Mile? A Critique of open Access Rules for Broadband Platforms," 17 *Yale Journal on Regulation* 39 (2000).

Barry Turner, ed., *The Statesman's Yearbook: The Politics, Cultures and Economies of the World,* 139th ed. (Houndmills, Basingstoke, UK: Palgrave, 2001).

Wireless Philadelphia Executive Committee, *A 21st Century Opportunity,* available at http://www.phila.gov/wireless/briefing.html (visited October 12, 2004).

❖ BUDAPEST OPEN ACCESS INITIATIVE ❖

Academic articles, as original works of authorship fixed in a tangible medium of expression, are protected by copyright, yet the copyright in these articles is generally of little or no monetary value. The authors publish the articles for the purpose of sharing the results of their research with other scholars; they receive no payment for the articles. Locating the copyright holder for an academic article is not always easy; in the case of a deceased copyright holder or an institution that no longer exists, it can be nearly impossible. The right holder might be the author, the journal in which the work was published, the university or university press that published it, the university or other institution that employed the author at the time the article was written, the foundation or other donor that provided a grant that made the article possible, or some other person. Even when the copyright holder can be located, permission to reprint may be unavailable; a small academic journal may arbitrarily refuse permission to reprint part of a work or may demand an unrealistic fee.

In theory the Internet should simplify increased sharing of academic work. Yet often attempts to reprint or otherwise share academic work founder—even when the author wants the work to be shared—because of the complexities of copyright law. A system designed to protect valuable property rights in books, movies, songs, and other commercial works is overkill when applied to works written for free and published to an audience of a few hundred readers.

One attempt to address this problem is the Budapest Open Access Initiative. The Open Society Institute (OSI) created the Budapest Open Access Initiative in 2002. The Initiative grew out of OSI's December 2001 meeting in Budapest, thus its name; OSI is the central administrative entity of the Soros Foundations network. The initiative's goal is, as the title implies, open access: "free and unrestricted availability" of works that "scholars give to the world without expectation of payment." This goal is to be achieved by two mechanisms: open-access journals and self-archiving.

Open-access journals are journals that do not "invoke copyright to restrict access. . . . Instead they will use copyright and other tools to ensure permanent open access to all the articles they publish. Because price is a barrier to access, these new journals will not charge subscription or access fees" (Budapest Open Access Initiative 2002). This does not mean that the journals will not restrict their content; the journals will apply their own peer review or other standards in deciding what to publish.

Self-archiving is the depositing of articles in open-access electronic archives. The goal of the initiative is to preserve the author's moral rights of integrity and paternity while taking away the economic right to control reproduction of the material:

> There are many degrees and kinds of wider and easier access to this literature. By "open access" to this literature, we mean its free availability on the public internet, permitting any users to read, download, copy, distribute, print, search, or link to the *full texts* of these articles, crawl them for indexing, pass them as data to software, or use them for any other lawful purpose, without financial, legal, or technical barriers other than those inseparable from gaining access to the internet itself. The only constraint on reproduction and distribution, and the only role for copyright in this domain, should be to give authors control over the integrity of their work and the right to be properly acknowledged and cited. (Budapest Open Access Initiative 2002)

Although this makes sense in the context of academic articles, where the economic rights are in most cases worth nothing and the main incentive for authors, other than sharing knowledge, is to enhance their reputations, it does not reflect current U.S. copyright law. Instead of seeking to effect change through legislation, the initiative seeks a voluntary change on the part of academic journals and authors; they are called upon to opt out of the protection guaranteed them under copyright law, in the interest of making their work and other academic work more widely available.

Initiative
- Budapest Open Access Initiative, Feb. 14, 2002, available at http://www. soros.org/openaccess/read.shtml (visited October 4, 2004)

See also: Copyright

❖ BUENOS AIRES CONVENTION ❖

See Berne Convention; Copyright

❖ BUSINESS METHODS PATENT ❖

A business methods patent is, as the name states, a patent on a method of doing business; it grants a right to the patent holder to exclude others from using a particular method of doing business. Historically courts rejected the idea that business methods were patentable (*Hotel Security Checking,* 160 F. at 469). This changed in 1998 with the decision in *State Street Bank & Trust v. Signature Financial Group.* The *State Street* court held that an invention did not become unpatentable merely because it was a business method (149 F.3d at 1375). The years since *State Street* have seen the granting of many business methods patents, some of which have become objects of ridicule and have been held up as examples of the United States Patent Office's apparent abandonment of the requirements of novelty and nonobviousness.

Among the most famous business methods patents is Amazon.com's patent on one-click ordering, issued in 1999. During the 1999 Christmas shopping season, Amazon succeeded in obtaining an injunction prohibiting a competitor, Barnes & Noble, from using one-click ordering on its Web site (239 F.3d 1343).

State Street raised fears, especially among small businesses, that someone else might succeed in obtaining a patent on a method that the small business had been using all along. The small business would then be faced with costly patent litigation to establish that the patent should not have been granted in the first place. In 1999, as Amazon was pursuing an injunction against Barnes & Noble, Congress enacted the First Inventor Defense Act (FIDA). The FIDA provides that:

> It shall be a defense to an action for [patent] infringement . . . with respect to any subject matter that would otherwise infringe one or more claims for a method in the patent being asserted against a person, if such person had, acting in good faith, actually reduced the subject matter to practice at least 1 year before the effective filing date of such patent, and commercially used the subject matter before the effective filing date of such patent. (35 U.S.C. § 273)

In other words, a business that could show that it had reduced a method to practice a year before the filing date and had begun to use the method at some point before the filing date was protected from liability for patent infringement. *Reduction to practice* is a term of art in patent law that refers either to the filing of a patent application (constructive reduction to practice) or to the construction of an apparatus or carrying out of steps necessary for the invention; a trial run or set-up of the business method might satisfy this requirement. Of course, anyone actually using a method for at least a year would be protected; those who had used it for less than a year would have to demonstrate that they had taken the necessary steps to reduce the idea to practice at least a year earlier.

The recent change in U.S. law regarding business method patents, like the somewhat less recent change regarding the patentability of computer programs, has resulted in inconsistencies between U.S. law and the law of other countries. The European Patent Convention, for example, provides that "schemes, rules and methods for . . . doing business, and programs for computers" are not patentable subject matter (European Patent Convention, art. 52(2)(c)). On the other hand, the Agreement on Trade-Related Aspects of Intellectual Property Rights (TRIPS) provides that "patents shall be available for any inventions, whether products or processes, in all fields of technology," with certain exceptions, for at least "a period of twenty years counted from the filing date" (TRIPS arts. 27, 33). This has been interpreted as requiring parties to TRIPS to issue business methods patents. It remains to be seen whether TRIPS and the changes in U.S. law on this subject herald a worldwide change, or whether the inconsistency will persist; it seems unlikely, however, that the United States will return to a patent regime in which business methods are not patentable subject matter.

Treaties
- Agreement on Trade-Related Aspects of Intellectual Property Rights, Marrakesh Agreement Establishing the World Trade Organization, Annex 1C, Apr. 15, 1994, 33 I.L.M. 81 (1994)
- Convention on the Grant of European Patents, 5 Oct. 1973, 13 I.L.M. 276, text as amended through Dec. 10, 1998, available at http://www.european-patent-office.org/legal/epc/e/ma1.html (visited October 20, 2004) [European Patent Convention]

Statute
- First Inventor Defense Act, 35 U.S.C. § 273

Cases
- *Amazon.com, Inc. v. Barnesandnoble.com, Inc.,* 239 F.3d 1343 (Fed. Cir. 2001)
- *Hotel Security Checking Co. v. Lorraine Co.,* 160 F.467 (2d Cir. 1908)
- *State Street Bank & Trust v. Signature Financial Group, Inc.,* 149 F.3d 1368 (Fed. Cir. 1998)

See also: Computer Program; Patent; TRIPS (Patent)

Sources and further reading:
Matthew G. Wells, "Internet Business Method Patent Policy," 87 *Virginia Law Review* 729 (2001).

C

❖ CABLE ❖

Broadband Internet access can be provided to homes and businesses over special lines dedicated to the purpose, or much more cheaply over existing telephone or cable television lines. For home users the cost of a dedicated broadband connection other than a telephone or cable connection is almost always too high to be worthwhile, although the increasing availability of wireless broadband could change this, as could new technologies such as broadband over power lines. At present, though, telephone and cable television companies compete for the home broadband market. To date the cable television industry has proved more adept at reaching and exploiting this market.

Cable lines, like telephone lines, are owned by a relatively small number of companies. Typically homes will have access to the lines of only one cable company and one telephone company; the use of these lines for broadband Internet access provided these companies with a potential monopoly, or at least a potential local duopoly, on the provision of broadband access. Telephone companies have been compelled to allow other broadband services access to their lines. Local governments have attempted to impose similar requirements on cable broadband providers as a condition of granting a cable franchise. However, in 2000 the Court of Appeals for the Ninth Circuit held, in *AT&T Corporation v. City of Portland*, that cable broadband service is not a "cable service" within the meaning of the Communications Act and thus may not be regulated by local governments through their franchising authority (*AT&T*, 216 F.3d 871). The Federal Communications Commission (FCC) subse-quently classified cable broadband services as information services and not cable services or telecommunications services. Three years later a divided three-judge panel of the same court, in three separate opinions, vacated that part of the FCC's ruling, stating that cable modem services were not also telecommunications services; the court felt itself to be bound by its earlier decision (*Brand X*, 345 F.3d at 1132); the panel's decision, however, was later reversed by the Supreme Court (*National Cable*, 125 S.Ct. 2688).

The FCC continues to review the competitive situation to determine whether cable companies, like telephone companies, should be compelled to share their lines with competitors. For the time being the FCC seems less willing to enforce sharing of cable lines than sharing of telephone lines. The current regulatory structure seems unstable at best, and further change seems likely.

Statute
- Telecommunications Act of 1996, 47 U.S.C. § 151 et seq.

Cases
- *AT&T Corp. v. City of Portland*, 216 F.3d 871 (9th Cir. 2000)
- *Brand X Internet Services v. FCC*, 345 F.3d 1120 (9th Cir. 2003), reversed sub nom. *National Cable and Telecommunications Association v. Brand X Internet Services*, 125 S.Ct. 2688 (2005)

See also: Broadband; Federal Communications Commission; Internet

Sources and further reading:

Mark Robichaux, *Cable Cowboy: John Malone and the Rise of the Modern Cable Business* (New York: John Wiley & Sons, 2002).

Steven Semeraro, "The Antitrust-Telecom Connection," 40 *San Diego Law Review* 555 (2003).

Roderick W. Smith, *Broadband Internet Connections: A User's Guide to DSL and Cable* (Boston: Addison-Wesley Publishing Company, 2002).

Phil Weiser, "Paradigm Changes in Telecommunications Regulation," 71 *University of Colorado Law Review* 819 (2000).

Tim Wu, "Network Neutrality, Broadband Discrimination," 2 *Journal on Telecommunications and High Technology Law* 141 (2003).

❖ CAN-SPAM ACT ❖

See Spam

❖ CENSORSHIP ❖

Censorship is the act or process of inspecting expressive content, such as books, movies, recorded music, or Web pages, and deleting or restricting access to material deemed offensive by the person or organization doing the inspecting. The Internet provides new problems for censorship because of its international nature, the ease with which it provides children as well as adults with access to information, the widespread availability of encryption technology, and the quantity of information exchanged. The law of the United States and of the individual states, in accordance with the First and Fourteenth Amendments to the U.S. Constitution, severely restricts the censorship powers of governments.

State action: The First Amendment protects against censorship by the government and not ordinarily against censorship by private parties; state action, rather than private action, is the target of the amendment. It is perfectly legal, for instance, for a private Internet service provider (ISP) such as America Online to block certain mass-mailed e-mail messages, even if it would be impermissible for the government to do so; America Online's action is not state action (*America Online*, 948 F.Supp. 456).

Testing the limits: In 2004 a Web site called Re-code.com chose an unusual way to test the limits of freedom of expression. The site offered not endorsements of terrorism, instructions on how to make chemical weapons, pornography, or MP3s, but something perhaps even more subversive: product bar codes. Re-code, conceived as a prank, offered a database of UPC product codes that users could print as stickers—and, perhaps, stick over the UPC codes on products in stores. This might allow the users to buy those products at a lower price, although doing so would be illegal. Merely providing the bar codes was sufficient to alarm retailers, however, and Re-code's Web site no longer offers them. Instead, it currently announces "The site is temporarily down while we decide how to deal with the latest threat from WalMart attorneys."

Source

Re-code.com Web site, www.re-code.com (visited January 8, 2005).

Three distinct tests are used in determining whether acts by private parties can be classified as state action for First Amendment purposes: the exclusive public function test, the state-assisted action test, and the joint participant test. The exclusive public function test looks at whether the private entity has exercised powers that are traditionally the exclusive prerogative of the state. The state-assisted action test looks at whether the private entity has acted with the help of or in concert with state officials. The joint participant test looks at whether the state has insinuated itself so far into a position of interdependence with the private entity that the state must be recognized as a joint participant in the challenged activity. If the answer to any one of these three questions is "yes," there is state action (*America Online*, 948 F.Supp. 456).

Strict scrutiny for broad content-based prohibitions: Governments or state actors may impose broad content-based restrictions upon expression only in certain narrowly defined situations; most such restrictions are subject to strict constitutional scrutiny. Governments may impose such restrictions when doing so is necessary to achieve a compelling state interest. This interest must be unrelated to the message being communicated; in other words, a government's interest in preventing a message from being heard is not in itself sufficient basis for restricting that message. The means chosen to restrict the expression must also be the least restrictive alternative available (*Reno v. ACLU*, 521 U.S. 844).

Less-scrutinized restrictions: Non-content-based restrictions on the time, place, and manner in which expression is permitted must be narrowly tailored to further an important or significant government interest; such restrictions are generally constitutionally permissible unless they unduly constrict the flow of free speech.

Certain types of content-based restrictions are likely to be constitutionally permissible. Governments may prohibit expression such as shouting "Fire!" in a crowded theater, as well as speech that is intended to create a likelihood of imminent violence. Speech or expression may form an element of certain crimes—conspiracy and solicitation, for example—and thus may be prohibited. Defamation and invasion of privacy may be prohibited or made the basis for civil liability, although the scope of this exception is limited when public figures or public officials are involved. The right to duplicate and distribute the expressions of others may be limited by intellectual property rights, particularly copyright. And obscenity, discussed in more detail under the subheading "Pornography" in this entry and in the section of this encyclopedia titled "Obscenity," may be prohibited (*Miller*, 413 U.S. 15).

Broadcast media are traditionally entitled to a lower level of protection than print media, because of the government's role in allocating broadcast frequencies and the limited number of such frequencies available. Courts have held, however, that the Internet is not a broadcast medium and is thus entitled to the highest level of First Amendment protection (*Reno v. ACLU*, 521 U.S. 844). Commercial speech (speech that proposes a commercial transaction) is afforded protection under the First Amendment, although it may be subject to time, place, and manner restrictions, and may be prohibited if it is untruthful, misleading, or deceptive or if its subject matter or presentation is illegal.

Special problems for the Internet: The two categories of online speech that have been the subject of the greatest number of private and governmental attempts at censorship are pornography and mass e-mail advertising. Free speech that may undermine copyright protections, such as the publishing of encryption/decryption code, is also an Internet-related problem.

Pornography: The term *pornography* covers a variety of sexually explicit material, some of it protected by the First Amendment and some, including child pornography and obscenity, not protected. Although the First Amendment's protection does not extend to obscenity, the term *obscenity* is difficult to define. After wrestling with the problem for some time, the Supreme Court in *Miller v. California* set down the definition that is generally used in U.S. law. Under the *Miller* test, material is obscene if (a) "the average person, applying contemporary community standards would find that the work taken as a whole appeals to the prurient interest"; (b) "the work depicts or describes, in a patently offensive way, sexual conduct specifically defined by the applicable state law; and" (c) "the work, taken as a whole, lacks serious literary, artistic, political, or scientific value" (413 U.S. at 39).

Child pornography involving images of actual children is banned even if it does not meet all three prongs of the *Miller* test, because it is a record of the actual sexual abuse of children and the government has a compelling interest in preventing such abuse (*Ferber*, 458 U.S. 747).

Material that is not obscenity or child pornography may not be banned outright merely on the basis of indecency or offensiveness; much pornographic material is thus protected. The extent to which access to pornographic material may be restricted or controlled has been the subject of much congressional activity and subsequent litigation.

Access by minors: It is permissible for governments to control minors' access to some material that is permissible for adults. In the pre-Internet era the access of minors to sexually explicit material could be controlled at the point of sale, by verifying the age of the purchaser. On the Internet it is impossible to determine the age of any user with certainty; any child who can read can access any portion of the Internet accessible to adults. The U.S. legal system has not yet found an effective way to deal with this problem. Statutes enacted by Congress to restrict the access of minors to some Internet content, such as the Child Online Protection Act and the Communications Decency Act of 1996, have been struck down by the Supreme Court on constitutional grounds. Among other flaws, they impermissibly restricted the access of adults to information (*Reno v. ACLU*, 521 U.S. 844).

Software solutions: In the absence of an effective legal solution to the problem of the accessibility of Internet pornography to minors, market-based solutions have emerged. Many filtering programs are available. Although the constitutionality of the required use of these programs by schools and public libraries has been heavily litigated and has not yet been resolved with any degree of finality, filtering programs can be and are used on home computers. However, such programs are a less-than-perfect solution for several reasons. They tend to miss some sites, especially foreign-language sites, containing content that the purchasers of the programs would undoubtedly deem offensive. They also err in the other direction and screen many sites with innocuous content. Finally, they rely to a great degree on the willingness of the child using the computer to comply with the restrictions. Many children are more technologically adept than their parents and can circumvent the programs if they are determined to do so. Even if they are unable to do so, they have the option of using another computer.

International communication: From a U.S. perspective, the international nature of the Internet presents two distinct censorship problems. One is that content that is illegal under U.S. law or the law of a state or local government within the United States might be legal in a foreign country. There is no practical way for a local government to restrict its inhabitants' access to the illegal content (see *Reno v. ACLU*, 521 U.S. at 878 n. 45). It would be difficult for the national government to do so, and such restriction would probably require the blocking of all or most content from that foreign country; this in turn presents constitutional prob-

lems because it restricts the access of persons in the United States to non-prohibited information. In addition, other countries that have tried such draconian measures have found them to be of only limited effectiveness; clever users easily find ways to circumvent the controls. A second problem is that content that is legal in the United States—the advertising for sale of Nazi memorabilia, for example—might be illegal in another country, such as France. United States Web publishers may thus unwittingly violate the laws of other countries, risking civil sanctions and even criminal prosecution (*Yahoo!*, 169 F.Supp.2d 1181).

Encryption: The widespread availability of encryption technology poses additional problems. Users can exchange encrypted files over the Internet; even if the communication is being monitored, those monitoring it will have no means to determine whether the encrypted file contains illegal obscene materials, legal but highly confidential corporate secrets, or a collection of recipes. Although breaking the encryption is usually possible, it is time consuming and thus expensive.

Too much information: Finally, the sheer volume of information exchanged on the Internet makes universal monitoring impossible, and thus censorship is a hit-or-miss affair. To some extent this also is being addressed with software, which can be instructed to search for particular types of content. But any time savings gained through the use of such software is offset by the use of encryption.

The state of Internet censorship today: First Amendment advocates continue to battle with opponents of pornography in a struggle that is ultimately without resolution because it pits widely held and incompatible sets of values against each other. The struggle to protect spam, or unsolicited commercial e-mail, is a lonelier one; unsolicited commercial advertising is almost universally detested, while civil liberties advocacy groups may prefer to devote their resources to the defense of noncommercial speech. In December 2003 the U.S. Congress enacted anti-spam legislation, authorizing the Federal Trade Commission (FTC) to create a "do not spam" registry similar to the widely popular anti-telemarketing "do not call" registry. The FTC has so far declined to do so, pointing out that although such an action might withstand the constitutional scrutiny given to restrictions on commercial speech, it is also likely to prove futile. Unlike telemarketers, spammers incur no cost savings by sending their messages from within the United States; the sources of spam will simply move outside the country's borders. Only action against the companies whose products and services are advertised by spam, rather than against spammers, is likely to prove effective, and even then only against companies with a presence in the United States.

At this point serious attempts to censor the Internet are focused on a few areas: Governments aggressively pursue and prosecute child pornographers and consumers of child pornography (see 18 U.S.C. §§2251–2260); the wider campaign against pornography as a whole, though, must be regarded as lost, or at least abandoned for the time being. In response to consumer outrage, governments are now, as Internet service providers have been doing for some time, taking actions to restrict the activities of spammers (bulk e-mail advertisers). And speech that creates a private right of action, such as defamation, invasion of privacy, the commercial appropriation of one's name or likeness, or infringement of an intellectual property right, may be the subject of lawsuits brought by the individuals affected.

Statutes
- CAN-SPAM Act of 2003, 15 U.S.C. §§ 7701–7713
- Child Online Protection Act, 47 U.S.C. § 231
- Child Pornography Prevention Act of 1996, 18 U.S.C. §§2251–2260
- Children's Internet Protection Act, 47 U.S.C. § 254(h)
- Communications Decency Act of 1996, Pub. L. No. 104–104, § 502, 1996 U.S.S.C.A.N. (110 Stat.) 56,133 (later codified at 47 U.S.C. § 223)

Cases
Supreme Court
- *Ashcroft v. American Civil Liberties Union*, 124 S. Ct. 2783 (2004)

- *Brandenburg v. Ohio*, 395 U.S. 444 (1969)
- *Miller v. California*, 413 U.S. 15 (1973)
- *New York v. Ferber*, 458 U.S. 747 (1982)
- *Reno v. American Civil Liberties Union*, 521 U.S. 844 (1997)
- *United States v. American Library Association, Inc.*, 539 U.S. 194 (2003)

Federal Appellate Courts
- *Yahoo!, Inc. v. La Ligue Contre le Racisme et L'Antisemitisme*, 169 F.Supp.2d 1181 (N.D. Cal. 2001), reversed by *Yahoo! Inc. v. La Ligue Contre Le Racisme et L'Antisemitisme*, 379 F.3d 1120 (9th Cir. 2004)

Federal Trial Courts
- *America Online v. Cyber Promotions*, 948 F.Supp. 456 (E.D. Pa. 1996)
- *Mainstream Loudoun v. Board of Trustees of the Loudoun County Library*, 2 F.Supp.2d 783 (E.D. Va. 1998)

See also: Activism and Advocacy Groups; Child Online Protection Act; Child pornography; Children's Internet Protection Act; Communications Decency Act; Data Haven; Declaration of the Independence of Cyberspace; DeCSS; Defamation; Encryption; First Amendment; French Yahoo! Case; Indecency; Obscenity; Pornography; Spam

Sources and further reading:
Terry Gillespie, "Virtual Violence? Pornography and Violence against Women on the Internet," in *Women, Violence and Strategies for Action*, Jill Radford et al., eds. (Buckingham, UK: Open University Press, 2000).
Mike Godwin, *Cyber Rights: Defending Free Speech in the Digital Age* (Cambridge, MA: MIT Press, 2003).
Tim Jordan, *Cyberpower: The Culture and Politics of Cyberspace and the Internet* (New York: Routledge, 1999).
Kathryn Kolbert and Zak Mettger, eds., *Justice Talking: Censoring the Web: Leading Advocates Debate Today's Most Controversial Issues* (New York: The New Press, 2002).
Lawrence Lessig, *The Future of Ideas* (New York: Random House, 2001).

Jeremy Lipschultz, *Free Expression in the Age of the Internet: Social and Legal Boundaries* (Boulder, CO: Perseus Books, 1999).

Kevin W. Saunders, *Saving Our Children from the First Amendment* (New York: New York University Press, 2004).

Madeleine Schachter, *Law of Internet Speech,* 2d ed. (Durham, NC: Carolina Academic Press, 2002).

Sources and further reading:

Frank Mosuch and Susan B. Hillson, "Technical Security Measures," in Kevin P. Cronin and Ronald N. Weikers, eds., *Data Security and Privacy Law: Combating Cyberthreats* (St. Paul, MN: West, 2004).

❖ CERTIFICATE ❖

Digital certificates can be used to establish the identity of persons doing business over the Internet. The certificate is issued by a trusted third party, known as a certification authority, and includes the name of the party to whom it is issued along with a serial number, an expiration date, and the party's public encryption key and digital signature. Digital certificates commonly use some form of the X.509 standard; because the standard is informal rather than formally defined and approved, implementations of the standard may differ. The simplest way for companies to avoid difficulties in verifying certificates is to use a third-party verification authority, such as VeriSign, Inc. (Mosuch and Hillson 2004, § 3.13).

Digital certificates can be used for a variety of purposes. They can enable secured communications through a virtual private network by identifying persons eligible to use the network. They can verify the identity of buyers and sellers in a transaction in which the parties never meet face-to-face. They can be used to determine eligibility to view particular content on a Web site, in order to screen the content from certain persons or to ensure that access is limited to authorized persons; these might be persons who have paid a subscription fee, or who work for a particular company, or who are working on a particular project. The Child Online Protection Act of 1998 envisioned the use of digital certificates verifying a user's age as one means to shield children from online pornography (47 U.S.C. § 231(c)(1)(B)).

Statute

- Child Online Protection Act, 47 U.S.C. § 231(c)(1)(B)

See also: Child Online Protection Act; Encryption

❖ CHILD ONLINE PROTECTION ACT ❖

Following the Supreme Court's 1997 decision striking down the Communications Decency Act (CDA), Congress made a second attempt to regulate the availability of indecent material to minors with the 1998 Child Online Protection Act (COPA). COPA attempted to address the specific constitutional concerns raised by the Supreme Court when it struck down the CDA. COPA imposed penalties on anyone who "knowingly and with knowledge of the character of the material, in interstate or foreign commerce by means of the World Wide Web, ma[de] any communication for commercial purposes that [was] available to any minor and that include[d] any material that [was] harmful to minors" (47 U.S.C. § 231(a)(1)). COPA included a three-part test for determining whether material was harmful to minors. Material was harmful if and only if all three of the following requirements were met:

> (a) The "average person, applying contemporary community standards, would find" that the material taken as a whole, with respect to minors, was designed to appeal or pander to the prurient interest;
> (b) The material depicted, described, or represented, "in a manner patently offensive with respect to minors, an actual or simulated sexual act or sexual contact, an actual or simulated normal or perverted sexual act, or a lewd exhibition of the genitals or post-pubescent female breast; and"
> (c) The material, taken as a whole, lacked "serious literary, artistic, political, or scientific value for minors." (47 U.S.C. § 231(e)(6))

Unlike the CDA's definition, struck down in *Reno v. American Civil Liberties Union,* COPA's definition closely tracked the definition of obscenity set out by the Supreme Court in the 1973 case of *Miller v. California*. Under the *Miller* test, material is obscene if:

> (a) "the average person, applying contemporary community standards would find that the work taken as a whole appeals to the prurient interest;"
> (b) "the work depicts or describes, in a patently offensive way, sexual conduct specifically defined by the applicable state law; and"
> (c) "the work, taken as a whole, lacks serious literary, artistic, political, or scientific value."
> (413 U.S. at 39)

The first prong of the COPA definition was essentially identical to the first prong of the *Miller* test, with the exceptions of the addition of the words "with respect to minors" and the qualification that the average person must find that the work is *designed to* appeal or pander to the prurient interest, rather than merely that it does appeal to the prurient interest.

The second prong still differed in one major respect: Miller refers to applicable state law for its definitions of the types of conduct whose depiction is prohibited, but COPA attempted to establish its own definition, and this definition extended beyond the depiction of sexual conduct.

The third prong of the COPA definition, other than the addition of the words "for minors," was identical to the third prong of the *Miller* test.

Like the CDA, COPA provided safe harbors for Web publishers and Internet service providers (ISPs). Under COPA, ISPs were not liable for material merely passing through their systems. And Web publishers were not liable under COPA if they restricted access by minors through the use of a "credit card, debit account, adult access code, adult personal identification number, . . . a digital certificate that verifies age, . . . or by any other reasonable measures that are feasible under available technology." (47 U.S.C. § 231(c)(1)). Inevitably some minors would be able to circumvent these measures, but COPA insulated complying Web publishers from liability nonetheless.

COPA was immediately challenged by First Amendment advocates; the American Civil Liberties Union (ACLU) and others brought suit in the federal district court for the Eastern Dis-

---

Blocking unlawful content at the state level: In September 2004 the federal district court for the Eastern District of Pennsylvania struck down a Pennsylvania state law that had required ISPs to block access to Web sites containing child pornography. Without questioning Pennsylvania's right to add its own laws to federal laws against child pornography, the court found that the effect of the statute had been to block access to a large number of Web sites containing only lawful content, not only in Pennsylvania, but also across the Web. At the time, Pennsylvania was the only state with such a law, although at least three other states were considering similar laws. The prospect of fifty states each enacting different Web censorship laws presents a compliance nightmare for ISPs, who would surely prefer a single federal regulatory structure.

Source
"Judge Strikes Child Porn-Blocking Law,"
    CNN.com, Sept. 10, 2004, www.cnn.com
    (visited September 11, 2004).

---

trict of Pennsylvania to enjoin (prevent) enforcement of COPA. The district court granted the request for an injunction, reasoning that the ACLU had shown that their attack on the constitutionality of COPA was likely to succeed on the merits; in other words, the District Court ordered that COPA not be enforced pending a decision on its constitutionality.

After the grant of the injunction, the government appealed the case to the U.S. Court of Appeals for the Third Circuit, which decided in June 2000 that the District Court had acted correctly in issuing the preliminary injunction. In its opinion the Circuit Court focused on the problem of applying "community standards" to the World Wide Web. The nature of the Web renders it impossible for a Web publisher to know where, in the real world, the viewer of the published material is located. In contrast, providers of printed pornographic material, pornographic cable television programs, and sexually explicit telephone messages know where the materials are being sent; they can choose not to send or transmit them to certain communities if the content would violate the standards of those communities. Web publishers cannot restrict access to their published content on the basis of geography; they must publish it to the whole world or not at all.

Thus, to apply "community standards" to Web content would require each Web publisher to tailor the content to the standards of the least broad-minded community. The parties conceded that the "contemporary community standards" prong was inapplicable to communities outside the United States, so that there was no need to consider, as the circuit court put it, "the more liberal community standards of Amsterdam or the more restrictive community standards of Tehran." Even within the United States, however, there is a wide range of community standards; enforcement of COPA would in effect allow the United States' most puritanical community to determine what was acceptable Web content for the entire population of the United States. (This anomalous result is also produced by the current law governing obscenity generally, but in an Internet context, when every person connected to the Internet is potentially connected to all communities simultaneously, the problem becomes even more pronounced.)

The Third Circuit's decision had the interesting effect of granting a higher degree of First Amendment protection to Web content than is enjoyed by print content. It also raised, by implication, an obvious problem with congressional attempts to censor the Web: It is as easy to publish content outside the United States as within its borders and as easy to access foreign content from within the borders of the United States as to access domestic content. There is little Congress can do to regulate what is published outside the United States and little it can do to regulate the access of persons within the United States to foreign Web sites, short of unconstitutionally heavy-handed intervention.

The Third Circuit's decision was not the last word on COPA. In May 2001 the U.S. Supreme Court granted certiorari (a writ directing a lower court to deliver the record in a case for review by a higher court, and the mechanism by which a majority of cases come to the Supreme Court) to review the Third Circuit's decision (*ACLU v. Reno*, 217 F.3d 162).

In 2002 the Supreme Court, in *Ashcroft v. American Civil Liberties Union*, vacated (nullified) the decisions of the Third Circuit and the Eastern District of Pennsylvania enjoining enforcement of COPA. The Court held that the reference to "contemporary community standards" did not in and of itself render COPA facially unconstitutional. A three-justice plurality, with five justices concurring in the result, stated "community standards need not be defined by reference to a precise geographic area," adding that a

> publisher's burden does not change simply because it decides to distribute its material to every community in the Nation. . . . Nor does it change because the publisher may wish to speak only to those in a 'community where avant garde culture is the norm,' . . . but nonetheless utilizes a medium that transmits its speech from coast to coast. If a publisher wishes for its material to be judged only by the standards of particular communities, then it need only take the simple step of utilizing a medium that enables it to target the release of its material into those communities. (*Ashcroft v. ACLU*, 535 U.S. at 583)

In other words, COPA might well have the effect of limiting expression on the Web in accordance with the standard of the most puritanical community, but to do so was not unconstitutional.

The Supreme Court remanded (sent back) the case to the Third Circuit for further proceedings. On remand the Third Circuit held that the plaintiffs had established a substantial likelihood of prevailing on their claim that COPA was not narrowly tailored to achieve a compelling government interest and that they had also established a substantial likelihood of prevailing on their claim that COPA was unconstitutionally overbroad.

As a restraint on expression in a unique nonbroadcast medium, COPA is subject to strict scrutiny, the highest level of constitutional scrutiny. In order to withstand strict scrutiny a law or other government action must:

(1) serve a compelling governmental interest;

(2) be narrowly tailored to achieve that interest; and

(3) be the least restrictive means of advancing that interest.

It had been agreed by the parties throughout the litigation that the protection of minors from harmful online content was a compelling state interest. However, the Third Circuit found that the statute was not narrowly tailored both because holding all communities to the standard of one would mean that much material that was acceptable in some or all communities would nonetheless be banned in those communities, and because of the difficulty of ascertaining the meaning of the term *as a whole* in the statute "when everything on the Web is connected to everything else" (*ACLU v. Ashcroft*, 322 F.3d at 252). And blocking and filtering software provided a less restrictive means than COPA to achieve the same result; indeed, such software might be more effective, because it could block foreign Web sites beyond the reach of COPA. The Third Circuit once again affirmed the issuance of the injunction.

The matter did not end there. The Supreme Court once again granted certiorari to consider the matter. On June 29, 2004, a three-justice plurality, with two justices concurring in the result, issued a decision affirming the preliminary injunction and remanding the case for trial. The Court reasoned that the preliminary injunction should stand because the government had not shown that it would be likely to rebut the ACLU's contention that filtering software, a less restrictive alternative to COPA, can protect children from online pornography without infringing the First Amendment rights of adults. A trial was necessary to determine the present-day effectiveness of filtering technology, five years after the grant of the initial injunction.

The Court also reasoned that COPA's "effectiveness is likely to diminish even further if COPA is upheld, because the providers of the materials that would be covered by the statute simply can move their operations overseas" (*Ashcroft v. ACLU*, 124 S.Ct. at 2786). Filtering software can block content originating outside the United States; COPA cannot.

The Internet may ultimately bring the entire issue of "community standards," the linchpin of the *Miller* definition of obscenity, into question. Even without the Internet, the increasing mo-bility of the United States populace and the fragmentation of society, especially in large cities, make "community standards" difficult to determine. On any street in any town in the United States one may encounter values both more conservative than those in Tehran and more liberal than those in Amsterdam, to use the Third Circuit's examples. Indeed, any person using a computer in any U.S. household can be virtually present in Tehran or in Amsterdam, or in both at once.

Statute
- Child Online Protection Act, 47 U.S.C. § 231

Cases
- *American Civil Liberties Union v. Reno*, 217 F.3d 162 (3d Cir. 2000); rev. sub nom *Ashcroft v. American Civil Liberties Union*, 535 U.S. 564 (2002); on remand, *American Civil Liberties Union v. Ashcroft*, 322 F.3d 240 (3d Cir. 2003); cert. granted, *Ashcroft v. American Civil Liberties Union*, 124 S. Ct. 399 (2003); affirmed and remanded, 124 S. Ct. 2783 (2004)
- *Miller v. California*, 413 U.S. 15 (1973)

See also: Censorship; Children's Internet Protection Act; Communications Decency Act; Constitutional Law; First Amendment; Indecency; Obscenity; Pornography

Sources and further reading:
Mike Godwin, *Cyber Rights: Defending Free Speech in the Digital Age* (Cambridge, MA: MIT Press, 2003).
Lawrence Lessig, *Code and Other Laws of Cyberspace* (New York: Basic Books, 1999).
Kevin W. Saunders, *Saving Our Children from the First Amendment* (New York: New York University Press, 2004).

❖ CHILD PORNOGRAPHY ❖

The Supreme Court has long held that child pornography is not protected speech under the First Amendment, at least where actual children are involved (*Ferber*, 458 U.S. 747). In 1996 Congress enacted the Child Pornography Prevention Act, which prohibited the possession or distribution of any image that was, "or appeared to be, of a minor engaging in sexually explicit conduct." This covered not only depictions of actual children, but computer-generated images in which no actual children were involved.

A major component of the underlying rationale for Supreme Court decisions on child pornography, particularly *New York v. Ferber*, had been that child pornography is intrinsically related to the sexual abuse of children. It is a record of sexual abuse; actual children are involved in its production and are harmed thereby; and it creates a market for the material, which in turn fuels the problem of sexual abuse of children. When no actual children are involved, the first two of these components are no longer present; the Child Pornography Prevention Act thus presented the Supreme Court with a new question of law. In *Ashcroft v. Free Speech Coalition*, the Court found that the prohibition was unconstitutionally overbroad because it could prohibit expression that was not intrinsically related to the sexual abuse of actual children and was not obscene under the test set out in *Miller v. California* (535 U.S. 234). The Court rejected other arguments offered by the government regarding the potential for harm from virtual child pornography on the grounds that they were speculative and did not justify curtailing First Amendment protections (535 U.S. 234).

The Court's decision in *Ashcroft v. Free Speech Coalition* does not mean that all images containing virtual child pornography are necessarily protected by the First Amendment, or even that any are. Such images may be, and probably are, obscene under the *Miller* test and may thus be prohibited.

Statute

- Child Pornography Prevention Act, 18 U.S.C. §§ 2251–2260

Cases

- *Ashcroft v. Free Speech Coalition*, 535 U.S. 234 (2002)

- *Miller v. California*, 413 U.S. 15 (1973)
- *New York v. Ferber*, 458 U.S. 747 (1982)
- *Osborne v. Ohio*, 495 U.S. 103 (1990)

See also: Censorship; Child Online Protection Act; Children's Internet Protection Act; Children's Online Privacy Protection Act; Communications Decency Act; Constitutional Law; Encryption; First Amendment; Obscenity; Pornography

❖ CHILDREN'S INTERNET PROTECTION ACT ❖

The Children's Internet Protection Act (CIPA) of 1998 was a companion act to the Child Online Protection Act (COPA). While COPA attempts to control all access to certain types of material by certain persons, CIPA attempts to control access from certain computers by requiring schools and libraries receiving federally subsidized discounted Internet access to install filtering and blocking software.

The federally funded E-rate, or School and Libraries Discount program, enables qualifying schools and libraries to obtain access to the Internet at discounts of up to 90 percent, depending on economic need. Under the Telecommunications Act, the E-rate is only available to schools and libraries if administrators certify that the school or library

(1) is enforcing a policy of Internet safety for minors that includes monitoring the online activities of minors and the operation of a technology protection measure with respect to any of its computers with Internet access that protects against access through such computers to visual depictions that are
(I) obscene;
(II) child pornography; or
(III) harmful to minors; and
(2) is enforcing the operation of such technology protection measure during any use of such computers by minors. (47 U.S.C. § 254(h)(5)(B))

With respect to adults, the school or library must make an identical certification, except that item III (protection against material harmful to minors) is not required. In addition, a school or library administrator or authorized person "may disable the technology protection measure concerned, during use by an adult, to enable access for bona fide research or other lawful purpose" (47 U.S.C. § 254(h)(5)(D)).

CIPA was signed into law in December 2000 by then-President Clinton, who expressed disappointment with the statute. Clinton's misgivings included concerns about the efficacy of filtering software and the conflict with First Amendment rights; he stated that he would have preferred locally developed and implemented alternatives.

CIPA required elementary and secondary schools and public libraries providing Internet access to meet two additional requirements for federal funding and benefits. First, schools and libraries were required to purchase and install "technology protection measures"—filtering programs—to filter or block Internet access to specified "visual depictions." In addition, each institution was required to hold a minimum of one public meeting on Internet safety policies to gather input and feedback from community members.

The specified visual depictions to be blocked were those that were obscene or constituted child pornography; the First Amendment protects neither obscenity nor child pornography, and the requirement of one meeting was at least a nod to the "community standards" element of the *Miller* test for obscenity. "Harmful to minors" is defined in CIPA as meaning

any picture, image, graphic image file, or other visual depiction that—
(i) taken as a whole and with respect to minors, appeals to a prurient interest in nudity, sex, or excretion;
(ii) depicts, describes, or represents, in a patently offensive way with respect to what is suitable for minors, an actual or simulated sexual act or sexual contact, actual or simulated normal or perverted sexual acts, or a lewd exhibition of the genitals; and
(iii) taken as a whole, lacks serious literary, artistic, political, or scientific value as to minors. (47 U.S.C. § 254(h)(5)(G))

Interestingly, this definition differs somewhat from the definition of "harmful to minors" in CIPA's companion act, COPA (47 U.S.C. § 231(e)(6)).

CIPA also includes a subtitle, Neighborhood Children's Internet Protection, that requires schools and libraries to adopt policies that address areas such as minors' access to inappropriate matter on the Web, their safety when using e-mail, chat rooms, and other direct electronic communications (such as instant messaging), and hacking. The term *inappropriate for minors* is to be determined by a "school board, local educational agency, library, or other authority," rather than by an "agency or instrumentality of the United States Government," nor are these locally adopted policies subject to review by these federal agencies or instrumentalities (47 U.S.C. § 254(l)).

Not surprisingly, CIPA was immediately challenged by First Amendment advocates. Plaintiffs, including the American Civil Liberties Union (ACLU) and the American Library Association (ALA), filed suit in the federal District Court for the Eastern District of Pennsylvania to enjoin enforcement of CIPA on the grounds that it was an unconstitutional abridgement of First Amendment rights, at least as far as libraries and their adult patrons were concerned. With regard to libraries, the plaintiffs argued that CIPA required the imposition of content-based restrictions on library patrons' access to constitutionally protected speech. Although patrons could request that blocked content be unblocked, placing the burden on the library patron to make the request, which might be embarrassing, was likely to discourage many patrons from doing so, which would have a consequent chilling effect on free speech. And because existing filtering and blocking programs are imperfect, much speech that Congress intended to permit is blocked, and much speech that Congress intended to restrict gets through. In addition, the plaintiffs claimed, the imposition of controls on freedom of expression as a prerequisite to the receipt of federal funds was an impermissible use of the spending power. The district court agreed (201 F. Supp.2d 401).

The case was appealed directly to the United States Supreme Court, which reversed the district court's decision in June 2003. A four-justice plurality of the Supreme Court, with two justices concurring in the result, stated that CIPA was not unconstitutional either as a violation of First Amendment rights or as an impermissible condition attached to congressional exercise of the spending power. Writing for the plurality, Chief Justice Rehnquist pointed out that "a library reviews and affirmatively chooses to acquire every book in its collection," and that most libraries choose not to acquire pornographic books. The nature of the Web renders it impossible for a library to engage in a similar selection process with the Web content, but the purpose of a library is not to provide a First Amendment forum for Web content publishers. It is to facilitate learning and cultural enrichment, and this process of facilitation invariably involves the making of choices about what material the library will provide to its patrons (123 S. Ct. 2297).

Statute
- Children's Internet Protection Act, 47 U.S.C. § 254(h)
- Neighborhood Children's Internet Protection Act, 47 U.S.C. § 254(l)

Case
- *American Library Association v. United States*, 201 F.Supp.2d 401 (E.D. Pa. 2002); reversed sub nom *U.S. v. American Library Association, Inc.*, 123 S. Ct. 2297 (2003)

See also: Censorship; Child Online Protection Act; Communications Decency Act; Constitutional Law; First Amendment; Indecency; Obscenity; Pornography

Sources and further reading:
Kathryn Kolbert and Zak Mettger, eds., *Justice Talking: Censoring the Web: Leading Advocates Debate Today's Most Controversial Issues* (New York: The New Press, 2002).

Kevin W. Saunders, *Saving Our Children from the First Amendment* (New York: New York University Press, 2004).

Madeleine Schachter, *Law of Internet Speech*, 2nd ed. (Durham, NC: Carolina Academic Press, 2002).

❖ CHILDREN'S ONLINE PRIVACY PROTECTION ACT ❖

The Children's Online Privacy Protection Act (COPPA) was enacted in 1998; the Federal Trade Commission (FTC) promulgated implementing regulations that took effect in April 2001 (16 C.F.R. § 312). COPPA was enacted in response to concerns that information about children's use of the Web, routinely gathered by the Web sites the children visited, could be misused. COPPA sets guidelines for operators of commercial Web sites that target children under the age of thirteen and for operators of other Web sites who know that they collect information from children under the age of thirteen.

COPPA requires such operators to provide notice of what information they collect from children, how they use the information, and their practices regarding disclosure of the information. Operators may not collect, use or disclose personal information obtained from a child without the verifiable consent of the child's parents. Information that will trigger COPPA, if gathered, includes information that could identify or permit communication with the child, such as a first or last name, address, e-mail address, telephone number, or social security number. The parents must be provided with a reasonable means to review the information and to refuse to permit its further use or maintenance. A child's participation in a game, promotional sweepstakes or contest, or any other activity may not be conditioned upon the collection of any information other than that which is reasonably necessary to enable the child to participate in the activity. Web site operators must establish privacy policies that adopt reasonable procedures to protect the confidentiality, security, and integrity of any personal information collected from children (15 U.S.C. § 6502).

COPPA contains a safe harbor provision for certain organizations, but it must be affirmatively applied for; if not previously applied for and granted, it cannot be raised as a defense (15 U.S.C. § 6503). Only two organizations, so far, have been granted exceptions from COPPA under the safe harbor provision: the Children's Advertising Review Unit of the Better Business

Bureau (CARU) and the Entertainment Software Ratings Board.

The Federal Trade Commission, aided by independent watchdogs such as CARU, has actively pursued COPPA violators, often imposing significant fines. In 2003 Hershey's Foods and Mrs. Fields Cookies agreed to settle COPPA charges brought by the FTC for $85,000 and $100,000, respectively ("Hershey" 2003).

Statute

- Children's Online Privacy Protection Act, 15 U.S.C. § 6501–6506

Regulation

- Children's Online Privacy Protection Rule, 64 Fed. Reg. 59,888 (Nov. 3, 1999) (codified at 16 C.F.R. § 312 (2001))

See also: Advertising; Adware and Spyware; Anonymity; Privacy

Sources and further reading:

Tsan Abrahamson, "Coping with COPPA: The Practical Aspects of Children's Privacy," *Practical Lawyer,* Jan. 2002, at 49.

Melanie L. Hersh, "Is COPPA a Cop-Out? The Child Online Privacy Protection Act as Proof that Parents, Not Government, Should be Protecting Children's Interests on the Internet," 28 *Fordham Urban Law Journal* 1831 (2001).

"Hershey, Mrs. Fields Fined for Violating Children's Online Privacy," ConsumerAffairs. com, Feb. 27, 2003, http://www. consumeraffairs.com/news03/candy_fines.html (visited November 18, 2004).

❖ CHOICE OF LAW ❖

A choice of law problem arises when the law of more than one jurisdiction may be applicable to a particular situation. Choice of law problems arise even in the absence of the Internet. If, for example, a California employee of a California corporation travels to Nevada on business and is injured there by a resident of Arizona, it is not instantly apparent whether California, Nevada, or Arizona tort and workers' compensation laws should apply to a suit for damages brought by the injured employee. The answer might depend on where the suit was brought; courts in California, Arizona, and Nevada, each employing their own choice of law rules, might reach three different results.

Although states tend, either through stated policy or through their practice over a period of time, to prefer their own law, the preference is not absolute. A Nevada court might well decide that California workers' compensation law should apply and that, if the California workers' compensation law did not bar the tort suit, that Nevada's own tort law should apply.

The Internet increases the possibility of choice of law problems. On the Internet, most transactions and interactions involve multiple jurisdictions. With a single click, and without consulting an attorney or reviewing the law of the various jurisdictions involved, a surfer sitting at home in Vermont can purchase and download music from an Australian company with its principal place of business in the Netherlands. The download might take place via a server located in Virginia; the server might belong to an Internet service provider incorporated in the Cayman Islands but with its principal place of business in Louisiana. The order might be paid for with a credit card issued by a bank in Delaware. Without the knowledge of the purchaser, the music downloads might have been illegally copied in Switzerland from disks purchased in Spain by a Norwegian citizen; the copyright owner might be a Mexican corporation with its principal place of business in Florida, which in turn has authorized a California organization to enforce its rights. If the organization in California sues the Norwegian copier, the Dutch/Australian seller, and the Vermont purchaser, and the purchaser in turn sues the seller, the various disputes might conceivably be governed by the laws of Vermont, Australia, the Netherlands, Virginia, the Cayman Islands, Louisiana, Delaware, Switzerland, Spain, Norway, Mexico, Florida, or California. (Although the latter three are the places where the plaintiff, rather than any of the defendants, are located, choice of law clauses in the music licensing agreements might dictate the application of the laws of one of these places against the purchaser of the disks. Such clauses might also dictate the application of the law of some other jurisdiction.)

The question of choice of law is separate from, although related to, the question of jurisdiction. The fact that a court in, say, California has jurisdiction over the case does not necessarily mean that the case will be decided under California law. The California court might apply the laws of Vermont, Australia, the Netherlands, Virginia, the Cayman Islands, Louisiana, Delaware, Switzerland, Spain, Norway, Mexico, or Florida, instead. Which state's or nation's law is to be applied will be determined under the forum state's choice of law rules; these vary widely among states. Special problems occurring in the resolution of conflicts of laws problems include problems of characterization, *renvoi, ordre public* and *depéçage,* and the difficulty of proving the content and meaning of foreign law (Richman and Reynolds 2002, 165–172).

Characterization: In any choice of law problem the issues of characterization of the subject matter, characterization of the problem as substantive or procedural, and characterization of the applicable law must be addressed. The forum state's law is generally applied to problems of characterization.

Characterization of the subject matter and applicable law can affect the outcome because a state's choice of law rules may end up dictating that one state's law is applicable if the problem is characterized as a tort problem and another's is applicable if the problem is characterized as a contract problem. This result might be indirect; for instance, even though a state's law may apply superficially similar rules to torts and contracts conflicts, it may define the locus of a tort as the place where the injury was suffered and the locus of a contract as the place where performance was to take place. If these two loci are not in the same state, the focus of the litigation may be on whether the case is more properly characterized as one in tort or in contract, with each litigant urging the characterization that results in the application of the law most favorable to that litigant's position.

Characterization of the problem as substantive or procedural may also affect the outcome.

When a forum's choice of law rule refers to the law of another state, it will apply the substantive law of that state but will still use its own procedural law. Thus, in a case in which the law of another state or country may be applied to some issues, the court must characterize each issue as substantive or procedural (Richman and Reynolds 2002, 160–165).

Renvoi: Occasionally, a court will be directed by statute or prior case law to apply the "whole law" of another jurisdiction, meaning that other state's substantive law and its choice of law rules. This is *renvoi,* so called because it may result in a "sending back" to the law of the original state: The second state's choice of law rules might refer the case back to the law of the first state, whose own choice of law rules originally referred the case to the law of the second state. Applying the second state's choice of law rules might also result in a "sending on" to the law of some third state. Even in the absence of a statutory or other directive to apply the whole law of some other state, a question may arise as to whether a court should consider the other state's conflicts law, either in circumstances where the other state's law would refer back to the forum (remission) or to yet another state (transmission). *Renvoi* is rare in the United States; when it does occur, the original state must either accept or reject the *renvoi* to avoid an endless loop in which each state's law dictates the application of the other state's law rather than its own.

Ordre public/Public policy: A state will not apply another state's law if that law offends its own public policy. However, through the process of *depéçage* ("dismemberment," or applying the laws of different states to different issues in a case), the state's court may apply that part of the law that does not offend the state's public policy, eliminating only the part that offends.

Proof of foreign law: At common law, foreign law (including the law of other U.S. states) had to be pleaded and proved as fact, and the determination of the foreign law was therefore not ordinarily subject to review on appeal. (Appellate courts ordinarily review only a trial court's conclusions of law, not its findings of fact.) Statutory changes now provide for judicial notice of the law of other states of the United

States, although not of the law of foreign countries. A uniform act and a federal rule provide that the court, with the assistance of the parties, is to determine foreign law and that its decision is subject to review. When proof fails or the foreign law cannot be determined, a court may presume that the foreign law is the same as the forum's law (Richman and Reynolds 2002, 173–176).

Cases
Supreme Court
- *Alabama Great Southern Railroad Company v. Carroll*, 97 Ala. 126, 11 So. 803 (1892)

State Courts
- *In re Schneider's Estate*, 96 N.Y.S.2d 652 (N.Y. Sup. Ct. 1950)
- *Kilberg v. Northwest Airlines, Inc.*, 9 N.Y.2d 34, 211 N.Y.S.2d 133, 172 N.E.2d 526 (Ct. App. N.Y. 1961)
- *University of Chicago v. Dater*, 277 Mich. 658 (1936)

Restatement
- American Law Institute, Restatement of the Law Second: Conflict of Laws (Philadelphia: American Law Institute, 1971)

Sources and further reading:
William M. Richman and William L. Reynolds, *Understanding Conflict of Laws*, 3d ed. (New York: Matthew Bender, 2002).
David D. Siegel, *Conflicts in a Nutshell* (St. Paul, MN: West, 1994).
Russell J. Weintraub, *Commentary on the Conflict of Law*, 4th ed. (New York: Foundation Press, 2000).

❖ CIPHER AND CIPHERTEXT ❖

See Encryption

❖ CIRCUMVENTION OF TECHNOLOGICAL MEASURES ❖

See DeCSS; Digital Millennium Copy Act, Title I

❖ CLASS ACTION ❖

A class action lawsuit is one in which a small number of named parties—possibly as few as one—represents the interest of a large class. In order for a class action to be brought under rule 23 of the Federal Rules of Civil Procedure, the class must be "so numerous that joinder of all members is impracticable," there must be "questions of law or fact common to the class," "the claims or defenses of the representative parties" must be "typical of the claims or defenses of the class," and the representative parties must "fairly and adequately protect the interests of the class" (Fed. R. Civ. P. 23(a)). In addition to these four basic elements, certain additional elements are necessary to maintain a class action. There are three ways in which these additional elements may be met: A class action may be maintained if the first four elements are met and

(1) Separate actions by or against the class members would create a risk of inconsistent results or would dispose of or impair the interests of other class members, or
(2) The party opposing the class has acted or refused to act on grounds generally applicable to the class, thereby making appropriate final injunctive relief or corresponding declaratory relief with respect to the class as a whole, or
(3) There are questions of law or fact common to the members of the class that predominate over any questions affecting only individual members so that a class action is the fairest and most efficient means of adjudication available. (Fed. R. Civ. P. 23(b))

The information technology revolution has brought about no fundamental change in the law of class actions, but class actions have been used as a tool to ensure fairness to consumers. The settlement of a class action brought on behalf of users of Toshiba laptop computers on the grounds that a flaw in the computers could cause incorrect recording of data has been particularly influential (see 91 F.Supp.2d 942). The settlement, for over two billion dollars, led to the immediate filing of class action suits against NEC, Compaq, Hewlett-Packard, and other computer manufacturers. It has also encouraged the use of class actions as a tool for the litigation of mass torts: If the number of plaintiffs in the class is large, lawyers can earn substantial fees even when the amount of damage suffered by each individual plaintiff is very, very small. The legal fees for the lawyers representing the class in the Toshiba case, for example, came to $147.5 million.

For this reason class actions have been criticized as being more valuable in providing employment for lawyers than in protecting consumer rights. A class action plaintiff who receives an eight-page notice of class action in the mail, spends fifteen minutes filling out the enclosed form, mails it back, and finally receives a check for three cents might feel that the reward was not justified by the amount of effort involved.

Against this argument is balanced the argument that some harms too small to motivate individual plaintiffs might thus go unchecked in the absence of class action litigation. For example, an Internet service provider (ISP) with ten million subscribers might, either through a deliberate intent to mislead the subscribers or through sheer inefficiency, overbill each subscriber by ten cents per month. It would not be worth any subscriber's time to take the effort to correct the error, and most would probably not even notice. Yet the ISP would receive a substantial benefit: a million dollars a month in unearned revenue. This hardly seems fair, yet the government lacks the resources to pursue all cases of such minor injustice. Rule 23 has the effect of enabling private parties—in this case class action lawyers—to enforce public rights where the government is unable or unwilling to do so.

The Internet can also affect class actions by reducing some of the costs involved: Defendants and plaintiff/class lawyers can use Web sites as a means of communicating with class members; in the Toshiba case, for example, Toshiba Corporation used a Web site to communicate with the plaintiffs, presumably reducing printing and mailing costs.

Rule
- Rule 23 of the Federal Rules of Civil Procedure

Case
- *Shaw v. Toshiba America Information Systems, Inc.,* 91 F.Supp.2d 942 (E.D. Tex. 2000)

See also: Activism and Advocacy Groups; Enforcement

Sources and further reading:
Robert H. Klonoff, *Class Actions and Other Multi-Party Litigations in a Nutshell* (St. Paul, MN: West, 1999).

❖ CLICKWRAP AGREEMENT ❖

When software is downloaded over the Internet or when an Internet user registers for an online service, it is generally necessary for the user to click a box indicating that he or she accepts the terms of a licensing agreement. The first few lines of the licensing agreement generally appear in the scroll window of a dialog box. The agreements are almost never read in their entirety by the users and are rarely read at all. Nonetheless, they purport to affect the rights of the users of the software or the service. The extent to which they actually do so depends on general principles of contract law and law regarding end-user license agreements in particular.

Clickwrap agreements may be adhesion contracts: contracts prepared by one party, in which the other party has no opportunity to negotiate and has no option but to take the contract as written or forgo the transaction. The Uniform Commercial Code, the body of contract law adopted, with slight modifications, by the legislatures of all fifty states, looks upon adhesion contracts without favor. Although adhesion contracts are not prohibited by the code, they are not enforceable if they defeat the reasonable expectations of the adhering party or are oppressive or unconscionable (Stone 2001).

Clickwrap and shrinkwrap agreements have been the subject of intensive lobbying by the software industry, which would like them to be free of the restrictions placed on adhesion contracts. This approach is embodied in the Uniform Computer Information Transactions Act, which like the Uniform Commercial Code is a body of law proposed for adoption by all fifty states, but unlike the code has been adopted by only two (Maryland and Virginia). Consumer advocates and several state governments have united to oppose the adoption of the act on the grounds that it would unfairly tilt the balance of bargaining power in favor of software companies (Letter from Attorneys General 1999).

Uniform Act
- Uniform Computer Information Transactions Act, available at http://www.law.upenn.edu/bll/ulc/ucita/ucita200.htm (visited November 14, 2004)
- Uniform Commercial Code, available at http://www.law.cornell.edu/ucc/ucc.table.html (visited November 14, 2004)

See also: Choice of Law; Contracts; Copyright; Uniform Computer Information Transactions Act

Sources and further reading:
Letter to NCCUSL from Attorneys General Opposing UCITA, July 23, 1999, available at http://www.arl.org/info/frn/copy/agoppltr.html (visited November 14, 2004).
Bradford Stone, *Uniform Commercial Code in a Nutshell* (St. Paul, MN: West, 2001).

❖ CLIPPER CHIP ❖

See Encryption

❖ CODES AND CODE-BREAKING ❖

See Encryption

❖ .COM ❖

".com" is the most universally familiar of the top-level domains; it is intended to indicate the address of a commercial enterprise, but many noncommercial organizations and individuals use .com addresses as well. The phrase "dot-com" or "dot.com" is also used to refer to Internet-based businesses as a category, particularly in reference to the stock market bubble of the late 1990s.

The .com domain name was originally created in 1984–1985 by Jon Postel and Joyce Reynolds of the Network Working Group, along with five other generic top-level domains: .edu, .gov, .mil, .net, and .org (Postel and Reynolds 1984). The .com domain name is now administered by VeriSign (VeriSign 2004).

As the best-known and most popular top level domain, .com has been especially plagued by cybersquatting and domain name disputes. These disputes can be resolved under the Uniform Domain Name Dispute Resolution Policy of the Internet Corporation for Assigned Names and Numbers, or in court under the Anticybersquatting Consumer Protection Act of 1999 (15 U.S.C. § 1125(d)). The .com top-level domain is also experiencing resource depletion; all or nearly all of the desirable domain names within it have already been registered.

See also: Cybersquatting; Domain Name Registration; Internet Corporation for Assigned Names and Numbers

Sources and further reading:
Jon Postel and Joyce Reynolds, "Domain Requirements," Network Working Group Request for Comments: 920, Oct. 1984, available at http://www.ietf.org/rfc/rfc920.txt (visited November 18, 2004).
VeriSign, "Corporate Overview: The More the World Moves to a Digital Infrastructure, the More It Turns to One Company," http://www.verisign.com/verisign-inc/corporate-overview/index.html (visited November 18, 2004).

❖ COMMUNICATIONS DECENCY ACT ❖

The Communications Decency Act of 1996 (CDA) was the first law passed by Congress attempting to address the availability of pornography and obscene materials to minors over the Internet. The CDA was unsuccessful; it was ultimately struck down by the Supreme Court as unconstitutional, and even had it been enforced would have been ineffective against pornography originating outside the United States.

The CDA attempted to restrict the access of minors to pornography in two ways, each of which raised First Amendment issues. The first restrictive provision imposed a penalty on any person who knowingly transmitted "obscene" or "indecent" material to recipients known to the sender to be under eighteen years of age. The second imposed a penalty on any person who used an "interactive computer service" to transmit to specific persons under eighteen years of age, or to "display in a manner available to persons under eighteen, any comment, request, suggestion, proposal, image, or other communication that, in context, depict[ed] or describe[d], in terms patently offensive as measured by community standards, sexual or excretory activities or organs" (47 U.S.C. § 223(d); amended in 2003 to read "any comment, request, suggestion, proposal, image, or other communication that, is obscene or child pornography" in an attempt to conform to the Supreme Court's holding discussed below; *superfluous comma in original*).

The constitutional problem posed by the first prohibition involved the definition of "indecent"; the Supreme Court had long since established that obscene material was not entitled to First Amendment protection. The Court had also, however, distinguished indecent speech from obscenity and stated that indecent speech among adults, even though offensive, was constitutionally protected.

The constitutional problem posed by the second prohibition involved the scope of "patently offensive" content covered by the statute. The test developed by the Supreme Court in 1973 in *Miller v. California* provides that material is obscene if

(a) "the average person, applying contemporary community standards would find that the work taken as a whole appeals to the prurient interest;"

(b) "the work depicts or describes, in a patently offensive way, sexual conduct specifically defined by the applicable state law; and"

(c) "the work, taken as a whole, lacks serious literary, artistic, political, or scientific value." (413 U.S. at 39)

The CDA's prohibition incorporated portions of this test: the "community standards" prong and part of the "patently offensive" prong (although it omitted *Miller*'s reference to "applicable state law"). Nothing was said about works that might have "serious literary, artistic, political, or scientific value."

The CDA provided a safe harbor for content providers and Internet service providers who took "good faith, reasonable, effective and appropriate actions under the circumstances to restrict or prevent access by minors . . . including any method which [was] feasible under available technology" (47 U.S.C. § 223(d)(5)).

The CDA was immediately challenged by First Amendment advocates, including the American Civil Liberties Union (ACLU). In a lengthy (175 pages) opinion, a three-judge panel of the U.S. District Court for the Eastern District of Pennsylvania unanimously found the restrictive provisions of the CDA unconstitutional because it had the effect of banning constitutionally protected, albeit "indecent," adult speech over the Internet. Two of the three judges also found that the CDA was unconstitutionally vague under the Fifth Amendment because it did not enable content providers to reasonably distinguish between permitted and prohibited speech (*ACLU v. Reno*, 929 F.Supp. 824).

On appeal, the United States Supreme Court affirmed. Seven justices joined in the majority opinion; two (O'Connor and Rehnquist) wrote separate opinions, concurring in part and dissenting in part. The Court affirmed the district court's finding that the Internet, as a unique communications medium that had never been subject to government regulation, was entitled to the highest level of constitutional protection.

The Court found that the terms *indecent* and *patently offensive* were unconstitutionally vague under the First Amendment. (The Court did not reach the Fifth Amendment vagueness issue addressed by the district court because it struck down the provisions on First Amendment grounds.) As a result of this vagueness, the CDA functioned as a content-based blanket restraint and could not be analyzed as a time, place, and manner restriction. The CDA's purpose was to regulate children's access to "indecent" material; its effect, however, was to restrict constitutionally protected adult speech. The goal of regulating children's access to indecent material could have been achieved by a less-restrictive alternative; the burden on adult speech thus was not justified by the goal of the CDA (*Reno v. ACLU,* 521 U.S. 844).

Statute
- Communications Decency Act of 1996, Pub. L. No. 104-104, § 502, 1996 U.S.S.C.A.N. (110 Stat.) 56,133 (later codified at 47 U.S.C. § 223)

Cases
- *American Civil Liberties Union v. Reno,* 929 F.Supp. 824 (E.D. Pa. 1996); affirmed sub nom. *Reno v. American Civil Liberties Union,* 521 U.S. 844 (1997)
- *Miller v. California,* 413 U.S. 15 (1973)

See also: Censorship; Child Online Protection Act; Children's Internet Protection Act; Constitutional Law; Declaration of the Independence of Cyberspace; First Amendment; Indecency; Obscenity; Pornography

Sources and further reading:
Robert Cannon, "The Legislative History of Senator Exon's Communications Decency Act: Regulating Barbarians on the Information Superhighway," 49 *Federal Communications Law Journal* 51 (1996).
Kevin W. Saunders, *Saving Our Children from the First Amendment* (New York: New York University Press, 2004).
Madeleine Schachter, *Law of Internet Speech,* 2nd ed. (Durham, NC: Carolina Academic Press, 2002).
Cass R. Sunstein, *Republic.Com* (Princeton, NJ: Princeton University Press, 2002).

❖ COMPUTER MAINTENANCE COMPETITION ASSURANCE ACT ❖

See Digital Millennium Copyright Act, Title III

❖ COMPUTER PROGRAM ❖

The Copyright Act of 1976 (as amended in 1980) defines a computer program as "a set of statements or instructions to be used directly or indirectly in a computer in order to bring about a certain result." The definition of copyrightable computer programs extends to operating systems as well as applications.

In 1966 the President's Commission on the Patent System issued a report opposing the grant of patents for computer programs. The President's Commission was influenced by the United States Patent and Trademark Office (USPTO), which had been overwhelmed with computer hardware patents and opposed the idea of software patents. Although in 1969 the Court of Customs and Patent Appeals had held that software for an analog computer was patentable, in 1972 the United States Supreme Court, relying heavily on the President's Commission report, held that a mathematical algorithm used in a computer program was not patentable (*Gottschalk,* 409 U.S. 63). This was widely, if incorrectly, understood in the United States and Europe as a statement that computer programs themselves were unpatentable, and the USPTO suspended all pending computer program patent applications. As a result copyright rather than patent became the main mechanism for protecting intellectual property rights in software. This has had significant consequences: It is much easier to obtain a copyright than to obtain a patent, and once obtained a copyright lasts for far longer than a patent; in information technology industry terms, copyright, which can easily endure for over a century, might as well be eternal.

It was not until 1981 that the Supreme Court backtracked from this position; the USPTO began to accept applications for, and issue, software patents (*Diamond,* 450 U.S. 175). But the USPTO remained, if not overtly hostile, at least skeptical toward the idea. Only after a 1994 decision of the Court of Appeals for the Federal Circuit did the USPTO publish guidelines recognizing the patentability of a wide range of computer programs and related inventions (*In re Alappat,* 33 F.3d 1526).

How would you design a new form of intellectual property protection for computer programs? Subject matter, exclusive rights, exceptions, and the term of protection would all need to be defined. How would you define "computer program"? Would all programs be treated equally, or would some (operating systems, for example) be treated differently? What exclusive rights would you grant to the right-holder? Would the adaptation of an application to a new operating system or machine be treated as a translation, as some other type of derivative work, or as a new work? How would you define fair use to avoid existing copyright law's difficulties with copies made during operation and routine backups while still protecting the interests of the right-holder? How long would the right-holder's monopoly last? Would you grant a different term for operating systems than for applications?

The U.S. position regarding the patentability of computer programs influences the development of patent law elsewhere; the subsequent reversal of the U.S. position led to inconsistencies between U.S. law and the law of those countries and regions that had followed the U.S. lead. For example, the European Patent Convention still provides that computer programs are not patentable subject matter (European Patent Convention, art. 52(2)(c)), although a recent decision of the European Patent Office has held otherwise (*International Business Machines* 1999).

Treaty
- Convention on the Grant of European Patents, 5 Oct. 1973, 13 I.L.M. 276, text as amended through Dec. 10, 1998, available at http://www.european-patent-office.org/legal/epc/e/ma1.html (visited October 20, 2004) [European Patent Convention]

Statutes
- Copyright Act of 1976, 17 U.S.C. § 114

- Patent Act, 35 U.S.C. §§ 101 et seq.

Cases
Supreme Court
- *Diamond v. Diehr*, 450 U.S. 175 (1981)
- *Gottschalk v. Benson*, 409 U.S. 63 (1972)

Federal Appellate Courts
- *Apple Computer, Inc. v. Franklin Computer Corp.*, 714 F.2d 1240 (3d Cir. 1983)
- *In re Alappat*, 33 F.3d 1526 (Fed. Cir. 1994)

European Patent Office, Technical Board of Appeal
- *International Business Machines Corporation*, Technical Board of Appeal of the European Patent Office, Case No. T 0935/97-3.5.1 (1999)

See also: Copyright; Copyright Infringement; Digital Millennium Copyright Act, Title III; International Patent Protection; Patent

Sources and further reading:
Stephen Fishman, *Copyright Your Software*, 3d ed. (Berkeley: Nolo Press, 2001).
Pamela Samuelson et al., "A Manifesto Concerning the Legal Protection of Computer Programs," 94 Columbia Law Review 2308 (1994).

❖ CONSTITUTIONAL LAW ❖

Several areas of the U.S. Constitution touch upon problems arising in computer and Internet law. Two areas that have attracted a great deal of legislative activity and litigation are the Patent and Copyright Clause and the First Amendment. The Patent and Copyright Clause (Art. I, § 8, clause 8) provides that Congress shall have the power "To promote the Progress of Science and useful Arts, by securing for limited Times to Authors and Inventors the exclusive Right to their respective Writings and Discoveries"; this clause provides the basis for U.S. copyright and patent law.

The First Amendment provides a guarantee of freedom of expression that is at the heart of the ongoing debate over a variety of unpopular uses of the Internet, ranging from spam to pornography and racist hate Web sites. Other areas of constitutional law may also be affected by technological advances. For example, the scope of the Fourth Amendment's protection against unreasonable searches and seizures is growing increasingly difficult to assess as information technology makes it possible for law enforcement officials to view information kept on home computers or exchanged over the Internet.

See also: Censorship; Child Online Protection Act; Child Pornography; Children's Internet Protection Act; Communications Decency Act; Copyright; Digital Millennium Copyright Act; Digital Millennium Copyright Act, Title I; First Amendment; Indecency; Obscenity; Patent; Pornography; Privacy; Spam

Sources and further reading:
Jerome A. Barron and C. Thomas Dienes,
    Constitutional Law in a Nutshell (St. Paul, MN:
    West, 2002).

❖ CONSUMER BROADBAND AND DIGITAL TELEVISION PROMOTION ACT ❖

The Consumer Broadband and Digital Television Promotion Act was a proposed law that would greatly enhance the content industry's control over digital recordings purchased by consumers. Senator Fritz Hollings (D-SC) introduced the act, originally drafted as the Security Systems and Standards Certification Act, in the Senate in 2002. The act was another salvo on the content industry's ongoing fight against digital piracy in general and online file-sharing in particular. Had it been enacted, it would have required equipment manufacturers, including PC manufacturers, to incorporate piracy detection and prevention technology into all playback equipment, including PCs. The act would also have outlawed the sale or shipment of any digital devices not incorporating this security technology and would have prohibited the re-

moval or alteration of the security technology (Consumer Broadband and Digital Television Promotion Act, §§ 3-6). Violations would be punishable under the scheme set by Title I of the Digital Millennium Copyright Act, which includes fines of up to one million dollars and prison terms of up to ten years (17 U.S.C. § 1204).

The act was unpopular not only with consumer advocates, who resist anything that would further restrict users' already-restricted ability to make copies within the limits of fair use, but also with the equipment manufacturers. The law proposed to impose an expense on manufacturers in order to add a feature to their product—even though the consumers would have preferred not to have that feature. An emotionally heated debate arose between equipment makers and the content industry; at one point Leslie L. Vadasz, then senior vice president of Intel Corporation, described the entertainment industry as "a pimple on the elephant's rear end," the elephant being the computer industry.

In a victory for equipment manufacturers and consumers, the Recording Industry Association of America, representing the music content industry, agreed to withdraw its support for the bill in exchange for concessions on the part of the computer industry. Other sectors of the content industry, however, were not involved, notably the movie industry, which intends to continue lobbying for mandatory security technology ("Unexpected Harmony" 2003).

Proposed Act
- Consumer Broadband and Digital Television Promotion Act, S. 2048, 107th Cong., 2d Sess., Mar. 21, 2002, available at http://thomas.loc.gov/cgi-bin/query/z?c107:S.2048: (visited October 22, 2004)

Statute
- Digital Millennium Copyright Act, §§ 1201–1204

See also: Content Industry; Copyright; Digital Millennium Copyright Act, Title I; Fair Use

(Copyright); INDUCE Act; Macrovision; Piracy

Sources and further reading:
"Unexpected Harmony: The Music and Computer Industries Make Peace, but Differences Remain," *The Economist,* Jan. 23, 2003.
"We've Won, for Now," www.stoppoliceware.org (visited October 22, 2004).

❖ CONTENT INDUSTRY ❖

The content industry is composed of those businesses deriving their profits from the control of intellectual property rights, especially copyright in books, music, and movies. Although it could be said to include the creators of content, the term is usually used to refer to the owners of intellectual property rights in that content, who may be but often are not the content creators. Typically the content industry purchases or licenses intellectual property rights from the creators or acquires the rights because the content is created for hire. The content industry then reproduces the content—a music CD, for example—and sells it to the public.

The business model of the content industry, especially the music sector, has been under stress in recent years. The music industry's pre-Internet model involves the bundling of a dozen or more songs in a single package; in order to purchase one song, the consumer must also purchase a dozen or so other songs that he or she might not want.

The Internet makes it possible to exchange and record copies of individual songs. Companies not part of the traditional content industry have made varying uses of this capability. In the early days of the Internet a company called MP3.com placed tens of thousands of copyrighted songs on its servers and made them available to subscribers who could demonstrate, by placing a recorded CD in the disk drive of their computers, that they owned, or at least had access to, a legitimate (licensed) copy of the copyrighted version of the material. Representatives of the content industry sued MP3.com; the federal district court for the Southern District of New York found that MP3.com's use of its CDs exceeded the limits of fair use of copyrighted material (*UMG Recordings,* 92 F. Supp.2d 349).

The content industry faced its next serious threat in Napster, a service that enabled users to view directories of music files on other users' computers and to download those files (*Napster,* 239 F.3d 1004). After intensive litigation Napster was shut down. The demise of Napster, however, led immediately and predictably to the rise of numerous imitators. Industry attempts at using the Internet to sell music failed to win consumer approval not only because of the cost of the music (which might have been counterbalanced by the greater availability of music on record company sites and the greater reliability of those sites) but because of restrictions placed on the content, such as a restriction that the downloaded file could only be played on the computer to which it was downloaded

© *Zits partnership. King Features Syndicate.*

and could not be copied for use in a home audio system or car stereo.

The first successful large-scale attempt to offer copyrighted music content with few restrictions was Apple Computer's iTunes.com; iTunes offered (and continues to offer) individual songs, not bundled as albums, for 99 cents each, and has been popular with the public.

The long-term threat to the music content industry is not file-sharing, but the fact that it is no longer necessary for artists to sell songs to a record company for bundling and distribution to the public. Aside from preexisting contract obligations for some established artists, there is nothing to stop musicians from offering their songs directly to an online retailer such as iTunes. The music content industry could eventually find that the most valuable service it can offer musicians is not distribution but publicity.

Eventually most sales of music could take place directly from the content creators to the consumers through such intermediaries as iTunes; however, the future of other forms of content such as books and movies is more difficult to predict. Music, after all, is cheap to create; while artistic inspiration is priceless, the actual cost of making a studio recording of a song is within the reach of most aspiring musicians. And music files are relatively small; an MP3 of a three-minute popular song can be stored in only three megabytes or so, while a noncompressed, twenty-minute digital recording sufficient to satisfy the most demanding audiophile can fit in a few hundred megabytes.

Movies are a different matter; at this point even compressed versions of a two-hour movie are too large to be worth the effort of downloading, for several reasons. First, movies are not bundled; they are sold as individual works, and the consumer is not forced to buy unwanted movies in order to buy the desired one. Second, movies recorded on DVD or videotape are relatively cheap; a movie that costs tens of millions of dollars to make typically sells for about the same price as a CD that costs tens of thousands of dollars to make. After taking into account the value of the time spent downloading a DVD and the higher cost of recordable DVD media, most Internet users will save little or no money by downloading and recording the movie rather than buying it. Third, the movie industry has been quicker to realize the possibilities of digital recording than has the music industry; movie DVDs typically fill the otherwise unused space on the disk with additional content such as alternate language tracks, scenes that ended up on the cutting-room floor, interviews with the cast, video games, and assorted trivia. Fourth, only about 30 percent of U.S. households currently have broadband Internet access (although the percentage is projected to grow to 70 percent by 2008); for those using a dial-up connection, the size of movie files renders downloading them impracticable. Fifth, most movies on DVD, but few music albums on CD, contain copy protection that it is illegal, if not particularly difficult, to circumvent.

At present there is little economic incentive for most users to download most movies. Increases in Internet speed or improvements in compression technology could change the situation in the future, however. But because motion picture studios, unlike record companies, are creators as well as marketers of content, they are in a better position than the record companies to offer content directly to the public via the Internet.

Books are the form of mass-produced and mass-marketed content least threatened by the Internet. An entire book will fit in a quite small file, easily downloadable even by dial-up users. But few consumers want to read a book at the computer, even a small laptop computer. E-book readers, bulky, expensive, and breakable, have not caught on. Most consumers seem to prefer printed books, and the cost of printing, let alone binding, a downloaded book generally exceeds that of purchasing the generally higher-quality printed version. The relative lack of online book piracy is thus related to the relative lack of success of the e-book industry. Challenges posed by future technologies, such as e-paper, that might alter this balance seem more remote than those currently faced by the music and movie industries. Reference works, however, are more threatened, because few people read them in their entirety. High-cost reference works such as the *Oxford English Dictionary* have addressed this problem with copy protection on their software versions and by offering online subscription versions.

Statutes

- Copyright Act of 1976, 17 U.S.C. § 101-1332

Cases

Federal Appellate Courts

- *A&M Records, Inc. v. Napster, Inc.*, 239 F.3d 1004 (9th Cir. 2001)

Federal District Courts

- *MGM Studios, Inc. v. Grokster, Ltd.*, 259 F.Supp.2d 1029 (C.D. Cal. 2003)
- *UMG Recordings, Inc. v. MP3.com, Inc.*, 92 F. Supp.2d 349 (S.D. N.Y. 2000)

See also: Audio Home Recording Act; Copyright; Copyright Infringement; DeCSS; Digital Audio Works; Digital Millennium Copyright Act, Title I; Digital Rights Management; E-books; File-Sharing; Macrovision; P2P; Piracy; Protecting Intellectual Rights against Theft and Expropriation Act; Recording Industry Association of America; Sonny Bono Copyright Term Extension Act

Sources and further reading:

Lawrence Lessig, *The Future of Ideas: The Fate of the Commons in a Connected World* (New York: Random House, 2001).
"The Meaning of iPod," *Economist Technology Quarterly,* June 12, 2004, at 16.
Trevor Merriden, *Irresistible Forces: The Business Legacy of Napster and the Growth of the Underground Internet* (New York: John Wiley and Sons, 2002).

❖ CONTENT SCRAMBLE SYSTEM ❖

See DeCSS

❖ CONTRACTS ❖

A contract is an agreement between two or more parties that creates legally binding and enforceable rights and obligations. The advent of computer technology and Internet commerce has probably resulted in an increase in the number of contracts formed across state and national boundaries, with consequent conflict-of-laws issues. The two areas in which the law of contracts has been most heavily impacted, however, are e-commerce—now a new area of contracts law—and end user license agreements: agreements that purport to limit the intellectual property and other rights of consumers of software.

The contracts laws of the states of the United States are for the most part based on the Uniform Commercial Code (UCC). The UCC limits the enforceability of end-user license agreements of the "take it or leave it" variety, such as shrinkwrap or clickwrap agreements. Contracts of this sort, which are prepared by one party and in which the other party is in a weaker bargaining position and has no opportunity to negotiate terms, are known as adhesion contracts and are disfavored under the UCC. Although not automatically invalid, adhesion contracts will generally not be enforced if their terms are oppressive or unconscionable or if they defeat the reasonable expectations of the weaker (or "adhering") party. Ambiguities are generally strictly construed against the drafter and in favor of the adhering party.

The rise of e-commerce has also required changes in contract law, particularly to deal with the problem of signatures when the parties never exchange any physical documents. A federal statute, the Electronic Signatures in Global and National Commerce Act addresses this problem by providing that in most cases "a signature, contract, or other record relating to such transaction may not be denied legal effect, validity, or enforceability solely because it is in electronic form" (15 U.S.C. § 7001(a)(1)).

Statute

- Electronic Signatures in Global and National Commerce Act (E-Sign), 15 U.S.C. § 7001 et seq.

Uniform Acts

- Uniform Commercial Code, available at http://www.law.cornell.edu/ucc/ucc.table.html (visited November 14, 2004)

- Uniform Computer Information Transactions Act, available at http://www.law.upenn.edu/bll/ulc/ucita/ucita200.htm (visited November 14, 2004)
- Uniform Electronic Transactions Act, available at http://www.law.upenn.edu/bll/ulc/fnact99/1990s/ueta99.htm (visited November 14, 2004)

See also: Choice of Law; Clickwrap Agreement; E-commerce; Jurisdiction; Recognition and Enforcement of Judgments

Sources and further reading:
Jeffrey Ferriell and Michael Navin, *Understanding Contracts* (New York: Matthew Bender, 2004).
Christina Ramberg, *Internet Marketplaces: The Law of Auctions and Exchanges Online* (Oxford: Oxford University Press, 2002).
Claude D. Rohwer et al., *Contracts in a Nutshell* (St. Paul, MN: West, 2000).
Bradford Stone, *Uniform Commercial Code in a Nutshell* (St. Paul, MN: West, 2001).

❖ COOKIES ❖

A cookie is a small file (usually a text file) placed by a Web page on computers visiting that page. Cookies generally contain information about the visiting computer; they can store information such as passwords and preferences or pages previously viewed. Because cookies collect information about Web browsing by individual users and because they may remain on a computer long after a page is visited, they can raise security and privacy concerns.

Cookies can be used in conjunction with adware and spyware to track a user's online and off-line computer use; cookies can track Web pages viewed and documents opened, and the adware or spyware can then transmit that information to some third party. Cookies can also be used by Web sites to track a user's behavior in that particular site: the documents viewed, the number of times the user visits the site, and so forth. This information might have benign or even beneficial uses; it can help a commercial site to direct a viewer to products the viewer might find interesting, and it can eliminate the

necessity for retyping usernames, passwords, and addresses.

Users who feel uncomfortable with cookies can set their Web browser to refuse cookies or to notify them when a cookie is being placed on their computer. The former choice will mean that some Web pages cannot be viewed at all; the latter provides a compromise for privacy-conscious Web surfers. Because cookies are within users' control to accept or reject, there is nothing illegal about their use to collect information about users' Web browsing habits, even when it is done without the users' knowledge (*DoubleClick*, 154 F.Supp.2d 497). An exception is made when the users are children, however: The Children's Online Privacy Protection Act requires Web sites that collect information from children under the age of thirteen to provide notice of what information they collect from children, how they use the information, and what their practices are regarding disclosure of the information. When the Web sites gather information that might identify or permit communication with the child, they must first obtain the verifiable consent of the child's parents (15 U.S.C. § 6502).

Case
- *In re DoubleClick, Inc. Privacy Litigation*, 154 F.Supp.2d 497 (S.D. N.Y. 2001)

Statute
- Children's Online Privacy Protection Act, 15 U.S.C. § 6501–6506

See also: Adware and Spyware; Children's Online Privacy Protection Act; DoubleClick; Privacy

❖ COPYLEFT ❖

See Open-Source

❖ COPYRIGHT ❖

Copyright is the main form of protection of the rights of authors of computer programs and Internet content; as the name implies, it provides the holder, for a limited time, with a monopoly on the right to make copies of the copyrighted work. Under the Copyright Act of 1976, "original works of authorship fixed in any tangible medium of expression" may be copyrighted (17 U.S.C. § 102(a)); there is no copyright in U.S. government works (17 U.S.C. § 105). In other words, in order to be eligible for copyright protection the thing to be protected must be original, it must be a work of authorship, and it must be fixed in a tangible medium. If a work meets these three requirements, the copyright holder will have the exclusive right to reproduce, distribute, and publicly display or perform the work (including, in the case of sound recordings, performance by digital audio transmission), as well as to prepare derivative works based on the work (17 U.S.C. §§ 103, 106). For works created after January 1, 1978, this exclusive right will endure for seventy years after the death of the author or, in the case of a work with multiple authors, for seventy years after the death of the last surviving author. For works made for hire and works published anonymously or under a pseudonym, the copyright will endure for ninety-five years from the date of first publication or 120 years from the date of creation, whichever is shorter (17 U.S.C. § 302).

History: The concept of copyright in modern law owes its existence to an early revolution in information technology: the invention of the printing press. Anglo-American law's first sweeping attempt to control the reproduction of books came in the century after the introduction of the printing press to Britain, with the granting of a royal monopoly on book publishing to the Stationer's Company in 1557. This monopoly lasted until 1695. In the next fifteen years alternative publishers flourished; the Stationer's Company lobbied for further legal protection, and in 1710 the British Parliament passed its first copyright act, the Statute of Anne (Leaffer 1999, 4–5).

The Statute of Anne preserved the rights of the Stationer's Company in works already published for an additional 21 years, until 1731. But it effectively undermined the position of

Does intellectual property law shape societies? Developing a new pharmaceutical product costs, on the average, about ten times as much as making a Hollywood movie—and thousands of times as much as publishing a book. Yet the makers of the movie will enjoy a monopoly for about five times as long as the inventors of the pharmaceutical; the author of the book might enjoy an even longer monopoly. Inventors have to take their profits quickly; movie studios and publishing houses can coast through a string of flops for years, buoyed by royalties from past successes.

Has this imbalance led to a diversion of talent and resources away from science and engineering and into the entertainment industry? Many scientists and engineers arrive in the United States as immigrants, often from countries in which copyright law has only recently been widely enforced, or from small countries whose works of entertainment are less likely to reach a global audience. On the other hand, the United States also imports actors, entertainers, and literary, cinematic, and musical works. If intellectual property law has been structured to divert talent toward entertainment and away from science, is this the result of a conscious societal choice that entertainment is more valuable? Or is it a perverse and unanticipated result of the opposite choice—a belief that it is more important for society to have access to medicines and other useful inventions than to be able to make copies of books, songs, and movies? Or is the entertainment industry simply more organized than the science and technology industries and more effective in promoting its interests?

the Stationer's Company by viewing copyright as stemming from the act of creation of the work, rather than from the act of publishing; the purpose of the statute was to encourage "learned men to compose and write useful work." For works created after the date of the statute, copyright was to endure for fourteen years and was renewable for a second fourteen-year term if the author was still alive at the end of the first. For the next sixty-four years, however, the Stationer's Company managed to convince the British courts that its rights in the works it published, at least, were perpetual; it was not until 1774 that the House of Lords established, in the case of *Donaldson v. Beckett,* that the term of copyright is invariably finite (Leaffer 1999, 4–5).

In the United States, the establishment of a law of copyrights was one of the powers granted to Congress by the Constitution. The Patent and Copyright Clause provides that Congress shall have the power "To promote the Progress of Science and useful Arts, by securing for limited Times to Authors and Inventors the exclusive Right to their respective Writings and Discoveries" (Art. I, § 8, cl. 8). In the following year, 1790, the country's first Copyright Act established a fourteen-year copyright, renewable once for an additional fourteen years, in books, charts, and maps. This copyright was held by the author or those to whom the author might assign it. The act was readily adapted to cover new forms of material in response to rapid technological change; for example, in 1865 photographs became copyrightable. Nonetheless, over the following century or so the act, despite two major overhauls, became increasingly unworkable. The United States law of copyright was increasingly out of step with that developing in the rest of the world, and trade in information was increasingly becoming international (Leaffer 1999, 6–7).

The Copyright Act of 1909, the culmination of a work begun four years earlier at the urging of President Theodore Roosevelt, failed to solve these problems. It doubled the term of copyright protection—from two fourteen-year terms to two twenty-eight-year terms—but failed to bring U.S. copyright law into compliance with the international norms set forth in the 1886 Berne Convention. Major areas of difference were that U.S. law continued to require compliance with certain formalities before a copyright could be claimed, and that U.S. law granted a shorter term of copyright than the Berne Convention's minimum of the lifetime of the author plus fifty years. A domestic problem was created by the 1909 act's grant of copyright to only a few narrowly defined categories of unpublished works; as a result, an unwieldy parallel system of state common-law copyright protection was necessary to protect copyrights in most unpublished works (Leaffer 1999, 39).

As with the 1790 act, the 1909 act evolved to take into account new forms of recorded information. Motion pictures, for example, were added to the list of copyrightable works in 1912. But the difficulties of the 1909 act were apparent from its inception, and in 1955 Congress began a two-decades-long revision process, culminating in the passage of the Copyright Act of 1976 (Leaffer 1999, 9).

The 1976 act was designed to bring U.S. law more into line with international practice. The United States, as the world's largest exporter of intellectual property, had far more to gain than to lose from complying with international norms and joining the Berne Convention; its failure to do so had been costly and inconvenient for the U.S. content industry.

The 1976 act preempted state law, eliminating the problem of common-law copyright (17 U.S.C. § 301). It eliminated the renewable twenty-eight-year term of copyright, replacing it with the Berne Convention minimum of the lifetime of the author plus fifty years, and with a term of seventy-five years from publication or one hundred years from creation, whichever was less, for anonymous or pseudonymous works and works for hire. It established the broad and flexible subject matter categories still in use. It defined the rights granted to copyright holders, and the limitations on those rights, far more clearly than had been done previously. It failed in one notable respect to bring U.S. law into compliance with Berne Convention standards: Formalities regarding registration and the affixing of copyright notice were still required. This problem was resolved with the Berne Convention Implementation Act of 1988, however, and the United States finally joined the Berne Convention, more than a century after it first came into existence. Legislative tinkering has continued; revisions include the Sonny Bono Copyright Term Extension Act, which increases the duration of copyright terms to the lifetime of the author plus seventy years, with a term of ninety-five years from publication or 120 years from creation, whichever is less, for anonymous or pseudonymous works and works for hire (17 U.S.C. §§ 320, 304); the No Electronic Theft Act, which allows the government to prosecute those who give away copies of copyrighted material as well as those who sell it (17 U.S.C. §§ 101, 506, and 507); and the Digital Millennium Copyright Act, which makes many changes to accommodate the increase in electronic exchange of information (17 U.S.C. §§ 512, 1201–1204).

The last of these three reforms was at least partially driven by the need to keep U.S. law in compliance with international agreements, while the first was partially driven by concerns about the value of U.S. intellectual property exports and the duration of copyright protection in the European Union. To allow valuable copyrights to fall into the public domain in the United States after a term of life plus fifty years would bring them into the public domain in Europe as well, because even though the European Union has adopted a term of life plus seventy years, the Berne Convention allows it to adopt another state's term when that state's copyright law provides a term that is in compliance with the Berne Convention but shorter than its own. These recent changes to U.S. copyright law in response to international concerns demonstrate the increasingly international nature of copyright law. Because information can now be exchanged quite freely across international borders, protection of copyright must be international in nature if it is to succeed at all.

The 1909 and the original 1976 acts remain important, however, as they may affect rights to works created before January 1, 1978. Determining exactly which copyright term applies to a particular work is complex and depends on a variety of factors, including the exact date the work was first created or published, whether copyright notice was affixed, and whether the original copyright was renewed.

Originality: The level of originality required for copyright protection is low, but not nonexistent. For example, an alphabetical listing of names in a telephone directory is not copyrightable. The arrangement and page numbering of cases in a case reporter may be, however. The mere fact that an author has put effort into assembling a collection of information does not confer copyright; originality, rather than the "sweat of the brow," is what is protected (*Feist,* 499 U.S. 340).

The *scènes a fàire* doctrine provides that work that is too dependent on basic, common ways of treating particular subject matter is not copyrightable. For example, a movie about Germany in the 1930s might include images of German soldiers drinking in beer halls, saying "Heil Hitler" and singing the German national anthem. Because these images are a standard part of any depiction of Germany in that era, they cannot be copyrighted (*Hoehling,* 618 F.2d 972). Similarly, any video game about baseball, football, or basketball will necessarily follow a certain sequence of play and a certain point scoring system; any martial arts video game will include certain moves. These elements are *scènes a fàire* and not copyrightable (*Data East,* 862 F.2d 204).

Works of authorship: Works of authorship include literary, musical, and dramatic works, pantomimes and choreographic works, works traditionally thought of as "art" (pictorial, graphic, and sculptural works), motion pictures and other audiovisual works, and sound recordings. Copyright will not protect ideas, although when an idea can be expressed in only a limited number of ways, the idea and the expression merge and the expression is uncopyrightable. Nor will copyright protect procedures, processes, systems, or methods of operation (17 U.S.C. § 102). Computer operating systems, however, are not "mere methods of operation" within the meaning of the Copyright Act and are thus copyrightable (*Apple Computer,* 714 F.2d 1240). The exact boundary between a copyrightable computer program and an uncopyrightable "method of operation" is not always easy to determine. For example, threshold values used to determine the best time to replace a hard disk drive are not mere methods of operation and are copyrightable, but the menu command hierarchy of a computer program is a method of operation and not copyrightable (*Compaq,* 908 F.Supp. 1409; *Lotus,* 49 F.3rd 807).

Fixed in a tangible medium of expression: The most common forms in which computer programs are recorded—magnetic and optical storage—cannot be read without mechanical aid. Information recorded in such a way is nonetheless "fixed in a tangible medium of expression."

International copyright protection: Even before the advent of the Internet, copyright required international protection. Copyrights are granted by national governments; in the absence of a treaty obligation to do so, countries can and will disregard copyrights issued by their neighbors. Entire industries depend on international recognition of copyrights; if the copyright to the Harry Potter series were honored only in Britain, or copyrights on Hollywood films were honored only in the United States, the greater part of the value of those pieces of intellectual property would be lost.

The need for an international copyright regime was already evident by 1878, when Victor Hugo and others began lobbying for the adoption of an international convention. As a result, the Berne Convention for the Protection of Literary and Artistic Works was adopted in 1886 and has evolved through numerous revisions to become the cornerstone of the modern international copyright regime. For more than a century, however, the United States was unable to join the convention because of differences between U.S. copyright law and the Berne Convention's requirements. As a result, a parallel system of bilateral and multilateral treaties arose to protect U.S. copyright interests abroad and foreign copyright interests in the United States; these treaties, some of which are still in force, are now chiefly of historical interest.

The Internet era, with its greatly expanded exchange of copyrighted information across national borders, has seen the adoption of several new international copyright treaties. Important treaties to which the United States is a party include the Agreement on Trade-Related Aspects of Intellectual Property Rights (TRIPS) and two World Intellectual Property Organization (WIPO) treaties. TRIPS is an annex to the World Trade Organization (WTO) treaty; it addresses many types of intellectual property and provides, through the WTO, enforcement and dispute resolution mechanisms that other treaties lack. The two 1996 WIPO treaties, although they did not enter into force until 2002,

led to the adoption of Title I of the Digital Millennium Copyright Act of 1998, perhaps the most significant change to U.S. copyright law in recent years.

Statute
- Copyright Act of 1976, 17 U.S.C. §§ 101–1332

Constitution
- United States Constitution, Article I, Section 8, Clause 8

Treaties
- Agreement on Trade-Related Aspects of Intellectual Property Rights, Marrakesh Agreement Establishing the World Trade Organization, Annex 1C, Apr. 15, 1994, 33 I.L.M. 81 (1994)
- Convention Concerning the Creation of an International Union for the Protection of Literary and Artistic Works (Berne Convention), Sept. 9, 1886, as last revised at Paris, July 24, 1971 (amended 1979), 25 U.S.T. 1341, 828 U.N.T.S. 221
- WIPO Copyright Treaty, Dec. 20, 1996, 36 I.L.M. 65 (1997)
- WIPO Performance and Phonograms Treaty, Dec. 20, 1996, 36 I.L.M. 76 (1997)

European Union Materials
- Council Directive 93/98/EEC of 29 October 1993 Harmonizing the Term of Protection of Copyright and Certain Related Rights

Cases
England
- *Donaldson v. Beckett,* 2 Bro. P.C. 129, 1 Eng. Rep. 837 Burr. (4th ed.) 2408, 98 Eng. Rep. 257 (H.L. 1774)

Supreme Court
- *Eldred v. Ashcroft,* 123 S. Ct. 769 (2003)
- *Feist Publications v. Rural Telephone Service Co.,* 499 U.S. 340 (1991)
- *Wheaton v. Peters,* 33 U.S. (8 Pet.) 591 (1834)

Federal Appellate Courts

- *Apple Computer v. Franklin Computer,* 714 F.2d 1240 (3d Cir. 1983)
- *Atari v. JS & A,* 747 F.2d 1422 (Fed. Cir. 1984)
- *Data East USA v. Epyx,* 862 F.2d 204 (9th Cir. 1988)
- *Hoehling v. Universal City Studios, Inc.,* 618 F.2d 972 (2d Cir. 1980)
- *Lewis Galoob Toys v. Nintendo of America,* 964 F.2d 965 (9th Cir. 1992)
- *Lotus Development Corporation v. Borland International, Inc.,* 49 F.3rd 807 (1st Cir. 1995), affirmed, 516 U.S. 233 (1996)
- *Sega Enterprises v. Accolade,* 977 F.2d 1510 (9th Cir. 1992)
- *Williams Electronics v. Arctic International,* 685 F.2d 870 (3d Cir. 1982)

Federal Trial Courts

- *Compaq Computer Corp. v. Procom Technology,* 908 F.Supp. 1409 (S.D. Tex. 1995)
- *Oasis Publishing Co. v. West Publishing Co.,* 924 F.Supp. 918 (D. Minn. 1996)

See also: Berne Convention; Content Industry; Copyright Infringement; DeCSS; Digital Millennium Copyright Act; Digital Millennium Copyright Act, Title I; Digital Millennium Copyright Act, Title II; Digital Millennium Copyright Act, Title III; Digital Millennium Copyright Act, Title IV; Digital Millennium Copyright Act, Title V; Digital Rights Management; Fair Use (Copyright); File-Sharing; International Copyright Protection; Moral Rights; Open-Source; Piracy; Public Domain; Public Domain Enhancement Act; Sonny Bono Copyright Term Extension Act; TRIPS (Copyright); Universal Copyright Convention; WIPO; WIPO Copyright Treaty; WIPO Performances and Phonograms Treaty

Sources and further reading:

Mary E. Carter, *Electronic Highway Robbery: An Artist's Guide to Copyrights in the Digital Era* (Berkeley, CA: Peachpit Press, 1996).

Richard Chused, ed., *A Copyright Anthology: The Technology Frontier* (Cincinnati, OH: Anderson Publishing, 1998).

"Copyrights: A Radical Rethink," *The Economist,* Jan. 25, 2003, at 15.

Anthony D'Amato and Doris Estelle Long, eds., *International Intellectual Property Anthology* (Cincinnati, OH: Anderson Publishing, 1996).

Michael H. Davis and Arthur Raphael Miller, *Intellectual Property: Patents, Trademarks, and Copyright in a Nutshell* (St. Paul, MN: West, 2000).

Stephen R. Elias, *Patent, Copyright & Trademark: An Intellectual Property Desk Reference,* 6th ed. (Berkeley, CA: Nolo Press, 2003).

"A Fine Balance: How Much Copyright Protection Does the Internet Need?" *Economist Technology Quarterly,* Jan. 25, 2003, at 12.

Jane C. Ginsburg, "No 'Sweat'? Copyright and Other Protection of Works of Information after *Feist v. Rural Telephone,*" 92 *Columbia Law Review* 338 (1992).

Marshall Leaffer, *Understanding Copyright Law,* 3d ed. (New York: Matthew Bender, 1999).

Lawrence Lessig, *Free Culture: How Big Media Uses Technology and the Law to Lock Down Culture and Control Creativity* (New York: Penguin, 2004) (also available as a free download).

Jessica Litman, *Digital Copyright: Protecting Intellectual Property on the Internet* (Amherst, NY: Prometheus, 2000).

Pamela Samuelson, "Will the Copyright Office Be Obsolete in the Twenty-First Century?" 13 *Cardozo Arts and Entertainment Law Journal* 55 (1994).

Richard Stim, *Getting Permission: How to License & Clear Copyrighted Materials Online & Off* (Berkeley: Nolo Press, 2001).

Adam D. Thierer and Wayne Crews, *Copy Fights: The Future of Intellectual Property in the Information Age* (Washington, DC: Cato Institute, 2002).

Siva Vaidhyanathan, *Copyrights and Copywrongs: The Rise of Intellectual Property and How It Threatens Creativity* (New York: New York University Press, 2001).

❖ COPYRIGHT INFRINGEMENT ❖

A copyright is infringed when someone not authorized by the copyright holder reproduces, distributes, or publicly displays or performs a copyrighted work (including, in the case of sound recordings, performance by digital audio transmission), or prepares a derivative work (17 U.S.C. § 106), unless the use of the copyrighted material falls within one of the permissible exceptions: the right to make backup copies, fair use, the first sale doctrine, and the four safe harbors for Internet service providers (ISPs)(17 U.S.C. §§ 107–122, 512). Infringement may be direct, contributory, or vicarious.

Reproduces, distributes, or publicly displays: The making, distribution or public display of a single copy may be sufficient to constitute a copyright infringement if the other elements of infringement are also present.

Derivative works: The copyright holder has the exclusive right to make or license derivative works, but a device (or perhaps program) that enhances the operation of a computer program may not be a derivative work (*Lewis Galoob Toys,* 964 F.2d 965).

Backup copies: The purchaser of a recording of copyrighted material, such as a computer program, has the right to make a backup copy of the copyrighted material as a safeguard against the destruction of the original recording. However, Title I of the Digital Millennium Copyright Act (DMCA) has the practical effect, although ostensibly not the purpose, of prohibiting the making of digital backup copies of media recordings containing some form of copy protection.

Privileges of ISPs: Under Title II of the DMCA, Internet service providers (ISPs) are not liable for copyright infringement for material passing through their servers if their connection to the infringing material falls within one of the four statutory safe harbors established by the act. There are safe harbors for ISPs for transitory communications, system caching, storage of information on systems or networks at the direction of users, and information location tools (17 U.S.C. § 512). The safe harbors are necessary to enable ISPs to function; policing all content transmitted over, cached on, stored on, or located via a network for possible copyright infringement would be extremely costly, if not impossible. The four statutory safe harbors are not absolute, however, and ISPs may be required to remove or block infringing

content if the copyright owner complies with certain notice procedures.

Fair use: The right of the copyright owner to prevent unauthorized copying is limited by the fair use doctrine. The exact parameters of fair use are poorly defined and are currently the subject of a multisided conflict among the varied interests of content producers, copyright holders, equipment manufacturers, and consumers. The definition created by Congress in section 107 of the Copyright Act allows considerable latitude for interpretation:

> [T]he fair use of a copyrighted work, including such use by reproduction in copies or phonorecords or by any other means specified by that section, for purposes such as criticism, comment, news reporting, teaching (including multiple copies for classroom use), scholarship, or research, is not an infringement of copyright. In determining whether the use made of a work in any particular case is a fair use the factors to be considered shall include –
> - the purpose and character of the use, including whether such use is of a commercial nature or is for nonprofit educational purposes;
> - the nature of the copyrighted work;
> - the amount and substantiality of the portion used in relation to the copyrighted work as a whole; and
> - the effect of the use upon the potential market for or value of the copyrighted work. (17 U.S.C. § 107)

Among the established fair uses of computer software is the right to disassemble or decompile a computer program to reverse-engineer for compatibility. Copying a music recording that one has purchased onto one's own computer for one's own listening is fair use, but copying music so that large numbers of anonymous individuals can access it over the Internet is not (*Napster,* 239 F.3d 1004). This latter type of online file-sharing of copyrighted material is perhaps the most hotly contested area in the ongoing battle between the content industry and consumers.

The traditional fair use doctrine provides that the purchaser or licensee of copyrighted software may make backup copies, as noted previously, and may make copies necessary for the use of the program or for diagnostic purposes. Many media recordings, however, especially movies, contain copy protection that prevents the making of digital backup copies. Although this copy protection can be circumvented relatively easily, doing so violates the provisions of the DMCA forbidding the circumvention of technological copy-protection measures (17 U.S.C. § 1201).

First sale doctrine: The first sale doctrine, set out in section 109 of the Copyright Act, limits the copyright holder's control over the copyrighted material to its first sale. Once a copy of a work has been sold or given away, the purchaser or recipient may dispose of that copy as he or she wishes. The first sale doctrine does not create a right to make copies, but only to freely dispose of an authorized copy and to display that copy at the place where it is located. It does not include the right to display the copy at some other place than the place where it is located, whether by broadcasting, posting on the Internet, or some other means.

Distributors and resellers of copyrighted materials, such as bookstores, must be permitted to resell the copies they purchase in order to function; similarly libraries must be able to lend out copies of books, and individuals who purchase books must be permitted to give them away as gifts. The first sale doctrine permits all of these persons to do so without infringing on the copyright.

Exceptions to the doctrine have been carved out for holders of copyrights in audio recordings and computer software, who retain the right to control rentals of the copyrighted material. Curiously, no similar exception exists for motion picture recordings. One possible explanation could be that the exceptions for audio recordings and computer programs are designed more to deter piracy than to generate revenue directly for copyright holders. The average consumer watches most motion pictures only once, whereas the average consumer might listen to a favorite audio recording hundreds of times, so the incentives for piracy are much higher, while the costs in time and recording media or disk storage space are much lower. However, Title I of the Digital Millennium

Copyright Act (DMCA) provides motion picture copyright holders with additional antipiracy protections through its provisions prohibiting the circumvention of anti-copying technological measures.

The exceptions for computer programs and sound recordings are themselves subject to exceptions for lending by nonprofit libraries and educational institutions, and rentals of computer programs "embodied in a machine or product and which cannot be copied during the ordinary operation or use of the machine or product; or embodied in or used in conjunction with a limited purpose computer that is designed for playing video games and may be designed for other purposes" (17 U.S.C. §§ 109(b), 109(e)). Section 117 of the Copyright Act adds a further exception for copies of computer programs made as a necessary part of using the program, for archival purposes, or in the course of maintenance or repair.

Contractual limitations on purchasers' rights: The software end-user license agreement (EULA) can affect these rights, but its effect will be limited by applicable state law, including restrictions on adhesion contracts, and may be preempted by federal copyright law (*Vault Corp.*, 847 F.2d 255).

Contributory infringement: The sale of devices or programs enabling the copying of copyrighted material may become contributory infringement if the primary use of such devices or programs is copyright infringement. The operation of file-sharing services might also be contributory infringement. Contributory infringement requires a direct infringement by someone other than the contributory infringer. The contributory infringer must have actual or constructive knowledge of the violation; that is, the contributory infringer must either know of it or be in such a position that a reasonable person similarly situated would know that direct infringement was taking place. This knowledge requirement is essential to both contributory and vicarious liability, but there is no knowledge requirement for liability for direct infringement. Finally, contributory infringement also requires that the contributory infringer make a material contribution to the direct infringer's activities (*Fonovisa*, 76 F.3d 259).

For example, under Title I of the DMCA it is illegal to distribute to others software or hardware designed to enable users to overcome technological measures designed to prevent copying. A reasonable person distributing software or hardware that had no other use than to overcome these technological protective measures should know that direct infringement is taking place, and the distribution of the software or hardware is a material contribution to the direct infringement. A person distributing such hardware or software might thus be liable for contributory infringement as well as for violation of Title I's anticircumvention provisions.

Vicarious infringement: Like contributory infringement, vicarious infringement is defined by case law rather than by statute. Also like contributory infringement, vicarious infringement requires actual or constructive knowledge of a direct infringement by some other person. In addition, the vicarious infringer must have the right and ability to control the direct infringer's actions, and a direct financial benefit from the infringing activity (*Fonovisa*, 76 F.3d 259). The right and ability to control the infringer's actions may result from a continuing relationship such as an employment relationship; for example, officers and directors of a corporation may be liable for copyright infringement committed by employees of the corporation. It may also result from a contract in which the vicarious infringer retains the right to restrict the direct infringer's actions—for example, a contract between an on-line file-sharing service and a user of the service in which the file-sharing service reserves the right to restrict access. The direct financial benefit from the infringing activity need not be actual payment; if the possibility of engaging in direct copyright infringement brings more users to a file-sharing service, there is a direct financial benefit for vicarious infringement purposes.

Statute
- Copyright Act of 1976, 17 U.S.C. §§ 101–1332

Cases
Supreme Court
- *Sony Corp. of America v. Universal City Studios, Inc.,* 464 U.S. 417 (1984)

Federal Appellate Courts
- *A & M Records, Inc. v. Napster, Inc.,* 239 F.3d 1004 (9th Cir. 2001), on remand, 2001 WL 227083 (N.D. Cal. 2001), aff'd, 284 F.3d 1091 (9th Cir. 2002)
- *Apple Computer v. Franklin Computer,* 714 F.2d 1240 (3d Cir. 1983)
- *Atari v. JS & A,* 747 F.2d 1422 (Fed. Cir. 1984)
- *Computer Associates International v. Altai,* 126 F.3d 365 (2d Cir. 1997)
- *Data East USA v. Epyx,* 862 F.2d 204 (9th Cir. 1988)
- *Fonovisa, Inc. v. Cherry Auction, Inc.,* 76 F.3d 259 (9th Cir. 1996)
- *Gershwin Publishing Corporation v. Columbia Artists Management, Inc.,* 443 F.2d 1159, 1162 (2d Cir. 1971)
- *In re Aimster Copyright Litigation (Aimster II),* 334 F.3d 643 (7th Cir. 2003)
- *Lewis Galoob Toys v. Nintendo of America,* 964 F.2d 965 (9th Cir. 1992)
- *Lotus Development Corp. v. Borland International,* 140 F.3d 70 (1st Cir. 1998)
- *Recording Industry Association of America v. Diamond Multimedia Systems, Inc.,* 180 F.3d 1072 (9th Cir. 1999)
- *Vault Corp. v. Quaid Software,* 847 F.2d 255 (5th Cir. 1988)

Federal Trial Courts
- *Intellectual Reserve, Inc. v. Utah Lighthouse Ministry, Inc.,* 75 F.Supp.2d 1290 (D. Utah 1999)
- *MGM Studios, Inc. v. Grokster, Ltd.,* 259 F.Supp.2d 1029, 1046 (C.D. Cal. 2003)
- *NEC v. Intel,* 10 U.S.P.Q. 2d 1177 (N.D. Cal. 1989)
- *Religious Technology Center v. Netcom On-Line Communication Services, Inc.,* 907 F.Supp. 1361 (N.D. Cal. 1995)
- *UMG Recordings, Inc. v. MP3.Com, Inc.,* 92 F.Supp.2d 349 (S.D. N.Y. 2000)
- *UMG Recordings, Inc. v. Sinnott,* 300 F.Supp.2d 993 (E.D. Cal. 2004)

- *Universal City Studios, Inc. v. Reimerdes,* 111 F.Supp.2d 294 (S.D. N.Y. 2000), aff'd by *Universal City Studios, Inc. v. Corley,* 273 F.3d 429 (2nd Cir. 2001)

See also: Berne Convention; Clickwrap Agreement; Content Industry; Copyright; DeCSS; Digital Millennium Copyright Act; Digital Millennium Copyright Act, Title I; Digital Millennium Copyright Act, Title II; Digital Millennium Copyright Act, Title III; Digital Rights Management; Encryption; File-Sharing; International Copyright Protection; Piracy; Steganography; WIPO Copyright Treaty; WIPO Performances and Phonograms Treaty

Sources and further reading:
Mary E. Carter, *Electronic Highway Robbery: An Artist's Guide to Copyrights in the Digital Era* (Berkeley, CA: Peachpit Press, 1996).
Richard Chused, ed., *A Copyright Anthology: The Technology Frontier* (Cincinnati, OH: Anderson Publishing, 1998).
Michael H. Davis and Arthur Raphael Miller, *Intellectual Property: Patents, Trademarks, and Copyright in a Nutshell* (St. Paul, MN: West, 2000).
Marshall Leaffer, *Understanding Copyright Law,* 3d ed. (New York: Matthew Bender, 1999).
J. Thomas McCarthy et al., *McCarthy's Desk Encyclopedia of Intellectual Property,* 3d ed. (Washington, DC: Bureau of National Affairs, 2004).
Richard Stim, *Getting Permission: How to License & Clear Copyrighted Materials Online & Off* (Berkeley, CA: Nolo Press, 2001).

❖ COURT OF APPEALS FOR THE FEDERAL CIRCUIT ❖

The United States Court of Appeals for the Federal Circuit has jurisdiction to hear appeals from a variety of specialized federal courts and administrative tribunals. From a computer and Internet law perspective, its most important function is that it is the court in which patent appeals are heard and decided.

From 1929 until 1982, customs and patent appeals were heard in the aptly named United States Court of Customs and Patent Appeals. The court served this function until 1982, when it was abolished and its functions were taken over by the newly created Court of Appeals for the Federal Circuit. The Court of Appeals for the Federal Circuit was created in 1982 by a merger of most of the functions of the United States Court of Customs and Patent Appeals and the United States Court of Claims. The trial jurisdiction of the United States Court of Claims was spun off to the newly created and confusingly named United States Claims Court, later renamed (without reducing the likelihood of confusion to any significant degree) the United States Court of Federal Claims. Decisions of the Federal Circuit have had a profound effect on computer and Internet law; for example, the court's decision in *In re Alappat* led the United States Patent and Trademark Office to adopt rules for the patenting of computer programs (33 F.3d 1526).

Cases
- *Atari v. JS & A,* 747 F.2d 1422 (Fed. Cir. 1984)
- *In re Alappat,* 33 F.3d 1526 (Fed. Cir. 1994)

See also: Computer Program; Patent

❖ CRACKING ❖

See Hacking

❖ CRYPTOGRAPHY ❖

See Encryption

❖ CSS ❖

See DeCSS

❖ CYBER- ❖

The prefix "cyber" is derived by back-formation from the term *cybernetics,* first used in 1948 by

Norbert Wiener, the coiner of the word *cybernetics,* was a child prodigy who grew up to become, in the opinion of many of his contemporaries, the archetypal absentminded professor. Wiener entered Tufts College at the age of eleven, graduated with a degree in mathematics at fourteen, and completed a doctorate in mathematical logic at Harvard by the age of eighteen, in 1912. Eventually he settled, more or less, at the Massachusetts Institute of Technology. His academic work, though brilliant, was often frustrating to his colleagues in its disorganized presentation; fellow mathematician Hans Freudenthal commented that Wiener "spoke many languages but was not easy to understand in any of them." His former student C. K. Jen relates that "Professor Wiener would . . . face the blackboard, standing very close to it because he was extremely near-sighted. Although I usually sat in the front row, I had difficulty seeing what he wrote. Most of the other students could not see anything at all. It was most amusing to the class to hear Professor Wiener saying to himself, 'This was very wrong, definitely.' He would quickly erase all he had written down. He would then start all over again, and sometimes murmur to himself, 'This looks all right so far.' Minutes later, 'This cannot be right either,' and he would rub it all out again. This on-again, off-again process continued until the bell signaled the end of the hour. Then Professor Wiener would leave the room without even looking at his audience."

In addition to *Cybernetics* and numerous academic works, Wiener also wrote fiction. In 1952 he published a disturbing short story, "The Brain," in which a neurosurgeon named Cole is called upon to perform brain surgery on a man named Macaluso, who had previously injured Cole's family in an auto accident. The accident left Cole's wife paralyzed and his son not only paralyzed but blind, deaf, and without "a trace of intelligence to be seen." While operating on Macaluso for a skull fracture sustained in another auto accident, Cole deliberately performs a lobotomy, which later leads to Macaluso's death during an attempted robbery. Cole then suffers a mental breakdown. The unnamed narrator of the story describes himself as "something in between a mathematician and an engineer"—a fitting description, perhaps, for the information technology profession Wiener helped to create.

Source

Norbert Wiener, *Cybernetics: Or the Control and Communication in the Animal and the Machine,* 2d ed. (Cambridge, MA: MIT Press, 1965); C. K. Jen, *Recollections of a Chinese Physicist* (Los Alamos, NM: 1990); *Norbert Wiener (Biography),* http://www-groups.dcs.st-and.ac.uk/~history/Mathematicians/ Wiener_Norbert.html (visited January 3, 2005); Norbert Wiener, "The Brain," in *Great Science Fiction by Scientists* 298, edited by Groff Conklin (New York: Collier-MacMillan, 1962).

mathematician and computer pioneer Norbert Wiener in the book *Cybernetics: Or the Control and Communication in the Animal and the Machine.* Popular imagination seized on the term not so much to describe the general concept of guided feedback systems but as a shorthand reference for Wiener's conception of the *machinea rationcinatrix,* the reasoning machine. Wiener derived the word *cybernetics* from the Greek word *kybernetes,* meaning the helmsman, or steersman, of a boat.

The use of the term *cyber* enjoyed its media heyday in the 1990s, when it became an almost automatic indicator of media hype; since then its use in new words has declined considerably, and such new cyber-terms as do appear are often ironic.

Sources and further reading:

Norbert Wiener, *Cybernetics: Or the Control and Communication in the Animal and the Machine,* 2d ed. (Cambridge, MA: MIT Press, 1965).

❖ CYBERLAW ❖

The varied areas of law having to do with computers and the Internet are sometimes lumped together under the heading "cyberlaw." Cyberlaw might include, for example, areas of business entity law, constitutional law, contract law, criminal law, intellectual property law, and tort law. The use of the term and the sense that it describes something new in the law has generated a cyberskeptic reaction from many legal theorists, who take the view that the law applicable to computer hardware and software and especially to the Internet is in no way separate from the law applicable to off-line situations. Most or all of the legal problems posed by the Internet, the argument runs, are different in degree rather than in kind from the problems posed by previous technologies (Gomes 2002).

The use of the term *cyberlaw* is thus to some extent associated with a particular ideological approach to problems of computer and Internet law. In the minds of some it is associated with a libertarian, laissez-faire approach that can perhaps be summed up succinctly in the adage that "information just wants to be free" or somewhat less succinctly in the Declaration of the Independence of Cyberspace, which concludes "We will create a civilization of the Mind in Cyberspace. May it be more humane and fair than the world your governments have made before" (Barlow 1996).

See also: Declaration of the Independence of Cyberspace

Sources and further reading:
John Perry Barlow, *A Declaration of the Independence of Cyberspace*, Feb. 8, 1996, available at http://www.eff.org/~barlow/Declaration-Final.html (visited September 30, 2004).

Gerald R. Ferrera et al., *Cyberlaw: Your Rights in Cyberspace* (Mason, OH: South-Western College Publications, 2001).

Lee Gomes, "Hot Field of Cyberlaw Is So Much Hokum, Some Skeptics Argue," *Wall Street Journal*, July 1, 2002, at B-1.

David R. Koepsell, *The Ontology of Cyberspace: Law, Philosophy and the Future of Intellectual Property* (Chicago: Open Court, 2000).

Lawrence Lessig, *Code and Other Laws of Cyberspace* (New York: Basic Books, 1999).

Joseph H. Sommer, "Against Cyberlaw," 15 *Berkeley Technology Law Journal* 1145 (2000).

Timothy Wu, "When Law and the Internet First Met," 3 *Green Bag 2d* 171 (2000).

❖ CYBERPUNK ❖

Cyberpunk is a genre of popular literature, generally thought of as a subgenre of science fiction (or, more properly, SF), which explores the possible evolution of information technology and human society in the relatively near future. Computer technology in general and data networks in particular form the central component of the scientific extrapolation involved, and provide the "cyber" in cyberpunk. A pervading sense of weltschmerz, often overdone to the point of bathos, provides the "punk" component. Cyberpunk flourished in the 1980s; although it is still being written, most of its best-known practitioners have moved on.

Although proto-cyberpunk works can be traced as far back as the 1950s and perhaps earlier (a late entry is the stylistically definitive 1982 movie *Bladerunner*), the term *cyberpunk* was probably first used by author Bruce Bethke in his short story of that title, although long before Bethke's story was published, the term had been picked up by editor Gardner Dozois (of *Isaac Asimov's Science Fiction Magazine*) and widely used by others. Cyberpunk burst out of the narrow world of SF magazines and into the broader popular imagination with William Gibson's 1984 novel *Neuromancer*.

Neuromancer's astonishing cultural impact probably results as much from its timing as its content; it came out at the beginning of the home computing revolution in the developed world. It provided names for things that the world was just beginning to realize existed, or might soon exist. It provided cultural context and cachet to what otherwise was no more than office equipment. And it was adopted into the canon by the reigning academic elite of the day, providing a body of referents for scholarly discourse on the culture of information.

Cyberpunk's adoption by the mass media resulted in the 1990s habit of tagging anything vaguely connected with information technology with a "cyber" prefix, and in some memorably bad movies. Postmodernists adored cyberpunk (e.g., Jameson 1991); as a literary genre, however, it was necessarily short-lived. Its heavy dependence on artifice, particularly on a created slang, meant that it moved from innovation to cliché almost instantly. Many of the writers most closely associated with cyberpunk in its early days—Gibson, Bruce Sterling, Neal Stephenson—are still actively exploring, in their

Cyberpunk, which in its day was so successful in print, has translated poorly to the screen. Hollywood's attempt to bring a William Gibson story to the big screen, *Johnny Mnemonic,* may have suffered from the fact that the original story is only twenty-two pages long. About fifteen minutes in, it seems to run out of material and becomes incoherent. (Gibson has said that Ridley Scott's *Bladerunner* embodied his vision of a cyberpunk future; *Johnny Mnemonic* strives to imitate that vision, but ultimately fails.) Keanu Reeves's persona from *Johnny Mnemonic* is reprised in all three *Matrix* movies—a pointless trilogy in which the *Bladerunner*/Gibson stylistic vision is reduced to a world in which everything is made of unpainted metal, everything is filmed through a green filter with insufficient lighting, and it rains a lot. The *Matrix* movies also suffer from Hollywood's ongoing problem with science fiction: bad science. In an unintentionally amusing scene Lawrence Fishburne holds up a battery and explains to Keanu that the evil machines keep humans alive to use them as a power source—unnecessarily undermining whatever credibility the movie might have had up to that point, because keeping humans alive in pods would use far more energy than the machines can possibly get out of the process. It would have been far better to explain that the machines, like the sinister TechnoCore in Dan Simmons's *Hyperion* novels, are using the processing power of human brains, or better yet that, like the machines in the *Terminator* movies, they are motivated by sheer malice—or to have said nothing at all.

work, the "cyber" side of cyberpunk: the conjoined evolution of human society and information technology. But though some remain pessimistic, the highly stylized "punk" component has been largely or entirely abandoned. Interesting postcyberpunk works by these authors include William Gibson's *Pattern Recognition,* Neal Stephenson's *Cryptonomicon,* and some of the short stories collected in Bruce Sterling's *A Good Old-Fashioned Future;* stories in the latter collection range from the distinctly cyberpunk

Deep Eddy (1993) to the upbeat *Maneki Neko* (1998), which, despite the shift in attitude, addresses the same underlying concern: the ways in which human society will change to adapt to information technology.

See also: Cyber-; Cyberspace; Data Haven; Encryption

Sources and further reading:
Nonfiction:
Thomas M. Disch, *The Dreams Our Stuff Is Made Of: How Science Fiction Conquered the World* (New York: Touchstone, 1998).
Carl Freedman, *Critical Theory and Science Fiction* (Hanover, CT: Wesleyan University Press, 2000).
Fredric Jameson, *Postmodernism, or the Cultural Logic of Late Capitalism* (Durham, NC: Duke University Press, 1991).
Brian McHale, *Postmodernist Fiction* (London: Methuen Press, 1987).
Fiction:
Bruce Bethke, "Cyberpunk," *Amazing Science Fiction,* Nov. 1983.
William Gibson, *Neuromancer* (New York: Ace, 1984) [*Neuromancer* is actually the first book in a trilogy; the second and third volumes are *Count Zero* (New York: Arbor House, 1986) and *Mona Lisa Overdrive* (New York: Bantam, 1988). *Burning Chrome* (New York: Arbor House, 1986) is a collection of thematically linked short stories].
William Gibson, *Pattern Recognition* (New York: Putnam Publishing Group, 2003).
Neal Stephenson, *Snow Crash* (New York: Bantam, 1992).
Neal Stephenson, *Cryptonomicon* (New York: HarperCollins, 1999).
Bruce Sterling, *Islands in the Net* (New York: Arbor House, 1988).
Bruce Sterling, *A Good Old-Fashioned Future* (New York: Bantam, 1992).
Bruce Sterling, ed., *Mirrorshades: The Cyberpunk Anthology* (New York: Arbor House, 1986).

❖ CYBERSPACE ❖

Although the idea had been a staple of speculative fiction for decades, the term *cyberspace* was first used by William Gibson in his 1984 novel *Neuromancer* to describe a data network as perceived by a human mind connected directly to it: "the consensual hallucination that [is] the matrix." (Gibson 1984, 5). The idea of a direct connection between a human brain and a computer had been a staple of SF and a goal of researchers for some time. The term captured the popular imagination, however, and for a while it became fashionable to refer to the Internet, the World Wide Web, a local area network, or any data network as "cyberspace." Early users began to think of cyberspace as a physical place; importantly, this place was *terra nullius*, not yet under the control of any government. The attitudes of these earlier "settlers" of cyberspace tended toward the libertarianism expressed in the Declaration of the Independence of Cyberspace or more succinctly in the aphorism "information just wants to be free."

A contrasting view was provided by Lawrence Lessig's revolutionary 1999 book *Code and Other Laws of Cyberspace* and further developed in his later work. Lessig proposed that the architecture of data networks was an architecture of control; liberty is not the natural condition of information systems, and to keep information free requires constant vigilance.

While the term *cyberspace* itself has become passé, the attitudes of its early settlers continue to shape and inform debate about the exchange, use, and ownership of information on the Internet today.

See also: Cyber-; Cyberpunk; Declaration of the Independence of Cyberspace

Sources and further reading:

William Gibson, *Neuromancer* (New York: Ace, 1984).

David R. Koepsell, *The Ontology of Cyberspace: Law, Philosophy and the Future of Intellectual Property* (Chicago: Open Court, 2000).

Lawrence Lessig, *Code and Other Laws of Cyberspace* (New York: Basic Books, 1999).

Brian Loader, *The Governance of Cyberspace: Politics, Technology and Global Restructuring* (Basingstoke, Hampshire, UK: Routledge, 1997).

Vernor Vinge, *True Names and the Opening of the Cyberspace Frontier* (James Frenkel, ed., New York: Tor, 2001).

Timothy Wu, "Cyberspace Sovereignty? The Internet and the International System," 10 *Harvard Journal of Law and Technology* 647 (1997).

The return of cyberspace? The original Gibsonian vision of cyberspace seems to have receded into yesterday's tomorrow, becoming one with the autogiro, food pills, androids, Cavorite, and cities under the sea. Yet online communities—cyberpopulations for cyberspaces, as it were—are undergoing a renaissance. Though many of the old, BBS-based communities were swept away by the advent of the World Wide Web, new Web-based communities are slowly emerging to replace them. Some communities—the community of product reviewers on Amazon.com, for example—are open marketplaces of ideas; they bear more resemblance to a notional downtown business district than to a neighborhood. In other communities users of a certain mind-set have gathered to create a community with a distinctly individual character; thus the community of LiveJournal.com users is different from the community of Fark.com users, and no visitor is likely to mistake one for the other.

Yet no set of rules, other than unwritten social rules, sends one user to Fark and another to LiveJournal. In fact, there are no doubt users who maintain a presence in both communities, using a different persona for each. This flexibility of personality—the ability to change identities as quickly as Clark Kent could in the days when there were still phone booths—might account in part for the appeal of online communities. Like Superman, though, users have reason to keep their true identities secret. Although there are probably few people who believe that billclintondailydiary.blogspot.com is actually the diary of the former president, there are probably more who have been at least briefly taken in by Snoop Doggy Blog. When the assumed identity is not a famous one, many or most other users will take it at face value, and might feel deeply wronged when the subterfuge is discovered, as when Minneapolis lesbian blogger Layne Johnson turned out to be a fictional character; Layne's creator's family has been harassed as a result.

❖ CYBERSQUATTING ❖

Cybersquatting is the act of registering a domain name that includes or resembles a trade or service mark with the intent of later selling or licensing that domain name to the owner of the mark. Cybersquatting was rampant in the early days of the Internet, leading to the passage of the Anticybersquatting Consumer Protection Act of 1999 (ACPA). Despite its name, the ACPA's primary aim is to protect the interests of trademark owners. It provides that one who, with a bad faith intent to profit, registers, traffics in, or uses a domain name that at the time of registration is (1) identical to or confusingly similar to a *distinctive* mark, or (2) identical to or confusingly similar to or dilutive of a *famous* mark, is liable in a civil action by the owner of the mark. (There are also special protections for words associated with the International Red Cross and the Olympic symbol.) Remedies may include the transfer of the domain name (15 U.S.C. § 1125(d)).

Bad faith intent to profit: In a typical cybersquatting case the focus is not so much on whether the domain name is identical or confusingly similar to a mark, or whether that mark is famous or distinctive. The distinction would only be important if what was at issue was dilution of the mark rather than a more direct form of infringement; in the early days of cybersquatting, at least, the infringement was generally direct. Many registrants may seek to register domain names similar to the marks of others unwittingly or without malice, however; for example, a person might register his own name for a personal Web site without being aware that the name was used as a trademark by another. To address this problem, the ACPA includes a list of nine factors to consider in assessing bad faith. These include

(I) the trademark or other intellectual property rights of the person, if any, in the domain name;

(II) the extent to which the domain name consists of the legal name of the person or a name that is otherwise commonly used to identify that person;

(III) the person's prior use, if any, of the domain name in connection with the bona fide offering of any goods or services;

Even Harry Potter has been used as bait for a typosquatter's mousetrap. In 2004 the World Intellectual Property Organization (WIPO) ordered a Uruguayan typosquatter to transfer the domain names kjkrowling.com and www-jkrowling.com to the Gryffindor Seeker's creator, J. K. Rowling. Rowling had complained to WIPO after learning that users who accidentally typed either name were bombarded with pop-up ads unrelated either to Harry Potter or to the domain name registrar, dot.registrar.com. The person who registered the names had a previous history of typosquatting, having registered names such as expediua.com and bankofamericq.com.

Source
Joanne Rowling v. Alvaro Collazo, WIPO Arbitration and Mediation Center, Administrative Panel Decision, Case No. D2004-0787, available at http://arbiter.wipo.int/domains/decisions/html/2004/d2004-0787.html Nov, 22, 2004 (visited January 8, 2005).

(IV) the person's bona fide noncommercial or fair use of the mark in a site accessible under the domain name;

(V) the person's intent to divert consumers from the mark owner's online location to a site accessible under the domain name that could harm the goodwill represented by the mark, either for commercial gain or with the intent to tarnish or disparage the mark, by creating a likelihood of confusion as to the source, sponsorship, affiliation, or endorsement of the site;

(VI) the person's offer to transfer, sell, or otherwise assign the domain name to the mark owner or any third party for financial gain without having used, or having an intent to use, the domain name in the bona fide offering of any goods or services, or the person's prior conduct indicating a pattern of such conduct;

(VII) the person's provision of material and misleading false contact information when applying for the registration of the domain name, the person's intentional failure to maintain accurate contact information, or the person's prior conduct indicating a pattern of such conduct;

(VIII) the person's registration or acquisition of multiple domain names which the person knows are identical or confusingly similar to marks of others that are distinctive at the time of registration of such domain names, or dilutive of famous marks of others that are famous at the time of registration of such domain names, without regard to the goods or services of the parties; and

(IX) the extent to which the mark incorporated in the person's domain name registration is or is not distinctive and famous. (15 U.S.C. § 1125(d))

Finally, a catch-all exception provides that bad faith intent shall not be found in any case in which the court determines that the person reasonably believed that the use of the domain name was a fair use or otherwise lawful.

The ACPA has succeeded in rendering traditional cybersquatting unprofitable. It is effective against non-U.S. parties as well as those within the United States, because when it is not possible to proceed in personam (personally) against the person who registered the domain name, the trademark holder may proceed in rem (against a thing rather than a person) against the domain name itself; if the suit is successful, the domain name registration will be transferred to the trademark holder. In addition, many other countries have taken similar measures against cybersquatting.

The "sucks" problem: Some Web site operators register domain names that include a trademark but clearly indicate that they are intended to criticize the trademark owner, such as www.aolsucks.org. The operator of this site does not wish to steal business from America Online (AOL), but probably does wish to harm AOL's reputation. However, the registration of the name is not cybersquatting under the ACPA, both because there is no likelihood of confusion and because criticizing a company, so long as there is no defamation, is protected speech; for a court to enjoin the use of the domain name would be state action in violation of the First Amendment (*Bally*, 29 F.Supp. at 1167). If, however, the site is used for some unprotected form of speech, such as the tarnishing of a famous trademark by posting pornographic images unrelated to the mark, use of the site for

that purpose may be enjoined to prevent dilution of the famous trademark (*Lucent Technologies v. Johnson*, 2000 WL 1604055).

Typosquatting: The decline in traditional, direct cybersquatting has been accompanied by a rise in a form of indirect cybersquatting known as typosquatting. A typosquatter attempts to cash in on the traffic generated by high-volume Web sites. Inevitably, many people will type domain names incorrectly. People also commonly substitute the ".com" top level domain name for other top level domain names, or forget the period after "www." A typosquatter registers domain names that are likely to be entered accidentally by persons seeking to visit a popular Web site. A technique known as mousetrapping can then be used to profit from the visitor's mistake.

The mousetrapped visitor will be trapped in a blizzard of pop-up and pop-under advertisements, often pornographic; inexperienced Web surfers might be unable to extricate themselves from the mousetrap without shutting off the computer. Other, less readily apparent harm can be done: Personal information on the user's computer may be revealed. The mousetrap might reset the user's Internet browser home page to the mousetrap site or some other site typically owned by or paying a fee to the mousetrapper. Adware, spyware, and Trojans may be downloaded to the user's computer, resulting in a loss of privacy, impaired system performance, endless pop-up ads, and vulnerability to hackers. Mousetrapping is an unethical practice to begin with, and mousetrappers may make improper use of personal information gleaned from mousetrapped users' computers.

Some typosquatters, like some cybersquatters, have other motives than purely financial ones. Persons who have a dispute with the operator of a particular Web site may typosquat in order to express their side of the dispute. Typosquatting has been used for political purposes, for example, especially during presidential election campaigns and in such highly emotionally charged areas as the debate over reproductive rights. Such typosquatting, to the extent that it is not actually trademark infringement, raises First Amendment concerns not raised by the more common mousetrapping typosquatters.

Statute
- Anticybersquatting Consumer Protection Act, 15 U.S.C. § 1125(d)

Cases
Federal Appellate Courts
- *Interstellar Starship Services, Ltd. v. Epix, Inc.,* 304 F.3d 936 (9th Cir. 2002)
- *Shields v. Zuccarini,* 254 F.3d 476 (3rd Cir. 2001)
- *Sporty's Farm L.L.C. v. Sportsman's Market, Inc.,* 202 F.3d 489 (2nd Cir. 2000)
- *Virtual Works, Inc. v. Volkswagen of America, Inc.,* 238 F.3d 264 (4th Cir. 2001)

Federal Trial Courts
- *Bally Total Fitness Holding Corp. v. Faber,* 29 F.Supp. 1161 (C.D. Cal. 1998)
- *E. & J. Gallo Winery v. Spider Webs Ltd.,* 129 F.Supp.2d 1033 (S.D. Tex. 2001)
- *International Bancorp, L.L.C. v. Société des Baines de Mer et du Cercle des Etrangers a Monaco,* 192 F.Supp.2d 467 (E.D. Va. 2002)
- *Lucent Technologies v. Johnson,* 2000 WL 1604055 (C.D. Cal. 2000)
- *Lucent Technologies, Inc. v. Lucentsucks.com,* 95 F.Supp.2d 528 (E.D. Va. 2000)
- *Pinehurst, Inc. v. Wick,* 256 F.Supp.2d 424 (M.D. N.C. 2003)
- *Victoria's Cyber Secret Ltd. Partnership v. V Secret Catalogue, Inc.,* 161 F.Supp.2d 1339 (S.D. Fla. 2001)

See also: Domain Name Registration; Fair Use (Trademark); Internet; Internet Corporation for Assigned Names and Numbers; Trademark; Trademark Dilution; Trademark Infringement; World Wide Web

Sources and further reading:
John Brogan, "Much Ado about Squatting: The Constitutionally Precarious Application of the Anticybersquatting Consumer Protection Act," 88 *Iowa Law Review* 163 (2002).
Zohar Efroni, "A Guidebook to Cybersquatting Litigation: The Practical Approach in a Post-Barcelona.com World," 2003 *University of Illinois Journal of Law, Technology and Policy* 457 (2003).
Dara B. Gilwit, "The Latest Cybersquatting Trend: Typosquatters, Their Changing Tactics, and How to Prevent Public Deception and Trademark Infringement," 11 *Washington University Journal of Law and Policy* 267 (2003).
Elizabeth D. Lauzon, "Validity, Construction, and Application of Anticybersquatting Consumer Protection Act, 15 U.S.C.A. § 1125 (D)," 177 *American Law Reports Federal* 1 (2002).
Barbara A. Solomon, "Domain Name Disputes: New Developments and Open Issues," 91 *The Trademark Reporter* 833 (2001).
Rebecca S. Sorgen, "Trademark Confronts Free Speech on the Information Superhighway: 'Cybergripers' Face a Constitutional Collision," 22 *Loyola of Los Angeles Entertainment Law Review* 115 (2001).
Bettina Wendlandt, *Cybersquatting, Metatags und Spam* (München: Beck Juristischer Verlag, 2002) (in German).

❖ CYPHERPUNK ❖

See Data Haven; Encryption

❖ DATA HAVEN ❖

The term *data haven* was introduced by author Bruce Sterling in a 1988 novel, *Islands in the Net;* the concept appears even earlier, for example, in John Brunner's mid-1970s novel *The Shockwave Rider.* A data haven is a "place" both on the Internet and in the physical world in which data can be safe, especially from government control. All or nearly all national governments attempt to regulate exchange of information within their jurisdiction. The United States, for example, attempts to control or prohibit the exchange over the Internet of child pornography, obscenity, unauthorized reproductions of copyrighted material, and software that can be used to circumvent copyright protections. Other countries may attempt to control political dissent through controlling the exchange of information that criticizes the government or shows it in a bad light.

There are two aspects to keeping data safe in a data haven: a technical aspect and a legal aspect. The technical side of the problem is addressed with computer security tools, especially encryption, and by maintaining the physical security of the servers on which the information is stored. The legal aspect is addressed by locating the data haven in a country that imposes few or no legal restrictions on the information stored in the data haven. (All or nearly all countries prohibit the use of data havens for child pornography or the furtherance of terrorism or violent crime, so data havens specializing in content of this sort are presumably outside the law wherever they are located and rely on a combination of encryption and lax enforcement to protect their data.)

Because one of the uses of a data haven is the avoidance of copyright restrictions, the countries suitable for data havens are those that are outside the treaty regime governing international copyright law. The Berne Convention, an international copyright protection agreement, includes as parties most of the countries of the world; some of the few that are not parties to the Berne Convention are parties to the Agreement on Trade-Related Aspects of Intellectual Property Rights (TRIPS) or the Universal Copyright Convention (U.C.C.). The few countries remaining are mostly small. Sterling's novel anticipated this; the data havens in the story are located in Grenada and Singapore. Neither of these countries was a party to the Berne Convention at the time; both became parties in 1998. Another novel developing the concept, Neal Stephenson's *Cryptonomicon,* locates its data haven in a fictional country bearing some resemblance to Brunei. Brunei is not a party to the Berne Convention but has been a member of the WTO since 1995 and is thus bound by TRIPS. Another favored hypothetical site for data havens, Taiwan, became a WTO member in 2002, under the confusing name "Chinese Taipei," or more formally the "Separate Customs Territory of Taiwan, Penghu, Kinmen and Matsu." (Taipei is the capital city of Taiwan.)

Only a few countries are not either WTO members or Berne parties: Afghanistan, Comoros, East Timor, Eritrea, Iran, Kiribati, Marshall Islands, Nauru, Palau, San Marino, Somalia, Turkmenistan, and Tuvalu. Many of these countries lack the Internet infrastructure to support a data haven; others lack the inclination or requisite atmosphere of legal tolerance. The world's most famous data haven, HavenCo, is located in the world's most famous imaginary country, Sealand. Sealand is a fortified platform in the North Sea; it was built by the United Kingdom for military purposes during World War II and later abandoned. It was occupied by a former British military officer and pirate radio entrepreneur, Paddy Roy Bates, after he was fined for pirate radio broadcasting from another abandoned fortress within the United Kingdom's territorial sea. Although he never used the platform for broadcasting, Bates proclaimed it to be the independent Principality of Sealand in 1967; he became Prince Roy, and his wife became Princess Joan. Their son, Prince Regent Michael, now administers the "principality"; his parents no longer live on the platform. No country has recognized the sovereignty of Sealand (Garfinkel 2000).

There are obvious similarities between pirate radio and data havens; both attempt to deliver information to the populace of developed countries from outside the territory of those countries, thus avoiding censorship and copyright laws. A place like Sealand is a natural venue for both. Further advances in wireless broadband might also make it possible for data havens to be based on ships in international waters, as European pirate radio broadcasters once were.

In theory, HavenCo prohibits only three uses: child pornography, spamming, and "black hat" hacking. As a practical matter, HavenCo is constrained by the ability of mainland governments to shut off its Internet connections; data stored on servers on a platform in the North Atlantic is useless without a connection to the outside world. As a result, HavenCo reserves the right to drop any Web site or service that might threaten its access to the Net; use of HavenCo to assist terrorist activities, for instance, would not be allowed (Garfinkel 2000).

Although in theory the idea of a data haven located outside the jurisdiction of any state might be appealing, in practice it has not succeeded. HavenCo is still operating, but the company apparently has not enjoyed financial success (McCullagh 2003). This could be because of internal conflicts and difficulty serving customers, but is more likely to have resulted from lack of demand; apparently few customers currently feel the need of a data haven not bound by the laws of existing countries.

Treaties

- Agreement on Trade-Related Aspects of Intellectual Property Rights (TRIPS), Marrakesh Agreement Establishing the World Trade Organization, Annex 1C, Apr. 15, 1994, 33 I.L.M. 81 (1994)
- Convention Concerning the Creation of an International Union for the Protection of Literary and Artistic Works (Berne Convention), Sept. 9, 1886, as last revised at Paris, July 24, 1971 (amended 1979), 25 U.S.T. 1341, 828 U.N.T.S. 221
- Universal Copyright Convention, Sept. 6, 1952, 6 U.S.T. 2731, revised at Paris July 24, 1971, 25 U.S.T. 1341
- WIPO Copyright Treaty, Dec. 20, 1996, 36 I.L.M. 65 (1997)

See also: Anonymity; Berne Convention; Copyright; Cyberpunk; Encryption; File-Sharing; International Copyright Protection; Privacy; TRIPS

Sources and further reading:
Fiction:
John Brunner, *The Shockwave Rider* (New York: Ballantine, 1976).
Neal Stephenson, *Cryptonomicon* (New York: HarperCollins, 1999).
Bruce Sterling, *Islands in the Net* (New York: Arbor House, 1988).
Nonfiction:
Warwick Ford and Michael S. Baum, *Secure Electronic Commerce: Building the Infrastructure for Digital Signatures and Encryption,* 2d ed. (Upper Saddle River, NJ: Prentice Hall, 2001).
Simson Garfinkel, "Welcome to Sealand. Now Bugger Off," *Wired,* July 2000, available at http://www.wired.com/wired/archive/8.07/haven.html?pg=1&topic=&topic_set= (visited June 27, 2004).
Stephen Graham and Simon Marvin, *Splintering Urbanism: Networked Infrastructures, Technological Mobilities and the Urban Condition* (Basingstoke, Hampshire, UK: Brunner-Routledge, 2001).

Declan McCullagh, "Has 'Haven' for Questionable Sites Sunk?" C/Net News.com, Aug. 4, 2003, available at http://news.com.com/2100–1028_3–5059676.html?tag=fd_top (visited June 27, 2004).

❖ DATA MINING ❖

Data mining, also known as knowledge discovery in databases (KDD) is a statistical technique that has been rapidly developing since the pioneering work of Usama Fayyad on General Motors defects in the early 1990s. The term *data mining*, however, has come to be increasingly and somewhat inaccurately applied in the popular press to a wide range of techniques for extracting information from databases (Zarsky 2002–2003). Data mining has raised privacy concerns, particularly in three areas: consumer behavior, security, and medical records.

The first step in data mining is the compilation of a database. Everything that is done online is at least potentially recordable, although much of it is not actually recorded in any permanent form. Every credit card or ATM transaction is recorded. Nearly every boarding pass issued in the United States is recorded in an airline computer, and nearly every time a prescription is filled, a record is made. Commuters who use FastPass cards to avoid tollbooths may have their movements recorded, as may Web surfers who have a Global Positioning System (GPS) receiver attached to or built into their portable computers. Telephone companies keep records of all numbers dialed from each telephone, and it is possible to track the movement of cellular telephones. Private and government surveillance cameras store images of people passing by a given location.

Just a few years ago the gathering of this information was of little concern, for two reasons: There was too much of it, and it was too scattered. Statistical techniques were not yet sophisticated enough to extract meaningful information from all this data, and even if they had been, computers capable of crunching so much data were not widely available. Even with improved computers and KDD algorithms, the information described in the preceding paragraph was inaccessible because it was stored in many different databases, most of them not available to anyone but the owner: Telephone company databases could not easily be combined with airline, credit card, pharmacy, or highway authority databases for data mining.

For the most part this is still true; the privacy advocates' nightmare of a world in which Big Brother is aware of every move that every individual takes has not yet arrived. It has become possible, however. Computers continue to become faster, and KDD techniques continue to advance. Corporate mergers and information-sharing agreements create combined databases of information on disparate areas of activity. As more and more companies realize that their databases are worth money, this process is likely to accelerate. And the government engages in data mining of government and perhaps private databases ("Homeland Security" 2003). The Food and Drug Administration (FDA) uses information on pharmaceutical use to identify adverse drug interactions that might not otherwise be detected ("FDA to Use Data Mining" 2003).

Proponents of data mining argue that these uses are benign. Detecting and avoiding adverse drug reactions is surely a noble cause; it helps many and harms none. In the wake of September 11, most travelers are willing to sacrifice some degree of privacy in order to keep air travel safe. And the marketing companies that engage in commercial data mining do not want to use that information for any purpose more sinister than trying to sell goods and services.

Privacy advocates are not convinced, however. Although avoiding adverse drug interactions is a good thing, data mining of a patient's medical records could make it possible to draw conclusions about the patient's medical history that might not otherwise be obvious—and this information might become available to persons other than pharmacists, physicians, and the FDA. And security-based and consumer data mining are greeted with outright alarm. The Computer Assisted Passenger Prescreening System program (CAPPS II), for example, would allow the Transportation Security Administration (TSA) to use data mining techniques in commercial databases to assign air passengers a score, similar to a credit rating, "to determine whether a passenger is a known terrorist, or has identifiable links to known terrorists" ("Aviation Criticism Prompts GAO Review" 2003). Credit-rating agencies have done the same thing for years, of course, and in the process they have made many errors. Credit-rating agencies are sued constantly and are also forced to compete in the marketplace with other companies; the TSA would not be competing with any other terror-threat-rating companies or agencies and would probably be immune from suit for errors. In addition, an incorrect identification as a terrorist could do far more harm to an individual than a bad credit rating.

Private data mining could also be used in ways more sinister than merely designing junk-mail lists. Private data could conceivably assign scores purporting to reveal the likelihood that a particular individual would be an unsatisfactory employee, for instance. Inevitably, some individuals would be placed in that category incorrectly—yet the low score would make them effectively unemployable. And use of private database information by private individuals and companies is harder to control than use of that information by the government.

Individuals already have some protection against government use of information in electronic databases under a 1988 statute, the Computer Matching and Privacy and Protection Act. And the CAPPS II program and similar security-related proposals have brought a prompt response from Congress and the General Accounting Office. In addition, two Democratic senators have introduced legislation to stop data mining related to individuals by the Department of Defense, particularly the controversial Total Information Awareness program ("Sens. Feingold, Wyden Begin Effort to Stop 'Data Mining'" 2003). On the other hand, Department of Defense data mining could have benefits aside from the sometimes-disputed security benefits: In August 2004 data mining of government purchase card data by the Defense Criminal Investigative Service resulted in the indictment of four people, including a senior Defense Information Systems Agency Contracting Officer, who had allegedly improperly awarded over eleven million dollars in contracts to a business in which the Contracting Officer had a financial interest ("Purchase Card Data Mining" 2004).

Statutes
- Computer Matching and Privacy Protection Act of 1988, 5 U.S.C. § 552a(o)
- Privacy Act of 1974, 5 U.S.C. § 552a

See also: Advertising; Adware and Spyware; Anonymity; DoubleClick; Privacy

Sources and further reading:

Usama M. Fayyad et al., eds., *Advances in Knowledge Discovery and Data Mining* (Menlo Park, CA: AAAI Press 1996).

Joseph S. Fulda, "Data Mining and Privacy," 11 *Albany Law Journal of Science and Technology* 105 (2000).

David Hand et al., *Principles of Data Mining* (Cambridge, MA: MIT Press 2001).

"Investigations: Aviation Criticism Prompts GAO Review of TSA Data Mining Program," *Cybercrime Law Report,* Sept. 22, 2003, at 6.

"Legislation—Homeland Security: Senate Funding Bill Requires Review of DHS Data Mining," *Cybercrime Law Report,* Aug. 11, 2003, at 4.

"National Security—Government Databases: Pentagon Concludes DOD Data Mining Plan Doesn't Threaten Privacy Rights," *Cybercrime Law Report,* June 2, 2003, at 3.

"Privacy Legislation: Sens. Feingold, Wyden Begin Effort to Stop 'Data Mining' by Department of Defense," *Cybercrime Law Report,* Jan. 27, 2003, at 3.

"Purchase Card Data Mining Leads to Co. Indictment," *Government Contractor,* Aug. 25, 2004, 330.

"Regulatory Affairs—Pharmaceutical: FDA to Use Data Mining to Monitor Adverse Events," 22 *Biotechnology Law Report* 481 (2003).

Tal Z. Zarsky, "'Mine Your Own Business!' Making the Case for the Implications of the Data Mining of Personal Information in the Forum of Public Opinion," 5 *Yale Journal of Law and Technology* 4 (2002–2003).

Tal Z. Zarsky, "Desperately Seeking Solutions: Using Implementation-Based Solutions for the Troubles of Information Privacy in the Age of Data Mining and the Internet Society," 56 *Maine Law Review* 13 (2004).

❖ DECLARATION OF THE INDEPENDENCE OF CYBERSPACE ❖

In early 1996, as the Internet exploded into popular consciousness, the Declaration of the Independence of Cyberspace appeared. It was well timed; mainstream media were fascinated by the Internet, governments everywhere were reacting to its advent more with apprehension than with appreciation of the opportunities, and the general public was beginning to log on. The prevailing sentiment of the more experienced users—the Internet old-timers—was that there was such a "place" as cyberspace, and that it should remain forever free of interference from real-world governments. John Perry Barlow, a songwriter for the Grateful Dead and co-founder of the Electronic Frontier Foundation, captured this cyber-libertarianism in the Declaration of the Independence of Cyberspace.

The declaration is reproduced in full in appendix II of this volume. It makes eight basic points:

1. The Internet ("Cyberspace") should not be subject to existing governments, nor is it likely to produce a government of its own; "ethics, enlightened self-interest, and the commonweal" will produce the governance (not government) of cyberspace.
2. Cyberspace grows through the cooperation of its users; it cannot be built by governments, "as though it were a public construction project."
3. Internet users, rather than governments, will resolve the problems that have arisen from some users' online activities.
4. Real-world "legal concepts of property, expression, identity, movement, and context" are inapplicable in cyberspace.
5. In cyberspace, all users are equal.
6. Attempts by national governments to control their citizens' access to cyberspace will ultimately prove unsuccessful.
7. Government should not take the place of parents in regulating children's access to Internet content.
8. Intellectual property law, particularly copyright law, is oppressive; information can and should "be reproduced and distributed infinitely at no cost."

A decade later, some of these points seem prescient, others naive. The first point is largely a matter of opinion, not fact, and thus cannot be definitively shown to be true or untrue. The second seems to ignore the history of the Internet, which after all had its origins in projects of the United States Department of Defense and National Science Foundation. The third seems, thus far, to be an open question: The community of Internet users, rather than governments, has been relatively successful in addressing problems such as viruses and spyware. Governments and users have both played a role in suppressing malicious hacking. And neither governments nor users have been notably successful in suppressing annoyances (such as spam) or some crimes (such as child pornography).

The fourth point—that real-world legal concepts are inapplicable in cyberspace—represents a viewpoint that must now be considered extreme. Real-world law governs a wide variety of online activities and problems, among them the sale of goods and services; defamation; fraud and identity theft; and malicious hacking and the creation of worms and viruses. And this situation seems to be widely accepted by the overwhelming majority of users. Only in a few areas, notably the area of file-sharing, is there still widespread opposition to the application of "real-world" law to cyberspace; in most other areas it now seems to be accepted that online activities are subject to the same laws as off-line activities.

The fifth point (that all users are equal) states a truth that is, as Thomas Jefferson put it, self-evident. The sixth has also proved true, so far: National governments have for the most part been unable to control their citizens' access to cyberspace. The seventh and eighth serve to draw the lines in two fiercely fought and still ongoing battles: the battle over freedom of expression and the battle over intellectual property rights.

The U.S. government, in particular, has made three notable attempts to restrict children's access to Internet content. Two of these, the Communications Decency Act and the Child Online Protection Act, attempted to impose a direct governmental prohibition between children and certain forms of content; both statutes were unfavorably received by the courts. The third, the Children's Internet Protection Act, required computers in certain places—schools and libraries—to use filtering software available from private parties. This hybrid approach has been more favorably received; although it might be said that this shows a rejection of the idea of direct government control over children's access to "cyberspace," there is now near-universal acceptance of the idea that children should be shielded from some Internet content. The constitutional problems with the Communications Decency Act and the Child Online Protection Act came not from their shielding of children but from the difficulty of doing so without simultaneously blocking or otherwise interfering with the Internet access of adults to the same content.

The declaration is somewhat contradictory, as well. On the one hand it scorns governments, or perhaps parents, who would impose laws restricting children's access: "you entrust your bureaucracies with the parental responsibilities you are too cowardly to confront yourselves." The declaration acknowledges that there is some bad content out there: "In our world, all the sentiments and expressions of humanity, from the debasing to the angelic, are parts of a seamless whole, the global conversation of bits. We cannot separate the air that chokes from the air upon which wings beat." But while castigating parents who would entrust the government with parental responsibilities, the declaration also acknowledges that many or most parents lack the skills to police their own children's Internet access: "You are terrified of your own children, since they are natives in a world where you will always be immigrants."

The battle over intellectual property rights also persists. Trademark, patent, and copyright law are all battlegrounds. The Internet Corporation for Assigned Names and Numbers, perhaps the closest analogue "cyberspace" has produced to a real-world government institution, has been mired in controversy. "Business method" patents for such inventions as one-

click online ordering have been much maligned, but they have been granted nonetheless by the real-world United States Patent and Trademark Office. The U.S. government, via the Anticybersquatting Consumer Protection Act, has also stepped in to protect trademark rights online. And courts in many nations have entertained suits by holders of intellectual property rights to protect those rights against online infringement. Suits over online file-sharing of copyrighted information have gained the most attention. From the viewpoint of the declaration this file-sharing is not a problem: "In our world, whatever the human mind may create can be reproduced and distributed infinitely at no cost." Information, in other words, just wants to be free, and the Internet has given it the keys to its cage.

A large number, possibly even a majority, of Internet users still share the declaration's opinion of the content industry: "Your increasingly obsolete information industries would perpetuate themselves by proposing laws, in America and elsewhere, that claim to own speech itself throughout the world. These laws would declare ideas to be another industrial product, no more noble than pig iron . . .. The global conveyance of thought no longer requires your factories to accomplish." Nonetheless laws to protect the content industry persist, and their spirit has entered "cyberspace" through the use of such technological copy-protection and digital rights management measures as encryption and trusted computing.

Although some of its points are now accepted aspects of Internet law, and others continue to be debated, the overall sense of community present in the declaration seems to have vanished. In 1996 the Internet was a new thing to the majority of its users; a core of technically sophisticated, more experienced users was able to guide debate and discourse. The idea of an Internet "community" made far more sense than it does today, when experienced Internet users number in the hundreds of millions, perhaps billions. Cyberspace has vanished as connecting to the Internet has become a part of daily life for the people of North America, Europe, East Asia, and increasingly the rest of the world as well. In this sense, the declaration's goal of "a civilization of the Mind in Cyberspace" has been achieved; Internet users have "spread [them]selves across the Planet so that no one can arrest [their] thoughts"—or, rather, the Internet has spread itself across the world, entering into the life of people everywhere; what was revolutionary has become mundane.

Declaration

- John Perry Barlow, A Declaration of the Independence of Cyberspace, Feb. 8, 1996, available at http://www.eff.org/~barlow/Declaration-Final.html (visited September 30, 2004)

See also: Activism and Advocacy Groups; Censorship; Child Online Protection Act; Children's Internet Protection Act; Communications Decency Act; Cyberspace; Cybersquatting; Encryption; File-Sharing; Hacking

Sources and further reading:
Brian Loader, *The Governance of Cyberspace: Politics, Technology and Global Restructuring* (Basingstoke, Hampshire, UK: Routledge, 1997).

❖ DECRYPTION ❖

See Encryption

❖ DECSS ❖

DeCSS is a computer program that can be used to decrypt motion picture files encrypted with Content Scramble System (CSS, often incorrectly called Content Scrambling System), used on commercially manufactured DVDs. CSS uses a 40-bit encryption algorithm that is relatively easy to break. Content owners in the United States were initially prevented from using stronger encryption by U.S. export-control regulations; now that a huge number of DVDs and DVD players incorporating the CSS keys have already been sold, there are market pressures against changing the encryption system used on commercial DVDs.

In order to play back movies encrypted with CSS, DVD players must contain a decryption key. The DVD Copy Control Association (DVDCCA), a motion-picture industry trade association, licenses CSS decryption keys to equipment manufacturers (*Reimerdes*, 111 F.Supp.2d 308; *Bunner*, 113 Cal.Rptr.2d 341). The manufacturers themselves were always a potential source of leakage, but in fact DeCSS and similar programs have been developed by reverse engineering rather than by any compromise of the equipment-makers' security. As a further defense, CSS uses multiple layers of encryption, in which an authentication key

Apple's iTunes provides individually packaged music files, rather than albums, and provides them with fewer restrictions than previous online content-industry offerings. But iTunes songs are not completely free of restrictions. Chief among these is that music files in the proprietary iTunes AAC format can only be played back on Apple and Windows computers and on Apple's iPod and other devices licensed by Apple; they cannot be played back on ordinary CD players in home or car stereos. In order to play iTunes songs on these players, users must convert the AAC format to another format, either by making an analog recording of the playback or by circumventing Apple's protective technology. Although there is no shortage of clever users capable of doing so, trafficking in devices or software for the circumvention of technological protective measures is illegal in the United States under the Digital Millennium Copyright Act. It is not illegal in all countries, however, and programs such as iOpener, PlayFair (later HYMN), and DeDRMS have appeared on non-U.S. (and some U.S.) Web sites. DeDRMS, or iTunes DRM (Digital Rights Management) Stripper, first appeared on a blog headed "So sue me," apparently maintained by Jon Lech Johansen of DeCSS fame.

Source
Jon Lech Johansen, *So Sue Me (blog)*, Apr. 16–Nov. 16, 2004 (visited January 7, 2004).

ensures that the CSS decryption module can only be used with the DVD drive to which it was originally connected, as a defense against hardware hacking. Each equipment manufacturer is allotted one of the several hundred available player keys; these can be used to decrypt disc keys on DVDs. The disc keys in turn are used to decrypt the title keys, which are used to decrypt the titles—the actual content on the DVD: movies, trailers, and special features. If one has access to the title keys, however, the intermediate steps can be bypassed.

CSS has been used since the mid-1990s. On October 6, 1999, Jon Lech Johansen, a fifteen-year-old Norwegian citizen, posted the program to a mailing list. Johansen was arrested and tried for violation of Norwegian law. The publicity surrounding the trial made "DVD Jon" an instant Internet celebrity. He was acquitted in January 2003, but the prosecution appealed the verdict. (In many countries, although not in the United States, the prosecution may appeal a verdict of acquittal.) In December an appellate court upheld the acquittal (*Sunde v. Johansen* (appeal) 2003). In January 2004 Økokrim, the Economic Crimes Unit of the prosecutor's office, announced that it was dropping the case rather than appealing it to Norway's highest court.

Johansen's reason for using (and perhaps writing) DeCSS fell within the boundaries of what in the United States, in the absence of the Digital Millennium Copyright Act (DMCA), might have been called fair use: CSS-encrypted discs could not be played on Linux systems; DeCSS could decrypt those disks in order to play the movies they contained on Linux systems. The Norwegian appellate court found this use permissible (*Sunde v. Johansen* [appeal] 2003).

Despite the intense interest of the U.S. content industry in the Johansen case, and despite the fact that as a result of Johansen's actions DeCSS became available in the United States, Johansen himself remained effectively outside the reach of the DMCA and the U.S. justice system. The legal test for DeCSS in the United States came when persons within the borders of the United States became involved in the distribution of the program.

In November 1999 activists Shawn Reimerdes, Roman Kazan, and Eric Corley made DeCSS available on their Web sites. They also encouraged others to do the same as an act of civil disobedience. Eight movie studios immediately filed suit against the three. At trial, the federal district court for the Southern District of New York held that CSS effectively controlled access to copyrighted works and that DeCSS was a means of circumventing that control. Thus distribution of DeCSS was unlawful under the DMCA's prohibition against circumvention of technological measures, contained in 17 U.S.C. § 1201(a)(2)(A).

The court rejected the defendants' contention that their conduct was protected under the reverse engineering, encryption research, or security testing exceptions. It also rejected the defendants' two First Amendment arguments. The defendants had argued that Title I's anticircumvention provisions were either an unconstitutional restraint on free speech or that they were unconstitutionally overbroad because they restricted the fair use of encrypted works. Although the district court agreed that a computer program "is a means of expressing ideas," and that therefore "the First Amendment must be considered before its dissemination may be prohibited or regulated," it then decided that the DMCA's restriction in this expression was content neutral, because it was aimed at the function of the program rather than at the ideas expressed within the code itself. Applying the intermediate standard of review appropriate to a content-neutral restriction of this sort, the court held that the anticircumvention provisions were constitutional. The interest in freely expressing whatever expressive content was contained within the program was outweighed by the interest in protecting copyrights and reducing video piracy, and the potential harm to those interests from the program's function. The trial court also rejected the overbreadth argument, finding that other, not unlawful alternative methods were already available that would allow such fair uses as the making of backup copies, although the image quality would not be as high as that made by the use of DeCSS (*Reimerdes,* 111 F.Supp.2d 294).

Corley appealed the decision to the Second Circuit Court of Appeals. The Second Circuit largely agreed with the trial court. DeCSS was "speech" within the meaning of the First Amendment, but the focus of the DMCA's restriction was on the functional rather than expressive aspect of the program. The anticircumvention provisions and the injunction against distribution of DeCSS were thus content-neutral and subject only to intermediate scrutiny. Applying this scrutiny, the court found the injunction (and thus Tiltle I of the DMCA) constitutional. In addition, the Second Circuit pointed out that fair use does not guarantee "copying by the optimum method or in the identical format of the original." Title I, the court noted,

> does not impose even an arguable limitation on the opportunity to make a variety of traditional fair uses of DVD movies, such as commenting on their content, quoting excerpts from their screenplays, and even recording portions of the video images and sounds on film or tape by pointing a camera, a camcorder, or a microphone at a monitor as it displays the DVD movie. The fact that the resulting copy will not be as perfect or as manipulable as a digital copy obtained by having direct access to the DVD movie in its digital form, provides no basis for a claim of unconstitutional limitation of fair use. (*Corley*, 273 F.3d at 459)

On the heels of the case against Reimerdes and Corley came a state law case, *DVD Copy Control Association v. Bunner*. Bunner, like Reimerdes and Corley, had made DeCSS available for download on his Web site. (Another of the named defendants in *Bunner* was "Emmanuel Goldstein," an Internet alias for Corley. The name is drawn from George Orwell's classic dystopian novel *1984*; Orwell's novel suggests that Goldstein, who never appears, probably does not actually exist.) The DVDCCA brought a case against Bunner under California's trade secrets law, arguing that CSS was a trade secret. After the trial court issued a preliminary injunction against Bunner, the California Court of Appeal for the Sixth District reversed. The California appellate court agreed that computer software could be protected as a

trade secret. Unlike the *Reimerdes* court, however, it found that the defendant's distribution of DeCSS was protected by the First Amendment. In an opinion that was later reversed by the California Supreme Court, the appellate court stated that DeCSS was "a written expression of the author's ideas and information about decryption of DVDs without CSS," and therefore "the trial court's preliminary injunction barring Bunner from disclosing DeCSS [could] fairly be characterized as a prohibition of 'pure' speech" (*Bunner*, 4 Cal.Rptr.3d 69 (2003)).

The California Supreme Court, in reversing the appellate court's decision, did not have to address the question before the *Reimerdes* court—the characterization of the DMCA's prohibition on DeCSS and similar programs as content-based or content-neutral. The California courts were applying California trade secrets law, not the DMCA, and the particular issue in *Bunner* was the preliminary injunction issued to prevent Bunner from continuing to distribute DeCSS pending the resolution of the trade secrets dispute. The court observed that it was in the nature of any such injunction that it would burden a particular type of content—that which the defendant sought to disclose. The purpose of such an injunction, however, was not to suppress the expression of a particular idea, but to protect the plaintiff's property interest in its trade secret. The injunction could thus be viewed as content-neutral, and under the level of scrutiny applied to content-neutral regulations it was constitutional (*Bunner*, 4 Cal.Rptr.3d 69 (2003)).

DeCSS was neither the first nor the only program capable of making unencrypted copies of titles on encrypted DVDs. A few weeks earlier a more limited program, DVD Speed Ripper, had been released. And the release of the DeCSS source code has made possible the development of hundreds of alternative programs, some of them considerably more powerful and effective than DeCSS itself. DeCSS has become a cause célèbre, and the program has been expressed as a series of haiku, as graphic art, and even as a 1,401-digit prime number. Suppression of DeCSS in these forms would seem to invite reexamination of the question of functionality versus expressive content, but that has not stopped the DVDCCA from suing (as a code-fendant in *Bunner*) a New Jersey T-shirt company. The T-shirt company, Copyleft, sold shirts with the DeCSS code printed on them. Because DeCSS itself is still widely available on the Internet, and because typing in the code from a T-shirt would be a slow, laborious, and unnecessary process for anyone wishing to de-crypt CSS-encrypted DVDs, it seems far more likely that the T-shirts are worn as a form of po-litical protest and sold to enable that protest. The fact that the T-shirt company donates $4 to the Electronic Frontier Foundation for each T-shirt sold would seem to support this inter-pretation, as does the name of the company, drawn from the open-source movement. DeCSS and programs like it continue to pres-ent a potential for conflict between the DMCA and the First Amendment, and further litiga-tion seems likely. DeCSS has also inspired a decoy program, the perfectly innocuous but confusingly named DeCSS, which can remove Cascading Style Sheets (thus the CSS) tags from HTML documents.

In the meantime, restrictions on DeCSS and similar programs continue to affect individual users without affecting commercial-scale video piracy. Large-scale video-pirating operations can mechanically reproduce all of the informa-tion on a DVD, encryption included, and place it on a new DVD. This new DVD can then be played on a standard DVD player.

Statute

- Digital Millennium Copyright Act, 17 U.S.C. § 1201

Cases

Federal

- *Universal City Studios, Inc. v. Reimerdes,* 111 F.Supp.2d 294 (S.D. N.Y. 2000), affirmed by *Universal City Studios, Inc. v. Corley,* 273 F.3d 429 (2nd Cir. 2001)

State

- *DVD Copy Control Association, Inc. v. Bunner,* 113 Cal.Rptr.2d 338 (2001), rev'd, 4 Cal.Rptr.3d 69 (2003)

Norway

- *Sunde (for Norway) v. Johansen,* Oslo First Instance Trial Court, January 7, 2003, No. 02-507 M/94, English translation by Professor Jon Bing available at http://www.eff.org/IP/ Video/DeCSS_prosecutions/Johansen_ DeCSS_case/20030109_johansen_ decision.html (visited July 27, 2004); on appeal, Borgarting Appellate Court, Dec. 22, 2003, No. LB-2003-00731, English translation by Professor Jon Bing available at http://www.efn.no/ DVD-dom-20031222-en.html (visited July 27, 2004)

See also: Activism and Advocacy Groups; Ad-vanced Access Content System; Censorship; Content Industry; Copyright; Copyright In-fringement; Digital Millennium Copyright Act, Title I; Digital Rights Management; Encryp-tion; File-Sharing; First Amendment; Interna-tional Copyright Protection; WIPO Copyright Treaty

Sources and further reading:

Lawrence Lessig, *Free Culture: How Big Media Uses Technology and the Law to Lock Down Culture and Control Creativity* (New York: Penguin, 2004)(also available as a free download).

Steven Levy, *Crypto: How the Code Rebels Beat the Government—Saving Privacy in the Digital Age* (New York: Penguin Putnam, 2002).

Kerry Segrave, *Piracy in the Motion Picture Industry* (Jefferson, NC: McFarland and Company, 2003).

Siva Vaidhyanathan, *Copyrights and Copywrongs: The Rise of Intellectual Property and How It Threatens Creativity* (New York: New York University Press, 2001).

❖ DEFAMATION ❖

The tort of defamation is defined in the United States by state law; the elements of the tort thus vary depending on the jurisdiction. The tort will almost invariably include these elements, however: There must be a false statement that is harmful, either because it causes actual damages or because it falls into a category that is deemed harmful per se, even in the absence of any proof of damages. The statement must be published—that is, it must be communicated to some third party, not merely to the person described in the statement (Restatement § 558). Statements that are privileged are not defamatory; the privileges that may be asserted as a defense also vary from state to state, but the First Amendment imposes a nationwide uniform privilege protecting certain types of statements. Defamation may be either libel (written) or slander (spoken). There are several related torts, including injurious falsehood, false light, publicizing of private facts, and appropriation of another's name or likeness (see Restatement §§ 623–629, 652).

By itself, defamation creates no particular legal issues specific to the Internet. The global nature of the Internet, however, means that a statement made in one jurisdiction may be received everywhere in the world. What is defamatory under the laws of one jurisdiction may be acceptable under the laws of another; questions of jurisdiction, choice of law, and recognition and enforcement of judgments then arise.

Jurisdictional issues arise when a statement made in one jurisdiction defames a person located in another, and may be complicated if the message is received in yet a third jurisdiction. The jurisdiction in which the statement is made, as well as the jurisdiction in which the person making the statement is located, will generally be acknowledged as having jurisdiction over the tort. The location where the harm is felt and the location where the defamatory communication is received may also have jurisdiction; in the United States a combination of state and federal law is applied to this problem.

Where the defendant does not have systematic and continuous contacts with the forum state (the state seeking jurisdiction) sufficient to establish general jurisdiction over the defendant, U.S. states can only obtain jurisdiction if there is grounds for specific jurisdiction: jurisdiction over the defendant for that particular matter, rather than all matters. Specific jurisdiction requires a two-step analysis. First, the state's long-arm statute (a statute providing jurisdiction over out-of-state defendants) must be examined to determine whether it supports ju-

risdiction over the defendant for the particular defamation claim. Second, if the long-arm statute does support jurisdiction, the application of the statute must be examined to determine whether the defendant has "certain minimum contacts with [the forum], such that the maintenance of the suit does not offend 'traditional notions of fair play and substantial justice'" (*International Shoe*, 326 U.S. 310).

In the United States this rule has been applied to give jurisdiction in Internet defamation cases when the defendant knew or reasonably should have known that the injury caused by the defamatory statement would be suffered in a particular state. It has also been applied to give jurisdiction in the state where the server that stores and transmits the statement is located (*Bochan*, 68 F.Supp.2d 692). The logic underlying this latter application is somewhat more questionable, because the server in question could be located almost anywhere and its location is generally neither known to the parties nor significant to the communication.

The concerns that apply to jurisdiction also apply to choice of applicable substantive law: Once a court in, say, Virginia has decided that it has jurisdiction over a case, should it apply its own law to the case? Should it apply the law of the state in which the statement was made, or the law of the state in which the server on which the statement was stored is located, or the state in which the harm caused by the statement was felt? Here, though, there is no uniformity even among the states of the United States; there is a wide variety of choice of law rules.

Courts in other countries may be quicker to take jurisdiction over foreign defendants than U.S courts are. In 2002 an Australian court decision caused considerable controversy: The Australian High Court decided that it could exercise personal jurisdiction in a defamation suit against a U.S. publishing company, Dow Jones. The allegedly defamatory article was available on the Dow Jones Web site, from which it could be, and was, viewed in Australia. Had the situation been reversed, these facts alone would not have permitted a court in the United States to exercise jurisdiction over an Australian defendant. The Australian court, though, found that it did have jurisdiction (*Gutnick*, [2002]

H.C.A. 56). The reasoning in *Gutnick* has been much criticized as having a potentially chilling effect on Internet speech: If all countries were to be as liberal in granting themselves jurisdiction as Australia, everything posted on the Internet would have to first be checked against the laws of nearly two hundred countries and hundreds or even thousands of states, provinces, territories, dependencies, and colonies.

The problem posed by *Gutnick* is limited by the problem of enforcement of foreign judgments, however. The U.S. courts are unlikely to enforce a foreign judgment in a situation in which the foreign court did not acquire jurisdiction over the defendant in a way that would also have sufficed for jurisdiction in a U.S. court. Most Americans thus have nothing to fear from a judgment in Australia, and even Dow Jones's exposure to Australian judgments is limited to the extent of its assets in Australia.

In addition to the unenforceability of judgments obtained without what U.S. courts regard as proper jurisdiction, U.S. defendants have an additional protection from foreign defamation suits: the First Amendment. Speech protected by the First Amendment includes some speech that in other countries would be considered defamatory. As a result, U.S. courts have refused to apply those countries' defamation laws, or to enforce those countries' defamation judgments. In *Bachchan v. India Abroad Publications,* for example, a state court in New York refused to enforce a British defamation judgment on First Amendment grounds, while in *Matusevitch v. Telnikoff* a federal trial court in the District of Columbia did the same. Another nondefamation case, the French Yahoo! case, also stated that a foreign judgment could not be enforced where the First Amendment would have prevented the judgment from being obtained in the United States (*Yahoo! Inc.,* 169 F.Supp.2d 1181).

Although the First Amendment provides some protection against foreign defamation suits for U.S. Internet publishers, the problem is likely to continue to grow. The countries that have already been involved in litigation of this sort are early adopters of the Internet; Australia and the United Kingdom share a legal history and legal culture with the United States, yet incompatibilities between the systems arise. As the Internet continues to increase communication between people from radically different legal cultures, further cross-border disputes over defamation and other real or perceived insults are inevitable.

Cases
Australia
- *Gutnick v. Dow Jones & Co.,* [2002] H.C.A. 56

United States Supreme Court
- *International Shoe v. Washington,* 326 U.S. 310 (1945)

Federal Appellate Court
- *Cybersell, Inc. v. Cybersell, Inc.,* 130 F.3d 414 (9th Cir. 1997)

Federal Trial Court
- *Bochan v. La Fontaine,* 68 F.Supp.2d 692 (E.D. Va. 1999)
- *Matusevitch v. Telnikoff,* 877 F.Supp. 1 (D.D.C. 1995)
- *Yahoo!, Inc. v. La Ligue Contre le Racisme et L'Antisemitisme,* 169 F.Supp.2d 1181 (N.D. Cal. 2001), reversed by *Yahoo! Inc. v. La Ligue Contre Le Racisme et L'Antisemitisme,* 379 F.3d 1120 (9th Cir. 2004)

State Courts
- *Bachchan v. India Abroad Publications,* 585 N.Y.S.2d 661 (N.Y. Sup. Ct. 1992)

Restatement
- Restatement (Second) of Torts (Washington, D.C.: American Law Institute, 1984 and Supp. 2003)

See also: Censorship; Choice of Law; First Amendment; French Yahoo! Case; Jurisdiction; Recognition and Enforcement of Judgments

Sources and further reading:
Cherie Dawson, "Creating Borders on the Internet: Free Speech, the United States, and

International Jurisdiction," 44 *Virginia Journal of International Law* 637 (2004).

Nathan W. Garnett, "*Dow Jones & Co. v. Gutnick:* Will Australia's Long Jurisdictional Reach Chill Internet Speech World-Wide?" 13 *Pacific Rim Law and Policy Journal* 61 (2004).

Uta Kohl, "Defamation on the Internet—Nice Decision, Shame about the Reasoning," 52 *International and Comparative Law Quarterly* 1049 (2003).

Ken Kraus and Dan Polatsek, "Enforcement of Foreign Media Judgments in the Aftermath of *Gutnick v. Dow Jones & Co.*," 21 *Communications Lawyer* 1 (2003).

Bryan P. Werley, "Aussie Rules: Universal Jurisdiction over Internet Defamation," 18 *Temple International and Comparative Law Journal* 199 (2004).

Gary Chan Kok Yew, "Internet Defamation and Choice of Law In *Dow Jones & Company Inc. v. Gutnick*," 2003 *Singapore Journal of Legal Studies* 483 (2003).

❖ DENIAL-OF-SERVICE ATTACK ❖

A denial-of-service attack is an attack on an information service—for example, a Web site—that seeks to deny other users access to the service. In the simplest form, a denial-of-service attack can be launched on a telephone number by setting another telephone to dial that number repeatedly; anyone else trying to reach the same number will receive a busy signal. If the number against which the denial-of-service attack is launched is a toll-free number, the attack will cost the victim not only the loss of the resource, but the cost of the telephone calls.

Internet information resources, such as Web sites, are generally not capable of being overwhelmed by repeated requests for access from a single user. In order to deny service, a large number of requests must be sent from several different locations. Internet denial-of-service attacks launched simultaneously from multiple locations are called distributed denial-of-service (DDoS) attacks; their goal is to deny access to other users. In contrast to a cracker attack, a denial-of-service attack does not

Spamming spammers: The same techniques used by spammers can be used against them, especially by ISPs. ISPs can collect intercepted spams and return millions at a time to the sender as an "e-mail bomb"—that is, if the ISP can identify the true sender. Or an ISP can use its subscribers' computers, with their permission, to bombard spammers' Web sites with traffic, as Lycos Europe tried to do with its 2004 "Make Love Not Spam" campaign.

Lycos offered users a screensaver that would use idle computer time to send requests for pages to spammers' servers—and then, of course, rejecting the requested pages. This would increase spammers' bandwidth costs, slow down their servers, and perhaps knock some off the Web altogether, for a while. There were only two problems with the idea: It was unsafe and, in many countries, illegal.

The "Make Love Not Spam" screensaver was unsafe because the spammers, more technically sophisticated than the vast majority of users, might retaliate. As computer technology consultant Graham Cluley observed, "Attacking a spammer's Web site is like poking a grizzly bear sleeping in your back garden with a pointy stick." It could also harm innocent Web sites hosted on the same servers as spammers' sites. And "Make Love Not Spam" might be illegal as a distributed denial-of-service attack in those countries (such as the United States) that have laws prohibiting such attacks.

Source

"Freeze on Anti-Spam Campaign," BBC News/Technology, Dec. 3, 2004, available at http://news.bbc.co.uk/go/pr/fr/-/2/hi/technology/4065751.stm (visited December 3, 2004).

attempt to gain entry. Distributed denial-of-service attacks often use zombies—computers that have been backdoored by worms or Trojans, without the consent or knowledge of their users. Smurf attacks and related attacks such as the "ping of death," in which the attacker spoofs the address of the target server and sends a large number of pings to which the recipients then reply, flooding the network, are now easily preventable and thus are largely a thing of the past (Allot 2001).

The 1996 National Information Infrastructure Protection Act creates a private right of action against persons launching a DDoS attack against "protected computers" if the attack meets certain criteria (18 U.S.C. 1030(g)). Nearly all computers in the United States are likely to fall within the statute's definition of "protected computers" (Jordan 2000). The victim may bring an action against the attacker if any of the five factors in § 1030(a)(5)(B) is present. Section 1030(a) provides in part that:

> (a) Whoever –
> ***
> (5)(A)(i) knowingly causes the transmission of a program, information, code, or command, and as a result of such conduct, intentionally causes damage without authorization, to a protected computer;
> (ii) intentionally accesses a protected computer without authorization, and as a result of such conduct, recklessly causes damage; or
> (iii) intentionally accesses a protected computer without authorization, and as a result of such conduct, causes damage; and
> (B) by conduct described in clause (i), (ii), or (iii) of subparagraph (A), caused (or, in the case of an attempted offense, would, if completed, have caused) –
> (i) loss to 1 or more persons during any 1-year period . . . aggregating at least $5,000 in value;
> (ii) the modification or impairment, or potential modification or impairment, of the medical examination, diagnosis, treatment, or care of 1 or more individuals;
> (iii) physical injury to any person;
> (iv) a threat to public health or safety; or
> (v) damage affecting a computer system used by or for a government entity in furtherance of the administration of justice, national defense, or national security;
> shall be punished as provided in subsection (c) of this section.

Subsection (c) then sets out a schedule of fines and prison sentences for various violations.

At first glance, a denial-of-service attack does not seem to fit readily within the terms of § 1030(a)(5). The denial-of-service attack does not allow the attacker to gain entry to the victim's computer, nor does it cause actual damage to any computer; when the denial-of-service attack is over, the victim's computer will continue to operate as before. There is unauthorized access to the zombie computers used in a DDoS, but the zombies' users do not suffer any appreciable economic harm as a result. However, the unauthorized access to the zombies, and the transmission of commands from the zombies, might cause economic harm to the victim. The unauthorized access and transmission of commands satisfies the requirements of either § 1030(a)(5)(A)(ii) or § 1030(a)(5)(A)(iii) and of § 1030(a)(5)(A)(i); only one of these three is needed. And an attack on a business Web site could well cause more than $5,000 in damage, in the form of lost business and the cost of measures taken to end the DDoS attack, thus satisfying the requirement of § 1030(a)(5)(B)(i). In fact, merely "impairing the availability of [the target] computer to other systems in the network" can constitute damage, although the $5,000 threshold must still be met (*Four Seasons*, 267 F.Supp. at 1323). Attacks on hospital computers, emergency 911 systems, and government computers may satisfy the requirements of subsections (ii) through (iv) of § 1030(a)(5)(B). DDoS attacks may also result in prosecution and lawsuits under state law, particularly under the tort of trespass to chattel. The chattels in this case might be the zombie computers or, on somewhat more tenuous reasoning, the target computer; the trespass consists of the unauthorized access to the zombies or the excessive requests and taking up of bandwidth of the target (*eBay*, 100 F.Supp. at 1070).

The problem with private lawsuits as protection against DDoS attacks, however, is that the victim must first identify the attacker. In *Four Seasons* and *eBay*, the partial denial of service was only one of the harms alleged; an attack in which denial of service is the attacker's only goal would be more difficult to trace. Section 1030 includes a statute of limitations of two years from either the date of the act causing damage or the date of discovery of the damage (18 U.S.C. § 1030(g)). Denial-of-service attacks that result in, for example, the disabling of an air traffic control tower are likely to result in criminal investigations (Nemerofsky 2000, 11). Once the government has located the attacker, the injured parties may pursue private actions. But where the denial-of-service attack results in the loss of a few thousand dollars' worth of business to a small company, the attacker is less likely to be apprehended, and the victim will be less likely to have sufficient resources to discover the identity of the attacker on its own.

A final category of denial-of-service attacks includes politically motivated "attacks" launched not with the use of zombies but through large numbers of users, by prearrangement, simultaneously attempting to access a political opponent's Web site at the same time. Such an "attack" might fall outside the scope of Section 1030 and might also be protected by the First Amendment.

Statute

- National Information Infrastructure Protection Act (NII) of 1996, codified at 18 U.S.C. § 1030

Cases

- *eBay v. Bidder's Edge*, 100 F.Supp.2d 1058 (N.D. Cal. 2000)
- *Four Seasons Hotels and Resorts B.V. v. Consorcio Barr, S.A.*, 267 F.Supp.2d 1268 (S.D. Fla. 2003)

See also: Hacking; Malware; Worm; Zombie

Sources and further reading:

William H. Jordan, "Going after Internet Hackers: Civil and Criminal Responses to Denial of Service Attacks," *Electronic Banking Law and Commerce Report*, Mar. 2000, at 6.

Jeff Nemerofsky, "The Crime of 'Interruption of Computer Services to Authorized Users': Have You Ever Heard of It?" 6 *Richmond Journal of Law and Technology* 23 (2000).

Protecting Networks from DoS Attacks and Malicious Traffic, Allot Communications, 2001, available at http://www.allot.com/html/solutions_enterprise_dos_attacks.shtm (visited October 19, 2004).

Margaret Jane Radin, "Distributed Denial of Service Attacks, Who Pays? Part I," *Cyberspace Lawyer*, Dec. 2001, at 2.

Margaret Jane Radin, "Distributed Denial of Service Attacks, Who Pays? Part II," *Cyberspace Lawyer*, Jan. 2002, at 2.

❖ DERIVATIVE WORKS ❖

The holder of copyright in a work has the exclusive right to make or authorize derivative works. For copyright purposes, a derivative work is a work that builds upon or incorporates a preexisting work. If a Russian novel is translated into English, the translation is a derivative work. If the English translation is adapted for a stage production, the stage play is yet another derivative work. A movie made of the play is derivative, as are a video game based on the movie and a novelization of the movie. To bring the work full circle, the Russian translation of the novelization (which would probably differ substantially from the original) would also be a derivative work. Each of the authors of these derivative works acquires a copyright in the derivative work, but no copyright in the underlying work. If the underlying work is copyrighted and the derivative work infringes upon that copyright, the author of the derivative work acquires no copyright in the infringing portion of the work; derivative works that are substantially similar to the copyrighted works upon which they are based require the permission of the copyright holder. If the underlying work is in the public domain, only those parts of the derivative work that differ from the underlying work may be copyrighted.

The exact level of originality required to make a derivative work copyrightable in its own right is unclear. There must be some difference; otherwise, as soon as any work came into the public domain, the first person to copy it could claim to have created a derivative work and the work would once again be copyrighted (see *L. Batlin & Son*, 536 F.2d at 492).

The copyright holder's exclusive right to authorize derivative works is subject to limitations imposed by fair use and the First Amendment. This is particularly evident in the case of parodies, which are necessarily derivative of the work they parody. A parody may use as much of the original material as necessary to conjure up the original in the mind of the viewer or listener; otherwise the point of the parody would be lost. The exact extent beyond that to which the parody may incorporate material from the original is unclear (510 U.S. at 588). In many cases the copyright holder may be unwilling to grant permission to use the material in a parody at any price; parodies are often unwelcome.

Parodies are popular on the Web, but the law regarding derivative works is equally important to computer and Internet law because of something that is *not* a derivative work. Many companies sell "helper" programs or programs that work jointly with popular programs, such as Microsoft Office: antivirus programs, citecheckers, document makers, metadata cleaners, printer drivers, and many others. These programs may add icons to the taskbars and pulldown menus of the various Microsoft Office programs, making it possible to use the helper program with a single click. If the combined program (Office with one-click helper function) were a derivative work, software makers would be unable to offer this convenient function without prior licensing permission from Microsoft (many, of course, nonetheless take the precaution of obtaining such permission). Similarly, every program loaded onto a Windows system adds information about itself to the Windows Explorer screen; the altered screen does not become a derivative work, however.

The test for whether such programs are derivative works, and thus require permission, was set out by the Ninth Circuit in *Lewis Galoob Toys v. Nintendo of America*. The plaintiff, Lewis Galoob Toys, made a device called the Game Genie for use with the Nintendo video game system. The Game Genie was inserted between the Nintendo system and the game cartridge; the program on the game cartridge was loaded into the Game Genie, which in turn loaded it onto the system—but allowed the player to increase the number of lives of the player's character and the speed at which the character moved and allowed the character to float above obstacles (964 F.2d at 967). The Ninth Circuit, in holding that the altered copy of the video game thus created was not a derivative work, pointed out that the Game Genie itself did not physically incorporate any portion of a work copyrighted by another, and that it did not sup-

plant or diminish demand for Nintendo video games (964 F.2d at 969). In addition, the altering of characteristics of the video game for the game-player's enjoyment and convenience was fair use (964 F.2d at 970–972).

This reasoning has been applied to Internet software cases. In an unreported decision, *RealNetworks, Inc. v. Streambox, Inc.*, the federal district court for the Western District of Washington issued an injunction against the distribution of the Streambox Ferret. The Ferret added a button to RealNetworks' RealPlayer graphical user interface (GUI), allowing users to use Streambox's search engine rather than RealNetworks'. The district court considered *Lewis Galoob Toys* and seemed to suggest that the altered GUI might be a derivative work, but reached no definite conclusion; it issued the injunction on other grounds (*RealNetworks*, 2000 WL 127311, *11–12). In another battleground area, adware and spyware, the federal district court for the Southern District of New York has held that the creation of a program that triggers pop-ups whenever a particular Web page is viewed does not create a derivative work, and thus does not violate the Web page owner's copyright (*1-800-Contacts*, 309 F.Supp.2d 467).

Statute
- Copyright Act of 1976, Exclusive Rights, 17 U.S.C. § 106(2)

Cases
Supreme Court
- *Campbell v. Acuff-Rose Music, Inc.*, 510 U.S. 569 (1994)

Federal Appellate Courts
- *Lewis Galoob Toys v. Nintendo of America*, 964 F.2d 965 (9th Cir. 1992)
- *L. Batlin & Son, Inc. v. Snyder*, 536 F.2d 486 (2d Cir. 1976)

Federal District Courts
- *RealNetworks, Inc. v. Streambox, Inc.*, 2000 WL 127311 (W.D. Wash. 2000)
- *1-800-Contacts, Inc. v. WhenU.com*, 309 F.Supp.2d 467 (S.D. N.Y. 2003)

See also: Copyright; Copyright Infringement; Fair Use (Copyright); File-Sharing

Sources and further reading:
Gregory M. Duhl, "Old Lyrics, Knock-Off Videos, and Copycat Comic Books: The Fourth Fair Use Factor in U.S. Copyright Law," 54 *Syracuse Law Review* 665 (2004).

❖ DIGITAL AUDIO WORKS ❖

In 1986, digital audio recording technology became commercially available to the general public, sending unease through the music content industry. (An earlier attempt to introduce digital recording in the 1970s had failed.) Digital audio recordings, like all digital recordings, can be copied an unlimited number of times with no degradation in quality. The advent of the Internet and of file-compression formats meant that these recordings could then be distributed in moments to countless individuals around the globe. Recorded music is generally sold at prices that make unlawful copying far more attractive than is the case with books and movies; in addition, the music content industry is largely a middleman business, and is thus particularly vulnerable to piracy. As a result, the music content industry successfully lobbied for additional legislation to protect it, including the Audio Home Recording Act of 1992.

The Audio Home Recording Act (AHRA) imposed royalties—in effect, taxes—on digital audio recorders and media, and required digital audio recorders to incorporate electronic rights management technology. These provisions may have succeeded in killing off the digital audiotape (DAT) technology at which the statute was originally aimed, but they have been rendered irrelevant by technological advance. By the terms of the statute and subsequent court decisions, home computers are not digital audio recorders; they are not "designed or marketed for the primary purpose of" making digital audio recordings and thus are not covered by the AHRA (17 U.S.C. § 1001(3); *RIAA v. Diamond Multimedia*, 180 F.3d at 1078; *Napster*, 239 F.3d at 1024). The AHRA did, however, provide for immunity from copyright liability for private, noncommercial recording of copyrighted music.

Digital audio recording, by itself, was a threat to the music content industry's revenues. Two newer technologies transformed this to a threat to the industry's existence. These new technologies were file compression, especially the MP3 file format, and the Internet. It is now possible for anyone, anywhere on the globe, to make a digital recording and distribute it worldwide, at no significant cost in time or money. The ongoing battle over this online file-sharing has become the defining struggle of the content industry and of Internet copyright law; it is discussed in detail under the heading "File-Sharing" in this encyclopedia.

Statute

- Audio Home Recording Act, 17 U.S.C. §§ 1001–1003, 1008

Cases

- *A&M Records, Inc. v. Napster, Inc.*, 239 F.3d 1004 (9th Cir. 2001)
- *Recording Industry Association of America v. Diamond Multimedia Systems, Inc.*, 180 F.3d 1072 (9th Cir. 1999)

See also: Audio Home Recording Act; Content Industry; Copyright; Digital Performance Right in Sound Recordings Act; Digital Rights Management; File-Sharing

Sources and further reading:
Rachel Gader-Shafran, "Confessions of a Serial Infringer: Can the Audio Home Recording Act of 1992 Protect the Consumer from Copy-Protected CDs?" *Intellectual Property Law Newsletter*, Winter 2003, at 10.
Aaron L. Melville, "The Future of the Audio Home Recording Act of 1992: Has It Survived the Millennium Bug?" 7 *Boston University Journal of Science and Technology Law* 372 (2001).
Eric Smith, "The DAT Tax," http://www.brouhaha.com/~eric/bad_laws/dat_tax.html (visited October 19, 2004).

❖ DIGITAL DIVIDE ❖

The term *digital divide* refers to a gap between rich and poor individuals, communities, or nations in access to information technologies. The origin of the term is uncertain; it has been variously credited to several people, including former president Bill Clinton, the assistant secretary for Communications and Information in

THE BOONDOCKS © 2004 Aaron McGruder. Dist. By UNIVERSAL PRESS SYNDICATE. Reprinted with permission. All rights reserved.

Clinton's Commerce Department, and *Los Angeles Times* reporters Jonathan Webber and Amy Harmon. (Foster and Borkowski, n.d.). It came into widespread popular use around the time of its use by Bill Clinton in 1995.

At the individual and community level, wealthy individuals and wealthier or more privileged communities tend to have better access to information technology. In the early days of the Internet there was widespread concern that this would result in the poor being left behind and missing out on economic and educational opportunities, even in wealthy countries such as the United States. This fear has proved, if not totally unfounded, exaggerated. In 1998 only 26.2 percent of U.S. households had Internet access; a mere three years later, by 2001, the percentage had nearly doubled, to 50.5 percent (*Statistical Abstract* 2003, 736). Internet access is now available to all, even in most remote rural communities, at little or no cost; debate over the digital divide in the United States now focuses not merely on access but on the quality of access. Broadband access is still relatively expensive, at around $30–$50 per month, and not available in all areas. Free broadband access is available in schools and libraries, although it may be subject to content restrictions and does not provide the convenience of home access. Cheap, less-restricted access is available in Internet cafés and copy centers. Many businesses provide free wireless Internet access for patrons, and some U.S. cities are considering plans to provide free city-wide wireless access. Children without computers at home have the opportunity to learn to use them at school: By 2003, 89 percent of schools in the United States had computers, with an average of one computer for every five students (*World Almanac* 2004, 289–290).

But if the digital divide is narrowing in the United States, it still exists among nations. In Europe and East Asia the divide has also closed rapidly, with some countries surpassing the United States; South Korea, for example, leads the world in the percentage of homes with broadband Internet access—78 percent and growing (Shameen 2004). The island of Niue in the South Pacific now provides free wireless Internet access island-wide. But parts of the world are being left behind. As late as 1998 only one-tenth of one percent of African households had Internet access (Kenny 2000).

To aid in measuring the digital divide the International Telecommunications Union has created the Digital Access Index (DAI). The DAI attempts to reduce the imprecision of measures such as Internet connections per household, which are useful when making comparisons within a society but not so useful when comparing between societies that have radically different patterns of work and recreational Internet use, not to mention different concepts of "household." The DAI is based on eight variables drawn from five areas: availability of infrastructure, affordability of access, educational level, quality of information technology and communications technology services, and Internet usage. The results are not surprising in the aggregate: The dozen nations or territories with the highest DAI are the five Scandinavian countries, plus Canada, Hong Kong, the Netherlands, South Korea, Taiwan, the United Kingdom, and the United

States. The thirty with the lowest DAI are all poor countries, all but two of them (Bhutan and Haiti) in sub-Saharan Africa (ITU 2003).

This correlation has led some to dismiss the digital divide as a symptom, rather than a cause, of poverty. Michael Powell, chairman of the Federal Communications Commission, has compared it to a "Mercedes divide" (Lemann 2002). Powell's point seems to be that some people can afford to drive a Mercedes, whereas others cannot, but this is a product of the wealth of the Mercedes drivers, not a cause of it. Driving a Mercedes does not make the Mercedes driver still wealthier, nor do Mercedes drivers have greater access to the roads and highways than Volkswagen drivers, Hyundai drivers, or drivers of rusted 1984 Ford Escorts.

The analogy could be carried yet further: Part of the reason for limited Internet access in Niger or Bhutan is its limited usefulness to countries at that stage of development. A dweller on a roadless island has no use for a Mercedes; in Niger, where only 14.7 percent of the population is literate, 85.3 percent would be unable to make use of an Internet connection if they had one. Nor is literacy the only requirement; Niger has only 1.8 telephones per 1,000 people, and as of 1998 there were only about 100 mobile telephones in the entire country (Turner 2001, 1224). Even those who are literate and able to connect to the Internet will find few Web pages written in Djerba or Fulani, and perhaps a few more in Hausa, although most potential users will also be fluent in French. But even the 3,000 Internet users in the country cannot make the same use of the Internet as users in Tokyo or Toronto. For example, Niger's commercial and physical infrastructure cannot yet support the lively online commerce, with overnight delivery of goods to the user's front door, that is just one of the appealing features of the Internet.

Whether the ongoing international digital divide is a cause or effect of poverty remains subject to debate; however, there are ongoing efforts by developing-country governments, international organizations, and aid groups to narrow this divide by building infrastructure and providing training and free or subsidized Internet access to schools and villages.

See also: Broadband, Internet

Sources and further reading:
Sharon Foster and Adrianna Borkowski, *Who Coined the Term? Origin of 'Digital Divide' Escapes Even the Experts,* Access Denied, available at http://www1.soc.american.edu/students/ij/co_3/digitaldivide/history.htm (no date)(visited June 2, 2005).
International Telecommunications Union, "World Telecommunication Development Report 2003: Access Indicators for the Information Society" (2003).
Charles J. Kenny (World Bank), *Expanding Internet Access to the Rural Poor in Africa,* International Telecommunications Union, African Internet and Telecom Summit, Banjul, The Gambia, June 5–9, 2000.
Nicholas Lemann, "Letter from Washington: The Chairman: He's the Other Powell, and No One Is Sure What He's Up To," *New Yorker,* October 7, 2002, available at http://www.newyorker.com/fact/content/?021007fa_fact (visited October 1, 2004).
Assif Shameen, "Korea's Broadband Revolution: What Korea Is Doing Will Have Global Impact," *Chief Executive Magazine,* Apr. 2004, available at http://www.chiefexecutive.net/depts/technology/197a.htm (visited October 1, 2004).
Barry Turner, ed., *The Statesman's Yearbook: The Politics, Cultures and Economies of the World,* 139th ed. (Houndmills, Basingstoke, UK: Palgrave, 2001).
U.S. Census Bureau, *Statistical Abstract of the United States: 2003* 123rd ed (Washington, DC: Government Printing Office, 2003).
World Almanac and Book of Facts 2004 (New York: World Almanac Books, 2004).

❖ DIGITAL MILLENNIUM COPYRIGHT ACT ❖

The Digital Millennium Copyright Act (DMCA), enacted in 1998 and signed into law by then-President Clinton, amended several sections of Title 17 of the United States Code, the portion that contains laws governing copyright. The DMCA as enacted contained five titles, four of which addressed various copyright issues. Title I, the WIPO Copyright and Performances and Phonograms Treaties Implementation Act, was designed to bring U.S. law into conformity with the obligations imposed by two World Intellectual Property Organization

(WIPO) treaties. The most controversial aspect of Title I is probably its prohibition of the circumvention of copy-protection measures (17 U.S.C. §§ 1201–1204). Title II, the Online Copyright Infringement Liability Limitation Act, addressed the problem of potential liability of online service providers for copies made in the routine course of storing and transmitting information, hosting Web sites, and providing search services. Copying of information is necessary to the activities of service providers; Title II insulates these service providers from liability for such routine activities so long as they comply with certain conditions (17 U.S.C. § 512). Title III, the Computer Maintenance Competition Assurance Act, was enacted in response to a federal court decision that had exposed third-party computer maintenance and repair companies to copyright infringement liability for copies of computer programs made by the mere act of starting up a computer in the course of maintenance and repair operations (17 U.S.C. §117). Title IV addressed several issues: functions of the Copyright Office, ephemeral recordings, copies made for distance education purposes, copies made by nonprofit libraries and archives for preservation or interlibrary loan purposes, webcasting, and the assumption of collective bargaining agreement obligations in the case of transfers of rights in motion pictures (17 U.S.C. §§ 106, 108, 110, 112). Title V created a new form of intellectual property protection for vessel hull designs (17 U.S.C. §§ 1301–1332).

Copyright law, once obscure, has become a battleground on which content owners, equipment manufacturers, and consumers all struggle to preserve what each group perceives as its rights. The DMCA, especially Title I, remains among the most controversial of the several controversial developments in copyright law in recent years. In what is surely a rare honor for a federal copyright statute, it even has an activist group, Anti-DMCA, specifically dedicated to its repeal. Congressional efforts to modify the DMCA in ways more friendly to users than to content owners include the Digital Media Consumers' Rights Act (DMCRA), introduced by users' rights advocate Richard Boucher (D-VA).

Statutes

- Copyright Act of 1976 (as amended by DMCA), §§ 101, 104, 104A, 106–10, 112, 117, and 411
- Digital Millennium Copyright Act, 17 U.S.C. §§ 512, 1201–1205

See also: Activism and Advocacy Groups; Copyright; Copyright Infringement; Digital Millennium Copyright Act, Title I; Digital Millennium Copyright Act, Title II; Digital Millennium Copyright Act, Title III; Digital Millennium Copyright Act, Title IV; Digital Millennium Copyright Act, Title V; File-Sharing; WIPO Copyright Treaty; WIPO Performances and Phonograms Treaty

Sources and further reading:

David Nimmer, *Copyright: Sacred Text, Technology, and the DMCA* (The Hague: Kluwer Academic/ Plenum Publishers, 2004).

Marcia Wilbur, *DMCA: The Digital Millennium Copyright Act* (San Jose, CA: Writers Club Press, 2001).

Christopher Wolf, *Digital Millennium Copyright Act: Text, History, and Caselaw* (Silver Spring, MD: Pike and Fischer, 2003).

❖ DIGITAL MILLENNIUM COPYRIGHT ACT, TITLE I ❖

Title I of the Digital Millennium Copyright Act (DMCA), the WIPO Copyright and Performances and Phonograms Treaties Implementation Act, was designed to bring U.S. law into conformity with the obligations imposed by two World Intellectual Property Organization (WIPO) treaties. The two treaties referred to in the name of the Act, the WIPO Copyright Treaty and the WIPO Performances and Phonograms Treaty, were adopted in 1996 but did not enter into force until 2002. In order to implement the treaties, Title I created new prohibitions against the circumvention of technological protective measures used to prevent unauthorized copying and against tampering with or removing digital rights management information, made technical amendments to various sections of the copyright code, and required the Copyright Office to perform two joint studies with the

National Telecommunications and Information Administration of the Department of Commerce (NTIA). The anticircumvention and rights-management provisions have been the focus of nearly all opposition to Title I and of much of the opposition to the DMCA as a whole.

The anticircumvention provisions: Article 11 of the WIPO Copyright Treaty and Article 18 of the WIPO Performances and Phonograms Treaty both require the United States, as a party to the treaties, to "provide adequate legal protection and effective legal remedies against the circumvention of effective technological measures that are used" to prevent unauthorized reproduction of protected works.

Section 103 of the DMCA adds a new chapter 12 to the copyright code. The first section of this new chapter, section 1201, carries out the mandate of Articles 11 and 18 and is titled "circumvention of copyright protection systems." Ostensibly it aims to prevent circumvention of technological protective measures that prevent unauthorized *access* to a copyrighted work rather than those that prevent *copying* of the work, thus retaining fair use. In practice, however, access is necessary for copying, and section 1201 is widely perceived as having narrowed the scope of fair use. Although it is still possible to make a copy of the analog output of a motion picture or music file, and this copying may be permitted by fair use, this means of copying is less convenient and there will inevitably be some loss of quality.

In addition to the provision that, with a few narrow exceptions, "no person shall circumvent a technological measure that effectively controls access to a work," section 1201 also prohibits the enabling of circumvention by others:

> No person shall manufacture, import, offer to the public, provide, or otherwise traffic in any technology, product, service, device, component, or part thereof, that—
> (A) is primarily designed or produced for the purpose of circumventing a technological measure that effectively controls access to a work protected under this title;
> (B) has only limited commercially significant purpose or use other than to circumvent a technological measure that effectively controls access to a work protected under this title; or
> (C) is marketed by that person or another acting in concert with that person with that person's knowledge for use in circumventing a technological measure that effectively controls access to a work protected under this title. (17 U.S.C. § 1201(a)(2))

In other words, it is unlawful under the DMCA to distribute hardware or software that will enable the user to violate the underlying prohibition on circumventing a technological measure that effectively controls access to a work, if the hardware or software is designed for that purpose, if it has little other purpose, or if it is marketed for use in circumvention. Only one of these conditions must be met, not all three. It is only permissible to distribute a device or program capable of circumvention if it is not primarily designed for that purpose, it has another commercially significant purpose or use, and it is not marketed for that purpose.

This might seem to create problems for a wide range of equipment manufacturers. Apple's famous advertisement ("Rip. Mix. Burn. After all, it's your music.") could easily be seen as marketing Apple's iMac for circumvention of technological measures, a use of which the iMac is capable. And consumers, even those who have no intention of violating copyright laws, will generally prefer a computer capable of copying protected works to a computer without that capability. The concerns of equipment manufacturers led to the "no mandate" rule of section 1201(c)(3): equipment manufacturers are not required to design their products to "provide for a response to any particular technological measure." There is an exception to this exception, however: Within eighteen months of the enactment of the DMCA, all analog videocassette recorders were required to conform to "the automatic gain control copy control technology" distributed by Macrovision Corporation and used to prevent unauthorized copying of analog videocassettes and some analog signals. The statute prohibits the use of Macrovision's technology to prevent copying of free analog broadcast television and basic and extended basic tier cable broadcasts.

In addition to the "no mandate" provision, there are also two savings clauses in section 1201. Section 1201(c)(1) provides that nothing in section 1201 "shall affect rights, remedies, limitations, or defenses to copyright infringement, including fair use, under this title."

And section 1201(c)(2) provides that nothing in section 1201 "shall enlarge or diminish vicarious or contributory liability for copyright infringement[.]" Aside from the "no mandate" provision and these savings clauses, section 1201 also includes an exception for law enforcement, intelligence, and other governmental activities. There are also exceptions, under certain circumstances, for nonprofit library, archive, and educational institutions; reverse engineering to achieve interoperability; encryption research; protection of minors; personal privacy, when the technological measure or the work it protects is capable of collecting or disseminating personally identifying information about the online activities of a natural person; and security testing. There is also an ongoing administrative rule-making proceeding, described in section 1201(a)(1)(B)–(E), to evaluate the impact of the anticircumvention provisions.

Challenges to Section 1201: The anticircumvention provisions have been challenged repeatedly in the courts by activists, as well as by the practice of large numbers of users. These challenges are discussed in detail in the entries on DeCSS and file-sharing elsewhere in this encyclopedia. The DeCSS saga can be regarded as a challenge by technically sophisticated activists seeking to protest Title I, while file-sharing, although it contains a not insignificant element of protest, is primarily of concern to content owners because of its ubiquity rather than its ideological underpinnings.

Not long after the anticircumvention provisions came into effect, copies of a program called DeCSS became available on Web sites in the United States. DeCSS could be used to decode the encryption used to control access to material recorded on DVDs. The operators of these Web sites were immediately sued by the motion picture industry. The case was heard at trial before the federal district court for the Southern District of New York as *Universal City Studios v. Reimerdes,* and on appeal before the federal Court of Appeals for the Second Circuit as *Universal City Studios v. Corley.* Both the trial court and the appellate court found for the movie-industry plaintiffs, rejecting the defendants' constitutional challenge to section 1201.

The DeCSS case presented § 1201 with two major challenges: The defendants questioned the constitutionality of the anticircumvention provisions, which could have resulted in the striking down of § 1201 altogether, and the applicability of § 1201 to software as well as hardware, which could have opened a gigantic loophole, effectively eviscerating the statute. The courts found that, although DeCSS contained expression subject to First Amendment protection, the prohibition against its distribution contained in § 1201 was content-neutral, furthered an important governmental interest (protecting copyrighted works stored on digital media), and was no broader than necessary to further this interest. Nor was there a First Amendment violation in applying the statute to enjoin the defendants from posting links to websites from which DeCSS could be downloaded. As to the potential loophole, the things included in the categories of "technology, product, service, device, component, or part thereof" listed in the statute were not limited to hardware, but included software as well. And, although CSS was a relatively weak form of encryption (movie studios had been unable to use stronger encryption because of U.S. export control regulations), it was nonetheless a measure that "effectively controlled access" within the meaning of the statute; a technological measure would be deemed to effectively control access so long as controlling access was its function. (273 F.3d 429) (Note that this interpretation raises a question as to whether the word "effectively" in the statute has any effect.)

The federal courts again considered the application of section 1201 to traditionally copyrighted works on digital media in *United States v. Elcom Ltd.* Elcom made a program capable of circumventing access controls on Adobe e-books. The court found that the application of section 1201 to ban distribution of Elcom's program was, like the ban on distribution of DeCSS, not unconstitutional. The court cited extensively from the opinions of the district and circuit courts in the DeCSS case. (In the federal court system district courts are bound by the holdings of the Circuit Courts to which their decisions may be appealed, but are not bound by the decisions of other Circuit Courts. The court that decided *Elcom* was a federal district court located in California; appeals from it are heard by the Ninth Circuit. Although the decision of the Second Circuit on a question that had not yet been decided by the Ninth Circuit would carry considerable weight, it was quite possible for the *Elcom* court to have disagreed with the Second Circuit, and for the Ninth Circuit to have affirmed the decision. The Ninth Circuit and the Second Circuit would then have been in disagreement. This sort of conflict between the circuits actually happens quite often; if the situation persists, the Supreme Court may eventually resolve the conflict. The resolution would probably come relatively quickly in a case such as this, if two circuits were to disagree as to the constitutionality of a federal statute.)

> In holding that section 1201 as applied to Elcom's program was constitutional, the district court explained that "while it is not unlawful to circumvent for the purpose of engaging in fair use, it is unlawful to traffic in tools that allow fair use circumvention." In other words, fair use of protected materials is still available, but only to those who are technically savvy enough to circumvent the protective measures themselves. (203 F.Supp 1111)

The anticircumvention provisions, originally envisioned as a way to prevent piracy of movies recorded on DVDs, have also been applied to technological protective measures in things as diverse as printer cartridges, garage door openers, and an investment firm's virtual private network (VPN). This expansion of the application of the DMCA's anticircumvention provisions could ultimately have more far-reaching effects than the application of those provisions to movies, music, and e-books. No one questions, after all, that movies, music, and books are copyrightable; these are traditional subjects of copyright law, and debate over the anticircumvention provisions has tended to focus on the extent to which the DMCA restricts fair use. But printer cartridges, for example, are not traditional subjects of copyright law. Copyright could give printer manufacturers a powerful tool to ensure that those who buy their printers must use their cartridges and no others, bringing about the demise of the printer cartridge aftermarket.

In *Lexmark International v. Static Control Components,* a maker of printers and printer cartridges sued a manufacturer of components for remanufactured printer cartridges. One of these components was the SMARTEK chip, which could be used to allow remanufactured cartridges to work with Lexmark printers. Lexmark had installed chips containing a toner loading program on some of its cartridges; the printers, meanwhile, contained a printer engine program. Neither the toner loading program nor the printer engine program would function unless the printer and the microchip on the toner cartridge "recognized" each other by successfully executing an authentication sequence. Static Control Components ("SCC") designed the SMARTEK chip to enable cartridges remanufactured by persons other than Lexmark to mimic this authentication sequence, thus fooling the printer into believing that it was working with an authentic Lexmark-remanufactured cartridge. SCC reverse engineered a means of bypassing the authentication sequence, but copied the toner loading program on to the SMARTEK chip. The first of these actions gave rise to Lexmark's anticircumvention claim, while the second gave rise to an infringement claim (253 F.Supp.2d 943).

The federal district court for the Eastern District of Kentucky agreed with Lexmark that Lexmark was likely to prevail upon both its anticircumvention and its copyright infringement claims on the merits and granted injunctive relief against SCC. On appeal, however, the Sixth Circuit Court of Appeals vacated the decision and remanded the case for further proceedings. The Sixth Circuit found that Lexmark had failed to establish a likelihood of success on the merits and that the bypassing of the lockout code was not necessarily a copyright violation:

> Generally speaking, "lock-out" codes fall on the functional-idea rather than the original-expression side of the copyright line. Manufacturers of interoperable devices such as computers and software, game consoles and video games, printers and toner cartridges, or automobiles and replacement parts may employ a security system to bar the use of unauthorized components. To "unlock" and permit operation of the primary device (i.e., the computer, the game console, the printer, the car), the component must contain either a certain code sequence or be able to respond appropriately to an authentication process. To the extent

compatibility requires that a particular code sequence be included in the component device to permit its use, the merger and scènes à faire doctrines generally preclude the code sequence from obtaining copyright protection. (*Lexmark,* 387 F.3d at 536)

This was in direct contrast to the trial court's rejection of SCC's argument that Lexmark had improperly used copyright law to provide protection to a thing not otherwise copyrightable—the printer cartridge (253 F.Supp.2d 943). The Sixth Circuit pointed out that there were public policy interests favoring interoperability—the "Progress of Science and Useful Arts" mentioned in the Constitution's copyright clause (U.S. Constitution, Art. I, § 8, cl. 8). Congress took these interests into account in designing the DMCA, apparently with things like printer cartridges in mind: "Congress added the interoperability provision in part to ensure that the DMCA would not diminish the benefit to consumers of interoperable devices 'in the consumer electronics environment.'"

The garage door opener case, *Chamberlain Group v. Skylink Technologies,* had superficially similar facts. Chamberlain is a manufacturer of garage door openers; Skylink is a distributor of garage door opener components. Modern garage door openers, including Chamberlain's, use a rolling code signal for added security. (In the absence of the rolling code method, a burglar could leave recording equipment near the garage door, wait until the door opener was used, and then retrieve the door-opening code from the recording equipment.) Because the rolling codes in the remote control and the garage door opener might become desynchronized if the remote control were pressed several times while out of range of the door opener, Chamberlain's door openers also included a process to allow resynchronization of the door opener and the remote control. Skylink distributed universal remotes that used the resynchronization process to operate the Chamberlain garage door openers, thus compromising the rolling code security feature. Chamberlain claimed that the rolling code component of its copyrighted garage door opener program protected the portion of the software that actually operated the door opener and thus fell within the protection of section 1201. The federal district court for the Northern District of Illinois disagreed and denied Chamberlain's motion for summary judgment. A motion for summary judgment is a legal mechanism that can be used to resolve a case without trial; it can be granted only if there is no genuine issue of material fact and if, based on those undisputed facts, the moving party is entitled to judgment as a matter of law. The court found that there were genuine issues as to two material facts: whether the garage door opener program was in fact protected by copyright, and whether owners of Chamberlain rolling code garage door openers were authorized to use Skylink's remote control (292 F.Supp.2d 1023).

In the virtual private network (VPN) case, *Pearl Investments v. Standard I/O,* defendants improperly gained access to the plaintiff's VPN by unauthorized use of access protocols. The federal district court for the District of Maine held that because a "VPN is the 'electronic equivalent' of a locked door" it is a "technological protection measure." This decision, if widely adopted, would represent a further expansion of the scope of section 1201. The district court seems to be willing to apply section 1201 to any unauthorized access to a VPN or similar encryption-protected system and perhaps to any password-protected Web site, file, folder, or disk, even though no device or program—only a password—is used to gain that access (257 F.Supp.2d 326).

Digital rights management: Article 12 of the WIPO Copyright Treaty and Article 19 of the WIPO Performances and Phonograms Treaty require the parties to prohibit not only the circumvention of technological measures used to prevent actual copying, but also any other circumvention of an electronic rights management scheme. The parties must "provide adequate and effective legal remedies against any person knowingly" removing or altering "any electronic rights management information," or distributing, importing for distribution, broadcasting, or communicating to the public any works from which such information has been removed, if in either case the person does not have the authority to do so and knows or has reason to know that doing so "will induce, enable, facilitate or conceal an infringement of any right covered by" the treaties.

The second section of chapter 12, section 1202, carries out the mandate of Articles 12 and 19 and is titled "integrity of copyright management information." Copyright management information is defined in section 1202(c) as information identifying and about the title, author, and copyright owner and, with the exception of audiovisual works and broadcasts of public performance, the performer of a work; the writer, performer, or director credited in an audiovisual work, with the exception of broadcast public performances; "terms and conditions for use of the work"; and "identifying numbers or symbols referring to such information or links to such information." There is also a catch-all category: Copyright management information may also include "such other information as the Register of Copyrights may prescribe by regulation, except that the Register of Copyrights may not require the provision of any information concerning the user of a copyrighted work." The text at the beginning of section 1202(c) also specifically excludes "personally identifying information about a user of a work" from the definition of copyright management information.

Section 1202(a) prohibits the knowing use of false copyright management information "with the intent to induce, enable, facilitate, or conceal infringement." Section 1202(b) provides that

> No person shall, without the authority of the copyright owner or the law—
> (1) intentionally remove or alter any copyright management information, [or]
> (2) distribute or import for distribution copyright management information knowing that the copyright management information has been removed or altered without authority of the copyright owner or the law, or
> (3) distribute, import for distribution, or publicly perform works, copies of works, or phonorecords, knowing that copyright management information has been removed or altered without authority of the copyright owner or the law.

Section 1202, like section 1201, includes a general exemption for law enforcement, intelligence, and other governmental activities. It also provides exceptions for broadcast stations and cable systems if there is no intent "to induce, enable, facilitate, or conceal infringement of a right" and, in the case of analog transmissions, "avoiding the activity that constitutes such violation is not technically feasible or would create an undue financial hardship on such person"; or, in the case of digital transmissions, certain conditions relating to digital transmission standards for the placement of copyright management information are present.

The next section of chapter 12, section 1203, provides civil remedies for violations of the provisions of the preceding two sections; section 1204 provides criminal penalties.

The technical amendments: The three technical amendments in Title I dealt with eligibility for national treatment, restoration of protection to some works that had fallen into the public domain in the United States, and copyright formalities.

The WIPO treaties, along with the Berne Convention, require what is called national treatment. Parties to the treaties must provide protection to works and authors from other member countries no less favorable than that accorded to works authored by their own nationals or published in their own territories. Title I amended sections 101 and 104 of the Copyright Act; section 101 deals with general definitions, and section 104 deals with subject matter and national origin. Title I added references to the WTO Agreement (which includes the Trade-Related Aspects of Intellectual Property Agreement, better known as TRIPS), the WIPO Copyright Treaty, and the WIPO Performances and Phonograms Treaty and struck out the definition of a "Berne Convention work." It also made changes to the language of several subsections and added a provision regarding simultaneous publication of works initially published in states not parties to the various copyright treaties.

The DMCA also amended section 104A of the Copyright Act, which restores copyright protection to certain works that had fallen into the public domain in the United States under earlier U.S. copyright law, but remained protected by copyright in their country of origin. The amendments changed the wording of section 104A to include those states that were parties to the WIPO treaties. The Berne Convention and TRIPS had already required restoration of copyright to works from parties to those treaties, and in 1995 the Uruguay Round Agreements Act, in furtherance of this obligation, had created section 104A. The DMCA's extension of this protection to parties to the WIPO treaties was necessary in order to reflect the treaty obligations accurately, but had no practical effect, as all of the parties to the WIPO treaties were already parties to the Berne Convention, TRIPS, or both.

The next technical amendment concerned section 411(a) of the Copyright Act, which requires that claims of copyright be registered with the Copyright Office before the copyright owner can initiate a lawsuit for copyright infringement. Prior to the DMCA, section 411(a) contained an exemption for Berne Convention works. The DMCA broadened the exception to include all foreign works. This was not actually required by the various treaty obligations of the United States; even though the Berne Convention, TRIPS, and the WIPO treaties contain "no formalities" requirements, there are a handful of countries that are not parties to any of these conventions; these countries also receive the benefit of the DMCA's "all foreign works" amendment, even though the United States was under no obligation to extend it to them. Note also that this amendment, like the restoration of copyright to some foreign works that have fallen into the public domain but not to some U.S. works identically situated, has the odd effect of giving greater protection to foreign works than to U.S. works.

The joint studies: Title I required the NTIA to prepare two reports. The first, to be completed within one year, was to focus narrowly on the effects of section 1201(g) of the copyright code, added by the DMCA, on encryption research. The second, to be completed within two years, had a somewhat broader mandate; it was to address the effects of statutory, technological, and commercial changes on the right of first sale and the right to make backup and other necessary copies of computer programs.

The first of these two required reports was mandated by section 1201(g)(5), which provided that:

Not later than 1 year after the date of the enactment of [the DMCA], the Register of

Copyrights and the Assistant Secretary for Communications and Information of the Department of Commerce shall jointly report to the Congress on the effect this subsection has had on—
(A) encryption research and the development of encryption technology;
(B) the adequacy and effectiveness of technological measures designed to protect copyrighted works; and
(C) protection of copyright owners against the unauthorized access to their encrypted copyrighted works.

The report was to "include legislative recommendations, if any." The report was completed before the provisions that would have affected encryption technology research went into effect and forwarded to Congress in May 2000. It concluded that "Every concern expressed [in response to the Copyright Office's and NTIA's solicitation] was prospective in nature, primarily because the prohibition and its attendant exceptions will not become operative until October 28, 2000." As a result, "we conclude that it is premature to suggest alternative language or legislative recommendations with regard to Section 1201(g) of the DMCA at this time" (United States Copyright Office 2000).

The second report was due a year later, twenty-four months after the enactment of the DMCA, and required the same parties to evaluate the effects of Title I and technological and e-commerce advances on the first sale doctrine (17 U.S.C. § 109) and on the exemption allowing owners of copies of computer programs to reproduce and adapt them for use on a computer (17 U.S.C. § 117). The report was also to evaluate the relationship between the operation of sections 109 and 117 on the one hand and existing and emergent technology on the other. The NTIA issued its report in August 2001 (United States Copyright Office 2001).

The right of first sale allows the owner of a lawful copy of a work to dispose of that copy. The right to dispose includes the right to sell, give away, or otherwise transfer the lawful copy, as well as the right to display it at the place where it is located. It does not include the right to display the copy other than where it is located by broadcasting it, transmitting it over the Internet, or by other means. Section 109 also makes exceptions for sound recordings and computer programs, which may not be rented, leased, or lent by the purchaser without the consent of the copyright owner. Further exceptions to the exceptions for computer programs and sound recordings permit such lending by nonprofit libraries and educational institutions, and exempt rentals of computer programs "embodied in a machine or product and which cannot be copied during the ordinary operation or use of the machine or product; or . . . embodied in or used in conjunction with a limited purpose computer that is designed for playing video games and may be designed for other purposes" (17 U.S.C. § 109). The exemption in section 117 provides that

> it is not an infringement for the owner of a copy of a computer program to make or authorize the making of another copy or adaptation of that computer program provided:
> (1) that such a new copy or adaptation is created as an essential step in the utilization of the computer program in conjunction with a machine and that it is used in no other manner, [or]
> (2) that such new copy or adaptation is for archival purposes only and that all archival copies are destroyed in the event that continued possession of the computer program should cease to be rightful.

There is an additional exception added to section 117 by Title III of the DMCA: the exception for copies of computer programs made for purposes of maintenance or repair. There is also an exception for performance and display of video games.

In its report, the NTIA observed that "the inclusion of section 109 in the study has a clear relationship to the digital first sale proposal contained in a bill introduced in 1997 by Congressmen Rick Boucher and Tom Campbell. The reasons for including section 117 in the study are less obvious." The NTIA speculated, though, that section 117 was included because of "a proposed exemption for incidental copies found in the Boucher-Campbell bill, which would have been codified in section 117" (United States Copyright Office 2001).

After soliciting and reviewing comments from the content industry, consumer advocates, and others, the NTIA concluded that the anticircumvention provisions of the DMCA had, as yet, no adverse effect on section 109. The concerns expressed to the NTIA about the use of technological measures, particularly Content Scramble System (CSS), were flawed: The fact that DVDs require a special decoding device in order to be viewed does not make them unique. All sound and motion picture recordings require some special device in order to be played back. There is no statutory guarantee of a secondary market for copyrighted works. In any event, although "tethering" a work to a particular hardware device was possible and permissible under the DMCA, the practice was not widespread except in the case of e-books. If the practice were to become widespread, though, there might be a negative impact on the first sale doctrine. There was at least a potential negative impact on section 117, however; technological protective measures might interfere with section 117's archival exception (United States Copyright Office 2001).

While the effect of the DMCA itself on the two sections was minimal, the effect of e-commerce and technological change was significant. With regard to the first sale doctrine, the advent of computers and the Internet had vastly increased the potential for the owner of a lawful copy of a work to harm the copyright holder's interest. The first sale doctrine creates a right of distribution, not a right to copy. But because of the ease with which digital copies can be made and distributed—a click of a mouse can send thousands of copies over the Internet, and posting the work on a Web site can make it accessible to billions—the danger of harm to the copyright holder's interest is greater than with, for example, hard copies of books. Technological protective measures deal with this harm without affecting the right protected by section 109: the right to dispose of the original copy of the work that the consumer has purchased. The NTIA recommended no change to section 109 at present, but suggested that problems requiring legislative correction might eventually arise with regard to use by libraries (United States Copyright Office 2001).

A tangentially related and highly controversial area was the making of buffer copies in the course of playing streaming media. Webcasters of streaming media expressed to the NTIA their concerns that they could be forced to pay double royalties on a single download—once for buffering and once for actual playback. The NTIA found that the making of such buffer copies is "copying" for copyright purposes, adding that a strong case could be made that the making of buffer copies, necessary for smooth playback, was fair use. But the outcome of the fair use argument was not certain; to protect webcasters, the NTIA recommended "that Congress enact legislation amending the Copyright Act to preclude any liability arising from the assertion of a copyright owner's reproduction right with respect to temporary buffer copies that are incidental to a licensed digital transmission of a public performance of a sound recording and any underlying musical work." It made a similar observation, without an explicit legislative recommendation, regarding "performance" of licensed digital music downloads (United States Copyright Office 2001).

The NTIA's recommendation regarding copies has not yet been adopted, however, and in 2002 an arbitral panel decided that music webcasters—"Internet radio stations"—should pay a 9-percent surcharge for buffer copies. This was coupled with the panel's decision that Web-only stations should pay royalties twice as high as those paid by broadcast stations retransmitting their programs via the Internet; the concerns the webcasters voiced to the NTIA have thus proved well founded (Copyright Arbitration Royalty Panel 2002). This amount was reduced only slightly in the final order of the Librarian of Congress, which set the surcharge for buffer copies at 8.8 percent (67 Federal Register 45,239; 37 C.F.R. 261.3(c)).

Section 117 was considerably more out of date than section 109, the NTIA found. The provision permitting the making of an archival copy of a program, provided that "all archival copies are destroyed in the event that continued possession of the computer program should cease to be rightful," did not reflect the realities of computer use. Consumers need to back up digital works in digital form because the digital nature of the works renders them vulnerable. Most system administrators and many individual users address this problem with periodic tape backups of all of the data on a system, even though section 117 does not permit this. It would be costly, time consuming, and inefficient to go through each file on a system and identify

it as a program or nonprogram file before backing up the system. Nor would it be practical to examine the contents of past tape backups and delete any program files for which a license might have expired. As a result, the NTIA stated, "There is a fundamental mismatch between accepted, prudent practices among most system administrators and other users, on the one hand, and section 117 on the other. As a consequence, few adhere to the law." But the NTIA saw no need for legislative action on this basis alone: "While there is no question that this mismatch exists, nobody was able to identify any actual harm to consumers as a result of the limited scope of the archival exemption." A problem, however, arose from the interaction of fair use (17 U.S.C. § 107) and first sale: The making of backup copies according to the usual practice is probably a fair use, and a court might conceivably conclude that a copy thus made could be sold or otherwise disposed of by the user under section 109. The NTIA therefore recommended that Congress either "amend section 109 to ensure that fair use copies are not subject to the first sale doctrine or . . . create a new archival exemption that provides expressly that backup copies may not be distributed" (United States Copyright Office 2001).

The NTIA also considered the issue of contract preemption that arises when end-user license agreements (EULAs) purport to give copyright-like protection that overrides user rights under copyright law. Enforcement of these contracts under state law raises the preemption issue, because the Copyright Act by its terms (17 U.S.C. § 301) preempts state attempts to make copyright law. Again the NTIA stopped short of making any legislative recommendation; the situation was evolving rapidly, and it was possible that market forces alone would correct the problem, preventing rightholders from using EULAs to impose unreasonable limits on consumers' use of copyrighted material. If not, statutory change might be appropriate at some point in the future (United States Copyright Office 2001).

Statutes

- Copyright Act of 1976 (as amended by DMCA, Title I), §§ 101, 104, 104A, 107, 109, 117, and 411

- Digital Millennium Copyright Act, 17 U.S.C. §§ 1201–1205

Regulation
- Determination of Reasonable Rates and Terms for the Digital Performance of Sound Recordings and Ephemeral Recordings, Final Rule, 67 Federal Register 45,239 (July 8, 2002)(codified at 37 C.F.R. § 261)

Cases
Federal Appellate Courts
- *Universal City Studios, Inc. v. Corley,* 273 F.3d 429 (2nd Cir. 2001), affirming *Universal City Studios, Inc. v. Reimerdes,* 111 F.Supp.2d 294 (S.D. N.Y. 2000)

Federal Trial Courts
- *Adobe Systems, Inc. v. Stargate Software Inc.,* 216 F.Supp.2d 1051 (N.D. Cal. 2002)
- *Arclightz and Films Pvt. Ltd. v. Video Palace Inc.,* 2003 WL 21290889 (S.D. N.Y.2003) (unreported case)
- *Chamberlain Group, Inc. v. Skylink Technologies, Inc.,* 292 F.Supp.2d 1023 (N.D. Ill. 2003)
- *Lexmark International, Inc. v. Static Control Components, Inc.,* 253 F.Supp.2d 943 (E.D. Ky. 2003); reversed, 387 F.3d 522 (6th Cir. 2004); see also *Static Control Components, Inc. v. Dallas Semiconductor Corp.,* 2003 WL 21666582 (M.D. N.C. 2003) (same issue)
- *Microsoft Corp. v. Software Wholesale Club, Inc.,* 129 F.Supp.2d 995 (S.D. Tex. 2000)
- *Pearl Investments, LLC v. Standard I/O, Inc.,* 257 F.Supp.2d 326 (D. Me. 2003)
- *RealNetworks, Inc. v. Streambox, Inc.,* 2000 WL 127311 (W.D. Wash. 2000)
- *U.S. v. Elcom Ltd.,* 203 F.Supp.2d 1111 (N.D. Cal. 2002)
- *Video Pipeline, Inc. v. Buena Vista Home Entertainment, Inc.,* 192 F.Supp.2d 321 (D. N.J. 2002)

Reports
- Copyright Arbitration Royalty Panel, Report to the Librarian of Congress, Feb. 20, 2002, Appendix A, available from http://www.copyright.gov/carp/webcast_regs.html#panel (visited November 19, 2004)
- United States Copyright Office, DMCA Section 104 Report: A Report of the Register of Copyrights Pursuant to § 104 of the Digital Millennium Copyright Act, August 2001
- United States Copyright Office, Joint Study of Section 1201(g) of The Digital Millennium Copyright Act, May 2000

See also: Activism and Advocacy Groups; Berne Convention; Censorship; Copyright; Copyright Infringement; DeCSS; Digital Millennium Copyright Act, Title II; Digital Millennium Copyright Act, Title III; Digital Millennium Copyright Act, Title IV; Digital Rights Management; Encryption; Fair Use (Copyright); File-Sharing; First Amendment; First Sale; International Copyright Protection; Moral Rights; Open-Source; Steganography; TRIPS; WIPO Copyright Treaty; WIPO Performances and Phonograms Treaty

Sources and further reading:
David Nimmer, *Copyright: Sacred Text, Technology, and the DMCA* (The Hague: Kluwer Academic/Plenum Publishers, 2004).

Pamela Samuelson, "Intellectual Property and the Digital Economy: Why the Anti-Circumvention Regulations Need to Be Revised," 14 *Berkeley Technology Law Journal* 519 (1999).

Pamela Samuelson, "Towards More Sensible Anti-Circumvention Regulations," *Cyberspace Lawyer,* July/Aug. 2000, at 2.

Christopher Wolf, *Digital Millennium Copyright Act: Text, History, and Caselaw* (Silver Spring, MD: Pike and Fischer, 2003).

❖ DIGITAL MILLENNIUM COPYRIGHT ACT, TITLE II ❖

Title II of the Digital Millennium Copyright Act (DMCA), the Online Copyright Infringement Liability Limitation Act, created limitations on the liability of online service providers for copyright infringement when engaging in certain types of activities. The act created a new section 512 of Title 17 of the United States Code (the copyright code). Section 512 set up and defined safe harbors for service providers for transitory communications, system caching, storage of information on systems or networks at the direction of users, and information location tools. Special rules were also delineated for nonprofit educational institutions. Service providers whose activities fall within the scope of the safe harbor provisions cannot be held liable for damages for copyright infringement arising from those activities, and the availability of injunctive relief against those service providers is limited. The definition of "service provider" in the statute is broad and could conceivably include online file-sharing services; however, a file-sharing service that deliberately blinds itself (through the use of encryption, for example) to copyright infringement using its services may not be able to claim the protection of the safe harbors.

In addition to the safe harbor provisions, § 512 also permits a copyright owner to obtain a subpoena from a federal court ordering a service provider to disclose the identity of a subscriber who is allegedly engaging in infringing activities (17 U.S.C. § 512(h)). The limits of this subpoena power were defined by the federal appellate court for the District of Columbia Circuit in its December 2003 decision in the case of *Recording Industry Association of America v. Verizon Internet Services*. The RIAA had obtained a subpoena under § 512(h) to compel Verizon to disclose the name of a subscriber who had allegedly shared copyrighted music files. The D.C. Circuit agreed with Verizon that the subpoena, issued before any lawsuit had been filed, could not compel Verizon to disclose the name of the subscriber. The D.C. Circuit distinguished between conduit Internet service providers, which are not subject to a § 512(h) subpoena, and hosting Internet service providers, which may be. In this case Verizon, acting as a mere conduit, was not subject to the subpoena (351 F.3d 1229). As a result, subsequent RIAA file-sharing suits must be brought as "John Doe" actions; once the litigation has been instituted, subpoenas may be obtained as

part of the discovery process. Such subpoenas are harder to obtain than § 512(h) subpoenas and require judicial oversight to prevent abuses.

Under § 512 service providers are not required to monitor their services or access material in violation of law (such as the Electronic Communications Privacy Act) in order to be eligible for the protection of any of the safe harbor provisions. A service provider, for purposes of the transitory communications safe harbor provision, is "an entity offering the transmission, routing, or providing of connections for digital online communications, between or among points specified by a user, of material of the user's choosing, without modification to the content of the material as sent or received" (17 U.S.C. § 512(k)(1)(A)). For the other three safe harbors, a service provider is more broadly defined as "a provider of online services or network access, or the operator of facilities therefor" (17 U.S.C. § 512(k)(1)(B)). To be eligible for protection, a service provider must have "adopted and reasonably implemented . . . a policy that provides for the termination in appropriate circumstances of . . . repeat infringers"; and it must also accommodate and not interfere with "standard technical measures" for copyright protection (17 U.S.C. § 512(i)(1)).

Transitory communications safe harbor: Under section 512(a), a service provider is not liable for damages or, except as provided in section 512(j), for injunctive or other equitable relief for copyright infringement where the provider merely acts as a conduit, transmitting digital information from one point on a network to another at someone else's request. The transitory communications safe harbor is available if five elements are present:

(1) the transmission . . . was initiated by or at the direction of a person other than the service provider;

(2) the transmission, routing, provision of connections, or storage is carried out through an automatic technical process without selection of the material by the service provider;

(3) the service provider does not select the recipients of the material except as an automatic response to the request of another person;

(4) no copy of the material made by the service provider in the course of such intermediate or transient storage is maintained on the system or network in a manner ordinarily accessible to anyone other than anticipated recipients, and no such copy is maintained on the system or network in a manner ordinarily accessible to such anticipated recipients for a longer period than is reasonably necessary . . .; and

(5) the material is transmitted through the system or network without modification of its content. (17 U.S.C. § 512(a))

The exception in section 512(j) limits injunctive relief in such cases to two types of orders: orders requiring the service provider to deny access to the infringing user by terminating that user's account and, where the infringing site is outside the United States, orders requiring the service provider to take "reasonable steps . . . to block access to a specific, identified, online location outside the United States." In granting injunctive relief when one of the section 512 safe harbors protects the service provider from an award of damages, the court shall consider four factors:

(A) whether [injunctive relief] would significantly burden either the provider or the operation of the provider's system or network;

(B) the magnitude of the harm likely to be suffered by the copyright owner in the digital network environment if steps are not taken to prevent or restrain the infringement;

(C) whether implementation of such an injunction would be technically feasible and effective, and would not interfere with access to noninfringing material at other online locations; and

(D) whether other less burdensome and comparably effective means of preventing or restraining access to the infringing material are available. (17 U.S.C. § 512(j))

System caching safe harbor: Under section 512(b), a service provider is not liable for damages or, except as provided in section 512(j), for injunctive or other equitable relief for copyright infringement where the copy is made for system caching purposes, that is, "by reason of the intermediate and temporary storage of material" on the service provider's system or network, if

(A) the material is made available online by a person other than the service provider;

(B) the material is transmitted from the person described in subparagraph (A) through the system or network to a person other than the person described in subparagraph (A) at the direction of that other person; and

(C) the storage is carried out through an automatic technical process for the purpose of making the material available to users of the system or network who, after the material is transmitted as described in subparagraph (B), request access to the material from the person described in subparagraph (A). (17 U.S.C. § 512(b))

Certain additional conditions must also be met: The content of the retained material must not be modified. The service provider must periodically refresh the material by replacing the cached copy with a new copy made from the original location, in accordance with a generally accepted industry protocol, and must not interfere with technology that returns "hit" information to the person who posted the material. Once the service provider has been notified that copyrighted material posted without authorization has been removed or blocked, or ordered to be removed or blocked, at the original site, it must promptly remove or block access to the cached copy. If the person who posted the material has imposed limitations on access, such as password protection, the service provider must also impose these limitations (17 U.S.C. § 512(b)).

The scope of injunctive relief permitted under section 512(j) for the other three safe harbors (system caching, information storage, and information location tools) differs slightly from that permitted with respect to the transitory communications safe harbor. Injunctive relief is limited to orders "restraining the service provider from providing access to infringing material or activity residing at a particular online site on the provider's system or network," and, as with the transitory communications safe harbor, orders requiring the service provider to deny access to the infringing user by terminating that user's account. (17 U.S.C. § 512(j))

Information storage safe harbor: Under section 512(c), a service provider is not liable for damages or, except as provided in section 512(j), for injunctive or other equitable relief for copyright infringement for infringing material stored at the direction of a user on Web sites (or other information repositories) hosted on their systems. The information storage safe harbor is available if the service provider:

(A)(i) does not have actual knowledge that the material or an activity using the material on the system or network is infringing; [or]

(ii) in the absence of such actual knowledge, is not aware of facts or circumstances from which infringing activity is apparent; or

(iii) upon obtaining such knowledge or awareness, acts expeditiously to remove, or disable access to, the material; [and]

(B) does not receive a financial benefit directly attributable to the infringing activity, in a case in which the service provider has the right and ability to control such activity; and

(C) upon notification of claimed infringement as described in paragraph (3), responds expeditiously to remove, or disable access to, the material that is claimed to be infringing or to be the subject of infringing activity. (17 U.S.C. § 512(c))

In order to receive the benefit of the information storage safe harbor, the service provider must also have filed with the Copyright Office a designation of an agent to receive notifications of claimed infringement.

Section 512(c) also provides a notice-and-takedown procedure. If infringing material is posted on a Web site, the copyright owner must first submit a notification to the service provider's designated agent. If the notice does not contain all of the information required by section 512(c), it will not be considered in determining whether the service provider had knowledge of the infringement. Courts have construed this requirement strictly. For example, if the owner of copyright in a movie notifies eBay, an online auction marketplace, that unauthorized copies of his movie are being listed on eBay, that act alone does not meet the notice requirement. The notification must be in writing and must contain information specific enough to enable eBay to distinguish between authorized and unauthorized listings.

If the service provider acts promptly, upon receipt of proper notification, to remove or block access to the infringing content, the provider is protected within the safe harbor both from monetary liability to the copyright holder and from liability for any claim arising from its having removed or blocked access to the material. The service provider must also promptly notify the user who initially posted the allegedly infringing material that the material has been taken down; if the user believes that the material was incorrectly or fraudulently identified as infringing, the user may then file a counternotification. Within ten to fourteen business days following the filing of a proper counternotification the service provider must restore access to the material, unless the service provider's designated agent first receives notice that the person who submitted the original notification has filed an action seeking a court order against the user. Knowing misrepresentation by anyone involved is subject to penalties (17 U.S.C. § 512(c)).

Information location tools safe harbor: Under section 512(d), a service provider is not liable for damages or, except as provided in section 512(j), for injunctive or other equitable relief for copyright infringement for referring or linking users to sites containing infringing material through tools such as directories, indexes, references, pointers, or hyperlinks. The information location tools safe harbor is available if the service provider does not have the requisite knowledge that the material or activity is infringing; the "knowledge" standard here is the same as that for the information storage safe harbor. In addition, the service provider must not receive a financial benefit directly attributable to the infringing activity, in a case in which the service provider has the right and ability to control such activity; this standard is drawn from the standard established by the courts for determining vicarious copyright infringement. And finally, section 512(d) provides the same notice-and-takedown procedure as that provided in section 512(c) for the information storage safe harbor.

Nonprofit educational institutions: Under section 512(e), the actions of a faculty member or graduate student employee performing a teaching or research function may affect the eligibility of a nonprofit educational institution for two of the four safe harbors. With regard to the transitory communications and system caching safe harbors, the faculty member or student is a "person other than the provider" and cannot affect the institution's eligibility. Nor will the knowledge or awareness of the faculty member or student be attributed to the institution with regard to the information storage and information location tools safe harbors, so long as

(A) such faculty member's or graduate student's infringing activities do not involve the provision of online access to instructional materials that are or were required or recommended, within the preceding 3-year period, for a course taught at the institution by such faculty member or graduate student; [and]

(B) the institution has not, within the preceding 3-year period, received more than two notifications described in subsection (c)(3) of claimed infringement by such faculty member or graduate student, and such notifications of claimed infringement were not actionable under subsection (f); and

(C) the institution provides to all users of its system or network informational materials that accurately describe, and promote compliance with, the laws of the United States relating to copyright. (17 U.S.C. § 512(e))

Statute
- Digital Millennium Copyright Act, 17 U.S.C. § 512

Cases
Federal Appellate Courts
- *ALS Scan, Inc. v. RemarQ Communities, Inc.*, 239 F.3d 619 (4th Cir. 2001)
- *In re Aimster Copyright Litigation*, 334 F.3d 643 (7th Cir. 2003)
- *Recording Industry Ass'n of America, Inc. v. Verizon Internet Services*, 351 F.3d 1229 (D.C. Cir. 2003)

Federal Trial Courts
- *Hendrickson v. Ebay, Inc.*, 165 F.Supp.2d 1082 (C.D. Cal. 2001)

See also: Copyright Infringement; Digital Millennium Copyright Act, Title I; File-Sharing; Internet Service Providers; Search Engine

Sources and further reading:
Christopher Wolf, *Digital Millennium Copyright Act: Text, History, and Caselaw* (Silver Spring, MD: Pike and Fischer, 2003).

❖ DIGITAL MILLENNIUM COPYRIGHT ACT, TITLE III ❖

Title III of the Digital Millennium Copyright Act (DMCA), the Computer Maintenance Competition Assurance Act, created an exception to liability for copyright infringement in cases in which a person who activates a computer for purposes of maintenance or repair makes a copy of a computer program by doing so. Title III modifies section 117 of the copyright code to permit the making of such copies if they are:

made solely by virtue of the activation of a machine that lawfully contains an authorized copy of the computer program, for purposes only of maintenance or repair of that machine, if—

- such new copy is used in no other manner and is destroyed immediately after the maintenance or repair is completed; and
- with respect to any computer program or part thereof that is not necessary for that machine to be activated, such program or part thereof is not accessed or used other than to make such new copy by virtue of the activation of the machine. (17 U.S.C. § 117(c))

Title III was a congressional response to the decision of the Ninth Circuit Court of Appeals in the 1993 case of *MAI Systems v. Peak Computer,* which had effectively given software providers the opportunity to use copyright law to retain a monopoly on maintenance of computers running their software (991 F.2d 511). Congress let stand the Ninth Circuit's underlying reasoning that making a RAM copy of a computer program is "copying" for copyright purposes. But it added a provision that made such copying for repair or maintenance purposes permissible, thus removing the potential for use of copyright suits to suppress independent repair and maintenance companies.

Statute
- Copyright Act of 1976 (as amended), 17 U.S.C. § 117

Case
- *MAI Systems Corp. v. Peak Computer,* 991 F.2d 511 (9th Cir. 1993)

See also: Copyright Infringement; Digital Millennium Copyright Act, Title I; Fair Use (Copyright)

Sources and further reading:
Christopher Wolf, *Digital Millennium Copyright Act: Text, History, and Caselaw* (Silver Spring, MD: Pike and Fischer, 2003).

❖ DIGITAL MILLENNIUM COPYRIGHT ACT, TITLE IV ❖

Title IV of the Digital Millennium Copyright Act (DMCA) contained miscellaneous provisions relating to the functions of the Copyright Office, the making of ephemeral recordings by broadcasters, distance education, nonprofit libraries and archives, webcasting of sound recordings, and the assumption of collective bargaining agreement obligations in the case of transfers of rights in motion pictures.

Ephemeral recordings: It is often more convenient for music broadcasters to record a set of songs and broadcast the recording than to broadcast the set from the original disks each time. Prior to the enactment of the DMCA, section 112 of the Copyright Act allowed radio broadcasters to make such recordings and retain them for up to six months. The Copyright Act as enacted in 1976 contained no general public performance right in sound recordings. In 1995, however, Congress had enacted the Digital Performance Right in Sound Recordings Act (DPRA), creating such a right in public performances by means of digital transmission, with an exemption for digital broadcasts

by terrestrial stations licensed by the Federal Communications Commission (FCC) and a statutory license for certain subscription transmissions; the status of some ephemeral recordings made to facilitate such exempt or licensed transmissions was unclear. The DMCA amended the section 112 exemption to include such recordings and even, in some circumstances, to allow broadcasters to circumvent technological protective measures in order to make the ephemeral recording. In some circumstances organizations may also make multiple ephemeral copies (17 U.S.C. § 112(a)).

Distance education: Prior to the enactment of the DMCA, section 110(2) of the Copyright Act contained an exception for instructional broadcasting. The Copyright Office had recommended changes to section 110(2) that would have updated the language of this exception without broadening the scope. Rather than adopt this proposal, Congress directed the Copyright Office to make recommendations on whether and to what extent exceptions should also be made for Internet-based distance education or other new distance education technologies. After consultation with the public and the affected parties, the Copyright Office issued its report in May 1999. The report suggested several amendments to sections 110(2) and 112 of the Copyright Act, amounting to a restatement of the Copyright Office's pre-DMCA proposal. The report recommended that "it should be clarified through legislative history that the term 'transmission' in section 110(2) covers transmissions by digital means as well as analog." In other words, "transmission" should cover class materials transmitted over the Internet as well as by older means such as television or radio. In addition, the rights covered by section 110(2) should be expanded to cover digital transmissions as well as performance and display; specifically, the rights of reproduction and distribution should be added to "the extent technologically required." And because Internet access to a work posted as part of a distance learning course could substitute for purchase of the work, the exception should emphasize mediated instruction: The statute might be amended to "specify that the performance or display must be made by or at the direction of an instructor to illustrate a point in, or as an integral part of, the equivalent of a class session in a particular course" (United States Copyright Office 1999).

The report also recommended that the requirement of a physical classroom be eliminated, because the Internet had rendered it obsolete. A requirement could be added, though, that materials posted for a class be restricted, "to the extent technologically feasible, [to] the defined class of eligible recipients." Transient copies "should be retained for no longer than reasonably necessary to complete the transmission," but an ephemeral copy exception similar to that for broadcasters should also be added to section 112. Institutions using distance education technology "should be required to institute policies regarding copyright; to provide informational materials to faculty, students, and relevant staff members that accurately describe and promote compliance with copyright law; and to provide notice to students that materials may be subject to copyright protection." In addition, "technological measures should be in place to control unauthorized uses" (United States Copyright Office 1999).

The Copyright Office was less certain whether the distance learning exception should be made available to for-profit educational institutions, but tentatively concluded that it should not. And if audiovisual works were to be added to the list of materials for which the exception was available, "it should be done in a limited way, with greater restrictions than section 110(2) currently imposes." Congress should also clarify the scope of fair use for distance education purposes. Licensing issues, particularly the problem of "orphan works" whose copyright owners cannot be located, should also be addressed (United States Copyright Office 1999).

Congress adopted some of the report's recommendations in the 2002 amendments to section 110(2), contained in the Technology, Education and Copyright Harmonization Act ("TEACH Act"). The TEACH Act adopted the report's recommendations concerning the addition of an ephemeral copy exception for educational uses to section 112. Because access to course information over the Internet requires

that a copy of the information also be made on the students' computers, the possibility of downstream infringements—unauthorized reproduction and distribution of the work by the students—arises. The TEACH Act adds a new subparagraph requiring the transmitting institution to use technological measures to prevent "retention of the work in accessible form by recipients . . . for longer than the class session" and "unauthorized further dissemination of the work" (17 U.S.C. § 110(2)(D)(ii)). As a practical matter this would seem to preclude the use of anything but encrypted streaming formats—a significant, even severe, limitation. And because the schools are required to use technological protective measures, the circumvention of which is prohibited by the DMCA, the student may be unable to lawfully make even a single copy of the work for future study.

The TEACH Act provides the educational institution with a safe harbor analogous to that provided to online service providers by Title II of the DMCA. If the school does not maintain copies of the work on its server "in a manner ordinarily accessible to anyone other than anticipated recipients," or "for a longer period than is reasonably necessary to facilitate the transmissions," it will not be responsible for infringing copies made by others.

The TEACH Act amendments to section 110(2) are not altogether draconian, however. The legislative history of the act reveals that the intent of Congress was to exclude or curtail the reproduction via the Internet of materials that would ordinarily find a market on the Internet; materials intended for use in the physical classroom would fall within the educational materials exception, unless the performance or display over the Internet was made from an unlawful copy with the knowledge of the institution. The making of digital copies of analog works is permitted when otherwise authorized by section 110(2) if no digital version is available to the institution, or the available digital version is protected by technological measures.

Overall, the TEACH Act limits the work that may be displayed via the Internet to a quantity similar to that typically displayed in a live classroom session. The work must be displayed as part of a class session that in turn is part of a mediated instructional activity—in other words, a course. Only accredited, nonprofit educational institutions, and only transmissions made by, at the direction of, or under the supervision of the instructor, are eligible for the educational use exception.

Nonprofit libraries and archives: One of the consequences of advances in information technology is that media used for information storage become obsolete. Although a book printed hundreds of years ago might remain perfectly readable today, hardly anyone—not even music archives—retains a music player capable of playing music recorded on wax cylinders. Players for vinyl LPs and eight-track cassettes are rare; players for cassette tapes are becoming so. Digital media, if anything, race to extinction even more rapidly. Information on 5.25-inch floppy disks requires a now-obsolete player—and there is more than one type of 5.25-inch floppy; each type requires its own player. Three-and-one-half-inch floppy disks are on their way out as well. Other media flourished only briefly, and finding players for them might prove impossible: Iomega Zip and Jazz drives and Imation 120-megabyte SuperDisk drives are still around, but players for other formats—removable hard disk cartridges of various sizes, flopticals, EPROM and EEPROM cartridges for Atari, Commodore, and other computers that are no longer made, and numerous others—have in many cases been orphaned by the demise of their original manufacturers, or by abandonment of a particular product line. Because no new players are being made for these media, information stored on them is in danger of being lost forever. If a library has information stored on, for example, 5.25-inch Apple II disks, it might be able to borrow an old 5.25-inch Apple drive, connect it to a newer Apple Macintosh, and transfer the information to the hard drive of the Macintosh. It would not be practical for the library to purchase the 5.25-inch drive, keep it permanently connected to the Macintosh, and train library staff to assist patrons in accessing the information from the original 5.25-inch disks. Not only would such an arrangement be costly and cumbersome, but the disks would deteriorate over time, and repeated use would accelerate the process.

Copying the information to another computer's hard drive is cheaper, more secure, and more practical.

Making such a copy, however, raises copyright issues. Even media that are not obsolete (including printed materials) deteriorate. Prior to enactment of the DMCA, section 108 of the Copyright Act permitted nonprofit libraries and archives to make a single facsimile copy of a work for purposes of preservation or interlibrary loan. Section 404 of the DMCA extends this exemption to digital information and takes into account the increasing use of digital technology for preservation of information, allowing for digital storage of analog (including hard-copy) information for preservation or interlibrary loan. Section 108, as amended by the DMCA, now permits nonprofit libraries and archives to make up to three copies of works in their collections. The copies may be digital but may not be made available to the public outside the library premises. When the original format in which a work is stored becomes obsolete, the library or archive may also copy the work into a new format (17 U.S.C. § 108).

Webcasting: The Digital Performance Right in Sound Recordings Act, as mentioned, created a performance right in digital transmissions of sound recordings. The DPRA exempted broadcast transmissions from this performance right and made subscription transmissions subject to a statutory license; on-demand transmissions were made subject to the full exclusive right. Between 1995, when the DPRA was enacted, and 1998, a new category of digital transmission of sound recordings began to appear: streaming audio transmissions over the Internet, or webcasting. Section 405 of the DMCA amends the DPRA to treat webcasting in the same manner as subscription transmissions, bringing it within the scope of the statutory license. A statutory or compulsory license is a license created by statute; it allows, in this instance, subscription transmissions and webcasts of audio recordings to be made without requiring the prior permission of the copyright holder. The transmitter or webcaster must still pay a usage fee, however.

Assumption of contractual obligations upon transfers of rights in motion pictures: Typically a motion picture is produced subject to a collective bargaining agreement between the producers and the actors, director, writers, and other persons involved in the making of the film. The producer or production company is contractually obligated to make residual payments to these persons. At some point the production company may transfer its rights in the film to a distributor; at this time it is typically obligated to transfer the duty to make residual payments as well. If the production company does not do so, the various persons entitled to residuals may have no recourse against the distributor, because they lack what is called privity of contract with the distributor: There is no contractual relationship between them that may be sued upon. And the production company might have no remaining assets, so that even though the film is wildly successful at the box office, the persons involved in making it receive nothing. Section 416 of the DMCA addresses this problem by making transferees (such as the distributor) liable in most cases for residual payments for which the producer or production company would have been liable.

Statutes
- Copyright Act of 1976 (as amended by DMCA Title IV), 17 U.S.C. §§ 106, 108, 110, 112
- Digital Performance Right in Sound Recordings Act, codified at 17 U.S.C. §§ 106, 114-15

Case
- *Bonneville International Corp. v. Peters,* 153 F.Supp.2d 763 (E.D. Pa. 2001)

Report
- United States Copyright Office, Report on Copyright and Digital Distance Education, May 1999

See also: Copyright; Copyright Infringement; Digital Millennium Copyright Act, Title I; Digital Millennium Copyright Act, Title II; Digital Millennium Copyright Act, Title III; Digital Performance Right in Sound Recordings Act; Fair Use (Copyright)

Sources and further reading:
Chris Priestman, *Web Radio: Radio Production for Internet Streaming* (Boston: Focal Press, 2001).
Christopher Wolf, *Digital Millennium Copyright Act: Text, History, and Caselaw* (Silver Spring, MD: Pike and Fischer, 2003).

❖ DIGITAL MILLENNIUM COPYRIGHT ACT, TITLE V ❖

Title V of the DMCA, the Vessel Hull Design Protection Act (VHDPA), creates a new type of intellectual property, with aspects of both copyright and patent, for hull designs for vessels of 200 feet or less in length (17 U.S.C. §§ 1301–1332). The VHDPA has no direct application to computer and Internet law, but like the protection granted to semiconductor manufacturing mask work registrations under the 1984 Semiconductor Chip Protection Act (17 U.S.C. §§ 901–914), it is an indicator of congressional willingness to create new categories of intellectual property when the traditional categories do not seem to fit. This has both worrisome and encouraging aspects: It has the potential to further shrink the public domain, yet the application of patent and copyright law to information technology has proved cumbersome and unwieldy; eventually Congress may see fit to create categories of intellectual property specifically tailored to information technology.

Statutes
- Vessel Hull Design Protection Act, codified at 17 U.S.C. §§ 1301–1332

See also: Semiconductor Manufacturing Mask Work Registrations

❖ DIGITAL PERFORMANCE RIGHT IN SOUND RECORDINGS ACT ❖

The Copyright Act of 1976 granted most copyright owners the exclusive right of public performance of their copyrighted works (17 U.S.C. § 106(4)). Holders of copyrights in sound recordings, however, received no such right. The 1995 Digital Performance Right in Sound Recordings Act (DPRSA) added a right for performance by digital audio transmission (17 U.S.C. § 106(6)). This is not a general performance right; it does not cover performance by analog audio transmission or by public performance of analog or digital recordings. The DPRSA was aimed not at these types of performances or at possible future digital radio broadcasts, but at so-called Internet radio stations, or webcasters. Internet music services could maintain a large library of music and transmit it to listeners on demand, possibly diminishing the market for sound recordings. A related problem was that consumers might copy the webcast music; this was addressed by the use of encrypted streaming audio. Titles I and IV of the Digital Millennium Copyright Act (DMCA) assisted webcasters by bringing streaming audio transmissions within the scope of the statutory license covering other music performance copyrights. Under the statutory license, webcasters were still required to pay royalties, but the copyright owners could not deny permission to transmit the work.

The DPRSA distinguishes between streaming audio, which it calls digital transmission, and making a song available for download, which it calls "digital phonorecord delivery" (17 U.S.C. §§ 114(j), 115(d)). Digital rights management technology can be used to reduce the danger that digitally delivered phonorecords will be pirated. The use of encrypted streaming audio for digital transmission, though necessary to avoid vicarious or contributory copyright infringement liability, created an additional problem: In the course of streaming, buffer copies of the work are created. Although these are temporary, partial copies, webcasters are now required to pay royalties twice on a single transmission: once for the buffer, and once for the copy actually played. The webcasters pay a surcharge for the buffer copies, and independent, nonbroadcast webcasters also pay royalties twice as high as those paid by broadcast stations retransmitting their programs via the Internet. The Small Webcasters Settlement Act of 2002 provides modified terms to prevent the cost of royalty payments from crushing small and nonprofit webcasters (17 U.S.C. 114(f)).

Interactive services, in which the users can choose the songs to be played, are more likely to displace sales of sound recordings. As a result, they are not included within the scope of the statutory compulsory license, but must obtain a voluntary license for each song played—a nearly insurmountable hurdle for webcasters who are not the copyright holders of the recordings they play (17 U.S.C. 114(d)(3)).

Statutes
- Digital Performance Right in Sound Recordings Act, amending and codified at 17 U.S.C. §§ 106(6), 114, 115
- Small Webcasters Settlement Act of 2002, amending and codified at 17 U.S.C. § 114(f)

See also: Content Industry; Copyright; Digital Audio Works; Digital Millennium Copyright Act, Title I; Digital Millennium Copyright Act, Title IV; Digital Rights Management; File-Sharing

Sources and further reading:

Ronald H. Gertz, "Client Memo Re: Summary of Sections 106, 112 and 114 of the Copyright Act of 1976 as Amended by the Digital Performance Right in Sound Recordings Act of 1995 and the Digital Millennium Copyright Act of 1998," in *Music on the Internet: Understanding the New Rights and Solving New Problems,* edited by Anthony V. Lupo and Mark F. Radcliffe (New York: Practising Law Institute, 2001).

Lynne B. Lubash, "How the Digital Performance Right in Sound Recordings Act of 1995 Protects Copyright Owners on the Internet," 14 *Santa Clara Computer and High Technology Law Journal* 497 (1998).

❖ DIGITAL RIGHTS MANAGEMENT ❖

Digital rights management (DRM) is the use of technological measures to protect copyrighted digitally recorded material. A typical DRM package might employ some or all of a variety of techniques, including encryption and steganography. DRM software can use encryption to ensure that only authorized users can view the protected data, to control the number of times the protected data can be viewed or copied, and to keep a record of when and by whom the data has been viewed or copied. DRM technology is incorporated into DVD players, HDTV receivers, MP3 players, and other commercially available hardware and software media players to control the playback of copyrighted information and to prevent the playing of unauthorized copies. This incorporated DRM technology works in combination with DRM information included in the recorded movie, music disk, or other copyrighted information.

Encryption is used to restrict the playback of copyrighted information. For example, the movies stored on DVDs are encrypted using a cipher called Content Scramble System (CSS). Keys to CSS are integrated into DVD players to enable them to play the encrypted DVDs. Even relatively simple encryption such as CSS adds a level of complexity to recording and playback; compatibility issues arise, irritating consumers. Eventually consumers may attempt to reduce their frustration by reverse engineering the encryption—in this case, the CSS keys. It was apparently a compatibility issue, rather than an attempt at video piracy, that led to the most notorious instance of this reverse engineering: the creation of DeCSS in order to play CSS-encrypted DVDs on Linux systems. Once decryption information has been leaked to the general public, there is little the content industry can do, other than to push for harsher penalties for digital piracy: The keys cannot be changed for future players and disks without rendering them incompatible with DVD players and disks already sold.

Title I of the Digital Millennium Copyright Act (DMCA) provides penalties for the circumvention of copy-protection encryption such as CSS (17 U.S.C. §§ 1201, 1203–1204). The combination of encryption, which stops the casual user from copying the movie, and criminal penalties, which deter the more sophisticated user, has managed to control, if not eliminate, piracy of movies within the United States. However, the movie industry has united with

Fritz Hollings: Senator Hollings is possibly the only elected U.S. official ever to have a computer chip named after him, albeit informally: the "Fritz chip" that stands at the center of the trusted computing initiative. Hollings's tireless advocacy on behalf of the content industry also earned him an unflattering sobriquet: "the Senator from Disney." Users' rights advocates portrayed Hollings as an agent of Big Brother, seeking to destroy privacy and ensure that users would be unable to control content on their own computers. In fact Hollings was a dedicated advocate of individual rights, who grew steadily more frustrated with the constant need to raise money for campaigning; this, he felt, left elected officials beholden to their major contributors—who, in his case, included the entertainment industry. He did not run for reelection in 2004 and retired from the Senate at the end of his term in January 2005. Shortly before his retirement he complained to Mike Wallace of CBS's *60 Minutes* that campaign contributions and lobbyists had so distorted the legislative process that "Today, you can't find the real interests of the country." Hollings's retirement, after thirty-eight years in the Senate, may have cost the content industry some influence, although they are not without other allies in Congress.

Source

"Parting Shots from Fritz Hollings," *CBSNews.com,* Dec. 12, 2004, http://www.cbsnews.com/ stories/2004/12/10/60minutes/main660368. shtml (visited January 7, 2005).

other content owners in pushing for more powerful DRM tools.

Steganography, the process by which a message can be concealed within and later extracted from another message, can be used to digitally watermark copyrighted content. Any file can include a digital watermark that can be used to detect and track unauthorized copying; the watermark will not be visible or audible to anyone playing back the file, but can easily be detected with the appropriate software. Removal of the watermark can be prevented by employing robust steganography: The watermark can be made impossible to remove without degrading or destroying the recording in which it is contained.

There are several commercially available DRM software packages. Consumer content such as movies and commercial music downloads is often protected with DRM software, but DRM has drawbacks from both a security and a marketing perspective. The security is limited by the fact that there will always be technologically adept users who can circumvent any copyright-protection safeguards, and by the fact that in order to be useful content must be capable of being played; anyone can always record a copy of the playback, although there will be some degradation in quality. The marketing disadvantage is that DRM irritates consumers. A consumer with a DVD player at home and a VCR in the vacation cottage he rents for a week each summer does not want to buy a DVD player to take to the cottage; he wants to copy a couple of his children's favorite DVDs to VHS tape. A consumer who pays to download a music file from a recording industry–approved Web site does not want to listen to that music only on her computer; she wants to listen to it on the stereo in her living room, on the CD player in her car, on the tape cassette player in her old truck, on her portable MP3 player, and on the computer in her office. All of these uses would ordinarily fall within the "fair use" exception to copyright infringement; both of these consumers would legally be entitled to make this use of the information they have purchased, but for two things: The DMCA makes it illegal for them to circumvent the DRM protections, and the consumer is probably contractually obligated, through some form of shrinkwrap or clickwrap agreement, not to make copies, or not to make more than a certain number of copies.

DRM software can also make some recorded movies and music unplayable on some players. A consumer who purchases a music CD to listen to on the computer in her office might find that the disk cannot be played on the computer. She is not likely to purchase a CD player for her office or ask her company to do so; instead she will return the disk to the store and demand a refund. Even if the content owner is willing to supply a computer-playable disk upon request, many or most consumers will not have the patience to make the request. Thus the market forces a balance between the desire of the content owner for copy-protection mechanisms and the desire of consumers for convenience in the form of universally playable recordings. Recent developments in copyright law, particularly the anticircumvention provisions of Title I of the DMCA (17 U.S.C. § 1201), have tilted this balance further in favor of the content industry than would otherwise be possible.

DRM also poses difficulties for equipment manufacturers who must design their equipment to play back content recorded with several different DRM techniques. The goal of the DRM and content industries is for newer generations of computer software and hardware to incorporate what is called trusted computing to control the computer owner's use of the information on the computer. Trusted computing (also called trustworthy or safer computing) would enable the identification of each Internet user (or at least of each computer connected to the Internet) and encryption of data transmitted between the user and commercial content servers. It is unappealing to consumers, many of whom value the anonymity of the Internet, but appealing to the content industry because of its potential use to curtail copyright infringement.

Four features of trusted computing would make this curtailment of copyright infringement possible: remote attestation, memory curtaining, secure input and output, and sealed storage. Remote attestation allows changes to a computer to be detected; it could be used by the copyright owner of a music or movie file, for example, to prevent the file from being downloaded except by computers that employ the full battery of "trusted computing" protections for copyright owners. Memory curtaining prevents programs from reading or writing in memory used by other programs, preventing the user from copying the file while it is being played. Secure input and output denies programs on the user's computer access to information being typed or displayed in other programs; it can be used to prevent the user from making a copy of the output that is sent to the speakers and video display. And sealed storage encrypts data so that it can only be read by the same program and on the same machine as it was originally recorded, so that the file cannot be played with another player that might not follow the restrictions. Although all four of these features have legitimate security uses, they can also be used to make it difficult or impossible to transfer some data (music downloads, for example) from one format, program, or computer to another. They could be used to make certain Web sites accessible only with certain browsers, or to make Web sites inaccessible to computers running ad-blocking software or running certain operating systems (Schoen 2003, 2–5).

To prevent users from simply bypassing the trusted computing features of their computers, a fifth component is needed. This fifth component is the Fritz chip, named for United States Senator Fritz Hollings (D-SC), a proponent of content-industry rights (Woodford 2004, 282). The Fritz chip can deny the user access to trusted computing data if the computer is run in non-trusted computing mode or if significant changes are made to the hardware or software environment.

An additional potential cost for consumers is that upgrading to a new computer, or even a significant hardware upgrade to an existing computer, could make downloaded media files unplayable. This imposes a significant burden even on consumers who do not wish to play the downloaded files on a home or car entertainment system, but plan to keep the downloaded files only on their personal computers. All over the United States and much of the rest of the world, countless vinyl records, cassette and 8-track tapes, Betamax tapes, VHS tapes, and increasingly CDs sit abandoned in cardboard boxes in attics, garages, and landfills. The consumers who purchased these media have now replaced them with newer media, such as DVDs and iTunes downloads stored on iPods. Many feel the cost has been worthwhile because of the superior sound and image quality of digital media. At some point, however, they will balk if asked to pay for the same copyrighted material yet again, especially if there is no improvement in quality yet less flexibility in how the material may be used.

Microsoft, the market leader in PC operating systems, is working on DRM technology using a trusted computing platform it originally called Palladium and then renamed the Next-Generation Secure Computing Base; as consumers currently have few alternatives to Microsoft operating systems, adoption of trusted computing by Microsoft will in effect impose it upon most of the public (Roemer 2003, n. 105; Woodford 2004, 279–282). Yet the problems with trusted computing are not limited to a loss of flexibility in the use of copyrighted information. Trusted computing can also enable spyware; for instance, music or movie files might be made available only to computers that notified the content owner each time the file was played. It could even be used to deny users access to information already on their computers; ultimate control of information on the individual users' computers would be in the hands of Microsoft rather than of the individual users.

The misuse of copyrighted information is prohibited by the Copyright Act of 1976 and the Digital Millennium Copyright Act of 1998 (DMCA). The DMCA prevents circumvention of technological protective measures—including DRM—even if the copies thus made would otherwise be permissible fair use of the copyrighted material. Apparently, however, the content industry is not satisfied that either the Copyright Act or the DMCA gives it sufficient control over consumers' uses of copyrighted material. DRM based on trusted computing would give all-but-absolute control to the content owners, while posing a threat to the privacy of consumers. For both of these reasons the battle over DRM and trusted computing is likely to be fiercely fought.

Trusted computing might be more palatable to consumers if they have the ability to override it when they wish; this would enable them to retain the security benefits while also retaining more flexibility in the use of copyrighted information. But concerns about access to copyrighted information are not the only reasons that some consumer advocates are apprehensive. Another worrisome feature of trusted computing is the opportunity for a vendor enjoying a sizable market share for a particular type of program to lock consumers in to using the most current versions of its products. The vendor could set the default "trust" settings for documents created with its word-processing program, for example, so that the documents could only be read with that program. If a large enough number of users already use a single vendor's program, other users will have to buy that program in order to read documents created using it.

DRM based on trusted computing would transfer a significant degree of control over copyrighted information (and much other information as well) on a user's computer from the user to the content owner, the software maker, and the hardware maker. The number of times any content could be accessed could be limited, or users could be required to pay each time they watch a movie or listen to a song.

A final problem with DRM, especially DRM based on trusted computing, is that it will continue to prevent copying after the copyright has expired. The DRM protection of a particular music recording or movie could be set to expire at a certain date, but in the absence of a legislative requirement that it do so (which does not presently exist), content owners have no incentive to set such a limitation on built-in copyright protection. (In the absence of trusted computing, a date limit would disable the copy protection, because the date could easily be spoofed.) And as Congress has frequently adjusted the length of the copyright term, it would be rational for the content owners to assume that the term will be increased yet again and thus avoid limiting their protection by shutting it off after a certain date.

Statutes
- Copyright Act of 1976, 17 U.S.C. §§ 101–1332
- Digital Millennium Copyright Act, §§ 1201–1205

See also: Advanced Access Content System; Clickwrap Agreement; Copyright; Copyright Infringement; DeCSS; Digital Millennium Copyright Act, Title I; Encryption; File-Sharing; Steganography

Sources and further reading:
Megan E. Gray and Will Thomas DeVries, "The Legal Fallout from Digital Rights Management Technology," *Computer and Internet Lawyer,* April 2003, at 20.

Lawrence Lessig, *Free Culture: How Big Media Uses Technology and the Law to Lock Down Culture and Control Creativity* (New York: Penguin, 2004) (also available as a free download).

"Music to Their Ears: With Compact-Disc Sales Plummeting, Record Companies Are Rethinking How to Distribute Music Online," *Economist Technology Quarterly,* Sept. 21, 2002, at 12.

Adam Petravicius and Joseph T. Miotke, "Beyond the NDA: Digital Rights Management Isn't Just for Music," 16 *Journal of Proprietary Rights* 1 (2004).

Ryan Roemer, "Trusted Computing, Digital Rights Management, and the Fight for Copyright Control on Your Computer," 2003 *UCLA Journal of Law and Technology* 8 (2003).

Bill Rosenblatt et al., *Digital Rights Management: Business and Technology* (New York: John Wiley and Sons, 2001).

Seth Schoen, "Trusted Computing: Promise and Risk," Electronic Frontier Foundation, 2003, at http://www.eff.org/Infrastructure/trusted_computing/20031001_tc.php (visited November 19, 2004).

Mark Tamminga, "The Sweeping Ambitions of Digital Rights Management: A Potential Hammerlock on Digital Content Has Plenty of Folks Scared," *Law Practice Management,* Oct. 2003, at 24.

Siva Vaidhyanathan, *The Anarchist in the Library: How the Clash between Freedom and Control Is Hacking the Real World and Crashing the System* (New York: Basic Books, 2004).

Chad Woodford, "Trusted Computing or Big Brother? Putting the Rights Back in Digital Rights Management," 75 *University of Colorado Law Review* 253 (2004).

❖ DMCA ❖

See Digital Millennium Copyright Act

❖ DOCTRINE OF EQUIVALENTS ❖

The doctrine of equivalents is a rule of patent law that provides for a finding of patent infringement even if the product or process complained of by the patent holder does not violate the literal terms of the patent. In order not to be infringing, a product or process must differ substantially, not merely slightly, from that described in the patent. The doctrine of equivalents is flexible; whether the difference between the patent and the alleged infringement is substantial depends on how revolutionary the patent is. The doctrine is applied with a wide scope to patents that break significant new ground, called pioneer patents, but with a narrow scope to relatively minor patents in an already crowded field. This flexibility is not unlimited, however; the doctrine of equivalents is limited by rules with colorful names, such as "file wrapper estoppel" and the "nose of wax" rule.

File wrapper estoppel, now more commonly called prosecution history estoppel, draws its name from the file wrapper—a folder in which the patent's prosecution history is stored in the United States Patent and Trademark Office. It prohibits a patent holder from asserting the doctrine of equivalents with regard to any matters that have been conceded during the application process to be outside the scope of the patent (Katz and Riddle 2004, 668).

The nose of wax rule comes from an 1886 patent case, *White v. Dunbar*:

> Some persons seem to suppose that a claim in a patent is like a nose of wax, which may be turned and twisted in any direction, by merely referring to the specification, so as to make it include something more than, or something different from, what its words express. The context may, undoubtedly, be resorted to, and often is resorted to, for the purpose of better understanding the meaning of the claim; but not for the purpose of changing it, and making it different from what it is. (119 U.S. at 51–52)

The doctrine of equivalents cannot be used to twist the nose so far that it is no longer recognizable as a nose, and indeed its limits fall somewhat short of that. Most of all, of course, the doctrine of equivalents is limited by the prior art: It cannot be applied to prevent others from doing something that they have already done, or thought of doing, before the patent was is-

sued, or that was obvious from the prior state of the art in the field.

Statutes
- Patent Code, 35 U.S.C. §§ 101–103

Cases
- *Festo Corp. v. Shoketsu Kinzoku Kogyo Kabushiki Co., Ltd.*, 535 U.S. 722 (2002)
- *White v. Dunbar*, 119 U.S. 47 (1886)

See also: Patent; Prosecution History Estoppel

Sources and further reading:
Paul N. Katz and Robert R. Riddle, "Designing around a United States Patent," 45 *South Texas Law Review* 647 (2004).
Debra D. Peterson, "The Hydra of Identity Tolerance: Patent Law Heresies Involving 35 U.S.C. § 102," 85 *Journal of the Patent and Trademark Office Society* 639 (2003).

❖ DOMAIN NAME REGISTRATION ❖

A domain name is a portion of the uniform resource locator (URL), the address that allows a computer to find a particular page, file, or document on the Internet. Domain names and nonnumeric URLs translate the strings of numbers actually used by computers into a form that is easier for humans to remember. A URL might look like this:

http://www.icann.org/

Within this URL is the domain name:

icann.org

This domain name has two parts: the top level domain, ".org," and the domain, "icann." The "www" in the URL is a subdomain; there may be many subdomains within the "icann" domain, just as there are many domains within the ".org" top-level domain. The Internet Corporation for Assigned Names and Numbers (ICANN), a nonprofit entity formed in 1998 by an agreement between an existing Internet administrative service and the United States Department of Commerce, is in charge of establishing and assigning top-level domains. Administrative responsibility for the ".org" top-level domain, designed for use by nonprofit and noncommercial organizations, has been assigned to the Public Interest Registry. Persons wishing to register a domain name within the ".org" top-level domain may do so by checking for the availability of the name at the Public Interest Registry's Web site at http://www.pir.org/register/ or at the Web site of a registrar approved by the Public Interest Registry, and then registering that name with one of the approved registrars. In the United States alone there are more than six dozen such registrars; some are companies whose primary business is domain names, while others are diversified Internet service companies such as America Online (Public Interest Registry 2005). An individual or organ-

ization that has registered a domain name then has authority over the creation and assignment of subdomains within that domain.

Inevitably, disputes arise. Although the number of potential domain names is extremely large, the most desirable domain names are those that spell out easily remembered words and names, especially in English. From 1995 through 1998, a company called Network Solutions, Inc., was responsible for resolving disputes regarding domain names within the popular ".com," ".net," and ".org" top-level domains (Gilwit 2003, 271). With the formation of ICANN in 1998, ICANN became responsible for the resolution of some domain name disputes; more than five thousand disputes have been resolved under ICANN's dispute resolution policy (ICANN Information 2004).

Private and administrative dispute resolution procedures are not always successful, however,

---

Canadian high school student Mike Rowe found his fifteen minutes of fame in 2004 when he registered a domain name—MikeRoweSoft.com—based on his own name. Microsoft's attorneys in Canada wrote to Rowe, advising him to transfer the domain name to Microsoft. When Rowe asked to be compensated, the attorneys offered him ten dollars; he wrote back and asked for ten thousand dollars, to which the attorneys responded with a twenty-five-page letter accusing him of the Canadian equivalent of cybersquatting.

Was Mike Rowe a cybersquatter? Could Microsoft have successfully proceeded in rem against the domain name in the United States? Probably not; several of the nine Anticybersquatting Consumer Protection Act factors weighed in his favor. The domain name incorporated his actual name, Mike Rowe. There was no evidence that Rowe had registered any other domain names, and he did not use the site (a gaming forum) to divert Microsoft's customers or tarnish Microsoft's image in any way. The likelihood of confusion was close to nonexistent: Spoken aloud the domain names may sound the same, but typed into the address bar of a Web browser they are quite different. For the few users who use voice-recognition software to navigate the Web, the confusion would be more likely to run in the opposite direction; the software would be more likely to "hear" the name as the more common "Microsoft" than as the less common "MikeRoweSoft." And although Rowe did ask for a large sum of money for the domain name, Microsoft had already offered a small amount of money; his request was presumably a negotiating position.

The story attracted more attention to Rowe's site than would otherwise have been possible, while at the same time making Microsoft look foolish. Rowe agreed to transfer the domain name in exchange for an Xbox, assistance in moving his site to a new address, and a few other benefits. Today, however, www.mikerowesoft.com mirrors the content at the new site, www.mikeroweforums.com.

Source

"Microsoft to Take Over MikeRoweSoft.com: Teen Settles with Tech Giant for, among Other Things, an Xbox," CNN.com/Technology, Jan. 26, 2004.

and disputes over domain names sometimes end up in court. A particular problem in the early days of the expansion of the Internet was cybersquatting: the act of registering a domain name that includes or resembles a trademark, service mark, or other distinctive or famous mark used by someone other than the registrant, with the intent of later selling or licensing the domain name to the owner of the mark. Cybersquatters registered large numbers of domain names; for example, a cybersquatter might register the name "vw.net" and then attempt to sell the name to Volkswagen, the automobile manufacturer (*Virtual Works,* 238 F.3d 262). Volkswagen's "VW" trademark is both distinctive and famous; "vw.net" would be a natural place for Web surfers to seek information about Volkswagen automobiles, and Volkswagen's image could be harmed if inappropriate content were placed at that site instead.

Existing trademark law, however, had not been designed with cybersquatting in mind. To resolve the problem, in 1999 Congress enacted the Anticybersquatting Consumer Protection Act (ACPA) to protect the interests of trademark owners (15 U.S.C. § 1125(d)). The ACPA has proven largely effective in controlling cybersquatting, even when the registrant is unknown or outside the United States: In addition to providing remedies against known registrants, it provides for proceedings against the domain name itself. Even if the cybersquatter cannot be found or brought into court, the trademark owner can obtain an order transferring the domain name to it (15 U.S.C. § 1125(d)(2)(A)).

Other problems arise when there is a conflict between legitimate claimants to a particular domain name. For example, a thirteen-year-old girl in England created a Web site discussing the plight of endangered species, particularly the South American jaguar. An adult family friend registered the name "jaguarcenter.com" for her site, and was sued by Ford Motor Company, the owner of the Jaguar automobile trademark (Newman 2001). The site at jaguarcenter.com has since been taken down.

New top-level domains have also been proposed as a solution to the continuing problem of Internet pornography. Providing a safe har-

bor for adult-content Web sites in a top-level domain such as ".xxx" and requiring pornographic sites to move to that domain would make it far easier for parents and schools to filter inappropriate content from computers used by minors (ICM Registry 2004). After many years of lobbying by an unlikely alliance of pornographers and their opponents, ICANN finally approved the ".xxx" top-level domain in June 2005.

Statute
- Anticybersquatting Consumer Protection Act, 15 U.S.C. § 1125(d)

Case
- *Virtual Works, Inc. v. Volkswagen of America, Inc.,* 238 F.3d 262 (4th Cir. 2001)

See also: Cybersquatting; Internet Corporation for Assigned Names and Numbers; Trademark; Trademark Infringement; World Wide Web

Sources and further reading:
W. David Gardner, "Unlikely Alliance Seeks .xxx Top-Level Domain," *TechWeb.com,* April 15, 2004, available at http://www.techweb.com/wire/26804584;jsessionid=5TKOK12O3IE50QSNDBCSKHSCJUMEKJVN (visited November 14, 2004).
Dara B. Gilwit, "The Latest Cybersquatting Trend: Typosquatters, their Changing Tactics, and How to Prevent Public Deception and Trademark Infringement," 11 *Washington University Journal of Law and Policy* 267 (2003).
ICM Registry Inc., "Application for New sTLD RFP Application.xxx," 2004, available at http://www.icann.org/tlds/stld-apps-19mar04/xxx.htm (visited November 14, 2004).
Internet Corporation for Assigned Names and Numbers, "ICANN Information," Jan. 13, 2004, http://www.icann.org/general/ (visited November 14, 2004).
Heather Newman, "Web Sites Charge up Ford's Ire: Owners Sued over Net Names," *Detroit Free Press,* Jan. 24, 2001, available at http://www.freep.com/money/tech/domain24_20010124.htm (visited November 14, 2004).
Public Interest Registry, Registrars by Country, May 5, 2005, http://www.pir.org/register/reg_country (visited June 2, 2005).

Sex Sites Get Dedicated Net Home, BBC News, June 2, 2005, available at http://news.bbc.co.uk/2/hi/technology/4602449.stm (visited June 2, 2005).

Barbara A. Solomon, "Domain Name Disputes: New Developments and Open Issues," 91 *The Trademark Reporter* 833 (2001).

❖ DOUBLECLICK ❖

DoubleClick, Incorporated is an Internet marketing and advertising company that collects information about Internet users' online activities. It then uses this information to target online advertising to particular users. DoubleClick's collection of information raises privacy concerns; although DoubleClick is not the only company to engage in such activities, it has a particularly high profile both as the market leader and as one of the first such firms to attract the attention of the media and privacy advocates. DoubleClick's 1999 merger with Abacus Direct, a similar firm, raised concerns that the two firms' databases would also be merged. This would make it possible for DoubleClick to match specific surfing profiles not only to individual IP addresses, but also to individual users' names (Macavinta 1999).

The controversial nature of DoubleClick's business, combined with its high profile, has led to a certain amount of regulatory attention and litigation. In 1999, the merger with Abacus prompted an investigation by the Federal Trade Commission (FTC) for possible unfair or deceptive trade practices. After receiving assurances from DoubleClick that the two databases would not, in fact, be merged, and that users' information was not being used in ways inconsistent with DoubleClick's privacy policy, the FTC ended its investigation (Weinberg 2002, 36). An FTC employee stated, "We have no grounds to challenge the merger based on privacy concerns." (Macavinta 1999).

Subsequently users filed suits against DoubleClick for privacy violations, both individually and as class actions. These suits were consolidated in the federal district court for the Southern District of New York as *In re DoubleClick, Inc. Privacy Litigation.* The Southern District of New York granted DoubleClick's motion to dismiss the federal claims against it; in the absence of a federal claim, it also declined to exercise jurisdiction over the remaining New York state law claim. The decision was seen as a defeat for privacy advocates, but although it was undeniably a victory for DoubleClick, it has not been followed elsewhere: It has been disagreed with by a federal district court in Florida (*In re America Online,* 168 F.Supp.2d 1359), and decisions of several district and circuit courts have distinguished *In re DoubleClick* on its facts—that is, they have not followed the decision, on the grounds that some factual, procedural, or legal difference makes *In re DoubleClick* inapplicable.

At more or less the same time attorneys general in ten states (Arizona, California, Connecticut, Massachusetts, Michigan, New Jersey, New Mexico, New York, Vermont, and Washington) were conducting investigations into DoubleClick's business practices. Ultimately these investigations led to a settlement in which DoubleClick, without admitting wrongdoing, agreed to pay $450,000 to cover some of the costs of the investigation and also agreed to certain restrictions on data use and retention, along with enhanced disclosure and notification requirements (Weinberg 2002, 63–64). This settlement has been criticized as being a step behind recent advances in data mining technology (Zarsky 2002, 4).

Cases

- *In re America Online,* 168 F.Supp.2d 1359 (S.D. Fla. 2001)
- *In re DoubleClick, Inc. Privacy Litigation,* 154 F.Supp.2d 497 (S.D. N.Y. 2001)
- *In re Pharmatrak, Inc. Privacy Litigation,* 220 F.Supp.2d 4 (D.Mass. 2002); 329 F.3d 9 (1st Cir. 2003)

See also: Advertising; Adware and Spyware; Privacy

Sources and further reading:

"Consumer Privacy: $450,000 Payment to States—DoubleClick Reaches Agreement with States on Visibility of Consumer Tracking Activities," *Cybercrime Law Report,* Sept. 9, 2002, at 6.

Courtney Macavinta, "DoubleClick, Abacus Merge in $1.7 Billion Deal," C/Net News.com, Nov. 24, 1999, available at http://news.com.com/2100-1023-233526.html?legacy=cnet (visited October 4, 2004).

Amy S. Weinberg, "These Cookies Won't Crumble—Yet: The Corporate Monitoring of Consumer Internet Activity, *In re DoubleClick Inc. Privacy Litigation,* 154 F.Supp.2d 497 (S.D.N.Y. 2001)," 21 *Temple Environmental Law and Technology Journal* 33 (2002).

Tal Zarsky, "Cookie Viewers and the Undermining of Data Mining: A Critical Review of the DoubleClick Settlement," 2001 *Stanford Technology Law Review* 1 (2002).

❖ E-BOOKS ❖

E-books are books in electronic form: large text files that can be read on computers or dedicated e-book readers. Because e-books are original works fixed in a tangible medium of expression, they are subject to copyright protection; because they are digitally recorded works, they can easily be copied and distributed over the Internet. As a result, they raise copyright issues similar to those raised by digital music and motion picture recordings, although the e-book industry is smaller in scale than the digital music and movie industries, and e-book piracy is correspondingly smaller in scale as well.

Many e-books can be freely copied and distributed over the Internet either because they are already in the public domain or because the authors have chosen to place few or no restrictions on their copying and distribution. Project Gutenberg, a nonprofit undertaking, offers more than thirteen thousand texts for download. Most of these works are in the public domain because their copyrights have expired; some are works that are still in copyright, but whose owners have chosen to make them available through Project Gutenberg ("Welcome to Project Gutenberg" 2004). Other authors choose to make their works freely available through other Web sites, often their own. The conditions that authors place on the use of e-books still in copyright vary, but the conditions (although not the style) of this copyright notice are typical:

> If you go and buy a print version of *The Hacker Crackdown,* an action I encourage heartily, you may notice that in the front of the book, beneath the copyright notice—"Copyright (C) 1992 by Bruce Sterling"—it has this little block of printed legal boilerplate from the publisher. It says, and I quote:
>
> No part of this book may be reproduced or transmitted in any form or by any means, electronic or mechanical, including photocopying, recording, or by any information storage and retrieval system, without permission in writing from the publisher. For information address: Bantam Books.
>
> This is a pretty good disclaimer, as such disclaimers go. I collect intellectual-property disclaimers, and I've seen dozens of them, and this one is at least pretty straightforward. In this narrow and particular case, however, it isn't quite accurate. Bantam Books puts that disclaimer on every book they publish, but Bantam Books does not, in fact, own the electronic rights to this book. I do, because of certain extensive contract maneuverings my agent and I went through before this book was written. I want to give those electronic publishing rights away through certain not-for-profit channels, and I've convinced Bantam that this is a good idea.
>
> Since Bantam has seen fit to peaceably agree to this scheme of mine, Bantam Books is not going to fuss about this. Provided you don't try to sell the book, they are not going to bother you for what you do with the electronic copy of this book. If you want to check this out personally, you can ask them; they're at 1540 Broadway NY NY 10036. However, if you were so foolish as to print this book and start retailing it for money in violation of my copyright and the commercial interests of Bantam Books, then Bantam, a part of the gigantic Bertelsmann multinational publishing combine, would roust some of their heavy-duty attorneys out of hibernation and crush you like a bug. This is only to be expected. I didn't write this book so that you could make money out of it. If

anybody is gonna make money out of this book, it's gonna be me and my publisher. (Sterling 1992, preface)

In other words, the author is reserving the right to commercial reproduction and use of the work, but not to noncommercial uses. In contrast, Project Gutenberg claims no right to commercial or noncommercial uses of the public domain works it distributes, although it claims trademark rights in the name "Project Gutenberg." The author is very clear about what the right of noncommercial reproduction and distribution of his work includes:

> You can copy this electronic book. Copy the heck out of it, be my guest, and give those copies to anybody who wants them . . . .. You can upload the book onto bulletin board systems, or Internet nodes, or electronic discussion groups. Go right ahead and do that, I am giving you express permission right now. Enjoy yourself.
> You can put the book on disks and give the disks away, as long as you don't take any money for it. (Sterling 1992, preface)

He also corrects a common misperception: the idea that a work distributed with few or no restrictions on copying is in the public domain.

> But this book is not public domain. You can't copyright it in your own name. I own the copyright. Attempts to pirate this book and make money from selling it may involve you in a serious litigative snarl. Believe me, for the pittance you might wring out of such an action, it's really not worth it . . . ..
> This electronic book is now literary freeware. It now belongs to the emergent realm of alternative information economics. You have no right to make this electronic book part of the conventional flow of commerce. (Sterling 1992, preface)

Authors permitting noncommercial copying and distribution of their works also frequently claim the moral rights of integrity and paternity. The right to integrity is the right to protect the work from changes that could damage the work's or the author's reputation; the right of paternity, also known as the right of attribution, is the right to be identified as the author of a

work and to prevent one's name from being associated with a modified version of the work. Sterling does not appear to claim these rights, except perhaps the right of paternity by implication in the statement "You can't copyright it in your own name. I own the copyright." He makes it clear that he does not see the book as an indivisible whole: "I've divided the book into four sections, so that it is less ungainly for upload and download; if there's a section of particular relevance to you and your colleagues, feel free to reproduce that one and skip the rest" (Sterling 1992, preface).

Most authors who wish to make their works available for public use and copying probably do not wish to create their own copyright licenses or do not feel confident doing so. A wide variety of licenses is offered by Creative Commons, which also offers a selection tool to let authors choose the license best suited to their wishes (Creative Commons 2004).

Public domain works, such as those distributed by Project Gutenberg, and works whose authors do not wish to restrict copying, such as *The Hacker Crackdown,* are generally delivered in plaintext format: They are not encrypted and can be read without a decryption key. E-book authors who wish to forbid unauthorized copying must, if they are to rely on anything beyond the good intentions of consumers, encrypt their works. Such encryption then becomes a "technological protective measure" within the meaning of Title I of the Digital Millennium Copyright Act (DMCA), and circumvention of that measure is illegal (17 U.S.C. §§ 1201, 1204). The works can also be digitally watermarked so that unlawfully made copies can be detected.

Although most of the attention given to the DMCA's anticircumvention provisions has focused on the protection of movies and the decryption program DeCSS, the protection of e-books has also given the world of activists, hackers, and encryption enthusiasts one of its causes célèbres: the July 2001 arrest of Dmitri Sklyarov. Sklyarov had written a program, the Advanced E-Book Processor, which made it possible for users to break the copy protection used by Adobe Systems, Inc. for its Acrobat E-Book Reader. Sklyarov was a Russian citizen and had written the program in Russia for a

Russian company, Elcom Ltd.; it does not appear that he violated any Russian law by doing so (Samuelson and Scotchmer 2002). Sklyarov then traveled to the United States to give a presentation on Adobe's security flaws at a conference. Acting on a complaint from Adobe, the Federal Bureau of Investigation arrested Sklyarov at his hotel in Las Vegas on the day after his presentation (Lemos 2001). The Justice Department prosecuted Sklyarov for violation of the DMCA's anticircumvention provisions; Sklyarov was detained in the United States for five months, free on bail but forbidden to leave the country, and was released only when the Justice Department decided not to pursue the prosecution further (*Pravda* 2001; Samuelson and Scotchmer 2002, 1647 n. 332).

The Sklyarov case attracted considerable media attention both within and outside the United States (Vaidhyanathan 2004, ix–x). In Russia it was used in the media to ridicule the commitment of the United States to free speech (*Pravda* 2001). Even after the government dropped its case against Sklyarov, it continued to pursue charges against Sklyarov's employer, Elcom. Elcom moved to dismiss the charges against it on the grounds that, among other flaws, § 1201(b) of the DMCA violated the First Amendment "because it constitutes a content-based restriction on speech that is not sufficiently tailored to serve a compelling government interest, because it impermissibly infringes upon the First Amendment rights of third parties to engage in fair use, and because it is too vague in describing what speech it prohibits, thereby impermissibly chilling free expression" (*Elcom*, 203 F.Supp.2d at 1122). The court rejected all of Elcom's First Amendment claims, as well as a due process claim. Section 1201(b) did not violate the First Amendment, the court explained. Even though computer code was speech subject to First Amendment protection, § 1201(b) was sufficiently tailored because it did not burden more speech than necessary to attain its goal of protecting copyrighted works, and it was not vague. With regard to the fair use argument, the court stated that "it is not unlawful to circumvent for the purpose of engaging in fair use, [but] it is unlawful to traffic in tools that allow fair use circumvention" (*Elcom*, 203

F.Supp.2d at 1125). Thus had Sklyarov circumvented the copy protection only for his own use, his actions would have been lawful; but for Elcom to distribute his program to those less skilled was unlawful.

Statutes
- Copyright Act of 1976, §§ 101–106
- Digital Millennium Copyright Act, 17 U.S.C. § 1201–1204

Case
- *United States v. Elcom Ltd.*, 203 F.Supp.2d 1111 (N.D. Cal. 2002)

See also: Activism and Advocacy Groups; Content Industry; Copyright; Copyright Infringement; DeCSS; Digital Millennium Copyright Act, Title I; Digital Rights Management; Encryption; Fair Use; File-Sharing; First Amendment; Moral Rights; Piracy; Project Gutenberg; Public Domain; Steganography

Sources and further reading:
Creative Commons, *Publish: Choose License*, http://creativecommons.org/license/ (visited November 16, 2004).
Edward Lee, "The Public's Domain: The Evolution of Legal Restraints on the Government's Power to Control Public Access through Secrecy or Intellectual Property," 55 *Hastings Law Journal* 91 (2003).
Robert Lemos, "FBI Nabs Russian Expert at DefCon," ZDNet UK, July 18, 2001, http://news.zdnet.co.uk/internet/security/0,39020375,2091458,00.htm (visited June 2, 2005).
"The Project Gutenberg License, Header and 'Small Print,'" http://www.gutenberg.net/license (visited October 5, 2004).
Project Gutenberg, "Welcome to Project Gutenberg," Oct. 7, 2004, http://www.gutenberg.net/ (visited November 15, 2004).
"Rally in Support of Russian Programmer Dmitry Sklyarov," *Pravda*, Aug. 30, 2001, available at http://english.pravda.ru/society/2001/08/30/13827.html (visited June 2, 2005).
Pamela Samuelson and Suzanne Scotchmer, "The Law and Economics of Reverse Engineering," 111 *Yale Law Journal* 1575 (2002).
Bruce Sterling, *The Hacker Crackdown* (Electronic edition 1992), available at http://stuff.mit.edu/

hacker/hacker.html (visited November 13, 2004).

Siva Vaidhyanathan, *The Anarchist in the Library: How the Clash between Freedom and Control Is Hacking the Real World and Crashing the System* (New York: Basic Books, 2004).

❖ E-COMMERCE ❖

Existing commercial law has had to adapt to E-commerce, or electronic commerce. Most e-commerce is still business-to-business rather than business-to-consumer (Cockfield 2003, 87 n. 8), but business-to-consumer sales have made e-commerce part of daily life for Internet users. Shoppers today are familiar with the process of viewing pictures of goods on a Web site, reading reviews of those goods on another Web site, using a service such as Yahoo! or Froogle to shop for the best price on the item selected, and then sending credit card information to an unknown person who claims to have the product available for sale. This convenience has only been made possible, however, by a uniform and uniformly applied body of commercial law. E-commerce has required changes to Article 9 of the preexisting Uniform Commercial Code, the body of law that, with minor variations from state to state, governs contracts in all fifty states of the United States. It has also required other changes, notably to tax laws, and to the laws of other countries, in order to transform the Internet into a true global marketplace (Kryczka 2004).

One of the first problems presented by e-commerce was the problem of electronic signatures, which arguably did not meet the "signature" requirement for contracts under the Uniform Commercial Code. In 1998 Congress enacted the Electronic Signatures in Global and National Commerce Act, better known as E-Sign. E-Sign provides that, subject to some exceptions, "a signature, contract, or other record relating to such transaction may not be denied legal effect, validity, or enforceability solely because it is in electronic form" (15 U.S.C. § 7001(a)(1)).

Most contract law, however, is state law; the federal government may legislate with regard to interstate and international commerce, which certainly includes e-commerce, but much of the evolution in commercial law to address e-commerce issues has taken place at the state level. Two uniform acts attempt to address e-commerce issues; these acts have been approved by the National Conference of Commissioners on Uniform State Laws, which then urges state legislatures to adopt them. The first of these, the Uniform Electronic Transactions Act (UETA), has been adopted in thirty-nine states and the District of Columbia. UETA's provisions on electronic signatures are similar to E-Sign's (Ring 2003).

The second of the uniform acts is the Uniform Computer Information Transactions Act (UCITA). In contrast to UETA, UCITA has proved controversial; it has been opposed by consumer advocates and many state attorneys general (Letter from Attorneys General 1999), and has been adopted in only two states, Maryland and Virginia (Ring 2003). The controversy comes down to a disagreement over consumer software license agreements; UCITA's opponents point out that UCITA places all of the power in forming such agreements in the hands of software vendors and none in the hands of consumers.

Statutes
- Electronic Signatures in Global and National Commerce Act (E-Sign), 15 U.S.C. § 7001 et seq.

Uniform Acts
- Uniform Computer Information Transactions Act, available at http://www.law.upenn.edu/bll/ulc/ucita/ucita200.htm (visited November 14, 2004)
- Uniform Electronic Transactions Act, available at http://www.law.upenn.edu/bll/ulc/fnact99/1990s/ueta99.htm (visited November 14, 2004)

See also: Clickwrap Agreement; Contracts; Taxation; Uniform Computer Information Transactions Act

Sources and further reading
Arthur J. Cockfield, "Jurisdiction to Tax: A Law and Technology Perspective," 38 *Georgia Law Review* 85 (2003).

Katarzyna Kryczka, "Ready to Join the EU Information Society? Implementation of E-Commerce Directive 2000/31/EC in the EU Acceding Countries—the Example of Poland," 12 *International Journal of Law and Information Technology* 55 (2004).

Letter to NCCUSL from Attorneys General Opposing UCITA, July 23, 1999, available at http://www.arl.org/info/frn/copy/agoppltr.html (visited November 14, 2004).

Christina Ramberg, *The Law of Auctions and Exchanges Online* (Oxford, UK: Oxford University Press, 2002).

Carlyle C. Ring Jr., *Understanding Electronic Contracting 2003 The Impact of Regulation, New Laws and New Agreements: Overview of the Legal Landscape of E-Commerce,* Practising Law Institute Patents, Copyrights, Trademarks, and Literary Property Course Handbook Series (New York: Practising Law Institute, April 2003).

Kurt M. Saunders, *Practical Internet Law for Business* (Norwood, MA: Artech House, 2001).

❖ ELECTRONIC RIGHTS MANAGEMENT ❖

See Digital Rights Management

❖ ENCRYPTION ❖

"Here is something that will sound very extreme but is at most, I think, a slight exaggeration: encryption technologies are the most important technological breakthrough in the last one thousand years."

—Lawrence Lessig

Professor Lessig's exaggeration may be more than slight; technological breakthroughs of the last thousand years have included the printing press, the automobile, the discovery of the circulation of blood and of disease-causing microorganisms, antibiotics, safe drinking water, the scientific method itself, the harnessing of electricity, the motion picture camera, and sliced bread. He is trying to call attention to the often-overlooked importance of encryption in general, and public-key encryption in particular, and specifically to its effects on the Internet.

What might those effects be? Most of us are far less aware of the effects of encryption on our Internet lives than of the effects of electricity or automobiles on our real-world lives. To what degree are you aware of encryption as you use the Internet? Does encryption make you feel more secure or less secure?

Source

Lawrence Lessig, *Code and Other Laws of Cyberspace* (New York: Basic Books, 1999).

Encryption is the process by which easily comprehended information, such as ordinary text, a photograph, or a motion picture, is converted into a form that can only be understood with the aid of a key. The process by which this key is used to convert the encrypted message back into its easily understood form is called decryption. The encrypted message is called a ciphertext; the unencrypted message is called plaintext. The method by which the plaintext message is encrypted is called a cipher; it is often incorrectly referred to as a code. Although a "code" also converts information into some other form, this is done for technical reasons rather than to keep the information secret. For example, a code such as the American Standard Code for Information Interchange (ASCII) or Unicode, both used to convert the letters and characters of ordinary text to binary numbers for use in computers, is necessary in order to allow human beings to use binary computers; the usefulness of these codes would be destroyed if the information were kept secret, however. Encryption, in which the existence of the message is not hidden but the content of the message is rendered incomprehensible, is also sometimes confused with steganography, in which the existence of the message is hidden; encryption and steganography may be combined, of course.

Most encryption methods can be classified as either symmetric or asymmetric key algorithms. The former and much older type requires that the sender and receiver share a key, kept secret from the rest of the world; the key is used both to encrypt and decrypt messages. The key can be very simple or very complex, but the system has two weaknesses: Only persons who know the key can send and receive encrypted messages, and anyone who has the key can decrypt all messages encoded with it. As the number of persons with whom the key is shared increases, the likelihood that one of them will inadvertently or deliberately allow the key to fall into the hands of an unauthorized person increases as well.

Simple and not-so-simple symmetric-key encryption has been in use for millennia. One of the simplest forms, the substitution cipher (in which each letter of the alphabet is represented by some other letter) was used by the ancient Romans. As both ciphers and the ability of cryptographers to break them grew more complex, mechanical devices were invented to encode and decode them. These devices, especially those developed by British and U.S. mathematicians to break German and Japanese ciphers during World War II, were among the early ancestors of modern computers.

The tremendous advances in cryptography for military and intelligence purposes during World War II led to government involvement in and regulation of cryptography. In 1952, during the Korean War, then-President Harry Truman created the National Security Agency (NSA). At the time the primary function of the NSA was cryptography and its counterpart, cryptanalysis, or the breaking of codes used by others. The NSA worked to maintain a U.S. lead in these areas, which it did successfully until the emergence of asymmetric or public-key cryptography.

Public-key cryptography (PKC) avoids the weakness of symmetric cryptography by using two keys: A public key, available to all, used to encrypt the message, and a private key, known only to the recipient, used to decrypt it. Once the public key is made available, anyone who wishes can use it to send encrypted messages to the recipient. The public key can be made available to anyone without increasing the likelihood that the private key will fall into the wrong hands, so anyone can encrypt messages but only the authorized recipient can decrypt them (Lessig 1999, 36–38).

The "invention" of public-key cryptography is generally credited to the team of Martin Hellman, a professor at Stanford University, and two graduate students, Whitfield Diffie and Ralph Merkle, and to the slightly later work of three Massachusetts Institute of Technology professors: Ron Rivest, Adi Shamir, and Len Adleman (Diffie and Landau 1998). The latter group patented their encryption method, known as RSA (the initial letters of the surnames of the inventors), and it forms the basis for asymmetric encryption methods in wide use today. The NSA and its British counterpart later claimed to have been aware of the possibility of public-key encryption for some time and to have kept it secret for security reasons.

The NSA initially attempted to prevent the public's use of PKC. Under the Arms Export Control Act (AECA) and the International Traffic in Arms Regulation (ITAR), cryptographic devices were classified as "significant military equipment." Exporting public-key encryption outside the United States was, at least in theory, a violation of AECA and ITAR. But privacy pioneers like Phil Zimmermann, the developer of the popular PKC program Pretty Good Privacy (PGP), made public-key encryption methods available over the Internet (including, inevitably, to people outside the United States) and e-mailed their public keys to persons outside the United States (Rubinstein 1995, 425–427). Providing information on the Internet, however, even for free, may constitute an export; after making PGP available as a free download, Zimmerman was investigated for violation of AECA but never prosecuted.

The NSA is a security agency; perhaps its institutional focus on the potential use of PKC by spies and terrorists blinded it to the commercial possibilities. PKC provides obvious advantages to businesses such as online retailers and financial institutions, who need an easy way to protect the privacy of communications with their customers; without it, Internet commerce could not have expanded to the extent it has. Thus business interests, as well as privacy advocates, had a strong interest in PKC. The NSA attempted to address the problem with the Clipper chip. The Clipper chip was intended to be included in all communications devices sold in the United States and would have added a third component to the public/private key pair—a "spare key" to any encrypted message sent or received with the device. This spare key would be transmitted to a government facility and held in escrow, from which it could be retrieved by court order. This would give the government access, subject to constitutional restraints, to all encrypted communications in the United States (Froomkin 1995, 752–763). Needless to say, neither businesses nor privacy advocates were enthusiastic. Neither trusted either the integrity or the competence of the government; the government might use its escrow powers improperly, or the escrow database might be hacked and the spare keys made available to criminals. And, of course, no one outside the United States would want to send encrypted communications using a device that made the content available to the U.S. government, and no non-U.S. manufacturer would incorporate the Clipper chip into devices for sale outside the United States. Consumers would presumably prefer devices made without the Clipper chip, which would also be cheaper to manufacture; the effect on U.S. manufacturers of communications equipment would be disastrous.

Opposition from nearly all sectors of society led to the demise of the Clipper chip (Pednekar-Magal and Shields 2003). The United States was not the only country to attempt such centralized control of encryption; in France, for instance, a Clipper-like program was instituted in the mid-1990s, but abandoned in 1999. Asymmetric encryption is now an accepted part of Internet commerce, transparent to most users. PKC is incorporated into Web browsers in the form of the Secure Socket Layer (SSL), which encrypts messages between the browser and a Web server. Most users will not be aware that SSL is in use unless the Web page tells them or unless they notice the tiny "lock" icon on their Web browser or look at the URL: Encrypted pages generally have an address starting with "https" rather than "http." SSL can also be used to confirm a server's or user's identity through the use of a digital certificate and can be used to ensure that the content of a message has not been altered in transit (Lessig 1999, 39–40).

Public key encryption is widely available and difficult to break; it has also become an indispensable part of the Internet economy. In addition, PKC has numerous other legitimate uses: It can be used to verify identity through digital certificates and signature, it can be used to preserve the confidentiality of business and personal communications, and it can be used to protect copyrighted information (such as a movie recorded on a DVD) from unauthorized copying. But PKC can also be used by terrorists, child pornographers, and other criminals. The challenge for lawmakers is to create a set of rules that permits the economically and socially beneficial uses of PKC—encryption of credit card numbers, bank account information, business records, confidential business and personal communications, and the like—while controlling the harmful uses.

The first problem is not easily solved; the same encryption tool that can be used to conceal a legal but confidential business plan can be used to conceal an illegal and dangerous terrorist plot. Encryption can create a virtual private network that can save businesses millions of dollars in infrastructure costs—or provide a hidden marketplace for child pornographers. In this situation the encryption technology is merely a tool, and the appropriate legislative approach is to enhance penalties for crimes committed using that tool. A knife that can be used for slicing melons can also be used to commit a robbery; the legislature has responded not by outlawing knives but by providing that the penalty for a crime committed with a knife is more severe than the penalty for a similar crime committed without one.

There seems to be no downside to allowing the use of encryption to verify the identity of Web servers and Internet users. Copy-protection encryption, however, has presented significant legislative difficulties in commercial transactions, aside from privacy concerns. The content industry has lobbied heavily for legislative protection for, and even mandate of, copyright protection encryption technologies. Yet users and equipment makers resent copy protection encryption; equipment must be designed to play encrypted material, sometimes with uneven results. And users might want to record protected material to other media for legitimate space-shifting purposes. The use of encryption thus diminishes utility while simultaneously raising the cost: Consumers end up with a more expensive but less useful media player.

Within the United States the problem is addressed by a combined legislative and technological approach. Movies could easily be recorded with nearly unbreakable encryption. But in order to make movies that can be played, the recording industry must share the decryption key with the equipment manufacturing industry; the more complex the encryption, the greater the chance of incompatibility, and the greater the number of keys distributed, the greater the chance that a decryption key will be leaked to the general public.

Instead, movies are recorded with relatively simple encryption, and the Digital Millennium Copyright Act (DMCA) provides penalties for the circumvention of this encryption. The combination of encryption to stop the casual user from copying the movie and criminal penalties to deter the more sophisticated user have managed to control, if not eliminate, piracy of movies within the United States.

The problem for the movie industry is the rest of the world. Foreign earnings represent between two-thirds and three-quarters of the U.S. film industry's total revenues in a typical year; about one-third of this amount comes from home video sales, although amounts vary from year to year. Only a relatively sophisticated user can break the encryption used to copy-protect DVDs. But once the encryption is broken, the key can be distributed to the world at large; anyone can use a program such as DeCSS (a CSS-decryption program, the distribution of which is unlawful in the United States) to make copies of encrypted movies. In the United States the DMCA provides penalties for doing so (17 U.S.C. §§ 1203–1204); outside the United States, however, the movie industry's remedies are limited to an action for copyright infringement under local law (which will generally conform to international treaties).

The film industry would prefer sophisticated encryption for exported films, but it has run into the government's, and particularly the NSA's, concerns that to export this sophisticated encryption (and, necessarily, the means of decrypting it) would create a national security problem by giving this technology to foreign governments and persons. There is also a market-based problem: A large number of people already have DVD players; if they buy movies that their players cannot play, they are more likely to return the movie and demand their money back than to go out and buy a new DVD player. This is the factor that has inhibited the development of effective copy protection for music CDs: A large number of people already have CD players that are not capable of playing encrypted CDs. Instead, protective measures for CDs have focused on technological tricks designed to prevent the CD from being played in a computer's CD-ROM drive. One such method can easily be circumvented by coloring over the "security track" on the disk with a black marker, and another by holding down the "shift" key while the disk is loaded. These acts may or may not be unlawful under the DMCA.

The trend from the introduction of PGP through the end of the twentieth century was toward lightening of controls on use and distribution of encryption software. The events of September 11, 2001, may have halted or even reversed that trend, at least temporarily.

An intriguing event, and a measure of the level of public fascination with encryption and cipher-breaking, has been the emergence of a subgenre of popular fiction on the topic. These novels tend to be multilayered; on the surface they may be read as straightforward adventure novels. On the next level they provide a series of puzzles, related to the story, which the reader can decipher as the plot moves forward. On subsequently deeper levels they provide clues that the reader can use to decipher a variety of messages that give additional information about the story, or about the author's future work, or about other things unrelated to the story. These novels range from formulaic stories with simple ciphers aimed at a mass market (Dan Brown's *The Da Vinci Code*) and cipher novels for children (the *Artemis Fowl* series) to the more complex (and thus more rewarding) work of Umberto Eco (*Foucault's Pendulum*) and to complex ciphers requiring a degree of mathematical sophistication (Neal Stephenson's *Cryptonomicon*).

Statutes

- Arms Export Control Act, 22 U.S.C. § 2778
- Digital Millennium Copyright Act, 17 U.S.C. § 1201
- Security and Freedom through Encryption (SAFE) Act, H.R. 850, 106th Cong. (1999)

Regulation

- International Traffic in Arms Regulation, 22 C.F.R. part 120

Case

- *U.S. v. Hsu*, 364 F.3d 192 (4th Cir. 2004)

See also: Copyright; Copyright Infringement; Cyberpunk; Digital Rights Management; File-Sharing; Hacking; Phreaking; Privacy; Steganography

Sources and further reading:

Nonfiction

Andre Bacard, *The Computer Privacy Handbook: A Practical Guide to E-Mail Encryption, Data Protection, and PGP Privacy Software* (Berkeley, CA: Peachpit Press, 1995).

Whitfield Diffie and Susan Landau, *Privacy on the Line: The Politics of Wiretapping and Encryption* (Cambridge, MA: MIT Press, 1998).

Niels Ferguson and Bruce Schneier, *Practical Cryptography* (Indianapolis, IN: Wiley Publishing, Inc., 2003).

Warwick Ford and Michael S. Baum, *Secure Electronic Commerce: Building the Infrastructure for Digital Signatures and Encryption*, 2d ed. (Upper Saddle River, NJ: Prentice Hall, 2001).

A. Michael Froomkin, "The Metaphor Is the Key: Cryptography, the Clipper Chip, and the Constitution," 143 *University of Pennsylvania Law Review* 709 (1995).

Eric Hughes, *A Cypherpunk's Manifesto*, Mar. 9, 1993, http://www.activism.net/cypherpunk/manifesto.html (visited November 13, 2004).

David Kahn, *The Codebreakers: The Story of Secret Writing* (New York: Scribner, 1996).

The Law and Practice of Digital Encryption (Amsterdam: Institute for Information Law, 1998).

Lawrence Lessig, *Code and Other Laws of Cyberspace* (New York: Basic Books, 1999).

Steven Levy, *Crypto: How the Code Rebels Beat the Government—Saving Privacy in the Digital Age* (New York: Viking, 2001).

Wenbo Mao, *Modern Cryptography: Theory and Practice* (Upper Saddle River, NJ: Prentice Hall, 2003).

Alfred J. Menezes, et al., *Handbook of Applied Cryptography* (Boca Raton, FL: CRC Press, 1997).

Vandana Pednekar-Magal and Peter Shields, "The State and Telecom Surveillance Policy: The Clipper Chip Initiative," 8 *Communication Law and Policy* 429 (2003).

Phillip E. Reiman, "Cryptography and the First Amendment: The Right to Be Unheard," 14 *John Marshall Journal of Computer and Information Law* 325 (1996).

Ira S. Rubinstein, "Export Controls on Encryption Software," in *Coping with U.S. Export Controls* (New York: Practising Law Institute, 1995).

Simon Singh, *The Code Book: The Evolution of Secrecy from Mary, Queen of Scots to Quantum Cryptography* (New York: Doubleday, 1999).

William Stallings, *Cryptography and Network Security: Principles and Practice*, 2d ed. (Upper Saddle River, NJ: Prentice Hall, 1999).

"Uncrackable Beams of Light: Quantum Cryptography—Hailed by Theoreticians as the Ultimate of Uncrackable Codes—Is Finally Going Commercial," *Economist Technology Quarterly*, Sept. 6, 2003, at 16.

Peter Wayner, *Disappearing Cryptography: Being and Nothingness on the Net* (Boston: AP Professional, 1996).

Fiction

Dan Brown, *The Da Vinci Code* (New York: Doubleday, 2003).

Eoin Colfer, Artemis Fowl series, beginning with *Artemis Fowl* (New York: Hyperion Books, 2001).

Umberto Eco, *The Name of the Rose* (New York: Harcourt Brace and Company, 1983).

Umberto Eco, *Foucault's Pendulum* (San Diego, CA: Harcourt Brace and Company, 1989).

Neal Stephenson, *Cryptonomicon* (New York: Avon Books, 1999).

Neal Stephenson, Baroque Cycle, beginning with *Quicksilver* (New York: William Morrow, 2003).

❖ ENFORCEMENT ❖

The enforcement of laws and legal rights having to do with computers and the Internet involves a wide variety of public and private mechanisms. Intellectual property rights, such as copyright, patent, and trademark rights, are for the most part protected by private lawsuits brought by the victims of infringement on those rights. The same is true of torts against individuals, such as defamation or invasion of privacy. It is the duty of individuals to detect violations of these legal rights and to pursue the violators. In certain cases, however, defamation or infringement of an intellectual property right can result in criminal prosecution.

Certain crimes are especially likely to be committed using the Internet, or are unique to the Internet. These crimes include distribution of unlawful content, identity theft, malicious hacking, phishing, and spamming. Federal and state governments have authority over some Internet crimes, while others are purely federal crimes. Although a number of agencies are involved in preventing and pursuing Internet crimes, two in particular—the Federal Trade Commission (FTC) and the Department of Justice (DOJ)—carry an especially heavy load.

Crimes related to content fall into five general categories: content that infringes on an intellectual property right; content that is defamatory or invades privacy; content that is obscene, pornographic, or indecent; content that is illegal, including child pornography and criminal conspiracy; and content that threatens national security.

Content that infringes on an intellectual property right is largely an area for private enforcement, and content industry groups actively pursue civil lawsuits against file-sharing networks (*Napster*, 239 F.3d 1004) and individual file-sharers (*Verizon*, 351 F.3d 1229), while trademark owners pursue online trademark violators. The federal government may become involved when the scope of the infringement meets certain requirements (e.g., No Electronic Theft Act, 17 U.S.C. §§ 506–507), or when there may be a violation of the anticircumvention provisions of the Digital Millennium Copyright Act (DMCA) (*Elcom*, 203 F.Supp.2d 1111); investigation of a possible crime and the making of arrests are the job of the Federal Bureau of Investigation (FBI), while prosecuting the case against the alleged criminal is a matter for the DOJ.

Content that infringes on a personal right of reputation or privacy may give rise to a private

The September 11, 2001, terrorist attacks raised fears of further attacks, including physical or hacker attacks on the information systems and Internet infrastructure of the United States. In October 2001 President Bush appointed Richard Clarke as chair of the President's Critical Infrastructure Board—or, as he was dubbed by the media, cybersecurity czar. A year and four months later Clarke resigned, emerging as an outspoken critic of the Bush administration, and Bush dissolved the position of cybersecurity czar. Many of Clarke's responsibilities were taken over by Howard Schmidt, who left after just four months to become head of security at eBay. In June 2003 an industry expert, Amit Yoran, became head of the National Cyber Security Division within the newly formed Department of Homeland Security. Yoran's division, however, was buried three administrative layers below then-Homeland Security chief Tom Ridge, and information industry leaders and some legislators felt frustrated at Yoran's lack of access and authority. So, apparently, did Yoran, who resigned in October 2004 with a single day's notice. Yoran, who lasted as long in the job as Clarke had, confided to colleagues that he was frustrated by the government's lack of attention to issues of computer security. Yoran's deputy, Andy Purdy, was appointed as acting director.

It is difficult for an outsider to read meaning into government-agency reshufflings, especially in a field where secrecy is a reflex, but a disturbing picture seems to emerge. First, the U.S. government may be the last remaining entity involved in Internet technology to use the prefix "cyber" without apparent irony. Second, the government's Internet security program may be in disarray: Two cybersecurity chiefs have left after very short stays—just over a year—and have left with some bitterness; a third lasted only months. None of this speaks well of the country's preparedness for an Internet attack.

Source

"U.S. Cybersecurity Chief Resigns: Amit Yoran Cited Frustrations in Private," CNN.com, Oct. 1, 2004, available at http://www.cnn.com/2004/US/10/01/cyber.chief.ap/index.html (visited October 1, 2004).

right of action (*Zeran,* 129 F.3d 327). Ordinarily such content, even if it results in a civil suit, does not lead to criminal prosecution; however, especially egregious defamation may be a crime under state law. Defamation laws in other countries are significantly different, and courts in the United States will not enforce defamation judgments from other countries if enforcement would conflict with the First Amendment (*Bachchan,* 585 N.Y.S.2d 661).

Content that is obscene, pornographic, or indecent has posed an especially difficult problem for U.S. law. Obscene content, as defined in *Miller v. California,* can be prohibited; however, the distinction between obscenity and mere indecency is not always an easy one to draw (413 U.S. 15). Conduct that is merely indecent may not be prohibited, but measures may be taken to render it inaccessible to minors. The difficulty of crafting measures to protect minors from such content without unconstitutionally interfering with the access of adults has occupied considerable congressional attention. The substantive provisions of the first attempt to do so, the Communications Decency Act of 1996, were subsequently struck down as unconstitutional (*Reno v. American Civil Liberties Union,* 521 U.S. 844). A second attempt, the Child Online Protection Act of 1998, also seems unlikely to withstand constitutional scrutiny; an injunction has prevented it from being enforced, and the U.S. Supreme Court has sent a lawsuit opposing it to a lower court for trial on the issue of whether current blocking and filtering software, rather than federal legislation, can protect minors from inappropriate content (*Ashcroft v. American Civil Liberties Union,* 124 S. Ct. 2783).

Such blocking and filtering software is required on computers in schools and libraries receiving discounted Internet access. The statute requiring the blocking and filtering software, the Children's Internet Protection Act (CIPA) of 1998, has fared better in the courts than statutes attempting to restrict Web content rather than Web access; its constitutionality has been upheld by the Supreme Court (*American Library Association,* 123 S. Ct. 2297). Enforcement of CIPA is simple: Schools and libraries that do not comply do not receive the discount (47 U.S.C. § 254(h)(5)(F)).

Pornographic content provides complex problems of regulation and enforcement because lawmakers wish to restrict access to such content for some users, but not for others. When Congress does not wish to discriminate between groups of users, the lawmaking task is greatly simplified. Some content is prohibited for all users. Child pornography is illegal (18 U.S.C. §§ 2251–2260). Detecting it and arresting violators is the job of the FBI, whose agents infiltrate child pornography rings online; violators are then prosecuted by the Department of Justice. Other illegal content includes content that is part of a crime—for instance, an e-mail soliciting murder for hire, or a Web site offering gambling or prostitution in a jurisdiction where such an offering is illegal, or messages between criminal coconspirators in which they plot to rob a bank. Criminal content of this sort could involve both state and federal law enforcement authorities.

Some content may also be regulated or prohibited on grounds of national security, even if it is not otherwise illegal. The USA PATRIOT Act of 2001 greatly enhanced the authority of federal agencies to conduct surveillance of e-mail and other electronic communications and, perhaps more importantly, to disclose the contents of those communications to other law enforcement, intelligence, defense, and national security agencies (18 U.S.C. § 2517(6)). It is possible that the persons sending or receiving the communications may then be detained.

Other crimes are not related to Internet content but to Internet conduct; crimes of this sort include identity theft, malicious hacking, phishing, and spamming. The motivation for these crimes is usually either malicious—a pure desire to cause mischief—or financial. The Federal Trade Commission (FTC) addresses financial crimes directed at consumers. The FTC does this in two ways: through education, outreach, and data collection projects designed to prevent consumers from being victimized, and through prosecutions of violators. It enforces and makes regulations under the Children's Online Privacy Protection Act (COPPA), which governs the collection of personal information from children over the Internet (15 U.S.C. § 6502). The FTC Division of Advertising Practices enforces laws against unfair, misleading, or false advertising, much of which can be found on the Internet, especially in spam; it also monitors e-commerce. The FTC's anti-scam office, the Division of Marketing Practices, shuts down Internet scammers (Muris 2004, 11–13), while its ID Theft project addresses the crime of identity theft, which has become far more common as a result of Internet use. The FTC is also responsible for enforcing the CAN-SPAM Act of 2003, an antispam law (15 U.S.C. § 7705(c)). And the FTC is likely to be the agency charged with enforcement of future antispyware laws.

Crimes of mischief, chiefly malicious hacking, are governed by a variety of state and federal statutes; the chief antihacker (or anticracker) statute is the federal Computer Fraud and Abuse Act of 1986, enforced by the Department of Justice (via the FBI) and the Department of Homeland Security (via the Secret Service, formerly part of the Department of the Treasury) (18 U.S.C. § 1030(d)).

Statutes

- CAN-SPAM Act of 2003, 15 U.S.C. § 7705(c)
- Child Pornography Prevention Act of 1996, 18 U.S.C. §§ 2251–2260
- Children's Internet Protection Act of 1998, 47 U.S.C. § 254(h)
- Children's Online Privacy Protection Act of 1998, 15 U.S.C. § 6502
- Communications Decency Act of 1996, Pub. L. No. 104-104, § 502, 1996 U.S.S.C.A.N. (110 Stat.) 56,133 (later codified at 47 U.S.C. § 223)
- Computer Fraud and Abuse Act of 1986, 18 U.S.C. § 1030
- Copyright Act of 1976, 17 U.S.C. §§ 101–1332
- Digital Millennium Copyright Act, 17 U.S.C §§ 512, 1201–1204
- Identity Theft and Assumption Deterrence Act, amending and codified at 18 U.S.C. § 1028
- No Electronic Theft Act, amending and codified at 17 U.S.C. §§ 101, 506 and 507 and 18 U.S.C. §§ 2319–2320
- USA PATRIOT Act of 2001, 18 U.S.C. § 2517(6)

Cases

Supreme Court

- *Ashcroft v. American Civil Liberties Union*, 124 S. Ct. 2783 (2004)
- *Miller v. California*, 413 U.S. 15 (1973)
- *Reno v. American Civil Liberties Union*, 521 U.S. 844 (1997)
- *United States v. American Library Association, Inc.*, 123 S. Ct. 2297 (2003)

Federal Appellate Courts

- *A&M Records, Inc. v. Napster, Inc.*, 239 F.3d 1004 (9th Cir. 2001)
- *Recording Industry Ass'n of America, Inc. v. Verizon Internet Services*, 351 F.3d 1229 (D.C. Cir. 2003)
- *Zeran v. America Online, Inc.*, 129 F.3d 327 (4th Cir. 1997)

Federal Trial Court

- *U.S. v. Elcom Ltd.*, 203 F.Supp.2d 1111 (N.D. Cal. 2002)

State Court

- *Bachchan v. India Abroad Publications*, 585 N.Y.S.2d 661 (N.Y. Sup. Ct. 1992)

See also: Adware and Spyware; Censorship; Child Pornography; Children's Internet Protection Act; Communications Decency Act; Copyright; Defamation; Digital Millennium Copyright Act; Federal Communications Commission; Federal Trade Commission; Hacking; Identity Theft; No Electronic Theft Act; Patent; Phishing; Spam; Trademark

Sources and further reading

Joe Anastasi, *The New Forensics: Investigating Corporate Fraud and the Theft of Intellectual Property* (Hoboken, NJ: John Wiley and Sons, 2003).

Stuart Biegel, *Beyond Our Control? Confronting the Limits of Our Legal System in the Age of Cyberspace* (Cambridge, MA: MIT Press, 2001).

Federal Trade Commission, *ID Theft, What's It All About?* Oct. 2003, available from http://www.consumer.gov/idtheft/ (visited November 6, 2004).

Timothy J. Muris, Federal Trade Commission Chair, "Guide to the Federal Trade

Commission," Apr. 2004, available at http://www.ftc.gov/bcp/conline/pubs/general/guidetoftc.htm (visited November 16, 2004).

Bill Nelson et al., *Computer Forensics and Investigations* (Boston: Thomson Learning, 2004).

Adam Thierer et al., eds., *Who Rules the Net? Internet Governance and Jurisdiction* (Washington, DC: Cato Institute, 2003).

Douglas Thomas and Brian D. Loader, eds., *Cybercrime: Law Enforcement, Security and Surveillance in the Information Age* (London: Routledge, 2000).

F

❖ FAIR USE (COPYRIGHT) ❖

Fair use is a doctrine of trademark and copyright law; fair use is a defense to a claim of copyright or trademark infringement. Copyright fair use is somewhat hazily defined by section 107 of the Copyright Code, which provides that

> the fair use of a copyrighted work . . . for purposes such as criticism, comment, news reporting, teaching (including multiple copies for classroom use), scholarship, or research, is not an infringement of copyright. In determining whether the use made of a work in any particular case is a fair use the factors to be considered shall include –
> (1) the purpose and character of the use, including whether such use is of a commercial nature or is for nonprofit educational purposes;
> (2) the nature of the copyrighted work;
> (3) the amount and substantiality of the portion used in relation to the copyrighted work as a whole; and
> (4) the effect of the use upon the potential market for or value of the copyrighted work.
> The fact that a work is unpublished shall not itself bar a finding of fair use if such finding is made upon consideration of all the above factors.

Copyright fair use is sometimes confused with the idea of the public domain. The distinction is simple: Works in the public domain are not copyrighted. Fair use applies to works that *are* copyrighted, but which nonetheless may be copied without the permission of the copyright holder under certain circumstances. Uses that may be protected as fair use include scholarly and "transformative" uses; parody, but not necessarily satire; noncommercial time-shifting and space-shifting, and possibly some commercial time-shifting and space-shifting as well; copying for classroom use; copying in order to reverse engineer computer software; and the use of thumbnail images of copyrighted works on a Web site. One significant Internet use that has been found not to fall within the fair use exception is file-sharing.

Scholarly and transformative uses: The copying of parts of works by scholars is usually fair use under the four section 107 factors. Scholarly works are written for educational purposes, not commercial purposes; the work copied may itself be a scholarly work, and the copying is a way of including the work in an ongoing process of discussion and critical examination of ideas by the scholarly community; the part used is generally a small portion of the whole; and the scholarly examination is unlikely to have an adverse effect on the market for the work—even if the treatment is negative, the attention drawn to the work is likely to enhance the market for the complete original.

Although scholarly works are one form of transformative work, they are not the only form. All parodies are transformative works, for example. In discussing one parody, the Supreme Court observed generally that, "the goal of copyright, to promote science and the arts, is generally furthered by the creation of transformative works" (*Campbell*, 510 U.S. at 579). The court went on to observe that transformative works "lie at the heart of the fair use doctrine's guarantee of breathing space within the confines of copyright . . . and the more transformative the new work, the less will be the significance of other factors, like commercialism, that may weigh against a finding of fair use."

Blogging and fair use: The logic of pursuing P2P file-sharing networks is obvious even to opponents of the content industry. With their enormous catalogues of available material and huge numbers of users, P2P networks present a significant potential for harm to the copyright holder's interests. How great that potential is, and whether it is outweighed by possible beneficial effects of file-sharing, is hotly debated by content-industry and file-sharing advocates, but it is solidly established that file-sharing with large numbers of unknown users of a file-sharing network is not fair use.

MP3 blogs present a more difficult question, however. Blogs such as Said the Gramophone, Fluxblog, Fruits of Chaos, Tofu Hut, Music for Robots, and Spoilt Victorian Child, among many others, include MP3 files along with text and images; typically some, but not all, of the text comments on the music. If a blogger chooses to include a copyrighted but ancient music file—perhaps They Might Be Giants performing "Santa's Beard"—in her December 24 blog entry, the file might be downloaded by some unknown persons. The effect on the market for the work would be insignificant, however. An application of the four "fair use" factors of 17 U.S.C. § 107 might lead to a finding of fair use. But what if the blog includes a new MP3 every day? Or a hundred new MP3s every day? If a new three-minute MP3 is posted every three minutes, does the blog in effect become an Internet radio station? If thousands of MP3s are posted, does the blog become the equivalent of the copyright-infringing MyMP3.com? The appearance and persistence of music blogs makes it inevitable that these questions will be addressed in court. Yet many, perhaps most, music blogs post MP3s with the goal of broadening their readers' listening horizons; they post relatively obscure music rather than Britney and Beyonce and may well enhance the market for the specific songs and musical genres they represent.

Parody and satire: In the United States, parody is a form of criticism protected by the First Amendment. Political parodies, literary parodies, and parodies of works of popular entertainment are a staple of discourse in the United States from childhood onward. The urge to parody seems innate; schoolchildren parody the words to the songs they sing in music class, and require no special training to chuckle over the movie "satires" (actually parodies) in *Mad Magazine*.

Parodies are transformative works, and in order to be protected as fair use a sufficient degree of transformation is necessary. In parodying a song, for example, the parodist may use only as much of the original lyrics as is necessary to conjure up the original in the reader's or listener's mind; without such conjuring up, the parody will not be recognized as such. In the case of *Campbell v. Acuff-Rose Music, Inc.*, discussing one such parody, the Supreme Court observed that:

> When parody takes aim at a particular original work, the parody must be able to "conjure up" at least enough of that original to make the object of its critical wit recognizable. . . . What makes for this recognition is quotation of the original's most distinctive or memorable features, which the parodist can be sure the audience will know. Once enough has been taken to assure identification, how much more is reasonable will depend, say, on the extent to which the song's overriding purpose and character is to parody the original or, in contrast, the likelihood that the parody may serve as a market substitute for the original. But using some characteristic features cannot be avoided. (510 U.S. at 588)

The song parodied in *Campbell* was Roy Orbison's 1964 song "Oh, Pretty Woman." The defendants were Luther Campbell and the notorious early rap group 2 Live Crew. (Campbell performed under the name Luke Skyywalker, which despite its extra Υ raised issues of trademark infringement and dilution.) The parody was, by 2 Live Crew's standards, fairly mild. Nonetheless, it was offensive, as are many parodies. Parodies may generate more litigation than they should, not because the copyright owner of the parodied work has suffered economic harm as a result, but because parodies can sting: They are often cruel, and the owner of the parodied work can become emotionally involved to a degree that leads him or her to pursue a lawsuit that does not make good economic or legal sense.

Satire is distinguished from parody for legal (as opposed to artistic) purposes by its target: The purpose of a parody is to make fun of or otherwise criticize the parodied work; the purpose of satire is to make fun of or criticize some other target, perhaps using a copyrighted work as an instrument. The court in *Campbell* pointed out that satire, unlike parody, does not require such an instrument: Satire "can stand on its own two feet and so requires justification for the very act of borrowing" (510 U.S. at 581).

Time-shifting and space-shifting: Time-shifting and *space-shifting* are terms applied to the copying of copyrighted works that require a player, such as a television screen or speakers, to make them intelligible to a human viewer or listener. Time-shifting occurs when a viewer records a copyrighted work (for example, a broadcast or cable television program) for later viewing or listening. Space-shifting occurs when a viewer records a copyrighted work to play in some other location (for example, making a cassette tape from a legally purchased music CD in order to play the music in a car with no CD player). The Supreme Court ruled in the landmark case of *Sony Corporation of America v. Universal City Studios* that time-shifting for noncommercial purposes was fair use. The Ninth Circuit applied this reasoning in *Recording Industry Association of America v. Diamond Multimedia Systems* to hold that noncommercial space-shifting was also fair use.

In the years since *Sony* it has become apparent that not all noncommercial space-shifting and time-shifting is fair use; the four factors of section 107 must be applied to each case. Online file-sharing of copyrighted music, for example, might be categorized as noncommercial space-shifting, but it is not fair use, not least because it drastically affects the market for the work (*Napster,* 239 F.3d 1004). At the same time, some commercial space-shifting and time-shifting may be fair use: The creation of fair-use transformative works may involve space-shifting and time-shifting, for example.

Classroom use: The 1976 Guidelines for Classroom Copying in Not-for-Profit Educational Institutions, prepared as part of the process of drafting the Copyright Act of 1976, provide a safe harbor for teachers who follow some fairly restrictive guidelines on photocopying materials to hand out in class. A more recent concern is the posting of copyrighted materials on course Web sites. Uses of this sort are addressed by Title IV of the Digital Millennium Copyright Act and by the Technology, Education and Copyright Harmonization Act. As amended by these acts, the copyright code now requires the teacher's employing institution to use technological measures to ensure that the work will not be retained by the students in accessible form after the class session ends, and to prevent "unauthorized further dissemination of the work." Schools complying with these rather severe restrictions will be able to avail themselves of a statutory safe harbor providing immunity for further downstream infringements by the students.

Reverse engineering: The copying or decompiling of a copyrighted computer program in order to reverse engineer the program is fair use. Reverse engineering might be necessary either to design a competing program or to achieve interoperability—that is, to ensure that one program can work with another. Congress and the courts have decided that both of these goals are socially desirable (*Sega,* 977 F.2d at 1510; *Sony,* 203 F.3d at 596).

Web site thumbnails: Thumbnails are tiny pictures used on a Web site, usually to provide links either to larger copies of the images, to descriptions of the thing depicted, or to places where the thing depicted may be purchased. In *Kelly v. Arriba Soft,* photographer Leslie Kelly posted copies of his photographs on his own Web site and, under license, on other Web sites. Arriba Soft operated a search engine that displayed results as thumbnails rather than text, like the "Images" search function on Google. The Ninth Circuit Court of Appeals held that this was a fair use of Kelly's photographs. The use, though commercial, was incidental and "not highly exploitative" (336 F.3d at 818).

The use was transformative because it "created a different purpose for the images": access to information rather than artistic expression (336 F.3d at 819). The artistic, rather than factual, nature of the works weighed slightly against a finding of fair use; the fact that the thumbnail was of the entire work rather than a part was necessary to the search engine's purpose and weighed neither for nor against fair use (336 F.3d at 820–821). The fourth factor, like the first, weighed in favor of a finding of fair use: The thumbnails did not adversely affect the market for Kelly's work; they were unsuitable for use as substitutes for the actual photographs, and if anything acted to increase the market by guiding users to Kelly's Web site. Considering all four factors, the court decided that the use of Kelly's photographs (and, by extension, similar uses of copyrighted materials by search engines generally) was fair use. (336 F.3d at 822).

The President Ford clause: The final clause of section 107 provides that "The fact that a work is unpublished shall not itself bar a finding of fair use if such finding is made upon consideration of all the above factors." This clause was added to the statute after *The Nation* magazine obtained and published excerpts from the then-unpublished memoirs of former president Gerald Ford. The book's publisher sued the magazine, and the United States Supreme Court held that "Under ordinary circumstances, the author's right to control the first public appearance of his undisseminated expression will outweigh a claim of fair use" (*Harper & Row*, 471 U.S. at 555). This was widely interpreted as meaning that no use of unpublished work could be fair use; Congress added the final clause to section 107 in 1992 to correct this impression and perhaps to step back a bit from the holding in *Harper & Row.* In an Internet context the applicability of the clause is limited: All work that is posted on the Internet is published by virtue of being posted. Cases involving unpublished work may still arise, though, if someone obtains a copy of an unpublished work and posts it.

Statutes
- Copyright Act of 1976, 17 U.S.C. §§ 107

- Digital Millennium Copyright Act, Title IV, 17 U.S.C. §§ 106, 108, 110, 112
- Technology, Education and Copyright Harmonization Act amendments, 17 U.S.C. §§ 110(2), 112

Guidelines
- Guidelines for Classroom Copying in Not-for-Profit Educational Institutions, H.R. Rep. No. 94-1476, 94th Cong., 2d Sess. 72 (1976)

Cases
Supreme Court
- *Campbell v. Acuff-Rose Music, Inc.,* 510 U.S. 569 (1994)
- *Harper & Row Pub. v. Nation Enterprises,* 471 U.S. 539 (1985)
- *Sony Corporation of America v. Universal City Studios, Inc.,* 464 U.S. 417 (1984)

Federal Appellate Courts
- *A&M Records, Inc. v. Napster, Inc.,* 239 F.3d 1004 (9th Cir. 2001)
- *Kelly v. Arriba Soft Corp.,* 336 F.3d 811 (9th Cir. 2003)
- *Recording Industry Association of America v. Diamond Multimedia Systems, Inc.,* 180 F.3d 1072 (9th Cir. 1999)
- *Sega Enterprises v. Accolade,* 977 F.2d 1510 (9th Cir. 1992)
- *Sony Computer Entertainment, Inc. v. Connectix Corp.,* 203 F.3d 596 (9th Cir. 2000)

See also: Copyright; Copyright Infringement; DeCSS; Digital Millennium Copyright Act; Digital Millennium Copyright Act, Title I; Digital Millennium Copyright Act, Title IV; Fair Use (Trademark); File-Sharing; Public Domain

Sources and further reading:
Marshall Leaffer, *Understanding Copyright Law,* 3d ed. (New York: Matthew Bender, 1999).

❖ FAIR USE (TRADEMARK) ❖

Trademark fair use is a defense to a claim of trademark infringement just as copyright fair use is a defense to a claim of copyright infringement. As with copyright fair use, trademark fair use does not mean that the trademark in question has fallen into the public domain; it means simply that a particular use is permissible. There are two categories of trademark fair use: classic fair use and nominative fair use.

Classic fair use: Classic fair use occurs when a trademark is also a descriptive term and is used by a person other than the trademark holder in its descriptive sense. For example, a company might obtain a trademark in the name "California's Best Web Hosting." For another company to use the name "California's Best Web Hosting" for its business would then be infringement. But a company with another name—XYZ Web Services Corporation, say—could still claim to offer "the best Web hosting in California"; XYZ would be using the terms in their descriptive sense. XYZ might even be able to claim to offer "California's best Web hosting." A majority of U.S. courts would find the latter use permissible only so long as there was no likelihood that consumers would be confused—that is, no likelihood that consumers would think that XYZ was offering the services of or was in some way associated with California's Best Web Hosting. This majority approach has the effect of making classic fair use a subset of the "no likelihood of confusion" defense to trademark infringement. A minority of courts, however, see the two defenses as separate, and are willing to find that an otherwise infringing use is fair use even if a likelihood of confusion exists (see *Cosmetically Sealed Industries,* 125 F.3d 28).

Nominative fair use: Nominative fair use occurs when the person using another's trademark does so not, or not exclusively, to identify his or her own product or service, but to identify the trademark holder's product or service. A software company that describes its software as "Windows XP compatible" is intending to identify the Windows XP operating system made by Microsoft. The use is fair: Potential purchasers of the software who use the Windows XP operating system will want to know whether the software is compatible with their systems; the "Windows XP" trademark is used only to the extent necessary to identify the operating system; and the software company is not suggesting that it is Microsoft, or that Microsoft has endorsed the product.

This analysis follows, more or less, the three-part test for nominative fair use developed by the Ninth Circuit Court of Appeals in *Playboy Enterprises v. Welles.* Playboy Enterprises is a publisher of mildly pornographic print and Internet content. Each year, Playboy selects one of its models as "Playmate of the Year," a title that can be seen as outrageously offensive, irritatingly condescending, or quaintly archaic, depending on one's point of view, but which apparently has commercial value. The defendant in the case, Terri Welles, had been awarded the title of "Playmate of the Year" in 1981; she operated a Web site containing commentary and images of herself. On the site, she used Playboy's trademarked terms in three ways: She used the term *Playmate of the Year* in banner advertisements and in the headline of the Web page; she used the terms *playboy* and *playmate* in metatags (text that does not appear to the viewer of a site but does appear to search engines); and she used the repeated term *PMOY 1981* as a wallpaper design. The trial court found that Ms. Welles's actions were not infringements; the Ninth Circuit agreed in part. The use of the term *Playmate of the Year* and of the metatags *playboy* and *playmate* was nominative fair use. In order to be nominative fair use, the court explained,

> First, the product or service in question must be one not readily identifiable without use of the trademark; second, only so much of the mark or marks may be used as is reasonably necessary to identify the product or service; and third, the user must do nothing that would, in conjunction with the mark, suggest sponsorship or endorsement by the trademark holder. (279 F.3d at 801)

The repeated use of the term *PMOY 1981* on the wallpaper was not a nominative fair use, however. It was not necessary to identify Welles, nor did it appear to do so, as her name or likeness did not appear before or after the term on the wallpaper (279 F.3d at 804–805).

Statute

- Lanham Trademark Act, 15 U.S.C. § 1115(b)

Cases

- *Cosmetically Sealed Industries, Inc. v. Chesebrough-Pond's USA Co.,* 125 F.3d 28 (2d Cir. 1997)
- *New Kids on the Block v. News America Publishing, Inc.,* 971 F.2d 302 (9th Cir. 1992)
- *Playboy Enterprises, Inc. v. Welles,* 279 F.3d 796 (9th Cir. 2002)

See also: Fair Use (Copyright); Metatags; Trademark; Trademark Dilution; Trademark Infringement

Sources and further reading:

G. Peter Albert Jr. and Rita A. Abbati, "Metatags, Keywords and Links: Recent Developments Addressing Trademark Threats in Cyberspace," 40 *San Diego Law Review* 341 (2003).

Douglas G. McCray, "Oh, What a Tangled Web: The Subtle Difference between Metatag Usage as 'Fair Use' and Invisible Infringement," *Michigan Bar Journal,* Aug. 2002, at 42.

Hope Viner Samborn, "Hiding in Plain Site: The Hunt for Metatags on the Internet Is Changing the Field of Trademark Law," *ABA Journal* Sept. 2000, at 80.

❖ FEDERAL COMMUNICATIONS COMMISSION ❖

Enforcement of federal laws regarding the Internet is divided among many government agencies, with the Federal Communications Commission (FCC) and the Federal Trade Commission (FTC) both playing major roles. In general the FCC is responsible more for the infrastructure aspect—the Internet itself, and access to it—and the FTC is responsible more for the content transmitted over that infrastructure—the World Wide Web and e-mail. The boundaries of the categories are indistinct, however. For example, the FCC is charged with the administration of the Children's Internet Protection Act (CIPA); although CIPA is an access-control statute, it is aimed more at a particular type of content than at Internet infrastructure.

The FCC, established in 1934, is charged with regulating interstate and international communications by radio, television, wire, satellite, and cable. This includes the Internet's hardware communications infrastructure. In the early years of the Internet, the FCC nurtured the Internet's growth by distinguishing computer and Internet uses of the telephone network from voice and other "basic" uses. The use of the telephone network for transmission of computer and Internet data was classified as "enhanced service," later renamed "information services," and was left unregulated. This lack of regulation made the rapid growth of the Internet possible. The FCC's determination that "enhanced service providers"—dial-up Internet service providers (ISPs)—were exempt from access charges paid by interexchange telephone service carriers kept the cost of dial-up access low, increasing the number of households with access to the Internet and thus also helping to drive the medium's growth. Another little-noted FCC decision, without which the Internet might still be in its infancy, was the requirement that telephone carriers allow users to connect their own terminal equipment to the network, rather than equipment leased from the carrier (Oxman 1999). Without this FCC action, modem technology would probably have developed very slowly, from lack of competition.

Although the FCC was essential to the Internet's early growth, its role in more recent years has been less clearly helpful. The FCC has been criticized for what many perceive as an uneven approach to the regulation of broadband Internet access services. Digital subscriber line (DSL) broadband access and cable-modem broadband access are regulated differently; critics feel that the difference in regulation is responsible for the lackluster performance of DSL in the marketplace. The lack of a feasible or attractive DSL alternative, coupled with local cable company monopolies, has meant that most consumers in the United States have only one choice of broadband provider; this in turn has kept competition low and prices high. As a result, the percentage of U.S. households with broadband access is lower than the percentages in some less wealthy countries that have come to the Internet more recently (International Telecommunications Union 2003). The continuing relatively high cost of broadband access also places broadband out of reach of some families, contributing to the digital divide in the United States.

Statute

- Communications Act of 1934, as amended by Telecommunications Act of 1996, 47 U.S.C. § 151 et seq.

Cases

- *AT&T Corp. v. City of Portland,* 216 F.3d 871 (9th Cir. 2000)
- *Brand X Internet Services v. FCC,* 345 F.3d 1120 (9th Cir. 2003)

See also: Broadband; Cable; Children's Internet Protection Act; Digital Divide; Federal Trade Commission

Sources and further reading:

Robert W. Crandall et al., "The Empirical Case against Asymmetric Regulation of Broadband Internet Access," 17 *Berkeley Technology Law Journal* 953 (2002).

International Telecommunications Union, "World Telecommunication Development Report 2003: Access Indicators for the Information Society" (2003).

Jason Oxman, "The FCC and the Unregulation of the Internet," FCC/OPP Working Paper 31, July 1999.

Assif Shameen, "Korea's Broadband Revolution: What Korea Is Doing Will have Global Impact," *Chief Executive Magazine,* Apr. 2004, available at http://www.chiefexecutive.net/depts/technology/197a.htm (visited October 1, 2004).

❖ FEDERAL TRADE COMMISSION ❖

The Federal Trade Commission (FTC) is one of the U.S. government agencies most heavily involved in regulation of the Internet. The FTC was originally founded in 1914 to enforce federal antitrust laws; in 1938 its scope was expanded to include enforcement of laws against unfair and deceptive trade practices. Subsequently the FTC has also been empowered by Congress to enforce laws against and make regulations to control a wide variety of trade practices (Muris 2004, 3). The FTC's Bureau of Competition carries out the FTC's original mandate, its antitrust and antimonopoly duties (Muris 2004, 16). The various divisions of the Bureau of Consumer Protection carry out a wide variety of enforcement and regulatory functions with particular significance to the Internet. The Division of Advertising Practices enforces laws against unfair, misleading, or false advertising, problems with which the Internet is severely afflicted. The FTC focuses on advertising for products or services claiming to offer health benefits or weight loss; advertising making performance claims for computers, Internet services, and similar products and services; tobacco and alcohol advertising; claims about product performance; and advertising aimed at children (Muris 2004, 7–8). The FTC is also charged with enforcement of the Children's Online Privacy Protection Act (COPPA) and with making regulations to carry out COPPA (15 U.S.C. § 6502). Other Bureau of Consumer Protection divisions include the Consumer and Business Education Program, the Division of Enforcement, the Division of Financial Practices, the Division of Marketing Practices, the Division of Planning and Information, and the International Division of Consumer Protection. The Consumer and Business Education Program educates consumers and businesses about consumer protection statutes and regulations and maintains a Web site at www.consumer.gov. The www.consumer.gov site attempts to provide a one-stop shop for consumer protection information.

The Division of Enforcement monitors business compliance with consumer protection laws, regulations, and court orders; conducts investigations; and institutes lawsuits when violations are found. A significant part of its workload involves the monitoring of e-commerce (Muris 2004, 8). The Division of Financial Practices is not specifically Internet-related, although the Internet can be a medium through which predatory and fraudulent lending take place. The Division of Marketing Practices pursues and shuts down scammers, including Internet scammers (Muris 2004, 11–13).

The Division of Planning and Information is, like the Consumer and Business Education Program, involved in consumer education and outreach. It operates a toll-free number, 1-877-FTC-HELP, to receive consumer complaints and provide information, and maintains a database of these complaints. It also operates the Identity Theft Data Clearinghouse, which provides information on how to avoid identity theft and counsels consumers on how to protect themselves from identity theft and how to respond if they become victims. The International Division of Consumer Protection negotiates consumer protection agreements with foreign governments and participates, along with similar agencies from more than twenty other countries, in the International Consumer Protection and Enforcement Network (Muris 2004, 15).

The FTC is also likely to be the federal agency charged with enforcement of antispyware laws when such legislation is enacted; one such law, the Securely Protect Yourself against Cyber Trespass Act, has passed the House and is currently before the Senate. The FTC has already taken action against spammers, although it has declined to create a probably futile "do not spam" registry.

Statutes and Proposed Legislation
- Children's Online Privacy Protection Act, 15 U.S.C. § 6501–6506
- Federal Trade Commission Act, 15 U.S.C. § 45
- Safeguard against Privacy Invasions Act, H.R. 2929, 108th Cong., 1st Sess. (2003), reported to and passed by House of Representatives as Securely Protect Yourself Against Cyber Trespass Act ("SPY ACT")

See also: Advertising; Adware and Spyware; Children's Online Privacy Protection Act; Federal Communications Commission; Identity Theft; Phishing; Spam

Sources and further reading:
Timothy J. Muris, Federal Trade Commission Chair, "Guide to the Federal Trade Commission," Apr. 2004, available at http://www.ftc.gov/bcp/conline/pubs/general/guidetoftc.htm

Paul M. Schwartz, "Property, Privacy, and Personal Data," 117 *Harvard Law Review* 2055 (2004).

❖ FILE-SHARING ❖

File-sharing is the sharing of files on one computer with other computers to which the computer is linked through some sort of network. Most file-sharing is routine and perfectly legal; however, one type of file-sharing that has created a great deal of controversy is the sharing of copyrighted information over the Internet. The term *file-sharing* is often used in intellectual property law to refer not to all file-sharing but to this particular type of file-sharing. A typical file-sharing network of this type consists of many users who do not know each other, making music files on their computers available for others to download, while also downloading music files from the computers of other users. Any type of information may be shared, but the exchange of compressed music files in the MP3 file format is the type of file-sharing that has aroused the most vehement industry response.

The legal problem created by this type of file-sharing is copyright infringement.

The power to grant and protect copyrights is granted to the federal government by article I, section 8, clause 8 of the U.S. Constitution (the Patent and Copyright Clause): "Congress shall have the power . . . To promote the Progress of Science and useful Arts, by securing for limited Times to Authors and Inventors the exclusive Right to their respective Writings and Discoveries[.]" Copyright is a private right; detection of and action against copyright infringement must be taken by the copyright holders or their agents, rather than by the state.

Liability for copyright infringement may be incurred in three ways: by direct infringement, by contributory infringement, or by vicarious infringement. The latter two categories are also referred to as third-party infringement.

Direct infringement requires the violation of a reserved use (typically unauthorized copying) of a work in which copyright is owned by another. Direct infringement is evaluated in accordance with a strict liability standard; in contrast to third-party infringement, there is no notice or knowledge requirement.

DOONESBURY © 2003 G. B. Trudeau. Reprinted with permission of UNIVERSAL PRESS SYNDICATE. All rights reserved.

Contributory infringement requires a direct infringement by someone else, actual or constructive knowledge of the violation, and a material contribution to the direct infringer's activities. Defining "material contribution" is a particular problem area, with various circuits setting varying standards. The Ninth Circuit Court of Appeals has set what may be the lowest standard: In *Fonovisa, Inc. v. Cherry Auction, Inc.* the Ninth Circuit held that merely providing facilities used in the infringement is a material contribution (76 F.3d 259). At the other end of the spectrum the Second Circuit Court of Appeals has set what is probably the highest standard: In *Gershwin Publishing Corporation v. Columbia Artists Management, Inc.* the Second Circuit held that substantial participation in the activity is required (443 F.2d 1159).

Vicarious infringement requires a direct infringement by someone else, the right and ability to control the infringer's actions, and a direct financial benefit from the infringing activity. The right and ability to control the infringer's actions may result from the continuing relationship between the parties or from the retention of a contractual ability to restrict the infringer's actions. The direct financial benefit from the infringing activity need not be actual payment; if the infringement brings in customers, it generates a financial benefit (*Fonovisa,* 76 F.3d 259).

Two lines of vicarious infringement cases establish the extremes between which the problem of file-sharing falls: The landlord-tenant cases and the dance hall cases. The landlord-tenant cases have held that a landlord who receives fixed rents from tenants regardless of the tenants' activities is not vicariously liable for the tenants' infringement. The dance hall cases, on the other hand, have held that a dance hall owner's relationship with persons hired to provide music to paying customers is analogous to an employer-employee relationship; the dance hall owner is vicariously liable for the musicians' infringement. File-sharing occupies the middle ground between these two lines of cases.

Fonovisa was a vicarious and contributory infringement case involving off-line rather than online pirating of copyrighted music. The defendant, Cherry Auction, was the host of a swap meet. Vendors, including music vendors, paid a daily rental fee to Cherry Auction. Cherry Auction supplied utilities, parking, advertising, plumbing, and customers; the customers paid a fee to Cherry Auction upon entrance to the premises. Cherry Auction knew that many of the vendors sold counterfeit music, infringing upon copyrights owned by the plaintiff, Fonovisa.

The Ninth Circuit held that Cherry Auction was liable for vicarious infringement because there was control and financial benefit. There was control because Cherry Auction could control admission and advertising and had contractually reserved the right to restrict market access and vendor behavior. And there was a financial benefit to Cherry Auction in the form of rental fees from vendors, admissions fees from customers, parking revenues, food sales, and other customer services. In addition, the availability of copyright-infringing materials probably enhanced the appeal of the swap meet to customers (*Fonovisa,* 76 F.3d 259).

Cherry Auction was also liable for contributory infringement because there was knowledge and material contribution. Cherry Auction had actual knowledge of the infringing activity and made a material contribution by providing the site and facilities for the sale of the unlawfully copied material. The court explained that express encouragement or protection of the identity of the infringers was not required (*Fonovisa*, 76 F.3d 259).

In addition to *Fonovisa*, another prequel to the file-sharing cases is *Sony Corp. of America v. Universal City Studios, Inc.* In 1984, when videocassette recorders (VCRs) were new, producers of television shows sought to have VCRs banned because they could be used to record copyrighted television shows. To this end Universal Studios, a content owner, brought suit against Sony, a manufacturer of VCRs. The Sony Betamax VCRs at issue in the case recorded one-hour tapes. The market for video rentals had not yet emerged, and home video camcorders were unknown. The expectation was that the recording function of the VCRs would be used mainly to record television programs.

The U.S. Supreme Court held that Sony was not contributorily liable for infringements committed with the VCRs it manufactured. There was no ongoing relationship between Sony and the end users; the relationship was limited to the sale itself, warranties notwithstanding. In addition, the VCRs were capable of "substantial noninfringing uses" and thus qualified as a "staple article of commerce." (This "staple article of commerce" doctrine applies only to contributory infringement, not to vicarious infringement.) The substantial noninfringing uses included time-shifting (recording programs to watch later), copying non-copyrighted works, and making authorized copies of copyrighted materials (*Sony*, 464 U.S. 417).

Liability for copyright infringement (direct, contributory, or vicarious) is always limited by the fair-use doctrine; the noninfringing uses of which the Sony Betamax VCRs were capable included fair uses of copyrighted material such as time-shifting. Four factors are applied to determine the fuzzy parameters of fair use: the nature of the use, especially whether it is personal or commercial; the nature of the protected work; the extent to which the work is copied; and the potential economic effect on the market (*Sony*, 464 U.S. 417; 17 U.S.C § 107).

The advent of the Internet led to disparate results among circuits regarding the liability of an online service provider for content made available on its servers. Congress addressed the disparity with the Digital Millennium Copyright Act (DMCA). Provisions of the DMCA relevant to file-sharing include the safe harbor provisions and the anticircumvention provisions (17 U.S.C. §§ 512, 1201).

Safe harbor provisions: The DMCA provides four types of safe harbor, two of which are relevant to file-sharing: the Transitory Digital Network Communications Safe Harbor and the Information Location Tools Safe Harbor. The Transitory Digital Network Communications Safe Harbor provides that a service provider is not liable simply because it transiently stores or transmits, routes, or provides connections for infringing material through a system or network it controls or operates, if:

1. Someone other than the service provider initiates transmission of the material;
2. The transmission, routing, provision of connections, or storage is carried out through an automatic technical process without selection of the material by the service provider;
3. The service provider does not select the recipients of the material except as an automatic response to the request of another person;
4. No copy of the material is maintained on the system or network in a manner ordinarily accessible to anyone other than anticipated recipients, or for longer than reasonably necessary; and
5. The material is transmitted through the system or network without modification of its content (17 U.S.C. § 512(a)).

The Information Location Tools Safe Harbor provides that a service provider is not liable simply because it refers or links users to an online location containing infringing content by using information location tools, including a directory, index, reference, pointer, or hypertext link, if it:

1. Does not actually know that the content is infringing, OR is not aware of facts or

circumstances from which the infringing content is apparent, OR upon obtaining such knowledge or awareness, acts expeditiously to remove or disable access to the infringing content, AND

2. Does not receive a financial benefit directly attributable to the infringing activity, in a case in which the service provider has the right and ability to control such activity, AND

3. Upon notification of claimed infringement acts expeditiously to remove or disable access to the infringing content (17 U.S.C. § 512(d)).

Notification must include identification of the reference or link that is to be removed or disabled and information reasonably sufficient to permit the service provider to locate that reference or link.

The safe harbor provisions protect a service provider even if the provider actually knows of the infringement, unless the service provider receives notice of the infringement from the copyright holder or the copyright holder's agent.

Anticircumvention provisions: The anticircumvention provisions of the Digital Millennium Copyright Act work independently of other copyright law protections. No direct or indirect copyright infringement is necessary for liability under the anticircumvention provisions, which prohibit:

1. Tampering with or attempting to circumvent a technological measure that effectively controls access to a copyrighted work;

2. Trafficking in any technology, product, service, device, component or part that is primarily designed or produced for the purpose of circumventing a [protected] technological protection measure (17 U.S.C. § 1201).

The DMCA's use of the word *effectively* calls the entire section into question, however: Some forms of "technological protection measures" can be circumvented with a black marker, or by holding down the "Shift" key. Most or even all measures can be circumvented, within days or weeks of their appearance in the marketplace,

by software that can be downloaded and used by even the most minimally technically savvy Internet user, often for free. It might be that such measures cannot be said to be "effective"; they create barriers to copying, but they are generally circumvented fairly easily by anyone with the patience and motivation to do so. But courts have held that a technological measure effectively controls access if its function is to control access, even if it can be circumvented. This "intent to control access" test seems perhaps broader than the congressional intent seen in the plain language of the statute, but Congress has not yet seen fit either to correct this interpretation or incorporate it into the text of the statute.

Two other important cases in the run-up to *Napster* were *Recording Industry Association of America v. Diamond Multimedia Systems, Inc.* and *UMG Recordings, Inc. v. MP3.com, Inc.* The defendant in the first of these, Diamond Multimedia, manufactured the Rio, the first commercially available MP3 player. MP3 files, previously playable by most users only on a computer, could now be transferred to the Rio and played anywhere. The Ninth Circuit Court of Appeals determined that this space-shifting was analogous to the time-shifting in *Sony* and was fair use. The Rio could be used to play music already owned and was thus capable of a substantial noninfringing use (*Diamond Multimedia*, 180 F.3d 1072).

The defendant in the second case, MP3.com, purchased CDs containing tens of thousands of copyrighted songs and placed these songs, as MP3 files, on its servers. It then made the songs on its servers available to subscribers who could demonstrate, by placing a recorded CD in the disk drive of their computers, that they owned, or at least had access to, a legitimate (licensed) copy of the copyrighted version of the material. The federal district court for the Southern District of New York found that MP3.com's use of its CDs exceeded the limits of fair use of copyrighted material (*MP3.com*, 92 F.Supp.2d 349).

Napster: On the heels of these two cases came the case that was to become copyright law's most celebrated file-sharing case, so far: *A&M Records v. Napster.* Napster was a hugely popular file-sharing service. Unlike MP3.com, which stored MP3 files on its own servers, Napster stored no MP3 files; thus Napster, again unlike MP3.com, was not a direct infringer. Instead, Napster's MusicShare software enabled peer-to-peer file-sharing. Files were traded directly between users without passing through Napster's computers. Napster did, however, maintain a central list of available songs; users wishing to download songs would locate them via Napster's list. This list, more than any other single factor, made it possible for A&M Records and others to sue Napster for contributory and vicarious infringement, and win.

The suit for contributory infringement required that there be an underlying direct infringement and that Napster materially contribute to and have actual or constructive knowledge of that direct infringement. The underlying direct infringement required for liability for contributory infringement was committed by Napster's users, many if not most of whom were direct infringers unprotected by the fair-use exception. Distribution of copies of copyrighted material to anonymous requesters, the Ninth Circuit held, is not a private, personal use. Transfer to unknown, anonymous persons is not mere time-shifting or space-shifting. Typically the entire work was copied, and distribution adversely affected the market for the songs; users received for free something they would ordinarily have to buy (*Napster, Inc.*, 239 F.3d 1004).

The material contribution was simple enough to establish, using the Ninth Circuit's "but for" test: but for Napster's provision of the list and the file-sharing software, the direct infringement would not have taken place, or would at least have been far more difficult. The "actual or constructive" knowledge element was a bit more difficult to establish. The Ninth Circuit in *Napster* interpreted *Sony* to mean that knowledge cannot be imputed where a product is capable of a substantial noninfringing use; evidence of *actual* knowledge of *specific* acts of infringement was required. This higher standard (actual rather than constructive knowledge) was met, though: An e-mail from Napster co-founder Sean Parker referred to the fact that Napster users were "exchanging pirated music," and Napster used screen shots showing copyrighted material to promote its service. The court stated that "the record supports the district court's finding that Napster has *actual* knowledge that *specific* infringing material is available using its system, that it could block access to the system by suppliers of the infringing material, and that it failed to remove the material" (*Napster, Inc.*, 239 F.3d at 1022).

The suit for vicarious infringement also required an underlying direct infringement. In addition, in order to be found vicariously liable, Napster must have had the right and ability to control the direct infringers' actions and must have received a direct financial benefit from the infringing activity. Napster met all of these requirements. There was direct infringement by Napster users. Napster had the right and ability to control the actions of these direct infringers, because Napster reserved the right to block access to the Napster Web site at its discretion. And Napster received a direct financial benefit in the form of an increased customer base, on which its future income depended (*Napster, Inc.*, 239 F.3d 1004).

File-sharing after Napster: At the heart of Napster's legal vulnerability was the list of available songs. This list, maintained on Napster's servers, involved Napster in the ongoing file-sharing activity. It gave Napster a financial benefit, by bringing customers to the site. It gave Napster control over the process. And it materially contributed to the process. Post-*Napster* file-sharing services have sought to avoid this vulnerability by decentralization. Two approaches to decentralization are supernode-based services and virtual private network (VPN)-based services.

Supernode: A "supernode" is an individual user's computer that maintains a list of files available for sharing over a file-sharing network. Supernode-based services are based on the Fast-Track program from Bluemoon Interactive, which allows these services to avoid the necessity of maintaining a centralized directory of available files. (The supernodes are not, except perhaps by coincidence, the same computers on which the files are available.) StreamCast Networks, KaZaA, and Grokster are supernode-based systems.

Virtual Private Network (VPN): A VPN piggybacks on an existing network using passwords, tunneling protocols, and encryption to create a virtual network inaccessible by unauthorized users from the larger network. In essence the VPN provides a web of "secret passages" through the main network.

The lack of centralization makes it more difficult for makers of file-sharing software, which is usually distributed for free, to make money. Some, such as KaZaA, make money by advertising generated on (or directed to) the user's computer by the software. Others are not seeking to make a profit, but create file-sharing networks for the sheer pleasure of doing so.

In response, the content industry, led by the Recording Industry Association of America (RIAA) has turned to self-help tactics such as spoofing and interdiction. "Spoofing" in an online file-sharing context is distributing fake or damaged copies of popular downloads, wasting users' time and bandwidth. The spoofed files can also contain admonitory messages, as the notorious Madonna files did. Interdiction is the repeated requesting of popular files that are then downloaded very slowly, thus making them inaccessible to others. Although the RIAA denies that interdiction is a denial-of-service (DOS) attack, the underlying principle is the same. Users, in turn, have developed software to detect RIAA spoofers and interdictors and bar them from P2P networks. The RIAA has also introduced legislation that would allow it to hack file-sharers' computers and delete any MP3s found; needless to say, this has provoked widespread public outcry. And, of course, the RIAA has continued to sue distributors of file-sharing software. Two important recent cases are *In re Aimster Copyright Litigation (Aimster II)* and *MGM Studios v. Grokster.*

Aimster: Aimster was a VPN-based file-sharing program that piggybacked on America Online's instant messaging system, AIM (thus the name). Aimster used encryption to prevent anyone other than the users from monitoring or discovering the contents of traded files. The first version of the software, Classic Aimster, identified, by default, all other Aimster users logged on to AIM as "buddies" and therefore members of the VPN. A later version, Club Aimster, charged a monthly fee and included a Web site that listed the forty most popular downloads and a one-click download option, eliminating the need for manual searching. The Club Aimster Web site also included a tutorial.

At trial, the federal district court for the Northern District of Illinois found Aimster contributorily and vicariously liable. Aimster did not contest the plaintiffs' contention that an underlying direct infringement had occurred (*Aimster II,* 252 F.Supp.2d 634).

Contributory infringement: The district court found Aimster contributorily liable. Aimster had actual or constructive knowledge of and materially contributed to its users' direct infringement. Various letters from the plaintiffs gave Aimster notice of the direct infringement. Also, the Club Aimster Web site identified and commented on copyrighted material. The court rejected the contention that Aimster could not know what was being traded because of encryption, because Aimster itself had made the encryption available and because specific knowledge of individual transfers was not required; the encryption did not prevent Aimster from having constructive knowledge of the direct infringement (*Aimster II,* 252 F.Supp.2d 634). Note that this arguably differs from the Ninth Circuit's interpretation of *Sony* as stated in *Napster;* however, the Northern District of Illinois lies in the Seventh Circuit and is not bound by the precedent of the Ninth Circuit.

In addition, Aimster materially contributed to the infringement by providing software and services that enabled users to connect with each other. The Club Aimster Web site also ranked songs and enticed would-be infringers, and Aimster's one-click download service made infringement easier for its users (*Aimster II,* 252 F.Supp.2d 634).

The district court also reasoned (incorrectly, as it turned out) that the staple article of commerce doctrine applied to the VCRs in *Sony* was inapplicable to Aimster. In the district court's view, Aimster was not an "article of commerce"; it was not a discrete product, but a bundle of services. The mere assertion that Aimster was capable of substantial noninfringing uses, in the absence of supporting evidence that those uses were actually being made of Aimster, was insufficient. And unlike the relationship between Sony and the VCR purchasers, the relationship between Aimster users and Aimster was ongoing. In addition, the Aimster users' activities were not private; each became a global distributor of music (*Aimster II,* 252 F.Supp.2d 634).

Although the federal Court of Appeals for the Seventh Circuit also found Aimster contributorily liable for its users' direct infringements, it rejected the district court's reasoning regarding the "staple article of commerce doctrine" and held that the doctrine was potentially applicable. The Seventh Circuit stated that the doctrine is not categorically inapplicable to services and that the Supreme Court's concern in *Sony* was to avoid granting copyright holders an undue degree of control over technology. File-sharing and instant messaging, the Seventh Circuit pointed out, are valuable technologies. And the ongoing relationship between Aimster and its users did not automatically render the doctrine inapplicable; what was at issue was the ability of a service provider or product manufacturer to affect the ability of the end users to infringe. However, although the staple article of commerce doctrine was potentially applicable, Aimster had not met its burden of showing that its service fell within the scope of the doctrine. If Aimster had met this burden and if the infringing use was also substantial, the Seventh Circuit would then have required a showing that reducing or eliminating the infringing use would be disproportionately costly (*Aimster II,* 334 F.3d 643).

Vicarious infringement: The district court found that Aimster had the right and ability to control the infringers' actions and that Aimster received a direct financial benefit from the directly infringing activity; thus Aimster was vicariously liable. The appellate court did not address the issue of vicarious liability; it neither affirmed nor reversed the trial court's findings on this issue. It said that it was "less confident" that the plaintiffs would prevail on the merits of the vicarious liability claim than on the merits of the contributory liability claim.

According to the trial court, Aimster met the first of the requirements for vicarious liability because it contractually retained the right to terminate individual users and to take down infringing works. The use of a user name and password to log on to the Club Aimster site was a further measure of control; the fact that communications were encrypted did not mean that Aimster lacked control over the users. In addition, there was a financial benefit because Club Aimster required payment of a monthly fee, because Aimster solicited donations for legal fees on its Web site, and because the infringing activities attracted customers.

The court also evaluated the applicability of the safe harbor provisions to Aimster. It found that Aimster met the threshold requirement: It was a service provider within the meaning of the DMCA. However, Aimster was ineligible for either the Transitory Digital Network Communications Safe Harbor or the Information Location Tools Safe Harbor because it had not implemented a policy to bar repeat copyright infringers.

(Although a policy existed, Aimster stated that it could not implement it because of the encryption.) Although Aimster stated that it would respond to notice of infringement, the court stated that a provider may not willfully create an encryption scheme hiding the information sought and then claim ignorance.

In addition, the Transitory Digital Network Communications Safe Harbor was inapplicable because it applies to materials traveling through a provider's system, and no materials were exchanged through Aimster's system. And the Information Location Tools Safe Harbor is inapplicable to a party who knows of the infringing material or activity or receives a financial benefit therefrom; Aimster was disqualified on both counts (*Aimster II,* 252 F.Supp.2d 634).

In January 2004 the U.S. Supreme Court rejected Aimster owner John Deep's petition for certiorari, declining to review the Seventh Circuit's decision (*Deep,* 124 S. Ct. 1069).

The *Grokster* case: Grokster is a FastTrack (supernode)-based file-sharing system. Launching the Grokster software on a computer connected to the Internet automatically connects the user to the Grokster P2P network. Some users of Grokster have committed direct copyright infringement by using the software to share copyrighted material with large numbers of fellow users unknown to them. In October 2001 Metro-Goldwyn-Mayer (MGM), a content owner, and others brought suit against Grokster for contributory and vicarious infringement.

Contributory infringement: Although there was an underlying direct infringement, the trial court (the federal district court for the Central District of California) found Grokster not liable for contributory infringement because neither the knowledge element nor the material contribution element was met. The trial

File-sharing update: On June 27, 2005, the U.S. Supreme Court reversed the Ninth Circuit's decision (and thus the district court's decision as well) in *MGM v. Grokster.* The reversal was on fairly narrow grounds and left intact the "staple article of commerce" doctrine in the Sony Betamax case; the Court did not say that file-sharing networks are necessarily illegal. It did, however, say that Grokster and co-defendant StreamCast could be liable for encouraging users to infringe copyrights: An "affirmative intent that the product be used to infringe, and a showing that infringement was encouraged overcomes the law's reluctance to find liability when a defendant merely sells a commercial product suitable for some lawful use[.]" This intent can be shown by "Evidence of 'active steps . . . taken to encourage direct infringement'[.]" The court found that MGM had introduced or alleged such evidence; among other points, the mere act of soliciting ex-Napster users might show an intent that the service be used to infringe. The question of what weight and validity to accord the evidence was one for a trial court, not an appellate court, and the Supreme Court thus remanded the case to the district court for further proceedings.

The Supreme Court's decision was a loss for the defendants, Grokster and StreamCast. In a trial applying the definitions set out by the Supreme Court, they are unlikely to prevail. This may not matter all that much to these and other file-sharing networks that have no real need for a corporate presence or assets in the United States; they can continue to operate from outside the U.S. The decision was also a loss for the technology industry as a whole, however. A great many devices and programs, from cell-phone cameras to card reader drivers, can conceivably be used to violate copyrights. The Supreme Court's decision increases the level of legal risk for innovative technology firms; too much risk may decrease the level of innovation or drive the innovators out of the U.S.

Source

Metro-Goldwyn-Mayer Studios Inc. v. Grokster, Ltd., 125 S. Ct. 2764 (2005), available at http://www.supremecourtus.gov/opinions/04slipopinion.html (visited July 8, 2005).

court (Central District of California) is located within the Ninth Circuit. Like the Ninth Circuit in *Napster* (and unlike the Northern District of Illinois in *Aimster*) it applied a high standard to the "knowledge" element: Grokster had to have had "actual knowledge of infringement at a time when [it could] use that knowledge to stop the particular infringement. In other words, Plaintiffs' notices of infringing conduct are irrelevant if they arrive when Defendants do nothing to facilitate, and cannot do anything to stop, the alleged infringement." The fact that Grokster marketed itself as "the next Napster" and knew that its software was being used for copyright infringement did not mean that Grokster knew of any *specific* infringement at a time when it could prevent the infringement.

The "material contribution" element was not met, either. Grokster originally had control over a root supernode, but by the time of the litigation no longer had such control. At the time of the litigation, searches and downloads were taking place without any information being transferred to or through any computers owned by Grokster. Grokster's contribution to the network was the provision of the software; Grokster was not capable of shutting down the P2P network. This was analogous to the provision of a VCR; the plaintiffs did not introduce "evidence of [Grokster's] active and substantial contribution to the infringement itself." Thus, Grokster was not liable for contributory infringement (*Grokster,* 259 F.Supp.2d 1029).

Vicarious infringement: The district court found Grokster not liable for vicarious infringement, either, even though there was an underlying direct infringement and the "direct financial benefit" element was met, because Grokster did not have the right and ability to control the direct infringers' actions. "Direct financial benefit" was defined quite broadly: The district court stated that "because a substantial number of users download the software to acquire copyrighted material, a significant proportion of [Grokster's] advertising revenue depends upon the infringement. [Grokster] thus derive[s] a financial benefit from the infringement" (*Grokster,* 259 F.Supp.2d at 1044).

Unlike Napster, though, Grokster lacked the right and ability to control its users' access to the file-sharing network. Its software included filters, but the difference between the Napster system architecture (with all searches going through a central server) and the decentralized Grokster architecture meant that there was no obligation on the part of Grokster to police the users' conduct, just as there was no obligation on the part of Sony to police the conduct of those who purchased its VCRs.

After Grokster: The *Grokster* court concluded that it was "not blind to the possibility that Defendants may have intentionally structured their businesses to avoid secondary liability for copyright infringement, while benefiting financially from the illicit draw of their wares." But, the court pointed out, the proper remedy lay with Congress rather than with the judiciary (*Grokster,* 259 F.Supp.2d at 1045).

Aimster II and *Grokster* show a possible split between the Seventh and Ninth Circuits on the "knowledge" element of contributory liability. Contributory and vicarious liability are not creatures of statute but of case law. *Grokster* follows the reasoning of the Ninth Circuit in *Napster* requiring "evidence of actual knowledge of specific acts of infringement." *Aimster*'s holding that constructive knowledge is sufficient follows another line of cases, including cases from the Second and Eleventh Circuits. However, *UMG Recordings, Inc. v. Sinnott,* another recent case from a district court within the Ninth Circuit, pointed out that the requirement of actual knowledge of a specific violation is strictly limited to cases involving Grokster-like (decentralized, noncontrolled) online services (*Sinnott,* 300 F.Supp.2d 993). The defendant in *Sinnott,* like Cherry Auction (the defendant in *Fonovisa*), was the operator of a real-world flea market at which unauthorized copies of copyrighted music were exchanged. Like Cherry Auction or Napster, Sinnott had the power to stop the infringing activity at any time after he became aware of it; Grokster, once it had distributed its software, could no longer control the uses of the software.

The *Grokster* and *Aimster II* courts seem to be in agreement on vicarious liability. The results reached in the two cases were different, but the most important factor leading to the different outcomes appears to be not a differing interpretation of the "knowledge" requirement but the existence of Club Aimster. Club Aimster gave Aimster a measure of control that Grokster lacked.

In both cases financial benefit was defined broadly; *Grokster* requires the broader definition, but it does not appear to be inconsistent with *Aimster* on this element.

Even with the Seventh Circuit's "constructive knowledge" approach, a Grokster-type file-sharing program might not provide a basis for contributory infringement. The point at which Grokster has the power to stop infringement is at the outset, when it distributes the software. It would have to have constructive knowledge that a particular user who downloads the software plans to use it for copyright infringement rather than for some noninfringing use, and it would have to have that knowledge at the time the prospective user seeks to download the software. Even if Grokster has this knowledge, the absence of a Club Aimster–like service means that Grokster makes no material contribution to the file-sharing process. Once the software is distributed, the P2P network functions without further input from Grokster.

Because there is no centralized service, Grokster retains no right or ability to control access to the P2P network. Thus, there would be no vicarious infringement under the Seventh Circuit's approach, either.

Anticircumvention actions: File-sharing software does not break copy protection. But it can enable trading of copies of copy-protected works on which the copy protection has already been broken. That is, one skillful user can break the copy protection and then share the unprotected copy with less skillful users.

RIAA suits against individual users: In addition to suing file-sharing services, the RIAA has filed thousands of suits against individual file-sharers. This has been the most controversial tactic in the RIAA's campaign to defend music copyrights. Among the first defendants was twelve-year-old Brianna LaHara, who lived with her mother in public housing in New York City. Brianna said, "I thought it was OK to download music because my mom paid a service fee for it." (Her mother had paid a fee to KaZaA.) (Younge 2003). Another of the first defendants was seventy-one-year-old Durwood Pickle of Richardson, Texas, whose visiting teenage grandchildren allegedly downloaded music to his computer. Widespread media coverage, including Internet coverage, of the suits was largely unfavorable to the RIAA. Brianna La-Hara and Durwood Pickle were portrayed as victims. The individual user suits have increased hostility toward the RIAA; it remains to be seen whether the RIAA's gains from this strategy will outweigh the public relations harm.

The RIAA has also met resistance from service providers who put their users' privacy interests ahead of the RIAA's copyright interests. In December 2003 the federal appellate court for the District of Columbia agreed with Verizon Internet Services that Verizon did not have to turn over the name of a subscriber who had allegedly shared copyrighted music files (*Verizon*, 351 F.3d 1229). The RIAA had previously obtained a subpoena issued pursuant to Title I of the Digital Millennium Copyright Act (DMCA). The D.C. Circuit's decision reversed the decision of the district court for the District of Columbia, which had ordered Verizon to identify the subscriber (*Verizon*, 240 F.Supp.2d 24). As a result, the RIAA must now bring suit against file-sharing defendants as "John Does" first, and then obtain a subpoena. A subpoena of this sort is harder to obtain than a DMCA subpoena and requires judicial oversight to prevent abuses. The Circuit Court's opinion distinguished between conduit Internet service providers (ISPs), which are not subject to a DMCA subpoena, and hosting ISPs, which may be.

The music content industry's business model—bundling songs in albums—will have to change to adapt to the Internet. Neither bundling nor recording on a physical medium is now necessary. Musicians can sell their works directly to the public over the Internet, without the need of any intermediary, through services such as Apple's iTunes; they can still receive payment for their intellectual property rights in the recording. Musicians who do this may retain a higher proportion of the total sales revenue. Without bundling, consumers with a set amount of money to spend can buy more of the songs they want and avoid having to buy songs they do not want. Total revenue will remain the same, musicians may receive a higher percentage of the proceeds, and consumers will be happier.

There are signs, though, that the industry is beginning to adapt, perhaps adopting a solution along the lines of the Voluntary Collective License proposed by the Electronic Frontier Foundation, an activist group (Electronic Frontier Foundation 2004). Vivendi's Universal Music Group has reportedly agreed to license its music copyright inventory to Snocap, run by Napster founder Shawn Fanning, and Sony-BMG is reportedly negotiating to license its inventory to Grokster (*Economist* 2004). Under such an agreement the file-sharing services might agree to pay the music companies either a per-song or flat licensing fee, which would then be passed along to customers as part of the cost of the software license. Consumers are already willing to pay fees for upgraded versions of file-sharing software in order to avoid adware and pop-ups; presumably they—and the file-sharing networks—would also be willing to pay a reasonable fee to avoid the risk of record-company lawsuits.

Other segments of the content industry are less threatened by file-sharing. Other forms of copyrighted material are not shared over the Internet to the same extent that MP3 files are.

Books: Books are not greatly threatened by the Internet. Even though an entire book will fit in a quite small file, few people want to read a book on a computer or E-book readers. Part of the appeal of a book is that the information in it can be accessed without mechanical assistance; it can be carried anywhere, requires no batteries, and can still be read even after being dropped on the floor. Technology (e-paper, perhaps) that can provide these advantages has not yet reached the marketplace.

A downloaded book can be printed, but the cost of printing usually exceeds the cost of the published version, which will also be bound and will probably be of higher quality. Occasional high-demand items—the latest Harry Potter book, for example— may be pirated before they become available in stores, but piracy of this sort seems likely to remain rare.

Reference works are more threatened because they are rarely read in their entirety. Most users read only one recipe or one encyclopedia entry at a time, or look up only one word in a dictionary. High-cost reference works such as the *Oxford English Dictionary* have addressed this problem both legally and economically. A legal approach is the inclusion of copy protection on software versions of the work. The presence of the copy-protection software not only increases the difficulty of copying the work, but perhaps more importantly triggers the anticircumvention provision of the DMCA. An economic, market-based approach is to offer the work online, with frequent enhancements and updates, by subscription.

Movies: At this point even compressed versions of a two-hour movie are too large to be worth the effort of downloading for most users. That could change in the future, though, and the movie industry is alarmed by the prospect of widespread movie file-sharing. The movie studios are in a more secure position than the recording industry, however, for several reasons: Movies are not bundled; the consumer is not forced to buy unwanted movies along with the desired one. Movies recorded on DVD or videotape are relatively cheap when compared with music; a movie may cost a thousand times as much to make as a record album, and be recorded on media costing ten times as much, yet it sells for about the same price. And instead of seconds or minutes as with MP3 files, DVD-quality movie files can take hours to download. In addition, DVD-quality movie files are too large to allow more than a couple of dozen movies to be stored conveniently on most home computers; they must be recorded onto external media, especially if they are to be played on a DVD player. Recordable DVD media are more expensive than recordable CD media, and each disk will hold at most a single movie; a single CD can hold more than a hundred high-quality MP3 recordings. The cost of external media for recording songs is negligible—perhaps a tenth of a cent per song. The cost of external media for movies is considerable—perhaps as much as a dollar per movie.

Movie DVDs typically fill the otherwise unused space on the disk with additional content such as alternate language tracks, deleted scenes, cast interviews, and games. And almost all movies on DVD contain copy protection, circumvention of which would violate the DMCA. Most music recordings currently in existence do not contain this protection. Those who circumvent this copy protection expose themselves to liability and legal penalties for violation of the anticircumvention provisions of Title I of the DMCA in addition to any liability or penalties for the underlying copyright infringement itself.

Motion picture studios, unlike record companies, are creators and producers of content, not merely distributors, and they have not yet alienated their customer base. With current technology, at least, movies seem to be less endangered by file-sharing than popular music, although perhaps more endangered than books.

Statutes
- Audio Home Recording Act of 1992, Pub.L. 102-563, § 1, Oct. 28, 1992, 106 Stat. 4237, amending 17 U.S.C. §§ 101, 801, 803, 912, and 19 U.S.C.A. § 1337
- Copyright Act of 1976, 17 U.S.C. §§ 101–1332
- Digital Millennium Copyright Act, 17 U.S.C. §§ 512, 1201

Cases
Supreme Court
- *Sony Corp. of America v. Universal City Studios, Inc.,* 464 U.S. 417 (1984)

Federal Appellate Courts
- *A&M Records, Inc. v. Napster, Inc.,* 239 F.3d 1004 (9th Cir. 2001)
- *Fonovisa, Inc. v. Cherry Auction, Inc.,* 76 F.3d 259 (9th Cir. 1996)
- *Gershwin Publishing Corporation v. Columbia Artists Management, Inc.,* 443 F.2d 1159 (2d Cir. 1971)
- *In re Aimster Copyright Litigation (Aimster II),* 252 F.Supp.2d 634 (N.D. Ill. 2002); affirmed in part, 334 F.3d 643 (7th Cir. 2003); certiorari denied sub nom *Deep v. Recording Industry Ass'n of America, Inc.,* 124 S. Ct. 1069 (2004)
- *Recording Industry Association of America v. Diamond Multimedia*

Systems, Inc., 180 F.3d 1072 (9th Cir. 1999)

- *Recording Industry Association of America, Inc. v. Verizon Internet Services,* 240 F.Supp.2d 24 (D.D.C. 2003); reversed, 351 F.3d 1229 (D.C. Cir. 2003); certiorari denied, 125 S.Ct. 309 and 125 S. Ct. 347 (2004)

Federal Trial Courts
- *MGM Studios, Inc. v. Grokster, Ltd.,* 259 F.Supp.2d 1029 (C.D. Cal. 2003), affirmed, 380 F.3d 1154 (2004)
- *Religious Technology Center v. Netcom On-Line Communication Services, Inc.,* 907 F.Supp. 1361 (N.D. Cal. 1995)
- *UMG Recordings, Inc. v. MP3.com, Inc.,* 92 F.Supp.2d 349 (S.D. N.Y. 2000)
- *UMG Recordings, Inc. v. Sinnott,* 300 F.Supp.2d 993 (E.D. Cal. 2004)

See also: Abandonware; Content Industry; Copyright; Copyright Infringement; Digital Audio Works; Digital Millennium Copyright Act, Title I; Digital Millennium Copyright Act, Title II; Encryption; Fair Use (Copyright); Internet Service Providers; KaZaA; MP3; No Electronic Theft Act; P2P; Piracy; Voluntary Collective License; Warez

Sources and further reading:
Abou, Telechargez *vos DIVX et MP3 avec KaZaA et eDonkey* (Paris: Micro Application, 2003)(in French).

Michael Albert and Lisa Vertinsky, "From Sony to Napster—and Back? Copyright Law Implications of Decentralized File-Sharing Technology," *Boston Bar Journal,* Jan./Feb. 2004, at 10.

John Alderman and Evan I. Schwartz, *Sonic Boom* (Boulder, CO: Perseus, 2002).

Michel Barreau, *KaZaA, iMesh, eDonkey et tous les autres* (Paris: CampusPress, 2003)(in French).

Fritz Effenberger, *Clever tauschen mit KaZaA und Co.* (Poing: Franzis, 2003)(in German).

Electronic Frontier Foundation, *A Better Way Forward: Voluntary Collective Licensing of Music File Sharing,* "Let the Music Play" White Paper, Feb. 2004, available from http://www.eff.org/share/collective_lic_wp.php (PDF download) (visited November 16, 2004).

"Face Value: The Quiet Iconoclast—With KaZaA, Niklas Zennstrom Undermined the Music Industry," *The Economist,* July 3, 2004, at 54.

Sheila M. Heidmiller, "RIAA's Latest Attack on P2P File-Sharing," *Intellectual Property Law Newsletter,* Summer, 2003, at 10.

"I Want My P2P: Record Labels Are Trying to Do Deals with File-Sharing Networks," *The Economist,* Nov. 20, 2004, at 65.

Jupiter Research Corporation, *File Sharing and the DMCA* [e-book] (MarketResearch.com, 2001).

Joseph Menn, *All the Rave: The Rise and Fall of Shawn Fanning's Napster* (New York: Crown Business, 2003).

Trevor Merriden, *Irresistible Forces: The Business Legacy of Napster and the Growth of the Underground Internet* (New York: John Wiley and Sons, 2002).

Seagrumn Smith, "From Napster to KaZaA: The Battle over Peer-to-Peer Filesharing Goes International," 2003 *Duke Law and Technology Review* 8 (2003).

Gary Younge, "US Music Industry Sues 261 for Online Song Copying," *The Guardian,* Sept. 10, 2003, available at http://www.guardian.co.uk/online/news/0,12597,1038979,00.html (visited November 19, 2004).

❖ FILE WRAPPER ESTOPPEL ❖

See Prosecution History Estoppel

❖ FIREWALL ❖

A firewall is a hardware device or software program that can insulate a computer or network from some or all communications with computers on the other side of the firewall. Firewalls are used to prevent the intrusion of hackers, spyware, Trojans, and other dangers, and to prevent any spyware or Trojans that have been installed from reporting back to the outside world. Completely severing all communications links between the computer or network and the outside world is an effective way of insulating it from the outside world, but rarely practical. Instead, firewalls are designed to be partially permeable, so that authorized programs can pass information through the firewall while unauthorized programs are blocked (Curtin and Ranum 2004).

A personal firewall protects a single computer; a network firewall protects a network of computers. The personal firewall is usually a software program, but can also be a hardware device. The network firewall is usually a dedicated hardware device running a firewall program. When the term *firewall* is used generically by information systems professionals, it generally refers to a network firewall. On the smallest scale, most routers for home networks include a hardware firewall; this protects the home network, usually consisting of no more than half a dozen computers. Much larger firewalls exist, of course; some governments have even attempted, with some success, to create firewalls for entire countries (Yu 2002). These national firewalls have been used for censorship as well as security; in Saudi Arabia, for example, a national firewall prevents access to sites not approved by the national government (Sussman 2001, 3). The United Arab Emirates (UAE) achieves the same result through the use of a national proxy server; users connect not to the global Internet but to the proxy server, through which all traffic to and from the UAE must run (Sussman 2001, 3). Although the use of firewalls in this manner has provoked some protests from free-speech advocates, firewalls are viewed mostly as a useful security tool for defending against hackers, spyware, and other Internet pests.

Sources and further reading:
Matt Curtin and Marcus J. Ranum, "Firewalls FAQ," http://www.faqs.org/faqs/firewalls-faq/ (visited October 15, 2004).
Stephen Northcutt et al., *Inside Network Perimeter Security: The Definitive Guide to Firewalls, Virtual Private Networks (VPNs), Routers, and Intrusion Detection Systems* (Indianapolis, IN: New Riders, 2002).
Leonard R. Sussman, "The Internet in Flux, in Freedom House, How Free?: The Web and the Press: The Annual Survey of Press Freedom" 4 (2001), available from www.freedomhouse.org/pfs2001/pfs2001.pdf (visited October 15, 2004).
Peter K. Yu, "Introduction to Symposium on Bridging the Digital Divide: Equality in the Information Age," 20 *Cardozo Arts and Entertainment Law* 1 (2002).

❖ FIRST AMENDMENT ❖

First Amendment issues are an inevitable consequence of the nature of the Internet. The Internet is a vehicle for information; it contains the sum of the expression of all of the individuals and groups who publish Web sites or post information on them, who send e-mail or post to newsgroups, or who otherwise provide content that is made available to others. The First Amendment to the Constitution of the United States provides that "Congress shall make no law . . . abridging the freedom of speech, or of the press; or the right of the people peaceably to assemble, and to petition the Government for a redress of grievances." The Fourteenth Amendment extends this prohibition to the governments of the states, as well, as has been explained in numerous Supreme Court decisions. It is also solidly established that "speech" and "press" are not narrow definitions; the First Amendment applies not only to the spoken and written word, but to expressive conduct. The four protected categories of speech, press, assembly, and petition are generally referred to jointly under the heading "freedom of expression," although there are, or historically have been, subtle differences in the treatment of the four.

The First Amendment regulates the actions of government and not ordinarily of individuals or private entities. Private actions may be constructively considered "state action," however, if they meet one of three tests: the exclusive public function test, the state-assisted action test, or the joint participant test. A private entity that has exercised powers that are traditionally the exclusive prerogative of the state meets the exclusive public function test. A private entity that has acted with the help of or in concert with state officials may meet the state-assisted action test. And when the state has insinuated itself so far into a position of interdependence with the private entity that it must be recognized as a joint participant in the challenged activity, the joint participant test is met. Note that

"Freedom of the press is guaranteed only to those who own one."

—A. J. Liebling

In 1960, when Mr. Liebling published his oft-misquoted sentence in the *New Yorker,* it could only be taken in the cynical spirit in which it was intended. Today blogging makes everyone with Internet access the owner of a press—and some bloggers have run into trouble because of the content of their blogs. Typically this trouble comes not in the form of traditional censorship, however. Delta Airlines flight attendant Ellen Simonetti created a personal blog, *Diary of a Flight Attendant,* that included photos of herself posing in airplanes in her Delta uniform, without showing the Delta insignia; Delta apparently objected to the use of its uniform and equipment and fired her in November 2004. She has since published a *Blogger's Bill of Rights* on her site (queenofsky.journalspace.com) and renamed her site *Diary of a Fired Flight Attendant.*

Has Ms. Simonetti been censored? Delta is not a state actor and can place conditions on the uses its employees make of its equipment. Whether Delta is within its rights to fire Ms. Simonetti is a question of employment law; the *Diary of a Fired Flight Attendant* includes information on that legal struggle.

A more difficult case is provided by the blog of Washingtonienne, a Capitol Hill staffer who maintained a lurid online journal. When Washingtonienne was discovered to be an employee of Republican Senator Mike DeWine, she was fired . . . but not, ostensibly, because of the content of her blog. She was fired for using Senate computers and work time to compile her blog. The moral for bloggers seems to be that if you can't afford to lose your day job, you should keep your employer and your blog as separate as possible.

Source

Diary of a Fired Flight Attendant, queenofsky.journalspace. com (visited January 6, 2005); Chris Taylor, "10 Things We Learned about Blogs," *Time,* Dec. 19, 2004, available at http://www.time.com/time/ personoftheyear/2004/poymoments.html (visited December 6, 2004);

Washintonienne Archive, http://washingtoniennearchive. blogspot.com/ (visited January 6, 2005).

only one, and not all three, of these requirements must be met to support a finding of state action subject to the First Amendment (*America Online,* 948 F.Supp. 456).

Even when state action exists, the First Amendment does not, as is sometimes believed, create a universal right for all people to say whatever they want, whenever they want, wherever they want. Some forums are entitled to a higher level of protection than others, as are some forms of expression. The government may ban expression in the schoolroom that it permits on the street corner; it may ban expression on broadcast television that it permits on cable television; it may ban expression on daytime television that it permits on late-night television. The Internet is accorded the highest level of First Amendment protection. Despite some superficial similarities between the Internet and broadcast media such as radio and television, the government does not have the censorship powers over the Internet that it does over broadcast media. The government does not allocate Web addresses or e-mail accounts as it does radio and television frequency; Internet communication more closely resembles the print media or an exchange of letters among individuals, both of which are also entitled to the highest level of protection.

Even in this highly protected forum, however, some government control is permitted by the First Amendment. Some types of expression, such as obscenity and child pornography, are not protected and may be prohibited by the government (*Miller,* 413 U.S. 15). Other types of expression may be subject to reasonable time, place, and manner restrictions if those restrictions are content-neutral, narrowly tailored to further an important or significant government interest, and do not unduly constrict the flow of free speech. Speech that proposes a commercial transaction may be subject to time, place, and manner restrictions and may be prohibited if it is untruthful, misleading, or deceptive or if its subject matter or presentation is illegal.

The government may issue other broad content-based prohibitions, but in a protected forum such as the Internet those prohibitions will be subject to strict constitutional scrutiny: They must be necessary to achieve a compelling state interest unrelated to the message being communicated. A government's interest in preventing a message from being heard is not in itself sufficient justification for restricting that message. And the means chosen to restrict the expression must be the least restrictive alternative available.

Speech or expression may constitute an element of certain torts or crimes. Speech in furtherance of a criminal conspiracy, or that solicits the commission of a crime by another, may itself be criminalized. Expression that harms another's reputation and meets certain other requirements may form the basis of a tort action for defamation or invasion of privacy. The copying of someone else's trademark or copyrighted material may give rise to an infringement action. In the latter examples the aggrieved party, rather than the state, will take action against the defamer or infringer, but the court will enforce a judgment if necessary; thus, there is state action. Computer programs that allow users to break the copy protection on commercial DVDs and other media are prohibited by the Digital Millennium Copyright Act, even though the programs are "expression." Expression such as shouting "Fire!" in a crowded theater or that is likely to lead to imminent violence (but is not otherwise criminal) may also be prohibited, although these seem unlikely to arise in an Internet context, where the communicating parties might be miles apart—perhaps even on different continents.

Expression that is indecent but not obscene is protected by the First Amendment, but may be subject to content-based restrictions. There is probably a compelling state interest, and certainly an important state interest, in preventing the dissemination of indecent, particularly pornographic, material to minors. The problem for Congress has been to design a ban that is the least restrictive means available, or a time, place, and manner restriction that is narrowly tailored, to further this interest. The first congressional attempt to do so, the Communications Decency Act of 1996, failed to meet these requirements and was declared unconstitutional by the Supreme Court. Congress's second at-

tempt, the Child Online Protection Act of 1998, has been declared unconstitutional by a federal appellate court and has recently been remanded for trial by the Supreme Court.

Spam, as noted, is commercial speech and may be subject to reasonable time, place, and manner restrictions. There is no First Amendment right to have e-mail delivered; an Internet service provider (ISP) may block mass-mailed messages even if it would be impermissible for the government to do so, because the ISP is not a state actor. The federal government probably also has considerable leeway to restrict spam under the First Amendment; its failure to do so probably stems not from any legislative timidity but from the technical difficulties of enforcing restrictions on spam, and from the fact that a great deal of spam originates outside the United States.

Statutes
- Child Online Protection Act, 47 U.S.C. § 231
- Communications Decency Act of 1996, Pub. L. No. 104-104, § 502, 1996 U.S.S.C.A.N. (110 Stat.) 56,133 (later codified at 47 U.S.C. § 223)

Cases
Supreme Court
- *Ashcroft v. American Civil Liberties Union*, 124 S. Ct. 2783 (2004)
- *Ashcroft v. Free Speech Coalition*, 535 U.S. 234 (2002)
- *Brandenburg v. Ohio*, 395 U.S. 444 (1969)
- *Miller v. California*, 413 U.S. 15 (1973)
- *Reno v. American Civil Liberties Union*, 521 U.S. 844 (1997)
- *United States v. American Library Association, Inc.*, 123 S. Ct. 2297 (2003)

Federal Trial Courts
- *America Online v. Cyber Promotions*, 948 F.Supp. 456 (E.D. Pa. 1996)
- *Mainstream Loudoun v. Board of Trustees of the Loudoun County Library*, 2 F.Supp.2d 783 (E.D. Va. 1998)

See also: Activism and Advocacy Groups; Censorship; Child Online Protection Act; Child Pornography; Children's Internet Protection Act; Communications Decency Act; Constitutional Law; Data Haven; Declaration of the Independence of Cyberspace; French Yahoo! Case; Indecency; Obscenity; Pornography; Spam

Sources and further reading:

Jerome A. Barron and C. Thomas Dienes, *Constitutional Law in a Nutshell* (St. Paul, MN: West, 2002).

Mike Godwin, *Cyber Rights: Defending Free Speech in the Digital Age* (Cambridge, MA: MIT Press, 2003).

Jeremy Lipschultz, *Free Expression in the Age of the Internet: Social and Legal Boundaries* (Boulder, CO: Perseus Books, 1999).

❖ FIRST SALE ❖

The first sale doctrine provides an exception to the exclusive right of a copyright owner to make and distribute copies of the copyrighted work. The doctrine provides that "the owner of a particular copy or phonorecord lawfully made under this title, or any person authorized by such owner, is entitled, without the authority of the copyright owner, to sell or otherwise dispose of the possession of that copy or phonorecord" (17 U.S.C. § 109(a)). In other words, once a lawfully made copy of a copyrighted work has been sold, it belongs to the buyer; the buyer can sell it, give it as a gift, throw it away, destroy it, or dispose of it in some other way. There are important rights the buyer does not gain, however: the rights of reproduction, adaptation, and display. The buyer does not gain the right to make copies of the work. The buyer of the printed script of a play does not gain the right to adapt the work or perform the play in public; those rights must be purchased or received separately. And the lawful purchaser of a lawfully recorded DVD does not gain the right to show (perform) that DVD in public. In addition, although the lawful buyer of an authorized copy gains the right to display that copy at the place where it is lo-

cated, the right does not extend to display at some remote location by means such as broadcast or the Internet.

The first sale doctrine is subject to exceptions of its own, and these exceptions have had a dramatic effect on the way computer software is marketed and distributed. Most significantly, the first sale doctrine applies only to sales, not to rentals. Computer software makers can thus retain greater control over the use of their products if they can structure the transaction with the consumer as a rental rather than as a sale.

The first sale rights apply only to purchasers of the work, not to renters:

> The privileges prescribed by subsections (a) and (c) do not, unless authorized by the copyright owner, extend to any person who has acquired possession of the copy or phonorecord from the copyright owner, by rental, lease, loan, or otherwise, without acquiring ownership of it. (17 U.S.C. § 109(d))

Another exception to the first sale doctrine covers "phonorecords"—sound recordings. The purchaser of a phonorecord does not gain the right to rent out that record commercially (17 U.S.C. § 109(b)). Section 109(b) was expanded by the 1990 Computer Software Rental Amendments Act to cover computer programs, but curiously, and despite intense lobbying by the movie industry, it does not cover video recordings.

The rental exception for computer software provides that:

> [U]nless authorized by . . . the owner of copyright in a computer program (including any tape, disk, or other medium embodying such program), [no] person in possession of a particular copy of a computer program . . . may, for the purposes of direct or indirect commercial advantage, dispose of, or authorize the disposal of, the possession of that . . . computer program . . . by rental, lease, or lending, or by any other act or practice in the nature of rental, lease, or lending. (17 U.S.C. § 109(b)(1)(A))

This exception prohibiting the rental of computer software even by the lawful buyer contains three exceptions of its own: for products containing computer programs, for video games, and for nonprofit schools and libraries. Products containing computer programs may be rented if the program itself is not the object of the rental:

> This subsection [109(b)(1)(A)] does not apply to –
> (i) a computer program which is embodied in a machine or product and which cannot be copied during the ordinary operation or use of the machine or product[.] (17 U.S.C. § 109(b)(1)(B)(i))

A car, for example, might contain many software programs: diagnostic programs, onboard navigation programs, noise-reduction programs for the stereo, a CSS decryption program for the DVD player, climate-control programs, antilock braking programs, and so forth. Yet although these programs may enhance the attractiveness of the rental car to prospective clients, it is not the programs they want to rent, but the car. Nor can the programs be copied during the ordinary operation of the car; few consumers would be able to copy the programs even if they wanted to.

The video games exception provides that

> This subsection [109(b)(1)(A)] does not apply to –
> ***
> (ii) a computer program embodied in or used in conjunction with a limited purpose computer that is designed for playing video games and may be designed for other purposes. (17 U.S.C. § 109(b)(1)(B)(ii))

The exception applies to arcade games rather than to video games for use on computers or home game systems; in addition to a rental right, the purchaser of the video game receives performance and display rights:

> [I]n the case of an electronic audiovisual game intended for use in coin-operated equipment, the owner of a particular copy of such a game lawfully made under this title, is entitled, without the authority of the copyright owner of the game, to publicly perform or display that game in coin-operated equipment[.] (17 U.S.C. § 109(e))

This statutory provision supersedes an earlier court decision holding that the sale of a video arcade game did not extinguish the seller's performance and display interests (*Red Baron*, 883 F.2d 275). Once again, there is an exception to the exception:

> [T]his subsection shall not apply to any work of authorship embodied in the audiovisual game if the copyright owner of the electronic audiovisual game is not also the copyright owner of the work of authorship. (17 U.S.C. § 109(e))

In other words, if the video game includes some other copyrighted work—a popular song, for example—purchase of the video game alone does not convey the performance right to the song; that must be conveyed separately.

The third exception to the prohibition on rentals of computer software under the first sale doctrine applies to nonprofit schools and libraries. Nonprofit schools are permitted to transfer lawful copies of computer programs to their own employees and students and to other nonprofit schools:

> The transfer of possession of a lawfully made copy of a computer program by a nonprofit educational institution to another nonprofit educational institution or to faculty, staff, and students does not constitute rental, lease, or lending for direct or indirect commercial purposes under this subsection. (17 U.S.C. § 109(b)(1)(A))

And nonprofit libraries are permitted to lend computer programs to the general public, provided that a copyright warning notice is attached:

> Nothing in this subsection shall apply to the lending of a computer program for nonprofit purposes by a nonprofit library, if each copy of a computer program which is lent by such library has affixed to the packaging containing the program a warning of copyright in accordance with requirements that the Register of Copyrights shall prescribe by regulation. (17 U.S.C. § 109(b)(2)(A))

The nature of computer programs is such that, when a consumer buys a program on disk, she will have to make at least one copy in order to run the program. Typically she will have to make two copies of at least portions of the program: one copy onto the computer's hard drive, and another into RAM (random access memory) when the program is run. The making of these copies is necessarily licensed, explicitly or implicitly, by the sale of the program, rather than permitted by the first sale doctrine.

Statute

- Copyright Act of 1976, Limitations on Exclusive Rights: Effect of Transfer of Particular Copy or Phonorecords, 17 U.S.C. § 109

Case

- *Red Baron-Franklin Park, Inc. v. Taito Corp.*, 883 F.2d 275 (4th Cir. 1989)

See also: Copyright; Copyright Infringement; Digital Millennium Copyright Act, Title I; Fair Use (Copyright); File-Sharing; WIPO Copyright Treaty; WIPO Performances and Phonograms Treaty

Sources and further reading:
G. M. Buechlein, "Burden and Sufficiency of Proof under First Sale Doctrine in Prosecution for Copyright Infringement," 94 *American Law Reports Federal* 101 (1989 and Supp. 2004).
Marshall Leaffer, *Understanding Copyright Law*, 3d ed. (New York: Matthew Bender, 1999).

❖ FREE SPEECH ❖

See First Amendment; Censorship

❖ FREEDOM OF EXPRESSION ❖

See First Amendment; Censorship

❖ FRENCH YAHOO! CASE ❖

The term *French Yahoo! case* refers to two related cases, one in France and one in the United States, arising from differences in French and U.S. law. Yahoo!, Inc. is a U.S. company with its headquarters in Santa Clara, California. Yahoo! offers a wide variety of Internet services, including an online auction service. Yahoo! auctions can be accessed from anywhere in the world, including France. During the 1990s some Yahoo! users offered Nazi memorabilia for sale on the Yahoo! auctions site; offering such memorabilia for sale is legal in the United States but illegal in France. Yahoo! itself was not a party to the transactions, but it made them possible, profited from them, and exhibited pictures of the merchandise offered for sale. This was sufficient to make them legally responsible for certain aspects of the transactions under both French and U.S. law.

The Yahoo! case in France: In 2000 two civil rights groups, the Ligue Contre le Racisme et L'Antisémitisme (League against Racism and Antisemitism, generally known by its French acronym LICRA) and the Union Des Étudiants Juifs De France (French Union of Jewish Students) sued Yahoo! in a French court, the Tribunal de Grande Instance de Paris. The plaintiffs claimed, correctly, that some of the goods offered for sale on the Yahoo! auction site could not be offered for sale in France without violating French law. On May 22, 2000, the French court ordered Yahoo! to block access by French citizens to the offending material and to post a warning to French citizens that searching the Yahoo! site might lead to prohibited material, which could in turn lead to criminal prosecution under French law. Yahoo! was given until July to demonstrate its compliance with the order. Yahoo! asked the French court to reconsider, explaining that complying with the order was technologically impossible. In the broadest sense this was true; there would be no possible way for Yahoo! to distinguish between a French citizen accessing its auction site from a computer in Manhattan and a U.S. citizen doing the same thing. But the French court was concerned with access from computers in France, and a panel of experts testified to the court that in fact approximately 70 percent of Internet addresses used by French users or users within France could be identified. An additional 20 percent of French users could be filtered out by a voluntary identification and registration scheme; in all, 90 percent compliance was possible—that is, Yahoo! could successfully block access to the prohibited material by 90 percent of French users (Solum and Chung 2004, 912).

The French court's reaffirmation of its order, and the reasoning accompanying it, sent tremors through the Internet world. The issue was far broader than France's ban on advertising Nazi memorabilia and propaganda; every Web site operator could conceivably be forced to design filters to comply with the laws of nearly two hundred sovereign nations and possibly of administrative subdivisions within those nations as well. Taken to its extreme, the French court's decision could prohibit all Internet speech that violated the law of any country; all Internet users would be held not to the standard of their own country, but to a composite standard forbidding all speech that was forbidden by any nation's law, and was thus far more restrictive than the law of any individual nation.

The Yahoo! case in the United States: Having failed in French court, Yahoo! filed suit against LICRA in a court in the United States, the federal district (trial) court for the Northern District of California. Yahoo! sought a declaratory judgment that the French court's order could not be enforced in the United States because enforcement would violate the First Amendment's guarantee of freedom of speech.

A jurisdictional issue arose: While Yahoo! had a substantial enough business presence in France, including many French users and a French-language site within the .fr (France) top-level domain, LICRA had no comparable presence in the United States. LICRA moved to dismiss the suit on the grounds that the federal court lacked jurisdiction over the organization; the court denied the motion, but its denial would later be reversed by the Ninth Circuit Court of Appeals.

The trial court went on to find that the French ban could not be enforced in U.S. courts. It began with the maxim that "No legal judgment has any effect, of its own force, beyond the limits of the sovereignty from which its authority is derived" (169 F.Supp.2d at 1192). Foreign judgments, the court pointed out, were enforced in the United States only on a basis of comity, or mutual respect by sovereign states of each other's sovereign acts. In addition, no foreign judgment would be enforced if it "violate[d] American public policy" or was "repugnant to fundamental notions of what is decent and just" in the United States. The French judgment failed this test. The court was careful to point out that the ban on advertising Nazi memorabilia and propaganda was within France's sovereign authority and that it was a perfectly reasonable restriction for France to impose, in light of its historical experience. However, the court was not concerned with the French government's undisputed authority to ban such conduct within France, but with the applicability of that ban to conduct in the United States. Applying the ban to a U.S. party violated the guarantee of freedom of expression in the First Amendment. In reaching this decision, the court followed precedents set in cases involving suits against U.S. parties for defamation allegedly committed in the United Kingdom. Because British laws impose liability for some statements that in the United States would be protected by the First Amendment, U.S. courts will not apply the British law in those situations (169 F.Supp. 1192–1193).

In addition to the jurisdiction and enforcement of judgment issues, the court was presented with a substantive choice of law issue: Should French or U.S. law be applied to the dispute? The court stated that "it must and will decide this case in accordance with the Constitution and laws of the United States" (169 F.Supp. 1187). Although this makes sense in a case where the conflict is between the foreign law and a provision of the United States Constitution, it would have been less convincing had the French law conflicted only with a U.S. statute, not with the Constitution.

Once the court had established that the First Amendment, not the French statute, was the applicable law, and that a foreign judgment could not be enforced if enforcement would violate the First Amendment, the conclusion was obvious: The French judgment could not be enforced against Yahoo! in the United States (169 F.Supp. 1194).

LICRA and the Union des Étudiants Juifs de France appealed, however. The appellate court focused not on the constitutional issue but on the narrow jurisdictional issue, and reversed the decision of the trial court. Because Yahoo! had brought the case in the United States without waiting for the French parties to bring an action in a U.S. court to enforce the French judgment, the French parties were the defendants in the action, not the plaintiff. The French parties had not purposely availed themselves of the U.S. forum. As a result, the court could only exercise jurisdiction over the French parties if California's long-arm statute permitted the exercise of jurisdiction and if the exercise of jurisdiction was constitutionally permissible. Even granting the former, jurisdiction could not constitutionally be exercised. LICRA and the Union des Étudiants Juifs de France had no connections to California other than those arising from the dispute. The French parties had done three things that could be considered contacts with the forum state, California: They had sent a cease-and-desist letter to Yahoo! in California; they had used the U.S. Marshals Service to serve process on Yahoo!; and they had asked the French court to require Yahoo! to remove listings of Nazi items from its Web site in California. Although the district court had found these three acts sufficient to satisfy the "minimum contacts" standard for the exercise of jurisdiction, the appellate court disagreed (379 F.3d 1124), on the grounds that the acts were not "wrongful conduct targeted at Yahoo!" (379 F.3d 1125). The appellate court seemed to recognize implicitly that, should the French parties bring suit to enforce the French judgment in a U.S. court, the First Amendment would bar enforcement; but, the court said, Yahoo! would have to wait until the French parties brought suit in the United States before raising the First Amendment claim. As the lower court had done, the appellate court pointed out that the French statute and the French court's decision were completely acceptable exercises of the sovereign authority of the French government within France; there was nothing wrongful about the French parties' pursuit of a remedy in French court under French law (379 F.3d 1126).

The aftermath of the Yahoo! case: The French Yahoo! case demonstrated the potential for differing applications of law regarding freedom of expression not only between countries with radically different approaches to expression, such as the United States and Saudi Arabia, but between countries with very similar approaches. France and the United States share a history of commitment to a particular concept of civil and political freedoms; the French and American revolutions shaped the concept of freedom of expression as it is generally applied in Europe and North America today. The concept of civil liberties in the two countries is the result not only of shared ideals, but of shared founders, including Thomas Jefferson and the Marquis de Lafayette.

The outcome of the two cases provides no satisfactory solution to the question of jurisdiction over Internet speech; jurisdiction can, at a minimum, be found where the speaker is located, and perhaps where the server storing the speech is located or where the damaging effects of the speech are felt. Internationally there is no uniformity of laws regarding jurisdiction, and further problems are likely to arise in the area of jurisdiction over Internet speech.

In the meantime, Yahoo! and other companies similarly situated have engaged in voluntary self-censorship. The list of "Items that are Prohibited by Yahoo!" in Yahoo's Auctions Guidelines now includes:

> Any item that promotes, glorifies, or is directly associated with groups or individuals known principally for hateful or violent positions or acts, such as Nazis or the Ku Klux Klan. Official government-issue stamps and coins are not prohibited under this policy. Expressive media, such as books and films, may be subject to more permissive standards as determined by Yahoo! in its sole discretion. (Yahoo! Auctions Guidelines 2004)

Although some free speech advocates have criticized Yahoo! for its policy, Yahoo! is not a state actor and its self-censorship raises no First Amendment concerns. If the policy is arbitrarily or unevenly enforced, however, it may give rise to lawsuits on other grounds. Other auction sites have adopted similar policies, and the search engine Google has blocked more than a hundred Internet sites containing Nazi or hate speech from its French and German versions (Solum and Chung 2004, 910).

Cases

- *Dow Jones & Co., Inc. v. Harrods, Ltd.*, 237 F.Supp.2d 394 (S.D. N.Y. 2002)
- *League against Racism and Antisemitism (LICRA), French Union of Jewish Students, v. Yahoo! Inc. (USA), Yahoo France,* Tribunal de Grande Instance de Paris, Interim Court Order, 20 Nov. 2000, available from http://www.gigalaw.com/library/france-yahoo–2000–11–20-lesecq.html (visited December 6, 2004)
- *Yahoo!, Inc. v. La Ligue Contre le Racisme et L'Antisemitisme,* 169 F.Supp.2d 1181 (N.D. Cal. 2001), reversed, 379 F.3d 1120 (9th Cir. 2004)

See also: Censorship; Choice of Law; First Amendment; Jurisdiction; Recognition and Enforcement of Judgments; Yahoo!

Sources and further reading:

Xavier Amadei, "Standards of Liability for Internet Service Providers: A Comparative Study of France and the United States with a Specific Focus on Copyright, Defamation and Illicit Content," 35 *Cornell International Law Journal* 189 (2001–2002).

Andreas Manolopoulos, "Raising 'Cyber-Borders': The Interaction Between Law and Technology," 11 *International Journal of Law and Information Technology* 40 (2003).

Lawrence B. Solum and Minn Chung, "The Layers Principle: Internet Architecture and the Law," 79 *Notre Dame Law Review* 815 (2004).

Richard S. Whitt, "A Horizontal Leap Forward: Formulating a New Communications Public Policy Framework Based on the Network Layers Model," 56 *Federal Communications Law Journal* 587 (2004).

Jonathan M. Winer, "If the U.S. Is from Mars and the EU Is from Venus, What Do You Do in Cyberspace?" *Privacy and Information Law Report,* Apr. 2001, at 8.

Yahoo! Auctions Guidelines, http://user.auctions.yahoo.com/html/guidelines.html (visited October 12, 2004).

G

❖ GAMBLING ❖

Among the most popular and controversial Internet businesses is gambling. Gambling is illegal or restricted in most of the United States, but there is little to stop individual users from sitting at home and gambling. In 2003, the value of the Internet gambling industry was estimated at $4.2 billion, with an annual growth rate of 20 percent; in comparison, the value of the legal offline gambling business in the United States was estimated at $50.9 billion (Gottfried 2004). More than half of the online gamblers were from the United States, perhaps because most U.S. states offer their citizens few opportunities for legal off-line gambling.

Online gambling is currently illegal in all fifty U.S. states, including Nevada (House Report 108-133 2003). As a result, online gambling sites operate outside the United States, beyond the reach of U.S. law. Considering the problems this situation presents, the Committee on Financial Services of the U.S. House of Representatives noted that these offshore sites "are not only vulnerable to criminal exploitation by money launderers; they also can easily abuse a customer's credit card information or manipulate the odds of a particular wager to the casino's advantage" (House Report 108-133 2003). In addition, off-line gambling is generally considered to represent a trade-off for the jurisdictions that legalize it: The social undesirability of gambling is generally taken as given and tolerated for the sake of the jobs and tax revenues it provides. Offshore Internet gambling operations provide none of these advantages, and they are not subject to the licensing and regulatory oversight that keeps legalized off-line gambling honest.

For some gamblers gambling is no more than a form of entertainment; for others it is an addiction. The use of credit cards and the ability to gamble in the privacy of one's home complicate the problem: Addicted gamblers can quietly run up debts to the maximum limit on all of their credit cards without anyone, even family members, being aware of what is happening until the bill arrives. Hockey player Jaromir Jagr's Internet gambling loss of $500,000 attracted national attention to the problem, but most online gamblers can be financially ruined by far smaller losses. Age verification is another problem; mere possession of a credit card number is not proof of adulthood, and some gambling sites have accepted bets from minors (House Report 108-133 2003).

Historically the regulation of gambling has been a matter left to the states; state levels of tolerance of gambling vary widely, so that Nevada, for example, allows most forms of gambling, subject to government regulation and licensing, while its neighbor Utah imposes a strict ban. Occasionally, however, a form of gambling arises that requires the states to seek federal assistance. Thus, in the nineteenth century, states found themselves unable to enforce state laws against mail-order lotteries originating in other states and outside the United States; Congress responded to state concerns with a series of laws culminating in the Federal Anti-Lottery Act, prohibiting the sending of gambling materials through the mails. In 1948 this prohibition was expanded to cover broadcast media, although an exception was later made for the

Antigua and Barbuda is one of the world's smallest countries, with a land area of only 171 square miles and a population of fewer than seventy thousand people. While the country is not poor, its 2002 gross domestic product totaled only $750 million—about one-sixth of the amount spent on online gambling in 2003. In such a small country, a single business can have a disproportionate effect. Antiguans are currently alarmed by a wealthy Texan immigrant's proposal to build a huge resort, at a cost of more than a billion dollars, on nearly 2 percent of the country's land area. The resort would provide jobs, but would also threaten coral reefs and mangroves. Online gambling, at least, does not harm the environment.

Source

"Antigua & Barbuda: Counting the Pennies," *The Economist,* Dec. 4, 2004, at 38; *World Almanac and Book of Facts 2005* (New York: World Almanac Books, 2005).

mailing and broadcasting of information relating to state-conducted lotteries. Although the Internet is not a broadcast medium, it does involve the transmission of information over wires and is thus within the scope of another federal antigambling statute, the 1961 Wire Act.

The various states have attempted to enforce their laws against online gambling through lawsuits. Because the online gambling Web site operators are generally beyond the reach of state attorneys general, the targets of these suits have often been credit card companies. New York State Attorney General Elliot Spitzer has been especially diligent in pursuing financial institutions that facilitate online gambling. In 2002 Spitzer's activities resulted in two major Internet financial service providers, Citibank and PayPal, prohibiting their services from being used to fund Internet gambling. In a settlement agreement in which it admitted no wrongdoing, Citibank agreed to stop allowing its cards to be used for Internet gambling; in doing so, it joined American Express, Bank of America, Chase Manhattan, Fleet, and MBNA. In February 2003 Spitzer's office reached similar settlements in which ten other banks agreed not to allow New York residents to use their cards for online gambling, and other credit card issuers have since followed suit on their own initiative. In August 2002 PayPal agreed, also without admitting wrongdoing, not to allow New York residents to use its services for online gambling. Two months later eBay acquired PayPal and expanded the Internet gambling ban to all PayPal users (Porter 2004, 16).

Actions by state attorneys general are a piecemeal approach to a nationwide problem, however. Like mail lotteries in the nineteenth century, Internet gambling is a nationwide problem that requires a nationwide solution. The United States cannot and should not do anything to regulate gambling operations in other countries aimed at citizens of those countries. When U.S. parties are involved, however, it can take action, as it did in *United States v. Cohen.*

In the late 1990s the FBI began investigating an offshore gambling operation run by Jay Cohen, a U.S. citizen. In 1996 Cohen had left the United States and moved to the Caribbean island nation of Antigua and Barbuda, where he opened an online gambling business. The business, World Sports Exchange (WSE) accepted wagers on U.S. sporting events; it had no other business. All of Cohen's partners in WSE were, like Cohen himself, citizens of the United States, and WSE accepted bets by telephone and Internet from the United States (*Cohen,* 260 F. 3d at 70). After undercover agents placed bets with WSE from New York, the FBI arrested Cohen and charged him with violation of the Wire Act. Cohen was convicted in the federal district court for the Southern District of New York, and his conviction was upheld on appeal.

An interesting feature of the Wire Act and similar laws is that they criminalize the use of interstate means of communication for acts in violation of *state* law. Conceivably, a state might decide to legalize Internet gambling; had WSE accepted bets from that state, it would have committed no violation of the Wire Act; acts that violate federal law in one state might not violate federal law in another.

Cohen was a U.S. citizen; had he been a foreigner who never set foot in the United States, it would have been difficult or impossible for the U.S. government to bring him to trial. Although individual prosecution of U.S. persons operating some of the world's two thousand or so sizeable online gambling operations might have some effect, the most likely result is that those persons will be driven out of the business and their places will be taken by non-U.S. persons. If, as it seems, the United States is committed to a policy of controlling and reducing online gambling, the logical point of attack is still the financial mechanisms that make it possible. Actions against banks that issue credit cards have produced results, but the number of banks is large. The number of credit card companies is small, but thus far litigation against them has been less successful: In 2001 a federal district court dismissed several actions against Visa and MasterCard that had been consolidated under the name *Mastercard International, Inc. Internet Gambling Litigation* (132 F.Supp.2d 468).

Several bills have been proposed in Congress to give the federal government a greater ability to control Internet gambling. Bills that would create a federal gambling law tend to be met with distrust from the states; a recent attempt, the Unlawful Internet Gambling Funding Prohibition Act, would make no changes in substantive gambling law but would strengthen the federal government's ability to attack the financial devices that enable illegal Internet gambling from within the United States. The act was passed by the House on June 10, 2003, and referred to the Senate on the following day. Meanwhile, the *Cohen* saga is not yet at an end; it has given rise to an international dispute between the United States and Antigua and Barbuda. Antigua and Barbuda hosts other Internet gambling businesses and feels that the Wire Act violates international law regarding trade in services. On November 10, 2004, a World Trade Organization (WTO) dispute resolution panel agreed, potentially making the United States subject to WTO sanctions; the United States plans to appeal the decision (*Economist* 2004).

Treaty

- General Agreement on Trade in Services, Marrakesh Agreement Establishing the World Trade Organization, Annex 1B, Apr. 15, 1994, 33 I.L.M. 1168 (1994)

Statutes and Proposed Legislation

- Federal Anti-Lottery Act, 18 U.S.C. §§ 1301–1304
- Wire Act, 18 U.S.C. § 1084
- Unlawful Internet Gambling Funding Prohibition Act, H.R. 2143, 108th Cong., 1st Sess. (2003)

Committee Report

- Report of the Committee on Financial Services on the Unlawful Internet Gambling Funding Prohibition Act, H.R. Rep. No. 133, 108th Cong., 1st Sess. (2003)

Cases

- *In re Mastercard International, Inc. Internet Gambling Litigation*, 132 F. Supp. 2d 468 (E.D. La. 2002)
- *United States v. Cohen*, 260 F.3d 68 (2d Cir. 2001)

See also: E-commerce; Enforcement

Sources and further reading:

Jack L. Goldsmith, "What Internet Gambling Legislation Teaches about Internet Regulation," 32 *International Lawyer* 1115 (1998).

Jonathan Gottfried, "The Federal Framework for Internet Gambling," 10 *Richmond Journal of Law and Technology* 26 (2004).

"House of Cards: Laws Banning Gambling Show the Strength of Sovereignty," *The Economist*, Nov. 20, 2004, at 66.

Mark D. Lynch, "The Smart Money Is on Prosecutions: Using the Federal Interstate Wire Act to Prosecute Offshore Telephone Gambling Services," 10 *Indiana International and Comparative Law Review* 177 (1999).

Rebecca Porter, "Prosecutors, Plaintiffs Aim to Curb Internet Gambling," *Trial*, Aug. 2004, at 14.

Lawrance Kimmel Spiller, "Credit Card Companies Crave More Money and Accumulate More through Illegal Gambling on the Internet," *In re Mastercard International, Inc. Internet Gambling Litigation, 132 F. Supp. 2d 468 (E.D. La. 2002)," 22 Temple Environmental Law and Technology Journal* 99 (2003).

❖ GNU/LINUX ❖

See Open-Source

❖ GUTENBERG PROJECT ❖

See Project Gutenberg

H

❖ HACKING ❖

The term *hacker* is often used to describe a person with sophisticated computer skills and a certain lack of regard for laws and other norms of conduct. The term has its probable origin in student slang at the Massachusetts Institute of Technology. The media and popular fiction have invested the term with a certain outlaw mystique; however, the application of the term *hacking* to illegal activities has aroused resentment among hackers who are careful to keep their activities within the bounds of the law, or to step outside those bounds only to make calculated statements. According to these "white hat" and sometimes "gray hat" hackers, outlaw hackers should properly be referred to as "crackers" or "black hat hackers."

Early computer networks, such as ARPANET and NSFNet, did not support a community of for-profit businesses. Most users were scientists and computer programmers—many, perhaps most, were or aspired to be hackers themselves. Mischievous hacking served a useful purpose; it identified weaknesses and security flaws (Lessig 1999, 194). As a result, legislators and law enforcement ignored it. But as businesses and ordinary people came to rely on the Internet, the potential for hacking to do harm increased, while its usefulness decreased: Users whose sites or computers were hacked lacked the technical sophistication to understand which security flaws had been exposed by the hack. The spread of the Internet also gave rise to a generation of "script kiddies"—hackers who in many cases did not actually understand the systems and programs they were hacking, but used hacking programs written by others and traded on hacking sites.

The criminalization of hacking coincided with the transformation of the Internet from an experimental network for sophisticated users to a universal information resource. In 1988, hacking was brought to an unprecedented level of public attention by a worm created by Robert Morris Jr., a graduate student at Cornell University in New York State and the son of National Security Agency data security expert Robert Morris Sr. (Lessig 1999, 282 n. 18). The worm spread across the Internet, shutting down hundreds or perhaps thousands of computers and causing millions of dollars in damage. Morris, in creating the worm, was acting as an old-school hacker: He was pointing out a security flaw in the open-source program Sendmail, which is used to transfer most of the e-mail on the Internet. Because Sendmail is an open-source program, there is no one person responsible for fixing flaws such as the one discovered by Morris; in a world in which all users were also capable of understanding and rewriting code, the logical way to point out a flaw in Sendmail would be to exploit that flaw in an obvious but harmless way, thus calling it to everyone's attention (Lessig 1999, 195).

Morris used a worm—a self-replicating program—to expose the flaw in Sendmail and another program, Fingerdaemon, as well as in computers' "trusted hosts" and password features (*Morris,* 928 F.2d at 506). He committed two errors of judgment, however: The worm replicated too quickly, and most of the new users of the Internet were not technically sophisticated enough to figure out what to do about it. Morris tried to stop the worm after he had released it, but was unable to do so. The worm and its consequences attracted considerable media attention; at the time the Internet was a new and unfamiliar medium, so much so that the appellate opinion in Morris's case referred to it throughout not as "the Internet" but as "INTERNET," in capital letters and without the definite article (*Morris*, 928 F.2d at 504–511). Morris was arrested and charged with violation of what was then a recently enacted statute, the Computer Fraud and Abuse Act (18 U.S.C. § 1030). Section 1030(a)(5)(A) as it then read (it has since been amended) provided for the imposition of penalties on anyone who:

> (5) intentionally accesses a Federal interest computer without authorization, and by means of one or more instances of such conduct alters, damages, or destroys information in any such Federal interest computer, or prevents authorized use of any such computer or information, and thereby
>
> (A) causes loss to one or more others of a value aggregating $1,000 or more during any one year period. (quoted in *Morris*, 928 F.2d at 506)

Morris was convicted of violating § 1030(a)(5)(A) and "sentenced to three years of probation, 400 hours of community service, a fine of $10,050, and the costs of his supervision" (*Morris*, 928 F.2d at 506).

Morris's worm attack coincided with growing fears on the part of telephone companies that telecommunications networks were vulnerable to attacks by phreakers. The phreaking and hacking communities overlapped to a considerable extent; while phreakers had been more of a nuisance than a threat to the phone companies, the possibility of a massive hacker attack shutting down large sections of the telecommunications network motivated federal law enforcement officials to undertake what author Bruce Sterling has called the hacker crackdown: Several raids by federal agents and New York state police on known and suspected hackers in 1990, including Operation Sundevil in May of that year; "Sundevil" came to be used as a shorthand in the media for all of the antihacker activity in 1990 (Sterling 1992, Part 3).

The Computer Fraud and Abuse Act, frequently amended, remains an important weapon in the federal government's antihacker arsenal. Other hacker activities may be prohibited by statutes not specifically aimed at hacking, but designed instead to control bank fraud (18 U.S.C. § 1344), credit card fraud (18 U.S.C. § 1029), and wire fraud (18 U.S.C. § 1343). Warez trading inspired the No Electronic Theft Act of 1997. And the Digital Millennium Copyright Act prohibits the use of hacker skills to circumvent technological measures used to protect copyrighted works from unauthorized copying.

Almost any kind of computer mischief is likely to be lumped by the media under the term *hacking*. Sundevil and the other 1990 raids led not only to a polarization of many hackers against the government, but also to divisions within the hacker community. White-hat hackers have made a partially successful attempt to take back the name "hacker" for themselves, encouraging the media to refer to lawbreaking hackers as "crackers" (Lessig 1999, 282 n. 25). Nonetheless, it is common to see media reports using the term *hacking* to refer not only to cracking, but also to a variety of other computer mischief, including phishing, piracy, and spamming.

Hacking has inspired a subculture of literature and movies in which the hackers are almost always seen as outlaw heroes, on the wrong side of the law but (occasionally) with hearts of gold. Most or all of the cyberpunk genre falls into this general category; for example, the protagonists of cyberpunk's most celebrated practitioner, William Gibson, tend to be computer users who, despite an astonishing level of technical virtuosity, are down on their luck and suffer from a basic incompatibility with society's notions of law and order. Cyberpunk is not the only genre to romanticize hackers, however. Hollywood has made utterly nonpunk heroes of hackers in movies as varied as *Sneakers*, starring Robert Redford and Sidney Poitier as white-hat computer security experts who foil black-hat hacker Ben Kingsley, and the James Bond movie *Goldeneye*, in which Izabella Scorupco and Alan Cumming play good and evil hackers, respectively; predictably, evil hacker Cumming is part of a plot to rule the world or, failing that, to destroy it, but is foiled by good hacker Scorupco with some help from 007.

As the hacker culture overlapped with and was to some extent an outgrowth of phreaker culture, it in turn overlaps with and has contributed to the growth of the cypherpunk movement. Cypherpunk is an essentially idealistic commitment to encryption as a means of preserving privacy in the age of the Internet (Hughes 1993). Cypherpunk, too, has inspired a literary subgenre, of which perhaps the best-known example is Neal Stephenson's *Cryptonomicon*. Stephenson's cryptographer protagonists are not, strictly speaking, hackers, but they resemble the hacker protagonists of many cyberpunk works in both their extraordinary computer skills and their general haplessness when faced with anything other than computers.

Perhaps the best-known voice of hacker culture in the real world is *2600: The Hacker Quarterly*, published by Eric Corley under the name Emmanuel Goldstein. The name "2600" is drawn from the 2600 hertz tone used by early phone phreakers; the "Goldstein" alias is drawn from George Orwell's classic novel of a totalitarian future, *1984*. In the novel Goldstein never actually appears, although the work attributed to him is quoted extensively; it gradually becomes apparent that Goldstein probably does not actually exist, but is being used by a totalitarian state to justify repression. Corley, both personally and as the editor of *2600*, has been involved in the litigation over the DeCSS decryption program (e.g., *Corley*, 273 F.3d 429). The choice of the "Goldstein" alias has proven particularly apt in the wake of September 11; the USA PATRIOT Act and other security legislation have imposed harsher sentences for criminal hacking, prompting *2600* to announce that "Those who would use the tragic events of September 11 to create repression will do far more lasting harm to our society than any terrorist ever could" ("Life Imprisonment" 2001).

Statutes
- Bank Fraud Act, 18 U.S.C. § 1344
- Computer Fraud and Abuse Act, 18 U.S.C. § 1030
- Credit Card Fraud Act, 18 U.S.C. § 1029
- Digital Millennium Copyright Act, 17 U.S.C. § 1201
- Wire Fraud Act, 18 U.S.C. § 1343
- No Electronic Theft Act, amending and codified at 17 U.S.C. §§ 101, 506, and 507 and 18 U.S.C. §§ 2319–2320

Cases
Federal Appellate Courts
- *United States v. Morris*, 928 F.2d 504 (2nd Cir. 1991)
- *Universal City Studios, Inc. v. Reimerdes*, 111 F.Supp.2d 294 (S.D. N.Y. 2000), affirmed by *Universal City Studios, Inc. v. Corley*, 273 F.3d 429 (2nd Cir. 2001)

Federal Trial Court
- *United States v. LaMacchia*, 871 F.Supp. 535 (D. Mass. 1994)

State Court
- *DVD Copy Control Association, Inc. v. Bunner*, 113 Cal.Rptr.2d 338 (2001), reversed, 4 Cal.Rptr.3d 69 (2003)

See also: Cyberpunk; Encryption; Internet; No Electronic Theft Act; Open-Source; Phreaking; Piracy; Protecting Intellectual Rights against Theft and Expropriation Act; Virus; Warez; World Wide Web; Worm

Sources and further reading:
Nonfiction:
Stuart Biegel, *Beyond Our Control? Confronting the Limits of Our Legal System in the Age of Cyberspace* (Cambridge, MA: MIT Press, 2001).
Eric Hughes, "A Cypherpunk's Manifesto," Mar. 9, 1993, http://www.activism.net/cypherpunk/manifesto.html (visited November 13, 2004).
Lawrence Lessig, *Code and Other Laws of Cyberspace* (New York: Basic Books, 1999).
Steven Levy, *Hackers: Heroes of the Computer Revolution* (New York: Penguin Putnam, 2001).
"Life Imprisonment for Hackers Could Be Imminent," *2600 News*, Sept. 25, 2001, http://www.2600.com/news/view/article/726 (visited November 13, 2004).
Kevin D. Mitnick et al., *The Art of Deception: Controlling the Human Element of Security* (Indianapolis, IN: Wiley Publishing, Inc., 2002).

Bruce Sterling, *The Hacker Crackdown* (Electronic edition, 1992), available at http://stuff.mit.edu/hacker/hacker.html (visited November 13, 2004).

Siva Vaidhyanathan, *The Anarchist in the Library: How the Clash between Freedom and Control Is Hacking the Real World and Crashing the System* (New York: Basic Books, 2004).

Vernor Vinge, *True Names and the Opening of the Cyberspace Frontier,* edited by James Frenkel (New York: Tor, 2001)(fiction and nonfiction).

Fiction:

John Brunner, *The Shockwave Rider* (New York: Ballantine, 1976).

William Gibson, *Neuromancer* (New York: Ace, 1984).

William Gibson, *Burning Chrome* (New York: Arbor House, 1986).

William Gibson, *Count Zero* (New York: Arbor House, 1986).

William Gibson, *Mona Lisa Overdrive* (New York: Bantam, 1988).

William Gibson, *Idoru* (New York: Putnam Publishing Group, 1996).

Jeff Moss, ed., *Stealing the Network: How to Own the Box* (Rockland, MA: Syngress, 2003).

Neal Stephenson, *Cryptonomicon* (New York: HarperCollins, 1999).

Bruce Sterling, ed., *Mirrorshades: The Cyberpunk Anthology* (New York: Arbor House, 1986).

Bruce Sterling, *Islands in the Net* (New York: Arbor House, 1988).

❖ ICANN ❖

See Internet Corporation for Assigned Names and Numbers

❖ IDENTITY THEFT ❖

Identity theft is the assumption of another's identity. The most common motive for identity theft is fraud; the criminal assumes the victim's identity in order to use the victim's credit cards, open new credit card accounts, make purchases, take out loans, or otherwise use the victim's identity to obtain money, goods, or services. Identity theft may also be used by terrorists and ordinary criminals hoping to avoid the authorities, by persons wishing to circumvent immigration laws, and by spies for companies and governments. In most cases the victim is targeted for identity theft for reasons of convenience: The victim might bear a physical resemblance to the thief or might be of the same age and gender, or the thief might choose a particular victim simply because that victim's personal identifying information is available to the thief. Occasionally identity theft is motivated by a wish to cause harm to a particular victim; the thief might use the victim's identity to make it appear that the victim has committed a crime or other reprehensible act. In addition, identity thieves are criminals who may commit other crimes than the identity theft itself, and their crimes may sometimes be blamed on the victim whose identity was being used at the time the crime was committed.

In order to steal another person's identity, the identity thief needs to assemble several pieces of information. The victim's name, birth date, gender, race, place of birth, father's name, and mother's name can all be obtained from public birth certificate records. The mother's maiden name, if different, can then be obtained from marriage records. If the victim is a homeowner, the victim's home address can be obtained from county property records, as can the price paid for the property, the victim's marital status, how much money has been borrowed against the property, and the names and addresses of the lenders.

This information alone is enough for a diligent identity thief to construct an entirely fictitious identity, which can then be used in fraudulent transactions. Most identity thieves are lazy, though, and prefer to take shortcuts. Identity theft is far easier if the thief has additional information about the victim, such as the victim's social security number, employer and salary information, bank account numbers, and credit card numbers and expiration dates. There are several ways in which thieves can acquire this information. They might steal the victim's wallet, purse, or checkbook; the theft could be temporary, so that the victim never notices that the item is missing. Thieves might steal employee records from a company in which they work, or raid dumpsters looking for documents with the desired information. They might steal or divert the victim's mail (FTC ID Theft 2003). A thief who can acquire a copy of a victim's tax return will have all of the information he or she needs.

The Internet can serve as a means of identity theft, as well. Hackers can obtain salary, credit card, and other information from the records of employers and retailers. Hacking of this sort, however, requires a high level of technical sophistication. Far simpler are phishing scams, in which the thief sends a message to the victim purporting to be from a bank or credit card company. Typically the message claims that for security reasons it is necessary for the victim to confirm his or her account number and other identifying information and warns that if this is not done within a certain time the victim's account will be suspended (FTC Phishing 2004). Phishers make use of spam techniques to send millions or hundreds of millions of copies of the message; if only one person in a million is gullible enough to respond to the message, the scam will still have succeeded.

Identity theft can cause damage that can take years for the victim to correct. Even if the thief is apprehended and the misuse of the victim's identity is halted, bills for purchases and loans initiated by the thief will continue to be reported to credit agencies. Victims may be refused jobs, loans, or rental housing, based on the actions of the identity thief, as reported to credit agencies under the victim's name. In extreme cases victims of identity theft might even be arrested for crimes committed by the thief (FTC ID Theft 2003).

Through its ID Theft Web site at http://www.consumer.gov/idtheft/, the Federal Trade Commission collects information on identity theft and offers advice both on preventing identity theft and on repairing the damage if one becomes a victim. A wide variety of federal and state laws also address identity theft. Many of these are preexisting laws regarding fraud, embezzlement, theft, wire fraud, and so forth. Others have been created specifically to deal with the problem of identity theft. Federal statutes in this latter category include the Identity Theft and Assumption Deterrence Act of 1998, the Internet False Identification Prevention Act of 2000, the Fair and Accurate Credit Transactions Act of 2003, and the SAFE ID Act of 2004.

The Identity Theft and Assumption Deterrence Act added a new paragraph to 18 U.S.C. § 1028(a), the statute forbidding the use or transfer of unauthorized or false identification documents. The new paragraph makes it unlawful for any person to "knowingly [transfer or use], without lawful authority, a means of iden-

tification of another person with the intent to commit, or to aid or abet, any unlawful activity that constitutes a violation of Federal law, or that constitutes a felony under any applicable State or local law" (18 U.S.C. § 1028(a)(7)). This defines the crime that is at the heart of identity theft: the use of false identification, whether in the form of a physical document or an electronic password and account number, to commit some other crime. While the preceding six subsections of § 1028(a) refer to "identification documents," § 1028(a)(7) refers to "means of identification," an apparent acknowledgment that Internet and telephone transactions usually rely on means of identification that do not involve physical documents. "Means of identification" is defined in the act as:

> any name or number that may be used, alone or in conjunction with any other information, to identify a specific individual, including any –
>
> (A) name, social security number, date of birth, official State or government issued driver's license or identification number, alien registration number, government passport number, employer or taxpayer identification number;
>
> (B) unique biometric data, such as fingerprint, voice print, retina or iris image, or other unique physical representation;
>
> (C) unique electronic identification number, address, or routing code; or
>
> (D) telecommunication identifying information or access device. . . . (18 U.S.C. § 1028(d)(5))

These are the types of information that might be obtained from tax returns or employee records, or by phishing.

The Internet False Identification Prevention Act criminalized some types of distribution of counterfeit identification documents and credentials over the Internet that had been left uncovered by loopholes in prior laws; among other things, the act made it a crime to transfer a false or unauthorized identification document by electronic means (Towle 2004, 268). The Fair and Accurate Credit Transactions Act (FACT) amends the Fair Credit Reporting Act in several ways; among its goals is the protection of consumers from the adverse credit consequences of identity theft and the protection of both consumers and credit card companies from the theft of identifying information that can be used in identity theft. There is potential for inconsistency or conflict between FACT and state law, and it may be some time before the complexities of the relationship between FACT and state laws are fully worked out (Towle 2004, 270–271).

The Secure Authentication Feature and Enhanced Identification Defense Act of 2003, or SAFE ID Act, was signed by President Bush on April 30, 2004. The SAFE ID Act adds yet another new paragraph to 18 U.S.C. § 1028, and further erases the distinction between "documents" and "means of identification" in the remaining paragraphs of § 1028(a) by adding the words *or authentication feature* to the word *document* in sections 1028(a)(1) through 1028(a)(6). This change brings these six paragraphs up to date with § 1028(7), added by the 1998 Federal Identity Theft and Assumption Deterrence Act, and recognizes that physical documents are no longer required for identity theft. The new paragraph added by the SAFE ID Act makes it a crime to "knowingly [traffic] in false authentication features for use in false identification documents, document-making implements, or means of identification" (18 U.S.C. § 1028(a)(8)). The "authentication features" addressed by the act include "any hologram, watermark, certification, symbol, code, image, sequence of numbers or letters, or other feature that either individually or in combination with another feature is used by the issuing authority on an identification document, document-making implement, or means of identification to determine if the document is counterfeit, altered, or otherwise falsified" (18 U.S.C. § 1028(d)(1)).

For consumers, avoiding identity theft remains a concern. Although there is no way to avoid a skilled and determined identity thief, there are ways to avoid being an easy target. Consumers should shred tax returns, credit card receipts, paycheck stubs, and similar identifying documents, rather than merely throwing them away. Credit card numbers and other financial information should never be given to unknown persons. Internet phishing is easy to detect: Le-

gitimate banks, credit card companies, retailers, Internet service providers, and so forth will never have any reason to e-mail customers asking for their account numbers. The same logic applies to phone phishing and mail phishing: Legitimate businesses and financial institutions will never have a reason to call a customer and ask for his or her account number, nor will they have a reason to send a letter requesting it. Any uncertainty as to whether a request is legitimate can be resolved with a telephone call to the credit card company or other business involved; of course, the consumer should call the telephone number provided on the credit card itself or obtained from the telephone directory, rather than a telephone number provided on the suspected phishing document. And any time a consumer sees charges on a credit card statement that she does not recognize, she should contact the credit card company.

Statutes

- Fair and Accurate Credit Transactions Act, 117 Stat. 1952, amending and codified at 15 U.S.C. §§ 1681a et seq.
- Identity Theft and Assumption Deterrence Act, amending and codified at 18 U.S.C. § 1028
- Internet False Identification Prevention Act, amending and codified at 18 U.S.C. § 1028
- Secure Authentication Feature and Enhanced Identification Defense (SAFE ID) Act, amending and codified at 18 U.S.C. § 1028

Cases

- *In re Crawford*, 194 F.3d 954 (9th Cir. 1999), cert. denied sub nom *Ferm v. U.S. Trustee*, 528 U.S. 1189 (2000)
- *Andrews v. TRW, Inc.*, 225 F.3d 1063 (9th Cir. 2000), rev'd, 534 U.S. 19 (2001)

See also: Federal Trade Commission; Phishing; Spam

Sources and further reading:
Federal Trade Commission, "FTC Releases Survey of Identity Theft in U.S.: 27.3 Million Victims

in Past 5 Years, Billions in Losses for Businesses and Consumers," Sept. 3, 2003, http://www.ftc.gov/opa/2003/09/idtheft.htm (visited November 6, 2004).

Federal Trade Commission, *ID Theft, What's It All About?* Oct. 2003, available from http://www.consumer.gov/idtheft/ (visited November 6, 2004).

Federal Trade Commission, *How Not to Get Hooked by a Phishing Scam,* FTC Consumer Alert, June 2004, available from http://www.consumer.gov/idtheft/ (visited November 6, 2004).

Federal Trade Commission, "FTC Releases Consumer Fraud Survey: More Than One in 10 Americans Fell Victim to Fraud," Aug. 5, 2004, http://www.ftc.gov/opa/2004/08/fraudsurvey.htm (visited November 6, 2004).

Holly K. Towle, "Identity Theft: Myths, Methods and New Law," 30 *Rutgers Computer and Technology Law Journal* 237 (2004).

❖ INDECENCY ❖

In a loosely defined area between expression entitled to the full protection of the First Amendment and obscenity, which is not protected, lies indecency. Indecent expression is expression that does not conform to "accepted standards of morality." It may be "vulgar, offensive and shocking" (*Pacifica*, 438 U.S. 728, 740, 747). It may meet some, but not all, of the elements of the Supreme Court's three-part test for obscenity. That is, it may be material that

(a) "the 'average person, applying contemporary community standards' would find, taken as a whole, appeals to the prurient interest," or
(b) "depicts or describes, in a patently offensive way, sexual conduct specifically defined by the applicable state law," or
(c) "taken as a whole, lacks serious literary, artistic, political, or scientific value."
(*Miller*, 413 U.S. at 39)

It cannot be all three of these, however; content that meets all three criteria is obscene, not merely indecent.

At the federal level the most significant and pervasive regulation of indecency is that of the Federal Communications Commission (FCC).

The FCC does not regulate the Internet, but does regulate broadcast media. Because many providers of mainstream Internet content are also providers of broadcast media, content on these providers' sites may conform to FCC guidelines regarding indecency.

In the Internet context there has been little or no effort to regulate indecency of the type exemplified by George Carlin's notorious "Filthy Words" (aka "Seven Deadly Words") monologue, the subject of the Supreme Court's decision in *Federal Communications Commission v. Pacifica.* Carlin's monologue is entirely speech, without pictures or other graphic content. It is satirical; it is not designed to appeal to an interest in sex, prurient or otherwise, but to make a point about censorship and, when played on the radio (as it was by the defendant in *Pacifica*) to challenge what the author and the defendant apparently believe to be unnecessarily heavy-handed censorship. It makes its points, however, by deliberate use of shocking and offensive language and examples.

The entire text of the "Seven Deadly Words" monologue is readily available on the Web; it can be found in, among other places, an appendix to the Supreme Court's opinion in *Pacifica.* The widespread availability of this "indecent" content and content like it has aroused no perceptible public or governmental opposition. Rather, concern about indecency has focused on pornography: material that is sexually exciting to some, offensive to others, not obscene or otherwise illegal (as child pornography is), but generally agreed to be inappropriate for minors. Because the Internet is not a broadcast medium, it is entitled to the highest level of First Amendment protection; the FCC may not regulate Internet content in the way it regulates broadcast television and radio content.

Congress has attempted to restrict the access of minors to pornography, although not necessarily to other forms of indecent content, such as Carlin's monologue, both by regulating the supply side (Web sites containing pornographic content) and the user side. To date, neither approach has proven notably effective, as is evident to even a casual Web surfer.

The first congressional attempt to regulate Internet content was the Communications Decency Act of 1996 (CDA), which, among other things, imposed penalties for the knowing transmission or display of "indecent" material, including depictions or descriptions, "in terms patently offensive as measured by community standards, [of] sexual or excretory activities or organs" to known minors (47 U.S.C. § 223). The Supreme Court held the CDA to be unconstitutional for several reasons, including the difficulty of defining "indecent," the difficulty of verifying the age of the recipient or viewer of the content, and the burden placed on noncommercial sites. These problems rendered it difficult or impossible for content providers to know whether they were violating the CDA, and placed a burden on the operators of some sites, especially noncommercial sites (*Reno v. ACLU,* 521 U.S. 844).

Congress's second attempt was the Child Online Protection Act (COPA)(47 U.S.C. § 231). The federal Third Circuit Court of Appeals has declared COPA unconstitutional (*ACLU v. Reno,* 217 F.3d 162; *ACLU v. Ashcroft,* 322 F.3d 240). The Third Circuit's opinion in *American Civil Liberties Union v. Ashcroft* suggested that user-side control, through blocking and filtering software, might be more effective than supply-side control (322 F.3d 240); the Supreme Court agreed that this was a significant factual question, and therefore remanded the case for trial (124 S. Ct. 2783).

Congress has also enacted legislation (the Children's Internet Protection Act, or CIPA), requiring the use of such software by schools and libraries receiving federally subsidized discounted Internet access (47 U.S.C. § 254(h)); CIPA's constitutionality has been upheld by the Supreme Court (*U.S. v. American Library Association,* 539 U.S. 194). In a purely private context, of course, such as a parent's installation of blocking and filtering software on a child's computer, there is no First Amendment issue, because there is no state action.

The current problems with blocking and filtering software are not legal but technical. Blocking and filtering software can operate by allowing access only to an approved list of sites ("whitelist") of sites, or by prohibiting access to sites on a proscribed list ("blacklist"). It can look for digital certificates of sites that comply with certain standards, or search a site for proscribed keywords. The first approach is effective, but extremely restrictive and suitable only for very young children. Serious online research requires access to a large number of Web sites, many of which will not be whitelisted even though their content is utterly innocuous. The blacklist approach presents the flip side of this problem; for a variety of reasons, many sites containing indecent material will be omitted from the blacklist. The proscribed-keyword approach presents both of these problems: Like the whitelist approach, it is over-inclusive; like the blacklist approach, it is under-inclusive. It is over-inclusive because keywords used to identify indecent content might appear on almost any Web site as part of otherwise innocuous content; the proscribed words might appear in academic journals, news stories, encyclopedias, dictionaries, judicial opinions, the text of novels or screenplays, or medical advice Web sites. And it is under-inclusive because Web sites might contain indecent images without containing any of the proscribed words; this is especially true of foreign-language sites.

A hybrid approach that holds promise is the creation of a new top-level domain to which pornographic content, although not other indecent content, could be restricted; children's Web browsers could then be set to block this domain. The Internet Corporation for Assigned Names and Numbers (ICANN), after many years of deliberation and often heated debate, decided in June 2005 to create a ".xxx" top-level domain for adult content. Other forms of indecency, such as the transcript of Carlin's monologue, would continue to be available, but there has been little expression of public concern over such a possibility.

The problem of indecent spam (unsolicited bulk-mailed e-mail advertising) is a more difficult one to address. Most providers of indecent content on the Web have no particular wish to make their content available to minors. Spammers, in contrast, are the outlaws of the Web; they know that no e-mail recipient wants to receive their message, and they know that individuals and ISPs employ software designed to screen out their messages. They design their messages to be as difficult to screen out as possible, and have no incentive to assist recipients in blocking indecent content. The problem of blocking indecent spam is thus inseparable from the problem of blocking all spam, a problem that has thus far defied both legislative and technical solution.

Statutes

- Child Online Protection Act, 47 U.S.C. § 231
- Children's Internet Protection Act, 47 U.S.C. § 254(h)
- Communications Decency Act of 1996, Pub. L. No. 104-104, § 502, 1996 U.S.S.C.A.N. (110 Stat.) 56,133 (later codified at 47 U.S.C. § 223)

Cases

Supreme Court

- *American Civil Liberties Union v. Reno*, 217 F.3d 162 (3d Cir. 2000); rev. sub nom. *Ashcroft v. American Civil Liberties Union*, 535 U.S. 564 (2002); on remand, *American Civil Liberties Union v. Ashcroft*, 322 F.3d 240 (3d Cir. 2003); cert. granted, *Ashcroft v. American Civil Liberties Union*, 124 S. Ct. 399 (2003); affirmed and remanded, 124 S. Ct. 2783 (2004)
- *Ashcroft v. Free Speech Coalition*, 535 U.S. 234 (2002)
- *Federal Communications Commission v. Pacifica*, 438 U.S. 726 (1978)
- *Miller v. California*, 413 U.S. 15 (1973)
- *Reno v. American Civil Liberties Union*, 521 U.S. 844 (1997)
- *United States v. American Library Association, Inc.*, 539 U.S. 194 (2003)

Federal Trial Courts

- *America Online v. Cyber Promotions*, 948 F.Supp. 456 (E.D. Pa. 1996)
- *Mainstream Loudoun v. Board of Trustees of the Loudoun County Library*, 2 F.Supp.2d 783 (E.D. Va. 1998)

See also: Censorship; Child Online Protection Act; Children's Internet Protection Act; Communications Decency Act; Constitutional Law; First Amendment; Obscenity; Pornography; Spam

Sources and further reading:
Jerome A. Barron and C. Thomas Dienes, *Constitutional Law in a Nutshell* (St. Paul, MN: West, 2002).
Madeleine Schachter, *Law of Internet Speech*, 2d ed. (Durham, NC: Carolina Academic Press, 2002).
Sex Sites Get Dedicated Net Home, BBC News, June 2, 2005, available at http://news.bbc.co.uk/2/hi/technology/4602449.stm (visited June 2, 2005).

❖ INDUCE ACT ❖

The Inducing Infringement of Copyrights Act, a proposed law that would strengthen copyright protections to benefit the content industry, draws its acronym (INDUCE Act) from its original unwieldy title, the Inducement Devolves into Unlawful Child Exploitation Act. The history of the INDUCE Act has followed a pattern by now familiar in the ongoing three-sided battle among consumers, equipment manufacturers, and the content industry: First, content industry lobbyists write a bill that makes it more difficult for consumers to make copies, including fair use copies, of digital content they have purchased, or imposing harsher penalties for copyright infringement; this threatens the fair use interests of consumers and the potential revenue of equipment manufacturers. Next, consumer advocates and equipment manufacturers join forces to defeat the bill. Sometimes, as with the Consumer Broadband and Digital Television Promotion Act, they are successful. At other times, as with the No Electronic Theft Act and several provisions of the Digital Millennium Copyright Act, they are not. The outcomes of some battles, such as those over the INDUCE Act and the Protecting Intellectual Rights against Theft and Expropriation (PIRATE) Act, are still in doubt.

The INDUCE Act was introduced by Senator Orrin Hatch (R-UT) in June 2004. If enacted, it would impose liability for copyright infringement not only on copyright infringers but also on anyone who induced another to infringe a copyright (INDUCE Act, § 2). This would be a far broader category than the two forms of third-party copyright infringement liability currently recognized by case law: contributory and vicarious liability. Contributory liability requires, in addition to the underlying direct infringement, two elements: The contributory infringer must have actual or constructive knowledge of the infringement, and must materially contribute to the direct infringer's activities (*Fonovisa*, 76 F.3d 259). Vicarious infringement also requires an underlying direct infringement and two additional elements: In this case the vicarious infringer must have the right and ability to control the infringer's actions and must receive a direct financial benefit (*Fonovisa*, 76 F.3d 259).

The INDUCE Act provides that "Nothing in this subsection shall enlarge or diminish the doctrines of vicarious and contributory liability for copyright infringement or require any court to unjustly withhold or impose any secondary liability for copyright infringement" (INDUCE Act, § 2). Instead, the act would create a third category of third-party liability for copyright infringement. This "inducement liability" would cast a far wider net than either vicarious or contributory liability. It would apply to any person who "intentionally aids, abets, induces, or procures," an infringement by another, "and intent may be shown by acts from which a reasonable person would find intent to induce infringement based upon all relevant information about such acts then reasonably available to the actor, including whether the activity relies on infringement for its commercial viability" (INDUCE Act, § 2).

Neither of the factors required for vicarious liability—the right and ability to control and the financial benefit—would be needed for inducement liability. Nor would the material contribution requirement for contributory liability be necessary; the inducer would only have to aid, abet, induce, or procure the underlying infringement, and there is no requirement in the act that the aiding, abetting, inducing, or procuring be material. Conceivably, even slight assistance could fall within the scope of the act. The "constructive knowledge" required for contributory infringement is also expanded:

The INDUCE Act's definition of intent includes, in addition to a general description of constructive intent, a provision for finding intent where "the activity relies on infringement for its commercial viability" (INDUCE Act, § 2). This is aimed particularly at online file-sharing services, especially supernode-based services on the distributed, centerless P2P model. The federal district court for the Central District of California held, in the 2003 case of *MGM Studios v. Grokster,* that a service of this sort was not a contributory or direct infringer (259 F.Supp.2d 1029). The INDUCE Act apparently aims to reverse the effect of that decision.

Equipment manufacturers and consumer advocates fear that the act would impose liability too broadly; for the sake of protecting a single industry, development of computer and Internet technology would be stifled by fear of "inducement liability" lawsuits. Former Intel executive Les Vadasz warned that the bill "will do serious harm to innovation" because it could be interpreted to impose liability on, for example, Apple for manufacturing and distributing the iPod (Vadasz 2004). The Electronic Frontier Foundation, a users' rights group, created a mock complaint (a document that institutes a lawsuit) showing how the INDUCE Act could be used to fine Apple $150,000 for each iPod it produced, and how Toshiba could be fined for making the hard drives used to build the iPods. In theory even a newspaper that published a favorable review of the iPod might be liable (Vadasz 2004), although at that point the INDUCE Act would come into conflict with the First Amendment, which would surely protect such speech.

Proposed Legislation
- Consumer Broadband and Digital Television Promotion Act, S. 2048, 107th Cong., 2d Sess., Mar. 21, 2002, available at http://thomas.loc.gov/cgi-bin/query/z?c107:S.2048: (visited October 22, 2004)
- Inducing Infringement of Copyrights Act of 2004, S. 2560, 108th Cong., 2d Sess., June 22, 2004
- Protecting Intellectual Rights against Theft and Expropriation (PIRATE) Act

of 2004, S. 2237, 108th Cong., 2d Sess., Mar. 25, 2004

Statutes
- Digital Millennium Copyright Act, §§ 1201–1204
- No Electronic Theft Act, amending and codified at 17 U.S.C. §§ 101, 506, and 507 and 18 U.S.C. §§ 2319–2320

Cases
- *Fonovisa, Inc. v. Cherry Auction, Inc.*, 76 F.3d 259 (9th Cir. 1996)
- *MGM Studios, Inc. v. Grokster, Ltd.*, 259 F.Supp.2d 1029 (C.D. Cal. 2003)

See also: Consumer Broadband and Digital Television Promotion Act; Content Industry; Copyright; Digital Millennium Copyright Act, Title I; Fair Use (Copyright) ; File-Sharing; Macrovision; No Electronic Theft Act; Protecting Intellectual Rights against Theft and Expropriation Act

Sources and further reading:
"Unexpected Harmony: The Music and Computer Industries Make Peace, but Differences Remain," *The Economist*, Jan. 23, 2003.
Les Vadasz, "A Bill That Chills," *Wall Street Journal*, July 21, 2004.

❖ INDUSTRIAL DESIGNS ❖

See TRIPS (Industrial Designs and Integrated Circuit Layouts).

❖ INTEGRATED CIRCUIT LAYOUTS ❖

See Semiconductor Manufacturing Mask Work Registrations; TRIPS (Industrial Designs and Integrated Circuit Layouts)

❖ INTELLECTUAL PROPERTY ❖

The right of originators of intellectual creations to a monopoly on the use and reproduction of their ideas for a certain period of time has acquired the status of a property right under the laws of the United States and of most other countries. All of these property rights in ideas, rather than in tangible objects, are collectively referred to as intellectual property. Intellectual property includes the well-known areas of copyright, patent, and trademark, as well as less well-known areas such as trade secrets and know-how (McCarthy 2004, 308). National governments may create new forms of intellectual property when a new category of ideas does not seem to fit into any of the existing categories of intellectual property. Two such new categories created by the U.S. government are discussed elsewhere in this encyclopedia: copyright-like protection for semiconductor manufacturing mask work registrations, used in the making of computer chips, and copyright-like protection for vessel hull designs (17 U.S.C. §§ 1301–1332).

The advent of personal computing and the Internet has raised a wide variety of intellectual property issues and threatened to undermine the existence of intellectual property in some areas. The first of these areas is copyright: The Internet has transformed the formerly staid world of copyright law into a battleground. File-sharing threatens to undermine copyright protection in certain types of works, especially recorded popular music, and to bring about the demise of the music content industry. The content industry in general, and the music content industry in particular, have responded to this threat with lawsuits and lobbying. Copyright protection has been strengthened and extended by statutes such as the Digital Millennium Copyright Act and the Sonny Bono Copyright Term Extension Act (17 U.S.C. §§ 301–304, 512, 1201–1204). Proposed legislation would strengthen copyright protection still further; for example, the Protecting Intellectual Rights against Theft and Expropriation (PIRATE) Act would allow the government to bring civil suits to enforce the rights of private property holders.

At the same time the content industry is pursuing technological anti-copying solutions that could potentially tie copies of copyrighted material to a single playback device and could continue to prevent copying even after the expiration of the copyright. Many consumers feel that these measures and legislative initiatives such as the PIRATE Act go too far; as a result, activists and advocacy groups have brought lawsuits to block enforcement of certain statutes or to challenge certain interpretations of those statutes and have engaged in lobbying efforts on behalf of consumers (e.g., *Eldred v. Ashcroft*, 537 U.S. 186). Equipment manufacturers, including computer makers, are caught between the two: On the one hand they are the owners of valuable intellectual property in their own right, but on the other hand their business success depends on pleasing consumers, not on pleasing content owners. Enhanced technological protective measures may increase the cost and complexity of playback equipment. Consumers will prefer simpler and cheaper equipment, even more so if the cheaper and simpler equipment can also play back and copy a wider range of material.

Although battles over copyright issues capture headlines, the Internet has also led to battles in other areas of intellectual property. In the early days of the Internet, cybersquatters registered domain names incorporating well-known trademarks and then tried to sell those domain names to the trademark owners. Congress responded with the Anticybersquatting Consumer Protection Act, restricting the practice and providing for the transfer of the domain names to the trademark holders when trademark holders were targeted by cybersquatters (15 U.S.C. § 1125(d)). In the mid- and late 1990s, metatag trademark infringement also became an issue: In order to improve their ranking on search engine result pages, Web site operators used trademarked terms as metatags, invisible to the person viewing the page but visible to the search engine. Lawsuits established the limits of trademark protection in such cases and prevented the use of infringing metatags (*Playboy*, 279 F.3d 796); changes in search engine technology have brought about a decline in the practice.

Business methods patents, such as a patent for a one-click ordering system on a retail Web site, have also proven controversial. The Internet has also been used to disclose trade se-

Intellectual property rights everywhere: Hundreds of millions of roses are imported into the United States each year, mostly from South America. For war-ravaged Colombia, in particular, the flower trade is a rare economic bright spot. But rose varieties can be protected by patent and trademark law; growers who export unauthorized protected varieties of roses to the United States risk having their roses confiscated at the border as "counterfeits." In the run-up to Valentine's Day, 2004, Customs confiscated and destroyed at least ten thousand counterfeit roses, prompting one blogger to comment sarcastically, "Can you feel the love?" To opponents of the expansion of intellectual property rights, the idea of patenting or trademarking a rose is as unwelcome as the idea of patenting one-click ordering or copyrighting a printer cartridge authentication sequence. To the flower breeders who come up with new varieties, however, patent and trademark law are as essential to the survival of their business as copyright law is to the entertainment industry.

Sources
The Stuff in My Head (blog), Feb. 13, 2004, http://nickciske.com/blog/index.php?p=115 (visited January 5, 2005);
"Thousands of Roses Destroyed at Border," ABC 7 News, Feb. 13, 2004, available at http://www.wjla.com/news/stories/0204/126063.html (visited January 8, 2005).

crets—a secret, once published on the Internet, is secret no more.

Statutes
- Anticybersquatting Consumer Protection Act, 15 U.S.C. § 1125(d)
- Copyright Act of 1976, 17 U.S.C. §§ 101–1332
- Digital Millennium Copyright Act, 17 U.S.C. §§ 512, 1201–1204
- Lanham Trademark Act, 15 U.S.C. §§ 1051 et seq.
- Patent Code, 35 U.S.C. §§ 1 et seq.
- Sonny Bono Copyright Term Extension Act, amending and codified at 17

U.S.C. §§ 101, 108, 110, 201,
301–304, 512
- Vessel Hull Design Protection Act,
codified at 17 U.S.C. §§ 1301–1332

Proposed Legislation
- Protecting Intellectual Rights against
Theft and Expropriation (PIRATE) Act
of 2004, S. 2237, 108th Cong., 2d
Sess., Mar. 25, 2004

Cases
- *Eldred v. Ashcroft*, 537 U.S. 186 (2002)
- *Playboy Enterprises, Inc. v. Welles*, 279
F.3d 796 (9th Cir. 2002)

See also: Activism and Advocacy Groups; Copyright; Cybersquatting; Digital Millennium
Copyright Act; Digital Millennium Copyright
Act, Title V; File-Sharing; Metatags; Patent;
Search Engine; Semiconductor Manufacturing
Mask Work Registrations; Sonny Bono Copyright Term Extension Act; Trademark

Sources and further reading:
Michael H. Davis and Arthur Raphael Miller,
*Intellectual Property: Patents, Trademarks, and
Copyright in a Nutshell* (St. Paul, MN: West,
2000).
Stephen R. Elias, *Patent, Copyright & Trademark:
An Intellectual Property Desk Reference*, 7th ed.
(Berkeley: Nolo Press, 2004).
J. Thomas McCarthy et al., *McCarthy's Desk
Encyclopedia of Intellectual Property*, 3d ed.
(Washington, DC: Bureau of National Affairs,
2004).

❖ INTERNATIONAL COPYRIGHT
PROTECTION ❖

Copyrights are granted and enforced, if at all,
by national governments. No international or
global copyright exists. However, most of the
countries of the world have entered into one or
more treaties by which they undertake to protect, within their national boundaries, the copyrights of foreign authors. The principal multilateral copyright agreements to which the
United States is a party are the Buenos Aires
Convention, the Universal Copyright Convention (U.C.C.), the Berne Convention, the
World Intellectual Property Organization
(WIPO) Copyright Treaty and the WIPO Performances and Phonograms Convention, the
Brussels Satellite Convention, the Geneva
Phonograms Convention, and the Agreement
on Trade-Related Aspects of Intellectual Property Rights (TRIPS).

From 1891 through 1955, the United States
entered into a series of bilateral copyright
agreements and one major multilateral agreement, the 1911 Buenos Aires Convention. (An
earlier treaty, the Mexico City Convention of
1902, continued to govern U.S. copyright relations with one country, El Salvador, until 1979;
other pan-American copyright conventions included the 1889 Montevideo Convention, the
1906 Rio de Janeiro Convention, the 1911
Caracas Agreement, the 1928 Havana Convention, and the 1946 Washington Convention.)
The Buenos Aires Convention, to which the
United States and seventeen Latin American
countries are parties, provides that once a work
obtains copyright protection in any member nation, copyright protection will be extended by
all of the other member nations without requiring further formalities other than a declaration
on the work that intellectual property rights are
reserved, typically by the words *all rights reserved*. These words probably have no legal significance today, but are included on most published copyrighted works through persistence
of prior practice. The Buenos Aires Convention
has been, in effect, replaced by the U.C.C. and
the Berne Convention, as all states now parties
to the Buenos Aires Convention are parties to
one or both of the later treaties as well.

The U.C.C. came into existence partly because of the need of the United States for a
multilateral copyright agreement at a time
when the Copyright Act of 1909 was still in
force, making it impossible for the United
States to become a party to the Berne Convention. Its principal requirement is that countries
accord national treatment to foreign copyrighted works; in other words, that they extend
to foreign copyright holders and works published in foreign countries the same copyright
protections that they extend to works of their
own nationals first published in their own terri-

tory. In addition, registration requirements for foreign copyright holders for works published outside the contracting state's territory are satisfied by the use of the symbol "©" upon the work together with the year of first publication and the name of the person claiming copyright.

The U.C.C. came into force for the United States in 1955 and went through a major revision in 1971 to take into account certain concerns of developing countries, many of which had not existed as independent nations in 1955. At the insistence of those countries who were already parties to the Berne Convention, the U.C.C. includes a Berne Safeguard Clause, which provides that no country that is a party to the Berne Convention may denounce that convention and choose instead to rely on the U.C.C. in copyright matters relating to other parties to the Berne Convention. Now that the United States and most other U.C.C. parties are also parties to the Berne Convention, the U.C.C. is of declining importance, although it continues to govern copyright matters between the United States and those countries that are parties to the U.C.C. but not to the Berne Convention: Cambodia and Laos. (A third U.C.C. party, Andorra, finally became a party to the Berne Convention on June 2, 2004.)

The Berne Convention, administered by WIPO, is the most important international agreement dealing solely with copyright. Since its creation in 1886 it has been revised six times, most recently in 1971; the United States and most other parties are parties to the 1971 revision as amended in 1979.

Like the U.C.C., the Berne Convention requires national treatment. States parties must grant protection to works first published in the territory of other states parties or created by nationals of those states without formalities. This protection must be granted for a minimum of the lifetime of the author plus fifty years or, for anonymously or pseudonymously authored works, for a minimum of fifty years; for cinematographic works, fifty years from the date the work is released to the public; for photographic works or works of applied art, twenty-five years. The Berne Convention's subject matter categories include "every production in the literary and artistic domain whatever shall be the mode or form of its expression." Enumerated types of subject matter include

> books, pamphlets and other writings; lectures, addresses, sermons and other works of the same nature; dramatic or dramatico-musical works; choreographic works and entertainments in dumb show; musical compositions with or without words; cinematographic works to which are assimilated works expressed by a process analogous to cinematography; works of drawing, painting, architecture, sculpture, engraving and lithography; photographic works to which are assimilated works expressed by a process analogous to photography; works of applied art; illustrations, maps, plans, sketches and three-dimensional works relative to geography, topography, architecture or science. (Berne Convention art. 2(1))

Note that this may conceivably be less broad than the definition of subject matter protected by the U.S. Copyright Act of 1976: "original works of authorship fixed in any tangible medium of expression" (17 U.S.C. § 102). It may also be more broad, however, in that it contemplates that some countries, unlike the United States, may wish to protect works that are not fixed in a tangible medium of expression.

The Berne Convention also defines the exclusive rights granted to copyright holders in a way similar to, but not entirely coextensive with, the Copyright Act. The important differences are that the Berne Convention does not address distribution and display rights, and U.S. law does not, for the most part, address what are known as moral rights: The right of the author to "integrity" (the right to protect the work from changes that damage the work's or the author's reputation) and "paternity" (the right to be identified as the author of a work and to prevent one's name from being associated with a modified version of the work; also known as the right of attribution). The United States has accorded limited protection of moral rights to some paintings, sculptures, and similar works under the Visual Artists' Rights Act (17 U.S.C. § 106A), but broader recognition of moral rights has not historically been a part of U.S. law. Recognition of moral rights could present constitutional problems as well; it may not be authorized under the Patent and Copyright Clause and in many situations is likely to conflict with the First Amendment.

The international regime of copyright protection includes two World Intellectual Property Organization (WIPO) treaties; the United States became a party to both treaties in 2002. The WIPO Copyright Treaty protects computer programs as literary works and protects original compilations of data. It provides a higher level of protection for these and, with some exceptions, for sound recordings. It includes a clause preventing parties from relying on the Berne Convention's lower level of protection for sound recordings. The second WIPO treaty, the WIPO Performances and Phonograms Treaty, provides for protection of the economic and moral rights of performers of "live aural performances or performances fixed in phonograms" (WIPO Performances and Phonograms Treaty art. 5(1)). Title I of the Digital Millennium Copyright Act of 1998 was designed to, among other things, bring U.S. law into compliance with these two treaties. In most respects it does so, but it does not address the issue of moral rights. U.S. law and practice remains significantly out of step with international norms in the area of moral rights.

The Brussels Satellite Convention, ratified by the United States in 1984, prohibits the hijacking of satellite transmission capability. The Geneva Phonograms Convention, in effect for the United States in 1974, provides international protection for sound recordings. A related convention to which the United States is not a party is the 1961 Rome Convention for the Protection of Performers, Producers of Phonograms and Broadcasting Organizations, which protects performance rights in sound recordings.

The agreement on Trade-Related Aspects of Intellectual Property Rights (TRIPS) is a comprehensive intellectual property treaty; it addresses not only copyright but also patent, trademark, and other areas of intellectual property. TRIPS is Annex 1C to the Marrakesh Agreement Establishing the World Trade Organization (WTO); it thus stands outside the WIPO treaty framework, but not aloof from or,

for the most part, opposed to it. Most of the world's countries are parties to both the WTO-administered TRIPS and the WIPO-administered Berne Convention.

Under TRIPS, members of the WTO agree to comply with the 1971 revision of the Berne Convention; the convention's main substantive provisions, with the exception of those dealing with moral rights, are incorporated into TRIPS by reference. The Berne Convention definitions determine the subject matter to be protected, the minimum term of protection, the rights to be conferred, and the permissible limitations to those rights. An appendix allows developing countries to make some exceptions under certain conditions. Developing countries are also given a longer period of time to phase in their TRIPS obligations.

TRIPS mandates national treatment and most-favored nation treatment (TRIPS arts. 3–4). Under the requirement of most-favored nation treatment, parties must accord to all other parties the same level of protection that they accord to any one party; no parties can be singled out for favorable or unfavorable treatment. In addition, TRIPS adds enforcement and dispute resolution procedures and provides that copyright protection shall extend to expressions and not to ideas, procedures, methods of operation, or mathematical concepts. As provided by the 1971 revision to the Berne Convention, computer programs are protected as literary works; TRIPS adds the clarification that the form in which the program is expressed, whether in source or object code, does not affect the protection (TRIPS art. 10). Databases are eligible for copyright protection if, by reason of the selection or arrangement of their contents, they constitute intellectual creations. The data itself, however, is not necessarily protected. Authors of computer programs and, in certain circumstances, of motion pictures are to be provided with the right to authorize or to prohibit the commercial rental of those works, although in the case of motion pictures ("cinematographic works") member states are exempt from the obligation unless motion picture rentals have led to widespread copying that materially impairs the exclusive right of reproduction. The obligation with regard to computer programs does not apply where the program itself is not the essential object of the rental; for example, a member state would probably not be required to provide the holder of the copyright to an onboard navigation program with the exclusive right to authorize a car-rental company to rent cars incorporating the onboard navigation software; it would certainly not be required to provide the holder of the copyright to an automotive diagnostic program incorporated in these same cars with that right.

States parties to TRIPS are required to provide copyright protection for, at a minimum, the duration set by the Berne Convention. TRIPS also requires member states to provide performers of live audio performances with the right to prevent unauthorized broadcasts and audio, but not audiovisual, recordings of their performances. Producers of sound recordings ("phonograms") are to be given the exclusive reproduction and rental rights to those recordings for a minimum term of fifty years, although many states with other protections for these producers in their domestic law will escape this requirement through a grandfather clause. Broadcasting organizations are to be given the right to prevent unauthorized recording of their broadcasts for a minimum term of twenty years, unless such protection is redundant with protections already granted to the holders of the copyright in the broadcasted material (TRIPS art. 14).

Treaties

- Agreement between the World Intellectual Property Organization and the World Trade Organization, Dec. 22, 1995, 35 I.L.M. 754 (1996)
- Agreement on Trade-Related Aspects of Intellectual Property Rights (TRIPS), Marrakesh Agreement Establishing the World Trade Organization, Annex 1C, Apr. 15, 1994, 33 I.L.M. 81 (1994)
- Buenos Aires Convention, Aug. 20, 1910, 38 Stat. 1785, 155 L.N.T.S. 179
- Convention Concerning the Creation of an International Union for the Protection of Literary and Artistic Works (Berne Convention), Sept. 9, 1886, as last revised at Paris, July 24,

1971 (amended 1979), 25 U.S.T. 1341, 828 U.N.T.S. 221
- Convention Establishing the World Intellectual Property Organization, July 14, 1967, as amended on Sept. 28, 1979 (WIPO Convention), 21 U.S.T. 1749, 828 U.N.T.S. 3
- Convention for the Protection of Producers of Phonograms against Unauthorized Duplication of Their Phonograms, Oct. 29, 1971, 25 U.S.T. 309
- Convention Relating to the Distribution of Programme-Carrying Signals Transmitted by Satellite, May 21, 1974, 13 I.L.M. 1444 (1976)
- Rome Convention for the Protection of Performers, Producers of Phonograms and Broadcasting Organizations, Oct. 26, 1961, 496 U.N.T.S. 43
- Universal Copyright Convention, Sept. 6, 1952, 6 U.S.T. 2731, revised at Paris July 24, 1971, 25 U.S.T. 1341
- WIPO Copyright Treaty, Dec. 20, 1996, 36 I.L.M. 65 (1997)
- WIPO Performances and Phonograms Treaty, Dec. 20, 1996, 36 I.L.M. 76 (1997)

Statutes

- Copyright Act of 1976, 17 U.S.C. § 102
- Visual Artists' Rights Act, 17 U.S.C. § 106A

European Union Materials

- Council Directive 93/98/EEC of 29 October 1993 Harmonizing the Term of Protection of Copyright and Certain Related Rights

See also: Berne Convention; Copyright; Copyright Infringement; Digital Millennium Copyright Act, Title I; TRIPS (Copyright); Universal Copyright Convention; WIPO; WIPO Copyright Treaty; WIPO Performances and Phonograms Treaty

Sources and further reading:
Daniel C. K. Chow, *A Primer on Foreign Investment Enterprises and Protection of*

Intellectual Property in China (The Hague: Kluwer Law International, 2002).

Anthony D'Amato and Doris Estelle Long, eds., *International Intellectual Property Anthology* (Cincinnati. OH: Anderson Publishing, 1996).

Mihaly Ficsor, *The Law of Copyright and the Internet: The 1996 WIPO Treaties, Their Interpretation and Implementation* (Oxford: Oxford University Press, 2002).

Paul Goldstein, *International Copyright: Principles, Law, and Practice* (Oxford: Oxford University Press, 2000).

Alfredo Ilardi and Michael Blakeney, eds., *International Encyclopedia of Intellectual Property Treaties* (Oxford: Oxford University Press, 2004).

"Imitation v. Inspiration: How Poor Countries Can Avoid the Wrongs of Intellectual-Property Rights," *The Economist*, Sept. 14, 2002, at 13.

Pascal Kamina, *Film Copyright in the European Union* (Cambridge: Cambridge University Press, 2002).

Marshall Leaffer, "International Copyright from an American Perspective," 43 *Arkansas Law Review* 373 (1990).

Makeen Fouad Makeen, *Copyright in a Global Information Society: The Scope of Copyright Protection under International, US, UK, and French Law* (New York: Aspen, 2001).

Sam Ricketson, *The Berne Convention for the Protection of Literary and Artistic Works: 1886–1986* (London: Centre for Commercial Law Studies, Queen Mary College, 1987).

Susan K. Sell, *Private Power, Public Law: The Globalization of Intellectual Property Rights* (Cambridge: Cambridge University Press, 2003).

Deli Yang, *Intellectual Property and Doing Business in China* (Amsterdam: Pergamon, 2003).

❖ INTERNATIONAL FEDERATION OF REPRODUCTION RIGHTS ORGANIZATIONS ❖

Few individual copyright holders possess the resources to detect and pursue violations of their copyrights in their own country, let alone worldwide; and it is not easy for persons wishing to make copies of copyrighted material to track down the author of each individual work. Reproduction rights organizations (RROs) have arisen to serve this function; the RROs track copyright violators and pursue equitable remedies (getting the violators to stop) and legal remedies (collecting damages). They also act as clearinghouses to authorize reproduction of the copyrighted material (IFRRO "Introduction, Operation and History"). The International Federation of Reproduction Rights Organizations (IFRRO) is, as its name states, an umbrella organization that unites and coordinates the activities of more than forty RROs and nearly sixty similar organizations (IFRRO Directory 2004).

IFRRO arose to address the problems posed by photocopying of copyrighted materials for internal use by schools, corporations, and other organizations. The licenses granted by IFRRO members are typically for internal institutional use (IFRRO "Introduction, Operation and History"); commercial clearinghouse operations serve the same function with regard to large-scale commercial copying and file-sharing. The Internet has posed new problems for the IFRRO. An institution might make copies of a copyrighted work available on a Web site intended for internal use, such as a course Web site, that is nonetheless accessible to the broader community of Internet users. The posted materials would be, in effect, posted to the entire world.

IFRRO coordinates the division of royalties involved in international reproduction of copyrighted works and sets standards for agreements regarding digital reproduction (See IFRRO 1996). It also coordinates its activities with the World Intellectual Property Organization and engages in lobbying in the various states in which it has member organizations.

See also: Copyright; International Copyright Protection

Sources and further reading:
International Federation of Reproduction Rights Organizations, "Introduction, Operation and History," http://www.ifrro.org/about/intro.html (visited November 8, 2004).
International Federation of Reproduction Rights Organizations, *Collective Management of Digital Rights*, Oct. 1996, http://www.ifrro.org/papers/pp-digi.html (visited November 8, 2004).

International Federation of Reproduction Rights Organizations, *Directory of IFRRO Membership*, July 9, 2004, http://www.ifrro.org/members/index.html (visited November 8, 2004).

❖ INTERNATIONAL PATENT PROTECTION ❖

A patent, like a copyright or trademark, is a territorially limited right. Patents are granted by governments and are valid only within the territory under that government's control. The holder of a patent on a particular device in Country A can bring an action to stop anyone else in Country A from manufacturing the device, but can do nothing to stop someone in Country B from doing so. If the infringer in Country B tries to export the devices to Country A, the patent holder in country A can request that Country A's customs officials confiscate the infringing devices and not allow them to enter Country A. But if the infringer in Country B wishes only to sell the devices in Country B, or wishes to export them to Countries C, D, E, and F, the patent holder in country A has no recourse.

The solution for the patent holder is to patent the device in every country in which it might be manufactured or sold; however, this might well be more than a hundred different countries, each with its own legal system and patent application and approval process, speaking fifty different languages. Patenting an invention in more than a handful of countries would probably pose an insurmountable bureaucratic obstacle to most inventors. To address this problem and the related problem of enforcing patents in other countries, several treaties have been adopted, including the Paris Convention for the Protection of Industrial Property, the Patent Cooperation Treaty, the Patent Law Treaty, and the Agreement on Trade-Related Aspects of Intellectual Property Rights (TRIPS).

The Paris Convention, administered by the World Intellectual Property Organization, requires its 168 member states to provide three forms of protection to patent applicants from other member states. First, member states must provide applicants from other member states with "national treatment"; that is, they must accord to applicants from other member states the same rights and protection that they would accord to their own nationals (Paris Convention, art. 2). Second, the Paris Convention requires that each of its members provide certain minimum levels of protection for all patents (Paris Convention, arts. 4*ter*–5*quater*). And third, the convention guarantees inventors a right of priority: An inventor who has filed a patent application in his or her home country, if that country is a party to the convention, will enjoy a right of priority in all other member states for twelve months from the date of that first filing. Should the inventor file a patent application for the same invention in any of the other member states during that twelve-month period, the later application will be treated as if it had been filed on the same date as the original application. The right of priority will enable the inventor to prevail even over another person who has filed a patent application in the second country for the same invention, so long as the second person's filing was later than the inventor's original filing.

Is Linux really open-source? SCO Group Inc., owner of intellectual property rights in the Unix operating system, claims that Linux infringes its rights in Unix and has taken its claims to court. SCO enjoys the support of Microsoft, whose chief executive officer, Steve Ballmer, recently warned Asian governments that Linux violated "more than 228" patents. Ballmer delivered his warning in Singapore a month after Singapore's Ministry of Defense had switched 20,000 computers from Windows to Linux. Other governments have taken or are considering similar measures, not so much for cost reasons as because of concerns about security.

Source

"Microsoft Warns Asian Governments of Linux Suits," CNN.com, Nov. 19, 2004, available at http://www.cnn.com/2004/T, 2004). ECH/biztech/11/19/tech.microsoft.linux3.reut/index.html (visited November 20, 2004).

Although the Paris Convention guarantees a certain degree of uniformity of protection, the Patent Cooperation Treaty (PCT) greatly streamlines the multination patent application process. It provides a process by which an inventor can file a patent application simultaneously in any or all of the 124 countries that are parties to the PCT. It does not create a global patent, however, and the mere filing of simultaneous applications does not mean that all of the countries in which the applications are filed will grant the patent (McCarthy 2004, 437–438).

The Patent Law Treaty, not yet in force, attempts to address a discrepancy between U.S. patent law and the patent law of other countries: U.S. patent law protects the first person to invent; other countries' patent laws protect the first person to file a patent application. Attachment to the first-to-invent system has emotional as well as legal and economic roots in the United States, and a true global patent system is unlikely to be achievable until some sort of harmony between U.S. and international approaches can be reached (Takenaka 2003, 261).

Instead of the harmonized system of international patent law sought through measures such as the Patent Law Treaty, an enforceable international system has been reached under TRIPS. All of the 148 members of the World Trade Organization are parties to TRIPS. TRIPS incorporates the basic protections of the Paris Convention and provides for a uniform patent term of twenty years (TRIPS, arts. 2, 33). A substantive provision of TRIPS with direct application to the Internet is found in Article 27, which has been interpreted as requiring WTO members to grant business method patents (Conley 2003, 8).

Treaties
- Agreement on Trade-Related Aspects of Intellectual Property Rights, Marrakesh Agreement Establishing the World Trade Organization, Annex 1C, Apr. 15, 1994, 33 I.L.M. 81 (1994)
- Budapest Treaty on the International Recognition of the Deposit of Microorganisms for the Purposes of Patent Procedure, Apr. 28, 1977, as amended on Sept. 26, 1980, 32 U.S.T. 1241, 1861 U.N.T.S. 361

- Paris Convention for the Protection of Industrial Property, Mar. 20, 1883, as revised at Brussels on Dec. 14, 1900, at Washington on June 2, 1911, at The Hague on Nov. 6, 1925, at London on June 2, 1934, at Lisbon on Oct. 31, 1958, and at Stockholm on July 14, 1967, and as amended on Sept. 28, 1979, 21 U.S.T. 1583, 828 U.N.T.S. 305
- Patent Cooperation Treaty, Washington on June 19, 1970, as amended on Sept. 28, 1979, and as modified on February 3, 1984, and October 3, 2001, 28 U.S.T. 7645, 9 I.L.M. 978 (1970)
- Patent Law Treaty, June 1, 2000, 39 I.L.M. 1047 (2000)
- Strasbourg Agreement Concerning the International Patent Classification, Mar. 24, 1971, as amended Sept. 1979, 26 U.S.T. 1793

Rule
- WIPO PCT Rule 19.1(a)(iii), available at http://www.wipo.int/pct/en/texts/rules/r19.htm (visited November 8, 2004)

Statutes
- Patent Code, Right of Priority, 35 U.S.C. § 119

See also: Paris Convention; Patent; Patent Cooperation Treaty; TRIPS (Patent); WIPO

Sources and further reading:
John M. Conley, "The International Law of Business Method Patents," *U.S. Patent and Trademark Office Economic Review,* Oct. 2003, available at http://www.findarticles.com/p/articles/mi_m3883/is_4_88/ai_113233352/pg_1 (visited November 8, 2004).
Graeme B. Dinwoodie et al., *International and Comparative Patent Law* (Newark, NJ: LexisNexis, 2002).
J. Thomas McCarthy et al., *McCarthy's Desk Encyclopedia of Intellectual Property,* 3d ed. (Washington, DC: Bureau of National Affairs, 2004).
Nuno Pires de Carvalho, *The TRIPS Regime of Patent Rights* (The Hague: Kluwer Law International, 2002).

Toshiko Takenaka, "The Best Patent Practice or Mere Compromise? A Review of the Current Draft of the Substantive Patent Law Treaty and a Proposal for a First-to-Invent Exception for Domestic Applicants," 11 *Texas Intellectual Property Law Journal* 259 (2003).

WIPO, "Basic Facts about the Patent Cooperation Treaty," Apr. 2002, available from http://www.wipo.int/pct/en/access/filing.htm (PDF download) (visited November 8, 2004).

WIPO, "Direct Filing of PCT Applications with the International Bureau as PCT Receiving Office," 2004, http://www.wipo.int/pct/en/filing/filing.htm#P20_2204 (visited November 8, 2004).

❖ INTERNATIONAL TRADEMARK PROTECTION ❖

A trademark, service mark, or other protected mark is, like all intellectual property rights, territorially limited. In the absence of international agreements to protect trademarks, each trademark would be protected only in the country or countries in which the holders took appropriate steps to secure trademark protection. The holder would then be able to prevent others in those countries from using the trademark, but would be helpless to prevent the use of the mark in other countries. Complying with the trademark laws of all or most of the world's countries would probably be impossibly burdensome for all but the largest corporate mark holders; however, a system of international agreements simplifies the international trademark registration process and guarantees certain universal norms of protection. These treaties include the Paris Convention for the Protection of Industrial Property, the Madrid Arrangement and Protocol, the Trademark Law Treaty, and the Agreement on Trade-Related Aspects of Intellectual Property Rights (TRIPS).

The Paris Convention, administered by the World Intellectual Property Organization, requires its 168 member states to provide two forms of protection to trademark holders from other member states. First, member states must accord "national treatment" to each other's nationals; that is, they must accord to nationals of other member states the same rights and protection that they would accord to their own nationals (Paris Convention, art. 2). Second, the Paris Convention requires that each of its members provide certain minimum levels of protection (Paris Convention, arts. 6–8).

The Madrid Arrangement (also know as the Madrid Agreement), to which the United States is not a party, and the 1989 Madrid Protocol, to which the United States is a party, make it possible for a mark holder to obtain protection in multiple countries without having to register or otherwise apply for protection in each individual country. The protocol provides a single filing process for trademark protections in all of the member states; only a single application, in a single language, is required, and only a single fee must be paid. The Trademark Law Treaty, to which the United States is also a party, further harmonizes the administrative requirements for obtaining trademark registration and reduces the cost of the process (McCarthy 2004, 613). And TRIPS brings trademark law within the World Trade Organization's enforcement and dispute resolution framework.

Treaties
- Agreement on Trade-Related Aspects of Intellectual Property Rights (TRIPS), Marrakesh Agreement Establishing the World Trade Organization, Annex 1C, Apr. 15, 1994, 33 I.L.M. 81 (1994)
- Madrid Agreement Concerning the International Registration of Marks, Apr. 14, 1891, as revised at Brussels, Dec. 14, 1900, at Washington, June 2, 1911, at The Hague, Nov. 6, 1925, at London, June 2, 1934, at Nice, June 15, 1957, at Stockholm, July 14, 1967, and as amended Sept. 28, 1979, available from http://www.wipo.int/madrid/en/legal_texts/ (PDF download)(visited November 9, 2004)
- Madrid Agreement for the Repression of False or Deceptive Indications of Source on Goods, Apr. 14, 1891, as revised at Washington on June 2, 1911, at The Hague on Nov. 6, 1925, at London on June 2, 1934, and at Lisbon on Oct. 31,

1958, and Additional Act, Stockholm, July 14, 1967, 828 U.N.T.S. 389

- Nice Agreement Concerning the International Classification of Goods and Services for the Purposes of the Registration of Marks, June 15, 1957, as revised at Stockholm on July 14, 1967, and at Geneva on May 13, 1977, and amended on Sept. 28, 1979, 23 U.S.T. 1336, 550 U.N.T.S. 45
- Protocol Relating to the Madrid Agreement Concerning the International Registration of Marks, June 27, 1989, available from http://www.wipo.int/ madrid/en/legal_texts/ (PDF download) (visited November 9, 2004)
- Trademark Law Treaty, Oct. 27, 1994, available at http://www.wipo.int/clea/ docs/en/wo/wo027en.htm (visited August 1, 2004)
- Vienna Agreement Establishing an International Classification of the Figurative Elements of Marks, June 12, 1973, as amended Oct. 1, 1985, available at http://www.wipo.int/clea/ docs/en/wo/wo031en.htm (visited November 9, 2004)

Statutes
- Lanham Trademark Act, 15 U.S.C. § 1126

See also: Madrid Agreement and Madrid Protocol; Paris Convention; Trademark; TRIPS (Trademark); WIPO

Sources and further reading:
Anthony D'Amato and Doris Estelle Long, eds., *International Intellectual Property Anthology* (Cincinnati, OH: Anderson Publishing, 1996).
J. Thomas McCarthy et al., *McCarthy's Desk Encyclopedia of Intellectual Property,* 3d ed. (Washington, DC: Bureau of National Affairs, 2004).

❖ INTERNET ❖

The Internet is a network connecting numerous computers and local networks, so that each connected computer can, in theory, send information to and receive information from every other connected computer. The term *Internet* refers to the physical infrastructure—the computers and transmission lines and facilities—and to the communications protocols that make this worldwide interconnection possible. This infrastructure supports a variety of types of information exchange: e-mail and instant messaging, the World Wide Web, P2P networks, and a long list of obsolete information exchange technologies from Gopher to Usenet. The term *Internet* is often used, however, to refer to these information exchange technologies, and especially to the World Wide Web (Wagner 1999).

The Internet's ancestry is usually traced to ARPANET, a computer network established by the Advanced Research Projects Agency (ARPA, thus the name) of the United States Department of Defense. ARPANET's humble beginning, in 1969, was as a network of four computers at the University of California at Los Angeles, the Stanford Research Institute, the University of California at Santa Barbara, and the University of Utah (Kristula 2001). ARPANET thrived; two years later, in 1971, it connected two dozen computers at fifteen sites, including the Massachusetts Institute of Technology (MIT) and Harvard University. Ten years later, by 1981, ARPANET connected more than two hundred host systems. The first e-mail program was created in 1972, and in 1978 the first mass e-mailed commercial message, promoting the Decsystem-20 computer from Digital Equipment Corporation (DEC), was sent to about 400 users over ARPANET, although the term *spam* was not in use at the time. In 1983 an important technological milestone was achieved, as ARPANET switched to TCP/IP networking protocols; inasmuch as the Internet can be said to have originated at any particular moment, the switch to TCP/IP probably marks that moment. In the same year ARPANET's military functions were moved to MILNET, and seven years later, in 1990, ARPANET ceased to exist (*World Almanac* 2004, 713).

The demise of ARPANET did not mean the end of the Internet, and it did not mean that the computers formerly connected to ARPANET ceased to be connected to each other. New networks had grown up; among the most historically important of these were NSFNet, established in the 1980s by the National Science Foundation; USENET, or Unix User Network; and BITNET, a multi-university network originating at the City University of New York, and whose acronym was variously explained as standing for "Because It's Time Network" and "Because It's There Network." These networks and many others were linked to each other, making it possible for any computer connected to any one of the networks to communicate, via a sometimes tortuous route, with any computer connected to any of the others. The Internet spread beyond universities, government, and businesses, and into private homes during the 1980s with the growth of proprietary networks such as CompuServe, Prodigy, and America Online. In 1989, a company called The World became the first to offer dial-up Internet access to the public.

In 1989 and 1990 Tim Berners-Lee and Robert Cailliau created a system they called ENQUIRE in order to find documents more quickly on computers at CERN, the European Organization for Nuclear Research in Switzerland. In 1990 and 1991 Berners-Lee expanded ENQUIRE into the storage, search, and retrieval tools essential to the operation of the World Wide Web, and created both the first Web page and the first Web browser. The World Wide Web was made accessible to the world, thus living up to its name, in 1992 (Kristula 2001).

In 1988 Jarkko Oikarinen, a Finnish student, had created the first Internet Relay Chat (IRC) program, and various Web browsers appeared during the early 1990s. The early Internet required a degree of technical sophistication to navigate, however; the dramatic expansion of the Internet became possible after Netscape introduced its browser, Netscape Navigator, in 1994, followed by Microsoft's Internet Explorer in 1995 (*World Almanac* 2004, 713). By October 1993, the number of World Wide Web servers had increased from Berners-Lee's original one to 228. By June 1994, that number had increased more than tenfold, to 2,738, and it leaped yet another order of magnitude, to

23,500, by June 1995, and yet again, to 252,000, by June 1996 (Zakon 2004). By April 1997, there were more than a million Web servers; by 2004 the number approached fifty million (Zakon 2004).

The growth of the Internet has raised legal issues at almost every stage. The Internet's potential as a vehicle for the infringement of intellectual property rights, especially copyrights, has led to a number of legislative adjustments to copyright laws in the United States and in other countries. The ease with which the Internet provides access to information has led to attempts to censor Internet content and restrict access. The battle for dominance in the market for Internet browsers led to antitrust litigation against Microsoft. The Internet has been used as a vehicle for scams and frauds. And Internet users and the Internet itself have come under repeated attack from viruses, worms, and hackers since the first major Internet worm attack in 1988. The Internet has become an accepted part of life for a large part of the world's population, but society and the legal system are still digesting its implications.

See also: Censorship; Copyright; File-Sharing; Hacking; Microsoft Antitrust Litigation; Spam; Virus; Web Browser; World Wide Web

Sources and further reading:

Dave Kristula, "The History of the Internet," Aug. 2001, http://www.davesite.com/webstation/net-history.shtml (visited November 8, 2004).

Ronald L. Wagner, *Guide to Cyberspace*, 9th ed. (Herndon, VA: Citapei Communications, 1999).

World Almanac and Book of Facts 2004 (New York: World Almanac Books, 2004).

Robert H. Zakon, "Hobbes' Internet Timeline v7.0," Jan. 1, 2004, http://www.zakon.org/robert/Internet/timeline/ (visited November 8, 2004).

❖ INTERNET CORPORATION FOR ASSIGNED NAMES AND NUMBERS ❖

As the Internet grew in the 1990s from an academic network to a global medium, some form of governance became necessary to ensure that the various sites and servers remained connected and accessible. In particular, some uniform way of allotting Internet addresses and domain names was needed. In the early and mid-1990s this function was carried out by relatively informal organizations such as the Internet Engineering Task Force. In 1998, at the time that the Internet Corporation for Assigned Names and Numbers (ICANN) was created, the function of assigning addresses and domain names was performed by the Internet Assigned Numbers Authority (IANA), the project of Dr. Jon Postel at the University of Southern California (Palfrey 2004, 419). Since 1995, Network Solutions, Inc. had been in charge of registering domain names within the popular ".com," ".net," and ".org" top-level domains (Gilwit 2003, 271).

Dr. Postel died in October 1998. In November 1998 representatives of IANA reached an agreement with the United States Department of Commerce under which a new entity, ICANN, took over the functions of IANA, as well as other functions relating to the operation of the Internet. ICANN was incorporated as a nonprofit organization under the laws of California; its guiding documents were its Articles of Incorporation and the Memorandum of Understanding between ICANN and the Department of Commerce (Palfrey 2004, 420–421).

In an industry that has grown as rapidly and as chaotically as the Internet information industry, it is not surprising that there has been controversy or that ICANN has frequently found itself embroiled in controversy; in fact, it is perhaps more surprising that ICANN has survived. Much of this controversy has centered on the issue of representation. Paragraph II.C.4 of the memorandum of understanding, under the heading "Representation," declares that:

> This Agreement promotes the technical management of the DNS in a manner that reflects the global and functional diversity of Internet users and their needs. This Agreement is intended to promote the design, development, and testing of mechanisms to solicit public input, both domestic and international, into a private-sector decision making process. These mechanisms will promote the flexibility needed to adapt to changes in the composition of the Internet user community and their needs. (Memorandum of Understanding 1998)

Although ICANN has maintained its commitment to transparency, openness, and public representation, the scale of the Internet has altered so dramatically since its inception that "Whereas one representative used to have a constituency of 100, now he or she has a constituency of hundreds of millions (in the case of North America), or even billions of people (in the case of Asia). Similarly, openness—particularly in the sense of transparency—becomes harder with scale, as not all decisions can be made by a small group of directors and officers in front of the world at large" (Palfrey 2004, 425).

ICANN's structure has undergone changes, most recently in 2003. In 2000 it held an online election to choose five geographically distributed board members from among the global community of Internet users. Thirty-four thousand Internet users voted, out of an estimated 375 million users at the time, or fewer than one in ten thousand (Palfrey 2004, 448). For this reason the election has been criticized as undemocratic, although those who voted are perhaps more likely than most Internet users to be deeply involved in the construction and maintenance of the Internet.

Today ICANN continues to administer the top-level domain name system. Top-level domains are the parts of a domain name that appear after the last dot in the URL, such as ".com," ".gov," ".de," and ".uk." It authorizes new top-level domains and authorizes private registrars to assign domain names to within some of those top-level domains (ICANN Information 2004; ICANN-Accredited Registrars 2004). Most top-level domains are country-code top level domains, such as ".uk." These are delegated in accordance with the wishes of the national governments concerned (ICANN 1999). The ICANN also performs a dispute resolution function: Under its Uniform Domain Name Dispute Resolution Policy it resolves disputes regarding rights to domain names. More than five thousand disputes have been thus resolved (ICANN Information 2004).

Not everyone is happy with a system in which the Internet is administered by an organization with links to the U.S. government, however. On November 23, the first meeting of the United Nations Working Group on Internet Governance opened in Geneva, Switzerland. Among the possibilities discussed by the working group are that ICANN should be placed under the control of the United Nations, or that the UN should create a new entity to replace ICANN. Although ICANN is scheduled to become fully independent of the U.S. Commerce Department in 2006, one possible U.S. tactic to prevent UN control over the Internet may be to increase U.S. control over ICANN (*Economist* 2004).

ICANN Governing Documents
- Articles of Incorporation of Internet Corporation for Assigned Names and Numbers, as revised Nov. 21, 1998, available at http://www.icann.org/general/articles.htm (visited November 14, 2004)
- Bylaws for Internet Corporation for Assigned Names and Numbers, a California Nonprofit Public-Benefit Corporation, as amended effective Apr. 19, 2004, available at http://www.icann.org/general/archive-bylaws/bylaws–13oct03.htm (visited November 14, 2004)
- Memorandum of Understanding between the U.S. Department of Commerce and the Internet Corporation for Assigned Names and Numbers, Nov. 1998, available at http://www.icann.org/general/icann-mou–25nov98.htm (visited November 14, 2004)

See also: Cybersquatting; Domain Name Registration; Internet; World Wide Web

Sources and further reading:
Stuart Biegel, *Beyond Our Control? Confronting the Limits of Our Legal System in the Age of Cyberspace* (Cambridge, MA: MIT Press, 2001).
A. Michael Froomkin, "Wrong Turn in Cyberspace: Using ICANN to Route Around the APA and the Constitution," 50 *Duke Law Journal* 17 (2000).
Dara B. Gilwit, "The Latest Cybersquatting Trend: Typosquatters, Their Changing Tactics, and How to Prevent Public Deception and Trademark Infringement," 11 *Washington University Journal of Law and Policy* 267 (2003).
Internet Corporation for Assigned Names and Numbers, "Internet Domain Name System Structure and Delegation (ccTLD Administration and Delegation)," May 1999, available at http://www.icann.org/icp/icp–1.htm (visited November 14, 2004).
Internet Corporation for Assigned Names and Numbers, "ICANN Information," Jan. 13, 2004, http://www.icann.org/general/ (visited November 14, 2004).
Internet Corporation for Assigned Names and Numbers, "ICANN-Accredited Registrars," Nov. 12, 2004, http://www.icann.org/registrars/accredited-list.html (visited November 14, 2004).
Christopher T. Marsden, ed., *Regulating the Global Information Society* (New York: Routledge, 2000).
Milton Mueller, *Ruling the Root: Internet Governance and the Taming of Cyberspace* (Cambridge, MA: MIT Press, 2002).
John Palfrey, *The End of the Experiment: How ICANN's Foray into Global Internet Democracy Failed*, 17 *Harv. J. L. & Tech.* 409 (2004)
"World v Web: America Does Not Want the United Nations to Run the Internet," *The Economist*, Nov. 20, 2004, at 65.

❖ INTERNET SERVICE PROVIDERS ❖

An Internet service provider (ISP) is, in the broadest sense, any company or organization that provides Internet services. The term *ISP* is generally used more narrowly, however, to refer to companies that provide Internet access and transmission, e-mail, and Web hosting services. Specialized service providers such as search engines are generally discussed separately.

Telecommunications and cable television companies may also function as Internet service providers. There are also companies that exist solely or primarily to provide Internet access, such as America Online; these are a subgroup in their own right, often referred to as online service providers or OSPs.

ISPs, in addition to confronting the same legal problems confronted by any business, face two categories of problems unique to the business of providing Internet services. The first of these is the so-called battle for the last mile, often pitting ISPs against each other and against federal regulators in the struggle to gain subscribers and improve infrastructure. The second problem is inherent in the business of providing Internet services; ISPs transmit and store enormous amounts of information, beyond the capacity of any person or organization to scrutinize; inevitably, some of this information violates intellectual property rights, censorship laws, or other laws.

The last mile: ISPs provide Internet access to their subscribers in a variety of ways: Home subscribers can connect through dial-up modem connections, cable modem broadband connections, wireless broadband connections, and use of new or existing phone lines as digital subscriber line (DSL) connections. Business subscribers, and a few home subscribers, may opt for costlier direct high-speed, high-bandwidth connections. Legal disputes have arisen over the allocation and required sharing of infrastructure, particularly in the area of broadband access (access at a speed of 512,000 bits per second or higher) through cable and DSL lines. The Federal Communications Commission (FCC) treats cable and telephone lines differently for regulatory purposes, although from the consumer's point of view the two offer similar levels of service. Cable modem services have done better in the marketplace, so far, and the FCC has been blamed for the relative underperformance of the DSL sector (Hundt 2004, 239). The FCC provides different regulatory structures for three different categories of information transmission services: information services, cable services, and telecommunications services. In the context of the Internet and ISPs, however, the categories are so arbitrary as to be nearly meaningless. From the consumer's point of view, either a cable or a telecommunications connection is also an Internet connection; and the function of the Internet is to provide information, communication, and entertainment.

The FCC's task has been complicated by the federal courts, which have at times marched in advance of the regulatory process. The Ninth Circuit's 2000 decision in *AT&T v. City of Portland* that cable broadband service is not a "cable service" has been criticized for hastiness. In a subsequent case on the same issue in the Ninth Circuit, the three judges deciding the case filed three separate opinions; one, Judge O'Scannlain, pointed out the damaging effect of the earlier case on the regulatory process:

> Our Portland decision, in essence, beat the FCC to the punch, leading to the strange result we are compelled to reach today: three judges telling an agency acting within the area of its expertise that its interpretation of the statute it is charged with administering cannot stand—and that our interpretation of how the Act should be applied to a "quicksilver technological environment," *Portland,* 216 F.3d at 876, is the correct, indeed the only, interpretation. (*Brand X,* 345 F.3d at 1133–1134)

In 2002, after *Portland* but before *Brand X,* the FCC had ruled that cable modem services were information services, not cable services or telecommunications services (17 F.C.C.R. at 4819). *Brand X* united various challenges to the FCC ruling; the Ninth Circuit, however, found itself obliged to give weight to its earlier precedent in *Portland,* leading to the bizarre result criticized by Judge O'Scannlain and the subsequent reversal of the Ninth Circuit's decision by the U.S. Supreme Court (125 S. Ct. 2688).

Internet service providers and unlawful content: Internet service providers deal in information; billions of users continually transmit enormous quantities of information around the globe, and this information passes over the networks and through the servers of the ISPs. Some of this information is illegal; some of it may infringe on the intellectual property rights of others or may defame others; other information may be inherently illegal because it is part of a criminal act or transaction or because it violates censorship laws. There is no way for the ISPs to police all of the content stored on and passing through their systems; if they were required to do so, they would be unable to operate, and the Internet would collapse. In order to prevent this, laws have been created to protect ISPs from liability and prosecution in cases where they are innocent of any wrongful intent—that is, cases in which information merely passes through or is stored on the ISP's system without the ISP being aware of the content.

Internet service providers and content that infringes copyright: Title II of the Digital Millennium Copyright Act (DMCA) was enacted in 1998 to shield ISPs from liability for copyright infringement by creating four safe harbors: the transitory communications safe harbor, the system caching safe harbor, the information storage safe harbor, and the information location tools safe harbor. Compliance with the terms of these safe harbors will shield an ISP from awards of damages and from most forms of injunctive relief (17 U.S.C. § 512(j)).

The transitory communications safe harbor shields a service provider from liability where the provider merely acts as a conduit, transmitting digital information from one point on a network to another at someone else's request. Five elements must be present for a service provider to avail itself of the transitory communications safe harbor: the transmission must be "initiated by or at the direction of a person other than the SP"; it must be "carried out through an automatic technical process without selection of the material by the" service provider; the service provider must "not select the recipients of the material except as an automatic response to the request of another person"; the service provider must not maintain a copy of the material "in a manner ordinarily accessible to anyone other than anticipated recipients" or "for a longer period than is reasonably necessary;" and the material must be transmitted "without modification of its content" (17 U.S.C. § 512(a)).

The system caching safe harbor shields a service provider from liability where the provider makes a copy of material for system caching purposes. In order for a service provider to be eligible for the system caching safe harbor, the material must be "made available online by a person other than the service provider"; it must

be transmitted from that person to another person at the direction of the second person; and the caching "must be carried out through an automatic technical process for the purpose of making the material available to users of the system or network who . . . request access" (17 U.S.C. § 512(b)). In addition, the ISP must not modify the retained material, must periodically refresh it, and must not interfere with technology that returns hit information to the person who posted the material. Finally, the system caching safe harbor includes a notice and takedown provision: Once the service provider has been notified that copyrighted material posted without authorization has been removed or blocked, or ordered to be removed or blocked, at the original site, the service provider must promptly remove or block access to the cached copy. If the person who posted the material has imposed limitations on access, such as password protection, the service provider must also impose these limitations (17 U.S.C. § 512(b)(2)).

The information storage safe harbor shields a service provider from liability where the service provider stores information at the direction of a user. The information storage safe harbor will then protect the ISP if it does not have actual or constructive knowledge that the content is infringing, and upon acquiring such knowledge acts "expeditiously to remove, or disable access to, the material" (17 U.S.C. § 512(c)). However, the information storage safe harbor is only available to a service provider that "does not receive a financial benefit directly attributable to the infringing activity, in a case in which the service provider has the right and ability to control such activity" (17 U.S.C. § 512(c)(1)(B)). This exception, drawn from the rule established by the federal courts for determining vicarious copyright infringement, rules out the use of this safe harbor by online file-sharing services, other than perhaps nonprofit enthusiast services (see *Fonovisa*, 76 F.3d 259).

The information storage safe harbor also includes a notice and takedown provision: In order to receive the benefit of the safe harbor, the ISP must "upon notification of claimed infringement," respond "expeditiously to remove, or disable access to, the material that is claimed to be infringing or to be the subject of infringing activity" (17 U.S.C. § 512(c)(1)(C)). This procedure has potential for abuse; it can be used maliciously to block access to innocent Web sites. The DMCA seeks to reduce the potential for abuses by setting forth detailed requirements for the "notice" portion of the notice and takedown process:

(3) Elements of notification. –

(A) To be effective under this subsection, a notification of claimed infringement must be a written communication provided to the designated agent of a service provider that includes substantially the following:

(i) A physical or electronic signature of a person authorized to act on behalf of the owner of an exclusive right that is allegedly infringed.

(ii) Identification of the copyrighted work claimed to have been infringed, or, if multiple copyrighted works at a single online site are covered by a single notification, a representative list of such works at that site.

(iii) Identification of the material that is claimed to be infringing or to be the subject of infringing activity and that is to be removed or access to which is to be disabled, and information reasonably sufficient to permit the service provider to locate the material.

(iv) Information reasonably sufficient to permit the service provider to contact the complaining party, such as an address, telephone number, and, if available, an electronic mail address at which the complaining party may be contacted.

(v) A statement that the complaining party has a good faith belief that use of the material in the manner complained of is not authorized by the copyright owner, its agent, or the law.

(vi) A statement that the information in the notification is accurate, and under penalty of perjury, that the complaining party is authorized to act on behalf of the owner of an exclusive right that is allegedly infringed. (17 U.S.C. § 512(c)(3)(A))

The protection of § 512(c)(3)(A) is not perfect, of course; a malicious person could still submit a false notification, complete with false contact information, and escape undetected. To protect innocent Web site operators from such actions, the DMCA also provides penalties for misrepre-

sentation (17 U.S.C. § 512(f)) and a procedure for counter-notification:

Contents of counter notification. –

To be effective under this subsection, a counter notification must be a written communication provided to the service provider's designated agent that includes substantially the following:

(A) A physical or electronic signature of the subscriber.

(B) Identification of the material that has been removed or to which access has been disabled and the location at which the material appeared before it was removed or access to it was disabled.

(C) A statement under penalty of perjury that the subscriber has a good faith belief that the material was removed or disabled as a result of mistake or misidentification of the material to be removed or disabled.

(D) The subscriber's name, address, and telephone number, and a statement that the subscriber consents to the jurisdiction of Federal District Court for the judicial district in which the address is located, or if the subscriber's address is outside of the United States, for any judicial district in which the service provider may be found, and that the subscriber will accept service of process from the person who provided notification under subsection (c)(1)(C) or an agent of such person.

The notification process is thus simpler for the Web site operator than for the copyright owner, perhaps because only one person—the Web site owner—is likely to file the counter-notification; other persons have nothing to gain by doing so maliciously or as a prank. Once the counter-notification is received, the ISP must restore the removed or blocked material within not less than ten and not more than fourteen business days, unless the copyright owner or other person alleging copyright infringement notifies the ISP that it has "filed an action seeking a court order to restrain the subscriber from engaging in infringing activity relating to the material on the service provider's system or network" (17 U.S.C. § 512(g)(2)(c)). This provision helps to protect the rights of Web site operators; in addition, a notice that fails to comply with the provisions of § 512(c)(3)(A) in any way has no effect on the rights of the ISP. In other words, if a copyright owner informs the ISP that a particular Web site contains infringing content, but fails to include any of the required elements of the notice—a signature, for example—the ISP has no duty to act; it can safely ignore the notice and continue to claim the protection of the safe harbor.

The information location tools safe harbor is designed with search engines, Internet portals, and similar services in mind, rather than the broader category of ISPs generally. Its provisions are substantially similar to those of § 512(c) (the information storage safe harbor).

Internet service providers and trademark law: Trademark law contains no safe harbor for ISPs along the lines of that provided for copyright violations under the DMCA; trademark is a much riskier area for ISPs than copyright is. Congress once attempted to provide a safe harbor for ISPs from liability for any content that they innocently transmitted or stored: 47 U.S.C. § 230(c)(1) provides that "No provider or user of an interactive computer service shall be treated as the publisher or speaker of any information provided by another information content provider." However, § 230(c)(1) seems to provide no protection from liability for trademark infringement; indeed, if it did, its safe harbor would be so broad that the four DMCA safe harbors would have been unnecessary. 47 U.S.C. § 230(e)(2) further provides that "Nothing in this section shall be construed to limit or expand any law pertaining to intellectual property." A federal district court has held that § 230(e)(2) prevents the use of § 230(c)(1) as a defense to trademark infringement (*Gucci*, 135 F.Supp.2d 409).

The exposure of ISPs to liability for trademark infringement is potentially vast; any Web site or any Internet communication might contain trademark-infringing content. The protection of ISPs from trademark infringement liability must rely on traditional doctrines of trademark law, however, particularly the innocent infringer defense (Walsh 2002). Ordinarily the ISP should not be held liable until it has had notice of the alleged infringement and an opportunity to act on it, but the law in this area remains in flux (Walsh 2002).

Internet service providers and tortious speech: A tort, to lawyers, is an injury that entitles the victim to receive some form of legal remedy from a person causing the injury. Tortious speech includes defamation, traditionally divided into libel, or written defamation, and slander, or spoken defamation, as well as injurious falsehood, false light, publicizing of private facts, and appropriation of another's name or likeness. Just as some of the content posted or transmitted on the Internet inevitably infringes on intellectual property rights, some of it is inevitably defamatory or otherwise tortious. The speech component of these torts must be "published"—communicated to someone other than the speaker and the person spoken about. Many tortious statements are published on the Internet; the question for ISPs then becomes whether they can be held liable as publishers for statements made over their networks or on their servers.

47 U.S.C. § 230(c)(1) protects ISPs from liability as publishers, for the most part; under § 230(c)(1), ISPs are not "treated as the publisher or speaker of any information provided by another information content provider." In the most celebrated harmful-speech case to date, *Zeran v. America Online,* 230(c)(1) was applied to shield an ISP from liability. Kenneth Zeran, the plaintiff in the case, had been the victim of a malicious prank committed using the services of America Online (AOL), an ISP. In 1995, a week after the bombing of the Alfred P. Murrah Federal Building in Oklahoma City, an unidentified person posted a message on an AOL bulletin board advertising T-shirts with tasteless slogans relating to the bombing; among the milder examples was "Visit Oklahoma—It's a Blast!" The message instructed interested persons to call "Ken" at Zeran's home telephone number; not surprisingly, Zeran received numerous angry and insulting calls and some death threats. Zeran relied on his telephone number for a business he ran from his home and could not change it without losing a significant amount of business; instead he called AOL and asked AOL to remove the notice and print a retraction. AOL said that it would remove the notice, although the parties disagreed as to the date on which this was done; AOL refused, as a

matter of policy, to print a retraction. Over the next several days another person or persons, using the name KenZZ03, posted many similar messages; Zeran called AOL repeatedly and was told that the individual account from which the messages were posted would soon be closed. By April 30, five days after the first message, Zeran was receiving an abusive phone call approximately every two minutes; on May 1 an announcer for Oklahoma City radio station KRXO was apparently taken in by the hoax and read the first AOL posting on the air. The announcer urged listeners to call "Ken," and the calls intensified; Zeran requested and received protection from the Seattle police. Two weeks later, by May 14, after an Oklahoma City newspaper published a story exposing the shirt advertisements as a hoax and after KRXO made an on-air apology, the number of calls subsided to fifteen per day (*Zeran,* 129 F.3d at 329).

Zeran, not surprisingly, sued AOL for defamation. He lost; under section 230, the case was not even a close one. The trial court granted AOL judgment on the pleadings; there was no need for a trial, since even if all of the facts were as alleged by Zeran, the law would entitle him to no relief against AOL. The Fourth Circuit Court of Appeals affirmed the trial court's decision. From the point of view of ISPs, the decision is beneficial; the defamation in *Zeran,* and its effects, were about as bad as they possibly could be, yet the ISP was immune from suit under § 230. From the point of view of individuals, the result is a bit unsettling; what happened to Kenneth Zeran could happen to anyone. Even a person without enemies could become the target of such an attack; the person making the statements might have picked Zeran's name, or some other name, out of a telephone book. Congress has apparently decided, however, that the potential harm to the development of the Internet from forcing ISPs to undertake the probably impossible task of policing Internet content for possible defamation outweighs the potential for harm to individuals through defamation.

Internet service providers and criminal speech: Some Internet content is illegal, either in its own right (such as child pornography) or because it is part of a crime (such as the crime of conspiracy). Different governments ban different speech, yet speech posted on or transmitted through ISPs can be received anywhere in the world. Internet content is thus potentially subject to the law of every jurisdiction on the planet. Within the United States ISPs are broadly protected under § 230. However, content that is legal in the United States might be illegal elsewhere, even in countries that share many of their legal, political, and cultural values with the United States. In France, for example, advertising Nazi artifacts and memorabilia for sale is illegal; the U.S. ISP Yahoo! has found itself in violation of French law for postings originating in the United States, where they are legal, but accessible in France, where they are not (*Yahoo,* 379 F.3d 1120). Although U.S. courts are likely to continue to refuse to enforce such judgments, U.S. ISPs with assets in other countries may have to modify their behavior to conform to the laws of those countries, or risk the seizure of those assets in satisfaction of judgments.

Internet service providers and privacy: One of the most valuable services an ISP can offer its customers is privacy; most, perhaps all, Internet users would prefer their Internet activities to remain private. Some concerns have been raised over the use of information by ISPs; ISPs could potentially sell user information for marketing purposes and could allow government agencies access to confidential user information. In these areas the interests of the ISPs may be opposed to those of the users, but more frequently the interests of the ISPs and their subscribers are aligned, as when an outside party attempts to compel the ISP to disclose information about a user.

The DMCA provides a subpoena process by which content owners seeking to enforce copyrights may obtain subpoenas to compel ISPs to disclose the identities of subscribers (17 U.S.C. § 512(h)). The subpoenas thus obtained require no judicial oversight; this streamlined subpoena process is aimed at file-sharing, the biggest single threat to music (and, to a lesser extent, movie) copyright interests. Its use has been significantly restricted by the courts, protecting the interests of both ISPs and users against the interests of the content industry: In 2003 the Recording Industry Association of America (RIAA) had obtained a § 512(h) subpoena requiring Verizon Internet Services to turn over the name of a subscriber who had allegedly shared copyrighted music files, and Verizon refused to comply. The federal appellate court for the District of Columbia held that Verizon did not have to comply with the subpoena; Verizon was a conduit ISP, rather than a hosting ISP; it served only to transmit the shared music files, rather than to store them for access by other users. The D.C. Circuit's holding appears to limit the use of § 512(h) subpoenas to a small number of cases.

Statutes
- Communications Decency Act (immunity), 47 U.S.C. § 230
- Digital Millennium Copyright Act, 17 U.S.C. § 512
- Telecommunications Act of 1996, 47 U.S.C. § 151 et seq.

Cases
Supreme Court
- *American Civil Liberties Union v. Reno,* 929 F.Supp. 824 (E.D. Pa. 1996); aff'd sub nom. *Reno v. American Civil Liberties Union,* 521 U.S. 844 (1997)

Federal Appellate Courts
- *AT&T Corp. v. City of Portland,* 216 F.3d 871 (9th Cir. 2000)
- *Brand X Internet Services v. FCC,* 345 F.3d 1120 (9th Cir. 2003), reversed sub nom. *National Cable and Telecommunications Association v. Brand X Internet Services,* 125 S. Ct. 2688 (2005)
- *Fonovisa, Inc. v. Cherry Auction, Inc.,* 76 F.3d 259 (9th Cir. 1996)
- *Name.Space, Inc. v. Network Solutions, Inc.,* 202 F.3d 573 (2nd Cir.2000)
- *Playboy Enterprises Inc. v. Netscape Communications Corp.,* 354 F.3d 1020 (9th Cir. 2004)
- *Playboy Enterprises, Inc. v. Welles,* 279 F.3d 796 (9th Cir. 2002)

- *Recording Industry Association of America, Inc. v. Verizon Internet Services,* 351 F.3d 1229 (D.C. Cir. 2003)
- *Yahoo! Inc. v. La Ligue Contre Le Racisme et L'Antisemitisme,* 379 F.3d 1120 (9th Cir. 2004)
- *Zeran v. America Online, Inc.,* 129 F.3d 327 (4th Cir. 1997)

Federal Trial Courts
- *Ford Motor Co. v. Greatdomains.com, Inc.,* 2001 WL 1176319 (E.D. Mich. 2001)
- *Gucci America, Inc. v. Hall & Associates,* 135 F.Supp.2d 409 (S.D. N.Y. 2001)
- *Perfect 10, Inc. v. Cybernet Ventures, Inc.,* 213 F.Supp.2d 1146 (C.D. Cal. 2002)

Agency Decision
- *In re Inquiry Concerning High-Speed Access to the Internet over Cable and Other Facilities,* 17 F.C.C.R. 4798, 2002 WL 407567 (2002)

See also: Broadband; Cable; Censorship; Child Pornography; Communications Decency Act; Copyright; Copyright Infringement; Data Mining; Digital Millennium Copyright Act, Title II; Federal Communications Commission; File-Sharing; French Yahoo! Case; Metatags; Search Engine; Trademark Dilution; Trademark Infringement

Sources and further reading:

Timothy D. Casey, *ISP Liability Survival Guide: Strategies for Managing Copyright, Spam, Cache, and Privacy Regulations* (New York: John Wiley and Sons, 2000).

Cherie Dawson, "Creating Borders on the Internet: Free Speech, the United States, and International Jurisdiction," 44 *Virginia Journal of International Law* 637 (2004).

Reed Hundt, "The Ineluctable Modality of Broadband," 21 *Yale Journal on Regulation* 239 (2004).

Mark A. Lemley and Lawrence Lessig, "The End of End-to-End: Preserving the Architecture of the

Internet in the Broadband Era," 48 *UCLA Law Review* 925 (2001).

"The Sociology of Cyberspace: Censorship, Privacy and Control," Manchester Metropolitan University, 2003, available at http://www.sociology.mmu.ac.uk/socyb03/censor.php (visited October 28, 2004).

Gregory C. Walsh, *Internet Service Provider Liability for Contributory Trademark Infringement after Gucci,* 2002 *Duke L. & Tech. Rev.* 25 (2002)

Alfred C. Yen, "Internet Service Provider Liability for Subscriber Copyright Infringement, Enterprise Liability, and the First Amendment," 88 *Georgetown Law Journal* 1833 (2000).

J

❖ JUNK E-MAIL ❖

See Spam

❖ JURISDICTION ❖

Even in the absence of the Internet it is possible for an act in one state or country to have legally significant consequences in another. But the advent of the Internet makes multiple-jurisdiction transactions the norm rather than the exception. In very little time, and with no review of the laws of the various jurisdictions involved, a person located in Canada can order goods from a company in New York via a server located in California; the server might belong to an Internet service provider incorporated in Delaware but with its principal place of business in Virginia. The order might be paid for with a credit card issued by a bank in South Dakota, and result in goods being shipped by a third party located in Illinois to a fourth party located in Singapore. If disputes arise from the transaction, any or all of the states and countries involved might conceivably have jurisdiction over the matter.

When the territorial jurisdiction of state courts of the United States is at issue, the first question that must be addressed is the reach of the state's long-arm statute. A long-arm statute is a state law that permits that state's courts to exercise jurisdiction over parties outside the state. If the long-arm statute, by its own terms, permits jurisdiction over the out-of-state party, the next step is to determine whether the long-arm statute's reach exceeds what is constitutionally permissible.

The territorial jurisdiction of a court may be either general or specific. A person who is subject to the general jurisdiction of a forum (that is, a court or other dispute-resolution body) may be compelled to defend any action in that forum, even if the action is unrelated to the defendant's contacts with the forum state. Nonresidents are only subject to the general jurisdiction of a forum if they have contacts that are sufficiently systematic and continuous that they might reasonably anticipate being required to defend an action in that forum. In other words, people who live in a state are subject to the general jurisdiction of that state's courts, as are other people closely connected to that state.

Problems are more likely to arise with specific jurisdiction. The U.S. Supreme Court established in *International Shoe v. Washington* that specific jurisdiction exists over a nonresident defendant only if that defendant has "certain minimum contacts with [the forum], such that the maintenance of the suit does not offend 'traditional notions of fair play and substantial justice.'" This "minimum contacts" standard requires that a defendant purposefully avail himself or herself of the privilege of conducting activities in the forum. Because the jurisdiction thus created is specific, not general, the suit against the defendant must arise from his or her activities in or related to the forum. Finally, in order to comport with traditional notions of fair play and substantial justice, the exercise of jurisdiction must be reasonable (326 U.S. 310).

Thus, among the states of the United States there are certain universally agreed upon and constitutionally mandated concepts regarding the territorial jurisdiction of courts. Among the nations of the world, however, there is no such universal agreement.

Cases

Supreme Court

- *International Shoe v. Washington*, 326 U.S. 310 (1945)

Federal Appellate Court

- *Cybersell, Inc. v. Cybersell, Inc.*, 130 F.3d 414 (9th Cir. 1997)

See also: Choice of Law; Defamation; French Yahoo! Case; Recognition and Enforcement of Judgments

Sources and further reading:

Kevin M. Clermont, *Civil Procedure: Territorial Jurisdiction and Venue* (New York: Foundation Press, 1999).

K

❖ KaZaA ❖

KaZaA, also written as Kazaa, is often used as a shorthand reference both for the popular file-sharing program Kazaa Media Desktop and for the complicated web of companies that owns it. Kazaa was originally created by the Dutch company Consumer Empowerment, but following a lawsuit Consumer Empowerment dispersed ownership of Kazaa Media Desktop. The major owner is now Sharman Networks, a company incorporated in Vanuatu and headquartered in Australia, with the original owners retaining some influence. The FastTrack software on which Kazaa is based was developed by Consumer Empowerment's founders and Bluemoon Interactive, an Estonian company. As a result of its controversial business model and its international nature, Kazaa has been involved in litigation presenting an astonishingly wide variety of legal issues: Kazaa has been involved in copyright disputes both as a defendant and as a plaintiff; it has been sued in the Netherlands, the United States, and Australia; it has alleged infringement of its trademark and has been targeted by users' rights groups as a source of spyware (Smith 2003, 2).

Kazaa Media Desktop is a P2P (peer-to-peer) supernode-based file-sharing service. Kazaa and other supernode-based services arose in the wake of the Ninth Circuit's decision in *A&M Records v. Napster,* which spelled the demise of networks using a centralized search list. Napster had maintained a list of available songs on its servers; the songs themselves were on the users' computers. The Ninth Circuit, however, found that the maintenance of the list involved Napster in the ongoing infringement of copy-rights through file-sharing among Napster's users; it also materially contributed to the infringement, provided Napster a financial benefit (by increasing traffic to Napster's site), and gave Napster control over the process.

Without the centrally maintained list, Napster would not have been liable for vicarious or contributory copyright infringement under the Ninth Circuit's reasoning. Even before the decision, P2P software developers had been working on ways to eliminate the necessity for a central list of available files; the solution was to create a decentralized network in which some computers are "supernodes." These supernodes are users' computers; they do not belong to the file-sharing service, but to users who have consented to have their computers act as repositories for lists of available files. (The files listed are not, or not merely, those on the supernode computer; they are all of the files available on the network.)

Kazaa and similar supernode-based systems, most of them using FastTrack, were designed to avoid the legal problems encountered by Napster. To a certain extent, they seem to have succeeded: At least one federal district court has held that a completely decentralized system, which is beyond the power of the originator to control or even to shut down, does not make the originator contributorily or vicariously liable for copyright infringement by the system's users (*MGM Studios,* 259 F.Supp.2d 1029). Kazaa has not been so fortunate in all jurisdictions, however.

As the market leader in P2P file-sharing and a pioneer of P2P technology, Kazaa has been a primary target for copyright infringement lawsuits. It fled the Netherlands, or at least its corporate form did, because of a decision against it in a lawsuit brought by Buma/Stemra, a Dutch music-copyright clearinghouse. That decision was subsequently reversed on appeal; the Dutch appellate court held that Kazaa's corporate parent could not be held liable for potential illegal use of the Kazaa software by Kazaa's customers (*Buma & Stemra* 2002; Smith 2003, 2).

Kazaa's flight from the Netherlands did not insulate it from further litigation, however. In January 2003 Judge Stephen Wilson of the U.S. District Court for the Central District of California ruled that Sharman Networks could be joined as a defendant in the *Grokster* litigation (McCullagh 2003). Sharman Networks had argued that, as a Vanuatuan corporation with its headquarters in Australia, it was not subject to the jurisdiction of a U.S. federal court located in California. Judge Wilson disagreed; employing the "minimum contacts" jurisdictional analysis appropriate to cases involving out-of-state defendants, he wrote that "many, if not most, music and video copyrights are owned by California-based companies" and that "it would be mere cavil to deny that Sharman engages in a significant amount of contact with California residents," as millions of California residents have downloaded Sharman's software (McCullagh 2003). But though Sharman Networks lost the battle, they won that particular war; the district court ultimately found Grokster, Kazaa, and their codefendants not liable for contributory or vicarious copyright infringement (*Grokster*, 259 F.Supp.2d 1029). The court's decision was upheld on appeal, and the RIAA has filed a petition for writ of certiorari (a procedural device by which many cases come before the Supreme Court).

Judge Wilson, in the *Grokster* decision, suggested that congressional intervention might be necessary and desirable:

> The Court is not blind to the possibility that Defendants may have intentionally structured their businesses to avoid secondary liability for copyright infringement, while benefitting financially from the illicit draw of their wares. While the Court need not decide whether steps could be taken to reduce the susceptibility of such software to unlawful use, assuming such steps could be taken, additional legislative guidance may be well-counseled. (*Grokster*, 259 F.Supp.2d at 1046)

Meanwhile the content industry's campaign against Kazaa continues. Inasmuch as an entity as diffuse as Kazaa/Sharman Networks can be said to have a home, that home is Australia. The Australian Record Industry Association (ARIA) brought a copyright infringement action against Sharman Networks in Australian federal court in February 2004 (Gray, Feb. 2004); the case is still ongoing.

Kazaa has not been a passive target, however. It has responded to the content industry's copyright infringement suits with litigation of its own. It brought an antitrust suit against the RIAA and other content-industry entities, alleging violations of the Sherman Antitrust Act and of California's unfair business competition laws. Sharman claimed that the content industry entities against which its claim was brought controlled 85 percent of the market for copyrighted works, and "together have acted monopolistically and in restraint of trade by refusing to license any copyrighted works" to Sharman (*Grokster [Antitrust]*, 269 F.Supp.2d at 1217). The district court dismissed Sharman's federal claim, but ordered additional briefing to determine whether Kazaa would be able to pursue the state law claims.

Kazaa has also been active in litigation against other P2P networks. Its success has inspired imitators, while at the same time it has been attacked by users' rights advocates for installing adware and spyware on users' computers. Installing Kazaa also installs three adware programs and a distributed computing program that some advocates fear has potential for abuse as a backdoor program. Although all of these programs are described in the click-through licensing agreement, few if any consumers actually read or understand such agreements (Asaravala 2004).

One solution was Kazaa Lite, a version of Kazaa Media Desktop that became available in April 2002. Kazaa Lite was Kazaa without the adware; it offered access to the Kazaa file-sharing network without any of the drawbacks. Add-ons to Kazaa Lite also gave users the enhanced service Kazaa ordinarily reserves for the most generous file-sharers. Kazaa succeeded in blocking Google search access to Kazaa Lite and another copycat program, Kazaa Gold (Lyman 2003). In an interesting twist, Kazaa even sued content-industry companies for using Kazaa Lite to access the Kazaa network (*Wired News* Sept. 2003).

Kazaa Lite was a version of Kazaa from which adware had been removed; the code almost certainly infringed on the Kazaa copyright, just as the name infringed on the Kazaa trademark. Although Kazaa's efforts to suppress Kazaa Lite in 2003 had some effect, in 2004 Kazaa alternatives reappeared across the Web. Programs such as Clean KMD, Kazaa Lite Tools K++, K-Lite v2.6, and Diet K differ from the original Kazaa Lite in that they do not incorporate Kazaa's copyrighted code. Rather, they function jointly with the user's authorized copy of Kazaa Media Desktop, eliminating adware and enhancing performance. This raises the question of whether the combined programs become a derivative work, requiring the authorization of the copyright holder. Names that incorporate the Kazaa name may also infringe Kazaa's trademark, if they are not permissible as nominative fair use. Kazaa has also sought to address the problem by offering its own ad-free version, Kazaa Plus. While Kazaa Media Desktop is free and makes its money from advertising, Kazaa Plus costs $29.95 and is ad-free (Kazaa Web site 2004).

Cases
Federal Appellate Court
- *A&M Records, Inc. v. Napster, Inc.*, 239 F.3d 1004 (9th Cir. 2001)
- *Metro-Goldwyn-Mayer Studios, Inc. v. Grokster, Ltd.*, 259 F.Supp.2d 1029 (C.D. Cal. 2003), *affirmed*, 380 F.3d 1154 (9th Cir. 2004)

Federal Trial Court
- *Metro-Goldwyn-Mayer Studios Inc. v. Grokster, Ltd. [Antitrust claims]*, 269 F.Supp.2d 1213 (C.D. Cal. 2003)

Netherlands Appellate Court
- *Buma & Stemra v. KaZaA*, Amsterdam Court of Appeal (2002), unofficial English translation available at www. eff.org/IP/P2P/BUMA_v_Kazaa/ 20020328_kazaa_appeal_judgment.html (visited November 2, 2004)

See also: Adware and Spyware; Copyright; Copyright Infringement; Fair Use (Trademark); File-Sharing; Internet Service Providers; Look and Feel; P2P; Piracy; Search Engine; Trademark; Trademark Infringement

Sources and further reading:
Amit Asaravala, "Sick of Spam? Prepare for Adware," *Wired News,* May 7, 2004, http:// www.wired.com/news/technology/ 0,1282,63345,00.html.
CD Fabriek Nederland, "What Is the Role of Buma/Stemra?" Nov. 3, 2003, http://www. cdfabriek.nl/cdfactory/buma_stemra.htm (visited November 2, 2004).
"Face Value: The Quiet Iconoclast—With KaZaA, Niklas Zennstrom Undermined the Music Industry," *The Economist,* July 3, 2004, at 54.
Patrick Gray, "Please Don't Squeeze the Sharman," *Wired News,* Feb. 10, 2004, http://www.wired. com/news/digiwood/0,1412,62232,00.html (visited November 2, 2004).
Patrick Gray, "Sharman Presses for Evidence," *Wired News,* May 18, 2004, http://www.wired. com/news/digiwood/0,1412,63509,00.html (visited November 2, 2004).
"The Hunter Becomes the Hunted," *Wired News,* Sept. 24, 2003, available at http://www.wired. com/news/digiwood/0,1412,60574,00.html (visited November 2, 2004).
Kazaa Web site, http://www.kazaa.com/us/ index.htm (visited November 2, 2004).
Letter from Sharman Networks to Google, Aug. 11, 2003, available at http://www. chillingeffects.org/dmca512/notice.cgi? NoticeID=789 (visited November 2, 2004).
Jay Lyman, "Google Pulls P2P Links over Kazaa Copyright Claims," *TechNewsWorld,* Sept. 2, 2003, http://www.technewsworld.com/ story/31481.html (visited November 2, 2004).
Declan McCullagh, "Judge: Kazaa Can Be Sued in U.S.," *CNET News.com,* Jan. 10, 2003, at http://news.com.com/2102–1023–980274. html (visited November 2, 2004).
Trevor Merriden, *Irresistible Forces: The Business Legacy of Napster and the Growth of the Underground Internet* (New York: John Wiley and Sons, 2002).
Seagrumn Smith, "From Napster to KaZaA: The Battle over Peer-to-Peer Filesharing Goes International," 2003 *Duke Law and Technology Review* 8 (2003).

L

❖ LAST MILE ❖

See Broadband

❖ LIBRARIES ❖

See Children's Internet Protection Act

❖ LIKELIHOOD OF CONFUSION ❖

See Trademark Infringement

❖ LINUX ❖

See Open-Source

❖ LOOK AND FEEL ❖

Computer programs and Web sites interact with users through a graphical user interface (GUI). The look and feel of a program or Web site are often distinctive. The "look" consists of the site's or program's graphics, fonts, colors, and so forth. The "feel" describes the way in which buttons, menus, links, dialog boxes, and the like help the user to navigate the site or use the program. A user who is familiar with one program or site may be reluctant to switch to another, even one that is better at performing the same functions, if the new site is unfamiliar. There is thus an incentive for developers of new software and new sites to copy the look and feel of popular existing programs and sites, whose

owners have turned to two areas of intellectual property law to protect what they see as their rights in the look and feel of those programs and sites: copyright and trade dress.

Copyrightability of look and feel: Copyright protects the expression of ideas rather than the underlying ideas themselves; when an idea can be expressed only in a very limited number of ways, those means of expression are not copyrightable. The copyrightability of look and feel has thus depended on whether a program or Web site looks and feels the way it does because there are only a few possible ways for it to look and feel, or whether it looks and feels the way it does because that look and feel is one of many possible expressions and reflects the designer's originality (see Terry 1994, 144). In the early days of personal computing, look and feel litigation was a major battleground, culminating in the dispute between Apple and Microsoft over Windows, which looks and feels a lot like Apple's operating system for the Macintosh.

In 1985 Apple and Microsoft had reached an agreement regarding the development of Windows, but the agreement fell apart after Microsoft granted Hewlett-Packard ("HP") a license to use Windows to develop HP's New Wave software desktop. The release of New Wave and Windows 2.03 in 1988 led to more than six years of litigation between Apple and Microsoft, culminating in a decision by the Ninth Circuit Court of Appeals (Cole 1995).

In *Apple v. Microsoft,* the Ninth Circuit affirmed the district court's opinion, in which the district court had used a two-step analysis for finding copyright infringement. The first step of the test (the "extrinsic test") was to compare the disputed works and to determine if, according to an objective standard, they were substantially similar. If they were, the second step (the "intrinsic test") was to apply a subjective standard to only the copyrightable elements of the work, in order to determine whether "the similarity of the works in suit stems solely from unprotectible features" (*Apple Computer,* 799 F.Supp. at 1020). Under this test, for example, two children's software programs might each employ a "Print" button without either infringing upon the other. One button might be shaped like a rabbit, and the other like a flower; each might have the word "Print" across the button. The use of a Print button and the use of the word *Print* to identify it are substantially similar, and meet the requirements of the extrinsic test. However, both are methods of operation and thus not copyrightable; there are few if any other practical ways to make it easy for a user to print from the program. The shapes of the buttons may well be copyrightable, but they are not at all similar; they fail the intrinsic test, and thus there is no infringement.

In the year following the Ninth Circuit's 1994 decision in *Apple,* the First Circuit, in a decision later affirmed by the Supreme Court, declared that the menu command hierarchy of a computer program was not copyrightable. This was seen as another blow to the copyrightability of look and feel (*Lotus Development,* 49 F.3d 807).

Look and feel as trade dress: Even as *Apple* and *Lotus* seemed to herald the decline of look and feel suits for computer software, the World Wide Web was growing and creating new ground for look and feel lawsuits. Popular Web sites, like popular programs, have a particular look and feel, and if that look and feel cannot be protected by copyright, perhaps it can be protected as trade dress. Trade dress is a form of trademark protection that protects the "total image and overall appearance of a product" (*Two Pesos,* 505 U.S. at 764–765 n. 1). The Restatement (Third) of Unfair Competition describes trade dress as the "manner in which the goods or services are presented to prospective purchasers[.]" Once trade dress has acquired significance as an identifier of the source of goods and images offered for sale, it functions as a trademark (Restatement § 16, comment a). The interface of a Web site such as Yahoo! or Amazon might well serve the requisite identifying function and thus be protectable as trade dress.

There are problems with the use of trade dress law to protect Web site designs, however. One is that the appearance of a Web site on a user's screen is the result not only of the Web design, but of the interaction of the site with the user's computer and browser. Not all users use the same computer or browser, and even two users of the same browser, running on the same computer, at the same connection speed, may have chosen quite different display settings; as a result, they may see the same Web site differently. (Nguyen 2000, 1250–1252). Another is that Web sites constantly change their appearance, although in many cases the changes might not be significant enough to affect the look and feel of the site. For example, the text and images on the news Web site www.cnn.com change several times a day, but the look and feel of the site have remained unchanged for years. Finally, just as methods of operation are not copyrightable, purely functional elements of the presentation of a product or service are not eligible for trade dress protection. "Print this screen" buttons and similar functional Web site elements are no more eligible for trade dress protection than they are for copyright protection. Attorneys advise clients as to how to avoid possible trade dress infringement, and scholars speculate as to how the novel trade dress issues raised by Web sites might be resolved, but at present possible trade dress infringement of Web site designs is an issue more anticipated than litigated (see Nguyen 2000, 1244).

Statutes

- Copyright Act of 1976, 17 U.S.C. §§ 101–105
- Lanham Trademark Act, 15 U.S.C. § 1125

Cases

Supreme Court

- *Lotus Development Corporation v. Borland International, Inc.,* 49 F.3d

807 (1st Cir. 1995), affirmed, 516 U.S. 233 (1996)

- *Two Pesos, Inc. v. Taco Cabana, Inc.*, 505 U.S. 763 (1992)

Federal Appellate Court

- *Apple Computer, Inc. v. Microsoft Corp.*, 799 F.Supp. 1006 (N.D. Cal. 1992), affirmed, 35 F.3d 1435 (9th Cir. 1994)

See also: Business Methods Patent; Copyright; Copyright Infringement; Menu Command Hierarchy; Trademark; Trademark Infringement

Sources and further reading:

Lisa M. Byerly, "Look and Feel Protection of Web Site User Interfaces: Copyright or Trade Dress?" 14 *Santa Clara Computer and High Technology Law Journal* 221 (1998).

Rodger R. Cole, "Substantial Similarity in the Ninth Circuit: A 'Virtually Identical' 'Look and Feel'? 11 *Santa Clara Computer and High Technology Law Journal* 417 (1995).

Lauren Fisher Kellner: "Trade Dress Protection for Computer User Interface 'Look and Feel,'" 61 *University of Chicago Law Review* 1011 (1994).

George Likourezos, "Trademark Law in the Computer Age: Applying Trademark Principles to the 'Look and Feel' of Software," 77 *Journal of the Patent and Trademark Office Society* 451 (1995).

Xuan-Thao N. Nguyen, "Should It Be a Free for All? The Challenge of Extending Trade Dress Protection to the Look and Feel of Web Sites in the Evolving Internet," 49 *American University Law Review* 1233 (2000).

Steven Schortgen, "'Dressing' up Software Interface Protection: The Application of *Two Pesos* to 'Look and Feel,'" 80 *Cornell Law Review* 158 (1994).

Nicolas P. Terry, "GUI Wars: The Windows Litigation and the Continuing Decline of 'Look and Feel,'" 47 *Arkansas Law Review* 93 (1994).

❖ MACROVISION ❖

Macrovision Corporation is a software company specializing in copy protection and digital rights management software. The term *Macrovision* is often used, however, to refer to a particular Macrovision product: a technique to prevent analog copying of video recordings. The Macrovision copy protection is remarkable because it can prevent analog copying of either an analog or digital recording, thus closing the "analog hole" in most digital rights management systems. It does this by sending a signal that manipulates the automatic gain control and automatic tracking control features built into most videocassette recorders (VCRs); in Macrovision's own words, this causes the "VCRs to make distorted copies, devoid of entertainment value" (Macrovision 2003, 2). VCRs without automatic gain and tracking control are unaffected, however. To address this problem, Congress included a requirement in section 1201(k) of the Digital Millennium Copyright Act (DMCA) that VCRs made in or imported to the U.S. after April 26, 2002, must contain automatic gain control, and thus be vulnerable to Macrovision's copy-protection:

(k) Certain Analog Devices and Certain Technological Measures. –

(1) Certain analog devices. –

(A) Effective 18 months after the date of the enactment of this chapter, no person shall manufacture, import, offer to the public, provide or otherwise traffic in any –

(i) VHS format analog video cassette recorder unless such recorder conforms to the automatic gain control copy control technology;

(ii) 8mm format analog video cassette camcorder unless such camcorder conforms to the automatic gain control technology;

(iii) Beta format analog video cassette recorder, unless such recorder conforms to the automatic gain control copy control technology, except that this requirement shall not apply until there are 1,000 Beta format analog video cassette recorders sold in the United States in any one calendar year after the date of the enactment of this chapter;

(iv) 8mm format analog video cassette recorder that is not an analog video cassette camcorder, unless such recorder conforms to the automatic gain control copy control technology, except that this requirement shall not apply until there are 20,000 such recorders sold in the United States in any one calendar year after the date of the enactment of this chapter; or

(v) analog video cassette recorder that records using an NTSC format video input and that is not otherwise covered under clauses (i) through (iv), unless such device conforms to the automatic gain control copy control technology.

(B) Effective on the date of the enactment of this chapter, no person shall manufacture, import, offer to the public, provide or otherwise traffic in—

(i) any VHS format analog video cassette recorder or any 8mm format analog video cassette recorder if the design of the model of such recorder has been modified after such date of enactment so that a model of recorder that previously conformed to the automatic gain control copy control technology no longer conforms to such technology; or

(ii) any VHS format analog video cassette recorder, or any 8mm format analog video cassette recorder that is not an 8mm analog video cassette camcorder, if the design of the model of such recorder has been modified after such date of enactment so that a model of recorder that previously conformed to the four-line colorstripe copy control technology no longer conforms to such technology.

Manufacturers that have not previously manufactured or sold a VHS format analog video cassette recorder, or an 8mm format analog cassette recorder, shall be required to conform to the four-line colorstripe copy control technology in the initial model of any such recorder manufactured after the date of the enactment of this chapter, and thereafter to continue conforming to the four-line colorstripe copy control technology. For purposes of this subparagraph, an analog video cassette recorder "conforms to" the four-line colorstripe copy control technology if it records a signal that, when played back by the playback function of that recorder in the normal viewing mode, exhibits, on a reference display device, a display containing distracting visible lines through portions of the viewable picture.

The statute is aimed primarily at VHS recorders, as the VHS format is the market leader, and at 8-mm analog camcorders for the same reason. But other formats are also included, in case equipment manufacturers might try to circumvent the intent of the statute by reviving the Betamax format or bringing in some other analog format.

Section 1301(k) and Macrovision have been criticized for infringing on fair use. Apologists for the DMCA's anticircumvention provisions had pointed out that, although individual users were prohibited from making digital copies of protected works, they could still make analog copies for fair use purposes such as space-shifting—recording the work onto a different medium in order to play it on a different device. Because of its simplicity, Macrovision can be circumvented fairly easily through the use of devices to disable the VCR's automatic gain control or to filter out the manipulating information sent by the playback device. Macrovision Corporation owns patents not only on its copyright protection technology, however, but also on many means of circumventing it; as a result, such devices usually disappear from the market as soon as Macrovision discovers them (see, e.g., "Macrovision Wins Preliminary Injunction" 2004).

Statute
- Digital Millennium Copyright Act, 17 U.S.C. §§ 1201(c)(3), 1201(k)

Case
- *Recording Industry Association of America v. Diamond Multimedia Systems, Inc.*, 180 F.3d 1072 (9th Cir. 1999)

See also: Analog Recording; Copyright; Copyright Infringement; Digital Millennium Copyright Act, Title I; Digital Rights Management; Fair Use (Copyright)

Sources and further reading:
Macrovision Corporation, "Preserving an Effective DVD Copy Protection System," Mar. 3, 2003, available at http://www.macrovision.com/pdfs/Preserving-an-effective-DVD-Copying-System_0303.pdf (visited October 21, 2004).

"Macrovision Wins Preliminary Injunction against 321 Studios in Patent and Copyright Infringement Lawsuit," Macrovision Press Release, May 20, 2004, available at http://www.macrovision.com/company/news/press/newsdetail.jsp?id=Thu%20May%2020%2010:28:39%20PDT%202004 (visited October 21, 2004).

❖ MADRID AGREEMENT AND MADRID PROTOCOL ❖

The Madrid Agreement Concerning the International Registration of Marks (Madrid Agreement), originally adopted in 1891, sets up the Madrid Union, an international system for the registration of trademarks and other marks. The United States, however, is not a party, nor are several other major manufacturers and exporters of trademarked goods, including Japan, Korea, Sweden, and the United Kingdom. All of these countries, including the United States, have since become parties to the Madrid Union under the Protocol Relating to the Madrid Agreement Concerning the International Registration of Marks (Madrid Protocol), originally adopted in 1989. Seventy-six countries and the European Community are now parties to the Madrid Union via the Madrid Agreement, the

Madrid Protocol, or both; the United States became a party in November 2003. Conspicuous by their absence are the countries of Latin America. In 2003 the Madrid Protocol adopted Spanish as a third official language, in addition to French and English, in the hopes of encouraging Latin American countries to join (Hines 2004). The Madrid Agreement, despite its name, has only French as its official language (Madrid Agreement art. 17).

The eleven countries that are parties to the agreement but not the protocol (Algeria, Azerbaijan, Bosnia and Herzegovina, Egypt, Kazakhstan, Liberia, San Marino, Sudan, Tajikistan, Uzbekistan, and Vietnam) and the twenty countries that are parties to the protocol but not the agreement, plus the European Community, are nonetheless all parties to the union (Madrid Protocol art. 1; Madrid Agreement art. 1).

Under the Madrid Protocol, persons who wish to seek protection for a trademark or other mark in any or all of the Madrid Union's member countries may do so with a single application (in English, Spanish, or French) at any office authorized to accept applications for protection in a member state; U.S. parties, for example, may do so with the U.S. Patent and Trademark Office (Madrid Protocol arts. 2–3). States that are parties only to the agreement, in contrast, must file a registration of the mark in French with the World Intellectual Property Organization (Madrid Agreement art. 1). The Madrid Protocol, unlike the agreement, also permits international registration as soon as an application is filed in the home country, rather than after the registration is granted in the home country (McCarthy 2004, 360). After a mark has been registered for five years, the protocol also allows the international protection to remain valid even if the home country registration lapses; after five years, the international registration becomes independent of the home country registration (Madrid Protocol art. 6).

Treaties
- Madrid Agreement Concerning the International Registration of Marks, Apr. 14, 1891, as revised at Brussels, Dec. 14, 1900, at Washington, June 2, 1911, at The Hague, Nov. 6, 1925, at London, June 2, 1934, at Nice, June 15, 1957, at Stockholm, July 14, 1967, and as amended Sept. 28, 1979, available from http://www.wipo.int/madrid/en/legal_texts/ (PDF download)(visited November 9, 2004)
- Protocol Relating to the Madrid Agreement Concerning the International Registration of Marks, June 27, 1989, available from http://www.wipo.int/madrid/en/legal_texts/ (PDF download) (visited November 9, 2004)

See also: International Trademark Protection; Paris Convention; Trademark; TRIPS; WIPO

Sources and further reading:
P. Jay Hines, "The Year That Was: Madrid Protocol Milestones in 2003," Oblon, Spivak, McClelland, Maier and Neustadt, P.C., 2004, available at http://www.oblon.com/Pub/display.php?TheYearThatWas0704.htm (visited November 16, 2004).
J. Thomas McCarthy et al., *McCarthy's Desk Encyclopedia of Intellectual Property*, 3d ed. (Washington, DC: Bureau of National Affairs, 2004).

❖ MALWARE ❖

Malware is a catchall term, a contraction of "malicious software." Malware includes viruses, worms, Trojans, backdoors, and spyware (and, to many users, adware as well). Viruses and worms can spread from one computer to another by replicating themselves. Trojans do not replicate themselves, but are disguised as legitimate software in order to trick the user into installing them. Viruses usually do little besides replicate themselves, infecting other programs and files to do so; however, they can destroy data on a computer and render the computer unusable. Worms and Trojans can serve as vehicles for a variety of programs, including spam mailers and backdoor programs that allow the computer to be used as a zombie in denial-of-service attacks. More malicious uses are also possible, and worms and Trojans can install or enable the installation of programs that allow "black-hat" (malicious) hackers to access information on another user's computer and to perform any action that the legitimate user of the computer would be able to perform. Users of dial-up Internet connections are also vulnerable to dialer programs, often installed via a drive-by download—one in which the user is not notified that a program is being installed. These dialers can switch the user's dial-up connection number to a 900 number or other number that will result in a hefty charge to the user's account. Adware and spyware can slow the user's computer by increasing the amount of advertising the user receives, and spyware can report information on the user's Web-surfing habits and computer use to persons unknown to the user without the user's consent (Symantec 2004).

Malware that enables one user to gain access to another's computer without that user's knowledge or consent is governed by the Computer Fraud and Abuse Act (CFAA) of 1986 (18 U.S.C. § 1030). Section 1030(a)(5) of the CFAA, as amended, deals with malware; it provides for criminal penalties for any person who:

(A)(i) knowingly causes the transmission of a program, information, code, or command, and as a result of such conduct, intentionally causes damage without authorization, to a protected computer;
(ii) intentionally accesses a protected computer without authorization, and as a result of such conduct, recklessly causes damage; or
(iii) intentionally accesses a protected computer without authorization, and as a result of such conduct, causes damage; and
(B) by conduct described in clause (i), (ii), or (iii) of subparagraph (A), caused (or, in the case of an attempted offense, would, if completed, have caused)—
(i) loss to 1 or more persons during any 1-year period (and, for purposes of an investigation, prosecution, or other proceeding brought by the United States only, loss resulting from a related course of conduct affecting 1 or more other protected computers) aggregating at least $5,000 in value;
(ii) the modification or impairment, or potential modification or impairment, of the medical examination, diagnosis, treatment, or care of 1 or more individuals;

(iii) physical injury to any person;
(iv) a threat to public health or safety; or
(v) damage affecting a computer system used by or for a government entity in furtherance of the administration of justice, national defense, or national security[.] (18 U.S.C. § 1030(a)(5))

This is sufficiently verbose and complex to be nearly incomprehensible even to lawyers. In plain English, however, at the risk of some oversimplification and loss of detail, it can be translated as prohibiting any person from doing two types of things with regard to another's computer: No one may knowingly transmit any "program, information, code or command" that intentionally damages another's computer; this covers the sending of harmful viruses, worms, and Trojans. And no person may intentionally or knowingly gain unauthorized access or exceed authorized access to another's computer; courts have interpreted this to cover not only the installation of backdoors and other remote access tools, but also the "access" gained by the worms and other programs themselves (*Morris*, 928 F.2d 504). However, for criminal penalties to attach for unauthorized access or exceeding authorized access, the damage must either be caused recklessly or must be nontrivial; § 1030(a)(5)(B) lists the various types of damage that will make the access a crime even if the damage done by the access was caused accidentally or negligently. These include a loss of more than $5,000; interference with medical examination, diagnosis, care, and treatment; physical injury; a threat (but not necessarily actual harm) to public health or safety; and even trivial damage to certain government computers, those related to the justice system, defense, and national security.

Other statutes may also be applicable to malware. Depending on the type of harm caused, malware users may violate federal statutes against bank fraud (18 U.S.C. § 1344), credit card fraud (18 U.S.C. § 1029), and wire fraud (18 U.S.C. § 1343). They may also violate state privacy and burglary statutes. One type of malware that is not yet well regulated is spyware; much spyware causes no actual damage other than some slowing of the user's computer, but demands from consumer groups are likely to lead to legislative efforts to restrict adware and spyware in the near future.

Statutes
- Bank Fraud Act, 18 U.S.C. § 1344
- Computer Fraud and Abuse Act, 18 U.S.C. § 1030
- Controlling the Assault of Non-solicited Pornography and Marketing (CAN-SPAM) Act of 2003, 15 U.S.C. §§ 7701–7713
- Credit Card Fraud Act, 18 U.S.C. § 1029
- Unfair Methods of Competition, 15 U.S.C. § 45
- Wire Fraud Act, 18 U.S.C. § 1343

Case
- *United States v. Morris,* 928 F.2d 504 (2nd Cir. 1991)

See also: Adware and Spyware; Denial-of-Service Attack; Hacking; Spam; Trojan; Virus; Worm; Zombie

Sources and further reading:
Symantec U.S., "Security Response Glossary," 2004, http://securityresponse.symantec.com/avcenter/refa.html (visited November 13, 2004).

❖ MENU COMMAND HIERARCHY ❖

The menu command hierarchy of a computer program consists of the commands by which a user tells the program to do certain things and the order in which those commands are arranged. When more than one program performs the same function, the commands and command hierarchies of those programs may be similar or identical, raising questions of copyright infringement.

Copyright does not protect ideas, but the expression of ideas. When an idea is capable of only one or a small number of means of expression, those means of expression are not copyrightable. In addition, methods of operation are not copyrightable (17 U.S.C. § 102). The copyrightability of menu commands and menu command hierarchies thus depends on whether there are multiple ways of expressing the same idea, whether the idea is original enough to merit copyright protection, and whether the idea is a method of operation. For example, every keyboard driver has some method by which users can type letters and have them appear on the screen. All of these programs use the same commands: The user types the key marked E, and a letter E appears on the screen. The use of the key marked E to enter the letter E fails the copyrightability test on all three counts. There are no other practical ways of expressing the same idea; for the user to strike some other key or combination of keys in order to enter the letter E would be nonsensical. The idea is not original; the reason the key is marked E is so that it can be used to enter the letter $E,$ an idea derived from typewriter keyboards that predate the advent of personal computing by more than a century. And the "idea" is a method of operation; it serves to operate the computer rather than to express any idea apart from the task of placing a letter E on the screen.

The non-copyrightability of menu commands and command hierarchies might not be so obvious, however. The use of "Control-S" as a command to save a document is intuitive and scarcely original; the use of the F10 key for the same purpose is not intuitive, and might meet the originality requirement for copyrightability. It also meets the "multiple means of expression" test; any of the function keys on the keyboard, or any other key, might be used for the same purpose. It is thus copyrightable unless it is a mere method of operation.

The U.S. Supreme Court addressed this problem in the case of *Lotus Development v. Borland* and concluded that the hierarchy of commands in Lotus Development's Lotus 1-2-3 spreadsheet program was a non-copyrightable method of operation. The Supreme Court affirmed the decision of the appellate court, which had compared the command hierarchy to the buttons on a videocassette recorder (VCR):

> Users operate VCRs by pressing a series of buttons that are typically labeled "Record, Play, Reverse, Fast Forward, Pause, Stop/Eject."

That the buttons are arranged and labeled does not make them a "literary work," nor does it make them an "expression" of the abstract "method of operating" a VCR via a set of labeled buttons. Instead, the buttons are themselves the "method of operating" the VCR.

When a Lotus 1-2-3 user chooses a command, either by highlighting it on the screen or by typing its first letter, he or she effectively pushes a button. Highlighting the "Print" command on the screen, or typing the letter "P," is analogous to pressing a VCR button labeled "Play." (*Lotus*, 49 F.3rd at 817)

Clicking "Print," like pressing "Play," is not an expressive act; its purpose is not to express the idea "Print" or "Play," but to perform the act of printing a document or playing a video. The set of commands that operate a computer program, as well as the hierarchy in which they are ordered, is also a method of operation and not copyrightable. Although the court's decision has been criticized on the grounds that "user interfaces, including menu commands," may be expressive, original works and thus "should receive at least narrow protection under copyright law," the issue has not been revisited (Stagnone 1997, 948).

Statute
- Copyright Act of 1976, 17 U.S.C. §§ 101–105

Case
- *Lotus Development Corporation v. Borland International, Inc.,* 49 F.3rd 807 (1st Cir. 1995), affirmed, 516 U.S. 233 (1996)

See also: Business Methods Patent; Copyright; Copyright Infringement; Look and Feel

Sources and further reading:
Lauren A. Stagnone, "Copyright Law—Computer Program Menu Command Hierarchy: An Uncopyrightable Method of Operation? *Lotus Development Corporation v. Borland International, Inc.,* 49 F.3rd 807 (1995), aff'd, 116 S. Ct. 804 (1996)," 30 *Suffolk University Law Review* 939 (1997).

❖ METATAGS ❖

Metatags are text inserted into an HTML document so as to be invisible when the document is viewed as a Web page. The metatag is inserted near the top of the HTML document, just after the title; it typically takes the form <META name="category" content="thing(s) in category">. Metatags on a Web page can be viewed from a Web browser by selecting "View/Source." There are several uses for metatags; they can contain copyright information or direct the viewer to a new Web page. Legally, however, the most problematic use of metatags has been to include terms that increase the page's chance of being located by search engines, and its rank when located. This by itself is perfectly acceptable, but trademark issues arise when trademarked terms are used as metatags.

The use of a trademark as a metatag by a person other than the trademark holder or someone licensed by the trademark holder is trademark infringement unless an exception applies. The exception most likely to be applicable is the defense of nominative fair use. The Ninth Circuit Court of Appeals set out the elements of nominative fair use as applicable to metatags in the case of *Playboy Enterprises, Inc. v. Welles:*

> First, the product or service in question must be one not readily identifiable without use of the trademark; second, only so much of the mark or marks may be used as is reasonably necessary to identify the product or service; and third, the user must do nothing that would, in conjunction with the mark, suggest sponsorship or endorsement by the trademark holder. (279 F.3d at 801)

The defendant in *Welles,* a former model for *Playboy* magazine, had used the words *playboy* and *playmate* in metatags. In holding this use to be nominative fair use, the Ninth Circuit explained that the first element was met because "Welles has no practical way of describing herself without using trademarked terms. In the context of metatags, we conclude that she has no practical way of identifying the content of her website without referring to PEI's trademarks" (279 F.3d at 803). The second element was met because "[t]he metatags use only so much of the marks as reasonably necessary," and the third element was met because "nothing is done in conjunction with them to suggest sponsorship or endorsement by the trademark holder" (279 F.3d at 804). Whereas a single use of each term was thus nominative fair use, repeated use of the terms might not be: "We note that our decision might differ if the metatags listed the trademarked term so repeatedly that Welles' site would regularly appear above [Playboy's] in searches for one of the trademarked terms" (279 F.3d at 804).

Playboy Enterprise's trademark has been particularly subject to infringement; in cases where the metatag infringement was accompanied by other, more egregious infringement, it has sometimes prevailed (*Playboy Enterprises, Inc. v. AsiaFocus, Int'l*, 1998). And though feuding pornographers should attract little sympathy, mainstream businesses have also been involved in metatag trademark infringement litigation. *Niton Corporation v. Radiation Monitoring Devices, Inc.* involved metatags on the Web pages of Radiation Monitoring Devices, Inc. (RMD) that said "The Home Page of Niton Corporation, makers of the finest lead, radon and multi-element detectors" (27 F.Supp.2d at 104). The district court issued an injunction prohibiting RMD from using this and similar metatags, holding that Niton had shown that it was likely to succeed on the merits of its trademark infringement claim (27 F.Supp.2d at 104–105).

Thus the use of trademarks as metatags solely to identify the user's products or services and not to mislead is generally permissible, but the use of the trademarks with the intent to mislead search engines and Web surfers or to harm the trademark holder seems not to be. There is one special case, however: Some Web sites use trademarks as metatags not because they wish to steal business that would otherwise have gone to the trademark owner, but because they wish to criticize the trademark owner. The problem is analogous to the "sucks" problem in cybersquatting, in which critics of, say, Lucent Technologies register the domain name www.lucentsucks.com in order to post their criticisms. Metatags are not covered by the Anticybersquatting Consumer Protection Act (*Computer and Internet Lawyer* 2000, 44);

Snow White and the search engine spammers: Search engine spammers can combine metatag or keyword abuse with typosquatting to lure users who mis-type common search terms. In early 2004 a U.S. typosquatter was sentence to two and a half years in prison for using misspelled trademarked terms, including trademarked names from Disney and Harry Potter works, to mousetrap surfers and lure them to pornographic Web sites. The use of search terms likely to be used—and misspelled—by children led to the prison term under the Truth in Domain Names Act, which criminalizes luring children to pornographic Web sites.

Source

Jo Best, "Disney-Porn Hook-Up Sends Typosquatter to Jail," Silicon.com, Mar. 1, 2004, available at http://www.silicon.com/networks/webwatch/0,39024667,39118757,00.htm (visited January 8, 2005);

"Man Accused of Luring Kids to Porn Sites," CNN.com, Sept. 3, 2003, available at http://www.cnn.com/2003/TECH/internet/09/03/trick.names/ (visited January 8, 2005).

---

such use of metatags is likely to meet the three prongs of the *Playboy Enterprises* test and thus is generally permissible, although the content of the site may give rise to other claims for trademark infringement and defamation.

With the advent of Google (which does not use metatags) and the resulting necessary improvements in the technology of its competitors, the problems relating to metatags may be about to solve themselves through technological obsolescence. Search engines now rarely use metatags. However, search term metatags are still often included in Web pages from force of habit.

Statute

- Lanham Trademark Act, 15 U.S.C. § 1115(b)

Case

Federal Appellate Courts

- *Playboy Enterprises, Inc. v. Welles*, 279 F.3d 796 (9th Cir. 2002)

Federal Trial Courts
- *Bihari v. Gross,* 119 F.Supp.2d 309 (S.D. N.Y. 2000)
- *Lucent Technologies, Inc. v. Lucentsucks.com,* 95 F.Supp.2d 528 (E.D. Va. 2000)
- *Niton Corp. v. Radiation Monitoring Devices, Inc.,* 27 F.Supp.2d 102 (D. Mass. 1998)
- *Playboy Enterprises, Inc. v. AsiaFocus, Int'l,* 1998 U.S. Dist. LEXIS 10359 (E.D. Va. 1998)

See also: Cybersquatting; Fair Use (Trademark); Trademark; Trademark Dilution; Trademark Infringement

Sources and further reading:
G. Peter Albert Jr. and Rita A. Abbati, "Metatags, Keywords and Links: Recent Developments Addressing Trademark Threats in Cyberspace," 40 *San Diego Law Review* 341 (2003).

Katherine Ivancevich, "*Promatek Industries, Inc. v. Equitrac Corporation:* Promoting the Metatag Fallacy," 12 *DePaul-LCA Journal of Art and Entertainment Law* 351 (2002).

Douglas G. McCray, "Oh, What a Tangled Web: The Subtle Difference between Metatag Usage as 'Fair Use' and Invisible Infringement," *Michigan Bar Journal,* Aug. 2002, at 42.

Alex Michael and Ben Salter, *Marketing through Search Optimization: How to Be Found on the Web* (Burlington, MA: Butterworth-Heinemann, 2003).

"No Lanham Act Claim Where Trademark Was Used in Metatags for Web Site Criticizing Trademark Owner," *Computer and Internet Lawyer,* Dec. 2000, at 44.

Hope Viner Samborn, "Hiding in Plain Site: The Hunt for Metatags on the Internet Is Changing the Field of Trademark Law," *ABA Journal* Sept. 2000, at 80.

Shari Thurow, *Search Engine Visibility* (Berkeley, CA: New Riders Press, 2002).

Bettina Wendlandt, *Cybersquatting, Metatags und Spam* (München: Beck Juristischer Verlag, 2002) (in German).

❖ MICROSOFT ANTITRUST LITIGATION ❖

Microsoft Corporation enjoys a near-complete monopoly in the personal computer operating system and Web browser markets, and its Works and Office packages dominate the markets for word-processing software, spreadsheets, and presentation software. Microsoft is an aggressive business competitor; many smaller businesses, including former market leaders such as Netscape, have been unable to thrive in the face of competition from Microsoft. Private companies and government attorneys have sought to restrain Microsoft with laws designed to prevent single business entities from monopolizing entire industries.

Chief among these laws are sections 1 and 2 of the Sherman Antitrust Act, which prohibit contracts in restraint of trade and monopolization respectively (15 U.S.C. § 1 & 2). Many state laws contain similar restrictions. The Federal Trade Commission (FTC) had taken an interest in possible monopolistic practices by Microsoft as early as 1991; the FTC closed its investigation in 1993 without bringing suit, and in the same year the Department of Justice (DOJ) began its own investigation. In July 1994 the government and Microsoft entered into a consent decree under which Microsoft agreed not to charge a per processor licensing fee or tie other Microsoft products to the Windows operating system (Software Publishers Association 1998). In 1995, however, the consent decree was rejected by a federal district court as too lenient; this decision was overturned by an appellate court, which transferred the case to a new judge, Penfield Jackson. Judge Jackson approved the consent decree just as the browser wars between Microsoft and Netscape were beginning. Microsoft began giving away Internet Explorer (IE), its Web browser, for free at a time when Netscape was still charging for its browser. Microsoft later incorporated IE into Windows, refusing to sell a version of Windows without it (Software Publishers Association 1998). In 1996 the DOJ began a new investigation, this time into whether Microsoft had violated the terms of the consent decree. The browser wars continued, and in 1997 Netscape's share of the browser market fell from 90% to 60%. At the same time Microsoft attracted other opponents: Sun Microsystems filed a suit accusing Microsoft of attempting to undermine Sun's Java technology by not using Java with IE

(*Sun*, 81 F.Supp.2d 1026). Not long after Sun filed its suit, the DOJ also filed suit alleging that Microsoft had violated the 1994 consent decree by forcing PC makers to use IE on new PCs as a condition of obtaining a Windows license. Judge Jackson agreed, and the court issued an injunction requiring Microsoft to "cease and desist . . . from [this] practice" (980 F. Supp. at 545). Six days later the DOJ asked the court to hold Microsoft in contempt after Microsoft allegedly offered computer makers old and defective copies of Windows 95. In January 1998 Microsoft signed an agreement permitting computer makers to install Windows without the IE icon (Software Publishers Association 1998).

The DOJ's suit centered on the bundling of IE with Windows in new computers; Microsoft appealed Judge Jackson's decision and sought the removal of the Special Master, Lawrence Lessig, appointed by Jackson. In 1998 the District of Columbia Circuit Court of Appeals reversed Judge Jackson's grant of an injunction against Microsoft because the consent decree had accepted as legitimate the integration of Windows with the basic operating system and the DOJ had not demonstrated that that the integration of Windows and IE was sufficiently different (147 F.3d at 956).

The DOJ and several state governments then brought suit against Microsoft. The District Court determined, after a trial, that Microsoft was in violation of section 2 of the Sherman Act (the anti-monopoly provision). The court ordered that Microsoft be divided into two companies, one producing Windows and the other applications software. On appeal, the D.C. Circuit upheld the section 2 holding, but overturned the order to split the company and remanded the case. The parties then agreed to a consent decree that allowed Microsoft to continue to operate as an integrated company. Microsoft retains its near-monopoly in browsers and operating systems. What may have been the final blow to the effort to break up Microsoft came on June 30, 2004, with the D.C. Circuit's decision in *Massachusetts v. Microsoft*. Massachusetts, along with several other states, had refused to join in an earlier consent decree, and had continued to pursue an "unbundling" solution, separating IE and other programs from the Windows operating system. Microsoft had rejected the solution as technically not feasible; opponents had hoped that the two-company solution would open up both fields, operating systems and applications, to increased competition (Cohen 2004). By rejecting Massachusetts' challenge to the consent decree, the D.C. Circuit seems to have eliminated any possibility that Microsoft will be split into two companies or otherwise forced to unbundle its operating systems and applications (See 373 F.3rd 1241-1242).

But as the antitrust suits against Microsoft in the United States slowly wound down, European Union regulators began to consider similar suits. The European Commission (EC) cannot impose the profound structural changes upon a company that a U.S. court might impose; it cannot break up Microsoft. Its powers are limited to enjoining future violations and imposing fines and other penalties related to the offending conduct (Cohen 2004, 356), such as requiring Microsoft to disclose previously confidential information about its products or to package competing programs, as well as its own, with Windows.

The EC has focused on two areas related to the Sun Microsystems complaint but largely overlooked by the U.S. DOJ's antitrust efforts: the effect of Microsoft's Windows Media Player on the market for streaming media technology, and Microsoft's creation of applications programs that can only achieve full interoperability when used with Microsoft server software. The first of these arises from concerns similar to Sun's, while the second directly follows on Sun's complaint. In March of 2004 the EC found against Microsoft on both charges (George 2004, 577). In the future the EC may also investigate "price increases for Windows upgrade licensing, leveraging of power in the operating system market into the market for mobile phone software, and predatory pricing aimed at retarding the growth of GNU/Linux in developing markets" (Cohen 2004, 356). Some of Microsoft's discounting practices may also be illegal in Europe even if they are legal in the U.S.

Statutes

- Sherman Antitrust Act, 15 U.S.C. § 1, 2

Cases

- *United States v. Microsoft Corp.*, 980 F. Supp. 537 (D.D.C. 1997), reversed, 147 F.3d 935 (D.C. Cir. 1998)
- *In re Microsoft Corporation Antitrust Litigation*, 127 F.Supp.2d 702 (D. Md. 2001)
- *United States v. Microsoft Corp.*, 87 F.Supp.2d 30 (D.D.C. 2000); affirmed in part, reversed in part, 253 F.3d 34 (D.C. Cir. 2001); cert. denied sub nom *Microsoft Corp. v. United States*, 534 U.S. 952 (2001); on remand, *U.S. v. Microsoft*, 231 F.Supp.2d 144; affirmed by *Massachusetts v. Microsoft Corp.*, 373 F.3d 1199 (D.C. Cir. 2004)
- *New York v. Microsoft Corp.*, 2002 WL 31961461 (D.D.C. 2002)
- *Sun Microsystems, Inc. v. Microsoft Corp.*, 81 F.Supp.2d 1026 (N.D. Cal. 2000)

Complaints

- *United States v. Microsoft Corp.*, 980 F. Supp. 537 (D.D.C. 1997), reversed, 147 F.3d 935 (D.C. Cir. 1998)
- Complaint of State Attorneys General against Microsoft, May 18, 1998, available at http://www.courttv.com/archive/legaldocs/cyberlaw/microsoft/state_suit.html (visited November 9, 2004)

See also: Internet; Open-Source; Web Browser; World Wide Web

Sources and further reading:
Amanda Cohen, "Surveying the Microsoft Antitrust Universe," 19 *Berkeley Technology Law Journal* 333 (2004).
Barbara Crutchfield George et al., "Increasing Extraterritorial Intrusion of European Union Law into U.S. Business Mergers and Competition Practices: U.S. Multinational Businesses Underestimate the Strength of the European Commission from G.E.-Honeywell to Microsoft," 19 *Connecticut Journal of International Law* 571 (2004).
Robert A. Levy, "Microsoft and the Browser Wars," 31 *Connecticut Law Review* 1321 (1999).
Ramona Mateiu, "*In re Microsoft Corporation Antitrust Litigation*," 17 *Berkeley Technology Law Journal* 295 (2002).
Holger Metzger, "Netscape History," 2004, http://www.holgermetzger.de/Netscape_History.html (visited November 9, 2004).
Netscape Press Release, "Mosaic Communications Corporation Changes Name to Netscape Communications Corporation," Nov. 14, 1994, available at http://www.holgermetzger.de/netscape/NetscapeCommunicationsNewsRelease.htm (visited November 9, 2004).
Software Publishers Association, "Timeline of Events Surrounding Microsoft Antitrust Case," 1998, http://www.procompetition.org/litigation/timeline.html (visited November 9, 2004).

❖ MORAL RIGHTS ❖

Traditionally European, but not U.S., copyright law protected the so-called moral rights of an author: the right to integrity (the right to protect the work from changes that could damage the work's or the author's reputation); the right of paternity (also known as the right of attribution: the right to be identified as the author of a work and to prevent one's name from being associated with a modified version of the work); and the right of withdrawal (the right to withdraw a work from distribution if it no longer represents the views of the author). Not only are these not economic rights of the author, they can actually harm the economic interests of others if exercised.

U.S. law has historically been unreceptive to moral rights, both because copyright is viewed as an economic right (and moral rights are noneconomic) and because of the potential for conflict with First Amendment freedom of expression. If, as Richard Wilbur wrote, "Edgar Degas purchased once/A fine El Greco, which he kept/Against the wall beside his bed/To hang his pants on while he slept," then Degas might conceivably have violated El Greco's moral rights (Wilbur 1987, 292; the point is moot, however, because El Greco had been dead for more than two centuries when Degas was born). After Armand Vaillancourt painted the slogan "Vive le Quebec libre" on his fountain-sculpture (named *Quebec Libre*) at Justin Herman Plaza in San Francisco, the city government sent workers to remove his words; when Vaillancourt re-painted the slogan, the workers erased it yet again. (The fountain was spray-painted again by the musician Bono in 1987, this time with the words "Rock and roll stops the traffic.") The removal of the slogan might have violated Vaillancourt's moral rights had they been recognized under U.S. law at the time.

The United States has accorded limited protection of moral rights to some paintings, sculptures, and similar works under the Visual Artists' Rights Act (17 U.S.C. § 106A). Recognition of moral rights can present constitutional problems as well; it may conflict with the First Amendment (expressing disregard for a painting by hanging one's pants on it is surely protected expression) and may not be authorized under the Patent and Copyright Clause. Taken to its extreme, the idea of moral rights, even in paintings, becomes untenable: Most people would probably be appalled at the idea that the estate of serial killer John Wayne Gacy might be able to recover damages from people who bought his paintings in order to burn them.

European legal systems have also recognized moral rights in trademarks. At one time U.S. law was willing to recognize the rights of integrity and attribution with regard to trademarks under the Lanham Trademark Act. The U.S. Supreme Court's recent decision in *Dastar v. Twentieth Century Fox* seems to have severely limited the enforceability of these rights, however (539 U.S. 23).

U.S. law and practice remains significantly out of step with international norms in the area of moral rights; because of the conflict between moral rights and First Amendment freedoms, this situation is likely to persist. Under TRIPS, members of the World Trade Organization agree to comply with the 1971 revision of the Berne Convention; its main substantive provisions, with the exception of Berne Convention Article 6bis (dealing with moral rights) are incorporated into TRIPS by reference. This exception takes into account the concerns of those countries, especially the United States, that are unwilling to impose broad protections of moral rights.

Treaties
- Agreement on Trade-Related Aspects of Intellectual Property Rights, Marrakesh Agreement Establishing the World Trade Organization, Annex 1C, Apr. 15, 1994, 33 I.L.M. 81 (1994)
- Convention Concerning the Creation of an International Union for the Protection of Literary and Artistic Works (Berne Convention), Sept. 9, 1886, as last revised at Paris, July 24, 1971 (amended 1979), 25 U.S.T. 1341, 828 U.N.T.S. 221

Statutes
- Copyright Act of 1976, 17 U.S.C. §§ 101–1332
- Visual Artists Rights Act, 17 U.S.C. § 106A

Case
- *Dastar v. Twentieth Century Fox, Inc.*, 539 U.S. 23 (2003)

See also: Berne Convention; Copyright; International Copyright Protection; Trademark; TRIPS (Copyright)

Sources and further reading:
Stephen R. Elias, *Patent, Copyright & Trademark: An Intellectual Property Desk Reference*, 7th ed. (Berkeley, CA: Nolo Press, 2004).
Marshall Leaffer, *Understanding Copyright Law*, 3d ed. (New York: Matthew Bender, 1999).
J. Thomas McCarthy et al., *McCarthy's Desk Encyclopedia of Intellectual Property*, 3d ed. (Washington, DC: Bureau of National Affairs, 2004).
"Some of John Wayne Gacy's Artwork Displayed in West Palm Beach," Associated Press, June 5, 2004, available at http://www.fadp.org/news/MGBIUQQU3VD.html (visited October 21, 2004).
Richard Wilbur, "Museum Piece," in *New and Collected Poems* 292 (Fort Washington, PA: Harvest Books, 1987).

❖ MOUSETRAPPING ❖

See Cybersquatting

❖ MP3 ❖

MP3 is both the name of a file format and the name of a dot-com company, MP3.com. The file format is actually MPEG-1/2 Audio Layer 3, but is abbreviated as MP3 when used in a Windows file suffix or referred to in a nontechnical sense. "MPEG," in turn, stands for "Moving Picture Experts Group," often incorrectly given as "Motion Picture Experts Group." The Moving Picture Experts Group is an organization that seeks to develop formats for video and multimedia storage and playback.

The MP3 format has proven to be especially well adapted to the compact storage of audio files of about three to five minutes in length that demand polyphony and a range of tones and intensities, but for which some loss during compression can be tolerated. This makes it ideal for compressing popular songs; large numbers of songs can be stored on a computer's hard drive, a portable MP3 player, a CD, or any other digital storage medium. The quality, compactness, and versatility of the MP3 format make it a consumer's dream: Once the consumer has purchased an authorized copy of a popular song, she may make an MP3 compressed copy and space-shift it to play it on just about any other device she owns.

Unfortunately, the same qualities that make the MP3 format a consumer's dream make it the music content industry's nightmare. Before the advent of the MP3 format and the Internet, the music content industry had learned to accept, if not like, the fact that home recording for space-shifting purposes was a fair use of copyrighted material. But MP3 files are small enough to be shared across the Internet in seconds; they can be e-mailed and posted on Web sites—or shared over file-sharing networks. Teenagers who might have to save their allowances for a month to buy a single album at the music content industry's retail price, and might want only one song on the album, can now download hundreds of songs in an evening for free—as long as they can find someone who has a copy of the song and is willing to share it online. Although sharing with a friend might still fall within the fuzzy parameters of fair use set by 17 U.S.C. § 107, sharing with large numbers of unknown strangers does not (*Napster*, 239 F.3d 1004).

MP3.com, a company based in San Diego, California, was an early entrant into the Internet music field. MP3.com purchased CDs containing tens of thousands of copyrighted songs and converted them to MP3 format. It then placed these MP3 files on its servers; any subscriber to MP3.com's MyMP3.com service could access the servers and obtain the MP3 files. To protect against copyright infringement, MyMP3.com customers were required to demonstrate that they owned, or at least had access to, an authorized copy of the work they wished to download; this was done by placing an authorized recorded CD in the subscriber's computer. Although this seems absurdly cumbersome today, it made a certain amount of sense in a time when not all users could simply prepare their own MP3s from the CD.

"We're a record label. But we're not evil."

—*Magnatune*

Music as shareware: Apple's iTunes and the Electronic Frontier Foundation's proposed Voluntary Collective License are two possible solutions to the problem of distributing music online with maximum convenience for consumers while still ensuring revenue for the artists. A small company called Magnatune takes a different approach: It treats MP3 files as files that just happen to contain music, and distributes music as shareware.

Magnatune's customers can listen to entire albums on the Magnatune site, whenever they wish, as often as they wish, and only buy the albums if they wish to. The selection is limited, of course, to those performers that will agree to such an arrangement, and so far the number is small, although Magnatune declares "Our selection is intentionally small: we never waste your time with mediocre music."

Source
Magnatune Web site, http://magnatune.com/ (visited January 6, 2005).

MP3.com's other line of business was the direct offering to the public of musical works; these were almost exclusively works of artists without record contracts with the music content industry. On the day of its initial public offering MP3.com's share price opened at an astonishing $92 per share (Nerney 1999). At the height of the dot-com madness MP3.com's stock was still trading at $44 a share with a total market capitalization of nearly three billion dollars—more than twenty-four hundred times its annual earnings (Casey 2001).

The music content industry reacted with alarm to MyMP3.com, and sued for copyright infringement. The federal district court for the Southern District of New York held that MP3.com's copying and posting of its CDs were not protected fair use. The district court's decision might have played a part in the collapse of MP3.com's share price and the bursting of the dot-com bubble, but the share prices were so inflated that the collapse was inevitable.

The music content industry's victory over MP3.com might have paved the way for other file-sharing networks. File-sharers took the decision as a sign that centralized file-sharing networks on the MP3.com model, rather than all file-sharing networks, were illegal, and began to design around the decision, eventually building today's P2P networks.

Cases
Federal Appellate Courts
- *A&M Records, Inc. v. Napster, Inc.,* 239 F.3d 1004 (9th Cir. 2001)
- *Recording Industry Association of America v. Diamond Multimedia Systems, Inc.,* 180 F.3d 1072 (9th Cir. 1999)

Federal Trial Court
- *UMG Recordings, Inc. v. MP3.com, Inc.,* 92 F.Supp.2d 349 (S.D. N.Y. 2000)

See also: .com; Content Industry; Copyright; Copyright Infringement; Fair Use (Copyright); File-Sharing; KaZaA; P2P

Sources and further reading:

Doug Casey, "Your 'Net' Investment: Then and Now," Feb. 22, 2001, *WorldNetDaily.com,* http://www.worldnetdaily.com/news/article.asp?ARTICLE_ID=21814 (visited October 21, 2004).

Bruce Haring, *Beyond the Charts: MP3 and the Digital Music Revolution* (Los Angeles, CA: JM Northern Media LLC, 2000).

Chris Nerney, "Early MP3.com Investors May Be Singing Sad Tune," Internetnews.com, July 26, 1999, http://www.internetnews.com/bus-news/article.php/168501 (visited October 21, 2004).

N

❖ NAPSTER ❖

See File-Sharing

❖ NCIPA ❖

See Children's Internet Protection Act

❖ NO ELECTRONIC THEFT ACT ❖

The No Electronic Theft Act (NET Act) was enacted in 1997 to address the specific problem of warez trading and the general problem of intellectual property piracy. The NET Act was a response to an early unsuccessful attempt to prosecute a warez trader, David LaMacchia, a twenty-one-year-old student at the Massachusetts Institute of Technology (MIT). LaMacchia operated a bulletin board system (BBS), making use of MIT's network to do so. In the early 1990s LaMacchia's BBS, Cynosure, enabled users to upload and download popular software of the day, such as WordPerfect 6.0, Excel 5.0, and SimCity 2000. Because LaMacchia did not operate Cynosure for financial gain, he could not be charged directly with criminal copyright infringement under the law at the time. In 1994 LaMacchia was arrested and charged with conspiracy to violate the federal wire fraud statute, 18 U.S.C. § 1343 (*LaMacchia*, 871 F.Supp. at 536). The federal district court for the District of Massachusetts dismissed the charges against LaMacchia. An earlier Supreme Court decision, *Dowling v. United States*, had held that intellectual prop-

erty, including copyright, could not be taken by fraud; thus LaMacchia could not have conspired to commit a fraud to take the copyright owners' property interests in the software (*LaMacchia*, 871 F.Supp. at 545). The district court was not particularly pleased with its own result and called LaMacchia's conduct "at best . . . heedlessly irresponsible, and at worst . . . nihilistic, self-indulgent, and lacking in any fundamental sense of values" (*LaMacchia*, 871 F. Supp. at 545). Congress, the court suggested, should modify the law: "Criminal as well as civil penalties should probably attach to willful, multiple infringements of copyrighted software even absent a commercial motive on the part of the infringer" (*LaMacchia*, 871 F. Supp. at 545).

It took three years for Congress, at the urging of content industry lobbyists, to make the modifications suggested by the court. In 1997 Congress enacted the No Electronic Theft Act in order, according to the House of Representatives report on the bill, "to reverse the practical consequences of *United States v. LaMacchia*" (House Report, 339). Eric Goldman, an expert commentator on the NET Act, describes its effects as follows:

> The Act effected six principal changes to criminal copyright law. First, the NET Act expanded the Copyright Act's definition of "financial gain" to include the receipt (or expectation of receipt) of anything of value, including other copyrighted works. Second, in addition to willful infringement for commercial advantage or private financial gain, the Act criminalized the reproduction or distribution, in any 180 day period, of copyrighted works with a total retail value of more than $1,000. Third,

the Act said that evidence of reproducing and distributing copyrighted works does not, by itself, establish willfulness. Fourth, the Act changed the punishments for criminal infringement. For infringements of more than $1,000, the punishment includes imprisonment of up to one year and a fine. For infringements of $2,500 or more, the punishment includes imprisonment of up to three years and a fine. For second or subsequent offenses involving commercial advantage or private financial gain, the punishment includes imprisonment of up to six years. Fifth, the Act permits copyright infringement victims to submit victim impact statements. Finally, the Act instructed the United States Sentencing Commission . . . to adjust the United States Sentencing Guidelines . . . for criminal copyright infringement to make the punishments sufficiently stringent to deter the crimes and to reflect the infringed items' retail value and quantity. (Goldman 2003, 373–374)

After reviewing the provisions and the legislative history of the act, Goldman concludes that "Congress specifically targeted warez trading" of the nonprofit, enthusiast type engaged in by LaMacchia and others (Goldman 2003, 375).

The first eighteen months after the passage of the NET Act brought no prosecutions, leading Congress to convene hearings to inquire as to the lack of activity. Following the hearings, the Justice Department began to pursue prosecutions under the NET Act, and by February 2004 at least eighty warez traders and pirates had been convicted. Many of these, including many enthusiast warez traders with no financial motive, were sent to prison (Goldman 2004, 427). Several of the prosecutions resulted from the 2001 Department of Justice crackdown on the long-running cracker/warez group DrinkOrDie (see Tresco *Slashdot* Interview 2002).

Statute
- No Electronic Theft Act, amending and codified at 17 U.S.C. §§ 101, 506, and 507 and 18 U.S.C. §§ 2319–2320

Legislative History
- House Report on the No Electronic Theft Act, H.R. Rep. No. 339, 105th Cong., 1st Sess. 1997, 1997 WL 664424

Cases
Supreme Court
- *Dowling v. United States,* 473 U.S. 207 (1985)

Federal District Court
- *United States v. LaMacchia,* 871 F.Supp. 535 (D. Mass. 1994)

See also: Abandonware; Copyright; Copyright Infringement; File-Sharing; Hacking; Warez

Sources and further reading:
"Former DrinkOrDie Member Chris Tresco Answers," *Slashdot,* Oct. 4, 2002, http://interviews.slashdot.org/interviews/02/10/04/144217.shtml?tid=123 (visited October 20, 2004).
Eric Goldman, "A Road to No Warez: The No Electronic Theft Act and Criminal Copyright Infringement," 82 *Oregon Law Review* 369 (2003).
Eric Goldman, "Warez Trading and Criminal Copyright Infringement," 51 *Journal of the Copyright Society of the U.S.A.* 395 (2004).
"Six Formerly Associated with Fox Cable Charged with Copyright Infringement for Running Warez Site that Had Pirated Movies, Software," *Cybercrime Law Report,* May 31, 2004, at 21.

❖ OBSCENITY ❖

Expression that is obscene is not protected by the First Amendment. Defining "obscene" in universally comprehensible and applicable terms has presented some difficulty, however. The legal definition currently in use, established by the U.S. Supreme Court in the 1973 case of *Miller v. California,* was arrived at only after much litigation and deliberation and many false starts. The Supreme Court's first attempt to address the problem came in the 1957 case of *Roth v. United States.* The *Roth* court defined expression as obscene if "to the average person, applying contemporary community standards, the dominant theme of the material, taken as a whole, appeals to prurient interest" and if it is "utterly without redeeming social importance" (354 U.S. 484, 489). This rule contains elements of the rule finally adopted; however, it proved difficult to apply and resulted in many erroneous decisions in lower courts. The Supreme Court revisited the issue in the 1964 case of *Jacobellis v. Ohio.* In *Jacobellis* the Court added a requirement that expression, in order to be obscene, must go "substantially beyond customary limits of candor in description or representation" (378 U.S. 191). The *Jacobellis* court also struggled with the difficulty of determining "community standards"; at that time it decided that the "community" referred to in the phrase "contemporary community standards" was a national, not local, community (378 U.S. 192). Nine years later the Supreme Court was to reverse itself on this point in *Miller v. California,* the case that set the standard currently in use.

In 1973 the Court decided *Miller v. California,* a case involving the mass-mailing of sexually explicit advertising. Miller is thus relevant not only to the general problem of Internet pornography and obscenity but also to the specific problem of sexually explicit spam. The *Miller* court created a three-part test. In order to determine whether content is obscene it must be determined

> (a) whether the "average person, applying contemporary community standards" would find that the work, taken as a whole, appeals to the prurient interest,
> (b) whether the work depicts or describes, in a patently offensive way, sexual conduct specifically defined by the applicable state law, and
> (c) whether the work, taken as a whole, lacks serious literary, artistic, political, or scientific value. (413 U.S. at 39)

This definition, with its "community standards" element, covers a broader range of material than the definitions in *Roth* and *Jacobellis.* It has also proven capable enough of application to endure, with occasional clarifications, for more than thirty years so far.

In making determinations as to obscenity, jurors are to apply the standards of the area from which they come as "community standards." An appeal to the prurient interest, under the California law addressed in *Miller,* was an appeal to "shameful or morbid interests" in sexual conduct, but not something that incites "normal" lust, despite the obvious problems of moral relativity and value judgments implicit in distinguishing between "shameful" and "normal" lusts.

The obscenity cases brought to the Supreme Court in the 1960s and early 1970s gave rise to one of the Court's more bizarre traditions: Movie Day. In *The Brethren,* Bob Woodward and Scott Armstrong describe the justices and their law clerks sitting down with bags of popcorn in the Court's screening room to watch the pornographic films at issue in cases before the Court. Only one, free-speech absolutist Justice Hugo Black, refused to attend Movie Days, saying, "If I want to go see that film, I should pay my money."

Sources
Judith Silver, "Movie Day at the Supreme Court or 'I Know It When I See It': A History of the Definition of Obscenity," FindLaw/Coollawyer Inc., 2003, available at http://library.lp.findlaw.com/articles/file/00982/008860/title/Subject/topic/Constitutional%20Law_First%20Amendment%20-%20Freedom%20of%20Speech/filename/constitutionallaw_1_86 (visited December 10, 2004);
Scott Armstrong, *The Brethren: Inside the Supreme Court* (New York: Simon and Schuster, 1979).

The term *average person* includes only adults, not children. "Serious artistic, political, or scientific value" is determined according to a national, not local, standard. Material that meets some, but not all, of the criteria of the Miller test may be indecent, but not obscene. According to the Supreme Court's opinion in *Federal Communications Commission v. Pacifica,* indecent material can be identified by its "nonconformance with accepted standards of morality." The objectionable material in the *Pacifica* case was comedian George Carlin's notorious "Filthy Words" (also known as "Seven Deadly Words") monologue. The monologue appeals to no prurient interest in sex; thus, it does not meet the first element of the *Miller* test. It is not about sex or intended to titillate; its apparent purpose is to make a point about censorship and about what makes certain speech offensive in some contexts but not in others. However, Carlin makes his points in part by explicit sexual and scatological descriptions apparently intended to shock (and, by extension, offend) at least part of his audience; thus, the monologue

may meet the second of the three elements of the *Miller* test. It probably does not meet the third element of the test: The monologue has at least some literary, artistic, and political value, perhaps even serious value. Because the three elements are not all met, the monologue is not obscene, even though it is vulgar, offensive, and shocking. It can be (and is) indecent, however, and thus subject to some restrictions (*Pacifica,* 438 U.S. 726).

Cases
- *Ashcroft v. Free Speech Coalition,* 535 U.S. 234 (2002)
- *Brockett v. Spokane Arcades Inc.,* 472 U.S. 491 (1985)
- *Federal Communications Commission v. Pacifica,* 438 U.S. 726 (1978)
- *Hamling v. United States,* 418 U.S. 87 (1974)
- *Jacobellis v. Ohio,* 378 U.S. 184 (1964)
- *Miller v. California,* 413 U.S. 15 (1973)
- *Mishkin v. New York,* 383 U.S. 502 (1966)
- *Paris Adult Theatre v. Slaton,* 413 U.S. 49 (1973)
- *Pinkus v. United States,* 436 U.S. 293 (1978)
- *Pope v. Illinois,* 481 U.S. 497 (1987)
- *Reno v. American Civil Liberties Union,* 521 U.S. 844 (1997)
- *Roth v. United States,* 354 U.S. 476 (1957)

See also: Censorship; Child Online Protection Act; Children's Internet Protection Act; Communications Decency Act; Constitutional Law; First Amendment; Indecency; Pornography; Spam

Sources and further reading:
Jerome A. Barron and C. Thomas Dienes, *Constitutional Law in a Nutshell* (St. Paul, MN: West, 2002).
Mike Godwin, *Cyber Rights: Defending Free Speech in the Digital Age* (Cambridge, MA: MIT Press, 2003).
Kevin W. Saunders, *Saving Our Children from the First Amendment* (New York: New York University Press, 2004).
Madeleine Schachter, *Law of Internet Speech,* 2d ed. (Durham, NC: Carolina Academic Press, 2002).

❖ ONLINE COPYRIGHT INFRINGEMENT LIABILITY LIMITATION ACT ❖

See Digital Millennium Copyright Act, Title II

❖ OPEN-SOURCE ❖

The term *open-source* originally referred to software whose source code is freely distributed and may be modified by users. *Open-source* is now used for other information resources as well, including the open-source encyclopedia Wikipedia (*Economist* 2004). Because computer software is too new to have fallen into the public domain through the expiration of copyright terms, it can only be made open-source by a deliberate act of the author. The author must make the software available under an open-source license, of which the best known is probably the GNU General Public License (GPL). An author's use of an open-source license is sometimes, but inaccurately, referred to as "placing the software in the public domain." Technically the software is still copyrighted and thus not in the public domain; a better term is *copyleft,* developed as an alternative to "copyright" to refer to the use of the GNU GPL.

Other fields have imitated, or are attempting to imitate, the open-source approach. Copyright restrictions are often seen as stifling creativity, which might be a fair exchange when the copyrighted work is valuable but serves to hinder the development of ideas in the case of articles in academic journals; the academic articles

Open-source news: The mainstream media dubbed 2004 the Year of the Blog; stories originating in the blogosphere found their way into the mainstream media, perhaps influencing the course of politics. Two factors have enabled the spread of news blogs: the Web, which enables everyone to become a publisher, and the fact that there is no copyright in news—that is, in the underlying facts upon which news reporting is based.

Blogger Russ Kick scooped the traditional media in April 2004 by publishing photos of military coffins returned from Iraq. Kick, concerned that the U.S. military was keeping such photos out of the mainstream media, had obtained the photos by filing a Freedom of Information Act request.

News and opinion blogs also made the 2004 political campaign different from all previous campaigns and might have contributed to the high voter turnout. Conservative bloggers publicized the claims of the anti-Kerry Swift Boat Veterans for Truth. Liberal bloggers focused attention on the theory that Bush was wearing some sort of communications device during his first debate with Kerry; eventually the mainstream media picked up the story.

are worth no money but subject to the same level of copyright protection as works worth millions of dollars. The term *open access* is used to refer to a process equivalent to copylefting, through which journals and scholars would make their works available with few restrictions,

FOXTROT © 2005 Bill Amend. Reprinted with permission of UNIVERSAL PRESS SYNDICATE. All rights reserved.

other than the acknowledgment of authorship and first publication (Budapest Open Access Initiative 2002). Open-source approaches to areas of intellectual property other than copyright have also been proposed, including open-source pharmaceuticals (*Economist* 2004).

The best-known open-source software program is the GNU/Linux operating system, but others abound. Two-thirds of the Web's fifty million or so servers run Apache, an open-source HTTP server program (*Economist* 2004; Apache 2004). The open-source e-mail program Sendmail is even more universal (*Economist* 2004); however, these programs tend to operate out of the sight of most users and have not attracted the same level of media attention as GNU/Linux.

Documents

• Budapest Open Access Initiative, Feb. 14, 2002, available at http://www. soros.org/openaccess/read.shtml (visited November 10, 2004)

See also: Budapest Open Access Initiative; Project Gutenberg; Public Domain

Sources and further reading:

Apache HTTP Server Project, "The Number One HTTP Server on the Internet," Oct. 2004, http://httpd.apache.org/.

"Open Source: Beyond Capitalism?" *The Economist,* June 10, 2004.

P
❖

❖ P2P ❖

P2P, an abbreviation for peer-to-peer, refers to a type of file-sharing network in which files are exchanged directly between users rather than through a central server. The use of P2P networks in the abstract is perfectly legal, and there are many perfectly innocuous P2P networks, such as SETI@home, which allows users to participate in the search for extraterrestrial intelligence by devoting unused computer resources to analyzing radio telescope data for possible transmissions from alien civilizations. These uses of P2P networks rarely grab headlines, however (although SETI@home surely will if it ever succeeds in its mission). Most attention to P2P networks focuses on the fact that they are often, perhaps primarily, used to trade unauthorized copies of copyrighted material, especially popular songs compressed as MP3 files. The volume of MP3 file-sharing has grown so large that, in the opinion of many in the music content industry, it threatens the industry's continued existence. The content industry has pursued P2P networks and their users with lawsuits for copyright infringement, but these lawsuits may have been counterproductive. The content industry's early victory over Napster led P2P services to design around existing law. The currently popular "supernode" systems avoid the centralization of search functions that made Napster vulnerable to suits for contributory and vicarious infringement. These systems designate certain computers in the network, with their users' consent, as supernodes; search lists are maintained on these machines rather than on a centralized server. The legality of this approach was affirmed by both the federal district court for the Central District of California and the Ninth Circuit Court of Appeals (*Grokster*, 380 F.3d 1154); however, these decisions were reversed by the U.S. Supreme Court in June 2005 (see "File-sharing update" sidebar on p. 147).

The legality of the P2P networks themselves, however, does not mean that using those networks to share copyrighted material is lawful. The P2P operators do not copy files themselves; if they are to be held liable, it must be as contributory or vicarious infringers, or through some new category of copyright infringement liability to be defined by Congress in future legislation. The users who copy files, however, may be committing direct copyright infringement, and the content industry has filed hundreds of lawsuits against individual users of P2P networks (Bergen 2004, 200).

The international nature of P2P networks poses legal issues as well. The United States has, for the moment, affirmed the legality of supernode P2P networks, as has a Dutch appellate court (*Buma & Stemra* 2002). Litigation currently pending in Australia, however, may yield a different result (Gray 2004). In the meantime U.S. Internet service providers have also won a legal battle to preserve the confidentiality of their subscribers, placing a further roadblock in the path of content industry suits against P2P file traders (*Verizon*, 351 F.3d 1229). The content industry has by no means exhausted all of the avenues available to it, however, and it seems likely to continue its attempts to shut down P2P networks, both by lawsuits and by legislative change, for the foreseeable future.

P2P networks could not have grown as swiftly as they have if not for the appeal of file-sharing. But now that they exist, they are finding legitimate uses as well. Just as the trade networks forged by vicious British opium smugglers (with, deplorably, the backing of the British government) later proved invaluable for legitimate trade between Europe and the Far East, P2P networks may have grown too valuable to shut down. A P2P network can provide a ready-made virtual private network for any company or individual in need of one. P2P networks are more robust and resistant to attack than the World Wide Web. They can be used to distribute lawful content more effectively than the Web and can be used for distributed computing, storage, and search functions.

P2P networks now account for more than half of all Internet traffic, with one open-source network, BitTorrent, accounting for 35 percent. BitTorrent can be used for copyright-infringing sharing of music files, but it can also be used for games and to transmit open-source software, such as the Linux operating system. P2P technology also enables Internet telephone services such as Skype, founded by the founders of KaZaA. P2P, if allowed to grow, could eventually become a more valuable use of the Internet than the Web itself, its pirate past no more than a source of colorful historical anecdotes.

Source

"In Praise of P2P," *The Economist Technology Quarterly*, Dec. 4, 2004, at 35.

Cases
Federal Appellate Court
- *A&M Records, Inc. v. Napster, Inc.*, 239 F.3d 1004 (9th Cir. 2001)
- *Metro-Goldwyn-Mayer Studios, Inc. v. Grokster, Ltd.*, 259 F.Supp.2d 1029 (C.D. Cal. 2003), affirmed, 380 F.3d 1154 (9th Cir. 2004), reversed 125 S. Ct. 2764 (2005)

- *Recording Industry Association of America, Inc. v. Verizon Internet Services*, 351 F.3d 1229 (D.C. Cir. 2003)

Netherlands Appellate Court
- *Buma & Stemra v. KaZaA*, Amsterdam Court of Appeal (2002), unofficial English translation available at www.eff.org/IP/P2P/BUMA_v_Kazaa/20020328_kazaa_appeal_judgment.html (visited November 2, 2004)

See also: Copyright; Copyright Infringement; File-Sharing; KaZaA

Sources and further reading:
David Barkai, *Peer-to-Peer Computing: Technologies for Sharing and Collaborating on the Net* (Santa Clara, CA: Intel Press, 2002).
Grace J. Bergen, "Litigation as a Tool against Digital Piracy," 35 *McGeorge Law Review* 181 (2004).
"Face Value: The Quiet Iconoclast—With KaZaA, Niklas Zennstrom Undermined the Music Industry," *The Economist*, July 3, 2004, at 54.
Patrick Gray, "Sharman Presses for Evidence," *Wired News*, May 18, 2004, http://www.wired.com/news/digiwood/0,1412,63509,00.html (visited November 2, 2004).
Jay Lyman, "Google Pulls P2P Links over Kazaa Copyright Claims," *TechNewsWorld*, Sept. 2, 2003, http://www.technewsworld.com/story/31481.html (visited November 2, 2004).
Andy Oram, *Peer-to-Peer: Harnessing the Power of Disruptive Technologies* (Sebastopol, CA: O'Reilly and Associates, 2001).
Seagrumn Smith, "From Napster to KaZaA: The Battle over Peer-to-Peer Filesharing Goes International," 2003 *Duke Law and Technology Review* 8 (2003).

❖ PALLADIUM ❖

See Digital Rights Management

❖ PARODY ❖

See Fair Use (Copyright)

❖ PARIS CONVENTION ❖

The Paris Convention creates the Paris Union, which governs issues among its members relating to trademarks, patents, and unfair competition in international law. The Paris Union is administered by the World Intellectual Property Organization (WIPO). As of September 24, 2004, 168 countries were parties to the Paris Convention; the United States has been a party since 1887. The Paris Convention provides three forms of protection to intellectual property right holders from member states. The first of these is national treatment. Article 2 of the convention requires member states to give national treatment to right holders from other member states:

> Nationals of any country of the Union shall, as regards the protection of industrial property, enjoy in all the other countries of the Union the advantages that their respective laws now grant, or may hereafter grant, to nationals; all without prejudice to the rights specially provided for by this Convention. Consequently, they shall have the same protection as the latter, and the same legal remedy against any infringement of their rights, provided that the conditions and formalities imposed upon nationals are complied with. (Paris Convention, art. 2(1))

Article 3 extends this protection to "[n]ationals of countries outside the Union who are domiciled or who have real and effective industrial or commercial establishments in the territory of one of the countries of the Union," as well.

Second, the Paris Convention requires each of its members to guarantee to provide a defined minimum level of protection for various types of intellectual property. Third, it requires its members to provide a right of priority to applicants for trademarks, patents, and utility model and design registrations from other member countries:

> Any person who has duly filed an application for a patent, or for the registration of a utility model, or of an industrial design, or of a trademark, in one of the countries of the Union, or his successor in title, shall enjoy, for the purpose of filing in the other countries, a right

of priority during the periods hereinafter fixed. (Paris Convention, art. 4(A)(1))

In other words, once the applicant has applied for a patent, utility model registration, trademark, or design registration in Country A, she may apply for the same form of protection in other member countries within a set period of time, and her application will be treated as if it had been filed on the same date as the filing in Country A—assuming that Country A is a party to the Paris Convention. For patents and utility models, the right of priority extends for twelve months; at any time within twelve months after filing the initial application in Country A, the inventor may file another application in Country B—even if someone else has filed an application for the same invention in the interim. So long as the second inventor's filing is dated later than the first inventor's original filing in Country A, the first inventor's filing in Country B will be treated as if it had been filed first in Country B as well. For trademarks and industrial design registrations the right of priority works in the same way, but for a period of six months rather than twelve months (Paris Convention, art. 4(C)(1)).

The Paris Convention is incorporated into the World Trade Organization's Agreement on Trade-Related Aspects of Intellectual Property Rights (TRIPS) by Article 2 of TRIPS:

> 1. In respect of Parts II, III and IV of this Agreement, Members shall comply with Articles 1 through 12, and Article 19, of the Paris Convention (1967).
> 2. Nothing in Parts I to IV of this Agreement shall derogate from existing obligations that Members may have to each other under the Paris Convention, the Berne Convention, the Rome Convention and the Treaty on Intellectual Property in Respect of Integrated Circuits.

Thus WTO members, even the handful not already parties to the Paris Convention, are required to abide by the Paris Convention's substantive terms. And in the event that the terms of TRIPS impose less of an obligation on a member state than the Paris Convention would, the member states may not use TRIPS as an excuse to avoid the Paris Convention obligation.

Treaties
- Agreement on Trade-Related Aspects of Intellectual Property Rights, Marrakesh Agreement Establishing the World Trade Organization, Annex 1C, Apr. 15, 1994, 33 I.L.M. 81 (1994)
- Paris Convention for the Protection of Industrial Property, Mar. 20, 1883, as revised at Brussels on Dec. 14, 1900, at Washington on June 2, 1911, at The Hague on Nov. 6, 1925, at London on June 2, 1934, at Lisbon on Oct. 31, 1958, and at Stockholm on July 14, 1967, and as amended on Sept. 28, 1979, 21 U.S.T. 1583, 828 U.N.T.S. 305

See also: International Patent Protection; International Trademark Protection; Patent; Patent Cooperation Treaty; Trademark; TRIPS; WIPO

Sources and further reading:

Graeme B. Dinwoodie et al., *International and Comparative Patent Law* (Newark, NJ: LexisNexis, 2002).
J. Thomas McCarthy et al., *McCarthy's Desk Encyclopedia of Intellectual Property*, 3d ed. (Washington, DC: Bureau of National Affairs, 2004).
Nuno Pires de Carvalho, *The TRIPS Regime of Patent Rights* (The Hague: Kluwer Law International, 2002).

❖ PARIS UNION ❖

See Paris Convention

❖ PATENT ❖

A patent is an intellectual property right that grants the right holder the right to exclude others from making an invention, as well as from selling it, using it, offering to sell it, or importing it into the United States. It does not, as is sometimes believed, grant the holder the right to make, sell, use, offer to sell, or import the invention. Patents are often granted for improvements upon already-patented previous technology, and the patent on the underlying invention would prevent the holder of the patent on the improvement from making, and so on, the improved invention (McCarthy 2004, 433–435).

In order to be patentable under United States law, an invention must meet three basic requirements: It must be useful (35 U.S.C. § 101). It must be novel (35 U.S.C. § 102). And it must not be obvious (35 U.S.C. § 103). Assessing the latter two requirements requires an examination of the "prior art"—the existing body of inventions and technical knowledge in the area.

An invention that meets these three requirements must go through a lengthy patent application process. Under U.S. law the first person to invent, rather than the first person to file an application, is entitled to patent protection. The law in other countries grants the patent to the first person to file; other countries also take different approaches to the process of granting patents and to the substantive rules applied. As a result, gaining international patent protection is considerably more complex than gaining international copyright or even trademark protection. The Patent Cooperation Treaty simplifies the subject somewhat, but both the U.S. and Patent Cooperation Treaty processes are time consuming, complex, arduous, and expensive, and should not be undertaken without the assistance of someone experienced in the process.

Patent protection in the United States lasts for twenty years from the date on which the patent application was filed, in accordance with the Agreement on Trade-Related Aspects of Intellectual Property Rights (TRIPS) (35 U.S.C. § 154(a)(2)). The TRIPS term replaces the earlier U.S. term of seventeen years from the date on which the patent is granted; because the law adopting the TRIPS standard specifies that no patent application shall remain pending for more than three years, the TRIPS term will in no case be shorter than the original seventeen-year term (35 U.S.C. § 154(b)(1)(B)). As with other intellectual property rights, it is the duty of the right holder, not of the government, to detect and pursue infringers.

Patent law played an important role in the early development of software by its absence; from the 1960s onward, the United States

Inventions in the fields of information technology, the Internet, and related electronics applications make up the biggest share of applications for and grants of patents, with several companies (or their employees) receiving more than a thousand patents each year. In 2003 the top ten recipients of U.S. patents (including patents assigned to the employer by employees) were:

IBM:	3,415 patents
Canon:	1,992 patents
Hitachi:	1,893 patents
Matsushita Electrical:	1,774 patents
Micron Technology:	1,707 patents
Intel:	1,592 patents
Koninklijke Philips Elec.:	1,353 patents
Samsung Electronics:	1,313 patents
Sony:	1,311 patents
Fujitsu:	1,302 patents

All ten are information technology and/or electronics companies; one, IBM, is the leader by a wide margin, with more than 70 percent more patents than its nearest rival, Canon. It is also tempting to draw certain conclusions about the "nationality" of the companies involved: Three (including IBM) have their roots in the United States, five in Japan, one in Korea, and one in the Netherlands. However, it would be a mistake to draw broad conclusions, such as that Europe is lagging behind in technology, from this fact alone. All ten companies are multinational, with operations in Europe, Asia, and North America; for example, Micron, an Idaho corporation, has design facilities in Japan. And skilled scientists and engineers are among the world's most mobile workers; the inventor of a product at a Japanese company's U.S. design facility might well be European, or from a continent with few multinational high-tech companies of its own.

Source

World Almanac and Book of Facts 2005 (New York: World Almanac Books, 2005).

Patent and Trademark Office (USPTO) opposed the idea of software patents. The report of the 1966 President's Commission on the Patent System adopted this approach, and the 1972 decision of the U.S. Supreme Court in *Gottschalk v. Benson,* holding that a mathematical algorithm used in a computer program was not patentable, was also widely understood as stating that computer programs were unpatentable. Although the Supreme Court appeared to soften its position on software patents in the 1981 case of *Diamond v. Diehr,* it was not until 1994 that the USPTO explicitly accepted the idea of software patents by publishing guidelines regarding the patentability of computer programs. The USPTO's reversal followed the 1994 decision of the Federal Circuit Court of Appeals in *In re Alappat,* specifically recognizing the patentability of certain types of computer programs (33 F. 3d 1526).

In the meantime, however, copyright, rather than patent, had become the main form of protection for computer software, and other countries had followed the U.S. lead in declaring software to be the subject of copyright rather than patent. Patent law has become important in an Internet context, not because of the patenting of computer software but because of the advent and proliferation of business method patents. Prior to the decision of the Federal Circuit in the 1998 case of *State Street Bank & Trust,* business methods had been viewed as unpatentable "methods of operation" under U.S. law (149 F.3d 1368). Article 27 of TRIPS has had the same effect internationally; it has been interpreted as requiring WTO members to grant business method patents (Conley 2003, 8).

Treaties

- Agreement on Trade-Related Aspects of Intellectual Property Rights, Marrakesh Agreement Establishing the World Trade Organization, Annex 1C, Apr. 15, 1994, 33 I.L.M. 81 (1994)
- Paris Convention for the Protection of Industrial Property, Mar. 20, 1883, as revised at Brussels on Dec. 14, 1900, at Washington on June 2, 1911, at The Hague on Nov. 6, 1925, at London on

June 2, 1934, at Lisbon on Oct. 31, 1958, and at Stockholm on July 14, 1967, and as amended on Sept. 28, 1979, 21 U.S.T. 1583, 828 U.N.T.S. 305

- Patent Cooperation Treaty, June 19, 1970, as amended on Sept. 28, 1979, and as modified on February 3, 1984, and October 3, 2001, 28 U.S.T. 7645, 9 I.L.M. 978 (1970)

Statute
- Patent Code, 35 U.S.C. §§ 1–376

Cases
Supreme Court
- *Diamond v. Diehr*, 450 U.S. 175 (1981)
- *Gottschalk v. Benson*, 409 U.S. 63 (1972)

Federal Appellate Courts
- *Apple Computer, Inc. v. Franklin Computer Corp.*, 714 F.2d 1240 (3d Cir. 1983)
- *In re Alappat*, 33 F.3d 1526 (Fed. Cir. 1994)
- *State Street Bank & Trust Co. v. Signature Financial Group*, 149 F.3d 1368 (Fed. Cir. 1998); certiorari denied, 525 U.S. 1093

See also: Business Methods Patent; Computer Program; International Patent Protection; Paris Convention; Patent Cooperation Treaty; Prosecution History Estoppel; TRIPS (Patent); WIPO

Sources and further reading:
John M. Conley, *The International Law of Business Method Patents*, U.S. Patent and Trademark Office Economic Review, Oct. 2003, available at http://www.findarticles.com/p/articles/mi_m3883/is_4_88/ai_113233352/pg_1 (visited November 8, 2004).
Graeme B. Dinwoodie et al., *International and Comparative Patent Law* (Newark, NJ: LexisNexis, 2002).
J. Thomas McCarthy et al., *McCarthy's Desk Encyclopedia of Intellectual Property*, 3d ed. (Washington, DC: Bureau of National Affairs, 2004).
Toshiko Takenaka, "The Best Patent Practice or Mere Compromise? A Review of the Current Draft of the Substantive Patent Law Treaty and a Proposal for a First-to-Invent Exception for Domestic Applicants," 11 *Texas Intellectual Property Law Journal* 259 (2003).

❖ PATENT COOPERATION TREATY ❖

The Patent Cooperation Treaty (PCT) greatly streamlines the multination patent application process. Prior to the adoption of the PCT, patenting an invention in multiple countries was a daunting task involving long, expensive, and complex application procedures in multiple languages, cultures, and legal systems. The PCT has simplified the process; through the PCT, an inventor can file a patent application simultaneously in any or all of the countries that are parties. One hundred and twenty-four states are now parties to the PCT, the most recent being San Marino, for which the treaty became binding on December 14, 2004.

The PCT does not, as is sometimes believed, create any sort of global patent, and it does not guarantee the success of patent applications in other countries (McCarthy 2004, 437–438). Different countries have different standards for granting patents and different histories of patents already granted and refused, and an invention that is patentable in one country might well be unpatentable in another. The United States Patent and Trademark Office is considered to be lenient, even lax, in granting patents; many patent applications that are denied elsewhere may be granted in the United States.

In order to gain the benefit of the PCT, the inventor must file a patent application with a designated receiving office; the national patent offices of PCT member states can function as receiving offices. A separate fee must eventually be paid for each country in which a patent is sought and for each language into which the application must be translated; fees are not payable at the time of filing, but much later in the process. Only one application is required; once the fees are paid, the receiving office will handle much of the complexity of separate national application processes and translations (PCT arts. 10, 12, 15, 22). The initial application, however, must be in Chinese, English, French, German, Japanese, Russian, or Spanish (WIPO 2004).

The World Intellectual Property Organization (WIPO) administers the PCT, and PCT filing fees provide a significant portion of WIPO's budget. The International Bureau of WIPO is also designated as a receiving office under the PCT (PCT Rule 19.1(a)(iii)). The PCT works in conjunction with regional patent agreements, so that an applicant from a PCT member state may apply for and receive a regional patent where some agreement permitting regional patents exists. Regional patent agreements under which patents may be granted under the PCT include the Eurasian Patent Convention, the European Patent Convention, the Harare Protocol of the African Regional Industrial Property Organization, and the agreement forming the Organisation Africaine de la Propriété Intellectuelle (WIPO 2002, 5).

Treaty
• Patent Cooperation Treaty, Washington, DC, June 19, 1970, as amended on Sept. 28, 1979, and as modified on February 3, 1984, and October 3, 2001, 28 U.S.T. 7645, 9 I.L.M. 978 (1970)

Rule
• WIPO PCT Rule 19.1(a)(iii), available at http://www.wipo.int/pct/en/texts/rules/r19.htm (visited November 8, 2004)

See also: International Patent Protection; Patent; WIPO

Sources and further reading:
Graeme B. Dinwoodie et al., *International and Comparative Patent Law* (Newark, NJ: LexisNexis, 2002).
J. Thomas McCarthy et al., *McCarthy's Desk Encyclopedia of Intellectual Property,* 3d ed. (Washington, DC: Bureau of National Affairs, 2004).
Nuno Pires de Carvalho, *The TRIPS Regime of Patent Rights* (The Hague: Kluwer Law International, 2002).
WIPO, "Basic Facts about the Patent Cooperation Treaty," Apr. 2002, available from http://www.wipo.int/pct/en/access/filing.htm (PDF download) (visited November 8, 2004).
WIPO, "Direct Filing of PCT Applications with the International Bureau as PCT Receiving Office," 2004, http://www.wipo.int/pct/en/filing/filing.htm#P20_2204 (visited November 8, 2004).

❖ PEER-TO-PEER ❖

See File-Sharing; P2P

❖ PHISHING ❖

Phishing is an Internet scam technique used to obtain credit card numbers, account numbers, passwords, and other confidential information, often as the first stage of identity theft. The word is derived from "password harvesting fishing," and has no connection to the band Phish or the chat site Phishy. Phishing and related techniques that aim at exploiting the gullibility or goodwill of other users are known as social engineering.

A phishing attack is typically carried out by e-mail or instant messaging. The attacker sends an e-mail or instant message to the victim; the message purports to be from Citibank, America Online, or some similar entity with which the phisher suspects the victim might have an account. The text of the message is designed to convince the victim to send the desired information to the phisher in the mistaken belief that he or she is sending it to a company that will use it to the victim's benefit. A sample phishing e-mail, no fewer than three copies of which appeared in the author's in-box this morning, is reproduced below:

> *Subject: Verify Your E-mail with Citibank*
> This email was sent by the Citibank server to verify your E-mail address. You must complete this process by clicking on the link below and entering in the small window your Citibank ATM/Debit Card number and PIN that you use on ATM.

This is done for your protection—because some of our members no longer have access to their e-mail addresses and we must verify it.

To verify your E-mail address and access your bank account, click on the link below:

***

Thank you for using Citibank

The top of the e-mail reproduces the blue and white Citibank logo. Clicking on the link takes the user to a site that also uses the Citibank logo and purports to be a Citibank site; the site may even spoof the Citibank URL in the browser's address bar. Choosing "Sign On to a Citi Account" from a list of options gives the user the opportunity to enter his or her Citibank account number and password. A search in the Lookup database at www.whois.com reveals that the site is not, in fact, owned by Citibank. (Given the nature of the site, the name that does appear as registrant, administrative contact, and technical contact is most likely either the name of a nonexistent person or the name of some innocent person chosen either at random or maliciously by the site's true operator.) The most likely explanation is that some person is deliberately attempting to trick people into believing that the site is a Citibank site and then harvesting any account numbers and passwords that are entered.

Phishing can be (and in the case of the e-mail above is) combined with spamming. Few people would be taken in by the letter above; if it is e-mailed to 100 million Citibank card holders, however, and only one one-hundredth of 1 percent are taken in, the phisher will still have harvested ten thousand credit card numbers. If an average of only $100 is stolen from each card, the phisher will have made a million dollars with only a couple of hours' effort, or less. (Creating the fake site actually requires little effort, as it can be copied from the real site, changing only the crucial links.)

The easiest way to avoid being phished is not to respond to any e-mails asking for confidential personal or financial information; the real Citibank will have no reason to request your credit card number by e-mail. The crimes involved in phishing, including fraud, wire fraud, and theft, have long been prohibited by state and federal law; phishers face long prison sentences if caught and convicted. Crimes involved in phishing scams include bank fraud (18 U.S.C. § 1344), computer fraud (18 U.S.C. § 1030(a)(4)), credit card fraud (18 U.S.C. § 1029), identity theft (18 U.S.C. § 1028(a)(7)), and wire fraud (18 U.S.C. § 1343). Phishing operations involving spamming also violate the CAN-SPAM Act (18 U.S.C. § 1037); phishing operations involving viruses, worms, or other malicious codes violate 18 U.S.C. § 1028(a)(5).

Phishers are also subject to civil lawsuits. In addition to the obvious suits by the victims for compensation, they can also be subject to suits by the companies whose names are used and whose Web sites and logos are copied. The misuse of the name may be trademark dilution by tarnishment, and the copying of the trademark and of material from the company's Web site involves trademark infringement and copyright infringement.

Phishers are actively pursued by the Federal Trade Commission and the Anti-Phishing Working Group formed by companies whose names have been abused, and whose customers have been targeted, by phishing scams. Copies of suspected phishing e-mails can be sent to these organizations at uce@ftc.gov and reportphishing@antiphishing.org, respectively (DOJ Report 2004).

Statutes
- Bank Fraud Act, 18 U.S.C. § 1344
- Computer Fraud and Abuse Act, 18 U.S.C. § 1030
- Controlling the Assault of Non-Solicited Pornography and Marketing (CAN-SPAM) Act, 18 U.S.C. § 1037
- Credit Card Fraud Act, 18 U.S.C. § 1029
- Identity Theft and Assumption Deterrence Act, 18 U.S.C. § 1028
- Wire Fraud Act, 18 U.S.C. § 1343

See also: Enforcement; Federal Trade Commission; Hacking; Identity Theft; Spam

Sources and further reading:
Michael Tonsing, "Have Scammers Gone Phishing for Your Data or That of Your Clients? Beware!" *Federal Lawyer,* May, 2004, at 14.

U.S. Department of Justice, Special Report on
Phishing, 2004 [DOJ Report], available at
www.usdoj.gov/criminal/fraud/
Phishing.pdf (visited November 2, 2004).

❖ PHREAKING ❖

Phreaking bears the same relationship to
telecommunications systems that hacking bears
to information systems. Like hacking, it is a
tech-counterculture phenomenon that originated, insofar as it can be traced to any one origin, at the Massachusetts Institute of Technology (MIT) in the 1960s. The term *phreaking* is
derived from "phone freaking"; it is important
to the Internet world both because of the effect
it has had on hacking and because many early
phreakers developed technical skills that they
later put to use to build home computing and
the Internet.

In the 1960s early phreakers at MIT used
computers to generate the tones used by the
then-existing telecommunications network for
billing, switching, and dialing calls. Early
phreakers at MIT were more interested in exploring the telecommunications system than in
stealing telephone services; they were technology enthusiasts. At the time, however, long-
distance telephone calls were very expensive,
and the phreaking techniques developed by
enthusiasts soon spread beyond the MIT cam-
pus into the 1960s counterculture (*Jammer*
1987, 30). Phreaking became widespread in
the early 1970s, when Abbie Hoffman's Youth
International Party devoted a newsletter,
Youth International Party Line, to teaching
and discussing phreaking techniques. Although phreakers did not damage or disrupt
the telecommunications network, they made
calls that arguably resulted in substantial lost
revenues to the phone companies; Hoffman
argued that free phone calls harmed no one
(Cronin and Weikers 2004, n. 4). As with the
music industry's arguments regarding lost
sales, the total value of calls made by phreakers
was probably far greater than the amount of
business lost, because most of those calls
would not have been made had the callers
been required to pay for them.

Nonetheless, the phone companies felt
threatened by phreaking and prevailed upon the
federal government to criminalize phreaking
(Cronin and Weikers 2004). Phreakers, including the celebrated Captain Crunch, were imprisoned for violation of the Wire Fraud Act
and other telecommunications statutes (Draper
2004). Eventually, for reasons related to technological advances rather than to phreaking,
the telephone companies replaced their voice
transmission and signal-transmission hardware,
rendering old-school phreaking impossible
(Draper 2004). At the same time, long-distance
telephone costs dropped dramatically, decreas-
ing the popular appeal of phreaking.

The phreaking culture had its own slang and
its own celebrities, foreshadowing the hacking
culture of today. Captain Crunch (John
Draper) took his name from a whistle found in
a box of Captain Crunch cereal. The whistle,
when blown, generated a 2,600-hertz tone,
necessary for phone phreaking; the use of the
whistle had been discovered by Joe the Whistler
(Joe Engressia), who was blind and could whistle the tone without the assistance of the cereal-
box toy. Many phreakers found their way into
Silicon Valley and the high-tech industry; Captain Crunch went to work for Apple, and Apple
founders Steve Wozniak and Steve Jobs were
rumored to have been phreakers (Freiberger
and Swaine 1999).

Although phreaking still goes on, it is largely
confined to enthusiast groups. One exception is
cell phone phreaking, or phone cloning, in
which phreakers copy the identifying digital
footprint of a cell phone in order to connect to
the telecommunications network on that
phone's account. Prankster phreaking of phone
networks, in which the purpose is to lock up
phones, also goes on, both through traditional
phreaking techniques and through denial-of-
service attacks. The growth of phones into
portable computing devices has also made cell
phone hacking possible; this hacking is sometimes, although incorrectly, referred to as
phreaking (Weingarten 2002). And Van Eck
phreaking, which has nothing to do with telephones, is a (perhaps largely hypothetical) technique for eavesdropping on computers from a
distance, using electromagnetic radiation given

off by now-obsolete cathode-ray tube monitors and possibly by printers and other devices (Van Eck 1985).

Statute

- Wire Fraud Act, 18 U.S.C. § 1343

See also: Encryption; Hacking

Sources and further reading:
Kevin P. Cronin and Ronald N. Weikers, "Electronic Security Risks and the Need for Privacy, § 1.17" in *Data Security and Privacy Law: Combating Cyberthreats* (St. Paul, MN: West, 2004).
John Draper, "The Story So Far . . . , http://www.Webcrunchers.com/crunch/story.html (visited November 3, 2004).
Paul Freiberger and Michael Swaine, *Fire in the Valley,* 2d ed. (New York: McGraw-Hill, 1999).
The Jammer and Jack the Ripper, The Official Phreaker's Manual, Feb. 14, 1987, available at http://www.morehouse.org/hin/blckcrwl/telcom/phreak_m.txt (visited November 3, 2004).
Wim Van Eck, "Electromagnetic Radiation from Video Display Units: An Eavesdropping Risk?" 4 *North-Holland Computers and Security* 269 (1985), available at www.shmoo.com/tempest/emr.pdf (visited November 3, 2004).
Marc Weingarten, "Phone Phreaks, The Feature," Feb. 25, 2002 http://www.thefeature.com/article?articleid=14318 (visited November 3, 2004).
Youth International Party Line (aka *TAP Magazine*) archive, http://flag.blackened.net/daver/misc/yipl/ (visited November 3, 2004).

❖ PIRACY ❖

To an international or admiralty lawyer, piracy is any of several crimes committed against ships at sea and their occupants, including robbery, theft, kidnapping, and murder. Piracy of this sort was for decades little more than a historical curiosity, romanticized by Hollywood; during the 1990s, however, pirate attacks on shipping began to rise, to more than 200 per year. Pirate attacks kill dozens of seamen a year (*Economist* 1999). Piracy is a crime against the law of nations; were Con-

gress today to exercise its constitutionally granted power to license privateers, or government-sponsored pirates, by "grant[ing] Letters of Marque and Reprisal, and mak[ing] Rules concerning Captures on Land and Water" (U.S. Constitution, art. I, § 8, cl. 8), the United States would almost certainly be in violation of international law.

The term *piracy* is also applied to the hijacking of aircraft; to intellectual property lawyers, however, and these days to the media, *piracy* refers to something far less violent: the infringement of intellectual property rights by large-scale unauthorized copying. Intellectual property pirates create and distribute unauthorized copies of things that are copyrighted, trademarked, or patented. In an Internet context most pirated material infringes on copyright, with trademark-infringing materials running a distant second. The term *piracy* can be used to refer to all unauthorized reproduction, but more often it is used to refer specifically to the operation of businesses specializing in the sale of unlawfully reproduced material. Thus software pirates make and sell copies of copyrighted software; video pirates make and sell DVDs; music pirates make and sell CDs with hundreds of unlawfully copied MP3 files on them; apparel pirates make and sell imitation designer-label clothes, complete with unlawfully reproduced labels; and so forth. These businesses involve the Internet only peripherally, for the most part. Spam (unsolicited mass e-mail advertising) is often used to advertise pirated goods, from unlawfully copied software to fake Rolex watches. Some pirated materials, especially computer programs, are offered for download over the Internet. But for the most part movies, music, and computer programs unlawfully copied over the Internet are exchanged for free via P2P file-sharing networks or through warez sites.

File-sharers and warez traders do not think of themselves as pirates. At first, the law agreed with them: The first warez trader prosecuted in the United States, David LaMacchia, was exonerated because criminal copyright infringement law at the time required that the act be undertaken for financial gain. Because LaMacchia had not undertaken his warez trading for financial gain, he was instead charged with conspiracy to commit wire fraud, and charges were dismissed

because an intellectual property interest could not be taken by fraud absent a specific statement to the contrary by Congress (*LaMacchia*, 871 F. Supp. at 545). The software content industry responded to the *LaMacchia* decision with alarm, however, and at the industry's urging Congress passed the No Electronic Theft Act (NET Act), which among other things expanded the requirement of financial gain for criminal copyright infringement to include "the receipt of other copyrighted works" (17 U.S.C. § 101), while removing the financial gain requirement altogether if the value of the works copied exceeded $1,000 (17 U.S.C. § 506). Thus the NET Act made warez traders into pirates.

File-sharing, especially music file-sharing, is far more widespread than warez trading. The proposed Protecting Intellectual Rights against Theft and Expropriation (PIRATE) Act of 2004 would, if enacted, establish file-sharers as pirates under U.S. law. The PIRATE Act has already passed the Senate and is currently before the House of Representatives. Although it would not impose criminal penalties on small-scale file-sharers, it would allow the government, rather than an injured private party, to maintain civil suits for damages against file-sharers even in the absence of any criminal copyright infringement (PIRATE Act 2004). Other countries have imposed drastic sanctions: Italy, for example, recently enacted a law that makes file-sharing of copyrighted material a crime punishable by a three-year prison sentence (Evansburg 2004).

Constitution
- United States Constitution, art. I, § 8, cl. 8

Proposed Legislation
- Protecting Intellectual Rights against Theft and Expropriation (PIRATE) Act of 2004, S. 2237, 108th Cong., 2d Sess., Mar. 25, 2004

Statute
- No Electronic Theft Act, amending and codified at 17 U.S.C. §§ 101, 506, and 507 and 18 U.S.C. §§ 2319–2320

Cases
Federal District Court
- *United States v. LaMacchia*, 871 F.Supp. 535 (D. Mass. 1994)

See also: Copyright; Copyright Infringement; DeCSS; File-Sharing; Internet Service Providers; KaZaA; Look and Feel; No Electronic Theft Act; P2P; Protecting Intellectual Rights against Theft and Expropriation Act; Search Engine; Trademark; Trademark Infringement; Warez

Sources and further reading:
"Dead Men Tell No Tales," *The Economist*, Dec. 16, 1999.

Amanda Evansburg et al., "Italian Anti-Piracy Law Includes Prison Term," *Journal of Proprietary Rights*, Aug. 2004, at 22.

Pascal Kamina, *Film Copyright in the European Union* (Cambridge, UK: University Press, 2002).

❖ PIRATE ACT ❖

See Protecting Intellectual Rights against Theft and Expropriation Act

❖ PORNOGRAPHY ❖

One of the most widely observable social effects of the Internet, and among those that has inspired the greatest amount of legislation and litigation, has been the ease with which it makes pornographic content available and the consequent expansion of the pornography industry. The Internet's early growth might have owed more to pornography than is generally acknowledged. Large media companies that had invested heavily in the provision of Internet services ran "hype" stories about Internet pornography, ostensibly decrying it as a menace but perhaps hoping to pique the prurient interest of the public and increase Internet use.

Pornographers have also played a significant role in the development of payment systems on the Web and have aggressively pursued copyright infringers. At the same time they have been the target of lawsuits, congressional legislation, and content-screening software. Pornographic Web sites were among the first profitable Internet businesses; even now, Web sites categorized as "adult" account for 18.8 percent, or just under one-fifth, of all Internet visits by users in the United States (*CNN Money* 2002). This is more traffic than all search engines combined, or about seven times as much traffic as Google alone. It is more than twice as many visits as are received by sites in the "shopping and classifieds" category that includes such universally known sites as Amazon and eBay (*CNN Money* 2002).

The pervasiveness of Internet pornography has caused concern for numerous reasons. A broad spectrum of social activists, from religious fundamentalists to radical feminists, see pornography as both a cause and a symptom of social problems. Almost everyone is concerned by the possible exposure of children to pornography.

Companies worry that employees waste work hours surfing pornography, potentially exposing their employers to liability in sexual harassment lawsuits brought by other employees who are exposed to unwelcome images. Some who are otherwise tolerant of pornography are disturbed not so much by the increase in the availability of "traditional" pornography as by the increase in overtly violent pornographic content.

One reason that it has been difficult to regulate pornography is the lack of agreement as to what, exactly, it is. Most people probably share the sentiments of Justice Potter Stewart, who, trying to define "hard-core pornography," said "perhaps I could never succeed in intelligibly doing so. But I know it when I see it" (*Jacobellis*, 378 U.S. 184). Some might define pornography as words or images that are sexually exciting to some while offensive to others, acknowledging that there might be a number of viewers—in some instances even a majority—who would be neither excited nor offended. Others reject this definition, preferring to separate "pornography," which in this definition includes an element of exploitation or degradation of the subject, from "erotica," which does not. Courts and lawmakers have for years attempted to define pornography by reference to particular body parts and particular acts; this tends to create a difficulty in distinguishing between materials produced as pornographic entertainment and materials produced for medical or scientific purposes.

Under current law, "pornography" (however defined) is not in itself illegal. Two categories that overlap with the category of pornographic material, however, are: obscenity and child pornography. A great deal of content that is "indecent" but not "obscene" and not child pornography may be permissibly distributed to adults but not to minors; this probably includes most of the material that most people would think of as pornographic.

The First Amendment protects neither material that is obscene nor child pornography. In modern U.S. law "obscenity" is defined according to the test set forth by the Supreme Court in *Miller v. California* in 1973. Child pornography is relatively easy to define when images of actual persons are involved: If the persons in "depictions of explicit sexual conduct" in photographs, film, or video are minors, the material is illegal as child pornography, even if not otherwise "obscene" under the *Miller* test. The Supreme Court has recently struck down a statute extending this prohibition to computer-generated images of minors engaged in sexually explicit conduct that are prepared without involving any actual children (*Ashcroft v. Free Speech Coalition,* 535 U.S. 234); Congress is currently considering new legislation to address computer-generated child pornography.

If material is not illegal as child pornography or obscenity, its transmission via the Internet presents an additional legal problem. Children use the Internet, and nothing about the architecture of the Internet makes it intrinsically more difficult for children to access pornographic materials than for adults. Most pornographic content cannot, for constitutional reasons, be banned outright. The protection of minors from pornographic Internet content thus requires the imposition of some sort of barrier between the minor's computer and the pornographic content.

There are two ways in which such barriers may be imposed: either by restricting access at the Web site containing the content, or by using blocking and filtering software on the minor's computer. Both approaches present problems; a hybrid approach might be the most effective.

Congress has twice attempted to control minors' access to pornography from the "supply" end. The first of these attempts was the Communications Decency Act of 1996 (CDA)(47 U.S.C. § 223). The CDA attempted to restrict the access of minors to pornography in two ways. The first restriction imposed a penalty for the knowing transmission of "obscene" or "indecent" material to recipients known to the sender to be under eighteen years of age. The second imposed a penalty for use of an "interactive computer service" to transmit to specific persons under eighteen years of age, or to "display in a manner available to" persons under eighteen, "any comment, request, suggestion, proposal, image, or other communication that, in context, depict[ed] or describe[d], in terms patently offensive as measured by community standards, sexual or excretory activities or organs"(47 U.S.C. § 223).

The second prohibition was clearly unconstitutional to a court applying the *Miller* test: Its prohibition of depictions or descriptions "in terms patently offensive as measured by community standards, sexual or excretory activities or organs" covers a much broader category of materials than the three-part test in *Miller,* because it incorporates only a portion of the *Miller* test.

The unconstitutionality of the first prohibition is less instantly obvious. Among the problems it presented were the difficulty of defining "indecent," the difficulty of verifying the age of the recipient or viewer of the content, and the burden placed on noncommercial sites. The lack of a clear definition of "indecent" (as opposed to "obscene") made it difficult or impossible for content providers to know exactly what material could permissibly be made available to minors. Actually verifying the age of any viewer on the Internet is as a practical matter impossible, although the senders were only required to avoid transmitting prohibited content to persons known to them to be minors. And though commercial sites could easily include age verification as one of the conditions of providing access (indeed, many already did so indirectly, by requiring credit cards for payment), requiring some form of documentary proof of age would impose a burden on noncommercial sites both by discouraging users from visiting the site and by increasing the cost of maintaining the site.

After the CDA was struck down in 1997, Congress tried again in 1998 with the Child Online Protection Act (COPA)(47 U.S.C. § 231). COPA included a definition of obscenity that was similar to, but oddly (in light of Congress's desire to enact a constitutional statute avoiding the problems of the CDA) not identical to, the *Miller* test. COPA has been declared unconstitutional by the federal Court of Appeals for the Third Circuit (*ACLU v. Reno,* 217 F.3d 162; *ACLU v. Ashcroft,* 322 F.3d 240). In addressing COPA, the Third Circuit suggested that blocking and filtering software, rather than supply-side control, might ultimately provide a more effective, as well as more constitutionally palatable, means of achieving the goal of protecting minors from exposure to pornography. The Supreme Court agreed that there were factual questions regarding the efficacy of such software, and remanded the case for trial to determine whether user-side control, through blocking and filtering software, might be more effective than supply-side control as a means of shielding minors from Internet pornography (*Ashcroft v. ACLU*, 124 S. Ct. 2783).

The problem with this solution is not primarily a constitutional one, but a technical one. The First Amendment protects freedom of expression against government interference; if a parent installs blocking and filtering software on her child's computer, there is no state action and thus no First Amendment issue. The use of blocking and filtering software by government entities such as libraries and schools, however, does present a constitutional issue. The Children's Internet Protection Act (CIPA), enacted as a companion statute to COPA, requires schools and libraries receiving federally subsidized discounted Internet access to install filtering and blocking software (47 U.S.C. § 254(h)). The constitutionality of CIPA has been upheld by the Supreme Court, which reasons that schools and libraries exist to facilitate learning and cultural enrichment rather than to provide a First Amendment forum for Web content publishers. This facilitation process inevitably involves selecting content (*U.S. v. American Library Association, Inc.*, 539 U.S. 194).

CIPA is not a supply-side control like COPA or the CDA. It regulates an intermediary (schools and libraries) but in effect it is more of a demand-side than a supply-side control. To date, then, Congress has been more successful in enacting laws intended to restrict access to pornography from the demand side, or at least the user side, than from the supply side.

The technical problems with blocking and filtering software are more difficult to address, however. There are at least three ways in which such software can operate: It can allow access only to an approved list ("whitelist") of sites, it can allow access to all sites other than those on a proscribed list ("blacklist"), or it can prohibit access to sites containing forbidden keywords. The first approach is the most effective, but also the most restrictive; as a practical matter it is suitable only for very young children who are just learning to use the Internet. Serious online research will require access to a very large number of Web sites; new sites are being created every day, and the whitelist cannot be updated quickly enough to keep track of all of them. A similar approach using digital certificates runs into the same problem: Most Web site creators do not bother to, or even know how to, create such certificates for their non-pornographic sites. The blacklist approach presents the problem from the opposite direction. New pornographic Web sites are created daily, and blacklists cannot be updated quickly enough to screen them all out.

The proscribed-keyword approach presents both the problem of overbreadth (as with the whitelist approach) and the problem of ineffective blocking (as with the blacklist approach). It is overbroad because keywords used to describe sexual behavior may appear on almost any Web site as part of otherwise innocuous content; the proscribed words could appear in academic journals, news stories, encyclopedias, dictionaries, the text of novels or screenplays, and medical advice sites. Even if the program looks for frequency of certain words or certain relationships between words, many non-pornographic sites are likely to be blocked. At the same time, sites that contain pornographic images might contain none of the proscribed words; this is especially true of foreign-language sites. At present there is no way for software to screen the content of the images themselves.

An approach that seems obvious, and that has been advocated for years by some both on the free speech and on the antipornography sides of the issue, is the creation of a "red-light district" on the Web. A top-level domain, such as ".xxx" or ".adult," could be created and made a safe haven for pornographic content, although not for obscenity or child pornography. Congress could then constitutionally restrict pornographic content, including pornographic Web advertising, to this top-level domain. Creating software to restrict access to certain top-level domains would be easy; in fact, it could be done using the security settings (rather than the less effective "content advisor" features) of existing Web browsers. In June 2005 the Internet Corporation for Assigned Names and Numbers (ICANN) approved a long-debated proposal to create a ".xxx" top-level domain for adult content. ICANN had opposed such proposals in the past, leading some companies to register such domains outside the ICANN domain-name registration system and distribute software enabling popular Internet browsers to access them.

Once the now-authorized .xxx top-level domain is created, the next step would be for Congress to enact legislation providing an incentive for pornographers to move their content to that domain, a disincentive for them to remain in the .com and other domains, or both. Few if any pornographers want their content to be available to minors, but there will be significant costs associated with moving the Web site. The costs of registering new domain names will be small, but measures may have to be taken to ensure that, for example, the owners of www.pornography.com have a right of first refusal to the domain name www.pornography.xxx. The Anticybersquatting Consumer Protection Act already provides some protection, but a problem may arise if different pornography businesses are currently using the same name in different top-level domains. There will also be labor costs, but these problems can be minimized by providing a phaseout period during which penalties will not be applied. Problems of definition will still arise, of course, and borderline cases will probably continue to be litigated for many years. It is to be hoped, though, that most pornographers will choose to self-define their content as pornographic and voluntarily transfer it to the .xxx domain, which may itself become a marketing tool.

Even effective and constitutional legislation restricting pornographic content to the .xxx domain will not completely solve the problem. Congress has legislative jurisdiction over actions, things, and persons within the territory of the United States and over some actions of U.S. persons outside the United States; it can thus, subject to the Constitution, regulate content on servers in the United States or published by persons within the United States or even by U.S. persons outside the United States. The scope of congressional authority to regulate actions of non-U.S. persons outside the United States is unclear and the subject of some debate; as a practical matter, however, there is little or nothing the U.S. government can do about Web content published in a foreign country by a foreign person. Yet such content is as accessible as any other content on the Web.

In addition, any screening software can be and will be circumvented by some clever minors. Attempts to restrict the availability of pornography to minors can never achieve absolute success. Just as laws prohibiting the sale of pornographic magazines to minors do not actually prevent all minors from gaining access to at least some of those magazines, screening software will not prevent some minors from gaining access to pornographic Internet content, or for that matter from sharing that content with other minors. The goal, rather, is to prevent pornography from becoming so pervasive that it becomes part of the cultural background noise, and to prevent the unsought exposure to pornography that is all too familiar to many Web surfers and e-mail users; attempts to restrict the access of minors to pornography are an exercise in control rather than in complete elimination of the problem.

A related problem, and a more difficult one to address, is the problem of sexually explicit spam (unsolicited bulk-mailed e-mail advertising). A high percentage of spam contains sexually explicit language; a smaller but not insignificant amount contains pornographic images. Spammers are already outside the rules of the Internet, if not outside the law. Whether they send advertisements for pornographic Web sites or non-pornographic advertisements for low-cost mortgages, they are often operating in violation of agreements with their own Internet service providers. A solution to the problem of pornographic spam must await a solution to the problem of spam generally.

Statutes

- Anticybersquatting Consumer Protection Act, 15 U.S.C. § 1125(d)

- Child Online Protection Act, 47 U.S.C. § 231
- Child Pornography Prevention Act of 1996, 18 U.S.C. §§ 2251–2260
- Communications Decency Act of 1996, Pub. L. No. 104-104, § 502, 1996 U.S.S.C.A.N. (110 Stat.) 56,133 (later codified at 47 U.S.C. § 223)

Cases
Supreme Court
- *American Civil Liberties Union v. Reno,* 217 F.3d 162 (3d Cir. 2000); rev. sub nom. *Ashcroft v. American Civil Liberties Union,* 535 U.S. 564 (2002); on remand, *American Civil Liberties Union v. Ashcroft,* 322 F.3d 240 (3d Cir. 2003); cert. granted, *Ashcroft v. American Civil Liberties Union,* 124 S. Ct. 399 (2003); aff'd and remanded, 124 S. Ct. 2783 (2004)
- *Ashcroft v. Free Speech Coalition,* 535 U.S. 234 (2002)
- *Jacobellis v. Ohio,* 378 U.S. 184 (1964)
- *Miller v. California,* 413 U.S. 15 (1973)
- *New York v. Ferber,* 458 U.S. 747 (1982)
- *Osborne v. Ohio,* 495 U.S. 103 (1990)
- *Reno v. American Civil Liberties Union,* 521 U.S. 844 (1997)
- *United States v. American Library Association, Inc.,* 539 U.S. 194 (2003)

Federal Trial Courts
- *America Online v. Cyber Promotions,* 948 F.Supp. 456 (E.D. Pa. 1996)
- *Mainstream Loudoun v. Board of Trustees of the Loudoun County Library,* 2 F. Supp.2d 783 (E.D. Va. 1998)

See also: Censorship; Child Online Protection Act; Children's Internet Protection Act; Communications Decency Act; Constitutional Law; First Amendment; Indecency; Obscenity; Spam

Sources and further reading:
Andrea Dworkin, *Pornography: Men Possessing Women* (New York: Perigee Books, 1981).
Terry Gillespie, "Virtual Violence? Pornography and Violence against Women on the Internet," in *Women, Violence and Strategies for Action: Feminist Research, Policy, and Practice,* edited by Jill Radford et al. (Buckingham, UK: Open University Press, 2000).
Mike Godwin, *Cyber Rights: Defending Free Speech in the Digital Age* (Cambridge, MA: MIT Press, 2003).
Kathryn Kolbert and Zak Mettger, eds., *Justice Talking: Censoring the Web: Leading Advocates Debate Today's Most Controversial Issues* (New York: The New Press, 2002).
Jeremy Lipschultz, *Free Expression in the Age of the Internet: Social and Legal Boundaries* (Boulder, CO: Perseus Books, 1999).
National Research Council, Technical, Business, and Legal Dimensions of Protecting Children from Pornography on the Internet: Proceedings of a Workshop (Washington, DC: National Academies Press, 2002).
Andy Patrizio, "XXX Domains May Be Hard Sell," *Wired News,* Mar. 6, 2001, available at http://www.wired.com/news/business/0,1367,42217,00.html (visited August 10, 2004).
"Porn 3x More Popular than Searches: Tracking Firm Finds that 18.8% of all U.S. Users went to 'Adult' Sites, 5.5% went to Search Engines," *CNN Money,* June 4, 2002, available at http://money.cnn.com/2004/06/04/technology/porn_search.reut/index.htm?cnn=yes (visited June 4, 2004).
Kevin W. Saunders, *Saving Our Children from the First Amendment* (New York: New York University Press, 2004).
Sex Sites Get Dedicated Net Home, BBC News, June 2, 2005, available at http://news.bbc.co.uk/2/hi/technology/4602449.stm (visited June 2, 2005).
Dick Thornburgh and Herbert S. Lin, *Youth, Pornography and the Internet* (Washington, DC: National Academies Press, 2002).

❖ PRIVACY ❖

The Internet is a two-way information tool; individuals use the Internet to locate information on the Web, to send and receive information by e-mail, and to upload and download information using FTP and file-sharing programs. All of this activity creates information about the user. Web sites collect information about visitors; copies of visited pages, e-mail messages, and uploads and downloads are stored on the user's computer and on servers through which they pass on their journey across the Internet. Together, all of this information can reveal things about the user that the user would prefer to keep private.

Many users prefer to maintain privacy, at least from the world at large, about their income and financial status, health and medical history, personal correspondence, sexual preference, employment history, and history of brushes with the law, if any. Yet information gained from observing the user's Internet use can reveal all of these things. Anyone who files an electronic tax return or uses online banking or bill payment is allowing detailed financial information to travel across the Internet and to be stored on Internet servers. The danger that this information will be accidentally disclosed is fairly low, because such information is always encrypted. More general information can also provide a thorough picture of an individual's financial status, however. A user who purchases a Patek Phillippe watch online has revealed information about his or her level of disposable income; one who purchases first-class tickets to Fiji can be placed in a different marketing category from one who flies coach class to Cleveland. A user who surfs debt-relief sites is announcing her indebtedness by doing so; one who uses a real estate site to shop for houses in the $300,000 price range and mortgages in the $250,000 range has given anyone familiar with real estate a fairly accurate idea of her wealth and annual income.

In the same way, visits to support groups for a particular disease, or searches for information on that disease, are usually a good indicator that the user or someone in the user's family suffers from the disease. Visits to pornographic Web sites can provide information about an individual's sexual orientation, as can purchasing a second-hand copy of *A Gay Guide to San Francisco and the Bay Area* on eBay. Few people would have difficulty deducing a great deal of information about a person who buys the following items:

- *Surviving Medical School,* by Robert H. Coombs
- *Irish Wedding Traditions: Using Your Irish Heritage to Create the Perfect Wedding,* by Shannon McMahon-Lichte
- Spiderman Halloween costume, size 8
- Little Mermaid Halloween costume, size 6
- Woman's sweatshirt, size S, reading "Catholic & Democrat: Because Jesus Didn't Ride into Town on an Elephant"

All of these items can be, and are, purchased over the Internet; the combination allows a casual observer to make fairly accurate guesses as to the user's age, education, marital status and plans, political affiliation, religion, and national origin, as well as the number, age, and gender of the user's children. It is not even necessary that the user actually purchase the items; the user leaves a trail of information simply by shopping for them. Of course, some or all of the items might be gifts for someone else, but an examination of a larger sample of the user's shopping and purchases would still

© *Zits partnership. King Features Syndicate.*

reveal patterns. Online marketing companies such as Doubleclick.com gather together far more pieces of data than the five items listed here. Data mining and advanced statistical techniques can then be used to come up with fairly accurate guesses about the user.

Many users feel uncomfortable at the idea that strangers can find out so much about them. The hypothetical shopper described above probably makes no effort to conceal her religion or political beliefs from her friends and acquaintances, but might be disconcerted to find the same information, matched to her name and home address, published on a Web site. In the same way, most people probably agree in the abstract with the idea that political campaign contributions should not be anonymous, but feel disconcerted when they visit www.fundrace.org and discover a record of the fact that they once donated $25 to the ill-fated presidential campaign of General Wesley Clarke. The feeling of unease is increased by the fact that the site's listings include the donors' home addresses and occupations.

Individual concerns about privacy fall into three general categories: privacy from the government, privacy from other legitimate private parties, and privacy from malicious users. Each of these types of privacy is protected in different ways.

Concerns about privacy from the government can in turn be divided into two categories: concerns about the government's use of information about individuals, and concerns about the government's disclosure of that information. The government collects a great deal of information about individuals, and that information is stored electronically. It can conceivably be used to create lists of individuals on the basis of race, national origin, or exposure to a certain disease. Worries about the uses of this information were raised in the aftermath of the September 11 attacks, when the FBI used existing information in government databases to identify and conduct interviews with thousands of Arabs and Muslims in the United States, including U.S. citizens (Sheridan 2004). In the minds of civil libertarians, the FBI's action was not only improper in its own right but also raised the specter of more sinister uses of the in-

Digital inheritance: What will happen to your online property when you die? Typically contractual arrangements between individuals and their ISPs, Web hosts, and other custodians of online property terminate on the death of the user. But the user's e-mail, Web pages, blogs, stored files, and other online assets might represent the product of thousands of hours of effort—and might be valuable, both sentimentally and financially, to the deceased user's family. Access to an online e-mail address book might be the only way to make sure that the user's friends and business associates are informed of his or her death. A password-protected Web site in the user's name may in fact have been a family project; it might be the only place where family photos and videos were stored, or could be necessary to an ongoing business.

ISPs must balance the interests of family members against the privacy interests of the deceased, however, as well as the privacy interests of those who might be discussed in e-mails in the deceased user's account, or whose photos or financial information might appear on the Web site, or who might otherwise be affected. The need to balance these interests is an issue that has only recently been brought to the attention of ISPs and the public, in part as the result of a dispute between Yahoo! and the family of a soldier killed in Iraq in November 2004.

Source
"Digital Inheritance Raises Legal Questions," CNN.Com, Dec. 24, 2004, available at http://www.cnn.com/2004/TECH/ptech/12/24/e.mailafterlife.ap/ (visited December 28, 2004).

formation, as in the case of the internment of Japanese-Americans during World War II.

The government may collect, use, and disclose data on individuals so long as the collection and use does not invade a constitutionally protected "zone of privacy." Protection of privacy requires that the government use both legal and technical safeguards to prevent improper use or disclosure of the information.

With these safeguards in place, the government may collect and use even quite personal information, such as the names and addresses of all persons who have received certain prescription drugs (*Whalen,* 429 U.S. 589). The government may also collect information that the individual cannot reasonably expect to remain private, such as postings in a chat room (*Charbonneau,* 979 F.Supp. 1177), and may subpoena records of electronic communications on private companies' servers (18 U.S.C. § 2703). And the government may conduct analysis and data mining of its own records, creating abstracts of existing information (*Pippinger,* 129 F.3d 519).

Collection of private information can be overt, as when a product registration screen asks for information about a consumer's hobbies, marital status, and income, or covert, as when spyware tracks a user's surfing habits. The overt collection of information usually arouses fairly little concern, because consumers have the option of refusing to provide the information. An exception is made in the case of the collection of information from children, however. Under the Children's Online Privacy Protection Act (COPPA), Web sites that collect information from children under the age of thirteen must provide notice of what information they collect from children, how they use the information, and what their practices are regarding disclosure of the information. Personal information, including information that might identify or permit communication with the child, may only be collected, used, or disclosed with the verifiable consent of the child's parents (15 U.S.C. § 6502).

Covert collection of information arouses greater concerns. Adware and spyware are almost universally despised by consumers and are a current target of legislative efforts. But much covert collection of information is less intrusive. Commercial Web sites track consumer purchases and shopping and then make suggestions as to further purchases. The Web sites are generally open about the process; consumer anxiety seems to be directed not at the maintenance of such information by retail Web sites but at the possibility that the information will be disclosed to third parties unknown to the consumer, without the consumer's knowledge or consent. Web sites post privacy policies, but reading and interpreting each site's policy would be a time-consuming task.

There are certain restrictions on private parties' collection, use, and disclosure of information about individuals even when those individuals are adults. However, the use of cookies to collect information about users' Web browsing habits is not illegal; concerned users can always block the cookies, at the cost of some browsing functionality (*DoubleClick,* 154 F.Supp.2d 497). And there is no reasonable expectation of privacy in workplace e-mail or Web surfing; workers who use their office e-mail to complain about the boss may be embarrassed, or worse, when the boss reads the messages (*Smyth,* 914 F.Supp. 97).

The third category of privacy worries, about disclosure of information to malicious users, is related to the first two. Information can be stolen from users' own computers, but users can take steps to prevent that. Once the information has been placed in a private or government database, however, the user can no longer protect it; a malicious hacker might crack the database's protection. Such unauthorized access to private records occurs frequently; sometimes the information is used by identity thieves, and sometimes it is gleefully posted on Web sites. The activities of the crackers and identity thieves are already illegal; privacy concerns focus more on the inadequate protection of many databases, especially government databases. The concern is that, although government agencies are required to use technical safeguards to protect the information (*Whalen,* 429 U.S. 589), those safeguards will not be updated quickly enough to keep pace with the development of cracking techniques.

Statutes
- Children's Online Privacy Protection Act, 15 U.S.C. §§ 6501–6506
- Electronic Communications Privacy Act, 18 U.S.C. § 2703

Cases
Supreme Court
- *Whalen v. Roe,* 429 U.S. 589 (1977)

Federal Appellate Court
- *Pippinger v. Rubin,* 129 F.3d 519 (10th Cir. 1997)

Federal Trial Court
- *Bohach v. City of Reno,* 932 F.Supp. 1232 (D. Nev. 1996)
- *In re DoubleClick, Inc. Privacy Litigation,* 154 F.Supp.2d 497 (S.D. N.Y. 2001)
- *Smyth v. Pillsbury,* 914 F.Supp. 97 (E.D. Pa. 1996)
- *United States v. Charbonneau,* 979 F. Supp. 1177 (S.D. Ohio 1997)

See also: Adware and Spyware; Children's Online Privacy Protection Act; Cookies; Data Mining; DoubleClick; Hacking; Identity Theft

Sources and further reading:
Michael A. Caloyannides, *Computer Forensics and Privacy* (Norwood, MA: Artech House, 2001).
Fred H. Cate, *Privacy in the Information Age* (Washington, DC: Brookings Institution Press, 1997).
Terry W. Posey Jr., "Tony Soprano's Privacy Rights: Internet Cookies, Wiretapping Statutes, and Federal Computer Crimes," 29 *University of Dayton Law Review* 109 (2003).
Paul M. Schwartz, "Property, Privacy, and Personal Data," 117 *Harvard Law Review* 2055 (2004).
Mary Beth Sheridan, "Interviews of Muslims to Broaden: FBI Hopes to Avert a Terrorist Attack," *Washington Post,* July 17, 2004, at A01.

❖ PROJECT GUTENBERG ❖

The duration of copyright protection is so long that by the time a work finally enters the public domain, it is often not only out of print but unavailable even from resellers. Project Gutenberg makes these works, and others in the public domain, available in electronic form. According to its mission statement, "The mission of Project Gutenberg is simple: 'To encourage the creation and distribution of eBooks.' This mission is, as much as possible, to encourage *ALL* those who are interested in making eBooks and helping to give them away." In furtherance of this mission Project Gutenberg makes more

than 13,000 e-books available for free download, with more constantly being added. For more than three decades the work of Project Gutenberg has been carried out entirely by volunteers. Although most of the available works are in English, Project Gutenberg also includes works in Chinese, Dutch, Finnish, French, German, Italian, and Spanish.

Most of the texts available via Project Gutenberg are in the public domain in the United States; a few are copyrighted texts that the copyright holders have licensed Project Gutenberg to distribute. Project Gutenberg in turn attaches restrictions to the copies it distributes, although the enforceability of these restrictions with regard to works already in the public domain is questionable. The main restrictions are on commercial uses, modification, and use of copyrighted materials. Project Gutenberg also attaches a warning that works in the public domain in the United States might still be protected by copyright in other countries. Other Project Gutenberg networks in Australia and the European Union (EU) distribute works that are in the public domain in Australia and the EU, respectively; some of these may still be in copyright in the United States.

Project Gutenberg cannot claim copyright in the public domain works it distributes. It cannot and does not demand royalties from commercial use of those works. It can and does claim a trademark in the name "Project Gutenberg," however, and the licensing agreement includes a royalty schedule for commercial use of the trademark.

The condition that "only unmodified copies of these eBooks may be redistributed without limitation" would be unenforceable as to works in the public domain, but is attached to use of the trademark rather than to use of the work: Altered works may not include the Project Gutenberg header or trademark, nor may they otherwise indicate that they are associated with Project Gutenberg.

Copyrighted works distributed via Project Gutenberg are, of course, subject to conditions attached by the copyright holder; these vary from work to work, but generally include restrictions on commercial use and protection of the moral rights of integrity and paternity.

A look at the most downloaded Project Gutenberg works raises some questions about Project Gutenberg's possible effect on the marketplace. Most of the most popular works are, or recently have been, in print and are readily available in print form: *Alice's Adventures in Wonderland, The Art of War, Grimm's Fairy Tales, The Notebooks of Leonardo Da Vinci, Pride and Prejudice, Relativity: the Special and General Theory, Ulysses,* and *Vanity Fair.* Even such unlikely favorites as an 1860 book on casting hand shadows (nearly 50,000 downloads in September 2004, or about as many as the next twenty most popular downloads combined) are still readily available. Printed editions of the work, *Hand Shadows to Be Thrown upon the Wall,* by Henry Bursill, can be purchased secondhand in the United States for under a dollar, and the work is currently in print in the United Kingdom, where it sells for £4.25, new. This does not mean that an additional 50,000 copies of the book could have been sold during September 2004; many or most of the downloaders probably chose the book because it was in the public domain and available for free. It does suggest, though, that public domain archives such as Project Gutenberg can be a source of information to commercial publishers as to which books it might be worthwhile to reprint.

See also: Budapest Open Access Initiative; Copyright; Open-Source; Public Domain

Sources and further reading:
Henry Bursill, *Hand Shadows to Be Thrown Upon the Wall: A Series of Novel and Amusing Figures Formed by the Hand* (Yorkletts, Whitstable, Kent, UK: Pryor Publications, 1993 (1860)), reviews and ordering information available from Amazon UK at http://www.amazon.co.uk/ exec/obidos/ASIN/0946014248/qid= 1097002589/ref=sr_8_xs_ap_i1_xgl/ 202–0143568–6564612 (visited October 5, 2004).
Edward Lee, "The Public's Domain: The Evolution of Legal Restraints on the Government's Power to Control Public Access through Secrecy or Intellectual Property," 55 *Hastings Law Journal* 91 (2003).
PG-EU, http://gutenberg.nl/ (visited October 5, 2004).

The Project Gutenberg License, Header and 'Small Print,' http://www.gutenberg.net/license (visited October 5, 2004).
Project Gutenberg of Australia: A Treasure-Trove of Literature, http://www.gutenberg.net.au/ (visited October 5, 2004).
Welcome to Project Gutenberg, http://www. gutenberg.net/ (visited October 5, 2004).

❖ PROSECUTION HISTORY ESTOPPEL ❖

Prosecution history estoppel, also called file wrapper estoppel, is a limit on the application of the patent law doctrine of equivalents. The "file wrapper" is the folder in which the United States Patent and Trademark Office keeps the papers filed during the process of a patent application. The doctrine of equivalents allows a patent holder or assignee to sue for patent infringement if the infringing conduct or product is not literally within the scope of the patent, but differs only insubstantially from the description in the patent. Prosecution history estoppel prevents a patent holder from asserting the doctrine of equivalents if the alleged infringement lies in an area that was given up by the patent holder during the prosecution of the patent. In order to obtain a patent, the patent holder may have conceded that certain processes or products were outside the scope of the patent even though they might have been substantially similar to those described in the patent. The patent holder is then *estopped*—prohibited—from attempting to recapture the area that was conceded; he or she may not later sue for infringement for activities within that area, even though those activities would otherwise be covered by the patent under the doctrine of equivalents.

File wrapper estoppel has been applied to many cases involving computer technology patents. Both *Texas Instruments v. U.S. International Trade Commission* and *Wang Labs v. Toshiba Corporation* involved arrangements of computer chips only slightly different from those described in allegedly infringed patents; in both cases prosecution history estoppel was applied to preclude the patent infringement claim. More recently, the Supreme Court has held that the doctrine is flexible: The range of subject matter surrendered by the patent applicant when submitting an amended application must be determined for each particular case, rather than by applying an inflexible complete bar (*Festo*, 535 U.S. at 737–738).

Cases
Supreme Court
- *Festo Corp. v. Shoketsu Kinzoku Kogyo Kabushiki Co., Ltd.*, 535 U.S. 722 (2002)

Federal Circuit
- *Texas Instruments Inc. v. U.S. International Trade Commission*, 988 F.2d 1165 (Fed. Cir. 1993)
- *Wang Labs v. Toshiba Corporation*, 993 F.2d 858 (Fed. Cir. 1993)

See also: Doctrine of Equivalents; Patent

Sources and further reading:
Stephen B. Maebius and Harold C. Wegner, "The Honeywell Nail in the Festo Coffin: A Narrowing Amendment Does Create a Presumption of Prosecution History Estoppel," 23 *Biotechnology Law Report* 417 (2004).

❖ PROTECTING INTELLECTUAL RIGHTS AGAINST THEFT AND EXPROPRIATION ACT ❖

The Protecting Intellectual Rights against Theft and Expropriation (PIRATE) Act of 2004 is a proposed law that would strengthen copyright protections. If enacted, it would allow the Department of Justice to bring civil as well as criminal actions in copyright infringement cases (Leahy 2004). This would be an extraordinary step; the government is not the injured party in civil copyright infringement, and historically it has been the task of the copyright holder to protect his or her own rights. The PIRATE Act is aimed specifically at peer-to-peer file-sharing networks. Because the value of the files traded is often quite small, most file-traders do not meet the $1,000 threshold requirement for criminal copyright infringement. This threshold itself

was set in 1997 by the No Electronic Theft (NET) Act; previously, criminal copyright infringement had required a financial motive. The NET Act aimed at the problem of nonprofit warez trading and created an alternative to the "financial gain" requirement in cases where the infringing copies had "a total retail value of more than $1,000" (17 U.S.C. § 506(a)(2)).

Songs are less expensive than software, however, and because music files are easy to copy, file-sharers tend to be individuals rather than groups like warez trading operations. The PIRATE Act would add a new Section 506a (not to be confused with Section 506(a)) to the copyright code:

> Sec. 506a. Civil penalties for violations of section 506
> (a) IN GENERAL- The Attorney General may commence a civil action in the appropriate United States district court against any person who engages in conduct constituting an offense under section 506. Upon proof of such conduct by a preponderance of the evidence, such person shall be subject to a civil penalty under section 504 which shall be in an amount equal to the amount which would be awarded under section 3663(a)(1)(B) of title 18 and restitution to the copyright owner aggrieved by the conduct.

This would allow the government to obtain civil damages in addition to any criminal penalties for copyright infringement. An additional provision is even more startling, however; the PIRATE Act would also amend 17 U.S.C. § 504(b) to allow the U.S. attorney general, in addition to the copyright holder, to maintain a suit for civil damages even in the absence of criminal copyright infringement.

The PIRATE Act has been opposed by users' rights advocates (Electronic Frontier Foundation 2004). These advocates question whether taxpayers should underwrite the legal costs of copyright holders. Existing law already allows the content industry to maintain civil actions against copyright infringers; the Recording Industry Association of America, a music content industry group, has filed thousands of such suits against individual file traders, as well as suits against bigger targets such as P2P networks. From an economic standpoint, it is worthwhile for the industry to bring suits against infringers so long as the value of the damage done to the copyright holder exceeds the legal costs. If the legal costs are too high or the damage is too small, the suits will no longer make economic sense, in which case subsidizing them might be unwise. However, the bill passed the Senate by unanimous consent on June 25, 2004, and was sent to the House and referred to the Judiciary Committee on the same day.

Proposed Act
- Protecting Intellectual Rights against Theft and Expropriation (PIRATE) Act of 2004, S. 2237, 108th Cong., 2d Sess., Mar. 25, 2004

Statutes
- Digital Millennium Copyright Act, Title I, §§ 1201–1204
- No Electronic Theft Act, amending and codified at 17 U.S.C. §§ 101, 506, and 507 and 18 U.S.C. §§ 2319–2320

Other Government Documents
- United States Department of Justice, The No Electronic Theft ("NET") Act: Relevant portions of 17 U.S.C. and 18 U.S.C. as amended (redlined), http://www.usdoj.gov/criminal/cybercrime/17–18red.htm

See also: Activism and Advocacy Groups; Copyright; Copyright Infringement; File-Sharing; No Electronic Theft Act; Warez

Sources and further reading:
Electronic Frontier Foundation, Sink the PIRATE Act, EFFector, May 27, 2004, http://www.eff.org/effector/17/19.php (visited October 21, 2004).
Office of Senator Patrick Leahy, "Leahy-Hatch Bill Takes Aim at Copyright Infringement: Proposal Allows DOJ Filing of Civil Actions in IP Piracy Cases," Mar. 25, 2004, http://leahy.senate.gov/press/200403/032504a.html (visited October 21, 2004).

❖ PSEUDONYMITY ❖

See Anonymity

❖ PUBLIC DOMAIN ❖

In intellectual property law, the public domain consists of those works and inventions unprotected by copyright or patent. Intellectual property rights protected by trademark or trade secret law are also spoken of as "falling into the public domain" if they lose that protection. The exact limits of the public domain are uncertain and are fiercely contested by the content industry on the one hand and users' and consumers' advocates on the other. The limits are also constantly changing: New works enter the public domain as copyrights and patents expire, and congressional modification of copyright and patent law can take works out of the public domain and restore intellectual property protection. Works created by the U.S. government are in the public domain, although the U.S. government may acquire ownership of copyrights in works created by others (17 U.S.C. § 105).

The concept of the public domain is inherent in the legislative creation of limited terms of copyright and patent protection. It was implicit in the 1710 Statute of Anne and the 1774 decision of the House of Lords in *Donaldson v. Beckett*. In the United States it is built into the Constitution: The Patent and Copyright Clause provides that Congress shall have the power "To promote the Progress of Science and useful Arts, by securing for limited Times to Authors and Inventors the exclusive Right to their respective Writings and Discoveries." After the "limited Times" set by Congress have expired, works fall into the public domain. Works that are unprotected by copyright from the outset, such as U.S. government works, are also in the public domain.

In the nineteenth century the federal courts fought off attempts by the content industry to invade the public domain using another form of intellectual property protection: trademark. In the 1890 case of *Merriam v. Holloway Publishing Company*, the publishers of an 1847 edition of *Webster's Dictionary*, on which the copyright had expired, brought suit against another publisher that had reproduced and distributed for sale the entire 1847 edition. Among the arguments advanced by Merriam was that even though the copyright had expired, the entire dictionary was still protected by trademark. Speaking for the court, Justice Miller stated that

> this proceeding is an attempt to establish the doctrine that a party who has had the copyright of a book until it has expired, may continue that monopoly indefinitely, under the pretense that it is protected by a trade-mark, or something of that sort. I do not believe in any such doctrine, nor do my associates. When a man takes out a copyright, for any of his writings or works, he impliedly agrees that, at the expiration of that copyright, such writings or works shall go to the public and become public property. I may be the first to announce that doctrine, but I announce it without any hesitation. If a man is entitled to an extension of his copyright, he may obtain it by the mode pointed out by law. The law provides a method of obtaining such extension. The copyright law gives an author or proprietor a monopoly of the sale of his writings for a definite period, but the grant of a monopoly implies that, after the monopoly has expired, the public shall be entitled ever afterwards to the unrestricted use of the book. (*Merriam,* 43 F. at 451)

Six years later, the U.S. Supreme Court addressed the same issue in a patent law context in the landmark case of *Singer Manufacturing Company v. June Manufacturing Company.* As Merriam had with its copyrighted dictionary, Singer asserted a trademark right in its patented sewing machine even after the patent had expired. The Supreme Court disagreed; although Singer could still claim a trademark in the name "Singer" and could require other manufacturers to identify themselves not Singer, as the manufacturer, it could not use its trademark in the Singer name to prevent others from manufacturing Singer machines on which the patent had expired, and from using the name "Singer" to identify those machines. Writing for the Court, Justice White explained:

> It is self-evident that on the expiration of a patent the monopoly created by it ceases to exist, and the right to make the thing formerly covered by the patent becomes public property. It is upon this condition that the patent is granted. It follows, as a matter of course, that on the termination of the patent there passes to the public the right to make the machine in the form in which it was constructed during the patent. . . . It equally follows from the cessation of the monopoly and the falling of the patented device into the domain of things public that along with the public ownership of the device there must also necessarily pass to the public the generic designation of the thing which has arisen during the monopoly in consequence of the designation having been acquiesced in by the owner, either tacitly, by accepting the benefits of the monopoly, or expressly by his having so connected the name with the machine as to lend countenance to the resulting dedication. To say otherwise would be to hold that, although the public had acquired the device covered by the patent, yet the owner of the patent or the manufacturer of the patented thing had retained the designated name which was essentially necessary to vest the public with the full enjoyment of that which had become theirs by the disappearance of the monopoly. In other words, that the patentee or manufacturer could take the benefit and advantage of the patent upon the condition that at its termination the monopoly should cease, and yet, when the end was reached, disregard the public dedication and practically perpetuate indefinitely an exclusive right.
>
> The public having the right, on the expiration of the patent, to make the patented article, and to use its generic name, to restrict this use, either by preventing its being placed upon the articles when manufactured or by using it in advertisements or circulars, would be to admit the right, and at the same time destroy it. It follows, then, that the right to use the name in every form passes to the public with the dedication resulting from the expiration of the patent. (*Singer,* 163 U.S. at 185–186)

The *Singer* opinion served both to clearly define the public domain and to introduce the term (as "the domain of things public") to American law. The public domain in *Singer* is more inclusive than the nineteenth-century concept of *domaine publique* in French law and in the Berne Convention, from which the term might have been drawn.

In contrast to copyrights and patents, which are of limited duration, trade secrets and trademarks are of potentially infinite duration. Trade secrets fall into the public domain as soon as they become public; the person who makes them public may be liable for penalties, but the protection cannot be regained once the secrecy is lost. Trademarks can fall into the public domain by coming into common use as a generic term for an item; words like *aspirin* and *shredded wheat* now suggest generic classes of products, rather than particular brand names; owners of trademarks such as Xerox and Frigidaire have battled valiantly—and successfully—to keep their trademarks from being similarly extinguished.

The battle over the limits of the public domain is particularly intense in the area of copyright law. Most recently, the Sonny Bono Copyright Term Extension Act, which extended most copyright terms by twenty years, has inspired a movement to defend the public domain against further encroachment. The act was challenged, unsuccessfully, in the case of *Eldred v. Ashcroft*. In the aftermath of *Eldred*, opponents of the act proposed a Public Domain Enhancement Act to require copyright registration and payment of a minimal fee in order to extend the copyright term beyond fifty years, thus allowing a great number of copyrighted works of no significant commercial value—most of them no longer in print—to fall into the public domain.

Constitution
- United States Constitution, Article I, Section 8, Clause 8

Statute
- Copyright Act of 1976, 17 U.S.C. § 105

Proposed Legislation
- Public Domain Enhancement Act, H.R. 2601, 108th Cong., 1st Sess., June 25, 2003, available at http://thomas.loc.gov/cgi-bin/query/z?c108:H.R.2601: (visited October 25, 2004)

Cases
England
- *Cheavin v. Walker*, 5 Ch. Div. 850 (1877)
- *Donaldson v. Beckett*, 2 Bro. P.C. 129, 1 Eng. Rep. 837 Burr. (4th ed.) 2408, 98 Eng. Rep. 257 (H.L. 1774)

United States
- *Eldred v. Ashcroft*, 537 U.S. 186 (2002)
- *Merriam v. Holloway Publishing Co.*, 43 F. 450 (C.C.E.D. Mo. 1890)
- *Singer Manufacturing Co. v. June Manufacturing Co.*, 163 U.S. 169 (1896)

See also: Budapest Open Access Initiative; Copyright; Patent; Project Gutenberg; Public Domain Enhancement Act; Sonny Bono Copyright Term Extension Act; Trademark

Sources and further reading:
James Boyle, "The Second Enclosure Movement and the Construction of the Public Domain," 66 *Law and Contemporary Problems* 33 (2003).
James Boyle, ed., *Collected Papers, Duke Conference on the Public Domain* (Durham, NC: Center for the Study of the Public Domain, 2003).
Stephen Fishman, *The Public Domain: How to Find and Use Copyright-Free Writings, Music, Art and More* (Berkeley, CA: Nolo Press, 2004).
Wendy J. Gordon, "A Property Right in Self-Expression: Equality and Individualism in the Natural Law of Intellectual Property," 102 *Yale Law Journal* 1533 (1993).
David Lange, "Recognizing the Public Domain," 44 *Law and Contemporary Problems* 147 (1981).
Marshall Leaffer, *Understanding Copyright Law*, 3d ed. (New York: Matthew Bender, 1999).
Lawrence Lessig, *Free Culture: How Big Media Uses Technology and the Law to Lock Down Culture and Control Creativity* (New York: Penguin, 2004) (also available as a free download).
Jessica Litman, "The Public Domain," 39 *Emory Law Journal* 965 (1990).
Edward Samuels, "The Public Domain Revisited," 36 *Loyola (Los Angeles) Law Review* 389 (2002).
Pamela Samuelson, "Mapping the Digital Public Domain: Threats and Opportunities," 66 *Law and Contemporary Problems* 147 (2003).
Symposium, "The Public Domain," 66 *Law and Contemporary Problems* (2003).
R. Polk Wagner, "Information Wants to Be Free: Intellectual Property and the Mythologies of Control," 103 *Columbia Law Review* 995 (2003).

❖ PUBLIC DOMAIN ENHANCEMENT ACT ❖

The Public Domain Enhancement Act was drafted by Stanford professor and information rights advocate Lawrence Lessig in response to the enactment of the Sonny Bono Copyright Term Extension Act (CTEA) and the subsequent decision of the U.S. Supreme Court in *Eldred v. Ashcroft*. The plaintiffs in *Eldred*, represented by Lessig, failed to have the CTEA declared unconstitutional. The battle to limit copyright and save the public domain shifted to the House of Representatives, where on June 25, 2003, Representatives Zoe Lofgren (D-CA) and John Doolittle (R-CA) introduced the Public Domain Enhancement Act (PDEA).

The PDEA's central provision is clearly set forth in its title, which declares it to be a bill "To amend title 17, United States Code, to allow abandoned copyrighted works to enter the public domain after 50 years." The "Findings" section of the bill sets forth its five underpinning arguments. First, the Constitution's copyright clause grants Congress the power to "promote the Progress of Science and useful Arts, by securing for limited Times to Authors . . . the exclusive Right to their respective Writings[.]" Second, the copyright clause gives authors an economic incentive to create new works by providing them with a monopoly on reproduction of their work, while at the same time making that monopoly temporary in order to promote "society's interest in the free flow of ideas, information and commerce." Third, "Both commercial and noncommercial creators depend on a healthy public domain." Fourth, "the vast majority of older works are no longer commercially available." Perhaps only 2 percent of works between fifty-five and seventy-five years old retain any commercial value, yet keeping those works out of the public domain "prevents commercial and noncommercial entities from building upon, cultivating, and preserving" them. And fifth, "the existing copyright system functions contrary to the intent of the Framers of the Constitution in adopting the copyright clause and the intent of Congress in enacting the Copyright Act." The PDEA seeks "to establish a mechanism by which abandoned American copyrights can enter the public domain."

The mechanism by which the PDEA would accomplish its goal is a "maintenance fee" of one dollar. All copyrights of U.S. works fifty years old or older would be required to be reg-

istered either fifty years after the date of first publication or on December 31, 2004, whichever is later; an additional one-dollar fee would be required every ten years thereafter until the expiration of the copyright term.

The fee itself is nominal, but the requirement of paying it would solve two problems with the current system: First, locating the copyright holder would become easier because that person would pay the fee, and contact information could be collected at the time the fee was paid. And second, abandoned works or works with no commercial value would enter the public domain more quickly because no one would pay the fee.

There are several practical obstacles to passage and implementation of the PDEA. First, the registration requirements are inconsistent with the obligations of the United States under the Berne Convention and other international copyright agreements. The PDEA gets around this difficulty by exempting foreign works; by its terms, it is applicable only to U.S. works. There are two drawbacks to this approach: It will have the effect of granting a longer term of protection to foreign works than to many U.S. works, and it will create confusion as to whether a work is protected—whether a work is a "United States work" or a "foreign work" is not always obvious to the person wishing to reproduce it.

In addition, the registration fee/renewal approach has already been rejected once by Congress: Such a system existed under the Copyright Act of 1909, and Congress chose to get rid of it when enacting the Copyright Act of 1976. Finally, the trend over the last hundred and twenty years or so of U.S. copyright law has been one of slowly, gradually bringing U.S. law into conformity with the law of most of the rest of the world. The PDEA would reverse that trend; perhaps the United States is enough of a market leader in copyrighted material that other countries would follow its lead, but that has not been the case in the past.

Another omission that has been noted, both in current copyright law and the PDEA, is the lack of any procedure for placing works into the public domain before the expiration of the copyright term. Because notice of a claim of copyright is not required under the Berne Convention and is no longer required under U.S. law, all original works of authorship fixed in a tangible medium of expression are copyrighted from the moment of their creation; although some authors may choose not to enforce that copyright, those who use the work without permission run the risk that the author will change her mind at some point in the future (West's Federal Administrative Practice 2004).

The Public Domain Enhancement Act seems unlikely to become law anytime soon. Immediately upon being introduced, the PDEA was referred to the House Committee on the Judiciary. On September 4, 2003, it was referred to the Subcommittee on Courts, the Internet, and Intellectual Property. As of October 2004 no further action had been taken.

Constitution
- United States Constitution, Article I, Section 8, Clause 8

Proposed Legislation
- Public Domain Enhancement Act, H.R. 2601, 108th Cong., 1st Sess., June 25, 2003, available at http://thomas.loc. gov/cgi-bin/query/z?c108:H.R.2601: (visited October 25, 2004)

Cases
- *Eldred v. Ashcroft*, 1537 U.S. 186 (2002)
- *Sony Corp. v. Universal City Studios, Inc.*, 464 U.S. 417 (1984)

See also: Copyright; Project Gutenberg; Public Domain; Sonny Bono Copyright Term Extension Act

Sources and further reading:
Dan Hunter, "Cyberspace as a Place and the Tragedy of the Digital Anticommons," 91 *California Law Review* 439 (2003).

Lawrence Lessig, *Free Culture: How Big Media Uses Technology and the Law to Lock Down Culture and Control Creativity* (New York: Penguin, 2004) (also available as a free download).

Mark S. Nadel, "How Current Copyright Law Discourages Creative Output: The Overlooked Impact of Marketing," 19 *Berkeley Technology Law Journal* 785 (2004).

West's Federal Administrative Practice § 4006, *Duration of Copyright Under the 1976 Act*, 3d ed. (Supp. 2004).

R

❖ RECOGNITION AND ENFORCEMENT OF JUDGMENTS ❖

The Internet increases the likelihood of international litigation. Material posted on a Web site in the United States that is completely legal and permissible under U.S. law might nonetheless expose the publisher to civil liability for defamation under some other country's law. Because the posted material is accessible from that other country, a plaintiff might bring an action in that country's court and obtain a judgment against the U.S. defendant. This could happen without the participation or even the awareness of the defendant. A problem could arise, however, if a court in the United States is asked to recognize or enforce the foreign court's judgment.

Recognition and *enforcement* are terms of art. A court *recognizes* the judgment of the courts of another state or nation when it acknowledges that the result reached by the foreign court was correct. It *enforces* a judgment when it takes some action, such as attaching assets or transferring property, as a result of a judgment reached by a court in another jurisdiction. The threshold required for enforcement of foreign judgments is, naturally, higher than that required for recognition. Although the Internet presents no fundamentally new problems in recognition and enforcement of foreign judgments, it may increase the number of cases in which courts are called upon to address the issue.

States of the United States are required by Article IV, § 1 of the U.S. Constitution to give full faith and credit to the judgments of the courts of other states, although certain limitations apply, particularly where real property is involved. The Full Faith and Credit Clause and Full Faith and Credit Statute also require the federal courts to recognize judgments of state courts, but interestingly do not require state courts to recognize federal judgments (28 U.S.C. § 1738). However, the Supreme Court has repeatedly stated that the states do have such an obligation, although the source upon which the Court bases this obligation is obscure.

No similar requirement of full faith and credit exists among nations, absent a treaty provision imposing it. This acts as a check on jurisdiction: The nation of Ruritania might decide that its courts should have jurisdiction over all parties and all controversies arising anywhere in the world, but the probable result would be that no court outside Ruritania would recognize Ruritania's judgments in the absence of some more concrete basis for jurisdiction.

There is no constitutional or statutory requirement for any court in the United States to recognize any foreign court's judgment. Two canons of construction apply to the recognition and enforcement of foreign judgments: (1) No law has any independent effect outside the territory of the government that creates it, and (2) No sovereign government is bound to recognize or enforce within its territory judgments rendered by the courts of other nations, absent some agreement to the contrary. Foreign country judgments are thus recognized and enforced in the United States, if at all, on a basis of comity, or mutual respect by sovereign states of each other's legislative, executive, and judicial acts (Richman and Reynolds 2002, 355–356).

U.S. federal courts will generally recognize and enforce foreign-country judgments on a basis of reciprocity, except where the foreign law is contrary to fundamental U.S. moral, legal, and policy principles (Richman and Reynolds 2002, 356–357). Default judgments seem to be less likely to be enforced. Where the foreign law conflicts with a fundamental constitutional right (such as freedom of expression) the foreign judgment will not be enforced. And U.S. courts may recognize, but need not enforce, penal and tax judgments of foreign countries.

The Uniform Foreign Money-Judgments Recognition Act (UFMJRA) has been adopted by twenty-eight states. Foreign money judgments (but not for taxes, fines, or penalties, or in family law matters) will be recognized unless one of the UFMJRA's mandatory or discretionary grounds for nonrecognition is present. Nonrecognition is mandatory (that is, a state in which the UFMJRA has been adopted is not permitted to recognize the judgment) where the judgment was rendered

(1) Under a system that does not provide impartial tribunals or procedures compatible with the requirements of due process of law;
(2) By a court that did not have personal jurisdiction over the defendant; or
(3) By a court that did not have jurisdiction over the subject matter. (UFMJRA § 4)

Note that the presence of any one of these three factors will prohibit recognition of the judgment; all three need not be present. Nonrecognition is discretionary (that is, a court in a state in which the UFMJRA has been adopted may choose not to recognize the judgment) where

(1) There was insufficient notice to the defendant, or fraud;
(2) The cause of action on which the judgment is based is repugnant to public policy;
(3) The judgment conflicts with another final and conclusive judgment;
(4) The judgment is contrary to the parties' choice of a forum (as expressed in a contract);
(5) Jurisdiction over the defendant was based only on personal service of process and the forum is an inconvenient one for the defendant. (UFMJRA § 4)

Because these factors render nonrecognition discretionary, a court might choose not to recognize a judgment if only one of the five factors were present; conversely, it might conceivably choose to recognize a judgment even if all five were present, so long as none of the three mandatory grounds were present.

Constitution
- United States Constitution, Art. IV, § 1

Statute
- Full Faith and Credit Statute, 28 U.S.C. § 1738

Uniform Act
- National Conference of Commissioners on Uniform State Laws, Uniform Foreign Money-Judgments Recognition Act, Aug. 4, 1962, available from www. law.upenn.edu/bll/ulc/fnact99/1920_69/ufmjra62.pdf (PDF download) (visited November 19, 2004)

Case
- *Hilton v. Guyot*, 159 U.S. 113 (1895)

See also: Choice of Law; Defamation; French Yahoo! Case; Jurisdiction

Sources and further reading:
John J. Barcelo III and Kevin M. Clermont, *A Global Law of Jurisdiction and Judgments: Lessons from the Hague* (Dordrecht, Netherlands: Kluwer Law International, 2002).
William M. Richman and William L. Reynolds, *Understanding Conflict of Laws*, 3d ed. (New York: Matthew Bender, 2002).
Mark D. Rosen, "Exporting the Constitution," 53 *Emory Law Journal* 171 (2004).

❖ RECORDING INDUSTRY ASSOCIATION OF AMERICA ❖

The Recording Industry Association of America (RIAA) is an industry association representing music content industry companies. The advent of home computing, digitally recorded music, and the Internet has threatened the music content industry's business model by making it far easier for consumers to copy and share recordings of popular music; in the past decade, the RIAA has been involved in ceaseless litigation to defend the interests of its members on several fronts. It has sued a maker of MP3 players, fearing that MP3 players might enable and encourage piracy of copyrighted music (*Diamond Multimedia*, 180 F.3d 1072). It has sued file-sharing services, usually as a co-plaintiff with music and motion picture content industry companies (e.g., *Napster*, 239 F.3d 1004). It has sued Internet service providers in an attempt to compel them to disclose the names of their subscribers who might be sharing copyrighted music files (*Verizon Internet Services*, 351 F.3d 1229). And it has filed thousands of suits against individual users of file-sharing services.

The RIAA has also pushed to protect its members' interests through changes in legislation. It has lobbied for increased copyright protection, particularly against online file-sharing. Its lawsuits and lobbying may have backfired, however, at least to some extent: The RIAA has acquired iconic status, representing to many consumer advocates the excesses of the current regime of copyright law. The RIAA has been sued in turn, for example, by distributors of the file-sharing software (*Grokster [Antitrust]*, 269 F.Supp.2d 1213). File-sharing service KaZaA has even sued the RIAA for copyright infringement, alleging that, while infiltrating the KaZaA file-sharing network, the

One of the lessons the RIAA may end up learning from its suits against individual users is not to bite anything that's capable of biting back. Users have lawyers, too: In February 2004 one user sued by the RIAA, Michele Scimeca, responded by bringing suit against the RIAA for violation of the Racketeer Influenced and Corrupt Organizations Act (RICO). Scimeca, who claims that the file-sharing for which her computer was allegedly used was part of her daughter's school research project, calls the RIAA's individual-user suits "scare tactics [that] amount to extortion." Her attorney, Bart Lombardo, adds that content owners are "banding together to extort money, telling people they're guilty and they will have to pay big bucks to defend their cases if they don't pony up now. It is fundamentally not fair."

Source

"RIAA Sued for RICO Violations—Racketeering and Extortion: Finally, Someone Is Standing up to the RIAA's Extortion Attempts," ZDNet, Feb. 18, 2004, http://news.zdnet.com/5208-3513-0.html?forumID=1&threadID=1768&messageID=37192&start=-1 (visited January 8, 2005), reprinting Kevin Coughlin;

"Morris Mom Turns Tables in Music Industry Lawsuit," [N.J.] *Star-Ledger*, Feb. 18, 2004, http://www.nj.com/news/ledger/jersey/index.ssf?/base/news-5/107708869350700.xml.

RIAA used copies of a program that infringed on the copyright in KaZaA's software (*Wired News* 2003). The RIAA Web site has become a

target for technically skilled pranksters, and the suits against individual file-sharers—especially when those file-sharers are children—have attracted considerable adverse publicity. For the time being, however, the RIAA seems committed to its current business model, although ultimately it might have to compromise with file-sharers, for example through a voluntary collective licensing agreement such as that proposed by the Electronic Frontier Foundation (EFF White Paper 2004).

Cases
Federal Appellate Courts
- *A&M Records, Inc. v. Napster, Inc.*, 239 F.3d 1004 (9th Cir. 2001)
- *In re Aimster Copyright Litigation (Aimster II)*, 334 F.3d 643 (7th Cir. 2003)
- *Recording Industry Association of America v. Diamond Multimedia Systems, Inc.*, 180 F.3d 1072 (9th Cir. 1999)
- *Recording Industry Association of America, Inc. v. Verizon Internet Services*, 351 F.3d 1229 (D.C. Cir. 2003)

Federal Trial Court
- *Metro-Goldwyn-Mayer Studios Inc. v. Grokster, Ltd. [Antitrust claims]*, 269 F.Supp.2d 1213 (C.D. Cal. 2003)

See also: Activism and Advocacy Groups; Content Industry; Copyright; File-Sharing; KaZaA; Open-Source; P2P; Piracy; Voluntary Collective License

Sources and further reading:

Electronic Frontier Foundation, *A Better Way Forward: Voluntary Collective Licensing of Music File Sharing,* "Let the Music Play" White Paper, Feb. 2004, available from http://www.eff.org/share/collective_lic_wp.php (PDF download) (visited November 16, 2004).

"The Hunter Becomes the Hunted," *Wired News,* Sept. 24, 2003, available at http://www.wired.com/news/digiwood/0,1412,60574,00.html (visited November 16, 2004).

Rich Menta, "RIAA Sues Music Startup Napster for $20 Billion," MP3 Newswire.net, Dec. 9, 1999, http://www.mp3newswire.net/stories/napster.html (visited November 16, 2004).

"RIAA Files News [*sic*] Lawsuits against 750 Illegal File Sharers," RIAA press release, Oct. 28, 2004, available at http://www.riaa.com/news/newsletter/102804.asp (visited November 16, 2004).

❖ RIAA ❖

See Recording Industry Association of America

S

❖ SAFE HARBOR ❖

See Digital Millennium Copyright Act, Title II

❖ SEARCH ENGINE ❖

A search engine is a computer program that locates files stored on one or more computers. The user specifies values, such as words, numbers, or dates, for the files sought; the search engine then examines the files in the location it is designed to search and returns a list of files containing those values. There are a wide variety of search engines for different tasks. The Windows Find function is a search engine that searches a single personal computer. Library online catalogs search a network of library computers, and may connect to search engines at other libraries or search a shared interlibrary database. Search engines make P2P networks possible. Search engines for large proprietary professional databases, such as Westlaw and Lexis, offer sophisticated search functions that require training to use. But the search engines that attract the greatest amount of attention, and are most likely to raise legal issues, are search engines that search the World Wide Web. Some of these search only a portion of the Web, whereas others attempt to search the entire Web, and actually do search a large portion of it. The most popular of these general-purpose search engines is Google, followed by MSN's and Yahoo!'s search engines. In addition to these and other proprietary search engines, there are also open-source search engines for a wide variety of purposes (see "Search Tools" 2004).

Internet search engine companies can become involved in legal disputes in several ways. Search engines can be vehicles for copyright and trademark infringement. Because they can be used from anywhere in the world, they may violate local censorship laws. And they are subject to abuse by search engine spammers.

Search engines and copyright infringement: Internet search engines are generally considered to be service providers within the meaning of Title II of the Digital Millennium Copyright Act (DMCA), although Title II as a whole seems not to have been designed with search engines in mind: References to "subscribers" and "account holders" have no application to search engines, for example (Walker 2004, 40). As service providers, search engines are eligible for the protection of the four statutory safe havens from liability for copyright infringement: the transitory communications safe harbor, the system caching safe harbor, the information storage safe harbor, and the information location tools safe harbor. The fourth of these, the information location tools safe harbor, is the one designed with search engines in mind; however, the nature of most search engines means that some search engine activities may also fall within the other three safe harbors. Most Internet search engines, including the most popular ones, work by crawling the Web and storing information about each crawled Web site in the search engine's database. Searches then take place in the database rather than in the Web as a whole, which makes the searches much faster. Some, such as Google, also make cached versions of Web sites available to the public.

The transitory communications safe harbor shields a service provider from liability where the provider merely acts as a conduit, transmitting digital information from one point on a network to another at someone else's request. Five elements must be present for a service provider to avail itself of the transitory communications safe harbor: the transmission must be "initiated by or at the direction of a person other than the" service provider; it must be "carried out through an automatic technical process without selection of the material by the" service provider; the service provider must "not select the recipients of the material except as an automatic response to the request of another person"; the service provider must not maintain a copy of the material "in a manner ordinarily accessible to anyone other than anticipated recipients" or "for a longer period than is reasonably necessary"; and the material must be transmitted "without modification of its content" (17 U.S.C. § 512(a)).

Many search engine activities are likely to meet these requirements: The search engine can be viewed as a conduit for conveying information about Web sites between Web site operators and users. The users initiate the search, which is carried out by an automatic technical process, although it might be difficult to establish that the process does not involve selection of the material by the service provider. The service provider does not select the recipients of the material; the recipients select themselves. The results of a particular search are accessible only to the person running that search, and are maintained only until the recipient closes the search window or runs another search. However, there are problems with this reasoning; it may well be that the automated process of selecting search results is "selection of material" within the meaning of the statute. The transitory communications safe harbor is not generally applied to search engine activities.

The system caching safe harbor shields a service provider from liability where the provider makes a copy of material for system caching purposes. This system caching is a necessary part of the operation of all search engines that rely on searching their own databases of crawled Web sites, which is to say nearly all In-

ternet search engines. In order for a service provider to be eligible for the system caching safe harbor, three requirements must be met: The material must be "made available online by a person other than the service provider"; it must be transmitted from that person to another person at the direction of the second person; and the caching "must be carried out through an automatic technical process for the purpose of making the material available to users of the system or network who . . . request access" (17 U.S.C. § 512(b)). These conditions appear to be met in the case of Internet search engines, although again the poorness of the fit between the statute and the reality of search engine operation is evident. Information about Web pages is made available online by the Web site operators, not by the search engines. It is "transmitted," or at least communicated in some way, to search engine users at their request. And the caching is done by an automatic process for the purpose of making the information available to search engine users.

Even if these requirements are met and the search engine service meets the threshold requirement of eligibility for the system caching safe harbor, however, additional conditions must be met before the search engine is shielded from liability. The search engine must not modify the retained material, must periodically refresh it, and must not interfere with technology that returns hit information to the person who posted the material. Search engines are likely to meet these conditions, but an additional condition has caused some controversy: Once the service provider has been notified that copyrighted material posted without authorization has been removed or blocked, or ordered to be removed or blocked, at the original site, the service provider must promptly remove or block access to the cached copy. If the person who posted the material has imposed limitations on access, such as password protection, the service provider must also impose these limitations (17 U.S.C. § 512(b)(2)). This provision may be necessary to protect the interests of the copyright owner, but it interferes with the use of large cached databases, such as Google's cache, as archives for research into the history of the Web.

The information storage safe harbor is not really applicable to search engines; it shields a service provider from liability where the service provider stores information at the direction of a user. Search engines store information provided by Web site operators, but on their own initiative rather than at the direction of the operators; this storage is more likely to fall within the system caching safe harbor or the information location tools safe harbor. Search engines may, however, store information provided by Web site operators for use in targeted advertising or paid search results, and conceivably this information could contain infringing content. The information storage safe harbor would then be available to the search engine if it does not have actual or constructive knowledge that the content was infringing, and upon acquiring such knowledge acts "expeditiously to remove, or disable access to, the material" (17 U.S.C. § 512(c)). However, the information storage safe harbor is not available to a service provider that receives "a financial benefit directly attributable to the infringing activity" (17 U.S.C. § 512(c)(1)(B)). The fact that the search engine is paid for the advertising is probably not a benefit attributable to the infringing content in the advertisement. The search engine's advertising revenue will be the same whether the advertisement does or does not include infringing content, although where the advertisement is for something that is inherently infringing, such as (arguably) an online music file-sharing service, the ad revenue would be directly attributable to the infringement, possibly making the search engine ineligible for this safe harbor. The question seems unlikely to arise, however, because this safe harbor is designed to protect services hosting Web pages from liability for infringement posted on those pages; as with the previous two safe harbors, it is a poor fit when applied to search engines.

The information location tools safe harbor is the safe harbor specifically designed with search engines in mind, although search engine operations have evolved and changed somewhat since the passage of the DMCA in 1998. The information location tools safe harbor shields a service provider from liability for referring or linking users to sites containing infringing material through tools such as directories, indexes, references, pointers, or hyperlinks. In order to be eligible for the information location tools safe harbor, the search engine or other service provider must not have actual or constructive knowledge that the located content is infringing; the "knowledge" standard here is the same as that for the information storage safe harbor. Again like the information storage safe harbor, the information location tools safe harbor requires that the search engine must "not receive a financial benefit directly attributable to the infringing activity, in a case in which the service provider has the right and ability to control such activity" (17 U.S.C. § 512(d)(2)). This standard is drawn from the rule established by the federal courts for determining vicarious copyright infringement (see *Fonovisa,* 76 F.3d 259). And the information location tools safe harbor includes the same notice-and-takedown procedure as the information storage safe harbor.

It is this notice-and-takedown procedure that has given rise to controversy. The importance of search engines cannot be overestimated; a site that is overlooked by search engines will receive little or no traffic. In order to guarantee themselves the protection of the information location tools safe harbor, search engines will take down any potentially infringing links as soon as they are informed of them. This gives actual and purported copyright holders tremendous power over Web use patterns. No court order is required; the person claiming to own certain content has merely to notify the search engine of the alleged infringement, and the site will be blocked without first giving the Web site operator a chance to argue that there is no infringement. There are several reasons why a use might not be infringing: perhaps because the material is in the public domain or because the use is a fair use, or because the person claiming to be the content owner is not, in fact, the owner, and the true owner has authorized the use. The Web site operator can make these arguments after the fact, but search engines are safer ignoring such arguments until they have been resolved by a court; the requirements of the information location tools safe harbor encourage the search engine to err on the side of protecting copyright interests, even at the cost of harm to the Web traffic (and thus the revenue) of the allegedly infringing Web site.

Here is an example of the operation of the notice-and-takedown procedure:

> On August 11, 2003, the owner of KaZaa, a popular file-sharing program, began sending a series of complaints to Google, a popular search engine, claiming that Google was providing links to sites offering unauthorized and infringing versions of its software. Without any determination by a court that the materials actually infringed on the owner's copyright, Google swiftly responded to these complaints by removing the specified links from its search results. Google replaced the links with a disclaimer at the bottom of each relevant search page stating that some results were removed and providing a link to the complaint. (Walker 2004, 1)

There is some irony in the idea of KaZaA, a file-sharing service that has been the target of numerous copyright-infringement lawsuits, complaining of copyright infringement. But the results are no different than they might have been in the case of a complaint by the Recording Industry Association of America: By removing the links, Google has cut off a sizable portion of the Web traffic that would otherwise have reached those sites. It is easy to imagine how such a procedure might be abused, especially by businesses seeking to block traffic to the Web sites of their competitors. To guard against such abuses, the DMCA establishes strict requirements for the notice that must be given to the service provider by the copyright owner:

> (3) Elements of notification. –
> (A) To be effective under this subsection, a notification of claimed infringement must be a written communication provided to the designated agent of a service provider that includes substantially the following:
> (i) A physical or electronic signature of a person authorized to act on behalf of the owner of an exclusive right that is allegedly infringed.
> (ii) Identification of the copyrighted work claimed to have been infringed, or, if multiple copyrighted works at a single online site are covered by a single notification, a representative list of such works at that site.
> (iii) Identification of the material that is claimed to be infringing or to be the subject of infringing activity and that is to be removed or access to which is to be disabled, and information reasonably sufficient to permit the service provider to locate the material.
> (iv) Information reasonably sufficient to permit the service provider to contact the complaining party, such as an address, telephone number, and, if available, an electronic mail address at which the complaining party may be contacted.
> (v) A statement that the complaining party has a good faith belief that use of the material in the manner complained of is not authorized by the copyright owner, its agent, or the law.
> (vi) A statement that the information in the notification is accurate, and under penalty of perjury, that the complaining party is authorized to act on behalf of the owner of an exclusive right that is allegedly infringed. (17 U.S.C. § 512(c)(3)(A))

All of the information required could be faked, of course; anyone could send a letter (or, with an electronic signature, an e-mail) claiming to be the owner of copyrighted material on a particular site. Although the person sending the letter must provide contact information, no duty is imposed on the service provider to use that contact information. A business could thus send a letter complaining of copyrighted content on its rival's site, claiming to be—and giving accurate contact information for—the true owner of the copyrighted material. Even though the copyright owner had actually authorized the use of its material on the site, the search engine might simply block the site without contacting the copyright owner. The business sending the letter would have violated requirements (v) and (vi), but would be unlikely to be caught; the rival's business would suffer harm until the confusion could be straightened out—and it would be the rival who would bear the cost in time and money of straightening out that confusion.

The alleged infringer may contest the allegation of infringement by submitting a counter-notification. Within ten to fourteen business days following the filing of a proper counter-notification the service provider must restore access, unless it first receives notice that the person who submitted the original notification has filed a court action against the user. A great deal of harm can be done to a business in ten to fourteen business days, however, and the counter-notification procedure has been criticized as inadequate (Yen 2000). The search engine is given every incentive to place a higher value on the interests of the copyright holder than on any harm to the business of the alleged infringer: The DMCA insulates the search engine from liability to the Web site owner for blocking the site, so there is no risk to the search engine in doing so (17 U.S.C. § 512(g)(1)). At the same time the DMCA shields the search engine from all monetary liability and most injunctive relief, other than orders "restraining the service provider from providing access to infringing material or activity residing at a particular online site on the provider's system or network" (17 U.S.C. § 512(j)).

Search engines and trademark law: The DMCA provides a safe harbor for search engines from liability for copyright infringement; it provides no similar safe harbor from liability for trademark infringement. Section 230(c)(1) of the Communications Decency Act provides that "No provider or user of an interactive computer service shall be treated as the publisher or speaker of any information provided by another information content provider." At one time this was thought to provide protection for service providers from liability for some trademark infringement along lines similar to those of the DMCA copyright infringement safe harbors. However, § 230(e)(2) of the same statute provides that "Nothing in this section shall be construed to limit or expand any law pertaining to intellectual property." Sections 230(c)(1) and 230(e)(2) survived the Supreme Court's decision in *Reno v. American Civil Liberties Union,* which struck down the Internet censorship portions of the Communications Decency Act as unconstitutional. The federal district court for the Southern District of New York has since explained that the effect of § 230(e)(2) is that § 230(c)(1) conveys no immunity upon service providers from liability for trademark infringe-

ment; in other words, there is no safe harbor (*Gucci,* 135 F.Supp.2d 409).

Search engines can be involved in trademark infringement and dilution in many ways. They can reproduce trademark infringing text or domain names on search result pages; search engines that show images as well as text can reproduce trademark logos exactly, and the trademarks may be used in a way that infringes upon or dilutes the mark holder's interest. And, as with copyright, search engines may provide links to sites with infringing content.

Abuse of search engines: Search engine results are crucial to the success of an online business; the higher a company shows up on a list of search results, the more hits it will receive. As a result, companies use a variety of tricks to increase search engine rank. Some of these tricks are simply sensible Web design, such as prominently displaying the terms most descriptive of the company's business on the Web site's front page, and publicizing the business to encourage other businesses to link to the Web site. Other tricks raise ethical questions: the use of terms, often repeated far more times than necessary simply for identification purposes, in metatags; paid placement; the use of competitors' trademarks as a part of either of these techniques; and link farming. Unethical use of these techniques to trick search engines into ranking a site higher than it ordinarily would is called search engine spamming.

Metatags are text inserted into an HTML document so as to be invisible when the document is viewed as a Web page. To view the metatags on a Web page, a user can select "View/Source" from the Web browser menu. Metatags, if any, will appear near the top of the HTML document, just after the title; they typically take the form <META name="category" content="thing(s) in category">. Although there are legitimate uses for metatags, such as identifying the Web page author and copyright holder, metatags have acquired notoriety for their abuse in search engine spamming. Although metatags are invisible to the viewer, they are visible to search engines; thus a term could be repeated thousands of times in metatags, potentially raising the page's rank, without changing the visible appearance of the page.

This use of metatags is not illegal, but it is unethical and is considered search engine spamming by Web professionals (Perkins 2002). A business can gain an advantage over its competitors, however, by using a competitor's name as a metatag; searches for one Web site will thus detect the other as well. This use of a competitor's name could be unlawful trademark infringement, subject to such exceptions as fair use: For example, it would probably not be infringement for an independent bicycle dealer, Citywide Bicycles, to use the trademarked name "Trek" as a metatag, if Citywide sells or repairs Trek bicycles; this use falls within the nominative fair use exception to trademark infringement. If, however, Citywide's chief competitor is Urban Cycles, it would be trademark infringement for Citywide to use the name Urban Cycles as a metatag; the tag is not being used to identify Urban Cycles, but to attempt to divert business from its Web site (see *Playboy v. Welles*, 279 F.3d at 801). Use of metatags is a nominative fair use so long as three conditions are met:

> First, the product or service in question must be one not readily identifiable without use of the trademark; second, only so much of the mark or marks may be used as is reasonably necessary to identify the product or service; and third, the user must do nothing that would, in conjunction with the mark, suggest sponsorship or endorsement by the trademark holder. (279 F.3d at 801)

The problem of use and abuse of metatags seems likely to subside without ever being fully resolved in the courts. The world's most popular search engine, Google, does not use metatags, and search engines that still use metatags have become aware of the problem and have designed filters to compensate for the effects of metatag spamming. As a result, metatag spamming is no longer worth the effort.

Paid placement is one way in which companies can obtain higher search result rankings for their Web sites: The company pays a sum of money to a search engine to move its site up the rankings when a particular search term is entered. The use of trademarks as search terms raises concerns similar to those raised by the use of metatags: If Citywide Bicycles pays to be ranked at or near the top of the list when the term "Trek" is entered, there is probably no problem; the use of the name "Trek" is nominative fair use. Applying the same factors applied to metatags yields the same result: Citywide cannot identify its business (selling and repairing Trek bicycles) without using the trademark; it is using no more of the mark than necessary to identify its service; and it is not using the mark in a way that suggests the sponsorship or endorsement of the bicycle maker, Trek.

However, if Citywide pays to be ranked first when the name of its competitor, Urban Bicycles, is entered as a search term, a problem arises. This use may well constitute trademark infringement, although the question is a new enough one that it has not yet been resolved by the courts (Padawer 2003). The business trend seems to be toward greater use of trademarks as search terms; for example, in April 2004 Google stopped screening paid advertising for the use of trademarks as keywords (Klein and Mazur 2004). Suits have already been filed by trademark owners; in the United States a company called Mark Nutritionals, owner of the trademark Body Solutions, recently sued search engines AltaVista, Overture, FindWhat, and Kanoodle for $440 million in damages for trademark infringement and unfair competition. Mark Nutritionals alleged that the search engines had accepted payment from its competitors to rank those competitors above Mark Nutritionals when users searched for the term *Body Solutions*. However, Mark Nutritionals subsequently filed for bankruptcy, and the suit was dismissed (Klein and Mazur 2004). The Ninth Circuit Court of Appeals recently reversed a lower court ruling in favor of Playboy Enterprises against Netscape and Excite, which had allowed advertisers of pornographic content to link their advertisements to search results for the trademarked terms *Playboy* and *Playmate;* the case has now been remanded for trial to the federal district court for the Central District of California (*Playboy v. Netscape,* 354 F.3d 1020). Similar lawsuits have been filed in federal courts in New Jersey, New York, and Virginia. In October 2003 in France, a court ordered Google to stop allowing the use of trademarks as keywords for paid advertising and to pay 75,000 euros to two French companies that had been injured by the practice. The French case is currently on appeal, but in the meantime similar suits have been filed against Google in Germany and Italy (Klein and Mazur 2004).

Link farming: A link farm is "a network of pages on one or more Web sites, heavily cross-linked with each other, with the sole intention of improving the search engine ranking of those pages and sites" (Perkins 2002). Link farming is aimed at Google and related search engines that rank pages by the number and type of links to those pages from other pages, just as metatag spamming was aimed at other search engines. Link farm spamming is considered unethical (Perkins 2002) but is not illegal; the best cure is probably not legislation but, as with metatags, advances in search engine technology that diminish the usefulness of the tactic.

Internet search engines and censorship: Search engines risk running afoul not only of copyright and trademark laws, but also of censorship laws. Search engines, like all Internet resources, are accessible from nearly everywhere in the world, and content that is legal, even accepted as mainstream, in one country might be illegal in another. The French Yahoo! case raised awareness of the fact that the actions of an Internet service provider in its home country can expose it to liability in another. In the aftermath of the Yahoo! case, Google has removed listings for Nazi and racist hate sites from the French and German versions of its search engines, www.google.fr and www.google.de ("Sociology of Cyberspace" 2003). The power of search engines over access to information on the Internet poses the problem of private censorship; although Google blocked sites from its French and German search engines in response to complaints from the French and German governments, it has also blocked search-engine access to sites critical of the Church of Scientology at the request of the church (McCullagh 2002). Search engines with a political agenda might even decide to remove sites from search results on their own initiative, rather than out of fear of litigation by some aggrieved outside party. Self-censorship of this sort poses no First Amendment concerns, because search engine operators are private companies and not state actors.

However, some users' rights advocates have begun to demand transparency in the process: Search engines, they say, may remove sites from search databases if they wish, but they should publish information about which sites have been removed (McCullagh 2002). At this point, however, search engine operators are not required to provide this information. Compromise steps include Google's promise to report legal threats (which, in the case of search engines, tend to be accompanied by demands to remove or block search access to certain sites) to the free-speech Web site www.chillingeffects.org.

Statutes
- Communications Decency Act, 47 U.S.C. § 230
- Digital Millennium Copyright Act, 17 U.S.C. § 512

Cases
Supreme Court
- *Reno v. American Civil Liberties Union,* 521 U.S. 844 (1997)

Federal Appellate Courts
- *Fonovisa, Inc. v. Cherry Auction, Inc.,* 76 F.3d 259 (9th Cir. 1996)
- *Name.Space, Inc. v. Network Solutions, Inc.,* 202 F.3d 573 (2nd Cir. 2000)
- *Playboy Enterprises Inc. v. Netscape Communications Corp.,* 354 F.3d 1020 (9th Cir. 2004)
- *Playboy Enterprises, Inc. v. Welles,* 279 F.3d 796 (9th Cir. 2002)
- *Yahoo! Inc. v. La Ligue Contre Le Racisme et L'Antisemitisme,* 379 F.3d 1120 (9th Cir. 2004)

Federal Trial Court
- *Gucci America, Inc. v. Hall and Associates,* 135 F.Supp.2d 409 (S.D. N.Y. 2001)

See also: Censorship; Communications Decency Act; Copyright; Copyright Infringement; Data Mining; Digital Millennium Copyright Act, Title II; File-Sharing; French Yahoo! Case; Metatags; Trademark Dilution; Trademark Infringement

Sources and further reading:

Sheldon H. Klein and Jason J. Mazur, "U.S. Trademark Cases Involving Keyword-Triggered Advertising on Internet Search Engines," Arent Fox, Sept. 15, 2004, available at http://www.arentfox.com/publications/alerts/alerts2004/alert2004–09–07.html (visited October 28, 2004).

Declan McCullagh, "Google Excluding Controversial Sites," CNET News.com, Oct. 23, 2002, http://news.zdnet.com/2100–1009_22–963132.html (visited October 28, 2004).

Heidi S. Padawer, "Google This: Search Engine Results Weave a Web for Trademark Infringement Actions on the Internet," 81 *Washington University Law Quarterly* 1099 (2003).

Alan Perkins, "The Classification of Search Engine Spam, Search Mechanics, 2002," available at http://www.ebrandmanagement.com/whitepapers/spam-classification/ (visited October 28, 2004).

"Search Tools Listing: Open Source Search Engines," June 22, 2004, http://www.searchtools.com/tools/tools-opensource.html (visited October 27, 2004).

"The Sociology of Cyberspace: Censorship, Privacy and Control," Manchester Metropolitan University, 2003, available at http://www.sociology.mmu.ac.uk/socyb03/censor.php (visited October 28, 2004).

Craig W. Walker, "Application of the DMCA Safe Harbor Provisions to Search Engines," 9 *Virginia Journal of Law and Technology* 1 (2004).

Alfred C. Yen, "Internet Service Provider Liability for Subscriber Copyright Infringement, Enterprise Liability, and the First Amendment," 88 *Georgetown Law Journal* 1833 (2000).

❖ SECURE SOCKET LAYER ❖

See Encryption

❖ SECURITY SYSTEMS STANDARDS AND CERTIFICATION ACT ❖

See Consumer Broadband and Digital Television Promotion Act

❖ SEMICONDUCTOR MANUFACTURING MASK WORK REGISTRATIONS ❖

A semiconductor manufacturing mask work is a design pattern used in the manufacture of computer chips.

These chips are manufactured in a three-stage process. The first stage is the manufacture of the blank wafers from which the chips will be etched; the wafers are usually made of silicon, gallium arsenide, or indium phosphide, and are made at a plant solely dedicated to wafer manufacturing; the second stage—the transformation of the blank wafer into a chip—generally takes place elsewhere. The third stage is the assembly and packaging; the etched wafers are cut apart and mounted in a ceramic or metal package, and leads are soldered on (Lee and Elliott n.d.).

The second stage of the process, the transformation of blank wafers into computer chips, is the most technically complex. The surface of the wafer is first oxidized by being exposed to oxygen at a high temperature. Much of the rest of the manufacturing process is devoted to selectively removing portions of this oxidized layer. This is done by first applying a coating of photoresist, a light-sensitive compound, over the oxidized layer. Portions of the photoresist are then exposed to light through a mask (Lee and Elliott n.d.). The mask is the informational portion of the manufacturing process; it determines which parts of the photoresist shall be exposed, in the same way, although not by the identical process, that a laser printer, photocopier, or photographic negative determines what part of a print drum or photographic paper shall be exposed. In essence, an image of the mask is being recorded on the photoresist-coated surface of the wafer.

Exposure to light causes a portion of the photoresist to either harden or soften. (Photoresist can be either positive or negative: Positive photoresist softens when exposed to light, and negative photoresist hardens.) A photoresist developing chemical is then used to strip away the soft portion of the photoresist; the hard portion remains. Where the photoresist has been removed, the silicon dioxide layer is exposed. This layer is then etched by exposure to acid or a reactive gas plasma. The channels left by the etching are then "doped"—conducting and semiconducting materials are deposited in them by one or more of several processes. A new layer of silicon is then deposited on the surface of the wafer, and the process begins again for as many layers as necessary. Finally, the wafers are polished and enter the third stage of production (Lee and Elliott n.d.).

The semiconductor manufacturing mask work is crucial to the process; the design of the mask is a long and complex process. Once designed, however, it can be imitated by reverse engineering. Conceivably a mask work could be made the subject of copyright or patent, but instead Congress has chosen to create a new category of intellectual property, giving the mask work copyright-like protection. The Semiconductor Chip Protection Act of 1984 provides for the registration of semiconductor mask work designs with the United States Copyright Office (17 U.S.C. § 908; 37 C.F.R. § 211.4). The registrant must then alert the world to the claim of an intellectual property right in the mask work by placing the words "mask work," the symbol "M," or the letter "M" in a circle in a visible location on the exterior surface of the finished chip or its receptacle (17 U.S.C. § 909; 37 C.F.R. § 211.6). The registrant will enjoy the exclusive right to reproduce the mask work and to import or distribute a semiconductor chip embodying the mask work, as well as the exclusive right to authorize, induce or knowingly cause any other person to do either of these things (17 U.S.C. § 905). This exclusive right will last for ten years from the date of registration or from "the date on which the mask work is first commercially exploited anywhere in the world, whichever occurs first" (17 U.S.C. § 904). The Act also includes a right of first sale (17 U.S.C. § 906(b)) and an exception to the exclusive rights for reverse engineering (17 U.S.C. § 906(a)). Innocent infringers are also protected (17 U.S.C. § 907).

Semiconductor manufacturing masks are not like other protected works such as MP3s; they are not subject to widespread piracy and infringement. Anyone can copy and use the MP3, but without a chip-manufacturing factory, the mask is useless. Chip factories are relatively rare, and setting up a new factory may require an investment of hundreds of millions of dollars. As a result, infringements of registered mask works are rare. The Semiconductor Chip Protection Act has given rise to relatively little litigation, resulting in only a handful of reported cases, only one of which—*Brooktree v. AMD*—deals with the substantive application of the Act. The others include *Anadigics v. Raytheon* and *Atari v. Nintendo*. The reported opinion in *Anadigics* dealt with procedural issues, however (903 F.Supp. 615), while the court in *Atari* concluded that the Act did not apply (975 F.2d at 842 n. 5).

Brooktree v. Advanced Micro Devices involved the reverse engineering exception. The defendant, Advanced Micro Devices (AMD) claimed to have reverse engineered the chip, resulting in a different chip that performed the same function. The court agreed that such reverse engineering would be permitted under the act. However, at trial a jury had found that AMD's chip design did infringe upon Brooktree's registered mask work; the appellate court held that a reasonable jury could have reached this conclusion, and declined to reverse the trial court's decision. The appellate court pointed out that, as a witness had testified to Congress in hearings on the act,

Whenever there is a true case of reverse engineering, the second firm will have prepared a great deal of paper—logic and circuit diagrams, trial layouts, computer simulations of the chip, and the like; it will also have invested thousands of hours of work. All of these can be documented by reference to the firm's ordinary business records. A pirate has no such papers, for the pirate does none of this work. Therefore, whether there has been a true reverse engineering job or just a job of copying can be shown by looking at the defendant's records. The paper trail of a chip tells a discerning observer whether the chip is a copy or embodies the effort of reverse engineering. (*Brooktree*, 977 F.2d at 1566)

The trial court had instructed the jury to "place great weight on the existence of the reverse paperwork trail" (977 F.2d at 1567); the jury had apparently done so. The trial court had also instructed the jury that AMD's mask work could be considered original if it incorporated new design elements either superior to or merely alternative to those in Brooktree's design; apparently the jury found that it did not. The appellate court announced that it would not revisit "these fact-dependent areas"; appellate courts are concerned with questions of law rather than fact, and based on the facts found by the jury, AMD had in fact infringed upon the rights of Brooktree under the act.

Anadigics aside, the twelve years since *Brooktree* have been quiet ones for the Semiconductor Chip Protection Act. Given the relatively small number of firms in the chip-making industry, industry self-regulation may have resolved most problems before they reached the litigation stage.

Statute
- Semiconductor Chip Protection Act, 17 U.S.C. §§ 901–914

Cases
Federal Appellate Courts
- *Atari Games Corp. v. Nintendo of America, Inc.*, 975 F.2d 832 (Fed. Cir. 1992)
- *Brooktree Corp. v. Advanced Micro Devices, Inc.*, 977 F.2d 1555 (Fed. Cir. 1992)

Federal Trial Court
- *Anadigics, Inc. v. Raytheon Co.*, 903 F.Supp. 615 (S.D. N.Y. 1995)

Code of Federal Regulations
- Mask Work Protection, 37 C.F.R. § 211

See also: Copyright; Digital Millennium Copyright Act, Title V; Intellectual Property

Sources and further reading:
Gerard V. Curtin Jr., "The Basics of ASICs: Protection for Semiconductor Mask Works in Japan and the United States," 15 *Boston College International and Comparative Law Review* 113 (1992).
The Industry Handbook—The Semiconductor Industry, Investopedia.com, http://www. investopedia.com/features/industryhandbook/ semiconductor.asp (visited October 27, 2004).
M. K. Carol Lee and J. Julian Elliott, "Semiconductor Manufacturing," available at http://www.baaqmd.gov/pmt/handbook/ s07c04pd.htm, in *Bay Area Air Quality Management District Permit Handbook* (no date), available at http://www.baaqmd.gov/ pmt/handbook/index.html (visited October 27, 2004).

❖ SMURF ATTACK ❖

See Denial-of-Service Attack

❖ SONNY BONO COPYRIGHT TERM EXTENSION ACT ❖

The Sonny Bono Copyright Term Extension Act (CTEA), named for the late singer, songwriter, and U.S. Representative Sonny Bono, extends the duration of copyrights in the United States by twenty years. The Copyright Act of 1976 had brought U.S. copyright terms into line with the Berne Convention requirements: the lifetime of the author plus fifty years for most individual works, and seventy-five years from publication or one hundred years from creation, whichever was less, for anonymous or pseudonymous works and works for hire. The CTEA extended these terms to life plus seventy years and ninety-five years, respectively (17 U.S.C. §§ 302, 304).

In the early 1990s the countries of the European Union had agreed among themselves to a longer term of copyright protection than that required by the Berne Convention. The copyright terms specified in the Berne Convention are minimum rather than maximum terms, and Article 20 of the convention specifically permits countries to agree among themselves to a longer term. The European Union directive extending copyright terms was applied to foreign works and foreign authors on a basis of reciprocity; that is, in order for a foreign author to receive the benefits of the EU directive, the author's country would have to offer works by EU authors the same term of copyright protection (Council Directive 93/98/EEC). The CTEA was ostensibly enacted, at least in part, to bring U.S. law into conformity with EU law. Although there was no treaty obligating the

United States to achieve this conformity, there is a benefit in that U.S. works and authors can now receive the same copyright term in the EU as EU works and authors do.

Its detractors, however, see another and more immediate purpose, and derisively refer to the CTEA as the Mickey Mouse Protection Act (*Economist* 2002, 67). Among those lobbying for the passage of the CTEA was the Walt Disney Corporation. Copyrights on early Mickey Mouse cartoons would have begun to expire in 2003, and the seventy-five-year term for works for hire would have become a moving terminator, constantly bringing more Disney works (and those of the other entertainment conglomerates that arose after Disney) into the public domain.

This does not mean that the characters themselves would fall into the public domain, allowing anyone who wished to make their own Mickey Mouse cartoons; Mickey Mouse is protected by trademark law as well as by copyright law, and trademarks are of potentially infinite duration. But Disney still receives substantial royalties from its early works; the first full-length animated feature, *Snow White and the Seven Dwarfs*, will be seventy-five years old in 2012, yet it remains among the best-selling movies of all time. Thanks to the CTEA, Disney will receive another twenty years of profits from *Snow White*. This provides a considerable windfall for Disney and is strikingly different from the way patents are treated. Pharmaceutical companies would surely be delighted to receive a twenty-year extension to the term of existing drug patents, which may be the product of far more expense and effort than even a Disney animated film. Yet Congress has quite wisely held the line against any such extension of patent terms, reasoning that the shorter patent term encourages greater effort devoted to research and development and thus greater and more rapid technological advance.

In the past four decades Congress has extended the copyright term eleven times. It is quite possible that in the next decade or two the copyright term will be extended yet again, creating a "limited" copyright term that never actually expires. Some consumer advocates fear that this is what the CTEA and future congressional action aim to achieve: Sonny Bono's widow, U.S. Representative Mary Bono, stated in the House of Representatives that "Sonny wanted the term of copyright protection to last forever." However, she said, because she was "informed by staff that such a change would violate the Constitution," Congress might instead consider a copyright term of "forever less one day" (Statement of Mary Bono 1998, H9952).

The "forever less one day" proposal has been attributed (by Mary Bono and many others) to Jack Valenti, content-industry advocate and, until his retirement in March 2004 at the age of eighty-two, president of the Motion Picture Association of America (MPAA). The constitutional problem to which Ms. Bono referred is the Patent and Copyright clause of the U.S. Constitution, which provides that Congress shall have the power "To promote the Progress

---

Although the Sonny Bono Copyright Term Extension Act was ostensibly enacted to make U.S. copyright terms equal in duration to European terms, it actually goes further than European law in protecting copyrighted music performances. European law protects the rights of performers for fifty years. Performances recorded before 1955 are now in the public domain in Europe, although not in the United States. This presents some possibility for harm to the interests of right-holders in the United States through cross-border sales, although the potential harm is probably small. But it also leaves European performers, from Cliff Richards to U2, feeling deeply wronged, and they are now lobbying the European Commission to extend the copyright term, to bring it into conformity with the U.S. term of ninety-five years. This presents the possibility of leapfrogging: If the European Commission decides to round off the ninety-five-year term to an even century, U.S. performers will soon be demanding a one hundred-year term as well.

Source

"Music Copyright: Not-So-Golden Oldies," *The Economist*, Jan. 8, 2005, at 55.

of Science and useful Arts, by securing for limited Times to Authors and Inventors the exclusive Right to their respective Writings and Discoveries." A perpetual copyright, even one of forever less one day, would not be for a limited time and would thus be unconstitutional.

The CTEA helps the content industry in the short term by protecting its revenues from already-created works. Opponents, however, point out that there is potential for long-term harm to the content industry by inhibiting creativity. Many of Disney's successful animated features have been based on works already in the public domain: *Snow White, Sleeping Beauty, Cinderella, Beauty and the Beast, The Little Mermaid, Mulan, Hercules,* and the *Hunchback of Notre Dame,* to name a few. Had the CTEA and the EU copyright directive been in force at the time, the copyright on the fairy-tale collections of the Brothers Grimm would have expired in 1933, seventy years after the death of Jakob Grimm; *Snow White* would just barely have fallen into the public domain. Had the 1857 edition of *Grimm's Fairy Tales* been a work for hire, the CTEA would have protected it until 1952.

In addition, holders of patents have enjoyed no similar extension of protection; patents have durations roughly similar to that which they had two centuries ago, while the term of copyright has increased from fourteen years, renewable once, to ninety-five years or life plus seventy years.

Although the CTEA passed Congress with little opposition, after its passage it became the subject of a lawsuit seeking to have it declared unconstitutional. The named plaintiff, Eric Eldred, operates Eldritch Press, an online publisher of out-of-copyright materials. The plaintiffs were represented by consumer advocate and Internet law guru Lawrence Lessig, of Stanford University.

The arguments of the plaintiffs were rejected, and the CTEA was upheld, both at trial in the federal district court and on appeal to the Circuit Court of Appeals for the District of Columbia. The U.S. Supreme Court granted certiorari to review the questions of whether Congress had the power under the Copyright Clause to retroactively extend the term of existing copyrights, and whether a law that extends the term of existing and future copyrights is categorically immune from challenge under the First Amendment. The plaintiffs did not challenge Congress's authority under the Copyright Clause to apply a longer copyright term to works created after the passage of the statute, but its ability to extend the term for works already in existence—the "Mickey Mouse Protection Act" aspect of the CTEA. The constitutional arguments advanced by Eldred and Professor Lessig were, first, that the "limited time" in the Copyright Clause is the time limit in effect when the copyright is granted, and subsequent congressional expansion of the term for existing works means, in effect, that the term is not "limited." The second argument was that the preambular language in the Copyright Clause—"To promote the Progress of Science and useful Arts"—was a substantive limitation on the length of the "limited time" for which Congress could grant copyright protection; any grant longer than that necessary to promote the progress of science and the useful arts was unconstitutional. This would prohibit extension of the terms of existing copyrights; as the longer copyright term would not have been in existence at the time of creation of the work, it could not have served as an incentive. The First Amendment argument was that the CTEA unconstitutionally restricted the right to make use of the copyrighted works of others (*Eldred*, 1537 U.S. 186).

The Supreme Court, like the lower courts, rejected the plaintiffs' arguments on both questions and held that the CTEA was constitutional. The term *limited* did not mean "fixed" or "inalterable." It meant "not unlimited." A perpetual term was prohibited, but Congress was free to adjust the limits. Historically Congress had repeatedly included existing works when extending the term of copyrights so that all copyrights would be governed evenhandedly. The Supreme Court had also previously found the extension of existing patents constitutional.

The Court evaluated the CTEA under a "rational basis" test and found that it was a rational exercise of legislative authority, with purposes including harmonizing U.S. copyright terms with those of the European Union in order to provide U.S. copyright holders with the same copyright term as European copyright holders under EU law. The Court rejected the First Amendment argument as well. The fact that the First Amendment and the Copyright Clause were adopted at about the same time showed that the framers of the Constitution viewed copyright protection as consistent with freedom of expression. In addition, copyright law incorporates First Amendment protections both by prohibiting copyright in an idea and through the fair use exception. The CTEA itself includes two additional exceptions to its twenty-year extension of copyright terms, one for reproduction by libraries and other institutions for scholarly purposes, if the work is not already being exploited commercially and further copies are unavailable at a reasonable price, and the other exempting small businesses from payment of royalties on music played from licensed broadcasting facilities. The Court noted that the goal of the First Amendment is to protect the individual's freedom to make his or her own speech rather than to protect the freedom to make someone else's speech (*Eldred*, 1537 U.S. 186).

Eldred v. Ashcroft has become a rallying point for consumer advocates and others who seek to resist further expansion of copyright law. These opponents of the CTEA have succeeded in having proposed legislation introduced in Congress that would restrict the scope of the CTEA. This bill, the Public Domain Enhancement Act, would require that in order to receive the extended term of the CTEA a copyright would first have to be registered. The Public Domain Enhancement Act would accomplish this through a de minimis copyright fee at a set time, such as a fee of one dollar to be paid fifty years after the initial publication of a work. Requiring payment of the tax for maintenance of copyright would avoid two problems with existing law: The search for the copyright owner, often difficult, would be greatly simplified. And under existing law, valuable works such as *Snow White* receive a term of copyright protection identical to that granted to works that provide no economic return to their creators; the copyright fee proposal would allow works in the latter category to fall into the public domain after a shorter term through nonpayment of the fee.

Constitution
- United States Constitution, Article I, Section 8, Clause 8

Statute
- Sonny Bono Copyright Term Extension Act, 17 U.S.C. §§ 302, 304

Proposed Legislation
- Public Domain Enhancement Act, H.R. 2601, 108th Cong. (2003)

Congressional Record
- Statement of Representative Mary Bono Regarding the Sonny Bono Copyright Term Extension Act, Oct. 7, 1998, 144 Cong. Rec. H9946-01, H9952

Cases
- *Eldred v. Ashcroft*, 1537 U.S. 186 (2002)
- *Harper & Row Publishers, Inc. v. Nation Enterprises*, 471 U.S. 539 (1985)

European Union Materials
- Council Directive 93/98/EEC of 29 October 1993 Harmonizing the Term of Protection of Copyright and Certain Related Rights

See also: Berne Convention; Constitutional Law; Copyright; International Copyright Protection; Public Domain

Sources and further reading:
"Face Value: Lawrence Lessig Wants Less Copyright Protection, Including for Disney's Famous Rodent," *The Economist*, Oct. 12, 2002, at 67.
Michael Jones, "*Eldred v. Ashcroft:* The Constitutionality of the Copyright Term Extension Act," 19 *Berkeley Technology Law Journal* 85 (2004).
Cecil C. Kuhne III, "Forcing the Copyright Genie Back into the Bottle: Public Policy Implications of Copyright Extension Legislation," 33 *Southwestern University Law Review* 327 (2004).
William M. Landes and Richard A. Posner, "Indefinitely Renewable Copyright," 70 *University of Chicago Law Review* 471 (2003).
Lawrence Lessig, *The Future of Ideas: The Fate of the Commons in a Connected World* (New York: Random House, 2001).

Lawrence Lessig, *Free Culture: How Big Media Uses Technology and the Law to Lock Down Culture and Control Creativity* (New York: Penguin, 2004) (also available as a free download).

Makeen Fouad Makeen, *Copyright in a Global Information Society: The Scope of Copyright Protection under International, US, UK, and French Law* (New York: Aspen, 2001).

Susan K. Sell, *Private Power, Public Law: The Globalization of Intellectual Property Rights* (Cambridge: Cambridge University Press, 2003). Symposium, Panel II: Mickey Mice? Potential Ramifications of *Eldred v. Ashcroft,* 13 *Fordham Intellectual Property, Media and Entertainment Law Journal* 771 (2003).

❖ SPAM ❖

No feature of the Internet arouses more widespread ire than spam, or unsolicited mass e-mail advertising. Everyone with an e-mail account has received unsolicited advertisements, many of them unsavory. E-mails offering generic Viagra, enlargement of various body parts, pornography, fake university degrees, and too-good-to-be-true interest rates have become a form of information pollution. Years of transparently fraudulent e-mails from purported Nigerian colonels proposing shady business transactions, or from phishers requesting credit card or bank account information, have prompted first outrage, then laughter, and finally resigned annoyance.

So why do the spammers bother? The answer lies in economics. The marginal cost of sending additional copies of a message is low; the cost of transmitting spam is borne by internet service providers (ISPs), not by the spammers; and the cost of deleting unwanted messages is borne by the users. By forcing others to bear these external costs, spammers are able to continue operating a business that results in a net loss to the overall economy. Suppose that a spammer spends $15 (including the cost of the spammer's time) writing and sending ten million copies of an e-mail message advertising the infamous "patch" for sale for $20. ISPs may spot and delete 99 percent of the messages before they arrive, but 100,000 messages will still be transmitted, and the ISPs will have incurred costs in transmitting and deleting the messages. Ninety-nine percent of the recipients might delete the message unread, but a thousand messages will still be read. Ninety-nine percent of those who read the message might ignore or delete it; if 1 percent of those who actually read the message order the product, the spammer will receive $200. If the spammer is a legitimate enough businessperson to actually ship some goods in exchange, there will be further costs—perhaps as much as 50 percent of the total. This leaves the spammer with a profit of $85: The $200 received, minus $100 for the cost of the goods and shipping, minus the original $15 cost of the advertisement.

The other economic actors involved, though, have much higher costs. If it costs one one-thousandth of a cent to transmit a message over the Internet or to delete the message before it reaches its intended recipient, the ISPs involved will have incurred costs of $100. If it

FOXTROT © 2004 Bill Amend. Reprinted with permission of UNIVERSAL PRESS SYNDICATE. All rights reserved.

takes the average user half a second to identify a message as spam and delete it, and the average user's time is valued at $10 per hour, the 99,000 messages deleted will have cost their recipients a total of $137.50. And if the average time spent by the 990 users who read the message but did not order the product was ten seconds, an additional $27.50 worth of time has been expended without recompense, assuming those users received no other value (such as entertainment) from the message. The users and their ISPs will thus have spent a total of $265 to support the spammer's $85 profit, representing a net loss to the Internet economy of $180. Expanding this to a larger scale reveals the scope of the problem: In 2002 advertisers spent an estimated $1.3 billion on spam marketing; this spam cost ISPs and corporations—not even taking into account individual users—an additional $11.9 billion (Alongi 2004). In effect, the ISPs and users unwillingly gave a twelve billion dollar subsidy to the spammers.

Similar arguments can be made with regard to other forms of advertising, but abuses are generally limited by the fact that other forms of advertising cost money. Spamming is very nearly free; after the initial set-up costs, unlimited copies of an advertisement can be sent at little or no additional cost. In addition, various tricks can be used to lower costs and increase profits. Many spam messages include a bogus "unsubscribe" option, saying something like "This e-mail has been sent to you because you have expressed an interest in receiving messages about low-interest loans. If you wish to unsubscribe, click here." When a recipient clicks on the "unsubscribe" message, the recipient's e-mail address will be identified to the spammer as a "live" address— one at which there is an actual person receiving and reading e-mail, and one naive enough to click on the bogus "unsubscribe" link. The e-mail address will then become more valuable and can be sold to other spammers at a higher rate.

Spammers may also trick users into installing spam-sending programs on their computers, often by clicking an e-mail attachment. Once installed, this program can send out copies of spam messages, and forward additional spam messages, to millions of other users. The user will be unaware that his or her computer has

The perils of spamming: Everyone hates spam. Spamming, as a profession, enjoys a level of respect and appreciation somewhere in the same range as crack-dealing and pocket-picking. Some spammers fear that the disesteem in which they are held could turn violent. Michigan e-mail marketer Alan Ralsky, dubbed the King of Spam by the media and antispam groups, has received threats and a packet of dog feces delivered to his house; as a result, he's taken his telephone number out of the directory and does not divulge his home address. The same Internet that has provided Ralsky and other spammers with their wealth, however, also undermines their attempts to stay out of the public eye: Antispam Web sites have posted Ralsky's home address and pictures of his house. Although some might feel that there is a measure of justice in this, the ease with which such information can be obtained and disseminated raises worrisome privacy and safety issues.

Source

Mike Wendland, "Spam King Lives Large off Others' E-mail Troubles: West Bloomfield Computer Empire Helped by Foreign Internet Servers," *Detroit Free Press,* Nov. 22, 2002, available at http://www.freep.com/money/tech/mwend22_20021122.htm (visited October 7, 2004).

been turned into a spam zombie; the spammer will be able to send far more messages at no additional cost. The zombie computer may also send out additional copies of the spam-sending program, further multiplying the number of spam messages.

The dubious honor of being the first spammers on the modern Internet goes to two users who, in 1994, sent an advertisement for legal services to eight thousand Usenet newsgroups, reaching twenty million users and crashing the spammers' ISP. The advertisement offered to assist would-be immigrants to the United States in applying for the Diversity Visa program, better known as the green card lottery. Application for the lottery is actually quite simple and requires no fee other than a postage stamp (Fogo

2000). Historical purists might put the origin of spam much earlier, though: In 1978 the first mass commercial e-mail (promoting Digital Equipment Corporation's Decsystem-20 computer) was sent over ARPANET, a predecessor to the Internet (*World Almanac* 2004, 713).

Spamming is a serious burden for users and ISPs alike. Users spend a great deal of time deleting spam and sometimes inadvertently delete important personal or business messages in the process. Children may be exposed to sexually explicit advertising. Some users are taken in by scams. Users sometimes find themselves unable to communicate with each other because one's ISP identifies the other's ISP as a source of spam; this is a particular problem for international e-mail. A user whose e-mail address is spoofed by a spammer may find himself or herself blocked or terminated by his or her ISP. Blind and visually impaired users suffer especially grievously from spam and may find themselves unable to use e-mail; where a sighted person can scan e-mail headers quite rapidly and delete spam with a fair degree of accuracy, a blind person must wait for screen-reading software to read the headers, one at a time, before identifying each message as spam.

ISPs are burdened by the sheer bulk of spam. Spam now makes up the majority of e-mail and has been steadily increasing. As recently as May 2003, 50 percent of e-mail was spam; two studies in May 2004 put the percentage at 64 percent and 78 percent (Greenspan 2004). In 2003 spammers sent an estimated 25.5 billion messages every day; in 2004 the number was expected to rise to more than 35 billion per day, but by the end of 2004 the actual total was probably over 50 billion per day—eight spam messages per day for every human being on the earth, or far more for those who receive e-mail (Hesseldahl 2004; MX Logic 2005). Unlike spammers, ISPs do incur additional costs in transmitting additional messages; the ISPs have to pass these costs along to users and legitimate advertisers, who are thus also subsidizing the spammers.

Spam is perhaps one of the two greatest operational threats the Internet faces, the other being malware. Yet a small number of people send most spam. According to the Register of

Known Spam Operations (ROKSO) maintained by Spamhaus, an antispam organization, a mere 200 spam operations, consisting of probably no more than 600 individuals, account for 90 percent of all spam (ROKSO 2004). Many of these individuals have been sued by ISPs; at least one, the Buffalo Spammer, has been sent to prison for identity theft and falsification of business records related to spamming (Roberts 2004). The techniques used by spammers often involve theft of services from ISPs; breaches of contracts with ISPs; illegal hacking, trespass, and theft of services to users whose computers are made into zombies; violation of the federal CAN-SPAM Act and an implementing federal regulation regarding adult e-mail; false advertising, false statements, fraud, identity theft, and a variety of other torts and crimes. Spammers often use stolen credit card numbers to set up accounts. Yet spam continues to grow; the legal system has not, so far, been able to deal with it effectively.

Recently legal efforts against spam have intensified. Jail sentences have been imposed on the Buffalo Spammer and on a North Carolina spammer, the latter under Virginia law (Swartz 2004). In 2003 and 2004 many ISPs, including America Online, Microsoft, and Yahoo!, brought suits against spammers. Earlier, in 2002, Verizon had reached a settlement with a company owned by one of the world's most notorious e-mail marketers. Around thirty states had enacted antispam statutes by the time of the federal Controlling the Assault of Non-solicited Pornography and Marketing (CAN-SPAM) Act of 2003; the federal statute superseded the state statutes, but so far has not proven significantly more effective. The CAN-SPAM Act requires that unsolicited mass-mailed commercial e-mail contain an opt-out provision, allowing the user to decline to receive future e-mails from the same sender, and a valid return e-mail address. The subject line must clearly indicate that the message is an advertisement and it may not be false or misleading. The message must also include the valid real-world address of the sender. In addition, an FTC regulation made under the authority of the CAN-SPAM Act requires that adult e-mails clearly indicate that they contain adult content and be designed so that the content will not be viewed accidentally.

By themselves, however, these provisions are likely to prove ineffective. Because spammers are already operating outside the law, they have no reason to comply with these additional rules. A spammer who uses stolen credit card information and plants spam Trojans on other users' computers is already facing serious legal penalties and is unlikely to be deterred by more. The CAN-SPAM Act's requirements may convince some of the more reputable mass e-mailers to comply, but are not likely to have a significant effect on the overall volume of spam without some additional measures.

The other point at which spam can be attacked is the demand side. Many businesses pay money to spammers; the CAN-SPAM Act makes these businesses responsible for violations by spammers. Persons or entities providing goods, products, property, or services to another person or entity that violates the statute may also be liable under two sets of circumstances: (1) if they have a greater than 50-percent ownership interest in the violator, or (2) if they have actual knowledge that the goods, products, property, or services are promoted in a prohibited spam message and they "receive, or expect to receive, an economic benefit from such promotion" (15 U.S.C. § 7705(b)). The CAN-SPAM Act provides for hefty damages of from $2,000,000 to $6,000,000 for violations. Aggravated violations such as address harvesting, automated creation of multiple e-mail accounts, and unauthorized use of a network for spamming purposes trigger the highest penalties.

The CAN-SPAM Act also authorizes the Federal Trade Commission (FTC) to create a "Do Not Spam" registry along the lines of the "Do Not Call" registry established to control telemarketing. The FTC has not done so because of the difficulties of putting such a registry into operation and its probable futility; only spammers who comply with the other requirements of CAN-SPAM can be reported for violations of the Do Not Spam registry.

Ultimately the CAN-SPAM Act and additional federal legislation might create a workable regime for U.S. spammers and U.S. advertisers. By itself, however, U.S. law can do little or nothing to solve the problem of spam originating outside the United States and advertising goods or services sold by non-U.S. parties. Spam is an international problem, and it will not be controlled until it can be addressed internationally. The e-mail marketer sued by Verizon now says, "I've gone overseas . . . I now send most of my mail from other countries. And that's a shame. I pay a fortune to providers to do this, and I'd much rather have it go to American companies. But I have to stay in business, and if I have to go out of the country, then so be it" (Wendland 2002).

Other countries have taken steps to outlaw spam, many of them more far-reaching than the CAN-SPAM Act. CAN-SPAM has been criticized as an "opt-out" rather than "opt-in" approach: All users are fair targets for commercial e-mail that otherwise complies with the statute unless and until they specifically request not to receive it. The European Union (EU), on the other hand, has chosen an "opt-in" approach: Its 2002 Directive on Privacy and Electronic Communications prohibits spam, telemarketing calls, and junk faxes unless consented to by the user or unless consent can be inferred from a preexisting business relationship; even when spam is sent, it must include an opt-out option. The EU directive also contains identification and valid e-mail address requirements similar to CAN-SPAM's. Many EU members have enacted domestic opt-in legislation along these lines, including Austria, Denmark, Finland, Germany, Greece, and Italy. At least two, Belgium and Spain, have chosen opt-out legislation similar to CAN-SPAM, as have South Korea and Japan; Australia, like the EU and many of its members, has adopted an opt-in law (Alongi 2004, 266–268). An opt-in law has obvious advantages in stopping spam, but in the United States and other countries it may conflict with constitutional protections of freedom of expression.

In the United Kingdom an older law, the 1990 Misuse of Computers Act, may prove useful in deterring spammers. The act prohibits unauthorized access to computers, potentially including the planting of spam Trojans and the use of zombies. Microsoft has filed two suits under the act against persons it alleges have engaged in illegal account name harvesting. The

United Kingdom is not the only major Internet country without an antispam law. Canada has not yet adopted any antispam legislation, preferring a market-based approach (Alongi 2004, 266–268).

Ultimately, international legal control of spam will probably require a multilateral treaty to set uniform antispam laws worldwide. In the United States even CAN-SPAM, an opt-out statute, is likely to come under constitutional attack, as the anti-telemarketing Do Not Call registry has. In the meantime users and ISPs must seek other means to reduce spam: denial of Internet access to known spammers, individual lawsuits, and interception and deletion of messages. Interception of messages, like detection of viruses and adware, involves an arms race, in this case between spammers on the one hand and ISPs and makers of antispam software on the other. But although antivirus and anti-adware software are relatively successful, antispam software is less so; a purely market-based solution may not be effective without government intervention to force spammers to internalize the costs they currently impose on others. One mechanism that has been proposed to achieve this is e-mail postage—charging a slight fee for each message sent. While this makes sense from an economic perspective, collecting the fee and enforcing violations would be a problem—spammers who use stolen credit card numbers to open e-mail accounts could use those numbers to pay the fee, and spam sent from zombie computers would be billed to that computer's Internet access account holder, not the spammer. Like the identification and opt-out provisions, e-mail postage would affect spammers who comply with the law but would do nothing to restrain outlaw spammers.

Statute

- Controlling the Assault of Non-Solicited Pornography and Marketing (CAN-SPAM) Act of 2003, 15 U.S.C. §§ 7701–7713

European Union Directive

- Directive on Privacy and Electronic Communications, Council Directive 2002/58/EC, 2002 O.J. (L 201) 37

Cases

- *Mainstream Marketing Service v. Federal Trade Commission,* 358 F.3d 1228 (10th Cir. 2004)
- *Cyber Promotions, Inc. v. America Online, Inc.,* 948 F.Supp. 436 (E.D. Pa. 1996)

See also: Advertising; Adware and Spyware; Censorship; Denial-of-Service Attack; First Amendment; Hacking; Malware; Privacy; Trademark; Trojan; Worm; Zombie

Sources and further reading:
Elizabeth A. Alongi, "Has the U.S. Canned Spam?" 46 *Arizona Law Review* 263 (2004).
Credence E. Fogo, "The Postman Always Rings 4,000 Times: New Approaches to Curb Spam," 18 *John Marshall Journal of Computer and Information Law* 915 (2000).
Robyn Greenspan, "The Deadly Duo: Spam and Viruses," May 2004, Internetnews.com, June 7, 2004, available at http://www.Internetnews.com/stats/article.php/3364421 (visited October 7, 2004).
Arik Hesseldahl, "Ten O'Clock Tech: D-Day in the Spam War," Forbes.com, Feb. 27, 2004, available at http://www.forbes.com/technology/2004/02/27/cx_ah_0227tentech.html (visited October 7, 2004).
MX Logic, Email Defense Industry Statistics, Feb. 3, 2005, available at http://www.mxlogic.com/PDFs/Industry_Stats_02_03_05.pdf (visited June 3, 2005).
Register of Known Spam Operations (ROKSO), The Spamhaus Project, http://www.spamhaus.org/rokso/index.lasso (visited October 7, 2004).
Paul Roberts, "'Buffalo Spammer' Convicted: Howard Carmack Was Convicted on Charges of ID Theft and Falsifying Business Records," *Computer World,* Apr. 1, 2004, available at http://www.computerworld.com/softwaretopics/software/groupware/story/0,10801,91823,00.html (visited October 7, 2004).
Jon Swartz, "Spammers Convicted: First Felony Case," USAToday.com, Nov. 3, 2004, available at http://www.usatoday.com/tech/news/2004-11-03-spam_x.htm (visited November 4, 2004).
"Verizon Reaches Favorable Settlement in Anti-Spam Lawsuit," Verizon Press Release, Oct. 28, 2002, available at http://www.spamhaus.org/

rokso/evidence.lasso?rokso_id=ROK2000 (visited October 7, 2004).

Mike Wendland, "Spam King Lives Large off Others' E-mail Troubles: West Bloomfield Computer Empire Helped by Foreign Internet Servers," *Detroit Free Press,* Nov. 22, 2002, available at http://www.freep.com/money/tech/mwend22_20021122.htm (visited October 7, 2004).

The World Almanac and Book of Facts 2004 (New York: World Almanac Books, 2004).

❖ SPYWARE ❖

See Adware and Spyware

❖ STEGANOGRAPHY ❖

The term *steganography* comes from *Steganographia*, a 1499 book by Johannes Trithemius. It refers to the process by which a message can be concealed within and later extracted from another message. The steganographic message can also be, but is not necessarily, encrypted. The fundamental difference between steganography and encryption is in the level of secrecy. In an encrypted message the content of the message is secret, but the existence of the message is not. In a steganographic message the very existence of the message is not readily apparent.

In the pre-digital age steganographic messages could be recorded with a variety of devices, including invisible ink, photographs compressed and used as the dot over the lower-case letter *i* in plaintext or encrypted messages, tattoos on the scalp, over which hair was allowed to grow back, and writing on the back of postage stamps and the inside of envelopes, among others. Digital data files, however, present a greatly expanded scope for steganography, so much so that the word *steganography* itself, which would probably have been unknown to almost every English speaker twenty-five years ago, has come back into use.

At the very simplest level, steganographic content might be included in a text file by typing a plaintext message in the same color as a document's background. This is the electronic equivalent of invisible ink; it offers no significant degree of security, but can be used for such things as concealing the answers to trivia quiz questions until after the reader has had a chance to guess the answer. But digital steganography offers greater possibilities: Data, in plaintext or encrypted, can be inserted into redundant or nonessential portions of files.

Any type of file can contain steganographic content; content can even be hidden in obscure areas, such as disk free space or print buffers. But data files, particularly text, image, sound, and motion picture files, are especially suited to containing steganographic content, for two reasons. First, text, image, sound, and motion picture files are well suited to serve as vehicles for steganographic content because they contain redundant or nonessential information that can easily be overwritten with steganographic content without either destroying the file's integrity or alerting the viewer to the presence of the hidden message. And because the files themselves contain information, the visible message distracts the viewer from the possible existence of a hidden message.

Second, text, image, sound, and motion picture files are also often copyrighted, or contain copyrighted content; steganographic content can be used to detect and track unauthorized copying of the files. This technique is not new to the digital age. Printed maps, for instance, often include one or two nonexistent features, such as cul-de-sacs, that do not affect the usefulness of the map. A publisher of telephone directories might include names and telephone numbers for a few nonexistent persons. If these nonexistent cul-de-sacs or phone listings show up in another map or phone directory, the only likely reason is that the later map or directory was copied from the earlier one. Similarly, a copyrighted JPEG file, for instance, might steganographically identify the photographer who took the picture; if copies of the JPEG are e-mailed around the Internet, posted on Web pages, and so forth, the hidden message will identify the JPEG as a copy. Text files created with Adobe Acrobat can be digitally signed by the author; these files might be copied and used by anyone else with a copy of the same program, but the signature will remain, although it is not visible in the text of the document. A programmer who illegally copies large chunks of another's code and incorporates it into his program may fail to notice the steganographic content the first programmer has included to identify the work as her own.

A file that contains a hidden message is called a container. Typically the container is unaffected by the inclusion of the steganographic content. In some cases, however, the steganographic content may be included in such a way as to make it impossible to remove without damaging or destroying the container. Steganography of this sort is called robust steganography. Robust steganography is useful for copyright protection because it prevents savvy users from removing the hidden copyright-protection information and sharing the "cleaned" file with others, and because it protects against inadvertent destruction of the hidden information through recompression of the file.

Because steganography can be used by criminals, terrorists, and spies, the government has an interest in steganalysis—the detection of steganographic content. And because steganography can be used to conceal malware, private individuals and companies also have an interest in steganalysis. As with encryption, there is an ongoing race between the development of increasingly sophisticated steganographic techniques and the development of steganalytic techniques to detect them. Advancements in steganalysis have decreased the usefulness of steganography alone as a copyright-protection tool; it will still identify the casual infringer, but protection from professional pirates requires more sophisticated digital rights management systems, in which steganography is only one element (see 17 U.S.C. § 1202).

See also: Copyright; Copyright Infringement; Digital Rights Management; Encryption

Sources and further reading:

Eric Cole, *Hiding in Plain Sight: Steganography and the Art of Covert Communication* (Indianapolis, IN: Wiley Publishing, Inc., 2003).

Neil F. Johnson et al., *Information Hiding: Steganography and Watermarking—Attacks and Countermeasures* (Boston: Kluwer Academic Publishers, 2000).

Stefan Katzenbeisser and Fabien A. P. Petitcolas, eds., *Information Hiding Techniques for Steganography and Digital Watermarking* (Norwood, MA: Artech House, 2000).

Gregory Kipper, *Investigator's Guide to Steganography* (Boca Raton, FL: Auerbach Publications, 2003).

Chun-Shien Lu, *Multimedia Security: Steganography and Digital Watermarking Techniques for Protection of Intellectual Property* (Hershey, PA: Idea Group Publishing, 2004).

Johannes Trithemius, *Steganographia* (1499; Darmstadt, Germany: Ioannis Berneri Bibliopolae, 1621), available in Latin at http://www.esotericarchives.com/tritheim/stegano.htm (visited June 16, 2004).

Peter Wayner, *Disappearing Cryptography—Information Hiding: Steganography and Watermarking*, 2d ed. (San Francisco, CA: Morgan Kaufmann Publishers, 2002).

❖ TAXATION ❖

E-commerce, like all commerce, is potentially subject to taxation; as e-commerce grows, so, too, does government's interest in taxing that commerce. However, e-commerce presents complex issues of jurisdiction; more than one government may claim authority to tax a single transaction. Even a very simple transaction can present complex tax issues. Suppose, for example, that a Web user in California purchases a copy of *Plan 9 from Outer Space* on DVD through an online auction site owned by a company incorporated in Delaware but located in Pennsylvania; the company listing the item for sale is located in Wyoming, but the copy of the DVD is actually located in, and shipped from, Nevada. At the seller's request, payment is made by a deposit into the seller's bank account in the Cayman Islands. In theory all five states, plus the Cayman Islands, might claim jurisdiction to tax the sale. In comparison with some inter-business transactions, this particular transaction is a fairly simple one, and catalog mail-order sales have forced the tax system to deal with similar problems for years.

The amount of tax revenue at stake is not trivial; about one hundred billion dollars per year is spent online (Swartz 2003, 143). When those sales take place within a single state, they are subject to sales taxes; when they take place across state lines, they are at least theoretically subject to use taxes imposed by the buyer's state. The Commerce Clause of the Constitution prevents states from passing laws that interfere with interstate commerce. The Supreme Court in *Quill Corp. v. North Dakota* interpreted this to mean that out-of-state re-tailers cannot charge sales taxes when they sell goods to consumers unless those retailers maintain a "substantial nexus" with the state, which usually means a physical presence in the taxing state. When the seller has a substantial nexus with the buyer's state, it becomes the seller's duty to collect and remit the use tax to the buyer's state; from the buyer's perspective, the process is identical to the collection of sales tax (*Quill*, 504 U.S. at 311). However, the Supreme Court has drawn a "sharp distinction . . . between mail-order sellers with [a physical presence in the taxing] State and those . . . who do no more than communicate with customers in the State by mail or common carrier as part of a general interstate business"; sellers in the latter category are not required to collect and remit the use tax (*Quill*, 504 U.S. at 311).

This does not mean that the state relinquishes its right to the use tax; the buyer remains obligated to calculate the use tax and pay it to the appropriate state authority (Swartz 2003, 144). As a practical matter, however, the tax is rarely paid; few buyers are aware of the obligation, and even those who are lack information on where and how to pay the tax. And the amounts involved in most transactions tend to be so small that the cost of education and enforcement would exceed the amount collected (Swartz 2003, 144), although enforcement might be worthwhile for high-value items such as automobiles, jewelry, and works of art.

The advent of e-commerce in the mid-1990s brought the problem of taxing interstate sales to the attention of state legislatures and Congress. State governments became concerned that they would lose tax revenues; e-commerce businesses were concerned that they would be unable to attract customers if they could not offer tax-free sales. In 1998, Congress, in order to simplify the situation and protect the nascent e-commerce industry, enacted the Internet Tax Freedom Act. The act prevents taxes that discriminate against e-commerce and taxes on Internet access (Internet Tax Freedom Act § 1101). It also declares that "It is the sense of Congress that no new Federal taxes . . . should be enacted with respect to the Internet and Internet access" during the act's moratorium period (Internet Tax Freedom Act § 1201) and that "the Internet should be free of foreign tariffs, trade barriers, and other restrictions" (Internet Tax Freedom Act § 1203 (header)). The act originally granted protection for a three-year period; in 2001 it was renewed by the Internet Tax Nondiscrimination Act until 2003, and in 2004, the act was modified and extended to 2008.

Bricks-and-mortar retailers, threatened by untaxed Internet sales, have united with state governors in pushing for the Streamlined Sales Tax and Use Tax Agreement, which would in effect eliminate the tax advantage that e-commerce retailers currently enjoy; e-commerce, consumer advocates, and technology industry groups favor legislation incorporating the *Quill* standard. In the meantime taxation of Internet services has also become a contentious issue, especially with the advent of voice-over-Internet telephone call technology; state governments estimate that they stand to lose up to eleven billion dollars in existing telecommunications tax revenues if the moratorium on taxing Internet services is extended (Feuchtwanger and LaPaille 2004).

Statutes
- Internet Tax Freedom Act, P.L. 105–277, Title XI

Cases
- *Quill Corp. v. North Dakota*, 504 U.S. 298 (1992)

See also: Choice of Law; E-commerce; Jurisdiction; Recognition and Enforcement of Judgments

Voice-over Internet protocol (VOIP) represents the completion of the circle of evolution: Internet telecommunications originally piggybacked on existing telephone network infrastructure, but the Internet has now grown to the point that it may become more profitable for telephone calls to piggyback on the Internet infrastructure. VOIP makes it possible to transmit voice and video conversations as packets, in the same way that e-mail and Web traffic are transmitted—and with sufficient speed and accuracy to allow voice and even video conversations to take place in real time. Unlike traditional phone calls, which require a dedicated line, VOIP calls are free from physical restraints on location. A VOIP phone can be connected to any broadband connection on the planet without requiring a change of phone number or area code. This makes it possible, for example, to make low-cost international calls: A traveling businessperson from San Diego, California, can carry a VOIP phone with San Diego's area code (619) and make telephone calls to San Diego from broadband connections in Seoul, Shanghai, Singapore, Sydney, São Paulo, Savannah, and Stockholm—all of which will be billed as local calls.

This represents a threat to phone companies' revenues, but not a disaster; long-distance international phone calls are already affordable, and not everyone will have either the opportunity or the incentive to use VOIP to lower their bills. The bigger threat could be to mobile phone companies, as a result of VOIP's mobility. Mobility has been the advantage mobile phone companies have offered their customers, but no mobile phone network can come close to offering the near-global availability of broadband Internet connections. Mobile phone companies still have one advantage: VOIP phones require a broadband connection, and wireless broadband is not yet widely available. It is not yet possible, in most of the world, to use a VOIP phone while driving to work or strolling in the park. But if universal wireless broadband becomes a reality, mobile phone companies could face a struggle for survival.

Source
"The Phone Call Is Dead; Long Live the Phone Call," *The Economist*, Dec. 4, 2004, at 61.

Sources and further reading:

Arthur J. Cockfield, "Jurisdiction to Tax: A Law and Technology Perspective," 38 *Georgia Law Review* 85 (2003).

Jason Feuchtwanger and Christine LaPaille, "Senate Offers a Reasonable Internet Access Tax Moratorium," National Governors' Association Press Release, May 12, 2004, available at http://www.nga.org/nga/legislativeUpdate/1,1169,C_ISSUE_BRIEF^D_6619,00.html (visted November 17, 2004).

Walter Hellerstein, "Jurisdiction to Tax Income and Consumption in the New Economy: A Theoretical and Comparative Perspective," 38 *Georgia Law Review* 1 (2003).

Brian Krebs, "Internet Sales Tax Effort on Hold for Now," *Washington Post,* Dec. 17, 2003, available at http://www.washingtonpost.com/wp-dyn/articles/A5949–2003Dec16.html (visited November 17, 2004).

Ryan J. Swartz, "The Imposition of Sales and Use Taxes on E-Commerce: A Taxing Dilemma for States and Remote Sellers," 2 *Journal of High Technology Law* 143 (2003).

❖ TECHNOLOGY, EDUCATION, AND COPYRIGHT HARMONIZATION ACT ❖

See Digital Millennium Copyright Act, Title IV

❖ TRADE-RELATED ASPECTS OF INTELLECTUAL PROPERTY RIGHTS ❖

See TRIPS

❖ TRADE SECRET ❖

Trade secrets are a difficult category of intellectual property to protect, because by their very nature they are secret and cannot be disclosed to any registering authority. To some extent, in fact, the protection of trade secrets runs contrary to one of the policy interests underpinning patent law: Patent law seeks to encourage inventors to share their inventions and discoveries with the public, in exchange for an economic benefit (the patent owner's limited-term mo-nopoly). Trade secret law, in contrast, seeks to protect those who do not wish to share their inventions and discoveries.

Trade secrets are protected in the United States primarily by the vigilance of their owners. State and federal law offer some protection, however. The first problem faced by lawmakers in dealing with trade secrets is the problem of defining them. The federal Economic Espionage Act of 1996, 18 U.S.C. §§ 1831 et seq., sets two requirements: The owner of the secret must have "taken reasonable measures to keep such information secret," and the material to be protected must derive "independent economic value, actual or potential, from not being generally known to, and not being readily ascertainable through proper means by, the public" (18 U.S.C. § 1839(3)). The definition of protected subject matter in the Uniform Trade Secrets Act, adopted in various modified forms in forty-five states, is virtually identical: A trade secret is information that "(i) derives independent economic value, actual or potential, from not being generally known to, and not being readily ascertainable by proper means by, other persons who can obtain economic value from its disclosure or use, and (ii) is the subject of efforts that are reasonable under the circumstances to maintain its secrecy." Although the order of the two elements is reversed, the only significant difference is that the federal statute requires that the secret derive its value from not being known to the public, whereas the Uniform Act requires that it derive its value from not being known to others in the same field.

The federal statute protects against economic espionage by any person who knowingly commits the espionage either "intending or knowing that the offense will benefit any foreign government, foreign instrumentality, or foreign agent" (18 U.S.C. § 1831) or "with intent to convert"—take—"a trade secret, that is related to or included in a product that is produced for or placed in interstate or foreign commerce, to the economic benefit of anyone other than the owner thereof, and intending or knowing that the offense will, injure any owner of that trade secret" (18 U.S.C. § 1832). The Uniform Act is not concerned with distinguishing between foreign and U.S. parties; it prohibits misappropriation of trade secrets, misappropriation being defined as: "(i) acquisition of a trade secret of another by a person who knows or has reason to know that the trade secret was acquired by improper means; or (ii) disclosure or use of a trade secret of another without express or implied consent by a person who" acquired the secret, directly or indirectly, by improper means, accident, or mistake, or subject to a duty to maintain the secrecy (Uniform Trade Secrets Act § 1(2)).

Trade secrets are inherently fragile. Other forms of intellectual property can survive infringement; the owner of a copyright, patent, or trademark may sue the infringer, bring a halt to the infringement, recover damages, and continue owning the right. Once a trade secret has been disclosed, however, it is no longer secret. The owner of the secret may recover damages from the person who disclosed it—but only from the first person to do so, or any other person who does so improperly. Once the secret has been widely disseminated, it is no longer a secret, and the original owner cannot reclaim it (*Religious Technology Center*, 908 F.Supp. 1362). In addition, trade secret law protects trade secrets only against improper means of discovery. It does not, as patent law does, protect the trade secret from independent rediscovery or reverse engineering (McCarthy 2004, 620).

Statute
- Economic Espionage Act of 1996, 18 U.S.C. §§ 1831 et seq.

Uniform Act
- National Conference of Commissioners on Uniform State Laws, Uniform Trade Secrets Act, as amended 1985, available at http://nsi.org/Library/Espionage/usta.htm (visited November 16, 2004)

Case
- *Religious Technology Center v. Lerma*, 908 F.Supp. 1362 (E.D. Va. 1995)

See also: Patent; TRIPS (Trade Secrets)

Sources and further reading:
J. Thomas McCarthy et al., *McCarthy's Desk Encyclopedia of Intellectual Property*, 3d ed.

(Washington, DC: Bureau of National Affairs, 2004).

❖ TRADEMARK ❖

Narrowly defined, a trademark is a mark that can be placed on goods to distinguish them from other goods. The term is often used in a broader sense, however, to refer to a wide range of distinguishing marks and indications of origin, including (in addition to trademarks) service marks, certification marks, collective marks, trade dress, and trade names. The body of law governing these marks and indications of origin is referred to as trademark law.

A trademark or other mark can be a design, motto, phrase, picture, shape, slogan, symbol, or word. It serves to identify the goods, services, or other thing to which the mark is attached, as well as to identify their source—that is, the person or entity that made or authorized them. It is used to connect goods and services to advertising promoting them, and it serves consumers by providing an indication of quality. Consumers learn to associate certain levels of quality with certain marks and are thus spared the effort of an exhaustive exploration of the quality of each particular good or service they wish to purchase. A consumer planning to buy a camera attaches certain expectations to the trademarks Vivitar, Olympus, and Hasselblad; each creates different expectations, and the owners of these trademarks have expended considerable effort to create those expectations and to ensure that their cameras match the expectations they have created.

There are limits on what may become a trademark. Generic names cannot become trademarks; Vivitar, Olympus, and Hasselblad cannot trademark the term *camera,* or even "digital camera." Descriptive terms, geographic terms, and personal names can only become trademarks if they acquire a secondary meaning—that is, if they become established among the public, or at least among the audience at whom the mark is named, as referring to the particular thing described and not to the broader class of things to which it belongs (*Abercrombie & Fitch*, 537 F.2d at 9). Once such a term acquires such a secondary meaning, however, it may become a protected mark; the name "Hasselblad" would fall into this category. And terms that are suggestive, arbitrary, or fanciful are always eligible to become trademarks; the name "Olympus" is arbitrary when attached to cameras, and the made-up name "Vivitar" is fanciful. However, as the court in *Abercrombie & Fitch v. Hunting World* pointed out, "the difficulties are compounded because a term that is in one category for a particular product may be in quite a different one for another": For example, the term "'Ivory' would be generic when used to describe a product made from the tusks of elephants but arbitrary as applied to soap" (*Abercrombie & Fitch*, 537 F.2d at 9 and fn. 6). In addition, "a term may shift from one category to another in light of differences in usage through time": The court's example here was "the coined word 'Escalator', originally fanciful, or at the very least suggestive," which by 1950 had become generic (*Abercrombie & Fitch*, 537 F.2d at 9 and fn. 7). In addition, "a term may have one meaning to one group of users and a different one to others," and "the same term may be put to different uses with respect to a single product" (*Abercrombie & Fitch*, 537 F.2d at 9).

Eligible trademarks and other marks are protected by both state and federal case law and statutes. The central federal trademark statute is the Lanham Trademark Act; in addition, trademarks may be registered in most states. State registration cannot narrow the protection granted to the trademark holder by the Lanham Act, but can grant broader protection within a particular state. Unregistered trademarks may also be protected in courts under state common law, and the Lanham Act provides that actions to protect unregistered marks may be brought in federal courts (15 U.S.C. § 1125). Foreign trademarks might also be entitled to special protection under international trademark protection agreements to which the United States is a party, including the Madrid Protocol, the Paris Convention, the Trademark Registration Treaty, and TRIPS.

Trademarks can be registered with the United States Patent and Trademark Office. However, registration does not create the

How long can trademarks last? Unlike copyrights and patents, which have limited durations, trademarks can be renewed without limit; a trademark is potentially everlasting. Finding the oldest trademark still in use, however, is not an easy task, because trademarks may be unregistered or may have been unregistered and used for years, decades, or even centuries before being registered. Changes in registration laws, back-dating registrations to application dates, reregistration, and changes in the form of the trademark make identifying even the oldest registered trademark difficult. Contenders for the title include the red triangle logo of Bass & Co. Pale Ale, the arcuate stitching pattern on the back pockets of Levi's jeans, and the crossed-swords logo of Meissen porcelain; all three have been in use and protected since the 1870s. This may reveal more about the development of trademark registration formalities than about the use of the trademarks themselves, though: Meissen's crossed swords have been used as a trademark, although not registered, since 1722; they are derived from the coat of arms of the German state of Saxony, which owns the company. Company names used as trademarks can be as old as the companies themselves. The Stationer's Company, which played so large a role in the development of copyright law in the sixteenth, seventeenth, and eighteenth centuries, is still around, in altered form, as are others far older. In Awazu, Japan, the Hoshi family has run an inn, the Hoshi Ryokan, for forty-six generations—nearly thirteen hundred years. Another Japanese family firm, construction firm Kongo Gumi, has been building temples and other things for more than fourteen hundred years—surely long enough to have acquired some rights in the name, which it has already claimed for its Web site: www.kongogumi.co.jp.

Source
"About LS&Co./Levi's 501 Jeans Facts," Levis Strauss & Co., http://www.levistrauss.com/about/history/501s.htm (visited January 5, 2005);
"275 Years under the Sign of the Crossed Blue Swords," Meissen Staatliche Porzellan-Manufaktur Meissen GmbH, http://www.meissen.de/engl/j275.htm (visited January 6, 2005);
"The World's Oldest Companies: The Business of Survival," *The Economist*, Dec. 16, 2004.

trademark; in the United States, trademark protection arises from the use of the mark rather than from its registration (*International Flavors*, 183 F.3d at 1366). Trademarks, unlike patents or copyrights, are of potentially infinite duration but must be renewed periodically; registrations issued after November 16, 1989, must be renewed every ten years (15 U.S.C. §§ 1058–1059). A somewhat similar renewable registration system for copyrights has been proposed in the Public Domain Enhancement Act, but is unlikely to be enacted because of opposition from the content industry and possible conflicts with international obligations.

Trademarks may be subject to infringement or dilution. All trademarks can be infringed upon; infringement occurs when someone other than the owner of the mark uses the mark without authorization in a way that creates a likelihood of confusion. Only strong and famous trademarks can be diluted; dilution occurs when someone other than the owner of the mark does something that tarnishes or blurs the distinctiveness of the mark (15 U.S.C. § 1125(c)(1)). As with all intellectual property rights, it is the duty of the mark owner rather than of the government to detect, pursue, and bring actions against violators. For the most part infringement and dilution actions involving the Internet involve no unique issues; sales of fake Rolex watches resulting from spam advertising involve essentially the same trademark issues as sales of fake Rolex watches at flea markets and on street corners, although the spam itself may result in dilution of the trademark: After receiving several hundred spam messages advertising fake Rolex watches, many users might be inclined to assume that most or all of the Rolex watches they see are fakes.

The Internet does provide some unique opportunities for trademark infringement and dilution, however. Metatags incorporating trademarks are invisible to the consumer, yet can guide search engine traffic to a particular site and thus infringe upon, dilute, or tarnish a trademark. And cybersquatting—the registration and use of trademarks owned by others as Internet domain names—posed a severe problem in the early days of the Internet. As a result, Congress enacted a statute, the Anticybersquat-ting Consumer Protection Act, especially to address this problem (15 U.S.C. § 1125(d)).

Statutes
- Anticybersquatting Consumer Protection Act, 15 U.S.C. § 1125(d)
- Lanham Trademark Act, 15 U.S.C. §§ 1052, 1058, 1059, 1125–1127

Proposed Legislation
- Public Domain Enhancement Act, H.R. 2601, 108th Cong., 1st Sess., June 25, 2003, available at http://thomas. loc.gov/cgi-bin/query/z?c108: H.R.2601: (visited October 25, 2004)

Cases
- *Abercrombie & Fitch Co. v. Hunting World, Inc.*, 537 F.2d 4 (2d Cir. 1976)
- *CPC International, Inc. v. Skippy Inc.*, 214 F.3d 456 (4th Cir. 2000)
- *In re International Flavors & Fragrances, Inc.*, 183 F.3d 1361 (Fed. Cir. 1999)

See also: Cybersquatting; Domain Name Registration; Fair Use (Trademark); Intellectual Property; International Trademark Protection; Madrid Agreement and Madrid Protocol; Metatags; Paris Convention; Trademark Dilution; Trademark Infringement

Sources and further reading:
Michael H. Davis and Arthur Raphael Miller, *Intellectual Property: Patents, Trademarks, and Copyright in a Nutshell* (St. Paul, MN: West, 2000).
Zohar Efroni, "A Guidebook to Cybersquatting Litigation: The Practical Approach in a Post-Barcelona.com World," 2003 *University of Illinois Journal of Law, Technology and Policy* 457 (2003).
Stephen R. Elias, *Patent, Copyright and Trademark: An Intellectual Property Desk Reference*, 7th ed. (Berkeley, CA: Nolo Press, 2004).
Christopher T. Marsden, ed., *Regulating the Global Information Society* (New York: Routledge, 2000).
J. Thomas McCarthy et al., *McCarthy's Desk Encyclopedia of Intellectual Property*, 3d ed. (Washington, DC: Bureau of National Affairs, 2004).

❖ TRADEMARK DILUTION ❖

Trademark dilution is a violation of an intellectual property right in famous marks; it does not apply to marks that are not famous. Dilution is addressed by federal and state trademark law; under the Federal Trademark Dilution Act, the owner of a famous mark may obtain "an injunction against another person's commercial use in commerce of a mark or trade name, if such use begins after the mark has become famous and causes dilution of the distinctive quality of the mark" (15 U.S.C. § 1125(c)). In other words, the owner of a famous mark may obtain a court order requiring anyone who is diluting the mark to cease doing so.

Famous marks: Determining whether a mark is famous presents a problem, of course, and the Trademark Dilution Act provides a list of factors:

> In determining whether a mark is distinctive and famous, a court may consider factors such as, but not limited to –
> (A) the degree of inherent or acquired distinctiveness of the mark;
> (B) the duration and extent of use of the mark in connection with the goods or services with which the mark is used;
> (C) the duration and extent of advertising and publicity of the mark;
> (D) the geographical extent of the trading area in which the mark is used;
> (E) the channels of trade for the goods or services with which the mark is used;
> (F) the degree of recognition of the mark in the trading areas and channels of trade used by the mark's owner and the person against whom the injunction is sought;
> (G) the nature and extent of use of the same or similar marks by third parties; and
> (H) whether the mark was registered under the Act of March 3, 1881, or the Act of February 20, 1905, or on the principal register. (15 U.S.C. § 1125(c)(1))

These are only factors, not indispensable elements. In determining whether a mark is famous a court must consider each factor; some factors may weigh in favor of finding that a mark is famous, while others may weigh against such a finding. A mark may still be famous even if some factors seem to point the opposite way; another mark may not be famous even though some of the factors indicate that it should be (McCarthy 2004, 175–176). Some marks (such as AOL, the trademark of America Online) may be generally famous; others may be famous only within a specific region or industry. If, for example, a trademark is famous in California but unknown elsewhere, it would be unlikely to be diluted by activities in New Jersey; similarly a trademark for a legal research service well-known to lawyers but unknown to the general public would be unlikely to be diluted by the use of a similar trademark for automobiles (*Mead Data Central*, 875 F.2d at 1031–1032).

Once a mark has been determined to be famous, the next question is whether any dilution has occurred. A trademark may be diluted in two ways: by blurring or by tarnishment.

Blurring: Dilution by blurring occurs when a mark similar to the famous mark is used on some other product, resulting in a diminution in the distinctiveness of the famous mark. Blurring is related, but not identical, to the "likelihood of confusion" requirement of trademark infringement (*Mead Data Central*, 875 F.2d at 1031). *Mead Data Central v. Toyota Motor Sales* was a suit brought by the owners of the Lexis computer-assisted legal research system against the makers of Lexus automobiles. Mead, the plaintiff and the owner of the Lexis trademark, sought to enjoin Toyota from using the name Lexus for luxury cars. The federal district court for the Southern District of New York issued the injunction, but the Second Circuit reversed, holding that Mead's Lexis mark was not diluted by Toyota's use of the name Lexus, for two reasons. First, although the Lexis mark was famous within its own niche market (attorneys and legal professionals), it was all but unknown to the general public; thus, there was no likelihood of blurring in the minds of the general public, because the general public was unaware of the Lexis mark. Second, blurring was not likely in the minds of attorneys, either, because "the recognized sophistication of attorneys" rendered it "unlikely that, even in the market where Mead principally operates, there [would] be any significant amount of blurring between the LEXIS and LEXUS marks" (*Mead Data Central*, 875 F.2d at 1031–1032).

Tarnishment: Tarnishment occurs when an unauthorized person uses a trademark in a way that casts disrepute upon a famous mark or otherwise interferes with the positive mental associations created in the minds of the public by the mark. For example, a poster imitating the appearance of a Coca-Cola advertisement, but substituting the words "Enjoy Cocaine" for "Enjoy Coca-Cola," tarnishes the Coca-Cola mark (*Coca-Cola,* 346 F.Supp. 1183). A cybersquatter who registers a domain name similar to a famous mark and posts pornographic content on the site is tarnishing the mark, presumably in the hope that the owner of the mark will pay for the domain name to avoid further tarnishment. Although conduct deliberately aimed at extorting money from the mark owner is prohibited by the Anticybersquatting Consumer Protection Act, some uses are protected, even if they would otherwise constitute trademark dilution. These uses include:

(A) Fair use of a famous mark by another person in comparative commercial advertising or promotion to identify the competing goods or services of the owner of the famous mark.
(B) Noncommercial use of a mark.
(C) All forms of news reporting and news commentary. (15 U.S.C. § 1125(c)(4))

Cybersquatting: The Anti-cybersquatting Consumer Protection Act (ACPA) provides that a cybersquatter is one who, with a bad faith intent to profit, registers, traffics in, or uses a domain name that –

(I) in the case of a mark that is distinctive at the time of registration of the domain name, is identical or confusingly similar to that mark;
(II) in the case of a famous mark that is famous at the time of registration of the domain name, is identical or confusingly similar to or dilutive of that mark. (15 U.S.C. § 1125(d)(1)(A)(ii))

The ACPA thus gives broader protection to famous marks than to other marks. A cybersquatter can safely register domain names that might blur or tarnish—that is, dilute—marks that are merely distinctive, so long as they are not actually identical or confusingly similar to those marks. Famous marks, however, are protected against blurring and tarnishing as well.

In effect, the ACPA reserves all of those potentially blurring or tarnishing domain names for the holder of the famous mark.

Relief granted and immunity: Ordinarily the holder of a famous mark is only entitled to injunctive relief in a dilution suit; that is, the court will make the person diluting the mark stop his or her diluting activity, but will not award money damages to the mark owner. However, money damages may be awarded when "the person against whom the injunction is sought *willfully intended* to trade on the owner's reputation or to cause dilution of the famous mark" (15 U.S.C. § 1125(c)(2))(emphasis added). And a person who holds a valid trademark registration is immune to a suit for dilution, even if brought by another person with an equal or superior right in the same mark (15 U.S.C. § 1125(c)(3)).

Statutes
- Anticybersquatting Consumer Protection Act, 15 U.S.C. § 1125(d)
- Federal Trademark Dilution Act of 1995, 15 U.S.C. § 1125(c)
- Lanham Trademark Act, 15 U.S.C. §§ 1117–1118

Cases
Federal Appellate Courts
- *Mead Data Central, Inc. v. Toyota Motor Sales, Inc.,* 875 F.2d 1026 (2d Cir. 1989)

Federal Trial Courts
- *Coca-Cola Co. v. Gemini Rising, Inc.,* 346 F.Supp. 1183 (E.D. N.Y. 1972)
- *Lucent Technologies, Inc. v. Lucentsucks.com,* 95 F.Supp.2d 528 (E.D. Va. 2000)
- *Lucent Technologies v. Johnson,* 2000 WL 1604055 (C.D.Cal. 2000)
- *Mattel, Inc. v. Internet Dimensions, Inc.,* 2000 WL 973745 (S.D. N.Y. 2000)

See also: Cybersquatting; Domain Name Registration; Fair Use (Trademark); Trademark; Trademark Infringement

Sources and further reading:
Kevin J. Greene, "Abusive Trademark Litigation and the Shrinking Doctrine of Consumer

Confusion: Rethinking Trademark Paradigms in the Context of Entertainment Media and Cyberspace," 27 *Harvard Journal of Law and Public Policy* (2004).

Martha Kelley, "Is Liability Just a Link Away? Trademark Dilution by Tarnishment under the Federal Trademark Dilution Act of 1995 and Hyperlinks on the World Wide Web," 9 *Journal of Intellectual Property Law* 361 (2002).

J. Thomas McCarthy et al., *McCarthy's Desk Encyclopedia of Intellectual Property,* 3d ed. (Washington, DC: Bureau of National Affairs, 2004).

Christopher R. Perry, "Trademarks as Commodities: The 'Famous' Roadblock to Applying Trademark Dilution Law in Cyberspace," 32 *Connecticut Law Review* 1127 (2000).

❖ TRADEMARK INFRINGEMENT ❖

Trademark infringement is the unauthorized use of a mark belonging to another, or the use of a similar mark in a manner that creates a likelihood of confusion (15 U.S.C. § 1114(1)). All marks, registered or unregistered, are protected against infringement creating a likelihood of confusion. Only famous marks are protected against dilution, however. When resolving claims arising under both state and federal law, courts will generally apply a single analysis to determine whether the alleged infringement creates a likelihood of confusion (McCarthy 2004, 301).

Likelihood of confusion: At the heart of most trademark infringement actions is the question of likelihood of confusion. In cases of deliberate counterfeiting of trademarked goods, the question is simple to answer; in other cases it is less so. The problem is complicated by the lack of a statutory guide or a uniform rule of case law; instead, the federal circuit courts have evolved different, but not necessarily contradictory, tests. The Second Circuit's list of factors set forth in *Polaroid v. Polarad* is typical, although neither exhaustive nor identical to the lists used by other circuits. The *Polaroid* factors are (1) the strength of the mark; (2) "the degree of similarity between the two marks"; (3) "the

proximity of the products"; (4) "the likelihood that the prior owner will bridge the gap" between his or her current products and the products of the alleged infringer; (5) "actual confusion"; (6) the "defendant's good faith in adopting its own mark"; (7) "the quality of defendant's product"; and (8) "the sophistication of the buyers" (*Polaroid,* 287 F.2d at 495). The *Polaroid* court noted, however, that "Even this extensive catalogue does not exhaust the possibilities" (*Polaroid,* 287 F.2d at 495). The Restatement (Third) of Unfair Competition sets forth a longer and more complex list of factors to be considered in common law trademark infringement cases. Some of these add clarifications to the *Polaroid* factors; for example, the restatement explains that subsidiary factors to be assessed in determining the degree of similarity between the conflicting marks include:

> (i) the overall impression created by the designations . . .
> (ii) the pronunciation of the designations;
> (iii) the translation of any foreign words contained in the designations;
> (iv) the verbal translation of any pictures, illustrations, or designs contained in the designations;
> (v) the suggestions, connotations, or meanings of the designations. (Restatement, § 21)

Actual confusion is not a requirement for likelihood of confusion; what the mark owner must show is that some significant amount of confusion is likely, not that anyone has actually been confused. When actual confusion can be shown, however, it tends to prove a likelihood of confusion (McCarthy 2004, 303).

Metatags: Two contentious areas of online trademark infringement are metatags and domain name registrations. Metatags are text inserted into an HTML document so as to be invisible when the document is viewed as a Web page. Because metatags can be used by search engines to locate a page, some Web site creators use metatags in an attempt to increase a page's search result rank. Trademarked terms may be used as metatags, triggering infringement suits when the mark holder discovers the use. Changes in search engine technology have rendered the use of metatags less profitable, however.

Cybersquatting: Cybersquatting—the registration and use of trademarks owned by others as Internet domain names—was once a serious problem. Cybersquatters would speculatively register large numbers of domain names, then attempt to sell those domain names. Many of the names registered were identical or confusingly similar to existing marks; the holders of these marks were the primary targets of the cybersquatters. In some cases the cybersquatter would simply wait for the mark holder to attempt to register its mark as a domain name; in others the cybersquatter would approach the mark holder and offer to sell the domain name. In especially egregious cases the cybersquatter would create a Web site containing offensive content in an attempt to pressure the mark owner into purchasing the name.

Existing trademark law was ill equipped to deal with this new form of trademark infringement, and the federal courts began to create a new form of trademark dilution—dilution by cybersquatting (*Panavision,* 141 F.3d 1316 (9th Cir. 1998)). This was an awkward fit, however, and did little to help the owners of marks that were distinctive but not famous. In 1999 Congress addressed the problem with the passage of the Anticybersquatting Consumer Protection Act (ACPA). The ACPA addresses both dilution of famous marks and infringement of all marks; it provides that a person who, with a bad faith intent to profit, registers, traffics in, or uses a domain name that at the time of registration is (1) identical to or confusingly similar to a *distinctive* mark, or (2) identical to or confusingly similar to or dilutive of a *famous* mark, is liable in a civil action by the owner of the mark. Remedies may include damages and the transfer of the domain name to the mark owner.

Fair use: Certain uses of the trademark of another, like certain uses of copyrighted material, are protected as fair use. The fact that a particular use of a trademark is fair use does not mean that the trademark has fallen into the public domain; it means simply that a particular use is permissible. Trademark fair use may be either classic fair use or nominative fair use. Classic fair use occurs when a trademark is also a descriptive term and is used in its descriptive sense. For most courts this analysis is inextricably linked to the "likelihood of confusion" analysis; if there is a classic fair use, there is no likelihood of confusion. Thus classic fair use in these courts is not truly an exception to the rule of liability for trademark infringement, but an instance of the requirements of the rule not being satisfied. Some courts, however, are willing to find fair use even if a likelihood of confusion exists (see *Cosmetically Sealed Industries,* 125 F.3d 28).

Nominative fair use is the use of a trademark to describe the thing trademarked in order to draw attention to some other product or service. The Ninth Circuit Court of Appeals has set out a three-part test for determining whether a particular use is nominative fair use:

> First, the product or service in question must be one not readily identifiable without use of the trademark; second, only so much of the mark or marks may be used as is reasonably necessary to identify the product or service; and third, the user must do nothing that would, in conjunction with the mark, suggest sponsorship or endorsement by the trademark holder. (*Playboy,* 279 F.3d at 801)

Under this test, for example, an independent automotive shop that specializes in Volkswagen repairs has no easy way to identify its services other than by using the trademarked name "Volkswagen"; this is fair use, although use of the Volkswagen logo (rather than merely the name) to advertise the repair shop's services would not be, because that would be more than reasonably necessary to identify the service and might suggest sponsorship or endorsement by Volkswagen corporation.

Internet Service Providers: As with copyright infringement, Internet service providers (ISPs) may be involved in trademark infringement without their knowledge if users of the ISP transmit or post infringing material. But although the Digital Millennium Copyright Act (DMCA) creates a safe harbor from copyright infringement liability, it contains no similar protection from trademark infringement liability. Nor does the safe harbor provision of the Communications Decency Act, 47 U.S.C. § 230(c)(1), provide such protection. Section

230(c)(1) provides that "No provider or user of an interactive computer service shall be treated as the publisher or speaker of any information provided by another information content provider." However, this is apparently inapplicable to trademark infringement: "Nothing in this section shall be construed to limit or expand any law pertaining to intellectual property" (47 U.S.C. § 230(e)(2)). One court has already found that the result of § 230(e)(2) is that § 230(c)(1) conveys no immunity to ISPs from liability for copyright infringement (*Gucci*, 135 F.Supp.2d at 413–414). The exact extent of potential ISP liability for trademark infringement remains unclear, although it is ultimately limited by the First Amendment (*Name.Space*, 202 F.3d at 585–586).

Statutes

- Anticybersquatting Consumer Protection Act, 15 U.S.C. § 1125(d)
- Communications Decency Act, 47 U.S.C. § 230
- Lanham Trademark Act, 15 U.S.C. § 1114
- Digital Millennium Copyright Act, 16 U.S.C. § 512

Cases

Federal Appellate Courts

- *Cosmetically Sealed Industries, Inc. v. Chesebrough-Pond's USA Co.*, 125 F.3d 28 (2d Cir. 1997)
- *Eclipse Associates Ltd. v. Data General Corp.*, 894 F.2d 1114 (9th Cir. 1990)
- *Falcon Rice Mill, Inc. v. Community Rice Mill, Inc.*, 725 F.2d 336 (5th Cir. 1984)
- *Frisch's Restaurants, Inc. v. Elby's Big Boy, Inc.*, 670 F.2d 642 (6th Cir.), cert. denied 459 U.S. 916 (1982)
- *Keds Corp. v. Renee Int'l Trading Corp.*, 888 F.2d 215 (1st Cir. 1989)
- *Kellogg Co. v. Pack'em Enterprises, Inc.*, 951 F.2d 330 (Fed. Cir. 1991)
- *Name.Space, Inc. v. Network Solutions, Inc.*, 202 F.3d 573 (2d Cir. 2000)
- *Panavision International L.P. v. Toeppen*, 141 F.3d 1316 (9th Cir. 1998)
- *Piper Aircraft Corp. v. Wag-Aero, Inc.*, 741 F.2d 925 (7th Cir. 1984)

- *Playboy Enterprises, Inc. v. Welles*, 279 F.3d 796 (9th Cir. 2002)
- *Polaroid Corp. v. Polarad Electronics Corp.*, 287 F.2d 492 (2d Cir. 1961)

Federal Trial Courts

- *Coca-Cola Co. v. Gemini Rising, Inc.*, 346 F.Supp. 1183 (E.D. N.Y. 1972)
- *Gucci America, Inc. v. Hall & Associates*, 135 F.Supp.2d 409 (S.D. N.Y. 2001)
- *Lucent Technologies v. Johnson*, 2000 WL 1604055 (C.D. Cal. 2000)
- *Lucent Technologies, Inc. v. Lucentsucks.com*, 95 F.Supp.2d 528 (E.D. Va. 2000)
- *Mattel, Inc. v. Internet Dimensions, Inc.*, 2000 WL 973745 (S.D. N.Y. 2000)
- *Ocean Bio-Chem, Inc. v. Turner Network Television, Inc.*, 741 F.Supp. 1546 (S.D. Fla. 1990)

Restatement

- Restatement (Third) of Unfair Competition §§ 21–23 (Washington, DC: American Law Institute, 1995 and Supp. 2004)

See also: Cybersquatting; Digital Millennium Copyright Act, Title II; Domain Name Registration; Fair Use (Trademark); Metatags; Trademark; Trademark Dilution

Sources and further reading:

James H. Aiken, "The Jurisdiction of Trademark and Copyright Infringement on the Internet," 48 *Mercer Law Review* 1331 (1997).

Katherine E. Gasparek, "Applying the Fair Use Defense in Traditional Trademark Infringement and Dilution Cases to Internet Meta Tagging or Linking Cases," 1 *George Mason Law Review* 787 (1999).

Lea Hall, "The Evolving Law of Personal Jurisdiction for Trademark Infringement on the Internet," 66 *Mississippi Law Journal* Winter 457 (1996).

Bryce J. Maynard, "The Initial Interest Confusion Doctrine and Trademark Infringement on the Internet," 57 *Washington and Lee Law Review* 1303 (2000).

J. Thomas McCarthy et al., *McCarthy's Desk Encyclopedia of Intellectual Property*, 3d ed.

(Washington, DC: Bureau of National Affairs, 2004).

Gregory C. Walsh, "Internet Service Provider Liability for Contributory Trademark Infringement after Gucci," 2002 *Duke Law and Technology Review* 95 (2002).

Gayle Weiswasser, "Domain Names, the Internet, and Trademarks: Infringement in Cyberspace," 13 *Santa Clara Computer and High Technology Law Journal* 137 (1996).

❖ TRADEMARK LAW TREATY ❖

The Trademark Law Treaty (TLT), promulgated by the World Intellectual Property Organization (WIPO), seeks to harmonize the trademark registration process. The treaty was concluded in 1994 and as of October 2004 had thirty-three parties; the United States became a party on August 12, 2000. In order to bring its law into compliance with the TLT the United States enacted the Trademark Law Treaty Act of 1998; the act simplified U.S. trademark registration and renewal formalities.

The TLT makes no distinction between trademarks and service marks (TLT art. 2(2)(a)), but does not apply to "collective marks, certification marks and guarantee marks" (TLT art. 2(2)(b)). Articles 3 and 13 set forth uniform filing and renewal processes to be followed by all member states. The TLT also incorporates by reference the terms of the Paris Convention (TLT art. 15) and makes the Paris Convention's terms regarding trademarks applicable to service marks as well (TLT art. 16).

Substantively, the TLT sets a uniform trademark term of ten years, renewable an indefinite number of times for ten-year periods (TLT art. 13(7)). Prior to the Trademark Law Treaty Act, U.S. law had required that each application for renewal be accompanied by a declaration or proof that the mark was actually being used; the TLT provides that no such proof may be required (TLT art. 13(6)), and the Trademark Law Treaty Act altered U.S. law accordingly. However, the substance of the requirement remains; trademark holders in the United States now have an obligation, independent of the renewal process, to file a declaration that the mark is being used (McCarthy 2004, 614).

Treaty
• Trademark Law Treaty, Oct. 27, 1994, available at http://www.wipo.int/clea/docs/en/wo/wo027en.htm (visited August 1, 2004)

Statute
• Trademark Law Treaty Act of 1998, 15 U.S.C. § 1051

See also: International Trademark Protection; Trademark; WIPO

Sources and further reading:
J. Thomas McCarthy et al., *McCarthy's Desk Encyclopedia of Intellectual Property,* 3d ed. (Washington, DC: Bureau of National Affairs, 2004).

Keith M. Stolte, "Functionality Challenges to Incontestable Trademark Registrations before and after the Trademark Law Treaty Implementation Act," 92 *The Trademark Reporter* 1094 (2002).

❖ TRADEMARK REGISTRATION TREATY ❖

See Madrid Agreement and Madrid Protocol.

❖ TRIPS ❖

The Agreement on Trade-Related Aspects of Intellectual Property Rights is almost invariably known by its acronym, TRIPS. In 1994, at the conclusion of the Uruguay Round of negotiations under the General Agreement on Tariffs and Trade (GATT) that gave rise to the World Trade Organization (WTO), TRIPS was adopted as Annex 1C to the Marrakesh Agreement Establishing the World Trade Organization (WTO). All countries that become parties to the WTO become parties to TRIPS.

TRIPS is a comprehensive intellectual property treaty: It covers the traditional areas of copyright, trademark, and patent, as well as other areas such as geographical indications, industrial designs, integrated circuit layouts, and trade secrets. Some of these rights, such as copyright, have both influenced and been influenced by changes in information technology; others, such as rights in geographical indications, have had little or no application to date in a computer and Internet law context.

Articles 3 and 4 of TRIPS require national treatment and most-favored nation treatment, respectively, with regard to all intellectual property rights covered by the agreement. "National treatment" means that states that are parties to TRIPS must accord to all other parties the same level of protection that they accord to their own nationals. "Most favored nation treatment" is a confusing term; it can create the incorrect impression that a country is being singled out for preferential treatment. In fact, most favored nation treatment has the opposite effect: All parties are required to give to each other party the same level of treatment that they give to the nation they most favor, so that in effect no country is favored over any other and all receive the same level of treatment. To avoid an undue hardship on developing countries, Part VI (Articles 65–67) of TRIPS contains transitional provisions; developing countries are permitted to make some exceptions to TRIPS standards under certain conditions and are given a longer period of time to phase in their TRIPS obligations.

Treaties
- Agreement between the World Intellectual Property Organization and the World Trade Organization, Dec. 22, 1995, 35 I.L.M. 754 (1996)
- Agreement on Trade-Related Aspects of Intellectual Property Rights, Marrakesh Agreement Establishing the World Trade Organization, Annex 1C, Apr. 15, 1994, 33 I.L.M. 81 (1994)

Statutes
- Copyright Act of 1976, 17 U.S.C. §§ 101–1332

See also: Copyright; International Copyright Protection; International Patent Protection; International Trademark Protection; Patent; Trademark; TRIPS (Copyright); TRIPS (Industrial Designs and Integrated Circuit Layouts); TRIPS (Patent); TRIPS (Trade Secrets); TRIPS (Trademark); WIPO

Sources and further reading:
Michael Blakeney, *Trade Related Aspects of Intellectual Property Rights* (London: Sweet and Maxwell Ltd., 1996).
Lonnie T. Brown and Eric A. Szweda, *Trade Related Aspects of Intellectual Property* (Buffalo, NY: William S. Hein, 1990).
Anthony D'Amato and Doris Estelle Long, eds., *International Intellectual Property Anthology* (Cincinnati, OH: Anderson Publishing, 1996).
Susan K. Sell, *Private Power, Public Law: The Globalization of Intellectual Property Rights* (Cambridge: Cambridge University Press, 2003).
Terence P. Stewart: *The GATT Uruguay Round: A Negotiating History (1986–1992): Trade-Related Aspects of Intellectual Property* (Dordrecht, Netherlands: Kluwer Academic Publishers, 1993).

❖ TRIPS (COPYRIGHT) ❖

The substantive copyright provisions of TRIPS take as their starting point the Berne Convention. Article 9(2) provides that copyright protection under TRIPS, as under U.S. copyright law, "shall extend to expressions and not to ideas, procedures, methods of operation or mathematical concepts as such." Article 9(1) of TRIPS provides that members of the WTO "shall comply with Articles 1 through 21 of the Berne Convention (1971) and the Appendix thereto," with one exception. The exception is Article 6bis of the Berne Convention, which deals with moral rights: Members of the WTO "shall not have rights or obligations under this Agreement in respect of the rights conferred under Article 6bis of that Convention or of the rights derived therefrom." Moral rights, in copyright law, include noneconomic rights such as the right not to have one's work mutilated or distorted, the right to be acknowledged as the author of the work, and the right to determine when and in what fashion the work shall be presented to the public. U.S. law, in contrast to European law, historically has not been receptive to the concept of moral rights. Under the pressure of international copyright agreements, notably the Berne Convention, the United States has begun to adopt limited moral rights protections such as the Visual Artists' Rights Act (17 U.S.C. § 106A). The protection of moral rights in the United States is hindered, however, both by reluctance to acknowledge a noneconomic dimension to copyright and by the First Amendment.

TRIPS reflects the concerns of the United States to a far greater degree than does the Berne Convention, as the exception of Article 6*bis* shows. The United States did not become a party to the Berne Convention for more than a century after its initial adoption; in contrast, the United States played a major role in the drafting of TRIPS.

The terms of the Berne Convention that are incorporated into TRIPS by the reference in Article 9(1) include provisions defining the subject matter to be protected, setting minimum terms of protection for various classes of materials, and defining the rights to be conferred and permissible limitations to those rights. Article 12 of TRIPS, like Article 7 of the Berne Convention, sets a minimum copyright term for most works of the lifetime of the author plus fifty years. Article 10 of TRIPS specifically gives protection to computer programs, and Article 11 deals with rental rights. The 1971 revision of the Berne Convention had previously provided that computer programs were to be protected as literary works. Article 10 of TRIPS adds detail: Computer programs are to be protected as literary works whether expressed in source code or object code. Compilations of data, electronic or otherwise, are also protected if (and only if) "by reason of the selection or arrangement of their contents" they "constitute intellectual creations." This could conceivably give wider protection to data compilations than is currently afforded under U.S. copyright law. In the 1991 case of *Feist Publications v. Rural Telephone Service*, the U.S. Supreme Court rejected the idea that mere effort in compiling data—the "sweat of the brow"—entitles the compiler to copyright protection. The Court held that under the Copyright Act originality, rather than mere effort, is required. The "intellectual" element of the term *intellectual creations* does not seem to require originality, although perhaps the "creations" element does (499 U.S. 340).

Copyright protection of a data compilation does not create any copyright in the data itself; if the data was originally within the public domain, it remains in the public domain, even if the compilation is protected by copyright. It would thus be permissible, for example, for someone else to arrange the data in a manner sufficiently different to constitute a new "intellectual creation" (TRIPS art. 10(2)).

Authors of computer programs, sound recordings, and, in certain circumstances, of motion pictures are to be provided with the right to authorize or to prohibit the commercial rental of those works, although in the case of motion pictures ("cinematographic works") member states are exempt from the obligation unless motion picture rentals have led to widespread copying that materially impairs the exclusive right of reproduction; in other words, this provision is meant to be applied only against states in which video piracy is widespread. With regard to computer programs, Article 11 provides that "this obligation does not apply to rentals where the program itself is not the essential object of the rental." In other words, a company that rents out equipment—cars, boats, aircraft, power tools, video camcorders—is in the business of renting equipment, not software. Even though the equipment may, and probably does, contain software, the software is not the object of the rental. TRIPS would thus not require its member states to require these equipment-rental companies to first obtain the software author's consent to the rental (TRIPS art. 11).

Article 14 deals with live performances, sound recordings, and broadcasting organizations. The performers of live audio performances "shall have the possibility" (the word *right* is not used) "of preventing the fixation" or broadcast of their performances. Producers of sound recordings ("phonograms") "shall enjoy the right to authorize or prohibit the direct or indirect reproduction of their phonograms." Performers and producers are to be given the exclusive reproduction and rental rights to their recordings for a minimum term of fifty years, although Article 14(4) provides that states that had "in force a system of equitable remuneration of right holders in respect of the rental of phonograms" are grandfathered in and do not need to alter their existing laws to conform to the Article 14 standard. Articles 14(3) and 14(5) set forth the right of broadcasting organizations to prevent unauthorized recording, reproduction, or rebroadcast of their broadcasts for a minimum term of twenty years.

It is Article 13, however, that represents the greatest departure from what has gone before and consequently has triggered the greatest controversy. Article 13 states, somewhat opaquely, "[m]embers shall confine limitations or exceptions to exclusive rights to certain special cases which do not conflict with a normal exploitation of the work and do not unreasonably prejudice the legitimate interests of the right holder." This provision was ostensibly intended to prevent nations with poor records of copyright enforcement from multiplying exceptions and limitations to the point that they effectively eviscerated those nations' copyright laws. However, it is also seen as an attack on the fair use exception. It benefits U.S. and other developed-country content owners at the expense of content consumers. Because the content industries of the developed countries provided input during the process of drafting TRIPS, some believe that the content industry used TRIPS as an "end run" to achieve through international law what could not be achieved through the domestic political process.

Article 13 is based on the three-step test in Article 9(2) of the Berne Convention, but goes further and can more readily be enforced. The three steps of the Article 13 test provide that exceptions to the exclusive rights of the copyright holder may be made in:

(1) Certain special cases

(2) Which do not conflict with a normal exploitation of the work, and

(3) Do not unreasonably prejudice the legitimate interests of the right holder.

In other words, a country that is a party to TRIPS can permit unauthorized reproduction of a work only in certain special cases. The permitted reproduction must not conflict with normal exploitation of the work and must not unreasonably prejudice the legitimate interest of the content owner. There are a number of abstractions here that beg for further definition.

It is not readily apparent, for example, what cases are "special," what degree of prejudice is "unreasonable," or what interests are "legitimate." A kindergarten teacher who copies a magazine article might or might not fall within the "special cases" category; the teacher's copying would conflict with the normal exploitation of the work (if, in the alternative, the teacher would have had to purchase copies of the work) and would consequently prejudice the interests of the right holder, although it is also unclear whether the right holder's interests in this case would be legitimate and even less clear whether the prejudice would be unreasonable.

Treaties

- Agreement on Trade-Related Aspects of Intellectual Property Rights, Marrakesh Agreement Establishing the World Trade Organization, Annex 1C, Apr. 15, 1994, 33 I.L.M. 81 (1994)
- Convention Concerning the Creation of an International Union for the Protection of Literary and Artistic Works (Berne Convention), Sept. 9, 1886, as last revised at Paris, July 24, 1971 (amended 1979), 25 U.S.T. 1341, 828 U.N.T.S. 221
- Universal Copyright Convention, Sept. 6, 1952, 6 U.S.T. 2731, revised at Paris July 24, 1971, 25 U.S.T. 1341
- WIPO Copyright Treaty, Dec. 20, 1996, 36 I.L.M. 65 (1997)
- WIPO Performances and Phonograms Treaty, Dec. 20, 1996, 36 I.L.M. 76 (1997)

Statutes

- Copyright Act of 1976, 17 U.S.C. §§ 101–1332
- Visual Artists' Rights Act, 17 U.S.C. § 106A

Case

- *Feist Publications v. Rural Telephone Service Co.*, 499 U.S. 340 (1991)

See also: Berne Convention; Copyright; Copyright Infringement; International Copyright Protection; Universal Copyright Convention;

WIPO; WIPO Copyright Treaty; WIPO Performances and Phonograms Treaty

Sources and further reading:
Paul Goldstein, *International Copyright: Principles, Law, and Practice* (Oxford: Oxford University Press, 2000).
Makeen Fouad Makeen, *Copyright in a Global Information Society: The Scope of Copyright Protection Under International, US, UK, and French Law* (New York: Aspen, 2001).

❖ TRIPS (INDUSTRIAL DESIGNS AND INTEGRATED CIRCUIT LAYOUTS) ❖

Industrial designs that are not eligible for patent, copyright, or trademark protection may nonetheless be protected as intellectual property; an example of such protection can be found in Title V of the Digital Millennium Copyright Act (DMCA). TRIPS provides that World Trade Organization (WTO) "Members shall provide for the protection of independently created industrial designs that are new or original" (TRIPS art. 25.1). The rights thus protected shall include "the right to prevent third parties . . . from making, selling or importing articles bearing or embodying a design which is a copy, or substantially a copy, of the protected design, when such acts are undertaken for commercial purposes" for a period of at least ten years (TRIPS art. 26).

The mask work used to create semiconductor chips is another category of intellectual property that doesn't fit neatly into conventional definitions; it is protected separately from industrial designs, but the protection granted under TRIPS is similar. Members of the WTO "agree to provide protection to the layout-designs (topographies) of integrated circuits . . . in accordance with" selected substantive provisions of the Treaty on Intellectual Property in Respect of Integrated Circuits (TRIPS art. 35). As with industrial designs, the protection lasts for a minimum of ten years (TRIPS art. 38). During that time, the owner of the right shall have the sole authority to authorize "importing, selling, or otherwise distributing for commercial purposes a protected layout-design, an integrated circuit in which a protected layout-design is incorporated, or an article incorporating such an integrated circuit only in so far as it continues to contain an unlawfully reproduced layout-design" (TRIPS art. 36), although innocent third parties are protected from liability for use of chips incorporating infringing designs (TRIPS art. 37).

Treaties
- Agreement on Trade-Related Aspects of Intellectual Property Rights, Marrakesh Agreement Establishing the World Trade Organization, Annex 1C, Apr. 15, 1994, 33 I.L.M. 81 (1994)
- Hague Agreement Concerning the International Deposit of Industrial Designs, Nov. 6, 1925, 74 L.N.T.S. 343, revised at London, June 2, 1934, 205 L.N.T.S. 179, revised at The Hague, Nov. 28, 1960; supplemented by the Additional Act of Monaco, Nov. 18, 1961, the Complementary Act of Stockholm, July 14, 1967, and the Protocol of Geneva, April 10, 1975, 26 U.S.T. 571; and as amended, Sept. 1979
- Locarno Agreement Establishing an International Classification for Industrial Designs, Oct. 8, 1968, as amended Sept. 28, 1979, 23 U.S.T. 1389
- Paris Convention for the Protection of Industrial Property, Mar. 20, 1883, as revised at Brussels on Dec. 14, 1900, at Washington on June 2, 1911, at The Hague on Nov. 6, 1925, at London on June 2, 1934, at Lisbon on Oct. 31, 1958, and at Stockholm on July 14, 1967, and as amended on Sept. 28, 1979, 21 U.S.T. 1583, 828 U.N.T.S. 305
- Treaty on Intellectual Property in Respect of Integrated Circuits, Washington, May 26, 1989, 28 I.L.M. 1477 (1989)

Statutes
- Digital Millennium Copyright Act, Title V, 17 U.S.C. §§ 1301–1332

- Semiconductor Chip Protection Act, 17 U.S.C. §§ 901–914

See also: Digital Millennium Copyright Act, Title V; Intellectual Property; Semiconductor Manufacturing Mask Work Registrations; TRIPS

❖ TRIPS (PATENT) ❖

TRIPS provides that "patents shall be available for any inventions, whether products or processes, in all fields of technology," with certain exceptions, for at least "a period of twenty years counted from the filing date" (TRIPS arts. 27, 33). The length of the patent term in the United States, originally seventeen years from the date the patent was granted, was changed to twenty years from the date of filing to conform to the TRIPS norm (35 U.S.C. § 154(a)(2)). The protection "for any inventions, whether products or processes" has been interpreted as requiring members to issue business methods patents, such as the controversial patent on one-click ordering. These patents were authorized in the United States by the decision of the Federal Circuit Court of Appeals in the 1998 case of *State Street Bank & Trust* (149 F.3d 1368).

Under TRIPS, WTO members must grant patent holders the exclusive right to prevent others from "making, using, offering for sale, selling, or importing" a patented product, or products made by a patented process (TRIPS art. 28). The patent holder's rights must be alienable—that is, the inventor must be able to sell, license, or give away the patent rights (TRIPS art. 28).

Treaties
- Agreement on Trade-Related Aspects of Intellectual Property Rights, Marrakesh Agreement Establishing the World Trade Organization, Annex 1C, Apr. 15, 1994, 33 I.L.M. 81 (1994)
- Paris Convention for the Protection of Industrial Property, Mar. 20, 1883, as revised at Brussels on Dec. 14, 1900, at Washington on June 2, 1911, at The Hague on Nov. 6, 1925, at London on June 2, 1934, at Lisbon on Oct. 31, 1958, and at Stockholm on July 14, 1967, and as amended on Sept. 28, 1979, 21 U.S.T. 1583, 828 U.N.T.S. 305
- Patent Cooperation Treaty, Washington on June 19, 1970, as amended on Sept. 28, 1979, and as modified on February 3, 1984, and October 3, 2001, 28 U.S.T. 7645, 9 I.L.M. 978 (1970)
- Patent Law Treaty, June 1, 2000, 39 I.L.M. 1047 (2000)

Statute
- Patent Code, 35 U.S.C. §§ 1–376

Case
- *State Street Bank & Trust Co. v. Signature Financial Group,* 149 F.3d 1368 (Fed. Cir. 1998); cert. denied, 525 U.S. 1093

See also: Business Methods Patent; International Patent Protection; Paris Convention; Patent; Patent Cooperation Treaty; TRIPS; WIPO

Sources and further reading:
Graeme B. Dinwoodie et al., *International and Comparative Patent Law* (Newark, NJ: LexisNexis, 2002).
Nuno Pires de Carvalho, *The TRIPS Regime of Patent Rights* (The Hague: Kluwer Law International, 2002).

❖ TRIPS (TRADE SECRETS) ❖

Article 39 of TRIPS governs the protection of trade secrets by members of the World Trade Organization. To qualify for protection as a trade secret under TRIPS information must meet four requirements: It must be lawfully within the control of a natural or legal person; it must be "secret in the sense that it is not, as a body or in the precise configuration and assembly of its components, generally known among or readily accessible to persons within the circles that normally deal with the kind of information in question;" it must have "commercial value because it is secret;" and it must have "been subject to reasonable steps under the circumstances, by the person lawfully in control of the information, to keep it secret" (TRIPS art. 39(2)).

A person who has a trade secret is entitled to keep the information from being "disclosed to, acquired by, or used by others . . . in a manner contrary to honest commercial practices" (TRIPS art. 39(2)). WTO members are thus obliged to enact laws preventing their nationals from stealing others' trade secrets through "practices such as breach of contract, breach of confidence and inducement to breach" (TRIPS art. 39 n. 10).

The provisions of Article 39 are broadly similar to the provisions of U.S. trade secret law, and are subject to the same difficulty in implementation: Because trade secrets are, by their very nature, unknown until after they have been disclosed, regulators do not know the exact nature of the content they are protecting. Instead they must focus on the owner's desire to keep the content secret and the conduct by which another person thwarts that desire.

Treaties

- Agreement on Trade-Related Aspects of Intellectual Property Rights, Marrakesh Agreement Establishing the World Trade Organization, Annex 1C, Apr. 15, 1994, 33 I.L.M. 81 (1994)

See also: Trade Secret; TRIPS

❖ TRIPS (TRADEMARK) ❖

TRIPS sets uniform standards for the subject matter eligible for trademark protection and for the conditions under which trademark registration may be granted or refused. "Any sign, or any combination of signs, capable of distinguishing . . . goods or services . . ., shall be capable of constituting a trademark" (TRIPS art. 15(1)). TRIPS includes a non-exhaustive list of signs that may be eligible for trademark protection: "words including personal names, letters, numerals, figurative elements and combinations

of colours as well as any combination of such signs" (TRIPS art. 15(1)). Even signs "not inherently capable of distinguishing the relevant goods or services" can be trademarks, although in that case "Members may make registrability depend on distinctiveness acquired through use." In addition, "Members may require, as a condition of registration, that signs be visually perceptible" (TRIPS art. 15(1)).

Use of a trademark may be made a prerequisite of trademark registration, but may not be made a prerequisite of trademark application, nor may certain types of goods or services be excluded from eligibility for trademark protection (TRIPS art. 15). Once a trademark is registered, the trademark owner shall have the right to prevent others from using the mark for similar goods and services (TRIPS art. 16), although WTO members may make an exception for fair use (TRIPS art. 17). TRIPS provides for a minimum trademark term of seven years (TRIPS art. 18); U.S. law currently provides for a term of ten years (15 U.S.C. §§ 1058–1059). Trademark registrations may be lost through nonuse of the trademark for at least three years (TRIPS art. 19). Trademarks are alienable— they may be transferred by the owner—and are not subject to compulsory licensing (TRIPS art. 21).

Treaties

- Agreement on Trade-Related Aspects of Intellectual Property Rights, Marrakesh Agreement Establishing the World Trade Organization, Annex 1C, Apr. 15, 1994, 33 I.L.M. 81 (1994)
- Lisbon Agreement for the Protection of Appellations of Origin and their International Registration, Oct. 31, 1958, as revised at Stockholm on July 14, 1967, and as amended on Sept. 28, 1979, 923 U.N.T.S. 205
- Madrid Agreement Concerning the International Registration of Marks, Apr. 14, 1891, as revised at Brussels, Dec. 14, 1900, at Washington, June 2, 1911, at The Hague, Nov. 6, 1925, at London, June 2, 1934, at Nice, June 15, 1957, at Stockholm, July 14, 1967, and as amended Sept. 28, 1979,

available from http://www.wipo.int/
madrid/en/legal_texts/ (PDF
download)(visited November 9, 2004)
- Nice Agreement Concerning the
International Classification of Goods
and Services for the Purposes of the
Registration of Marks, June 15, 1957, as
revised at Stockholm on July 14, 1967,
and at Geneva on May 13, 1977, and
amended on Sept. 28, 1979, 23 U.S.T.
1336, 550 U.N.T.S. 45
- Protocol Relating to the Madrid
Agreement Concerning the
International Registration of Marks,
June 27, 1989, available from http://
www.wipo.int/madrid/en/legal_texts/
(PDF download) (visited November 9,
2004)
- Trademark Law Treaty, Oct. 27, 1994,
available at http://www.wipo.int/clea/
docs/en/wo/wo027en.htm (visited
August 1, 2004)
- Vienna Agreement Establishing an
International Classification of the
Figurative Elements of Marks, June 12,
1973, as amended Oct. 1, 1985,
available at http://www.wipo.int/clea/
docs/en/wo/wo031en.htm (visited
August 1, 2004)

Statutes
- Lanham Trademark Act, 15 U.S.C. §§
1058–1059

See also: Fair Use (Trademark); International
Trademark Protection; Trademark; TRIPS;
WIPO

Sources and further reading:
Christopher Arup, editor. *The New World Trade
Organization Agreements: Globalizing Law
through Services and Intellectual Property*
(Cambridge: Cambridge University Press
2000).

❖ TROJAN ❖

A Trojan, or Trojan Horse program, is a piece
of malicious software, or malware, that dis-

guises itself as some other program in order to
trick a user into installing it. Trojans can arrive
as e-mail attachments or be downloaded from
Web sites; they may even perform the function
of the program they purport to be. However,
they also perform other, often harmful functions. They may backdoor the computer on
which they are installed, making the computer
into a zombie for use in spamming or denial-
of-service attacks (Symantec 2004). But because this is a function better suited to worms,
which can replicate themselves, than to Trojans, the purpose of a Trojan is often more sinister. Trojans can serve to provide a remote
user with complete access to the computer on
which they are installed; the user can then perform mischievous pranks, destroy or alter some
or all of the data on the computer, or steal data
from the computer that can then be used for
identity theft and other forms of fraud, or even
blackmail.

The federal Computer Fraud and Abuse Act
(CFAA) of 1986 prohibits the malicious use of
Trojan programs (18 U.S.C. § 1030). The installation of a Trojan violates the CFAA's prohibition on knowingly or intentionally obtaining unauthorized access or exceeding
authorized access to another's computer, because it is accomplished by subterfuge. The
subterfuge is necessarily knowing or intentional; it cannot be accomplished by accident.
And the access is necessarily unauthorized or in
violation of the authorization granted, because
the victim believes that s/he is consenting to
the installation of some other program. The
2001 USA PATRIOT Act has increased the
maximum penalties available under the CFAA
to imprisonment for ten years for first offenders, and twenty years for repeat offenders
(Klang 2003, 171–172).

Nonetheless, Trojans persist, largely because of the difficulty of catching and convict-
ing the perpetrators. Users can guard themselves against Trojans with a combination of
software and common sense. Antivirus programs will detect many, but not all, Trojans.
Antispyware programs such as AdAware, Pest-
Patrol, and SpyBot Search & Destroy will
catch most of the rest, as will antispyware offerings from antivirus leaders McAfee and

Symantec, often available with deluxe versions of those companies' antispyware programs. And even if a spyware or remote-access Trojan is installed, proper use of a firewall such as ZoneAlarm can render it ineffective by preventing the Trojan from communicating with the outside world.

In addition, common sense should be used when installing software. Programs contained in attachments to spam or messages from unknown persons should never be trusted. Even attachments to messages purporting to be from a friend, coworker, or acquaintance should be viewed with skepticism; the person purportedly sending the message may not actually have done so, or may have been taken in by the Trojan. And downloads offered by Web sites should be refused unless the user has made a point of seeking out that particular download and knows what is being downloaded and what conditions are attached to it.

Statute

- Computer Fraud and Abuse Act, 18 U.S.C. § 1030

See also: Advertising; Adware and Spyware; Denial-of-Service Attack; Hacking; Malware; Privacy; Spam; Trademark; Worm; Zombie

Sources and further reading:

Robyn Greenspan, "The Deadly Duo: Spam and Viruses," May 2004, internetnews.com, June 7, 2004, available at http://www.internetnews.com/stats/article.php/3364421 (visited October 7, 2004).

Mathias Klang, "A Critical Look at the Regulation of Computer Viruses," 11 *International Journal of Law and Information Technology* 162 (2003).

Symantec U.S., "Security Response Glossary," 2004, http://securityresponse.symantec.com/avcenter/refa.html (visited November 13, 2004).

❖ TRUSTED COMPUTING ❖

See Digital Rights Management

❖ TYPOSQUATTING ❖

See Cybersquatting

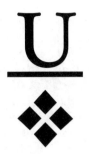

❖ UNIFORM COMPUTER INFORMATION TRANSACTIONS ACT ❖

The Uniform Computer Information Transactions Act (UCITA) is a uniform act approved and proposed (to the states) by the National Conference of Commissioners on Uniform State Laws. The commissioners have approved and proposed many such acts over the years; they play an important role in ensuring a relative uniformity of laws among the states of the United States. Of course, states may deliberately choose to adopt different laws, but the commissioners work to prevent the laws of the states from drifting too far apart by accident or inadvertence rather than by design.

UCITA has proven controversial; it has been opposed by consumer advocates, including the attorneys general of several states (Letter from Attorneys General, 1999). Maryland and Virginia are the only states to have adopted UCITA (Ring 2003); other states have apparently been swayed by arguments that UCITA would unfairly tilt the balance of bargaining power in software licensing agreements and related transactions, resulting in harm to consumers. In opposing UCITA, the state attorneys general constructed this scenario:

> Jane Consumer purchases a piece of software that promises analysis and advice concerning various investment options. When she installs the software, she learns from a message displayed during the installation process that she must subscribe to a proprietary information service to use it, rather than the competing service she already uses to obtain such information. Even though other similar software packages are available which do not impose such requirements, Jane is loathe to begin the shopping process over again in order to decide which of those packages to purchase, so she accepts the new terms. Jane subscribes to the new information service, selecting a discounted 1 year agreement rather than a full price month to month agreement, and logs onto the system for the first time. (Letter from Attorneys General, 1999)

This, it turns out, is a bad decision on Jane's part. As soon as Jane logs on, she is "presented a screen which contains a hyperlink in the upper left hand corner labeled 'important information.' She is also presented with a flashing icon calling her attention to a hot stock tip." The stock tip distracts her, and when she returns to the logon screen the "important information" button is gone. Six months later, "a package arrives in the mail. It is an upgrade to her investment analysis software. Because she did not order the upgrade and there is nothing contained in the package advising her otherwise, she assumes it is a free bug fix upgrade." It is not, of course, although it seems more likely that the upgrade, free or otherwise, would be downloaded rather than received in the mail. Jane misguidedly installs the upgrade and uses the upgraded software for the first time a few weeks later; this time she clicks the "important information" link and learns that "she will be billed $49.95 for the software because she failed to return it within 7 days of receipt as required by the upgrade service provisions of her original contract." She was unaware of this provision, because she never clicked the original "important information" link (Letter from Attorneys General, 1999).

Jane's problems continue to worsen, as the software vendor finds more ways of extracting more money from her than she ever believed she would pay; she cannot escape until her original twelve-month contract has run its course. The attorneys general point out that all of the vendor's actions would be legal under UCITA; all that would protect Jane would be the vendor's own scruples and its desire to maintain a good reputation. UCITA's advocates, on the other hand, argue that there is already a tendency in case law toward enforcement of contractual provisions of which consumers might be unaware, and that UCITA would actually curb this trend (Ring 2003, 35).

Uniform Act
- Uniform Computer Information Transactions Act, available at http://www.law.upenn.edu/bll/ulc/ucita/ucita200.htm (visited November 14, 2004)

See also: Clickwrap Agreement; Contracts; E-commerce

Sources and further reading:
Letter to NCCUSL from Attorneys General Opposing UCITA, July 23, 1999, available at http://www.arl.org/info/frn/copy/agoppltr.html (visited November 14, 2004).
Carlyle C. Ring Jr., *Understanding Electronic Contracting 2003 The Impact of Regulation, New Laws and New Agreements: Overview of the Legal Landscape of E-Commerce*, Practising Law Institute Patents, Copyrights, Trademarks, and Literary Property Course Handbook Series, April 2003.

❖ UNIVERSAL COPYRIGHT CONVENTION ❖

For twelve decades the primary multilateral treaty governing international copyright law has been the Berne Convention. For the first century of the Berne Convention's existence, however, U.S. copyright law diverged too greatly from the Berne Convention norm for the United States to become a party to the convention. Instead, U.S. copyright relations were governed by various bilateral treaties, by a multilateral treaty with the countries of Latin America (the Buenos Aires Convention), and, from the 1950s through the 1980s, by the Universal Copyright Convention (U.C.C.).

The U.C.C. was developed under the auspices of the United Nations Educational, Scientific and Cultural Organization and adopted in 1952; the drafters had to balance the divergent concerns of major nonparties to the Berne Convention such as the United States, which exported copyrighted information, and the Soviet Union, which was deeply suspicious of a copyright regime that would protect primarily the interests of capitalist countries. The U.C.C. came into force for the United States in 1955 and went through a major revision in 1971 to take into account certain concerns of developing countries, many of which had not existed as independent nations in 1955. The earlier and later versions of the U.C.C. are often referred to as the Geneva U.C.C. and the Paris U.C.C., respectively.

As with the Berne Convention, the core requirement of the U.C.C. is national treatment: Article II of both the Geneva U.C.C. and the Paris U.C.C. require parties to the convention to extend to foreign copyright holders and foreign copyrighted works the same copyright protections that they extend to works of their own nationals first published in their own territory.

In contrast to the Berne Convention, which requires no formalities for copyright registration other than the name of the author (and even makes allowances for works that are published without identifying the author), Article III of both the Geneva and the Paris U.C.C. includes a minimal but nonetheless real registration requirement: the use of the symbol "©" upon the work together with the year of first publication and the name of the person claiming copyright. This is all the registration that can be required for foreign works, even if a state requires a more formal registration process for its own nationals; the possibility thus exists that a state might treat foreign copyright holders more favorably than its own nationals. Not coincidentally, this was also, more or less, the notice required under the United States Copyright Act of 1909 and, before its amendment by the Berne Convention Implementation Act of 1988, under the Copyright Act of 1976.

Article IV deals with the duration of the copyright term. This was, at the time of the adoption of both the Geneva and the Paris U.C.C., the central and irreconcilable point of difference between U.S. law and the Berne Convention. U.S. law provided for a twenty-eight-year copyright term, renewable once; registration was required for both the initial and the renewal term. The Berne Convention required, for most printed works, a minimum term of the lifetime of the author plus fifty years. Article IV(3) of the Geneva and Paris U.C.C. requires a minimum term of the life of the author plus twenty-five years, but for countries (such as the United States) that computed the copyright term from the date of initial publication, the minimum term was twenty-five years from the date of publication. This made it possible for the United States to become a party to the convention without revising the copyright law then in effect, the Copyright Act of 1909.

Other protections provided by the U.C.C. are also generally less broad than those provided by the Berne Convention. It was anticipated that the Berne Convention parties would want to become parties to the U.C.C. as well, in order to gain the benefits of a multilateral copyright regime that included the United States and the other nonparties to the Berne Convention. To prevent these countries from picking and choosing those provisions of each convention that they found most congenial, Article XVII of the U.C.C. includes a Berne Safeguard Clause. This clause provides that no country that is a party to the Berne Convention may denounce that convention and choose instead to rely on the U.C.C. in copyright matters relating to other Berne Convention parties.

Ninety-eight states are now parties to the Geneva U.C.C., the Paris U.C.C., or both. However, ninety-six of those states are also parties to the Berne Convention, so the U.C.C. is very nearly a dead letter in international law: Once the United States, for example, became a party to the Berne Convention, the Berne Safeguard Clause prevented it from relying on the less stringent requirements of the U.C.C. in its relations with the other Berne Convention parties. The U.C.C. does, however, continue to govern U.S. copyright relations with Cambodia and Laos, because those countries are parties to the U.C.C. but not to the Berne Convention.

Treaties

- Convention Concerning the Creation of an International Union for the Protection of Literary and Artistic Works (Berne Convention), Sept. 9, 1886, as last revised at Paris, July 24, 1971 (amended 1979), 25 U.S.T. 1341, 828 U.N.T.S. 221
- Universal Copyright Convention, Sept. 6, 1952, 6 U.S.T. 2731, revised at Paris July 24, 1971, 25 U.S.T. 1341

Statutes

- Copyright Act of 1909, 17 U.S.C. §§ 1–216 (repealed 1976)
- Copyright Act of 1976, 17 U.S.C. §§ 101–1332

See also: Berne Convention; Copyright; International Copyright Protection

Sources and further reading:
Paul Goldstein, *International Copyright: Principles, Law, and Practice* (Oxford: Oxford University Press, 2000).

V

❖ VESSEL HULL DESIGN PROTECTION ACT ❖

See Digital Millennium Copyright Act, Title V

❖ VIRUS ❖

A computer virus is a program that replicates itself by inserting copies of itself into other programs or documents, much as a biological virus reproduces by inserting its genetic material into a host cell and causing the host cell to reproduce copies of the virus. The term *virus* is sometimes used in the media to refer to other types of malware as well, especially worms. Worms, however, make complete copies of themselves; they do not rely on other programs for reproduction or insert copies of themselves into other files.

The etymology of the term *virus* is more clouded than that of the term *worm*. By the early 1980s, however, the term was in everyday use in its present sense. In the United States the creation, use, or dissemination of viruses is governed by the Computer Fraud and Abuse Act (CFAA) of 1986 (18 U.S.C. § 1030). The CFAA, in extremely lengthy and, to nonlawyers, inscrutably complex terms, makes it unlawful for any person to intentionally or knowingly obtain unauthorized access to a computer, exceed authorized access, or transmit "a program, information, code, or command" that causes damage to another's computer. Viruses and other malware fall within this last prohibition; they can also, by replicating themselves or enabling other malware, gain access to a computer or exceed authorized access (see *Morris,* 928 F.2d 504).

The 2001 USA PATRIOT Act increased the range of penalties available for violations of § 1030, including those who spread computer viruses. At the lower end of the culpability scale, the act eliminated mandatory minimum sentences for relatively minor offenders. At the upper end, the act doubled the previous ceilings of five years for first offenses and ten years for repeat offenders; serious virus offenders can now receive prison sentences of ten years for a first offense and twenty years for repeat offenses (Klang 2003, 171–172).

As with biological viruses, many computer viruses do little or no harm. Some can be destructive, however, corrupting or deleting files on the computers they infect, or slowing down or crashing those computers. Because worms offer advantages to malicious users who wish to gain access to other users' computers, worms are replacing viruses as the Internet's most common malware; matters are confused by the media's habit of referring to worms as viruses. Like worms, viruses can best be avoided through the frequent use and updating of antivirus software and through common sense when opening attachments or downloading programs. Most antivirus programs scan incoming e-mail for viruses; however, even if the software detects no virus, there should never be a reason to open an attachment to a spam e-mail, or to click on any link (including, and especially, the bogus "unsubscribe" link in many spam messages). And no unfamiliar downloads, or downloads from unfamiliar Web sites, should ever be accepted.

Statute

- Computer Fraud and Abuse Act, 18 U.S.C. § 1030

Case

- *United States v. Morris*, 928 F.2d 504 (2nd Cir. 1991)

See also: Hacking; Malware; Trojan; Worm; Zombie

Sources and further reading:
Mathias Klang, "A Critical Look at the Regulation of Computer Viruses," 11 *International Journal of Law and Information Technology* 162 (2003).
Tiernan Ray, "E-mail Viruses Blamed as Spam Rises Sharply," *Seattle Times*, Feb. 18, 2004, available at http://seattletimes.nwsource.com/html/businesstechnology/2001859752_spamdoubles18.html (visited November 13, 2004).

❖ VOLUNTARY COLLECTIVE LICENSE ❖

A voluntary collective license is a license under which a copyright owner relinquishes the right to choose the licensee, without relinquishing the right to be paid. Anyone may copy and distribute a copyrighted work under a voluntary license, so long as he or she pays the fee set in the license (Ginsburg 1992, 383 n. 209). Open source works are generally distributed under some form of voluntary license, such as the GNU/Linux General Public License; under these licenses no payment is required, but certain other conditions are imposed. A voluntary collective license differs from a compulsory license, which requires owners of certain types of intellectual property rights to license those rights to all who pay a fee, and under which the fee is generally set and collected by a government agency (McCarthy 2004, 86–90).

Voluntary collective licensing has been proposed by the Electronic Frontier Foundation (EFF), an activist group, as a solution to the problem of file-sharing and music piracy. Under the EFF's proposal,

> the music industry forms a collecting society, which then offers file-sharing music fans the opportunity to "get legit" in exchange for a reasonable regular payment, say $5 per month. So long as they pay, the fans are free to keep doing what they are going to do anyway—share the music they love using whatever software they like on whatever computer platform they prefer—without fear of lawsuits. The money collected gets divided among rights-holders based on the popularity of their music. (EFF White Paper 2004)

The EFF explains that the music industry has used collective licensing in the past to confront new technology:

> Songwriters originally viewed radio exactly the way the music industry today views KaZaA users—as pirates. After trying to sue radio out of existence, the songwriters ultimately got together to form ASCAP [American Society of Composers, Authors and Publishers] . . . (and later BMI [Broadcast Music, Inc.] and SESAC [Society of European Stage Authors and Composers]). Radio stations interested in broadcasting music stepped up, paid a fee, and in return got to play whatever music they liked, using whatever equipment worked best. Today, the performing-rights societies ASCAP and BMI collect money and pay out millions annually to their artists. Even though these collecting societies get a fair bit of criticism, there's no question that the system that has evolved for radio is preferable to one based on trying to sue radio out of existence one broadcaster at a time. (EFF White Paper 2004)

The proposal may be reasonable; however, the current state of extreme polarization between the music content industry and enterprises involved in file sharing may make it difficult to reach agreement in the near future. There are signs that an agreement of some sort could eventually be reached, however, even if the terms differ from those in the EFF's proposal. Two major music companies are already reportedly in the process of reaching agreements with file-sharing networks: Sony-BMG is reportedly negotiating with Grokster, and Vivendi Universal Music Group will reportedly license its music to Snocap, a service run by Napster founder Shawn Fanning (*Economist* 2004).

See also: Activism and Advocacy Groups; Content Industry; Copyright; File-Sharing; Open-Source; P2P; Piracy; Recording Industry Association of America

Sources and further reading:

Electronic Frontier Foundation, *A Better Way Forward: Voluntary Collective Licensing of Music File Sharing,* "Let the Music Play" White Paper, Feb. 2004, available from http://www.eff.org/share/collective_lic_wp.php (PDF download) (visited November 16, 2004).

June C. Ginsburg, "No 'Sweat'? Copyright and Other Protection of Works of Information after Feist v. Rural Telephone," *Columbia Law Review* 338 (1992).

GNU/Linux General Public License, available at http://www.gnu.org/copyleft/gpl.html (visited November 16, 2004).

"I Want My P2P: Record Labels Are Trying to Do Deals with File-Sharing Networks," *The Economist,* Nov. 20, 2004, at 65.

J. Thomas McCarthy et al., *McCarthy's Desk Encyclopedia of Intellectual Property,* 3d ed. (Washington, DC: Bureau of National Affairs, 2004).

❖ WAREZ ❖

Warez are unauthorized copies of copyrighted computer software, unlawfully traded over the Internet or directly between users. The term is sometimes also used to refer to unauthorized copies of other types of copyrighted material, particularly movies. The term combines "ware" (short for software) with "wares" (goods). Warez trading begins with the cracking of the copy protection on the program or movie, if any, and the making of an unprotected copy. This copy can then be traded among warez groups, from which it will eventually leak into the mainstream Internet community through file-sharing services. It can also be recorded on disks and sold as a counterfeit of the original program.

There are distinctions among warezers. Those who create warez and distribute them for free tend to distinguish themselves from counterfeiters who sell pirated software for a profit, although their activities may still be illegal. These nonprofit warezers seem to be motivated primarily by an interest in demonstrating their technical prowess. An element of hostility to the copyright holders is also present, although some warezers argue that the distribution of warez actually increases demand for legitimate copies of the program.

A special subcategory of warez is abandonware—software that is no longer being sold or supported by its author, copyright owner, or licensed distributor. Abandonware traders seem to see themselves as archivists or historians rather than as pirates; many are motivated by enthusiasm for outdated software rather than by the technical rivalry that is evident in much of the rest of the warez community. They make the argument that, because the software is no longer being sold, the copyright holders are losing no sales as a result of the abandonware trading. Although this might be a convincing argument from an ethical standpoint, it is less so from a legal standpoint: Abandonware trading, like all warez trading, is illegal (Goldman 2004, 397).

The first warez trader to be prosecuted in the United States was David LaMacchia, a student. LaMacchia was an enthusiast, rather than a commercial warez trader, and thus could not be charged with criminal copyright infringement under the law of the time, which required that the infringement be done for financial gain. Instead, he was charged with conspiracy to commit wire fraud. The trial court dismissed the charge against him, though, because an earlier Supreme Court decision had held that an intellectual property interest in copyright could not be taken by fraud unless Congress had specifically stated otherwise (*LaMacchia*, 871 F.Supp. at 545). The dismissal of charges against LaMacchia ultimately led to the passage of the 1997 No Electronic Theft Act (NET Act), which was specifically intended "to reverse the practical consequences of United States v. LaMacchia" (House Report, 339). The NET Act was aimed at warez trading and greatly expanded the scope of actions subject to criminal copyright infringement penalties. It expanded the definition of "financial gain" to include "the receipt of other copyrighted works" (17 U.S.C. § 101); it criminalized the unauthorized reproduction of copyrighted works with a value in excess of $1,000 even if the infringement was *not* for financial gain (17 U.S.C. § 506); and it increased the statute of limitations for criminal copyright infringement from three years to five years (17 U.S.C. § 507).

After an initial period of inactivity, the Justice Department began to pursue warez traders aggressively, breaking up long-established groups such as the notorious DrinkOrDie (Tresco *Slashdot* interview 2002). By February 2004, at least eighty warez traders had been convicted; many, including enthusiast warez traders, were sent to prison (Goldman 2004, 427).

In addition to the NET Act, warez traders may be prosecuted under the Digital Millennium Copyright Act (DMCA), the Computer Fraud and Abuse Act (CFAA), and the Economic Espionage Act (EEA). Two provisions of the DMCA are applicable: the anticircumvention provisions codified at 17 U.S.C. § 1201 and the digital rights management provisions codified at 17 U.S.C. § 1202. The anticircumvention provisions prohibit the circumvention of "a technological measure that effectively controls access to a work" (17 U.S.C. § 1201(a)(1)(A)). Ostensibly this provision is aimed only at access, not at copying, but with some programs and most DVDs access is necessary for copying. Cracking, or circumventing copy protection, is an essential part of the warez process.

Copyrighted programs and other material also contain copyright management information; in the course of unauthorized copying this information may be removed or modified. Section 1202 is titled "integrity of copyright management information." Copyright management information that might be found on computer software and is protected by section 1202 includes information identifying and about the title, author, and copyright owner; terms and conditions under which the program may be used; "identifying numbers or symbols referring to such information or links to such information"; and "such other information as the Register of Copyrights may prescribe by regulation" (17 U.S.C. § 1202(c)).

The knowing use of false copyright management information "with the intent to induce, enable, facilitate, or conceal infringement" is prohibited by § 1202(a). The intentional removal or alteration of the copyright manage-

ment information is prohibited by § 1202(b)(1), and the unauthorized distribution of works from which the copyright management information has been removed or altered—a charge to which warez traders are particularly vulnerable—is prohibited by § 1202(3).

Section 1204 provides criminal penalties for violations of sections 1201 and 1202, while section 1203 provides civil remedies.

The antihacking Computer Fraud and Abuse Act, like the DMCA, contains provisions that may be used to prosecute warez traders. Obtaining copies of works for conversion to and distribution as warez often requires hacking, or unauthorized access to the copyright owner's computer or network. This is especially true in the case of zero-day and negative-day warez, which appear online on or before the day of their commercial release. Such unreleased works may also be trade secrets, protected by the Economic Espionage Act. The physical theft of a copy of a work from the copyright owner would, of course, be a crime under state law.

Statutes
- Computer Fraud and Abuse Act, 18 U.S.C. § 1030
- Digital Millennium Copyright Act, Title I, §§ 1201–1204
- Economic Espionage Act, 18 U.S.C. §§ 1831–1839
- No Electronic Theft Act, amending and codified at 17 U.S.C. §§ 101, 506, and 507 and 18 U.S.C. §§ 2319–2320

Legislative History
- House Report on the No Electronic Theft Act, H.R. Rep. No. 339, 105th Cong., 1st Sess., 1997, 1997 WL 664424

Cases
Supreme Court
- *Dowling v. United States*, 473 U.S. 207 (1985)

Federal District Court
- *United States v. LaMacchia*, 871 F.Supp. 535 (D. Mass. 1994)

See also: Abandonware; Copyright; Copyright Infringement; Digital Millennium Copyright Act, Title I; Digital Rights Management; File-Sharing; Hacking; No Electronic Theft Act; Protecting Intellectual Rights against Theft and Expropriation Act

Sources and further reading:
"Former DrinkOrDie Member Chris Tresco Answers," *Slashdot*, Oct. 4, 2002, http://interviews.slashdot.org/interviews/02/10/04/144217.shtml?tid=123 (visited October 20, 2004).

Eric Goldman, "A Road to No Warez: The No Electronic Theft Act and Criminal Copyright Infringement," 82 *Oregon Law Review* 369 (2003).

Eric Goldman, "Warez Trading and Criminal Copyright Infringement," 51 *Journal of the Copyright Society of the U.S.A.* 395 (2004).

"Six Formerly Associated with Fox Cable Charged with Copyright Infringement for Running Warez Site that had Pirated Movies, Software," *Cybercrime Law Report*, May 31, 2004, at 21.

❖ WEB ❖

See World Wide Web

❖ WEB BROWSER ❖

A Web browser is a computer program that allows the user to browse the World Wide Web. The first Web browser was created, along with the World Wide Web itself, by Tim Berners-Lee and Robert Cailliau at the European Organization for Nuclear Research (CERN) between 1989 and 1991. Other browsers appeared during the early 1990s, but like the early Web itself, they required either sophisticated computers or sophisticated users.

At the time, other technologies for locating and exchanging information over the Internet, such as Gopher, were not only difficult to use, but often incorporated proprietary technologies. Early Web browsers experimented with proprietary versions of Hypertext Markup Language (HTML), creating situations in which Web pages created with a particular vendor's software package could only be viewed using that vendor's browser. Much the same situation exists today with media players; format incompatibility, as well as copyright issues, has slowed the growth of Internet video and audio. By the mid-1990s, however, most Web browsers had abandoned this destructive format war, and the Web developed rapidly. The actions of CERN in making the underlying Web and browser technology available to all, free of charge, were a major reason a format war was avoided.

In 1993 the National Center for Supercomputing Applications (NCSA) at the University of Illinois released the Mosaic browser, which was easy to use and could run on the personal computers of the time (CERN n.d.). In April 1994 the leader of the team that developed Mosaic, Marc Andreessen, then left the NCSA to form Mosaic Communications, which released its browser, Mosaic Netscape 0.9, in October 1994 (Metzger 2004).

From the outset, Netscape was mired in legal disputes. The University of Illinois sued to prevent the company from using the name "Mosaic," and in November 1994 the company changed its name to Netscape Communications and the name of its browser to Netscape Navigator (Netscape 1994). Netscape Navigator was an immediate success, both coinciding with and contributing to the explosive growth of the World Wide Web in the mid-1990s. In mid-1994, before Mosaic Netscape 0.9 was introduced, there were fewer than three thousand Web servers; a year later there were more than twenty thousand (Zakon 2005) and Netscape's share of the browser market was more than 80 percent (Metzger 2004).

In August 1995 Microsoft released its own browser, Internet Explorer, and the browser wars began in earnest. Microsoft developed Internet Explorer from software purchased from Spyglass, Inc., which like Netscape was an offshoot of the NCSA at the University of Illinois. Internet Explorer was not initially bundled with Windows, but with Microsoft's Plus! 95 package. Plus! was an add-on package for Windows 95 that included extra utilities, of which Internet Explorer was the most important, and bells and whistles. In 1996 America Online began to bundle Internet Explorer with its software. Microsoft also used a strategy of bundling Internet Explorer with other Microsoft software installed on new computer systems; Netscape's market share steadily declined, but Microsoft's bundling strategy led the Justice Department and many state attorneys general to pursue antitrust litigation against Microsoft (Levy 1999).

The outcome of the Microsoft antitrust litigation was at best ambiguous; the outcome of the browser wars, however, was not. Netscape's decline in market share was irreversible; in 1998 Netscape programmers launched Mozilla.org, releasing Netscape's source code to the open-source community. In November 1998, America Online purchased Netscape; two years later it released Netscape 6.0, a version that disappointed many Netscape loyalists, leading them to switch to Internet Explorer (Metzger 2004). A year later America Online converted the Netscape site to a news and entertainment portal, more or less abandoning the primary identification of the Netscape brand with the Web browser. In an apparent turnaround, America Online released new versions of the browser, Netscape 7.1 in June 2003 and Netscape 7.2 in August 2004 (Metzger 2004). At that point, however, 95 percent of Web surfers were using Internet Explorer, with many of the remaining 5 percent using Mozilla or other programs in preference to America Online's Netscape Navigator (*BBC News* 2004). A recent Mozilla browser, Firefox 1.0, has proved popular, and Internet Explorer's market share dropped from 94.7 percent in July 2004 to 92.9 percent in October 2004. The Mozilla Foundation has announced a market share goal for Firefox of 10 percent, which by itself would not threaten Internet Explorer's market dominance but might open the door for other entrants into the browser market.

Case
- *United States v. Microsoft Corp.*, 980 F. Supp. 537 (D.D.C. 1997), reversed, 147 F.3d 935 (D.C. Cir. 1998)

Complaint
- Complaint of State Attorneys General against Microsoft, May 18, 1998, available at http://www.courttv.com/archive/legaldocs/cyberlaw/microsoft/state_suit.html (visited November 9, 2004)

See also: Internet; Microsoft Antitrust Litigation; World Wide Web

Sources and further reading:
CERN, "History of the WWW," http://public.web.cern.ch/Public/Content/Chapters/AboutCERN/Achievements/WorldWideWeb/WebHistory/WebHistory-en.html (visited June 3, 2005).

"Firefox Browser Takes on Microsoft," *BBC News,* Nov. 9, 2004, http://news.bbc.co.uk/2/hi/technology/3993959.stm (visited November 9, 2004).

Robert A. Levy, "Microsoft and the Browser Wars," 31 *Connecticut Law Review* 1321 (1999).

Holger Metzger, *Netscape History,* 2004, http://www.holgermetzger.de/Netscape_History.html (visited November 9, 2004).

Netscape Press Release, "Mosaic Communications Corporation Changes Name to Netscape Communications Corporation," Nov. 14, 1994, available at http://www.holgermetzger.de/netscape/NetscapeCommunicationsNewsRelease.htm (visited November 9, 2004).

Windows® 9x Abandonware, Dan's 20th Century Abandonware, http://home.pmt.org/~drose/aw-win9x–07.html (visited November 9, 2004).

Robert Hobbes Zakon, Hobbes' Internet Timeline v8.0, 2005, http://www.zakon.org/robert/internet/timeline/ (visited June 3, 2005).

❖ WIPO ❖

The World Intellectual Property Organization (WIPO) is an international organization dedicated to the international protection of the rights of creators and owners of intellectual property. WIPO had its origin in the late nineteenth century, which saw the emergence of an international regime of intellectual property rights protection. Notable cornerstones of this regime were the Paris Convention on patents, trademarks, and industrial designs in 1883 and the Berne Convention on copyrights in 1886. Each of these treaties created an organization for administrative purposes; these united in

1893 to form the Bureaux Internationaux Réunis pour la Protection de la Propriété Intellectuelle (United International Bureau for the Protection of Intellectual Property, or BIRPI), which also administered two other treaties. Over time the number of treaties administered and the size of the organization increased to its present level. BIRPI moved to Geneva (from Berne) in 1960; it became WIPO in 1967 and became a part of the United Nations in 1974. Today WIPO employs nearly a thousand people at its headquarters in Geneva, its Coordination Office in New York, and elsewhere.

In addition to the treaties regarding the structure and functions of WIPO itself (the WIPO Convention, the Agreement between the United Nations and WIPO, and the Agreement between WIPO and the WTO), WIPO is responsible in whole or in part for the administration of twenty-two treaties:

- Berne Convention for the Protection of Literary and Artistic Works
- Brussels Convention Relating to the Distribution of Programme-Carrying Signals Transmitted by Satellite
- Budapest Treaty on the International Recognition of the Deposit of Microorganisms for the Purposes of Patent Procedure
- Convention for the Protection of Producers of Phonograms against Unauthorized Duplication of Their Phonograms
- Hague Agreement Concerning the International Deposit of Industrial Designs
- International Convention for the Protection of New Varieties of Plants
- Lisbon Agreement for the Protection of Appellations of Origin and their International Registration
- Locarno Agreement Establishing an International Classification for Industrial Designs
- Madrid Agreement Concerning the International Registration of Marks
- Madrid Agreement for the Repression of False and Deceptive Indications of Source on Goods

- Nairobi Treaty on the Protection of the Olympic Symbol
- Nice Agreement Concerning the International Classification of Goods and Services for the Purposes of the Registration of Marks
- Paris Convention for the Protection of Industrial Property
- Patent Cooperation Treaty
- Patent Law Treaty
- Rome Convention for the Protection of Performers, Producers of Phonograms and Broadcasting Organizations
- Strasbourg Agreement Concerning the International Patent Classification
- Trademark Law Treaty
- Vienna Agreement Establishing an International Classification of the Figurative Elements of Marks
- Washington Treaty on Intellectual Property in Respect of Integrated Circuits
- WIPO Copyright Treaty
- WIPO Performances and Phonograms Treaty

One hundred and eighty states—nearly all of the world's countries—are members of WIPO. Although only states can be members, 172 international nongovernmental organizations (NGOs), 10 national NGOs, and 66 intergovernmental organizations (IGOs) have observer status (WIPO 2004). These observers overwhelmingly represent producers and owners of intellectual property rights rather than consumers; a few, such as the International Law Association, can be presumed to be neutral.

That does not mean, however, that WIPO exclusively represents the interests of content producers. WIPO's voting structure allots each member one vote, regardless of population or level of production or consumption of intellectual property. Although superficially this might seem equitable, it has the effect of giving the 33,000 people of Liechtenstein the same voting weight as the 1.1 billion people of India. It also gives the United States, the world's third most populous country and the largest producer and consumer of intellectual property, the same voting weight as the tiny island nation of Sao Tomé and Principe, with only 182,000 people and hardly any participation in the global intellectual property economy.

The breakup of the European overseas colonial empires has led to an increase in the number of developing countries. The concerns of developing countries, which have few or no intellectual property assets, tend to be the concerns of consumers rather than of producers. They tend to be opposed to the interests of developed country intellectual property rightholders, although not necessarily of developed country consumers. From the 1960s onward, it became apparent that an international intellectual property crisis was emerging in the area of pharmaceutical patents. Almost all pharmaceutical research and development is carried out by developed-world companies, and almost all pharmaceutical patents are held by developed-world persons. This research and development is expensive; costs are recouped during the period in which the drug is protected by patent. After the patent expires, the cost of the drug usually drops dramatically, because it can be manufactured by other companies and sold under a generic name; the cost of manufacture is usually less than the cost of research and development.

Many developing countries that lack the research and development resources necessary to create new drugs nonetheless have the resources to manufacture those drugs once developed. These countries are also often faced with desperate health problems; there is a strong temptation for these countries to ignore the drug developers' patents and simply manufacture the drug themselves, at far lower cost. People in these countries may feel that the lives and health of their compatriots outweigh the intellectual property interests of a handful of mostly European and North American corporations, and that no one should die because of inability to pay patent royalties. The pharmaceutical countries counter that in the absence of profits, there will be no incentive for further research and development; if the drug companies cannot recoup their costs, new drugs will not be created.

By the 1980s the strong representation of developing countries in WIPO had effectively stymied the efforts of the pharmaceutical companies, who then lobbied their governments, particularly the U.S. government, to include an intellectual property treaty in the General Agreement on Tariffs and Trade (GATT) negotiations then under way. The GATT negotiations ultimately led to the creation of the World Trade Organization (WTO), one of the components of which is the Agreement on Trade-Related Aspects of Intellectual Property (TRIPS). TRIPS created a separate framework for protection of international intellectual property rights outside the context of WIPO; the WTO and WIPO formalized this regime in the 1995 Agreement between the World Intellectual Property Organization and the World Trade Organization. The pharmaceutical companies, others with similar interests, and their developed-world backers thus achieved a result that might not have been possible within the WIPO process.

The emergence of TRIPS as the new standard by which international intellectual property rights are determined and national intellectual property laws are measured does not mean that WIPO is moribund, however. As international organizations go, it enjoys exceptional financial stability; it is not dependent on the dues or largesse of its members, but has a steady source of income in fees from the Patent Cooperation Treaty. It continues to maintain valuable education and outreach services, to serve a function as a forum for policy discussions, and to provide dispute resolution services. Its most important function, however, is probably the provision of registration services for patents, trademarks, and designs. All intellectual property rights are granted by national governments and have effect only within the territory governed by the granting government. Protection in other countries requires registration in other countries; without WIPO's registration services, the informational obstacles to patent, trademark, and design registration would probably prove prohibitive.

Treaties

- Agreement between the United Nations and the World Intellectual Property Organization, Dec. 17, 1974

- Agreement between the World Intellectual Property Organization and the World Trade Organization, Dec. 22, 1995, 35 I.L.M. 754 (1996)
- Agreement on Trade-Related Aspects of Intellectual Property Rights, Marrakesh Agreement Establishing the World Trade Organization, Annex 1C, Apr. 15, 1994, 33 I.L.M. 81 (1994)
- Brussels Convention Relating to the Distribution of Programme-Carrying Signals Transmitted by Satellite, May 21, 1974, 13 I.L.M. 1444
- Budapest Treaty on the International Recognition of the Deposit of Microorganisms for the Purposes of Patent Procedure, Apr. 28, 1977, as amended on Sept. 26, 1980, 32 U.S.T. 1241, 1861 U.N.T.S. 361
- Convention Concerning the Creation of an International Union for the Protection of Literary and Artistic Works (Berne Convention), Sept. 9, 1886, as last revised at Paris, July 24, 1971 (amended 1979), 25 U.S.T. 1341, 828 U.N.T.S. 221
- Convention Establishing the World Intellectual Property Organization, July 14, 1967, as amended on Sept. 28, 1979 (WIPO Convention), 21 U.S.T. 1749, 828 U.N.T.S. 3
- Convention for the Protection of Producers of Phonograms against Unauthorized Duplication of Their Phonograms, Oct. 29, 1971, 25 U.S.T. 309
- Hague Agreement Concerning the International Deposit of Industrial Designs, Nov. 6, 1925, 74 L.N.T.S. 343, revised at London, June 2, 1934, 205 L.N.T.S. 179, revised at The Hague, Nov. 28, 1960; supplemented by the Additional Act of Monaco, Nov. 18, 1961, the Complementary Act of Stockholm, July 14, 1967, and the Protocol of Geneva, April 10, 1975, 26 U.S.T. 571; and as amended, Sept. 1979
- Lisbon Agreement for the Protection of Appellations of Origin and their International Registration, Oct. 31, 1958, as revised at Stockholm on July 14, 1967, and as amended on Sept. 28, 1979, 923 U.N.T.S. 205
- Locarno Agreement Establishing an International Classification for Industrial Designs, Oct. 8, 1968, as amended Sept. 28, 1979, 23 U.S.T. 1389
- Madrid Agreement Concerning the International Registration of Marks, Apr. 14, 1891, as revised at Brussels on Dec. 14, 1900, at Washington on June 2, 1911, at The Hague on Nov. 6, 1925, at London on June 2, 1934, at Nice on June 15, 1957, and at Stockholm on July 14, 1967, and as amended on Sept. 28, 1979, 828 U.N.T.S. 389
- Madrid Agreement for the Repression of False or Deceptive Indications of Source on Goods, Apr. 14, 1891, as revised at Washington on June 2, 1911, at The Hague on Nov. 6, 1925, at London on June 2, 1934, and at Lisbon on Oct. 31, 1958, and Additional Act, Stockholm, July 14, 1967, 828 U.N.T.S. 389
- Nairobi Treaty on the Protection of the Olympic Symbol, Sept. 26, 1981, available at http://clea.wipo.int/ PDFFILES/English/WO/WO018EN. PDF (visited August 1, 2004)
- Nice Agreement Concerning the International Classification of Goods and Services for the Purposes of the Registration of Marks, June 15, 1957, as revised at Stockholm on July 14, 1967, and at Geneva on May 13, 1977, and amended on Sept. 28, 1979, 23 U.S.T. 1336, 550 U.N.T.S. 45
- Paris Convention for the Protection of Industrial Property, Mar. 20, 1883, as revised at Brussels on Dec. 14, 1900, at Washington on June 2, 1911, at The Hague on Nov. 6, 1925, at London on June 2, 1934, at Lisbon on Oct. 31, 1958, and at Stockholm on July 14, 1967, and as amended on Sept. 28, 1979, 21 U.S.T. 1583, 828 U.N.T.S. 305
- Patent Cooperation Treaty, Washington on June 19, 1970, as amended on Sept.

28, 1979, and as modified on February 3, 1984, and October 3, 2001, 28 U.S.T. 7645, 9 I.L.M. 978

- Patent Law Treaty, June 1, 2000, 39 I.L.M. 1047 (2000)
- Rome Convention for the Protection of Performers, Producers of Phonograms and Broadcasting Organizations, Oct. 26, 1961, 496 U.N.T.S. 43
- Strasbourg Agreement Concerning the International Patent Classification, Mar. 24, 1971, as amended on Sept., 1979, 26 U.S.T. 1793
- Trademark Law Treaty, Oct. 27, 1994, available at http://www.wipo.int/clea/docs/en/wo/wo027en.htm (visited August 1, 2004)
- Treaty on Intellectual Property in Respect of Integrated Circuits, Washington, May 26, 1989, 28 I.L.M. 1477 (1989)
- Universal Copyright Convention, Sept. 6, 1952, 6 U.S.T. 2731, revised at Paris July 24, 1971, 25 U.S.T. 1341
- Vienna Agreement Establishing an International Classification of the Figurative Elements of Marks, June 12, 1973, as amended Oct. 1, 1985, available at http://www.wipo.int/clea/docs/en/wo/wo031en.htm (visited August 1, 2004)
- WIPO Copyright Treaty, Dec. 20, 1996, 36 I.L.M. 65 (1997)
- WIPO Performances and Phonograms Treaty, Dec. 20, 1996, 36 I.L.M. 76 (1997)

Statutes

- Copyright Act of 1976, 17 U.S.C. §§ 101–1332

See also: Berne Convention; Copyright; Copyright Infringement; Domain Name Registration; International Copyright Protection; International Patent Protection; International Trademark Protection; Patent; Patent Cooperation Treaty; Trademark; Trademark Law Treaty; TRIPS; Universal Copyright Convention; WIPO Copyright Treaty; WIPO Performances and Phonograms Treaty

Sources and further reading:
Pamela Samuelson, "The U.S. Digital Agenda at WIPO," 37 *Virginia Journal of International Law* 369 (1997).
Hans Smit, ed., *WIPO Arbitration Rules: Commentary and Analysis* (Huntington, NY: Juris Publishing, 2000).
World Intellectual Property Organization, "Treaties and Contracting Parties," 2004, http://www.wipo.int/treaties/en/ (visited November 19, 2004).

❖ WIPO COPYRIGHT AND PERFORMANCES AND PHONOGRAMS TREATIES IMPLEMENTATION ACT ❖

See Digital Millennium Copyright Act, Title I

❖ WIPO COPYRIGHT TREATY ❖

The WIPO Copyright Treaty was adopted by the World Intellectual Property Organization (WIPO) in 1996 and entered into force, by its own terms, on March 6, 2002, three months after the deposit of the thirtieth instrument of ratification or accession. A total of fifty-two countries have now become parties to the convention, the most recent being Albania on May 6, 2005. The treaty extends copyright protections beyond those guaranteed by the Berne Convention or TRIPS.

Articles 2, 4, and 5 provide protection for computer programs and compilations of data equivalent to those provided by the Berne Convention and TRIPS; footnotes 3 and 4 provide that the protection accorded each "is consistent with Article 2 of the Berne Convention and on a par with the relevant provisions of the TRIPS Agreement." However, the WIPO Copyright Treaty's protection of rental and distribution rights, set forth in Articles 6 through 8, may exceed those contained in the Berne Convention and TRIPS. It is Articles 11 and 12, however, that represent the greatest departure from past treaties and have had the greatest impact on the domestic law of those states that have became parties to the treaty.

Article 11 requires the parties to the treaty to "provide adequate legal protection and effective legal remedies against the circumvention of effective technological measures that are used by authors in connection with the exercise of their rights under this Treaty or the Berne Convention." In other words, parties to the treaty must enact and enforce laws against the circumvention of copy-protection measures. Article 12 carries the idea a bit further, prohibiting not only the circumvention of technological measures used to prevent actual copying, but also any other circumvention of any part of a digital rights management scheme. Under Article 12, the parties must "provide adequate and effective legal remedies against any person knowingly" removing or altering "any electronic rights management information," or distributing, importing for distribution, broadcasting, or communicating to the public any works from which such information has been removed, if in either case the person does not have the authority to do so and knows or has reason to know that doing so "will induce, enable, facilitate or conceal an infringement of any right covered by this Treaty or the Berne Convention."

The anticircumvention provisions in Articles 11 and 12 of the WIPO Copyright Treaty have been enacted into U.S. law in the form of the anticircumvention provisions of Title I of the Digital Millennium Copyright Act (17 U.S.C. §§ 1201–1204), and into European Union law by EU Directive 2001/29/EC.

Treaty
- WIPO Copyright Treaty, Dec. 20, 1996, 36 I.L.M. 65 (1997)

Statute
- Digital Millennium Copyright Act, 17 U.S.C. § 1201

European Union Directive
- EU Directive 2001/29/EC on the harmonisation of certain aspects of copyright and related rights in the information society, 2001 O.J. (L 167) 10

See also: Berne Convention; Copyright Infringement; DeCSS; Digital Millennium Copyright Act, Title I; Digital Rights Management; Encryption; File-Sharing; International Copyright Protection; Steganography; TRIPS

Sources and further reading:
Mihaly Ficsor, *The Law of Copyright and the Internet: The 1996 WIPO Treaties, Their Interpretation and Implementation* (Oxford: Oxford University Press, 2002).

❖ WIPO PERFORMANCES AND PHONOGRAMS TREATY ❖

The WIPO Performances and Phonograms Treaty was adopted by the World Intellectual Property Organization (WIPO) in 1996 and entered into force, by its own terms, on May 20, 2002, three months after the deposit of the thirtieth instrument of ratification or accession. A total of forty-nine countries have now become parties to the convention, the most recent being the Former Yugoslav Republic of Macedonia on March 20, 2005.

With two exceptions, the WIPO Performances and Phonograms Treaty stands alone: Article 1(3) provides that "This Treaty shall not have any connection with, nor shall it prejudice any rights and obligations under, any other treaties." The first of these exceptions is set out in Article 1(1): "Nothing in this Treaty shall derogate from existing obligations . . . under the" Rome phonograms treaty (to which the United States is not a party). The second exception is more general: Article 1(2) adds that protection of phonograms under the treaty "shall leave intact and shall in no way affect the protection of copyright in literary and artistic works."

Article 3 of the treaty requires parties to provide protection under the treaty to nationals of other parties applying the Rome Convention's criteria for eligibility. Article 4 requires national treatment; that is, each party "shall accord to nationals of other Contracting Parties . . . the treatment it accords to its own nationals[.]"

Article 5 protects the moral rights of performers in sound recordings of live aural performances "independently of a performer's economic rights, and even after the transfer of those rights." In an inversion of the relative importance that the United States has traditionally accorded moral and economic rights, the article protecting moral rights precedes the article protecting economic rights. Moral rights, in copyright law, are the right not to have one's work mutilated or distorted, the right to be acknowledged as the author of the work, and the right to determine when and in what fashion the work shall be presented to the public. These rights are called, respectively, the rights of integrity, paternity, and disclosure. U.S. copyright law has traditionally been reluctant to acknowledge moral rights.

Article 6 of the treaty deals with the economic rights of performers in unfixed performances, requiring that parties to the treaty grant performers the sole right of authorizing the broadcasting, except in the case of performances that are already broadcast performances. Article 6 also requires the parties to grant performers the sole right of communication to the public and fixation of their unfixed performances. Articles 7 and 8 deal with the more familiar (from a U.S. copyright law standpoint) rights of reproduction and distribution; again, parties are required to grant these rights exclusively to the performers. Article 9 grants a similar monopoly on rental rights, whereas Article 10 provides that "Performers shall enjoy the exclusive right of authorizing the making available to the public of their performances fixed in phonograms, by wire or wireless means, in such a way that members of the public may access them from a place and at a time individually chosen by them." Articles 11 through 14 provide parallel rights to producers of phonograms. Article 15 provides performers and producers with a right of remuneration for the broadcasting or other communication to the public of their sound recordings. Article 17 sets the minimum term of protection at fifty years from the end of the year in which the performance was fixed (for performers and for producers of works fixed but not published), and fifty years from the end of the year of publication (for producers of published phonograms). Article 20 provides, in conformity with Berne Convention and TRIPS norms, that no formalities may be required for copyright protection.

Article 16 provides for limitations and exceptions such as the U.S. fair-use doctrine: "Contracting Parties may, in their national legislation, provide for the same kinds of limitations or exceptions with regard to the protection of performers and producers of phonograms as they provide for, in their national legislation, in connection with the protection of copyright in literary and artistic works." The treaty adopts the three-step test of Article 9(2) of the Berne Convention as expressed in Article 13 of TRIPS, confining the creation of limitations or exceptions to "certain special cases which do not conflict with a normal exploitation of the performance or phonogram and do not unreasonably prejudice the legitimate interests of the performer or of the producer of the phonogram." Article 18, like Article 11 of the WIPO Copyright Treaty, requires the parties to enact and enforce laws against the circumvention of copy-protection measures: Parties to the treaty "shall provide adequate legal protection and effective legal remedies against the circumvention of effective technological measures that are used by performers or producers of phonograms in connection with the exercise of their rights under this Treaty and that restrict acts, in respect of their performances or phonograms, which are not authorized by the performers or the producers of phonograms concerned or permitted by law." Article 19, like Article 12 of the WIPO Copyright Treaty, requires the parties to prohibit any other circumvention or spoofing of any part of an electronic rights management scheme. Under Article 19, the parties must "provide adequate and effective legal remedies against any person knowingly" removing or altering "any electronic rights management information," or distributing, importing for distribution, broadcasting, or communicating to the public any works from which such information has been removed, if in either case the person does not have the authority to do so and knows or has reason to know that doing so "will induce, enable, facilitate or conceal an infringement of any right covered by this Treaty."

The anticircumvention provisions in Articles 18 and 19 of the WIPO Performances and Phonograms Treaty, like the corresponding provisions of the WIPO Copyright Treaty, have been implemented in the United States by the anticircumvention provisions of the Digital Millennium Copyright Act (17 U.S.C. §§ 1201–1204) and in the European Union by EU Directive 2001/29/EC.

Treaties
- Rome Convention for the Protection of Performers, Producers of Phonograms and Broadcasting Organizations, Oct. 26, 1961, 496 U.N.T.S. 43
- WIPO Copyright Treaty, Dec. 20, 1996, 36 I.L.M. 65 (1997)
- WIPO Performances and Phonograms Treaty, Dec. 20, 1996, 36 I.L.M. 76 (1997)

Statute
- Digital Millennium Copyright Act, 17 U.S.C. § 1201

European Union Directive
- EU Directive 2001/29/EC on the harmonisation of certain aspects of copyright and related rights in the information society, 2001 O.J. (L 167) 10

See also: Berne Convention; Copyright Infringement; DeCSS; Digital Millennium Copyright Act, Title I; Digital Rights Management; International Copyright Protection; TRIPS

Sources and further reading:
Mihaly Ficsor, *The Law of Copyright and the Internet: The 1996 WIPO Treaties, Their Interpretation and Implementation* (Oxford: Oxford University Press, 2002).

❖ WORLD INTELLECTUAL PROPERTY ORGANIZATION ❖

See WIPO

❖ WORLD WIDE WEB ❖

The World Wide Web, or Web, is often but inaccurately referred to as the Internet. The Internet is the combination of physical infrastructure and communications protocols that supports the Web and other information networks. The Web is a collection of information, distributed on billions of hypertext pages scattered across millions of Internet-connected computers, which can be accessed using a Web browser. Any person with a Web browser and access to the Internet can view pages on the World Wide Web, interact with those pages, and follow links from one page to another (Wagner 1999). Information shared across the Web can be used to facilitate other Internet activities, such as e-mail, messaging, and file-sharing.

The Internet itself arose from a variety of sources and cannot readily be traced to a single inventor or originating event. The origins of the World Wide Web are less obscure, however. The Web was created in the late 1990s by an independent contractor and a researcher at CERN, the European Organization for Nuclear Research. (CERN is the French acronym for the organization's original name, Centre Européenne pour la Recherche Nucléaire; the organization is now the Organisation Européenne pour la Recherche Nucléaire.) The two, Tim Berners-Lee and Robert Cailliau, created a hypertext system they called ENQUIRE in order to find documents more quickly on CERN's computers. Hypertext systems existing at the time required two-way links; the system developed by Berners-Lee and Cailliau used unidirectional links, meaning that anyone creating a document could link to another document without the need for any alteration in that second document. By 1991 Berners-Lee had created both the first Web page and the first Web browser; the Web spread quickly, first among physics researchers and then to the world at large. In December 1991 the United States had its first Web server, at the Stanford Linear Accelerator Center in Menlo Park, California (CERN, n.d.).

Two factors contributed to the early growth of the World Wide Web: the ease with which unidirectional hypertext links could be created, and the fact that CERN made the underlying technology available to all, free of charge. This made the Web far more attractive than proprietary technologies for which content developers would have to obtain a license and pay a fee. Early Web browsers, however, either required sophisticated computers or were difficult to use for the technologically unsophisticated. The explosion of the Web beyond the scientific community began with the release of easy-to-use Web browsers that could run on the home computers of the time. The first of these was the Mosaic browser, released in 1993 by the National Center for Supercomputing Applications at the University of Illinois (CERN n.d.). Netscape released its browser, Netscape Navigator, in 1994. Netscape Navigator was followed by Microsoft's Internet Explorer in 1995, and the browser wars began. In October 1993, before Netscape Navigator appeared on the market, there were only 228 Web servers. Eight months later, in June 1994, there were 2,738. For a time during the mid-1990s the number of Web servers continued to grow at this astonishing rate, increasing an order of magnitude each year. In June 1995 there were 23,500 servers, and in June 1996 there were 252,000. The number of Web servers had topped a million by April 1997 and stands at around fifty million today, hosting billions of Web pages (Zakon 2004).

The World Wide Web, like the Internet, has been involved in controversy from its inception. The browser wars between Netscape and Microsoft led to federal and state government lawsuits against Microsoft. The ease with which the Web provides access to information has raised concerns about its use by criminal conspiracies and terrorist organizations. The relative anonymity of Web users has made it difficult to shield minors from indecent and pornographic content. These concerns have led to attempts to censor the Internet either by restricting content or by restricting access; these attempts have met with little success both because of the ease with which sophisticated users circumvent controls and, in countries such as the United States, because of constitutional protections of free speech and access to information.

Similarly, the ease with which material can be reproduced and published on the Web has also raised intellectual property concerns; holders of intellectual property rights have been more successful than censorship advocates, both in court

and in Congress, in achieving some measure of control over the Internet. Laws such as the Digital Millennium Copyright Act have greatly strengthened copyright protections, taking new technology into account. The Web has also revolutionized retailing through the advent of e-commerce, requiring changes to contract law.

Statute
- Digital Millennium Copyright Act, 17 U.S.C. §§ 512, 1201–1204

See also: Censorship; Copyright; Digital Millennium Copyright Act; E-commerce; File-Sharing; Hacking; Internet; Internet Corporation for Assigned Names and Numbers; Microsoft Antitrust Litigation; Spam; Virus; Web Browser

Sources and further reading:
CERN, "The World Wide Web," http:// public.web.cern.ch/Public/Content/Chapters/ AboutCERN/Achievements/WorldWideWeb/ WWW-en.html (visited November 8, 2004).
Dave Kristula, "The History of the Internet," Aug. 2001, http://www.davesite.com/webstation/ net-history.shtml (visited November 8, 2004).
Ronald L. Wagner, *Guide to Cyberspace*, 9th ed. (Herndon, VA: Citapei Communications, 1999).
Robert H. Zakon, "Hobbes' Internet Timeline v7.0," Jan. 1, 2004, http://www.zakon.org/ robert/internet/timeline/ (visited November 8, 2004).

❖ WORM ❖

A worm is a program that replicates itself until it has used up all of the available space on a computer. A worm is not a computer virus, although the two terms are often confused and worms can have the same effects as some viruses. The term *worm* was first used for such a program by the late British S.F. author John Brunner in his 1975 novel *Shockwave Rider*. Brunner's use of the term was adopted by researchers at Xerox PARC, who created the first computer worm in 1978 (*PARC History* 2003). It was not until a decade later, however, that computer worms burst into the popular consciousness, with the creation and distribution of a worm by Cornell University graduate student Robert Morris Jr. (Lessig 1999, 194–196).

Morris created the worm to point out security flaws in the then-new Internet, particularly in the open-source e-mail distribution program Sendmail:

> Morris identified four ways in which the worm could break into computers on the network:
>
> (1) through a "hole" or "bug" (an error) in SEND MAIL, a computer program that transfers and receives electronic mail on a computer;
>
> (2) through a bug in the "finger demon" program, a program that permits a person to obtain limited information about the users of another computer;
>
> (3) through the "trusted hosts" feature, which permits a user with certain privileges on one computer to have equivalent privileges on another computer without using a password; and
>
> (4) through a program of password guessing, whereby various combinations of letters are tried out in rapid sequence in the hope that one will be an authorized user's password, which is entered to permit whatever level of activity that user is authorized to perform. (*Morris,* 928 F. 2d at 506)

Morris, whose father was a data security expert for the National Security Agency, appeared to have no malicious intent; among old-school hackers, a prank like the one Morris planned was a proper and acceptable way to point out a security flaw in an open-source program such as Sendmail (Lessig 1999, 195, 282 n.18). Morris took steps to ensure that his worm would not do undue damage:

> Therefore, Morris designed the worm to "ask" each computer whether it already had a copy of the worm. If it responded "no," then the worm would copy onto the computer; if it responded "yes," the worm would not duplicate. However, Morris was concerned that other programmers could kill the worm by programming their own computers to falsely respond "yes" to the question. To circumvent this protection, Morris programmed the worm to duplicate itself every seventh time it received

a "yes" response. As it turned out, Morris underestimated the number of times a computer would be asked the question, and his one-out-of-seven ratio resulted in far more copying than he had anticipated. The worm was also designed so that it would be killed when a computer was shut down, an event that typically occurs once every week or two. This would have prevented the worm from accumulating on one computer, had Morris correctly estimated the likely rate of reinfection. (*Morris,* 982 F.2nd at 506)

Morris released his worm on November 2, 1988, from a computer at the Massachusetts Institute of Technology. The worm spread much faster than Morris had anticipated; alarmed, he tried to kill it, but could not. Morris and a friend sent an anonymous mass e-mail from a computer at Harvard, explaining how to kill the worm and prevent infection. Because the worm had grown so quickly, however, the fledgling Internet of the time was unable to cope with it, and much e-mail—including Morris's message—was unable to get through (*Morris,* 982 F.2nd at 506). Before it was brought under control, Morris's worm had infected thousands of computers, causing millions of dollars worth of damage (*World Almanac* 2004, 713). Morris was arrested and charged with violation of § 1030(a)(5)(A) of the Computer Fraud and Abuse Act. At the time, § 1030(a)(5)(A) imposed criminal penalties on anyone who:

> (5) intentionally accesses a Federal interest computer without authorization, and by means of one or more instances of such conduct alters, damages, or destroys information in any such Federal interest computer, or prevents authorized use of any such computer or information, and thereby
>
> (A) causes loss to one or more others of a value aggregating $1,000 or more during any one year period. (Quoted in *Morris,* 928 F.2nd at 506)

Morris was convicted of violating § 1030(a)(5)(A) (*Morris,* 928 F.2nd at 506); his conviction was affirmed on appeal. Since that time the statute has been amended many times, rendering obsolete the court's discussion of terms such as *Federal interest computer.* However, the basic elements of the crime of spreading a computer worm, as set forth by the court considering Morris's appeal, remain the same: intent and unauthorized access. Morris intended to create and spread the worm, even if he did not intend the effects to be as severe as they actually were. And by causing the worm to replicate itself on computers that he was not authorized to access, he obtained unauthorized access to these computers. This second part of the holding seems a bit more of a stretch, because Morris gained no control over the infected computers; he could not even prevent the worm from replicating itself on those computers, once he had started. Nonetheless, the court held that a reasonable jury could have found that Morris obtained access, for a variety of reasons: The worm's password-guessing function by itself was probably enough to support a finding of unauthorized access, as was the abuse of the "trusted hosts" function. Also, "he found holes in [Sendmail and Fingerdaemon] that permitted him a special and unauthorized access route into other computers" (*Morris,* 928 F.2nd at 510).

Although some worms simply replicate themselves, one virtue of worms, from a malicious user's point of view, is that they can be used as vehicles to install programs on other users' computers without the consent or knowledge of those other users. In recent years there have been Web-wide attacks by worms such as SoBig and MyDoom, which install Trojans or backdoor programs on the computers they infect (Stein 2004). These backdoors turn the infected computers into zombies; the zombies can then be turned to a variety of malicious uses. Zombies can be used to launch distributed denial-of-service (DDoS) attacks against Web sites and servers, to mail spam, or to mail other worms and viruses. Uses of this sort, of course, fit the definition of "unauthorized access" far more easily than did Morris's relatively innocuous worm.

The easiest way for users to avoid worms is to update and run antivirus software (which also checks for and removes known worms) frequently, and to exercise common sense when downloading unknown attachments. Although most antivirus programs scan incoming e-mail for worms and viruses, there is never a good reason for anyone other than a computer security professional to click on an attachment to a spam e-mail. Users should also be cautious about downloading programs from unknown Web sites.

Statute

- Computer Fraud and Abuse Act, 18 U.S.C. § 1030

Case

- *United States v. Morris,* 928 F.2d 504 (2nd Cir. 1991)

See also: Adware and Spyware; Denial-of-Service Attack; Hacking; Malware; Open-Source; Spam; Trojan; Virus; Zombie

Sources and further reading:
Nonfiction
Lawrence Lessig, *Code and Other Laws of Cyberspace* (New York: Basic Books, 1999).
PARC History, Aug. 12, 2003, http://www.parc.xerox.com/about/history/default.html (visited November 13, 2004).
Tiernan Ray, "E-mail Viruses Blamed as Spam Rises Sharply," *Seattle Times,* Feb. 18, 2004, available at http://seattletimes.nwsource.com/html/businesstechnology/2001859752_spamdoubles18.html (visited November 13, 2004).
Andrew Stein, "Microsoft Offers MyDoom Reward: No. 1 Software Firm Offers $250,000 for Information on Creator of Worm Seen Costing Firms $250M," *CNN Money,* Jan. 30, 2004, available at http://www.moneymag.com/2004/01/28/technology/mydoom_costs/ (visited November 13, 2004).
Bruce Sterling, *The Hacker Crackdown* (Electronic edition 1992), available at http://stuff.mit.edu/hacker/hacker.html (visited November 13, 2004).
World Almanac and Book of Facts 2004 (New York: World Almanac Books, 2004).
Fiction
John Brunner, *The Shockwave Rider* (New York: Ballantine, 1976).

X

❖ XUPITER ❖

See Adware and Spyware

❖ .XXX ❖

See Pornography

❖ YAHOO! ❖

Yahoo! Inc. is a company offering a wide range of Internet services, including news, e-mail, Web hosting, shopping, and search services. Its Web site at www.yahoo.com is the Internet's most-visited Web site ("Top 500," 2004). Yahoo! also has foreign-language sites aimed at markets in Argentina, Australia, Brazil, Canada, China, Denmark, France, Germany, Hong Kong, India, Italy, Japan, Mexico, Norway, Singapore, South Korea, Spain, Sweden, Taiwan, and the United Kingdom, as well as a Catalan-language site and Chinese and Spanish versions of the U.S. site.

The history of Yahoo! is the history of the commercial Internet in microcosm. Yahoo! began as the project of two Stanford University graduate students, Jerry Yang and David Filo, in 1994. Originally it was no more than a list of links to favorite Web sites: "Jerry's Guide to the World Wide Web." The list was divided into categories and eventually renamed Yahoo!; the etymology of the name has been variously given as an acronym for "Yet Another Hierarchical Officious Oracle," "Yet Another Hierarchically Organized Outline," and more simply as a term, originally derived from *Gulliver's Travels,* meaning a person who is uncouth and unsophisticated. This meaning is carried over into the name of Yahoo!'s children's site, Yahooligans.

The lists maintained by Filo and Yang began to attract first hundreds, then thousands of users. At the time, in 1994, the Internet was still used mostly by a relatively small number of technically sophisticated users; its transformation to a universal medium of communication had not yet taken place. Yahoo!'s popularity grew by word of mouth, and by fall of 1994 the site was attracting more than a hundred thousand unique visitors a day. Filo and Yang incorporated Yahoo! and raised about two million dollars from high-tech venture capital firm Sequoia Capital. The introduction of venture capitalists marked the transformation of Yahoo! from grad student hobby to serious business; the company hired professional managers and began to prepare for an initial public offering (IPO) of stock. At the time the IPO actually took place, on April 12, 1996, Yahoo! had forty-nine employees; its IPO raised about $34 million ("History of Yahoo!" 2004).

Yahoo!'s successful IPO and continuing post-IPO success, along with those of similar early-1990s Internet businesses, inspired wild investor enthusiasm for Internet IPOs. This led Federal Reserve Board Chairman Alan Greenspan to warn of "irrational exuberance" in the stock markets (Greenspan 1996), a warning that went largely unheeded until the dot-com meltdown nearly four years later.

Following its IPO, Yahoo! began to grow from a portal site to a comprehensive provider of Web services; it did this both by adding new features to its existing business and by acquiring other businesses. Among its significant acquisitions were the free Web-hosting service GeoCities and the search engines Inktomi and AltaVista.

Throughout its history Yahoo! has been involved in a significant amount of litigation that has contributed to the growth of Internet law in general; of the suits in which Yahoo! has been involved, the best-known and most influential is a case in a foreign country: the suits and decisions collectively referred to as the "French Yahoo! case." The French Yahoo! case involved Yahoo!'s U.S. auction site; some users offered Nazi memorabilia for sale on the site. The offering of such materials for sale is illegal in France, and the French Yahoo! cases, discussed in detail under their own heading in this encyclopedia, raised and addressed fundamental questions regarding freedom of expression in an international medium.

Cases

- *Yahoo!, Inc. v. La Ligue Contre Le Racisme et L'Antisemitisme,* 169 F.Supp.2d 1181 (N.D. Cal. 2001), reversed by *Yahoo!, Inc. v. La Ligue Contre Le Racisme Et L'Antisemitisme,* 379 F.3d 1120 (9th Cir. 2004)
- Yaman Akdeniz, *Case Analysis of League against Racism and Antisemitism (LICRA), French Union of Jewish Students, v. Yahoo! Inc. (USA), Yahoo France,* Tribunal de Grande Instance de Paris (The County Court of Paris), Interim Court Order, 20 November 2000, 1 Electronic Business Law

Reports 110 (2001), download available from http://www.cyber-rights.org/documents (visited October 11, 2004)

See also: .com; French Yahoo! Case

Sources and further reading:
Karen Angel, *Inside Yahoo! Reinvention and the Road Ahead* (New York: John Wiley and Sons, 2002).
"The History of Yahoo!—How It All Started . . . ," http://docs.yahoo.com/info/misc/history.html (visited October 11, 2004).
Andreas Manolopoulos, "Raising 'Cyber-Borders': The Interaction between Law and Technology," 11 *International Journal of Law and Information Technology* 40 (2003).
"Remarks by Chairman Alan Greenspan at the Annual Dinner and Francis Boyer Lecture of the American Enterprise Institute for Public Policy Research," Washington, DC, Dec. 5, 1996, available at http://www.federalreserve.gov/boarddocs/speeches/1996/19961205.htm (visited October 11, 2004).
"Top 500 Sites—The Most Popular Sites on the Web." Updated Daily! http://www.alexa.com/ (visited October 11, 2004).

Z

❖ ZOMBIE ❖

A zombie computer, or zombie, is a computer that has been backdoored for use in denial-of-service attacks, spamming, or other unethical or illegal Internet activity; that is, its security has been compromised and it has become available for use by an outside person. This backdooring is usually accomplished by the use of a worm or Trojan.

In a denial-of-service attack, the zombie sits quietly until it is activated; the user will not notice any difference in performance. If the backdoor is not first detected and removed, the person who created the backdoor, or some other person who is aware of it, can activate it by a signal from outside. The zombie will then attempt to access the Web site upon which the denial-of-service attack is being launched, as will a large number of other zombie computers that have been similarly backdoored and have received the same signal. The goal of a denial-of-service attack is to overwhelm the targeted Web site, which will then be inaccessible to legitimate users wishing to access it; the effect is analogous to constantly telephoning a certain telephone number so that anyone else trying to call that number will receive a busy signal or message service. A denial-of-service attack launched in this way is called a distributed denial-of-service attack.

Pulsing zombies can also be used in denial-of-service attacks. A pulsing zombie attempts to access the target site intermittently rather than continuously. This increases the target site's traffic, making access for legitimate users slower, but not making the site unavailable; an attack of this sort is also called a degradation-of-service attack. A denial-of-service attack is in-stantly noticeable, but a degradation-of-service attack might go on for months without being noticed. A mild "attack" by pulsing zombies can also be used to make a Web site look more popular than it actually is; like denial-of-service and degradation-of-service attacks, fraud of this sort is detectable.

Another popular use of zombies is as spam mailers. A zombie computer can be used to send e-mail advertising to large numbers of other computers without the user's knowledge; this will continue until the user notices and removes or disables the spamming program, or until the user's ISP notices (perhaps as a result of outside complaints) and shuts off the zombie's Internet access.

The use of zombies presents legal issues in all phases of the process: The installation and operation of the backdoor without the user's consent is illegal, and the purpose for which the zombie is used is often, although not always, illegal as well. Laws in many states criminalize various types of malicious hacking, often equating unlawful unauthorized access to another person's computer with burglary or criminal trespass. Federal statutes such as the Computer Fraud and Abuse Act (CFAA) impose penalties for computer-specific crimes that cannot readily be defined by analogy to traditional crimes (Schemmel 2003, 927–928). Under the CFAA, the use of worms (*Morris*, 928 F.2d 504) and Trojans is punishable by fines and jail sentences. The CFAA also prohibits the launching of denial-of-service attacks. Of course, proceeding under these statutes against a hacker outside the United States may be difficult.

The term *zombie* or *zombie site* is also sometimes used to refer to an abandoned but still accessible Web site, although such sites are more often called *ghost sites*.

Statute
* Computer Fraud and Abuse Act, 18 U.S.C. § 1030

Case
* *United States v. Morris*, 928 F.2d 504 (2nd Cir. 1991), certiorari denied 502 U.S. 817

See also: Denial-of-Service Attack; Hacking; Malware; Spam; Trojan; Virus; Worm

Sources and further reading:

Susan W. Brenner, "Toward a Criminal Law for Cyberspace: Distributed Security," 10 *Boston University Journal of Science and Technology Law* 1 (2004).

Marc D. Goodman and Susan W. Brenner, "The Emerging Consensus on Criminal Conduct in Cyberspace," 2002 *UCLA Journal of Law and Technology* 3 (2002).

Bruce P. Keller, "No More Junk! An Update on Spam," Practising Law Institute, 24th Annual Institute on Computer Law, Mar. 2004.

John Leyden, "Trojan Turns Victims into DDoS, Spam Zombies," *The Register,* July 17, 2003, available at http://www.theregister.co.uk/2003/07/17/trojan_turns_victims_into_ddos/ (visited October 10, 2004).

Rebecca Porter, "Smothered by Spam: More Than Half of All E-mail Messages Are Now 'Junk.' Recently Passed Legislation Should Bring Some Relief. Until Then, You Can Take Steps to Keep Spam from Clogging Your Computer System and Bogging Down Your Practice, *Trial,* Feb. 2004, at 50.

Tammy J. Schemmel, "WWW.STOPCYBER-CRIME.COM: How the USA PATRIOT Act Combats Cyber-Crime," 29 *William Mitchell Law Review* 921 (2003).

Bruce Sterling, *The Hacker Crackdown* (New York: Bantam, 1993); 1994 electronic edition available as a free download for noncommercial use from http://stuff.mit.edu/hacker/hacker.html (visited October 10, 2004).

Jon Swartz, "Hackers Hijack Federal Computers," *USA Today,* Aug. 30, 2004, available at http://www.usatoday.com/tech/news/computersecurity/2004–08–30-cyber-crime_x.htm (visited October 10, 2004).

Mark Tamminga, "Foot Soldiers and Attack Masters: Covert Demons that Can Crush Net Services," *Law Practice Management,* Oct. 2001, at 21.

❖ APPENDIX I: GLOSSARY ❖

This glossary includes selected legal and computer terms that may be unfamiliar; most are also defined where they appear in the text but do not have entries of their own (an exception is DeCSS). For definitions of other terms, please see the subject entries and the table of abbreviations in the front of this volume.

advergames, advertainment: Games and entertainment that serve as advertising, often through embedded product placement.

backdoor: Used as a noun, a backdoor is a means of accessing a program or computer that bypasses security measures. Used as a verb, to backdoor is to install or use a backdoor.

baud: A unit formerly used for measuring modem speeds, named after nineteenth-century French telegraph engineer Jean-Maurice-Émile Baudot. One baud is one electronic state change per second; for digital transmissions, however, it is more accurate to use bits per second (bps) as a measure, and that is the measure now used. The terms are sometimes, but incorrectly, used interchangeably.

black hat hacker: A person who gains unauthorized access to a computer system or network for purposes that are not innocuous; the black hat hacker might steal, destroy, or alter information, plant backdoors, or otherwise take advantage of the system's or network's vulnerability.

blog: A contraction of "weblog," a Web page in journal form to which content is added on a periodic, often daily, basis and which is generally intended for as wide a readership as possible.

blogger: The author of a blog.

captcha (completely automated public Turing test to tell computers and humans apart): A test used to prevent spamming, automated registrations of Web and e-mail addresses, and other abuses of the Internet; it consists of a task that is very simple for humans but impossible for software. For example, a captcha might present a picture of distorted text spelling out a word and ask the person or program viewing it to type the word; or it might present several images of kittens or airplanes and ask the viewer to type the word that best describes the subject of the images.

certiorari: A writ issued by an appellate or high court to a lower court, directing the lower court

Jean-Maurice-Émile Baudot, whose name is unknown to most people today, revolutionized the world's first electronic information network, the telegraph system. Baudot introduced multiplexing, allowing a single telegraph line to send and receive six messages simultaneously. To do this he had to invent the world's first truly digital electronic code; the Baudot code was a five-bit code, simpler than the ASCII or Unicode codes in use today—but telegraph operators using Baudot's equipment had no computers. The five-bit code allows for thirty-two combinations, an insufficient number to cover the twenty-six letters and ten digits needed for telegraph communications; Baudot added two special codes, LTRS and FIGS, which preceded and identified sequences of letters or numerals, thus allowing for thirty-two of each.

An interesting puzzle is to try to recreate Baudot's multiplexing: How would you send six messages simultaneously, using fairly simple mechanical devices and no computers?

Source
H. W. Pendry, *The Baudot Printing Telegraph System,* 2d ed. (London: Sir I. Pitman and Sons, Ltd., 1920).

to deliver the record in a particular case to the higher court for review; the most common procedural mechanism by which cases come before the United States Supreme Court.

constructive: A term used by courts and lawyers to mean that something will be treated in law as if it exists or has taken place, even if in fact it does not or has not; a person might have constructive knowledge of a fact that s/he does not, in fact, know, if a reasonable person similarly situated would have known the fact or would have been motivated to make further inquiries.

Content Scramble System (CSS): A form of encryption used to protect DVDs from unauthorized copying.

cracker: A black hat hacker; someone who breaks in to protected computers or networks. Also, a person who breaks the copy protection or security software on computer programs, often as part of a warez trading operation, or on DVDs or other protected content.

damages: Money sought by or awarded to the plaintiff in an action at law as compensation for a loss or injury.

DeCSS: A program for decrypting CSS-encrypted DVDs.

DivX: A method of compressing and decompressing video files that allows movies to be stored in relatively small files; DivX has caused some concern in the motion picture industry because smaller files can more easily be shared over file-sharing networks.

DSL: Digital subscriber line; a telephone line used to provide broadband Internet access.

enjoin: To issue an injunction prohibiting someone from doing something.

equitable relief: Relief awarded in equity rather than at law; as a practical matter, relief other than damages granted to a party in a lawsuit. An injunction is a form of equitable relief.

estoppel: A legal device that prevents parties from asserting, and courts from considering, certain claims, defenses, or issues.

File Transfer Protocol (FTP): A protocol used to transfer files from one computer to another.

GNU/Linux: An open-source operating system based on the Linux kernel developed by Linus Torvalds at the University of Helsinki.

gray hat: A hacker who, having identified a security vulnerability, does not exploit the vulnerability but publicizes it, possibly enabling black hat hackers (or crackers) to take advantage of it if the owner or the vulnerable system or computer does not address the problem promptly.

hacktivism: Hacking or cracking undertaken for purposes of political protest. Some definitions of hacktivism would exclude defacement of Web sites, such as replacing content on a music-content-industry Web site with content that criticizes or mocks the industry's lawsuits against individual file-sharers.

HTML: Hypertext Markup Language; the language in which Web pages are written.

HTTP: Hypertext Transfer Protocol; a protocol that runs on top of the TCP/IP layer and enables connected computers to send and receive Web pages.

HTTPS: A secure version of HTTP, in which all communications are encrypted.

information superhighway, information highway, infobahn: Outdated nicknames for the Internet.

injunction: A court order requiring or prohibiting a particular act or acts.

Linux: The kernel of Linux-based operating systems such as GNU/Linux; GNU/Linux is often, although not entirely correctly, referred to simply as "Linux." The first syllable should be pronounced "Lynn," not "line."

password cracker: A computer program used to break into password-protected systems, networks, programs, and files.

random access memory (RAM): A computer storage device whose contents can be accessed in any order, and which can be both written to and read from; the portion of a computer in which programs and information in use are stored while the computer is turned on.

read only memory (ROM): A computer storage device that can only be read from, not written to, by the user. Typically used to refer to chips storing BIOS or in game cartridges; also used in the term *CD-ROM* to refer to programs or data stored on nonrewritable CDs.

safe harbor: A provision in a statute or regulation that provides immunity from prosecution or liability for persons who meet certain requirements and comply with certain conditions.

script kiddies: Technically unskilled hackers who use programs written by others in hacking and cracking.

spim: Instant messenger spam.

sub nom.: Abbreviated form of *sub nomine,* Latin for "under the name [of]." Often a case on repeal or remand is decided under a different name than it had been given by the previous court; "sub nom." in a case cite, followed by the new name, indicates the name change.

subpoena: A court order requiring witnesses to appear or documents to be made available.

TCP/IP: Transmission Control Protocol/Internet Protocol; a two-layer system of protocols that enables internetworked computers, such as those connected to the Internet, to communicate with each other. The lower layer, IP, routes packets of information toward their correct destination. The upper layer, TCP, divides messages into packets for transmission and reassembles the packets into their original form at the receiving end. It also ensures the reliable delivery of messages by resending lost, dropped, or corrupted packets.

tort: A civil injury for which the victim may recover damages from the tortfeasor (the person causing the harm).

tortious: Action that constitutes a tort is tortious.

white hat: A hacker who, having identified a security vulnerability, notifies the owner of the vulnerable system or computer and does not exploit the vulnerability.

WTO: World Trade Organization; an international organization with limited governing authority over trade and economic relations between member states, and a forum for ongoing trade negotiations.

The documents in this section are just a sample of those referred to in this encyclopedia. For information on how to locate other documents, see "How to Find the Law" in the front of this volume.

The documents reproduced here trace parts of two of Internet law's stories: censorship and copy protection. The Declaration of the Independence of Cyberspace, the Communications Decency Act of 1996, and the Supreme Court's opinion in Reno v. ACLU *are part of the first story: The Declaration was written in part in response to the act, which was then struck down by the Supreme Court in* Reno. *The WIPO Copyright Convention, the Digital Millennium Copyright Act (DMCA), and* Universal City Studios v. Corley *are part of the second story: The WIPO Convention obligated the United States to adopt laws preventing the circumvention of copy-protection measures; § 1201 of the DMCA fulfilled this obligation, and an attempt by activists to have § 1201 limited or declared unconstitutional failed in* Corley. *Neither story has ended there; attempts to control offensive and harmful Internet content are likely to continue, as is the struggle to define the limits of copyright protection and fair use.*

A DECLARATION OF THE INDEPENDENCE OF CYBERSPACE

John Perry Barlow, Davos, Switzerland, February 8, 1996
Reprinted by permission of the author

In 1996 John Perry Barlow, Grateful Dead songwriter and cofounder of the Electronic Frontier Foundation, wrote the Declaration of the Independence of Cyberspace. At the time the first Web browsers for home computers had only recently appeared; while in a sense the Internet was years or decades old, as a mass medium it was something new. The Declaration embodied a libertarian approach to Internet communication and an idea of cyberspace as a place. Among its points was the futility and basic wrongness of government attempts to control Internet content: "In the United States, you have today created a law, the Telecommunications Reform Act, which repudiates your own Constitution and insults the dreams of Jefferson, Washington, Mill, Madison, De Tocqueville, and Brandeis." The Telecommunications Reform Act included the Communications Decency Act, which is re-produced after the Declaration as the next chapter in this particular story of Internet law. Other aspects of the Declaration are discussed in the entry "Declaration of the Independence of Cyberspace" in this volume.

Governments of the Industrial World, you weary giants of flesh and steel, I come from Cyberspace, the new home of Mind. On behalf of the future, I ask you of the past to leave us alone. You are not welcome among us. You have no sovereignty where we gather.

We have no elected government, nor are we likely to have one, so I address you with no greater authority than that with which liberty itself always speaks. I declare the global social space we are building to be naturally independent of the tyrannies you seek to impose on us. You have no moral right to rule us nor do you possess any methods of enforcement we have true reason to fear.

Governments derive their just powers from the consent of the governed. You have neither solicited nor received ours. We did not invite you. You do not know us, nor do you know our world. Cyberspace does not lie within your borders. Do not think that you can build it, as though it were a public construction project. You cannot. It is an act of nature and it grows itself through our collective actions.

You have not engaged in our great and gathering conversation, nor did you create the wealth of our marketplaces. You do not know our culture, our ethics, or the unwritten codes that already provide our society more order than could be obtained by any of your impositions.

You claim there are problems among us that you need to solve. You use this claim as an excuse to invade our precincts. Many of these problems don't exist. Where there are real conflicts, where there are wrongs, we will identify them and address them by our means. We are forming our own Social Contract. This governance will arise according to the conditions of our world, not yours. Our world is different.

Cyberspace consists of transactions, relationships, and thought itself, arrayed like a standing wave in the web of our communications. Ours is a world that is both everywhere and nowhere, but it is not where bodies live.

We are creating a world that all may enter without privilege or prejudice accorded by race, economic power, military force, or station of birth.

We are creating a world where anyone, anywhere may express his or her beliefs, no matter how singular, without fear of being coerced into silence or conformity.

Your legal concepts of property, expression, identity, movement, and context do not apply to us. They are all based on matter, and there is no matter here.

Our identities have no bodies, so, unlike you, we cannot obtain order by physical coercion. We believe that from ethics, enlightened self-interest, and the commonweal, our governance will emerge. Our identities may be distributed across many of your jurisdictions. The only law that all our constituent cultures would generally recognize is the Golden Rule. We hope we will be able to build our particular solutions on that basis. But we cannot accept the solutions you are attempting to impose.

In the United States, you have today created a law, the Telecommunications Reform Act, which repudiates your own Constitution and insults the dreams of Jefferson, Washington, Mill, Madison, De Tocqueville, and Brandeis. These dreams must now be born anew in us.

You are terrified of your own children, since they are natives in a world where you will always be immigrants. Because you fear them, you entrust your bureaucracies with the parental responsibilities you are too cowardly to confront yourselves. In our world, all the sentiments and expressions of humanity, from the debasing to the angelic, are parts of a seamless whole, the global conversation of bits. We cannot separate the air that chokes from the air upon which wings beat.

In China, Germany, France, Russia, Singapore, Italy and the United States, you are trying to ward off the virus of liberty by erecting guard posts at the frontiers of Cyberspace. These may keep out the contagion for a small time, but they will not work in a world that will soon be blanketed in bit-bearing media.

Your increasingly obsolete information industries would perpetuate themselves by proposing laws, in America and elsewhere, that claim to own speech itself throughout the world. These laws would declare ideas to be another industrial product, no more noble than pig iron. In our world, whatever the human mind may create can be reproduced and distributed infinitely at no cost. The global conveyance of thought no longer requires your factories to accomplish.

These increasingly hostile and colonial measures place us in the same position as those previous lovers of freedom and self-determination who had to reject the authorities of distant, uninformed powers. We must declare our virtual selves immune to your sovereignty, even as we continue to consent to your rule over our bodies. We will spread ourselves across the Planet so that no one can arrest our thoughts.

We will create a civilization of the Mind in Cyberspace. May it be more humane and fair than the world your governments have made before.

COMMUNICATIONS DECENCY ACT OF 1996, PUBLIC LAW 104-104, § 502(2), TITLE V, § 502, AS ORIGINALLY CODIFIED AT 47 U.S.C. § 223

When the Internet was new, as now, one of its most disturbing aspects was the amount and nature of pornographic content transmitted over it. In July 1995, Time magazine's controversial "Cyberporn" issue aggravated fears of Internet pornography. Congress was alarmed by the prospect of minors having unrestricted access to pornography. In 1996 Congress enacted the first of its attempts to control pornographic Internet content: the ill-fated Communications Decency Act (CDA). Although a House version of the act would have limited the prohibition on Internet transmissions to content not protected by the First Amendment, the Senate version was ultimately adopted. It seems almost to have been designed to fail constitutional scrutiny, or to attempt to force a change in U.S. First Amendment jurisprudence. The statute appears below as originally enacted; in 2003 it was amended in an attempt to bring it into conformity with the First Amendment and the Court's decision in Reno, reproduced below. The CDA is discussed in several entries in this encyclopedia, especially in the entry "Communications Decency Act."

(a) Whoever –
(1) in interstate or foreign communications –
* * *
(B) by means of a telecommunications device knowingly –
(i) makes, creates, or solicits, and
(ii) initiates the transmission of, any comment, request, suggestion, proposal, image, or other communication which is obscene or indecent, knowing that the recipient of the communication is under 18 years of age, regardless of whether the maker of such communication placed the call or initiated the communication;
* * *
(2) knowingly permits any telecommunications facility under his control to be used for any activity prohibited by paragraph (1) with the intent that it be used for such activity, shall be fined under Title 18, or imprisoned not more than two years, or both.

***

(d) Whoever –

(1) in interstate or foreign communications knowingly –

(A) uses an interactive computer service to send to a specific person or persons under 18 years of age, or

(B) uses any interactive computer service to display in a manner available to a person under 18 years of age, any comment, request, suggestion, proposal, image, or other communication that, in context, depicts or describes, in terms patently offensive as measured by contemporary community standards, sexual or excretory activities or organs, regardless of whether the user of such service placed the call or initiated the communication; or

(2) knowingly permits any telecommunications facility under such person's control to be used for an activity prohibited by paragraph (1) with the intent that it be used for such activity, shall be fined under Title 18, or imprisoned not more than two years, or both.

RENO V. AMERICAN CIVIL LIBERTIES UNION, 521 U.S. 844 (1997)

No sooner was the Communications Decency Act of 1996 (CDA) enacted than it was challenged by a coalition of First Amendment advocates, including the American Civil Liberties Union (ACLU). At the trial court level, three judges, in three separate opinions, agreed that the statute was unconstitutional. A seven-justice majority of the Supreme Court agreed; two other justices agreed only in part.

The decision below (from which the footnotes and citations have been omitted) is also discussed in the entry "Communications Decency Act." It is interesting not only for its effect on the law of the Internet, but also as a historical document. Many of the technical details that take up the first part of the Court's opinion, for example, would probably be dealt with far more quickly today; the Internet is more widely understood. Also interesting is the Court's acceptance of the concept of cyberspace as a place. This way of viewing information networks is essential to the Declaration of the Independence of Cyberspace, just as it is to Neuromancer *and other cyberpunk classics, but it is almost entirely absent today.*

Justice Stevens delivered the opinion of the Court.

At issue is the constitutionality of two statutory provisions enacted to protect minors from "indecent" and "patently offensive" communications on the Internet. Notwithstanding the legitimacy and importance of the congressional goal of protecting children from harmful materials, we agree with the three-judge District Court that the statute abridges "the freedom of speech" protected by the First Amendment.

I

The District Court made extensive findings of fact, most of which were based on a detailed stipulation prepared by the parties. The findings describe the character and the dimensions of the Internet, the availability of sexually explicit material in that medium, and the problems confronting age verification for recipients of Internet communications. Because those findings provide the underpinnings for the legal issues, we begin with a summary of the undisputed facts.

The Internet

The Internet is an international network of interconnected computers. It is the outgrowth of what began in 1969 as a military program called "ARPANET," which was designed to enable computers operated by the military, defense contractors, and universities conducting defense-related research to communicate with one another by redundant channels even if some portions of the network were damaged in a war. While the ARPANET no longer exists, it provided an example for the development of a number of civilian networks that, eventually linking with each other, now enable tens of millions of people to communicate with one another and to access vast amounts of information from around the world. The Internet is "a unique and wholly new medium of worldwide human communication."

The Internet has experienced "extraordinary growth." The number of "host" computers—those that store information and relay communications—increased from about 300 in 1981 to approximately 9,400,000 by the time of the trial in 1996. Roughly 60% of these hosts are located in the United States. About 40 million people used the Internet at the time of trial, a number that is expected to mushroom to 200 million by 1999.

Individuals can obtain access to the Internet from many different sources, generally hosts themselves or entities with a host affiliation. Most colleges and universities provide access for their students and faculty; many corporations provide their employees with access through an office network; many communities and local libraries provide free access; and an increasing number of storefront "computer coffee shops" provide access for a small hourly fee. Several major national "online services" such as America Online,

CompuServe, the Microsoft Network, and Prodigy offer access to their own extensive proprietary networks as well as a link to the much larger resources of the Internet. These commercial online services had almost 12 million individual subscribers at the time of trial.

Anyone with access to the Internet may take advantage of a wide variety of communication and information retrieval methods. These methods are constantly evolving and difficult to categorize precisely. But, as presently constituted, those most relevant to this case are electronic mail (e-mail), automatic mailing list services ("mail exploders," sometimes referred to as "listservs"), "newsgroups," "chat rooms," and the "World Wide Web." All of these methods can be used to transmit text; most can transmit sound, pictures, and moving video images. Taken together, these tools constitute a unique medium—known to its users as "cyberspace"—located in no particular geographical location but available to anyone, anywhere in the world, with access to the Internet.

E-mail enables an individual to send an electronic message—generally akin to a note or letter—to another individual or to a group of addressees. The message is generally stored electronically, sometimes waiting for the recipient to check her "mailbox" and sometimes making its receipt known through some type of prompt. A mail exploder is a sort of e-mail group. Subscribers can send messages to a common e-mail address, which then forwards the message to the group's other subscribers. Newsgroups also serve groups of regular participants, but these postings may be read by others as well. There are thousands of such groups, each serving to foster an exchange of information or opinion on a particular topic running the gamut from, say, the music of Wagner to Balkan politics to AIDS prevention to the Chicago Bulls. About 100,000 new messages are posted every day. In most newsgroups, postings are automatically purged at regular intervals. In addition to posting a message that can be read later, two or more individuals wishing to communicate more immediately can enter a chat room to engage in real-time dialogue—in other words, by typing messages to one another that appear almost immediately on the others' computer screens. The District Court found that at any given time "tens of thousands of users are engaging in conversations on a huge range of subjects." It is "no exaggeration to conclude that the content on the Internet is as diverse as human thought."

The best known category of communication over the Internet is the World Wide Web, which allows users to search for and retrieve information stored in remote computers, as well as, in some cases, to communicate back to designated sites. In concrete terms, the Web consists of a vast number of documents stored in different computers all over the world. Some of these documents are simply files containing information. However, more elaborate documents, commonly known as Web "pages," are also prevalent. Each has its own address—"rather like a telephone number." Web pages frequently contain information and sometimes allow the viewer to communicate with the page's (or "site's") author. They generally also contain "links" to other documents created by that site's author or to other (generally) related sites. Typically, the links are either blue or underlined text—sometimes images.

Navigating the Web is relatively straightforward. A user may either type the address of a known page or enter one or more keywords into a commercial "search engine" in an effort to locate sites on a subject of interest. A particular Web page may contain the information sought by the "surfer," or, through its links, it may be an avenue to other documents located anywhere on the Internet. Users generally explore a given Web page, or move to another, by clicking a computer "mouse" on one of the page's icons or links. Access to most Web pages is freely available, but some allow access only to those who have purchased the right from a commercial provider. The Web is thus comparable, from the readers' viewpoint, to both a vast library including millions of readily available and indexed publications and a sprawling mall offering goods and services.

From the publishers' point of view, it constitutes a vast platform from which to address and hear from a worldwide audience of millions of readers, viewers, researchers, and buyers. Any person or organization with a computer connected to the Internet can "publish" information. Publishers include government agencies, educational institutions, commercial entities, advocacy groups, and individuals.

* * *

Sexually Explicit Material

Sexually explicit material on the Internet includes text, pictures, and chat and "extends from the modestly titillating to the hardest-core." These files are created, named, and posted in the same manner as material that is not sexually explicit, and may be accessed either deliberately or unintentionally during the course of an imprecise search. "Once a provider posts its content on the Internet, it cannot prevent that content from entering any community." Thus, for example, "when the UCR/California Museum of Photography posts to its Web site nudes by Edward Weston and Robert Mapplethorpe to announce that its new exhibit will travel to Baltimore and New York

City, those images are available not only in Los Angeles, Baltimore, and New York City, but also in Cincinnati, Mobile, or Beijing—wherever Internet users live. Similarly, the safer sex instructions that Critical Path posts to its Web site, written in street language so that the teenage receiver can understand them, are available not just in Philadelphia, but also in Provo and Prague."

Some of the communications over the Internet that originate in foreign countries are also sexually explicit.

Though such material is widely available, users seldom encounter such content accidentally. "A document's title or a description of the document will usually appear before the document itself . . . and in many cases the user will receive detailed information about a site's content before he or she need take the step to access the document. Almost all sexually explicit images are preceded by warnings as to the content." For that reason, the "odds are slim" that a user would enter a sexually explicit site by accident. Unlike communications received by radio or television, "the receipt of information on the Internet requires a series of affirmative steps more deliberate and directed than merely turning a dial. A child requires some sophistication and some ability to read to retrieve material and thereby to use the Internet unattended."

Systems have been developed to help parents control the material that may be available on a home computer with Internet access. A system may either limit a computer's access to an approved list of sources that have been identified as containing no adult material, it may block designated inappropriate sites, or it may attempt to block messages containing identifiable objectionable features. "Although parental control software currently can screen for certain suggestive words or for known sexually explicit sites, it cannot now screen for sexually explicit images." Nevertheless, the evidence indicates that "a reasonably effective method by which parents can prevent their children from accessing sexually explicit and other material which parents may believe is inappropriate for their children will soon be widely available."

Age Verification
The problem of age verification differs for different uses of the Internet. The District Court categorically determined that there "is no effective way to determine the identity or the age of a user who is accessing material through e-mail, mail exploders, newsgroups or chat rooms." The Government offered no evidence that there was a reliable way to screen recipients and participants in such forums for age. Moreover, even if it were technologically feasible to block minors' access to newsgroups and chat rooms containing discussions of art, politics, or other subjects that potentially elicit "indecent" or "patently offensive" contributions, it would not be possible to block their access to that material and "still allow them access to the remaining content, even if the overwhelming majority of that content was not indecent."

Technology exists by which an operator of a Web site may condition access on the verification of requested information such as a credit card number or an adult password. Credit card verification is only feasible, however, either in connection with a commercial transaction in which the card is used, or by payment to a verification agency. Using credit card possession as a surrogate for proof of age would impose costs on non-commercial Web sites that would require many of them to shut down. For that reason, at the time of the trial, credit card verification was "effectively unavailable to a substantial number of Internet content providers." Moreover, the imposition of such a requirement "would completely bar adults who do not have a credit card and lack the resources to obtain one from accessing any blocked material."

Commercial pornographic sites that charge their users for access have assigned them passwords as a method of age verification. The record does not contain any evidence concerning the reliability of these technologies. Even if passwords are effective for commercial purveyors of indecent material, the District Court found that an adult password requirement would impose significant burdens on noncommercial sites, both because they would discourage users from accessing their sites and because the cost of creating and maintaining such screening systems would be "beyond their reach."

In sum, the District Court found: "Even if credit card verification or adult password verification were implemented, the Government presented no testimony as to how such systems could ensure that the user of the password or credit card is in fact over 18. The burdens imposed by credit card verification and adult password verification systems make them effectively unavailable to a substantial number of Internet content providers."

II

The Telecommunications Act of 1996 was an unusually important legislative enactment. As stated on the first of its 103 pages, its primary purpose was to reduce regulation and encourage "the rapid deployment of new telecommunications technologies." The major components of the statute have nothing to do with the Internet; they were designed to promote competition in the local telephone service market, the multichannel video market, and the market for over-the-air broadcasting. The Act includes seven Titles, six of which are the product of extensive committee hearings and the subject of discussion in Reports prepared by Committees of the Senate and the House of Representatives. By contrast, Title V—known as the "Communications Decency Act of 1996" (CDA)—contains provisions that were either added in executive committee after the hearings were concluded or as amendments offered during floor debate on the legislation. An amendment offered in the Senate was the source of the two statutory provisions challenged in this case. They are informally described as the "indecent transmission" provision and the "patently offensive display" provision.

The first, 47 U.S.C. § 223(a), prohibits the knowing transmission of obscene or indecent messages to any recipient under 18 years of age. It provides in pertinent part:

"(a) Whoever –

"(1) in interstate or foreign communications –

. . .

"(B) by means of a telecommunications device knowingly –

"(i) makes, creates, or solicits, and

"(ii) initiates the transmission of,

"any comment, request, suggestion, proposal, image, or other communication which is obscene or indecent, knowing that the recipient of the communication is under 18 years of age, regardless of whether the maker of such communication placed the call or initiated the communication;

. . .

"(2) knowingly permits any telecommunications facility under his control to be used for any activity prohibited by paragraph (1) with the intent that it be used for such activity,

"shall be fined under Title 18, or imprisoned not more than two years, or both."

The second provision, § 223(d), prohibits the knowing sending or displaying of patently offensive messages in a manner that is available to a person under 18 years of age. It provides:

"(d) Whoever –

"(1) in interstate or foreign communications knowingly –

"(A) uses an interactive computer service to send to a specific person or persons under 18 years of age, or

"(B) uses any interactive computer service to display in a manner available to a person under 18 years of age,

"any comment, request, suggestion, proposal, image, or other communication that, in context, depicts or describes, in terms patently offensive as measured by contemporary community standards, sexual or excretory activities or organs, regardless of whether the user of such service placed the call or initiated the communication; or

"(2) knowingly permits any telecommunications facility under such person's control to be used for an activity prohibited by paragraph (1) with the intent that it be used for such activity,

"shall be fined under Title 18, or imprisoned not more than two years, or both."

The breadth of these prohibitions is qualified by two affirmative defenses. See § 223(e)(5). One covers those who take "good faith, reasonable, effective, and appropriate actions" to restrict access by minors to the prohibited communications. § 223(e)(5)(A). The other covers those who restrict access to covered material by requiring certain designated forms of age proof, such as a verified credit card or an adult identification number or code. § 223(e)(5)(B).

III

On February 8, 1996, immediately after the President signed the statute, 20 plaintiffs filed suit against the Attorney General of the United States and the Department of Justice challenging the constitutionality of §§ 223(a)(1) and 223(d). A week later, based on his conclusion that the term "indecent" was too vague to provide the basis for a criminal prosecution, District Judge Buckwalter entered a temporary restraining order against enforcement of § 223(a)(1)(B)(ii) insofar as it applies to indecent communications. A second suit was then filed by 27 additional plaintiffs, the two cases were consolidated, and a three-judge District Court was convened pursuant to § 561 of the CDA. After an evidentiary hearing, that court entered a preliminary injunction against enforcement of both of the challenged provisions. Each of the three judges wrote a separate opinion, but their judgment was unanimous.

***

The judgment of the District Court enjoins the Government from enforcing the prohibitions in § 223(a)(1)(B) insofar as they relate to "indecent" communications, but expressly preserves the Government's right to investigate and prosecute the obscenity or child pornography activities prohibited therein. The injunction against enforcement of §§ 223(d)(1) and (2) is unqualified because those provisions contain no separate reference to obscenity or child pornography.

The Government appealed under the CDA's special review provisions, and we noted probable jurisdiction. In its appeal, the Government argues that the District Court erred in holding that the CDA violated both the First Amendment because it is overbroad and the Fifth Amendment because it is vague. While we discuss the vagueness of the CDA because of its relevance to the First Amendment overbreadth inquiry, we conclude that the judgment should be affirmed without reaching the Fifth Amendment issue. We begin our analysis by reviewing the principal authorities on which the Government relies. Then, after describing the overbreadth of the CDA, we consider the Government's specific contentions, including its submission that we save portions of the statute either by severance or by fashioning judicial limitations on the scope of its coverage.

IV

In arguing for reversal, the Government contends that the CDA is plainly constitutional under three of our prior decisions: (1) *Ginsberg v. New York;* (2) *FCC v. Pacifica Foundation;* and (3) *Renton v. Playtime Theatres, Inc.* A close look at these cases, however, raises—rather than relieves—doubts concerning the constitutionality of the CDA.

In *Ginsberg,* we upheld the constitutionality of a New York statute that prohibited selling to minors under 17 years of age material that was considered obscene as to them even if not obscene as to adults. We rejected the defendant's broad submission that "the scope of the constitutional freedom of expression secured to a citizen to read or see material concerned with sex cannot be made to depend on whether the citizen is an adult or a minor." In rejecting that contention, we relied not only on the State's independent interest in the well-being of its youth, but also on our consistent recognition of the principle that "the parents' claim to authority in their own household to direct the rearing of their children is basic in the structure of our society."

In four important respects, the statute upheld in *Ginsberg* was narrower than the CDA. First, we noted in *Ginsberg* that "the prohibition against sales to minors does not bar parents who so desire from purchasing the magazines for their children." Under the CDA, by contrast, neither the parents' consent—nor even their participation—in the communication would avoid the application of the statute. Second, the New York statute applied only to commercial transactions, whereas the CDA contains no such limitation. Third, the New York statute cabined its definition of material that is harmful to minors with the requirement that it be "utterly without redeeming

social importance for minors." The CDA fails to provide us with any definition of the term "indecent" as used in § 223(a)(1) and, importantly, omits any requirement that the "patently offensive" material covered by § 223(d) lack serious literary, artistic, political, or scientific value. Fourth, the New York statute defined a minor as a person under the age of 17, whereas the CDA, in applying to all those under 18 years, includes an additional year of those nearest majority.

In *Pacifica,* we upheld a declaratory order of the Federal Communications Commission, holding that the broadcast of a recording of a 12-minute monologue entitled "Filthy Words" that had previously been delivered to a live audience "could have been the subject of administrative sanctions." The Commission had found that the repetitive use of certain words referring to excretory or sexual activities or organs "in an afternoon broadcast when children are in the audience was patently offensive" and concluded that the monologue was indecent "as broadcast." The respondent did not quarrel with the finding that the afternoon broadcast was patently offensive, but contended that it was not "indecent" within the meaning of the relevant statutes because it contained no prurient appeal. After rejecting respondent's statutory arguments, we confronted its two constitutional arguments: (1) that the Commission's construction of its authority to ban indecent speech was so broad that its order had to be set aside even if the broadcast at issue was unprotected; and (2) that since the recording was not obscene, the First Amendment forbade any abridgment of the right to broadcast it on the radio.

In the portion of the lead opinion not joined by Justices Powell and Blackmun, the plurality stated that the First Amendment does not prohibit all governmental regulation that depends on the content of speech. Accordingly, the availability of constitutional protection for a vulgar and offensive monologue that was not obscene depended on the context of the broadcast. Relying on the premise that "of all forms of communication" broadcasting had received the most limited First Amendment protection, the Court concluded that the ease with which children may obtain access to broadcasts, "coupled with the concerns recognized in *Ginsberg,*" justified special treatment of indecent broadcasting.

As with the New York statute at issue in *Ginsberg,* there are significant differences between the order upheld in *Pacifica* and the CDA. First, the order in *Pacifica,* issued by an agency that had been regulating radio stations for decades, targeted a specific broadcast that represented a rather dramatic departure from traditional program content in order to designate when—rather than whether—it would be permissible to air such a program in that particular medium. The CDA's broad categorical prohibitions are not limited to particular times and are not dependent on any evaluation by an agency familiar with the unique characteristics of the Internet. Second, unlike the CDA, the Commission's declaratory order was not punitive; we expressly refused to decide whether the indecent broadcast "would justify a criminal prosecution." Finally, the Commission's order applied to a medium which as a matter of history had "received the most limited First Amendment protection," in large part because warnings could not adequately protect the listener from unexpected program content. The Internet, however, has no comparable history. Moreover, the District Court found that the risk of encountering indecent material by accident is remote because a series of affirmative steps is required to access specific material.

In *Renton,* we upheld a zoning ordinance that kept adult movie theaters out of residential neighborhoods. The ordinance was aimed, not at the content of the films shown in the theaters, but rather at the "secondary effects"—such as crime and deteriorating property values—that these theaters fostered: "'It is th[e] secondary effect which these zoning ordinances attempt to avoid, not the dissemination of "offensive" speech.'" According to the Government, the CDA is constitutional because it constitutes a sort of "cyberzoning" on the Internet. But the CDA applies broadly to the entire universe of cyberspace. And the purpose of the CDA is to protect children from the primary effects of "indecent" and "patently offensive" speech, rather than any "secondary" effect of such speech. Thus, the CDA is a content-based blanket restriction on speech, and, as such, cannot be "properly analyzed as a form of time, place, and manner regulation."

***

These precedents, then, surely do not require us to uphold the CDA and are fully consistent with the application of the most stringent review of its provisions.

V

In *Southeastern Promotions, Ltd. v. Conrad* we observed that "[e]ach medium of expression . . . may present its own problems." Thus, some of our cases have recognized special justifications for regulation of the broadcast media that are not applicable to other speakers. In these cases, the Court relied on the history of extensive Government regulation of the broadcast medium; the scarcity of available frequencies at its inception; and its "invasive" nature.

Those factors are not present in cyberspace. Neither before nor after the enactment of the CDA have the vast democratic forums of the Internet been subject to the type of government supervision and regulation that has attended the broadcast industry. Moreover, the Internet is not as "invasive" as radio or television. The District Court specifically found that "[c]ommunications over the Internet do not 'invade' an individual's home or appear on one's computer screen unbidden. Users seldom encounter content 'by accident.'" It also found that "[a]lmost all sexually explicit images are preceded by warnings as to the content," and cited testimony that "'odds are slim' that a user would come across a sexually explicit sight by accident."

We distinguished *Pacifica* in *Sable* on just this basis. In *Sable,* a company engaged in the business of offering sexually oriented prerecorded telephone messages (popularly known as "dial-a-porn") challenged the constitutionality of an amendment to the Communications Act of 1934 that imposed a blanket prohibition on indecent as well as obscene interstate commercial telephone messages. We held that the statute was constitutional insofar as it applied to obscene messages but invalid as applied to indecent messages. In attempting to justify the complete ban and criminalization of indecent commercial telephone messages, the Government relied on *Pacifica,* arguing that the ban was necessary to prevent children from gaining access to such messages. We agreed that "there is a compelling interest in protecting the physical and psychological well-being of minors" which extended to shielding them from indecent messages that are not obscene by adult standards, but distinguished our "emphatically narrow holding" in *Pacifica* because it did not involve a complete ban and because it involved a different medium of communication. We explained that "the dial-it medium requires the listener to take affirmative steps to receive the communication." "Placing a telephone call," we continued, "is not the same as turning on a radio and being taken by surprise by an indecent message."

Finally, unlike the conditions that prevailed when Congress first authorized regulation of the broadcast spectrum, the Internet can hardly be considered a "scarce" expressive commodity. It provides relatively unlimited, low-cost capacity for communication of all kinds. The Government estimates that "[a]s many as 40 million people use the Internet today, and that figure is expected to grow to 200 million by 1999." This dynamic, multifaceted category of communication includes not only traditional print and news services, but also audio, video, and still images, as well as interactive, real-time dialogue. Through the use of chat rooms, any person with a phone line can become a town crier with a voice that resonates farther than it could from any soapbox. Through the use of Web pages, mail exploders, and newsgroups, the same individual can become a pamphleteer. As the District Court found, "the content on the Internet is as diverse as human thought." We agree with its conclusion that our cases provide no basis for qualifying the level of First Amendment scrutiny that should be applied to this medium.

VI

Regardless of whether the CDA is so vague that it violates the Fifth Amendment, the many ambiguities concerning the scope of its coverage render it problematic for purposes of the First Amendment. For instance, each of the two parts of the CDA uses a different linguistic form. The first uses the word "indecent," while the second speaks of material that "in context, depicts or describes, in terms patently offensive as measured by contemporary community standards, sexual or excretory activities or organs," § 223(d). Given the absence of a definition of either term, this difference in language will provoke uncertainty among speakers about how the two standards relate to each other and just what they mean. Could a speaker confidently assume that a serious discussion about birth control practices, homosexuality, the First Amendment issues raised by the Appendix to our *Pacifica* opinion, or the consequences of prison rape would not violate the CDA? This uncertainty undermines the likelihood that the CDA has been carefully tailored to the congressional goal of protecting minors from potentially harmful materials.

The vagueness of the CDA is a matter of special concern for two reasons. First, the CDA is a content-based regulation of speech. The vagueness of such a regulation raises special First Amendment concerns because of its obvious chilling effect on free speech. Second, the CDA is a criminal statute. In addition to the opprobrium and stigma of a criminal conviction, the CDA threatens violators with penalties including up to two years in prison for each act of violation. The severity of criminal sanctions may well cause speakers to remain silent rather than communicate even arguably unlawful words, ideas, and images. As a practical matter, this increased deterrent effect, coupled with the "risk of discriminatory enforcement" of vague regulations, poses greater First Amendment concerns than those implicated by the civil regulation reviewed in *Denver Area Ed. Telecommunications Consortium, Inc. v. FCC.*

The Government argues that the statute is no more vague than the obscenity standard this Court established in *Miller v. California.* But that is not so. In *Miller,* this Court reviewed a criminal conviction against a commercial vendor who mailed brochures containing pictures of sexually explicit activities to individuals who had not requested such materials. Having struggled for some time to establish a definition of obscenity, we set forth in *Miller* the test for obscenity that controls to this day:

"(a) whether the average person, applying contemporary community standards would find that the work, taken as a whole, appeals to the prurient interest; (b) whether the work depicts or describes, in a patently offensive way, sexual conduct specifically defined by the applicable state law; and (c) whether the work, taken as a whole, lacks serious literary, artistic, political, or scientific value."

Because the CDA's "patently offensive" standard (and, we assume, *arguendo,* its synonymous "indecent" standard) is one part of the three-prong *Miller* test, the Government reasons, it cannot be unconstitutionally vague.

The Government's assertion is incorrect as a matter of fact. The second prong of the *Miller* test—the purportedly analogous standard—contains a critical requirement that is omitted from the CDA: that the proscribed material be "specifically defined by the applicable state law." This requirement reduces the vagueness inherent in the open-ended term "patently offensive" as used in the CDA. Moreover, the *Miller* definition is limited to "sexual conduct," whereas the CDA extends also to include (1) "excretory activities" as well as (2) "organs" of both a sexual and excretory nature.

The Government's reasoning is also flawed. Just because a definition including three limitations is not vague, it does not follow that one of those limitations, standing by itself, is not vague. Each of *Miller*'s additional two prongs—(1) that, taken as a whole, the material appeal to the "prurient" interest, and (2) that it "lac[k] serious literary, artistic, political, or scientific value"—critically limits the uncertain sweep of the obscenity definition. The second requirement is particularly important because, unlike the "patently offensive" and "prurient interest" criteria, it is not judged by contemporary community standards. This "societal value" requirement, absent in the CDA, allows appellate courts to impose some limitations and regularity on the definition by setting, as a matter of law, a national floor for socially redeeming value. The Government's contention that courts will be able to give such legal limitations to the CDA's standards is belied by *Miller*'s own rationale for having juries determine whether material is "patently offensive" according to community standards: that such questions are essentially ones of fact.

In contrast to *Miller* and our other previous cases, the CDA thus presents a greater threat of censoring speech that, in fact, falls outside the statute's scope. Given the vague contours of the coverage of the statute, it unquestionably silences some speakers whose messages would be entitled to constitutional protection. That danger provides further reason for insisting that the statute not be overly broad. The CDA's burden on protected speech cannot be justified if it could be avoided by a more carefully drafted statute.

VII

We are persuaded that the CDA lacks the precision that the First Amendment requires when a statute regulates the content of speech. In order to deny minors access to potentially harmful speech, the CDA effectively suppresses a large amount of speech that adults have a constitutional right to receive and to address to one another. That burden on adult speech is unacceptable if less restrictive alternatives would be at least as effective in achieving the legitimate purpose that the statute was enacted to serve.

In evaluating the free speech rights of adults, we have made it perfectly clear that "[s]exual expression which is indecent but not obscene is protected by the First Amendment." Indeed, *Pacifica* itself admonished that "the fact that society may find speech offensive is not a sufficient reason for suppressing it."

It is true that we have repeatedly recognized the governmental interest in protecting children from harmful materials. But that interest does not justify an unnecessarily broad suppression of speech addressed to adults. As we have explained, the Government may not "reduc[e] the adult population . . . to . . . only what is fit for children." "[R]egardless of the strength of the government's interest" in protecting children, "[t]he level of discourse reaching a mailbox simply cannot be limited to that which would be suitable for a sandbox."

The District Court was correct to conclude that the CDA effectively resembles the ban on "dial-a-porn" invalidated in *Sable*. In *Sable*, this Court rejected the argument that we should defer to the congressional judgment that nothing less than a total ban would be effective in preventing enterprising youngsters from gaining access to indecent communications. *Sable* thus made clear that the mere fact that a statutory regulation of speech was enacted for the important purpose of protecting children from exposure to sexually explicit material does not foreclose inquiry into its validity. As we pointed out last Term, that inquiry embodies an "overarching commitment" to make sure that Congress has designed

its statute to accomplish its purpose "without imposing an unnecessarily great restriction on speech."

In arguing that the CDA does not so diminish adult communication, the Government relies on the incorrect factual premise that prohibiting a transmission whenever it is known that one of its recipients is a minor would not interfere with adult-to-adult communication. The findings of the District Court make clear that this premise is untenable. Given the size of the potential audience for most messages, in the absence of a viable age verification process, the sender must be charged with knowing that one or more minors will likely view it. Knowledge that, for instance, one or more members of a 100-person chat group will be a minor—and therefore that it would be a crime to send the group an indecent message— would surely burden communication among adults.

The District Court found that at the time of trial existing technology did not include any effective method for a sender to prevent minors from obtaining access to its communications on the Internet without also denying access to adults. The Court found no effective way to determine the age of a user who is accessing material through e-mail, mail exploders, newsgroups, or chat rooms. As a practical matter, the Court also found that it would be prohibitively expensive for noncommercial—as well as some commercial—speakers who have Web sites to verify that their users are adults. These limitations must inevitably curtail a significant amount of adult communication on the Internet. By contrast, the District Court found that "[d]espite its limitations, currently available user-based software suggests that a reasonably effective method by which parents can prevent their children from accessing sexually explicit and other material which parents may believe is inappropriate for their children will soon be widely available."

The breadth of the CDA's coverage is wholly unprecedented. Unlike the regulations upheld in *Ginsberg* and *Pacifica*, the scope of the CDA is not limited to commercial speech or commercial entities. Its open-ended prohibitions embrace all nonprofit entities and individuals posting indecent messages or displaying them on their own computers in the presence of minors. The general, undefined terms "indecent" and "patently offensive" cover large amounts of nonpornographic material with serious educational or other value. Moreover, the "community standards" criterion as applied to the Internet means that any communication available to a nation wide audience will be judged by the standards of the community most likely to be offended by the message. The regulated subject matter includes any of the seven "dirty words" used in the *Pacifica* monologue, the use of which the Government's expert acknowledged could constitute a felony. It may also extend to discussions about prison rape or safe sexual practices, artistic images that include nude subjects, and arguably the card catalog of the Carnegie Library.

For the purposes of our decision, we need neither accept nor reject the Government's submission that the First Amendment does not forbid a blanket prohibition on all "indecent" and "patently offensive" messages communicated to a 17-year-old—no matter how much value the message may contain and regardless of parental approval. It is at least clear that the strength of the Government's interest in protecting minors is not equally strong throughout the coverage of this broad statute. Under the CDA, a parent allowing her 17-year-old to use the family computer to obtain information on the Internet that she, in her parental judgment, deems appropriate could face a lengthy prison term. Similarly, a parent who sent his 17-year-old college freshman information on birth control via e-mail could be incarcerated even though neither he, his child, nor anyone in their home community found the material "indecent" or "patently offensive," if the college town's community thought otherwise.

The breadth of this content-based restriction of speech imposes an especially heavy burden on the Government to explain why a less restrictive provision would not be as effective as the CDA. It has not done so. The arguments in this Court have referred to possible alternatives such as requiring that indecent material be "tagged" in a way that facilitates parental control of material coming into their homes, making exceptions for messages with artistic or educational value, providing some tolerance for parental choice, and regulating some portions of the Internet—such as commercial Web sites—differently from others, such as chat rooms. Particularly in the light of the absence of any detailed findings by the Congress, or even hearings addressing the special problems of the CDA, we are persuaded that the CDA is not narrowly tailored if that requirement has any meaning at all.

VIII

In an attempt to curtail the CDA's facial overbreadth, the Government advances three additional arguments for sustaining the Act's affirmative prohibitions: (1) that the CDA is constitutional because it leaves open ample "alternative channels" of communication; (2) that the plain meaning of the CDA's "knowledge" and "specific person" requirement significantly restricts its permissible applications; and (3) that the CDA's prohibitions are "almost always" limited to material lacking redeeming social value.

The Government first contends that, even though the CDA effectively censors discourse on many of the Internet's modalities—such as chat groups, newsgroups, and mail exploders—it is nonetheless constitutional because it provides a "reasonable opportunity" for speakers to engage in the restricted speech on the World Wide Web. This argument is unpersuasive because the CDA regulates speech on the basis of its content. A "time, place, and manner" analysis is therefore inapplicable. It is thus immaterial whether such speech would be feasible on the Web (which, as the Government's own expert acknowledged, would cost up to $10,000 if the speaker's interests were not accommodated by an existing Web site, not including costs for data base management and age verification). The Government's position is equivalent to arguing that a statute could ban leaflets on certain subjects as long as individuals are free to publish books. In invalidating a number of laws that banned leafletting on the streets regardless of their content, we explained that "one is not to have the exercise of his liberty of expression in appropriate places abridged on the plea that it may be exercised in some other place."

The Government also asserts that the "knowledge" requirement of both §§ 223(a) and (d), especially when coupled with the "specific child" element found in § 223(d), saves the CDA from overbreadth. Because both sections prohibit the dissemination of indecent messages only to persons known to be under 18, the Government argues, it does not require transmitters to "refrain from communicating indecent material to adults; they need only refrain from disseminating such materials to persons they know to be under 18." This argument ignores the fact that most Internet forums—including chat rooms, newsgroups, mail exploders, and the Web— are open to all comers. The Government's assertion that the knowledge requirement somehow protects the communications of adults is therefore untenable. Even the strongest reading of the "specific person" requirement of § 223(d) cannot save the statute. It would confer broad powers of censorship, in the form of a "heckler's veto," upon any opponent of indecent speech who might simply log on and inform the would-be discoursers that his 17-year-old child— a "specific person . . . under 18 years of age,"— would be present.

Finally, we find no textual support for the Government's submission that material having scientific, educational, or other redeeming social value will necessarily fall outside the CDA's "patently offensive" and "indecent" prohibitions.

IX

The Government's three remaining arguments focus on the defenses provided in § 223(e)(5). First, relying on the "good faith, reasonable, effective, and appropriate actions" provision, the Government suggests that "tagging" provides a defense that saves the constitutionality of the CDA. The suggestion assumes that transmitters may encode their indecent communications in a way that would indicate their contents, thus permitting recipients to block their reception with appropriate software. It is the requirement that the good-faith action must be "effective" that makes this defense illusory. The Government recognizes that its proposed screening software does not currently exist. Even if it did, there is no way to know whether a potential recipient will actually block the encoded material. Without the impossible knowledge that every guardian in America is screening for the "tag," the transmitter could not reasonably rely on its action to be "effective."

For its second and third arguments concerning defenses—which we can consider together—the Government relies on the latter half of § 223(e)(5), which applies when the transmitter has restricted access by requiring use of a verified credit card or adult identification. Such verification is not only technologically available but actually is used by commercial providers of sexually explicit material. These providers, therefore, would be protected by the defense. Under the findings of the District Court, however, it is not economically feasible for most noncommercial speakers to employ such verification. Accordingly, this defense would not significantly narrow the statute's burden on noncommercial speech. Even with respect to the commercial pornographers that would be protected by the defense, the Government failed to adduce any evidence that these verification techniques actually preclude minors from posing as adults. Given that the risk of criminal sanctions "hovers over each content provider, like the proverbial sword of Damocles," the District Court correctly refused to rely on unproven future technology to save the statute. The Government thus failed to prove that the proffered defense would significantly reduce the heavy burden on adult speech produced by the prohibition on offensive displays.

We agree with the District Court's conclusion that the CDA places an unacceptably heavy burden on protected speech, and that the defenses do not constitute the sort of "narrow tailoring" that will save an otherwise patently invalid unconstitutional provision. In *Sable,* we remarked that the speech restriction at issue there amounted to "'burn[ing] the house to roast the pig.'" The CDA, casting a far darker shadow over free speech, threatens to torch a large segment of the Internet community.

X

At oral argument, the Government relied heavily on its ultimate fall-back position: If this Court should conclude that the CDA is insufficiently tailored, it urged, we should save the statute's constitutionality by honoring the severability clause, see 47 U.S.C. § 608, and construing nonseverable terms narrowly. In only one respect is this argument acceptable.

A severability clause requires textual provisions that can be severed. We will follow § 608's guidance by leaving constitutional textual elements of the statute intact in the one place where they are, in fact, severable. The "indecency" provision, 47 U.S.C. § 223(a), applies to "any comment, request, suggestion, proposal, image, or other communication which is *obscene or indecent.*" Appellees do not challenge the application of the statute to obscene speech, which, they acknowledge, can be banned totally because it enjoys no First Amendment protection. As set forth by the statute, the restriction of "obscene" material enjoys a textual manifestation separate from that for "indecent" material, which we have held unconstitutional. Therefore, we will sever the term "or indecent" from the statute, leaving the rest of § 223(a) standing. In no other respect, however, can § 223(a) or § 223(d) be saved by such a textual surgery.

The Government also draws on an additional, less traditional aspect of the CDA's severability clause, 47 U.S.C. § 608, which asks any reviewing court that holds the statute facially unconstitutional not to invalidate the CDA in application to "other persons or circumstances" that might be constitutionally permissible. It further invokes this Court's admonition that, absent "countervailing considerations," a statute should "be declared invalid to the extent it reaches too far, but otherwise left intact." There are two flaws in this argument.

First, the statute that grants our jurisdiction for this expedited review . . . limits that jurisdictional grant to actions challenging the CDA "on its face." Consistent with § 561, the plaintiffs who brought this suit and the three-judge panel that decided it treated it as a facial challenge. We have no authority, in this particular posture, to convert this litigation into an "as-applied" challenge. Nor, given the vast array of plaintiffs, the range of their expressive activities, and the vagueness of the statute, would it be practicable to limit our holding to a judicially defined set of specific applications.

Second, one of the "countervailing considerations" mentioned in *Brockett* is present here. In considering a facial challenge, this Court may impose a limiting construction on a statute only if it is "readily susceptible" to such a construction. The open-ended character of the CDA provides no guidance what ever for limiting its coverage.

This case is therefore unlike those in which we have construed a statute narrowly because the text or other source of congressional intent identified a clear line that this Court could draw. Rather, our decision in *United States v. National Treasury Employees Union* is applicable. In that case, we declined to "dra[w] one or more lines between categories of speech covered by an overly broad statute, when Congress has sent inconsistent signals as to where the new line or lines should be drawn" because doing so "involves a far more serious invasion of the legislative domain." This Court "will not rewrite a . . . law to conform it to constitutional requirements."

XI

In this Court, though not in the District Court, the Government asserts that—in addition to its interest in protecting children—its "[e]qually significant" interest in fostering the growth of the Internet provides an independent basis for upholding the constitutionality of the CDA. The Government apparently assumes that the unregulated availability of "indecent" and "patently offensive" material on the Internet is driving countless citizens away from the medium because of the risk of exposing themselves or their children to harmful material.

We find this argument singularly unpersuasive. The dramatic expansion of this new marketplace of ideas contradicts the factual basis of this contention. The record demonstrates that the growth of the Internet has been and continues to be phenomenal. As a matter of constitutional tradition, in the absence of evidence to the contrary, we presume that governmental regulation of the content of speech is more likely to interfere with the free exchange of ideas than to encourage it. The interest in encouraging freedom of expression in a democratic society outweighs any theoretical but unproven benefit of censorship.

For the foregoing reasons, the judgment of the District Court is affirmed.

It is so ordered.

Justice O'Connor, with whom the Chief Justice [Rehnquist] joins, concurring in the judgment in part and dissenting in part.

I write separately to explain why I view the Communications Decency Act of 1996 (CDA) as little more than an attempt by Congress to create "adult zones" on the Internet. Our precedent indicates that the creation of such zones can be constitutionally sound. Despite the soundness of its purpose, however, portions of the CDA are unconstitutional be-cause they stray from the blueprint our prior cases have developed for constructing a "zoning law" that passes constitutional muster.

Appellees bring a facial challenge to three provisions of the CDA. The first, which the Court describes as the "indecency transmission" provision, makes it a crime to knowingly transmit an obscene or indecent message or image to a person the sender knows is under 18 years old. What the Court classifies as a single "'patently offensive display'" provision, see ante, at 2338, is in reality two separate provisions. The first of these makes it a crime to knowingly send a patently offensive message or image to a specific person under the age of 18 ("specific person" provision). The second criminalizes the display of patently offensive messages or images "in a[ny] manner available" to minors ("display" provision). None of these provisions purports to keep indecent (or patently offensive) material away from adults, who have a First Amendment right to obtain this speech. Thus, the undeniable purpose of the CDA is to segregate indecent material on the Internet into certain areas that minors cannot access.

The creation of "adult zones" is by no means a novel concept. States have long denied minors access to certain establishments frequented by adults. States have also denied minors access to speech deemed to be "harmful to minors." The Court has previously sustained such zoning laws, but only if they respect the First Amendment rights of adults and minors. That is to say, a zoning law is valid if (i) it does not unduly restrict adult access to the material; and (ii) minors have no First Amendment right to read or view the banned material. As applied to the Internet as it exists in 1997, the "display" provision and some applications of the "indecency transmission" and "specific person" provisions fail to adhere to the first of these limiting principles by restricting adults' access to protected materials in certain circumstances. Unlike the Court, however, I would invalidate the provisions only in those circumstances.

Our cases make clear that a "zoning" law is valid only if adults are still able to obtain the regulated speech. If they cannot, the law does more than simply keep children away from speech they have no right to obtain—it interferes with the rights of adults to obtain constitutionally protected speech and effectively "reduce[s] the adult population . . . to reading only what is fit for children." The First Amendment does not tolerate such interference. If the law does not unduly restrict adults' access to constitutionally protected speech, however, it may be valid. In *Ginsberg v. New York,* for example, the Court sustained a New York law that barred store owners from selling pornographic magazines to minors in part because adults could still buy those magazines.

The Court in *Ginsberg* concluded that the New York law created a constitutionally adequate adult zone simply because, on its face, it denied access only to minors. The Court did not question—and therefore necessarily assumed—that an adult zone, once created, would succeed in preserving adults' access while denying minors' access to the regulated speech. Before today, there was no reason to question this assumption, for the Court has previously only considered laws that operated in the physical world, a world that with two characteristics that make it possible to create "adult zones": geography and identity. A minor can see an adult dance show only if he enters an establishment that provides such entertainment. And should he attempt to do so, the minor will not be able to conceal completely his identity (or, consequently, his age). Thus, the twin characteristics of geography and identity enable the establishment's proprietor to prevent children from entering the establishment, but to let adults inside.

The electronic world is fundamentally different. Because it is no more than the interconnection of electronic pathways, cyberspace allows speakers and listeners to mask their identities. Cyberspace undeniably reflects some form of geography; chat rooms and Web sites, for example, exist at fixed "locations" on the Internet. Since users can transmit and receive messages on the Internet without revealing anything about their identities or ages, however, it is not currently possible to exclude persons from accessing certain messages on the basis of their identity.

Cyberspace differs from the physical world in another basic way: Cyberspace is malleable. Thus, it is possible to construct barriers in cyberspace and use them to screen for identity, making cyberspace more like the physical world and, consequently, more amenable to zoning laws. This transformation of cyberspace is already underway. Internet speakers (users who post material on the Internet) have begun to zone cyberspace itself through the use of "gateway" technology. Such technology requires Internet users to enter information about themselves—perhaps an adult identification number or a credit card number—before they can access certain areas of cyberspace, much like a bouncer checks a person's driver's license before admitting him to a nightclub. Internet users who access information have not attempted to zone cyberspace itself, but have tried to limit their own power to access information in cyberspace, much as a parent controls what her children watch on television by installing a lock box. This user-based zoning is accomplished through the use of screening software (such as Cyber Patrol or Sur-

fWatch) or browsers with screening capabilities, both of which search addresses and text for keywords that are associated with "adult" sites and, if the user wishes, blocks access to such sites. The Platform for Internet Content Selection project is designed to facilitate user-based zoning by encouraging Internet speakers to rate the content of their speech using codes recognized by all screening programs.

Despite this progress, the transformation of cyberspace is not complete. Although gateway technology has been available on the World Wide Web for some time now, it is not available to all Web speakers, and is just now becoming technologically feasible for chat rooms and USENET newsgroups. Gateway technology is not ubiquitous in cyberspace, and because without it "there is no means of age verification," cyberspace still remains largely unzoned—and unzoneable. User-based zoning is also in its infancy. For it to be effective, (i) an agreed-upon code (or "tag") would have to exist; (ii) screening software or browsers with screening capabilities would have to be able to recognize the "tag"; and (iii) those programs would have to be widely available—and widely used—by Internet users. At present, none of these conditions is true. Screening software "is not in wide use today" and "only a handful of browsers have screening capabilities." There is, moreover, no agreed-upon "tag" for those programs to recognize.

Although the prospects for the eventual zoning of the Internet appear promising, I agree with the Court that we must evaluate the constitutionality of the CDA as it applies to the Internet as it exists today. Given the present state of cyberspace, I agree with the Court that the "display" provision cannot pass muster. Until gateway technology is available throughout cyberspace, and it is not in 1997, a speaker cannot be reasonably assured that the speech he displays will reach only adults because it is impossible to confine speech to an "adult zone." Thus, the only way for a speaker to avoid liability under the CDA is to refrain completely from using indecent speech. But this forced silence impinges on the First Amendment right of adults to make and obtain this speech and, for all intents and purposes, "reduce[s] the adult population [on the Internet] to reading only what is fit for children." As a result, the "display" provision cannot withstand scrutiny.

The "indecency transmission" and "specific person" provisions present a closer issue, for they are not unconstitutional in all of their applications. As discussed above, the "indecency transmission" provision makes it a crime to transmit knowingly an indecent message to a person the sender knows is under 18 years of age. The "specific person" provision proscribes the same conduct, although it does not as explicitly require the sender to know that the intended recipient of his indecent message is a minor. § 223(d)(1)(A). The Government urges the Court to construe the provision to impose such a knowledge requirement, and I would do so.

So construed, both provisions are constitutional as applied to a conversation involving only an adult and one or more minors—e.g., when an adult speaker sends an e-mail knowing the addressee is a minor, or when an adult and minor converse by themselves or with other minors in a chat room. In this context, these provisions are no different from the law we sustained in *Ginsberg*. Restricting what the adult may say to the minors in no way restricts the adult's ability to communicate with other adults. He is not prevented from speaking indecently to other adults in a chat room (because there are no other adults participating in the conversation) and he remains free to send indecent e-mails to other adults. The relevant universe contains only one adult, and the adult in that universe has the power to refrain from using indecent speech and consequently to keep all such speech within the room in an "adult" zone.

The analogy to *Ginsberg* breaks down, however, when more than one adult is a party to the conversation. If a minor enters a chat room otherwise occupied by adults, the CDA effectively requires the adults in the room to stop using indecent speech. If they did not, they could be prosecuted under the "indecency transmission" and "specific person" provisions for any indecent statements they make to the group, since they would be transmitting an indecent message to specific persons, one of whom is a minor. The CDA is therefore akin to a law that makes it a crime for a bookstore owner to sell pornographic magazines to anyone once a minor enters his store. Even assuming such a law might be constitutional in the physical world as a reasonable alternative to excluding minors completely from the store, the absence of any means of excluding minors from chat rooms in cyberspace restricts the rights of adults to engage in indecent speech in those rooms. The "indecency transmission" and "specific person" provisions share this defect.

But these two provisions do not infringe on adults' speech in all situations. And as discussed below, I do not find that the provisions are overbroad in the sense that they restrict minors' access to a substantial amount of speech that minors have the right to read and view. Accordingly, the CDA can be applied constitutionally in some situations. Normally, this fact would require the Court to reject a direct facial challenge. Appellees' claim arises under the First Amendment, however, and they argue that the CDA

is facially invalid because it is "substantially overbroad"—that is, it "sweeps too broadly . . . [and] penaliz[es] a substantial amount of speech that is constitutionally protected." I agree with the Court that the provisions are overbroad in that they cover any and all communications between adults and minors, regardless of how many adults might be part of the audience to the communication.

This conclusion does not end the matter, however. Where, as here, "the parties challenging the statute are those who desire to engage in protected speech that the overbroad statute purports to punish, . . . [t]he statute may forthwith be declared invalid to the extent that it reaches too far, but otherwise left intact." There is no question that Congress intended to prohibit certain communications between one adult and one or more minors. There is also no question that Congress would have enacted a narrower version of these provisions had it known a broader version would be declared unconstitutional. I would therefore sustain the "indecency transmission" and "specific person" provisions to the extent they apply to the transmission of Internet communications where the party initiating the communication knows that all of the recipients are minors.

II

Whether the CDA substantially interferes with the First Amendment rights of minors, and thereby runs afoul of the second characteristic of valid zoning laws, presents a closer question. In *Ginsberg*, the New York law we sustained prohibited the sale to minors of magazines that were "harmful to minors." Under that law, a magazine was "harmful to minors" only if it was obscene as to minors. Noting that obscene speech is not protected by the First Amendment, and that New York was constitutionally free to adjust the definition of obscenity for minors, the Court concluded that the law did not "invad[e] the area of freedom of expression constitutionally secured to minors[.]" New York therefore did not infringe upon the First Amendment rights of minors.

The Court neither "accept[s] nor reject[s]" the argument that the CDA is facially overbroad because it substantially interferes with the First Amendment rights of minors. Ante, at 2348. I would reject it. *Ginsberg* established that minors may constitutionally be denied access to material that is obscene as to minors. As *Ginsberg* explained, material is obscene as to minors if it (i) is "patently offensive to prevailing standards in the adult community as a whole with respect to what is suitable . . . for minors"; (ii) appeals to the prurient interest of minors; and (iii) is "utterly without redeeming social importance for minors."

Because the CDA denies minors the right to obtain material that is "patently offensive"—even if it has some redeeming value for minors and even if it does not appeal to their prurient interests—Congress' rejection of the *Ginsberg* "harmful to minors" standard means that the CDA could ban some speech that is "indecent" (i.e., "patently offensive") but that is not obscene as to minors.

I do not deny this possibility, but to prevail in a facial challenge, it is not enough for a plaintiff to show "some" overbreadth. Our cases require a proof of "real" and "substantial" overbreadth, and appellees have not carried their burden in this case. In my view, the universe of speech constitutionally protected as to minors but banned by the CDA—i.e., the universe of material that is "patently offensive," but which nonetheless has some redeeming value for minors or does not appeal to their prurient interest—is a very small one. Appellees cite no examples of speech falling within this universe and do not attempt to explain why that universe is substantial "in relation to the statute's plainly legitimate sweep." That the CDA might deny minors the right to obtain material that has some "value," see ante, at 2348, is largely beside the point. While discussions about prison rape or nude art, may have some redeeming educational value for adults, they do not necessarily have any such value for minors, and under *Ginsberg,* minors only have a First Amendment right to obtain patently offensive material that has "redeeming social importance *for minors.*" There is also no evidence in the record to support the contention that "many e-mail transmissions from an adult to a minor are conversations between family members," and no support for the legal proposition that such speech is absolutely immune from regulation. Accordingly, in my view, the CDA does not burden a substantial amount of minors' constitutionally protected speech.

Thus, the constitutionality of the CDA as a zoning law hinges on the extent to which it substantially interferes with the First Amendment rights of adults. Because the rights of adults are infringed only by the "display" provision and by the "indecency transmission" and "specific person" provisions as applied to communications involving more than one adult, I would invalidate the CDA only to that extent. Insofar as the "indecency transmission" and "specific person" provisions prohibit the use of indecent speech in communications between an adult and one or more minors, however, they can and should be sustained. The Court reaches a contrary conclusion, and from that holding that I respectfully dissent.

WIPO COPYRIGHT TREATY, DECEMBER 20, 1996, 36 I.L.M. 65 (1997)

The WIPO Copyright Treaty, adopted in 1996, contained several articles addressing new forms of copyrightable content not addressed, or inadequately addressed, by prior treaties. Among these was Article 11, which required the parties to the treaty to "provide adequate legal protection and effective legal remedies against the circumvention of effective technological measures that are used" for copyright protection purposes. The United States fulfilled its obligation under Article 11 with §1201 of the Digital Millennium Copyright Act of 1998, enacted well before the treaty came into force on 2002. Other aspects of the treaty, including the other provisions reproduced here, are discussed in several entries in this encyclopedia, especially the "WIPO Copyright Treaty" and "Digital Millennium Copyright Act, Title I" entries.

Preamble

The Contracting Parties,

Desiring to develop and maintain the protection of the rights of authors in their literary and artistic works in a manner as effective and uniform as possible,
Recognizing the need to introduce new international rules and clarify the interpretation of certain existing rules in order to provide adequate solutions to the questions raised by new economic, social, cultural and technological developments,
Recognizing the profound impact of the development and convergence of information and communication technologies on the creation and use of literary and artistic works,
Emphasizing the outstanding significance of copyright protection as an incentive for literary and artistic creation,
Recognizing the need to maintain a balance between the rights of authors and the larger public interest, particularly education, research and access to information, as reflected in the Berne Convention,

Have agreed as follows:

Article 1: Relation to the Berne Convention
(1) This Treaty is a special agreement within the meaning of Article 20 of the Berne Convention for the Protection of Literary and Artistic Works, as regards Contracting Parties that are countries of the

Union established by that Convention. This Treaty shall not have any connection with treaties other than the Berne Convention, nor shall it prejudice any rights and obligations under any other treaties.

(2) Nothing in this Treaty shall derogate from existing obligations that Contracting Parties have to each other under the Berne Convention for the Protection of Literary and Artistic Works.

(3) Hereinafter, "Berne Convention" shall refer to the Paris Act of July 24, 1971 of the Berne Convention for the Protection of Literary and Artistic Works.

(4) Contracting Parties shall comply with Articles 1 to 21 and the Appendix of the Berne Convention. [See the agreed statement concerning Article 1(4)]

Article 2: Scope of Copyright Protection
Copyright protection extends to expressions and not to ideas, procedures, methods of operation or mathematical concepts as such.

Article 3: Application of Articles 2 to 6 of the Berne Convention
Contracting Parties shall apply *mutatis mutandis* the provisions of Articles 2 to 6 of the Berne Convention in respect of the protection provided for in this Treaty.

Article 4: Computer Programs
Computer programs are protected as literary works within the meaning of Article 2 of the Berne Convention. Such protection applies to computer programs, whatever may be the mode or form of their expression.

Article 5: Compilations of Data (Databases)
Compilations of data or other material, in any form, which by reason of the selection or arrangement of their contents constitute intellectual creations, are protected as such. This protection does not extend to the data or the material itself and is without prejudice to any copyright subsisting in the data or material contained in the compilation.

Article 6: Right of Distribution
(1) Authors of literary and artistic works shall enjoy the exclusive right of authorizing the making available to the public of the original and copies of their works through sale or other transfer of ownership.

(2) Nothing in this Treaty shall affect the freedom of Contracting Parties to determine the conditions, if any, under which the exhaustion of the right in paragraph (1) applies after the first sale or other transfer of ownership of the original or a copy of the work with the authorization of the author.

Article 7: Right of Rental
(1) Authors of
    (i) computer programs;
    (ii) cinematographic works; and
    (iii) works embodied in phonograms, as determined in the national law of Contracting Parties, shall enjoy the exclusive right of authorizing commercial rental to the public of the originals or copies of their works.

(2) Paragraph (1) shall not apply
    (i) in the case of computer programs, where the program itself is not the essential object of the rental; and
    (ii) in the case of cinematographic works, unless such commercial rental has led to widespread copying of such works materially impairing the exclusive right of reproduction.

(3) Notwithstanding the provisions of paragraph (1), a Contracting Party that, on April 15, 1994, had and continues to have in force a system of equitable remuneration of authors for the rental of copies of their works embodied in phonograms may maintain that system provided that the commercial rental of works embodied in phonograms is not giving rise to the material impairment of the exclusive right of reproduction of authors.

Article 8: Right of Communication to the Public
Without prejudice to the provisions of Articles 11(1)(ii), 11bis(1)(i) and (ii), 11ter(1)(ii), 14(1)(ii) and 14bis(1) of the Berne Convention, authors of literary and artistic works shall enjoy the exclusive right of authorizing any communication to the public of their works, by wire or wireless means, including the making available to the public of their works in such a way that members of the public may access these works from a place and at a time individually chosen by them.

Article 9: Duration of the Protection of Photographic Works
In respect of photographic works, the Contracting Parties shall not apply the provisions of Article 7(4) of the Berne Convention.

Article 10: Limitations and Exceptions
(1) Contracting Parties may, in their national legislation, provide for limitations of or exceptions to the rights granted to authors of literary and artistic works under this Treaty in certain special cases that do not conflict with a normal exploitation of the work and do not unreasonably prejudice the legitimate interests of the author.

(2) Contracting Parties shall, when applying the Berne Convention, confine any limitations of

or exceptions to rights provided for therein to certain special cases that do not conflict with a normal exploitation of the work and do not unreasonably prejudice the legitimate interests of the author. [See the agreed statement concerning Article 10]

Article 11: Obligations concerning Technological Measures

Contracting Parties shall provide adequate legal protection and effective legal remedies against the circumvention of effective technological measures that are used by authors in connection with the exercise of their rights under this Treaty or the Berne Convention and that restrict acts, in respect of their works, which are not authorized by the authors concerned or permitted by law.

Article 12: Obligations concerning Rights Management Information

(1) Contracting Parties shall provide adequate and effective legal remedies against any person knowingly performing any of the following acts knowing, or with respect to civil remedies having reasonable grounds to know, that it will induce, enable, facilitate or conceal an infringement of any right covered by this Treaty or the Berne Convention:

(i) to remove or alter any electronic rights management information without authority;

(ii) to distribute, import for distribution, broadcast or communicate to the public, without authority, works or copies of works knowing that electronic rights management information has been removed or altered without authority.

(2) As used in this Article, "rights management information" means information which identifies the work, the author of the work, the owner of any right in the work, or information about the terms and conditions of use of the work, and any numbers or codes that represent such information, when any of these items of information is attached to a copy of a work or appears in connection with the communication of a work to the public.

Articles 13 through 25 [omitted]

DIGITAL MILLENNIUM COPYRIGHT ACT ANTI-CIRCUMVENTION PROVISIONS, 17 U.S.C. § 1201

Few copyright statutes have aroused as much consumer and activist ire as the anticircumvention provisions of the Digital Millennium Copyright Act (DMCA). Consumers detest the provisions because they make content harder to use, harder to play back, harder to transfer from one medium or player to another—in short, *they limit its value as entertainment. Activists detest the provisions for these reasons and because they seem to be a symptom of a creeping loss of control over content, letting corporations dictate what consumers may do with content they have purchased and reducing the scope of fair use. Numerous battles have been fought over the provisions, which thus far have held up to constitutional scrutiny; the case of* Corley, *later in this appendix, is part of perhaps the most famous of these battles—the battle over DeCSS. More can be read about these issues in the entries "DeCSS," "Digital Millennium Copyright Act, Title I," and "Fair Use."*

§ 1201. Circumvention of copyright protection systems

(a) Violations regarding circumvention of technological measures

(1)

(A) No person shall circumvent a technological measure that effectively controls access to a work protected under this title. The prohibition contained in the preceding sentence shall take effect at the end of the 2-year period beginning on the date of the enactment of this chapter.

(B) The prohibition contained in subparagraph (A) shall not apply to persons who are users of a copyrighted work which is in a particular class of works, if such persons are, or are likely to be in the succeeding 3-year period, adversely affected by virtue of such prohibition in their ability to make noninfringing uses of that particular class of works under this title, as determined under subparagraph (C).

(C) During the 2-year period described in subparagraph (A), and during each succeeding 3-year period, the Librarian of Congress, upon the recommendation of the Register of Copyrights, who shall consult with the Assistant Secretary for Communications and Information of the Department of Commerce and report and comment on his or her views in making such recommendation, shall make the determination in a rulemaking proceeding for purposes of subparagraph (B) of whether persons who are users of a copyrighted work are, or are likely to be in the succeeding 3-year period, adversely affected by the prohibition under subparagraph (A) in their ability to make noninfringing uses under this title of a particular class of copyrighted works. In conducting such rulemaking, the Librarian shall examine –

(i) the availability for use of copyrighted works;

(ii) the availability for use of works for nonprofit archival, preservation, and educational purposes;

(iii) the impact that the prohibition on the circumvention of technological measures applied to copyrighted works has on criticism, comment, news reporting, teaching, scholarship, or research;

(iv) the effect of circumvention of technological measures on the market for or value of copyrighted works; and

(v) such other factors as the Librarian considers appropriate.

(D) The Librarian shall publish any class of copyrighted works for which the Librarian has determined, pursuant to the rulemaking conducted under subparagraph (C), that noninfringing uses by persons who are users of a copyrighted work are, or are likely to be, adversely affected, and the prohibition contained in subparagraph (A) shall not apply to such users with respect to such class of works for the ensuing 3-year period.

(E) Neither the exception under subparagraph (B) from the applicability of the prohibition contained in subparagraph (A), nor any determination made in a rulemaking conducted under subparagraph (C), may be used as a defense in any action to enforce any provision of this title other than this paragraph.

(2) No person shall manufacture, import, offer to the public, provide, or otherwise traffic in any technology, product, service, device, component, or part thereof, that –

(A) is primarily designed or produced for the purpose of circumventing a technological measure that effectively controls access to a work protected under this title;

(B) has only limited commercially significant purpose or use other than to circumvent a technological measure that effectively controls access to a work protected under this title; or

(C) is marketed by that person or another acting in concert with that person with that person's knowledge for use in circumventing a technological measure that effectively controls access to a work protected under this title.

(3) As used in this subsection –

(A) to "circumvent a technological measure" means to descramble a scrambled work, to decrypt an encrypted work, or otherwise to avoid, bypass, remove, deactivate, or impair a technological measure, without the authority of the copyright owner; and

(B) a technological measure "effectively controls access to a work" if the measure, in the ordinary course of its operation, requires the application of information, or a process or a treatment, with the authority of the copyright owner, to gain access to the work.

(b) Additional violations

(1) No person shall manufacture, import, offer to the public, provide, or otherwise traffic in any technology, product, service, device, component, or part thereof, that –

(A) is primarily designed or produced for the purpose of circumventing protection afforded by a technological measure that effectively protects a right of a copyright owner under this title in a work or a portion thereof;

(B) has only limited commercially significant purpose or use other than to circumvent protection afforded by a technological measure that effectively protects a right of a copyright owner under this title in a work or a portion thereof; or

(C) is marketed by that person or another acting in concert with that person with that person's knowledge for use in circumventing protection afforded by a technological measure that effectively protects a right of a copyright owner under this title in a work or a portion thereof.

(2) As used in this subsection –

(A) to "circumvent protection afforded by a technological measure" means avoiding, bypassing, removing, deactivating, or otherwise impairing a technological measure; and

(B) a technological measure "effectively protects a right of a copyright owner under this title" if the measure, in the ordinary course of its operation, prevents, restricts, or otherwise limits the exercise of a right of a copyright owner under this title.

(c) Other rights, etc., not affected

(1) Nothing in this section shall affect rights, remedies, limitations, or defenses to copyright infringement, including fair use, under this title.

(2) Nothing in this section shall enlarge or diminish vicarious or contributory liability for copyright infringement in connection with any technology, product, service, device, component, or part thereof.

(3) Nothing in this section shall require that the design of, or design and selection of parts and components for, a consumer electronics, telecommunications, or computing product provide for a response to any particular technological measure, so long as such part or component, or the product in which such part or component is integrated, does not otherwise fall within the prohibitions of subsection (a)(2) or (b)(1).

(4) Nothing in this section shall enlarge or diminish any rights of free speech or the press for activities using consumer electronics, telecommunications, or computing products.

(d) Exemption for nonprofit libraries, archives, and educational institutions

(1) A nonprofit library, archives, or educational institution which gains access to a commercially exploited copyrighted work solely in order to

make a good faith determination of whether to acquire a copy of that work for the sole purpose of engaging in conduct permitted under this title shall not be in violation of subsection (a)(1)(A). A copy of a work to which access has been gained under this paragraph –

(A) may not be retained longer than necessary to make such good faith determination; and

(B) may not be used for any other purpose.

(2) The exemption made available under paragraph (1) shall only apply with respect to a work when an identical copy of that work is not reasonably available in another form.

(3) A nonprofit library, archives, or educational institution that willfully for the purpose of commercial advantage or financial gain violates paragraph (1) –

(A) shall, for the first offense, be subject to the civil remedies under section 1203; and

(B) shall, for repeated or subsequent offenses, in addition to the civil remedies under section 1203, forfeit the exemption provided under paragraph (1).

(4) This subsection may not be used as a defense to a claim under subsection (a)(2) or (b), nor may this subsection permit a nonprofit library, archives, or educational institution to manufacture, import, offer to the public, provide, or otherwise traffic in any technology, product, service, component, or part thereof, which circumvents a technological measure.

(5) In order for a library or archives to qualify for the exemption under this subsection, the collections of that library or archives shall be –

(A) open to the public; or

(B) available not only to researchers affiliated with the library or archives or with the institution of which it is a part, but also to other persons doing research in a specialized field.

(e) Law enforcement, intelligence, and other government activities.—This section does not prohibit any lawfully authorized investigative, protective, information security, or intelligence activity of an officer, agent, or employee of the United States, a State, or a political subdivision of a State, or a person acting pursuant to a contract with the United States, a State, or a political subdivision of a State. For purposes of this subsection, the term "information security" means activities carried out in order to identify and address the vulnerabilities of a government computer, computer system, or computer network.

(f) Reverse engineering

(1) Notwithstanding the provisions of subsection (a)(1)(A), a person who has lawfully obtained the right to use a copy of a computer program may circumvent a technological measure that effectively controls access to a particular portion of that program for the sole purpose of identifying and analyzing those elements of the program that are necessary to achieve interoperability of an independently created computer program with other programs, and that have not previously been readily available to the person engaging in the circumvention, to the extent any such acts of identification and analysis do not constitute infringement under this title.

(2) Notwithstanding the provisions of subsections (a)(2) and (b), a person may develop and employ technological means to circumvent a technological measure, or to circumvent protection afforded by a technological measure, in order to enable the identification and analysis under paragraph (1), or for the purpose of enabling interoperability of an independently created computer program with other programs, if such means are necessary to achieve such interoperability, to the extent that doing so does not constitute infringement under this title.

(3) The information acquired through the acts permitted under paragraph (1), and the means permitted under paragraph (2), may be made available to others if the person referred to in paragraph (1) or (2), as the case may be, provides such information or means solely for the purpose of enabling interoperability of an independently created computer program with other programs, and to the extent that doing so does not constitute infringement under this title or violate applicable law other than this section.

(4) For purposes of this subsection, the term "interoperability" means the ability of computer programs to exchange information, and of such programs mutually to use the information which has been exchanged.

(g) Encryption research. –

(1) Definitions.—For purposes of this subsection –

(A) the term "encryption research" means activities necessary to identify and analyze flaws and vulnerabilities of encryption technologies applied to copyrighted works, if these activities are conducted to advance the state of knowledge in the field of encryption technology or to assist in the development of encryption products; and

(B) the term "encryption technology" means the scrambling and descrambling of information using mathematical formulas or algorithms.

(2) Permissible acts of encryption research.—Notwithstanding the provisions of subsection (a)(1)(A), it is not a violation of that subsection for a person to circumvent a technological measure as applied to a copy, phonorecord, performance, or display of a published work in the course of an act of good faith encryption research if –

(A) the person lawfully obtained the encrypted copy, phonorecord, performance, or display of the published work;

(B) such act is necessary to conduct such encryption research;

(C) the person made a good faith effort to obtain authorization before the circumvention; and

(D) such act does not constitute infringement under this title or a violation of applicable law other than this section, including section 1030 of title 18 and those provisions of title 18 amended by the Computer Fraud and Abuse Act of 1986.

(3) Factors in determining exemption.—In determining whether a person qualifies for the exemption under paragraph (2), the factors to be considered shall include –

(A) whether the information derived from the encryption research was disseminated, and if so, whether it was disseminated in a manner reasonably calculated to advance the state of knowledge or development of encryption technology, versus whether it was disseminated in a manner that facilitates infringement under this title or a violation of applicable law other than this section, including a violation of privacy or breach of security;

(B) whether the person is engaged in a legitimate course of study, is employed, or is appropriately trained or experienced, in the field of encryption technology; and

(C) whether the person provides the copyright owner of the work to which the technological measure is applied with notice of the findings and documentation of the research, and the time when such notice is provided.

(4) Use of technological means for research activities.—Notwithstanding the provisions of subsection (a)(2), it is not a violation of that subsection for a person to –

(A) develop and employ technological means to circumvent a technological measure for the sole purpose of that person performing the acts of good faith encryption research described in paragraph (2); and

(B) provide the technological means to another person with whom he or she is working collaboratively for the purpose of conducting the acts of good faith encryption research described in paragraph (2) or for the purpose of having that other person verify his or her acts of good faith encryption research described in paragraph (2).

(5) Report to Congress [omitted]

(h) Exceptions regarding minors.—In applying subsection (a) to a component or part, the court may consider the necessity for its intended and actual incorporation in a technology, product, service, or device, which –

(1) does not itself violate the provisions of this title; and

(2) has the sole purpose to prevent the access of minors to material on the Internet.

(i) Protection of personally identifying information. –

(1) Circumvention permitted.—Notwithstanding the provisions of subsection (a)(1)(A), it is not a violation of that subsection for a person to circumvent a technological measure that effectively controls access to a work protected under this title, if –

(A) the technological measure, or the work it protects, contains the capability of collecting or disseminating personally identifying information reflecting the online activities of a natural person who seeks to gain access to the work protected;

(B) in the normal course of its operation, the technological measure, or the work it protects, collects or disseminates personally identifying information about the person who seeks to gain access to the work protected, without providing conspicuous notice of such collection or dissemination to such person, and without providing such person with the capability to prevent or restrict such collection or dissemination;

(C) the act of circumvention has the sole effect of identifying and disabling the capability described in subparagraph (A), and has no other effect on the ability of any person to gain access to any work; and

(D) the act of circumvention is carried out solely for the purpose of preventing the collection or dissemination of personally identifying information about a natural person who seeks to gain access to the work protected, and is not in violation of any other law.

(2) Inapplicability to certain technological measures.—This subsection does not apply to a technological measure, or a work it protects, that does not collect or disseminate personally identifying information and that is disclosed to a user as not having or using such capability.

(j) Security testing. –

(1) Definition.—For purposes of this subsection, the term "security testing" means accessing a computer, computer system, or computer network, solely for the purpose of good faith testing, investigating, or correcting, a security flaw or vulnerability, with the authorization of the owner or operator of such computer, computer system, or computer network.

(2) Permissible acts of security testing.— Notwithstanding the provisions of subsection (a)(1)(A), it is not a violation of that subsection for a person to engage in an act of security testing, if such

act does not constitute infringement under this title or a violation of applicable law other than this section, including section 1030 of title 18 and those provisions of title 18 amended by the Computer Fraud and Abuse Act of 1986.

(3) Factors in determining exemption.—In determining whether a person qualifies for the exemption under paragraph (2), the factors to be considered shall include –

(A) whether the information derived from the security testing was used solely to promote the security of the owner or operator of such computer, computer system or computer network, or shared directly with the developer of such computer, computer system, or computer network; and

(B) whether the information derived from the security testing was used or maintained in a manner that does not facilitate infringement under this title or a violation of applicable law other than this section, including a violation of privacy or breach of security.

(4) Use of technological means for security testing.—Notwithstanding the provisions of subsection (a)(2), it is not a violation of that subsection for a person to develop, produce, distribute or employ technological means for the sole purpose of performing the acts of security testing described in subsection (2), provided such technological means does not otherwise violate section (a)(2).

(k) Certain analog devices and certain technological measures [omitted]

UNIVERSAL CITY STUDIOS, INC. V. CORLEY, 273 F.3D 429 (2ND CIR. 2001)

Not long after the passage of the Digital Millennium Copyright Act (DMCA), activists opposed it with the time-honored activist tactic of civil disobedience. In this case the civil disobedience was electronic; it involved no lying down in front of bulldozers or protest marches, but rather sharing copies of a program called DeCSS. DeCSS was capable of breaking the copy-protection encryption used on commercial DVDs; the movie studios claimed—correctly, as it turned out—that sharing the program, or even providing links to sites from which the program could be downloaded, violated the DMCA. In the case that follows (from which the footnotes, many of them quite lengthy, and the citations have been omitted), the federal Second Circuit Court of Appeals rejected the arguments of hacker activist and publisher Eric Corley. Corley had claimed that the anticircumvention provisions were unconstitutional or that, even if they were constitutional, Corley's acts in posting links to DeCSS did not violate the statute.

Jon O. Newman, Circuit Judge:

When the Framers of the First Amendment prohibited Congress from making any law "abridging the freedom of speech," they were not thinking about computers, computer programs, or the Internet. But neither were they thinking about radio, television, or movies. Just as the inventions at the beginning and middle of the 20th century presented new First Amendment issues, so does the cyber revolution at the end of that century. This appeal raises significant First Amendment issues concerning one aspect of computer technology—encryption to protect materials in digital form from unauthorized access. The appeal challenges the constitutionality of the Digital Millennium Copyright Act ("DMCA"), 17 U.S.C. § 1201 et seq. and the validity of an injunction entered to enforce the DMCA.

Defendant-Appellant Eric C. Corley and his company, 2600 Enterprises, Inc., (collectively "Corley," "the Defendants," or "the Appellants") appeal from the amended final judgment of the United States District Court for the Southern District of New York (Lewis A. Kaplan, District Judge), entered August 23, 2000, enjoining them from various actions concerning a decryption program known as "DeCSS." The injunction primarily bars the Appellants from posting DeCSS on their web site and from knowingly linking their web site to any other web site on which DeCSS is posted. We affirm.

Introduction

Understanding the pending appeal and the issues it raises requires some familiarity with technical aspects of computers and computer software, especially software called "digital versatile disks" or "DVDs," which are optical media storage devices currently designed to contain movies. Those lacking such familiarity will be greatly aided by reading Judge Kaplan's extremely lucid opinion, *Universal City Studios, Inc. v. Reimerdes, 111 F.Supp.2d 294 (S.D.N.Y.2000)*, beginning with his helpful section "The Vocabulary of this Case."

This appeal concerns the anti-trafficking provisions of the DMCA, which Congress enacted in 1998 to strengthen copyright protection in the digital age. Fearful that the ease with which pirates could copy and distribute a copyrightable work in digital form was overwhelming the capacity of conventional copyright enforcement to find and enjoin unlawfully copied material, Congress sought to combat copyright piracy in its earlier stages, before the work was even copied. The DMCA therefore backed with legal sanctions the efforts of copyright owners to protect their works from piracy behind digital walls such as encryption codes or password protections. In so doing, Congress targeted not only those pirates who would circumvent these digital walls (the "anti-circumvention provisions," contained in 17 U.S.C. § 1201(a)(1)), but also anyone who would traffic in a technology primarily designed to circumvent a digital wall (the "anti-trafficking provisions," contained in 17 U.S.C. § 1201(a)(2), (b)(1)).

Corley publishes a print magazine and maintains an affiliated web site geared towards "hackers," a digital-era term often applied to those interested in techniques for circumventing protections of computers and computer data from unauthorized access. The so-called hacker community includes serious computer-science scholars conducting research on protection techniques, computer buffs intrigued by the challenge of trying to circumvent access-limiting devices or perhaps hoping to promote security by exposing flaws in protection techniques, mischief-makers interested in disrupting computer operations, and thieves, including copyright infringers who want to acquire copyrighted material (for personal use or resale) without paying for it.

In November 1999, Corley posted a copy of the decryption computer program "DeCSS" on his web site, http://www.2600.com ("2600.com"). DeCSS is designed to circumvent "CSS," the encryption technology that motion picture studios place on DVDs to prevent the unauthorized viewing and copying of motion pictures. Corley also posted on his web site links to other web sites where DeCSS could be found.

Plaintiffs-Appellees are eight motion picture studios that brought an action in the Southern District of New York seeking injunctive relief against Corley under the DMCA. Following a full non-jury trial, the District Court entered a permanent injunction barring Corley from posting DeCSS on his web site or from knowingly linking via a hyperlink to any other web site containing DeCSS. The District Court rejected Corley's constitutional attacks on the statute and the injunction.

Corley renews his constitutional challenges on appeal. Specifically, he argues primarily that: (1) the DMCA oversteps limits in the Copyright Clause on the duration of copyright protection; (2) the DMCA as applied to his dissemination of DeCSS violates the First Amendment because computer code is "speech" entitled to full First Amendment protection and the DMCA fails to survive the exacting scrutiny accorded statutes that regulate "speech"; and (3) the DMCA violates the First Amendment and the Copyright Clause by unduly obstructing the "fair use" of copyrighted materials. Corley also argues that the statute is susceptible to, and should

therefore be given, a narrow interpretation that avoids alleged constitutional objections.

Background

For decades, motion picture studios have made movies available for viewing at home in what is called "analog" format. Movies in this format are placed on videotapes, which can be played on a video cassette recorder ("VCR"). In the early 1990s, the studios began to consider the possibility of distributing movies in digital form as well. Movies in digital form are placed on disks, known as DVDs, which can be played on a DVD player (either a stand-alone device or a component of a computer). DVDs offer advantages over analog tapes, such as improved visual and audio quality, larger data capacity, and greater durability. However, the improved quality of a movie in a digital format brings with it the risk that a virtually perfect copy, i.e., one that will not lose perceptible quality in the copying process, can be readily made at the click of a computer control and instantly distributed to countless recipients throughout the world over the Internet. This case arises out of the movie industry's efforts to respond to this risk by invoking the anti-trafficking provisions of the DMCA.

I. CSS

The movie studios were reluctant to release movies in digital form until they were confident they had in place adequate safeguards against piracy of their copyrighted movies. The studios took several steps to minimize the piracy threat. First, they settled on the DVD as the standard digital medium for home distribution of movies. The studios then sought an encryption scheme to protect movies on DVDs. They enlisted the help of members of the consumer electronics and computer industries, who in mid-1996 developed the Content Scramble System ("CSS"). CSS is an encryption scheme that employs an algorithm configured by a set of "keys" to encrypt a DVD's contents. The algorithm is a type of mathematical formula for transforming the contents of the movie file into gibberish; the "keys" are in actuality strings of 0's and 1's that serve as values for the mathematical formula. Decryption in the case of CSS requires a set of "player keys" contained in compliant DVD players, as well as an understanding of the CSS encryption algorithm. Without the player keys and the algorithm, a DVD player cannot access the contents of a DVD. With the player keys and the algorithm, a DVD player can display the movie on a television or a computer screen, but does not give a viewer the ability to use the copy function of the computer to copy the movie or to manipulate the digital content of the DVD.

The studios developed a licensing scheme for distributing the technology to manufacturers of DVD players. Player keys and other information necessary to the CSS scheme were given to manufacturers of DVD players for an administrative fee. In exchange for the licenses, manufacturers were obliged to keep the player keys confidential. Manufacturers were also required in the licensing agreement to prevent the transmission of "CSS data" (a term undefined in the licensing agreement) from a DVD drive to any "internal recording device," including, presumably, a computer hard drive.

With encryption technology and licensing agreements in hand, the studios began releasing movies on DVDs in 1997, and DVDs quickly gained in popularity, becoming a significant source of studio revenue. In 1998, the studios secured added protection against DVD piracy when Congress passed the DMCA, which prohibits the development or use of technology designed to circumvent a technological protection measure, such as CSS. The pertinent provisions of the DMCA are examined in greater detail below.

II. DeCSS

In September 1999, Jon Johansen, a Norwegian teenager, collaborating with two unidentified individuals he met on the Internet, reverse-engineered a licensed DVD player designed to operate on the Microsoft operating system, and culled from it the player keys and other information necessary to decrypt CSS. The record suggests that Johansen was trying to develop a DVD player operable on Linux, an alternative operating system that did not support any licensed DVD players at that time. In order to accomplish this task, Johansen wrote a decryption program executable on Microsoft's operating system. That program was called, appropriately enough, "DeCSS."

If a user runs the DeCSS program (for example, by clicking on the DeCSS icon on a Microsoft operating system platform) with a DVD in the computer's disk drive, DeCSS will decrypt the DVD's CSS protection, allowing the user to copy the DVD's files and place the copy on the user's hard drive. The result is a very large computer file that can be played on a non-CSS-compliant player and copied, manipulated, and transferred just like any other computer file. DeCSS comes complete with a fairly user-friendly interface that helps the user select from among the DVD's files and assign the decrypted file a location on the user's hard drive. The quality of the resulting decrypted movie is "virtually identical" to that of the encrypted movie on the DVD. And the file produced by DeCSS, while large,

can be compressed to a manageable size by a compression software called "DivX," available at no cost on the Internet. This compressed file can be copied onto a DVD, or transferred over the Internet (with some patience).

Johansen posted the executable object code, but not the source code, for DeCSS on his web site. The distinction between source code and object code is relevant to this case, so a brief explanation is warranted. A computer responds to electrical charges, the presence or absence of which is represented by strings of 1's and 0's. Strictly speaking, "object code" consists of those 1's and 0's. While some people can read and program in object code, "it would be inconvenient, inefficient and, for most people, probably impossible to do so." Computer languages have been written to facilitate program writing and reading. A program in such a computer language— BASIC, C, and Java are examples—is said to be written in "source code." Source code has the benefit of being much easier to read (by people) than object code, but as a general matter, it must be translated back to object code before it can be read by a computer. This task is usually performed by a program called a compiler. Since computer languages range in complexity, object code can be placed on one end of a spectrum, and different kinds of source code can be arrayed across the spectrum according to the ease with which they are read and understood by humans. Within months of its appearance in executable form on Johansen's web site, DeCSS was widely available on the Internet, in both object code and various forms of source code.

In November 1999, Corley wrote and placed on his web site, 2600.com, an article about the DeCSS phenomenon. His web site is an auxiliary to the print magazine, *2600: The Hacker Quarterly*, which Corley has been publishing since 1984. As the name suggests, the magazine is designed for "hackers," as is the web site. While the magazine and the web site cover some issues of general interest to computer users—such as threats to online privacy—the focus of the publications is on the vulnerability of computer security systems, and more specifically, how to exploit that vulnerability in order to circumvent the security systems. Representative articles explain how to steal an Internet domain name and how to break into the computer systems at Federal Express.

Corley's article about DeCSS detailed how CSS was cracked, and described the movie industry's efforts to shut down web sites posting DeCSS. It also explained that DeCSS could be used to copy DVDs. At the end of the article, the Defendants posted copies of the object and source code of DeCSS. In Corley's words, he added the code to the story because "in a journalistic world, . . . [y]ou have to show your evidence . . . and particularly in the magazine that I work for, people want to see specifically what it is that we are referring to," including "what evidence . . . we have" that there is in fact technology that circumvents CSS. Writing about DeCSS without including the DeCSS code would have been, to Corley, "analogous to printing a story about a picture and not printing the picture." Corley also added to the article links that he explained would take the reader to other web sites where DeCSS could be found.

2600.com was only one of hundreds of web sites that began posting DeCSS near the end of 1999. The movie industry tried to stem the tide by sending cease-and-desist letters to many of these sites. These efforts met with only partial success; a number of sites refused to remove DeCSS. In January 2000, the studios filed this lawsuit.

III. The DMCA

The DMCA was enacted in 1998 to implement the World Intellectual Property Organization Copyright Treaty ("WIPO Treaty"), which requires contracting parties to "provide adequate legal protection and effective legal remedies against the circumvention of effective technological measures that are used by authors in connection with the exercise of their rights under this Treaty or the Berne Convention and that restrict acts, in respect of their works, which are not authorized by the authors concerned or permitted by law." Even before the treaty, Congress had been devoting attention to the problems faced by copyright enforcement in the digital age. Hearings on the topic have spanned several years. This legislative effort resulted in the DMCA.

The Act contains three provisions targeted at the circumvention of technological protections. The first is subsection 1201(a)(1)(A), the anti-circumvention provision. This provision prohibits a person from "circumvent[ing] a technological measure that effectively controls access to a work protected under [Title 17, governing copyright]." The Librarian of Congress is required to promulgate regulations every three years exempting from this subsection individuals who would otherwise be "adversely affected" in "their ability to make noninfringing uses."

The second and third provisions are subsections 1201(a)(2) and 1201(b)(1), the "anti-trafficking provisions." Subsection 1201(a)(2), the provision at issue in this case, provides:

No person shall manufacture, import, offer to the public, provide, or otherwise traffic in any technology, product, service, device, component, or part thereof, that –

(A) is primarily designed or produced for the purpose of circumventing a technological measure that effectively controls access to a work protected under this title;

(B) has only limited commercially significant purpose or use other than to circumvent a technological measure that effectively controls access to a work protected under this title; or

(C) is marketed by that person or another acting in concert with that person with that person's knowledge for use in circumventing a technological measure that effectively controls access to a work protected under this title.

To "circumvent a technological measure" is defined, in pertinent part, as "to descramble a scrambled work . . . or otherwise to . . . bypass . . . a technological measure, without the authority of the copyright owner."

Subsection 1201(b)(1) is similar to subsection 1201(a)(2), except that subsection 1201(a)(2) covers those who traffic in technology that can circumvent "a technological measure that effectively controls access to a work protected under" Title 17, whereas subsection 1201(b)(1) covers those who traffic in technology that can circumvent "protection afforded by a technological measure *that effectively protects a right of a copyright owner* under" [17 U.S.C. § 1201(a)(2), (b)(1)] (emphases added). In other words, although both subsections prohibit trafficking in a circumvention technology, the focus of subsection 1201(a)(2) is circumvention of technologies designed to prevent access to a work, and the focus of subsection 1201(b)(1) is circumvention of technologies designed to permit access to a work but prevent copying of the work or some other act that infringes a copyright. Subsection 1201(a)(1) differs from both of these anti-trafficking subsections in that it targets the use of a circumvention technology, not the trafficking in such a technology.

The DMCA contains exceptions for schools and libraries that want to use circumvention technologies to determine whether to purchase a copyrighted product, 17 U.S.C. § 1201(d); individuals using circumvention technology "for the sole purpose" of trying to achieve "interoperability" of computer programs through reverse-engineering, § 1201(f); encryption research aimed at identifying flaws in encryption technology, if the research is conducted to advance the state of knowledge in the field, § 1201(g); and several other exceptions not relevant here.

The DMCA creates civil remedies, § 1203, and criminal sanctions, § 1204. It specifically authorizes a court to "grant temporary and permanent injunctions on such terms as it deems reasonable to prevent or restrain a violation." [Section 1203(b)(1)].

IV. Procedural History

Invoking subsection 1203(b)(1), the Plaintiffs sought an injunction against the Defendants, alleging that the Defendants violated the anti-trafficking provisions of the statute. On January 20, 2000, after a hearing, the District Court issued a preliminary injunction barring the Defendants from posting DeCSS.

The Defendants complied with the preliminary injunction, but continued to post links to other web sites carrying DeCSS, an action they termed "electronic civil disobedience." Under the heading "Stop the MPAA [(Motion Picture Association of America)]," Corley urged other web sites to post DeCSS lest "we . . . be forced into submission."

The Plaintiffs then sought a permanent injunction barring the Defendants from both posting DeCSS and linking to sites containing DeCSS. After a trial on the merits, the Court issued a comprehensive opinion, *Universal I,* and granted a permanent injunction, *Universal II.*

The Court explained that the Defendants' posting of DeCSS on their web site clearly falls within section 1201(a)(2)(A) of the DMCA, rejecting as spurious their claim that CSS is not a technological measure that "effectively controls access to a work" because it was so easily penetrated by Johansen, and as irrelevant their contention that DeCSS was designed to create a Linux-platform DVD player. The Court also held that the Defendants cannot avail themselves of any of the DMCA's exceptions, and that the alleged importance of DeCSS to certain fair uses of encrypted copyrighted material was immaterial to their statutory liability. The Court went on to hold that when the Defendants "proclaimed on their own site that DeCSS could be had by clicking on the hyperlinks" on their site, they were trafficking in DeCSS, and therefore liable for their linking as well as their posting.

Turning to the Defendants' numerous constitutional arguments, the Court first held that computer code like DeCSS is "speech" that is "protected" (in the sense of "covered") by the First Amendment, but that because the DMCA is targeting the "functional" aspect of that speech, it is "content neutral," and the intermediate scrutiny of *United States v. O'Brien* applies. The Court concluded that the DMCA survives this scrutiny, and also rejected prior restraint, overbreadth, and vagueness challenges.

The Court upheld the constitutionality of the DMCA's application to linking on similar grounds: linking, the Court concluded, is "speech," but the DMCA is content-neutral, targeting only the functional components of that speech. Therefore, its application to linking is also evaluated under *O'Brien,*

and, thus evaluated, survives intermediate scrutiny. However, the Court concluded that a blanket proscription on linking would create a risk of chilling legitimate linking on the web. The Court therefore crafted a restrictive test for linking liability (discussed below) that it believed sufficiently mitigated that risk. The Court then found its test satisfied in this case.

Finally, the Court concluded that an injunction was highly appropriate in this case. The Court observed that DeCSS was harming the Plaintiffs, not only because they were now exposed to the possibility of piracy and therefore were obliged to develop costly new safeguards for DVDs, but also because, even if there was only indirect evidence that DeCSS availability actually facilitated DVD piracy, the threat of piracy was very real, particularly as Internet transmission speeds continue to increase. Acknowledging that DeCSS was (and still is) widely available on the Internet, the Court expressed confidence in

> the likelihood . . . that this decision will serve notice on others that "the strong right arm of equity" may be brought to bear against them absent a change in their conduct and thus contribute to a climate of appropriate respect for intellectual property rights in an age in which the excitement of ready access to untold quantities of information has blurred in some minds the fact that taking what is not yours and not freely offered to you is stealing.

The Court's injunction barred the Defendants from: "posting on any Internet web site" DeCSS; "in any other way . . . offering to the public, providing, or otherwise trafficking in DeCSS"; violating the anti-trafficking provisions of the DMCA in any other manner, and finally "knowingly linking any Internet web site operated by them to any other web site containing DeCSS, or knowingly maintaining any such link, for the purpose of disseminating DeCSS."

The Appellants have appealed from the permanent injunction. The United States has intervened in support of the constitutionality of the DMCA. We have also had the benefit of a number of *amicus curiae* briefs, supporting and opposing the District Court's judgment. After oral argument, we invited the parties to submit responses to a series of specific questions, and we have received helpful responses.

Discussion
I. Narrow Construction to Avoid Constitutional Doubt

The Appellants first argue that, because their constitutional arguments are at least substantial, we should interpret the statute narrowly so as to avoid constitutional problems. They identify three different instances of alleged ambiguity in the statute that they claim provide an opportunity for such a narrow interpretation.

First, they contend that subsection 1201(c)(1), which provides that "[n]othing in this section shall affect rights, remedies, limitations or defenses to copyright infringement, including fair use, under this title," can be read to allow the circumvention of encryption technology protecting copyrighted material when the material will be put to "fair uses" exempt from copyright liability. We disagree that subsection 1201(c)(1) permits such a reading. Instead, it simply clarifies that the DMCA targets the circumvention of digital walls guarding copyrighted material (and trafficking in circumvention tools), but does not concern itself with the use of those materials after circumvention has occurred. Subsection 1201(c)(1) ensures that the DMCA is not read to prohibit the "fair use" of information just because that information was obtained in a manner made illegal by the DMCA. The Appellants' much more expansive interpretation of subsection 1201(c)(1) is not only outside the range of plausible readings of the provision, but is also clearly refuted by the statute's legislative history.

Second, the Appellants urge a narrow construction of the DMCA because of subsection 1201(c)(4), which provides that "[n]othing in this section shall enlarge or diminish any rights of free speech or the press for activities using consumer electronics, telecommunications, or computing products." This language is clearly precatory: Congress could not "diminish" constitutional rights of free speech even if it wished to, and the fact that Congress also expressed a reluctance to "enlarge" those rights cuts against the Appellants' effort to infer a narrowing construction of the Act from this provision.

Third, the Appellants argue that an individual who buys a DVD has the "authority of the copyright owner" to view the DVD, and therefore is exempted from the DMCA pursuant to subsection 1201(a)(3)(A) when the buyer circumvents an encryption technology in order to view the DVD on a competing platform (such as Linux). The basic flaw in this argument is that it misreads subsection 1201(a)(3)(A). That provision exempts from liability those who would "decrypt" an encrypted DVD with the authority of a copyright owner, not those who would "view" a DVD with the authority of a copyright owner. In any event, the Defendants offered no evidence that the Plaintiffs have either explicitly or implicitly authorized DVD buyers to circumvent encryption technology to support use on multiple platforms.

We conclude that the anti-trafficking and anti-circumvention provisions of the DMCA are not susceptible to the narrow interpretations urged by the Appellants. We therefore proceed to consider the Appellants' constitutional claims.

II. Constitutional Challenge Based on the Copyright Clause

In a footnote to their brief, the Appellants appear to contend that the DMCA, as construed by the District Court, exceeds the constitutional authority of Congress to grant authors copyrights for a "limited time," because it "empower[s] copyright owners to effectively secure perpetual protection by mixing public domain works with copyrighted materials, then locking both up with technological protection measures." This argument is elaborated in the *amici curiae* brief filed by Prof. Julie E. Cohen on behalf of herself and 45 other intellectual property law professors. For two reasons, the argument provides no basis for disturbing the judgment of the District Court.

First, we have repeatedly ruled that arguments presented to us only in a footnote are not entitled to appellate consideration. Although an amicus brief can be helpful in elaborating issues properly presented by the parties, it is normally not a method for injecting new issues into an appeal, at least in cases where the parties are competently represented by counsel. Second, to whatever extent the argument might have merit at some future time in a case with a properly developed record, the argument is entirely premature and speculative at this time on this record. There is not even a claim, much less evidence, that any Plaintiff has sought to prevent copying of public domain works, or that the injunction prevents the Defendants from copying such works. As Judge Kaplan noted, the possibility that encryption would preclude access to public domain works "does not yet appear to be a problem, although it may emerge as one in the future."

III. Constitutional Challenges Based on the First Amendment

A. Applicable Principles

Last year, in one of our Court's first forays into First Amendment law in the digital age, we took an "evolutionary" approach to the task of tailoring familiar constitutional rules to novel technological circumstances, favoring "narrow" holdings that would permit the law to mature on a "case-by-case" basis. In that spirit, we proceed, with appropriate caution, to consider the Appellants' First Amendment challenges by analyzing a series of preliminary issues the resolution of which provides a basis for adjudicating the specific objections to the DMCA and its application to DeCSS. These issues, which we consider only to the extent necessary to resolve the pending appeal, are whether computer code is speech, whether computer programs are speech, the scope of First Amendment protection for computer code, and the scope of First Amendment protection for decryption code. Based on our analysis of these issues, we then consider the Appellants' challenge to the injunction's provisions concerning posting and linking.

1. Code as Speech

Communication does not lose constitutional protection as "speech" simply because it is expressed in the language of computer code. Mathematical formulae and musical scores are written in "code," i.e., symbolic notations not comprehensible to the uninitiated, and yet both are covered by the First Amendment. If someone chose to write a novel entirely in computer object code by using strings of 1's and 0's for each letter of each word, the resulting work would be no different for constitutional purposes than if it had been written in English. The "object code" version would be incomprehensible to readers outside the programming community (and tedious to read even for most within the community), but it would be no more incomprehensible than a work written in Sanskrit for those unversed in that language. The undisputed evidence reveals that even pure object code can be, and often is, read and understood by experienced programmers. And source code (in any of its various levels of complexity) can be read by many more. Ultimately, however, the ease with which a work is comprehended is irrelevant to the constitutional inquiry. If computer code is distinguishable from conventional speech for First Amendment purposes, it is not because it is written in an obscure language.

2. Computer Programs as Speech

Of course, computer code is not likely to be the language in which a work of literature is written. Instead, it is primarily the language for programs executable by a computer. These programs are essentially instructions to a computer. In general, programs may give instructions either to perform a task or series of tasks when initiated by a single (or double) click of a mouse or, once a program is operational ("launched"), to manipulate data that the user enters into the computer. Whether computer code that gives a computer instructions is "speech" within the meaning of the First Amendment requires consideration of the scope of the Constitution's protection of speech.

The First Amendment provides that "Congress shall make no law . . . abridging the freedom of speech. . . ." "Speech" is an elusive term, and judges and scholars have debated its bounds for two centuries. Some would confine First Amendment protection to political speech. Others would extend it further to artistic expression.

Whatever might be the merits of these and other approaches, the law has not been so limited. Even dry information, devoid of advocacy, political relevance, or artistic expression, has been accorded First Amendment protection.

Thus, for example, courts have subjected to First Amendment scrutiny restrictions on the dissemination of technical scientific information, and scientific research, and attempts to regulate the publication of instructions.

Computer programs are not exempted from the category of First Amendment speech simply because their instructions require use of a computer. A recipe is no less "speech" because it calls for the use of an oven, and a musical score is no less "speech" because it specifies performance on an electric guitar. Arguably distinguishing computer programs from conventional language instructions is the fact that programs are executable on a computer. But the fact that a program has the capacity to direct the functioning of a computer does not mean that it lacks the additional capacity to convey information, and it is the conveying of information that renders instructions "speech" for purposes of the First Amendment. The information conveyed by most "instructions" is how to perform a task.

Instructions such as computer code, which are intended to be executable by a computer, will often convey information capable of comprehension and assessment by a human being. A programmer reading a program learns information about instructing a computer, and might use this information to improve personal programming skills and perhaps the craft of programming. Moreover, programmers communicating ideas to one another almost inevitably communicate in code, much as musicians use notes. Limiting First Amendment protection of programmers to descriptions of computer code (but not the code itself) would impede discourse among computer scholars, just as limiting protection for musicians to descriptions of musical scores (but not sequences of notes) would impede their exchange of ideas and expression. Instructions that communicate information comprehensible to a human qualify as speech whether the instructions are designed for execution by a computer or a human (or both).

Vartuli is not to the contrary. The defendants in *Vartuli* marketed a software program called "Recurrence," which would tell computer users when to buy or sell currency futures contracts if their computers were fed currency market rates. The Commodity Futures Trading Commission charged the defendants with violating federal law for, among other things, failing to register as commodity trading advisors for their distribution of the Recurrence software. The defendants maintained that Recurrence's cues to users to buy or sell were protected speech, and that the registration requirement as applied to Recurrence was a constitutionally suspect prior restraint. We rejected the defendants' constitutional claim, holding that Recurrence "in the form it was sold and marketed by the defendants" did not generate speech protected by the First Amendment.

Essential to our ruling in *Vartuli* was the manner in which the defendants marketed the software and intended that it be used: the defendants told users of the software to follow the software's cues "with no second-guessing," and intended that users follow Recurrence's commands "mechanically" and "without the intercession of the mind or the will of the recipient." We held that the values served by the First Amendment were not advanced by these instructions, even though the instructions were expressed in words. We acknowledged that some users would, despite the defendants' marketing, refuse to follow Recurrence's cues mechanically but instead would use the commands as a source of information and advice, and that, as to these users, Recurrence's cues might very "well have been 'speech.'" Nevertheless, we concluded that the Government could require registration for Recurrence's intended use because such use was devoid of any constitutionally protected speech.

Vartuli considered two ways in which a programmer might be said to communicate through code: to the user of the program (not necessarily protected) and to the computer (never protected). However, this does not mean that *Vartuli* denied First Amendment protection to all computer programs. Since *Vartuli* limited its constitutional scrutiny to the code "as marketed," i.e., as an automatic trading system, it did not have occasion to consider a third manner in which a programmer might communicate through code: to another programmer.

For all of these reasons, we join the other courts that have concluded that computer code, and computer programs constructed from code can merit First Amendment protection.

3. The Scope of First Amendment Protection for Computer Code

Having concluded that computer code conveying information is "speech" within the meaning of the First Amendment, we next consider, to a limited extent, the scope of the protection that code enjoys. As the District Court recognized, the scope of protection for speech generally depends on whether the restriction is imposed because of the content of the speech. Content-based restrictions are permissible only if they serve compelling state interests and do so by the least restrictive means available. A content-neutral restriction is permissible if it serves a substantial governmental interest, the interest is unrelated to the suppression of free expression, and the regulation is narrowly tailored, which "in this context requires . . . that the means chosen do not 'burden substantially more speech than is necessary to further the government's legitimate interests.'"

* * *

To determine whether regulation of computer code is content-neutral, the initial inquiry must be whether the regulated activity is "sufficiently imbued with elements of communication to fall within the scope of the First . . . Amendment." Computer code, as we have noted, often conveys information comprehensible to human beings, even as it also directs a computer to perform various functions. Once a speech component is identified, the inquiry then proceeds to whether the regulation is "justified without reference to the content of regulated speech."

The Appellants vigorously reject the idea that computer code can be regulated according to any different standard than that applicable to pure speech, i.e., speech that lacks a nonspeech component. Although recognizing that code is a series of instructions to a computer, they argue that code is no different, for First Amendment purposes, than blueprints that instruct an engineer or recipes that instruct a cook. We disagree. Unlike a blueprint or a recipe, which cannot yield any functional result without human comprehension of its content, human decision-making, and human action, computer code can instantly cause a computer to accomplish tasks and instantly render the results of those tasks available throughout the world via the Internet. The only human action required to achieve these results can be as limited and instantaneous as a single click of a mouse. These realities of what code is and what its normal functions are require a First Amendment analysis that treats code as combining nonspeech and speech elements, i.e., functional and expressive elements. ("[D]ifferences in the characteristics of new media justify differences in the First Amendment standards applied to them.")

We recognize, as did Judge Kaplan, that the functional capability of computer code cannot yield a result until a human being decides to insert the disk containing the code into a computer and causes it to perform its function (or programs a computer to cause the code to perform its function). Nevertheless, this momentary intercession of human action does not diminish the nonspeech component of code, nor render code entirely speech, like a blueprint or a recipe. Judge Kaplan, in a passage that merits extensive quotation, cogently explained why this is especially so with respect to decryption code:

> [T]he focus on functionality in order to determine the level of scrutiny is not an inevitable consequence of the speech-conduct distinction. Conduct has immediate effects on the environment. Computer code, on the other hand, no matter how functional, causes a computer to perform the intended operations only if someone uses the code to do so. Hence, one commentator, in a thoughtful article, has maintained that functionality is really "a proxy for effects or harm" and that its adoption as a determinant of the level of scrutiny slides over questions of causation that intervene between the dissemination of a computer program and any harm caused by its use.

The characterization of functionality as a proxy for the consequences of use is accurate. But the assumption that the chain of causation is too attenuated to justify the use of functionality to determine the level of scrutiny, at least in this context, is not.

Society increasingly depends upon technological means of controlling access to digital files and systems, whether they are military computers, bank records, academic records, copyrighted works or something else entirely. There are far too many who, given any opportunity, will bypass security measures, some for the sheer joy of doing it, some for innocuous reasons, and others for more malevolent purposes. Given the virtually instantaneous and worldwide dissemination widely available via the Internet, the only rational assumption is that once a computer program capable of bypassing such an access control system is disseminated, it will be used. And that is not all.

There was a time when copyright infringement could be dealt with quite adequately by focusing on the infringing act. If someone wished to make and sell high quality but unauthorized copies of a copyrighted book, for example, the infringer needed a printing press. The copyright holder, once aware of the appearance of infringing copies, usually was able to trace the copies up the chain of distribution, find and prosecute the infringer, and shut off the infringement at the source.

In principle, the digital world is very different. Once a decryption program like DeCSS is written, it quickly can be sent all over the world. Every recipient is capable not only of decrypting and perfectly copying plaintiffs'

copyrighted DVDs, but also of retransmitting perfect copies of DeCSS and thus enabling every recipient to do the same. They likewise are capable of transmitting perfect copies of the decrypted DVD. The process potentially is exponential rather than linear.

. . .

These considerations drastically alter consideration of the causal link between dissemination of computer programs such as this and their illicit use. Causation in the law ultimately involves practical policy judgments. Here, dissemination itself carries very substantial risk of imminent harm because the mechanism is so unusual by which dissemination of means of circumventing access controls to copyrighted works threatens to produce virtually unstoppable infringement of copyright. In consequence, the causal link between the dissemination of circumvention computer programs and their improper use is more than sufficiently close to warrant selection of a level of constitutional scrutiny based on the programs' functionality.

The functionality of computer code properly affects the scope of its First Amendment protection.

4. The Scope of First Amendment Protection for Decryption Code

In considering the scope of First Amendment protection for a decryption program like DeCSS, we must recognize that the essential purpose of encryption code is to prevent unauthorized access. Owners of all property rights are entitled to prohibit access to their property by unauthorized persons. Homeowners can install locks on the doors of their houses. Custodians of valuables can place them in safes. Stores can attach to products security devices that will activate alarms if the products are taken away without purchase. These and similar security devices can be circumvented. Burglars can use skeleton keys to open door locks. Thieves can obtain the combinations to safes. Product security devices can be neutralized.

Our case concerns a security device, CSS computer code, that prevents access by unauthorized persons to DVD movies. The CSS code is embedded in the DVD movie. Access to the movie cannot be obtained unless a person has a device, a licensed DVD player, equipped with computer code capable of decrypting the CSS encryption code. In its basic function, CSS is like a lock on a homeowner's door, a combination of a safe, or a security device attached to a store's products.

DeCSS is computer code that can decrypt CSS. In its basic function, it is like a skeleton key that can open a locked door, a combination that can open a safe, or a device that can neutralize the security device attached to a store's products. DeCSS enables anyone to gain access to a DVD movie without using a DVD player.

The initial use of DeCSS to gain access to a DVD movie creates no loss to movie producers because the initial user must purchase the DVD. However, once the DVD is purchased, DeCSS enables the initial user to copy the movie in digital form and transmit it instantly in virtually limitless quantity, thereby depriving the movie producer of sales. The advent of the Internet creates the potential for instantaneous worldwide distribution of the copied material.

At first glance, one might think that Congress has as much authority to regulate the distribution of computer code to decrypt DVD movies as it has to regulate distribution of skeleton keys, combinations to safes, or devices to neutralize store product security devices. However, despite the evident legitimacy of protection against unauthorized access to DVD movies, just like any other property, regulation of decryption code like DeCSS is challenged in this case because DeCSS differs from a skeleton key in one important respect: it not only is capable of performing the function of unlocking the encrypted DVD movie, it also is a form of communication, albeit written in a language not understood by the general public. As a communication, the DeCSS code has a claim to being "speech," and as "speech," it has a claim to being protected by the First Amendment. But just as the realities of what any computer code can accomplish must inform the scope of its constitutional protection, so the capacity of a decryption program like DeCSS to accomplish unauthorized—indeed, unlawful—access to materials in which the Plaintiffs have intellectual property rights must inform and limit the scope of its First Amendment protection.

With all of the foregoing considerations in mind, we next consider the Appellants' First Amendment challenge to the DMCA as applied in the specific prohibitions that have been imposed by the District Court's injunction.

B. First Amendment Challenge

The District Court's injunction applies the DMCA to the Defendants by imposing two types of prohibition, both grounded on the anti-trafficking provisions of the DMCA. The first prohibits posting DeCSS or any other technology for circumventing CSS on any Internet web site. The second prohibits knowingly linking any Internet web site to any other web site containing DeCSS. The validity of the posting and linking prohibitions must be considered separately.

1. Posting

The initial issue is whether the posting prohibition is content-neutral, since, as we have explained,

this classification determines the applicable constitutional standard. The Appellants contend that the anti-trafficking provisions of the DMCA and their application by means of the posting prohibition of the injunction are content-based. They argue that the provisions "specifically target . . . scientific expression based on the particular topic addressed by that expression—namely, techniques for circumventing CSS." We disagree. The Appellants' argument fails to recognize that the target of the posting provisions of the injunction—DeCSS—has both a non-speech and a speech component, and that the DMCA, as applied to the Appellants, and the posting prohibition of the injunction target only the non-speech component. Neither the DMCA nor the posting prohibition is concerned with whatever capacity DeCSS might have for conveying information to a human being, and that capacity, as previously explained, is what arguably creates a speech component of the decryption code. The DMCA and the posting prohibition are applied to DeCSS solely because of its capacity to instruct a computer to decrypt CSS. That functional capability is not speech within the meaning of the First Amendment. The Government seeks to "justif[y]," both the application of the DMCA and the posting prohibition to the Appellants solely on the basis of the functional capability of DeCSS to instruct a computer to decrypt CSS, i.e., "without reference to the content of the regulated speech." This type of regulation is therefore content-neutral, just as would be a restriction on trafficking in skeleton keys identified because of their capacity to unlock jail cells, even though some of the keys happened to bear a slogan or other legend that qualified as a speech component.

As a content-neutral regulation with an incidental effect on a speech component, the regulation must serve a substantial governmental interest, the interest must be unrelated to the suppression of free expression, and the incidental restriction on speech must not burden substantially more speech than is necessary to further that interest. The Government's interest in preventing unauthorized access to encrypted copyrighted material is unquestionably substantial, and the regulation of DeCSS by the posting prohibition plainly serves that interest. Moreover, that interest is unrelated to the suppression of free expression. The injunction regulates the posting of DeCSS, regardless of whether DeCSS code contains any information comprehensible by human beings that would qualify as speech. Whether the incidental regulation on speech burdens substantially more speech than is necessary to further the interest in preventing unauthorized access to copyrighted materials requires some elaboration.

Posting DeCSS on the Appellants' web site makes it instantly available at the click of a mouse to any person in the world with access to the Internet, and such person can then instantly transmit DeCSS to anyone else with Internet access. Although the prohibition on posting prevents the Appellants from conveying to others the speech component of DeCSS, the Appellants have not suggested, much less shown, any technique for barring them from making this instantaneous worldwide distribution of a decryption code that makes a lesser restriction on the code's speech component. It is true that the Government has alternative means of prohibiting unauthorized access to copyrighted materials. For example, it can create criminal and civil liability for those who gain unauthorized access, and thus it can be argued that the restriction on posting DeCSS is not absolutely necessary to preventing unauthorized access to copyrighted materials. But a content-neutral regulation need not employ the least restrictive means of accomplishing the governmental objective. It need only avoid burdening "substantially more speech than is necessary to further the government's legitimate interests." The prohibition on the Defendants' posting of DeCSS satisfies that standard.

2. Linking

In considering linking, we need to clarify the sense in which the injunction prohibits such activity. Although the injunction defines several terms, it does not define "linking." Nevertheless, it is evident from the District Court's opinion that it is concerned with "hyperlinks." A hyperlink is a cross-reference (in a distinctive font or color) appearing on one web page that, when activated by the point-and-click of a mouse, brings onto the computer screen another web page. The hyperlink can appear on a screen (window) as text, such as the Internet address ("URL") of the web page being called up or a word or phrase that identifies the web page to be called up, for example, "DeCSS web site." Or the hyperlink can appear as an image, for example, an icon depicting a person sitting at a computer watching a DVD movie and text stating "click here to access DeCSS and see DVD movies for free!" The code for the web page containing the hyperlink includes a computer instruction that associates the link with the URL of the web page to be accessed, such that clicking on the hyperlink instructs the computer to enter the URL of the desired web page and thereby access that page. With a hyperlink on a web page, the linked web site is just one click away.

In applying the DMCA to linking (via hyperlinks), Judge Kaplan recognized, as he had with DeCSS code, that a hyperlink has both a speech and a nonspeech component. It conveys information, the Internet address of the linked web page, and has the functional capacity to bring the content of the linked web page to the user's computer screen (or, as Judge Kaplan put it, to "take one almost instantaneously to the desired destination."). As he had ruled with respect to DeCSS code, he ruled that application of the DMCA to the Defendants' linking to web sites containing DeCSS is content-neutral because it is justified without regard to the speech component of the hyperlink. The linking prohibition applies whether or not the hyperlink contains any information, comprehensible to a human being, as to the Internet address of the web page being accessed. The linking prohibition is justified solely by the functional capability of the hyperlink.

Applying the *O'Brien/Ward/Turner Broadcasting* requirements for content-neutral regulation, Judge Kaplan then ruled that the DMCA, as applied to the Defendants' linking, served substantial governmental interests and was unrelated to the suppression of free expression. We agree. He then carefully considered the "closer call," as to whether a linking prohibition would satisfy the narrow tailoring requirement. In an especially carefully considered portion of his opinion, he observed that strict liability for linking to web sites containing DeCSS would risk two impairments of free expression. Web site operators would be inhibited from displaying links to various web pages for fear that a linked page might contain DeCSS, and a prohibition on linking to a web site containing DeCSS would curtail access to whatever other information was contained at the accessed site.

To avoid applying the DMCA in a manner that would "burden substantially more speech than is necessary to further the government's legitimate interests," Judge Kaplan adapted the standards of *New York Times Co. v. Sullivan* to fashion a limited prohibition against linking to web sites containing DeCSS. He required clear and convincing evidence

that those responsible for the link (a) know at the relevant time that the offending material is on the linked-to site, (b) know that it is circumvention technology that may not lawfully be offered, and (c) create or maintain the link for the purpose of disseminating that technology.

He then found that the evidence satisfied his three-part test by his required standard of proof.

In response to our post-argument request for the parties' views on various issues, including specifically Judge Kaplan's test for a linking prohibition, the Appellants replied that his test was deficient for not requiring proof of intent to cause, or aid or abet, harm, and that the only valid test for a linking prohibition would be one that could validly apply to the publication in a print medium of an address for obtaining prohibited material. The Appellees and the Government accepted Judge Kaplan's criteria for purposes of asserting the validity of the injunction as applied to the Appellants, with the Government expressing reservations as to the standard of clear and convincing evidence.

Mindful of the cautious approach to First Amendment claims involving computer technology expressed in *Name.Space*, we see no need on this appeal to determine whether a test as rigorous as Judge Kaplan's is required to respond to First Amendment objections to the linking provision of the injunction that he issued. It suffices to reject the Appellants' contention that an intent to cause harm is required and that linking can be enjoined only under circumstances applicable to a print medium. As they have throughout their arguments, the Appellants ignore the reality of the functional capacity of decryption computer code and hyperlinks to facilitate instantaneous unauthorized access to copyrighted materials by anyone anywhere in the world. Under the circumstances amply shown by the record, the injunction's linking prohibition validly regulates the Appellants' opportunity instantly to enable anyone anywhere to gain unauthorized access to copyrighted movies on DVDs.

At oral argument, we asked the Government whether its undoubted power to punish the distribution of obscene materials would permit an injunction prohibiting a newspaper from printing addresses of bookstore locations carrying such materials. In a properly cautious response, the Government stated that the answer would depend on the circumstances of the publication. The Appellants' supplemental papers enthusiastically embraced the arguable analogy between printing bookstore addresses and displaying on a web page links to web sites at which DeCSS may be accessed. They confidently asserted that publication of bookstore locations carrying obscene material cannot be enjoined consistent with the First Amendment, and that a prohibition against linking to web sites containing DeCSS is similarly invalid.

Like many analogies posited to illuminate legal issues, the bookstore analogy is helpful primarily in identifying characteristics that distinguish it from the context of the pending dispute. If a bookstore proprietor is knowingly selling obscene materials, the evil of distributing such materials can be prevented by injunctive relief against the unlawful distribution (and similar distribution by others can be deterred by punishment of the distributor). And if others publish the location of the bookstore, preventive relief against a distributor can be effective before any significant distribution of the prohibited materials has occurred. The digital world, however, creates a very different problem. If obscene materials are posted on one web site and other sites post hyperlinks to the first site, the materials are available for instantaneous worldwide distribution before any preventive measures can be effectively taken.

This reality obliges courts considering First Amendment claims in the context of the pending case to choose between two unattractive alternatives: either tolerate some impairment of communication in order to permit Congress to prohibit decryption that may lawfully be prevented, or tolerate some decryption in order to avoid some impairment of communication. Although the parties dispute the extent of impairment of communication if the injunction is upheld and the extent of decryption if it is vacated, and differ on the availability and effectiveness of techniques for minimizing both consequences, the fundamental choice between impairing some communication and tolerating decryption cannot be entirely avoided.

In facing this choice, we are mindful that it is not for us to resolve the issues of public policy implicated by the choice we have identified. Those issues are for Congress. Our task is to determine whether the legislative solution adopted by Congress, as applied to the Appellants by the District Court's injunction, is consistent with the limitations of the First Amendment, and we are satisfied that it is.

IV. Constitutional Challenge Based on Claimed Restriction of Fair Use

Asserting that fair use "is rooted in and required by both the Copyright Clause and the First Amendment," the Appellants contend that the DMCA, as applied by the District Court, unconstitutionally "eliminates fair use" of copyrighted materials. We reject this extravagant claim.

Preliminarily, we note that the Supreme Court has never held that fair use is constitutionally required, although some isolated statements in its opinions might arguably be enlisted for such a requirement. In *Stewart v. Abend*, cited by the Appellants, the Court merely noted that fair use "'permits courts to avoid rigid application of the copyright statute when, on occasion, it would stifle the very creativity which that law is designed to foster.'" In *Campbell v. Acuff-Rose Music, Inc.*, the Court observed, "From the infancy of copyright protection, some opportunity for fair use of copyrighted materials has been thought necessary to fulfill copyright's very purpose, '[t]o promote the Progress of Science and useful Arts. . . .'"

We need not explore the extent to which fair use might have constitutional protection, grounded on either the First Amendment or the Copyright Clause, because whatever validity a constitutional claim might have as to an application of the DMCA that impairs fair use of copyrighted materials, such matters are far beyond the scope of this lawsuit for several reasons. In the first place, the Appellants do not claim to be making fair use of any copyrighted materials, and nothing in the injunction prohibits them from making such fair use. They are barred from trafficking in a decryption code that enables unauthorized access to copyrighted materials.

Second, as the District Court properly noted, to whatever extent the anti-trafficking provisions of the DMCA might prevent others from copying portions of DVD movies in order to make fair use of them, "the evidence as to the impact of the anti-trafficking provision[s] of the DMCA on prospective fair users is scanty and fails adequately to address the issues."

Third, the Appellants have provided no support for their premise that fair use of DVD movies is constitutionally required to be made by copying the original work in its original format. Their examples of the fair uses that they believe others will be prevented from making all involve copying in a digital format those portions of a DVD movie amenable to fair use, a copying that would enable the fair user to manipulate the digitally copied portions. One example is that of a school child who wishes to copy images from a DVD movie to insert into the student's documentary film. We know of no authority for the proposition that fair use, as protected by the Copyright Act, much less the Constitution, guarantees copying by the optimum method or in the identical format of the original. Although the Appellants insisted at oral argument that they should not be relegated to a "horse and buggy" technique in making fair use of DVD movies, the DMCA does not impose even an arguable limitation on the opportunity to make a variety of traditional fair uses of DVD movies, such as commenting on their content, quoting excerpts from their screenplays, and even recording portions of the video images and sounds on film or tape by pointing a camera, a camcorder, or a microphone at a monitor as it displays the DVD movie. The fact that the resulting copy will not be as perfect or as manipulable as a digital copy obtained by having direct access to the DVD movie in its digital form, provides no basis for a claim of unconstitutional limitation of fair use. A film critic making fair use of a movie by quoting selected lines of dialogue has no constitutionally valid claim that the review (in print or on television) would be technologically superior if the reviewer had not been prevented from using a movie camera in the theater, nor has an art student a valid constitutional claim to fair use of a painting by photographing it in a museum. Fair use has never been held to be a guarantee of access to copyrighted material in order to copy it by the fair user's preferred technique or in the format of the original.

Conclusion

We have considered all the other arguments of the Appellants and conclude that they provide no basis for disturbing the District Court's judgment. Accordingly, the judgment is affirmed.

administering the law of the Internet
building the Internet
censorship and freedom of expression
consumers' and users' rights
copyright and the ownership of content
crimes and mischief
doing business: contracts and commerce
international problems and international law
the Internet in popular culture
Internet pests and other nuisances
keeping secrets: privacy and confidentiality of
   information
legislating change: federal statutes and
   proposed legislation
litigating change: landmark lawsuits
open-source and open-access
other forms of intellectual property: beyond
   traditional copyright, patent, and trademark
patent
trademark
whose Internet?—struggles for influence

ADMINISTERING THE INTERNET

broadband
cable
choice of law
class action
.com
cybersquatting
Declaration of the Independence of
   Cyberspace
domain name registration
enforcement
Federal Communications Commission
Federal Trade Commission
Internet Corporation for Assigned Names and
   Numbers
jurisdiction
recognition and enforcement of judgments

BUILDING THE INTERNET

broadband
cable
.com

cybersquatting
domain name registration
Federal Communications Commission
Internet
Internet Corporation for Assigned Names and
   Numbers
Web browser
World Wide Web

CENSORSHIP AND FREEDOM OF EXPRESSION

activism and advocacy groups
advertising
censorship
Child Online Protection Act
child pornography
Children's Internet Protection Act
Communications Decency Act
constitutional law
data haven
Declaration of the Independence of
   Cyberspace
DeCSS
defamation
encryption
First Amendment
French Yahoo! case
indecency
obscenity
pornography
search engine
spam

CONSUMERS' AND USERS' RIGHTS

activism and advocacy groups
advertising
adware and spyware
analog recording
anonymity
Audio Home Recording Act
backup copies
censorship
clickwrap agreement
Declaration of the Independence of Cyberspace

INDUCE Act
No Electronic Theft Act
Protecting Intellectual Rights against Theft
    and Expropriation Act
Public Domain Enhancement Act
semiconductor manufacturing mask work
    registrations
Sonny Bono Copyright Term Extension Act
Uniform Computer Information Transactions
    Act

LITIGATING CHANGE: LANDMARK LAWSUITS

broadband
Child Online Protection Act
Children's Internet Protection Act
Communications Decency Act
DeCSS
e-books
file-sharing
French Yahoo! case
look and feel
menu command hierarchy
microsoft antitrust litigation
warez

THE INTERNET IN POPULAR CULTURE

cyber-
cyberpunk
cyberspace
data haven
phreaking
worm

INTERNET PESTS AND OTHER NUISANCES

adware and spyware
cookies
Federal Trade Commission
firewall
hacking
malware
phishing
spam
Trojan
virus
worm

KEEPING SECRETS: PRIVACY AND CONFIDENTIALITY OF INFORMATION

activism and advocacy groups
adware and spyware
anonymity
certificate
Children's Online Privacy Protection Act
cookies
defamation
encryption
enforcement
Federal Trade Commission
identity theft
Internet service providers
privacy

OPEN-SOURCE AND OPEN-ACCESS

activism and advocacy groups
Budapest Open Access Initiative
class action
copyright
Declaration of the Independence of
    Cyberspace
DeCSS
open-source
Project Gutenberg
public domain
voluntary collective license

OTHER FORMS OF INTELLECTUAL PROPERTY: BEYOND TRADITIONAL COPYRIGHT, PATENT, AND TRADEMARK

Digital Millennium Copyright Act, Title V
intellectual property
semiconductor manufacturing mask work
    registrations
TRIPS
TRIPS (industrial designs and integrated
    circuit layouts)
TRIPS (trade secrets)

PATENT

business methods patent
computer program
court of appeals for the federal circuit
doctrine of equivalents
international patent protection
Paris Convention

❖ APPENDIX IV: BIBLIOGRAPHY ❖

NOLO PRESS

- Stephen R. Elias and Richard Stim, *Patent, Copyright and Trademark: An Intellectual Property Desk Reference*, 7th ed. (Berkeley, CA: Nolo Press, 2004).
- Richard Stim, *Getting Permission: How to License and Clear Copyrighted Materials Online and Off* (Berkeley, CA: Nolo Press, 2001).

Nolo Press is a publisher of do-it-yourself legal guides. Because Nolo's guides are written for non-lawyers, they are easy to understand. However, because they are designed to deal with immediate practical problems, they may have less theoretical depth than other works on the same subject. The two works listed here are good practical guides for anyone who operates a Web site or otherwise places content on the Web and is concerned about copyright or other intellectual property issues. *Getting Permission* focuses on the use of materials copyrighted by others, rather than on protection of one's own copyrighted Web content. The *Desk Reference* provides plain-English definitions for a wide range of intellectual property law terms.

WEST'S NUTSHELL SERIES

- Jerome A. Barron and C. Thomas Dienes, *Constitutional Law in a Nutshell* (St. Paul, MN: West, 2002).
- Michael H. Davis and Arthur Raphael Miller, *Intellectual Property: Patents, Trademarks, and Copyright in a Nutshell* (St. Paul, MN: West, 2000).
- Robert H. Klonoff, *Class Actions and Other Multi-Party Litigations in a Nutshell* (St. Paul, MN: West, 1999).
- Claude D. Rohwer et al., *Contracts in a Nutshell* (St. Paul, MN: West, 2000).
- David D. Siegel, *Conflicts in a Nutshell* (St. Paul, MN: West, 1994).
- Bradford Stone, *Uniform Commercial Code in a Nutshell* (St. Paul, MN: West, 2001).

West Publishing, based in St. Paul, Minnesota, is the largest, and among the oldest, legal publish-

ing companies in the United States. The Nutshell series includes volumes covering nearly every imaginable topic. Nutshells are small (5 inches by 7½ inches, and typically no more than one inch thick) paperback volumes providing an overview of the law on a particular topic. Although practicing attorneys use them, they are designed with law students in mind. As a result, they are less opaque than works aimed specifically at attorneys or law professors, if more challenging than the Nolo Press works. The titles of the books cited here are more or less self-explanatory. *Constitutional Law in a Nutshell* deals with a range of constitutional law issues, of which the ones most relevant to Internet law are those arising from the First Amendment's guarantee of freedom of expression. *Intellectual Property in a Nutshell* covers the three traditional areas: copyright, patents, and trademarks. All three of these are important to the Internet, but copyright most of all. *Class Actions and Other Multi-Party Litigations in a Nutshell* is much more specialized, dealing with a particular type of lawsuit; class actions might arise in a computer and Internet context when a business violates consumer rights. *Contracts in a Nutshell* and *Uniform Commercial Code in a Nutshell* deal with business transactions of all sorts, not merely e-commerce. And *Conflicts in a Nutshell* addresses the various conflicts of law that can arise when an action takes place in or affects persons, property, or interests in more than one jurisdiction, as often happens in Internet cases. These conflicts may include problems of choice of applicable law, recognition and enforcement of judgments, and territorial jurisdiction.

LEXISNEXIS'S UNDERSTANDING SERIES

- Jeffrey Ferriell and Michael Navin, *Understanding Contracts* (New York: Matthew Bender, 2004).
- Marshall Leaffer, *Understanding Copyright Law*, 3d ed. (New York: Matthew Bender, 1999).
- William M. Richman and William L. Reynolds, *Understanding Conflict of Laws*, 3d ed. (New York: Matthew Bender, 2002).

The Understanding series, from the Matthew Bender division of LexisNexis, is similar to the Nutshell series but provides somewhat more detailed source notes. The books are somewhat larger, and the footnotes provided for every point of law are a useful starting point for further research. However, although there is a Nutshell for nearly every legal topic, there are fewer volumes in the Understanding series. *Understanding Contracts* includes references to such Internet issues as electronic signatures and electronic transactions. The Internet affects and is affected by nearly every area of copyright law, making *Understanding Copyright Law* especially relevant. *Understanding Conflict of Laws* provides a thorough introduction to this often-misunderstood area of law and includes a section on jurisdiction and the Internet.

LEGAL REFERENCE WORKS

- Bryan A. Garner, ed., *Black's Law Dictionary*, 7th ed. (St. Paul, MN: West, 1999).
- J. Thomas McCarthy et al., *McCarthy's Desk Encyclopedia of Intellectual Property*, 3d ed. (Washington, DC: Bureau of National Affairs, 2004).

Black's Law Dictionary is a standard legal reference; anyone planning to spend any amount of time reading legal materials should keep *Black's* (or a similar work) handy as an aid in cutting through what at times might seem to be an impenetrable thicket of legal terminology.

McCarthy's Desk Encyclopedia of Intellectual Property is also a reference work, albeit a more specialized one. It covers all aspects of intellectual property, U.S. and international, online and off, with detailed explanations and references to statutes, cases, and other sources.

INTELLECTUAL PROPERTY IN DEPTH

- Richard Chused, ed., *A Copyright Anthology: The Technology Frontier* (Cincinnati, OH: Anderson Publishing, 1998).
- Anthony D'Amato and Doris Estelle Long, eds., *International Intellectual Property Anthology* (Cincinnati, OH: Anderson Publishing, 1996).

The editors of Anderson's anthologies take excerpts from books and law review articles by dozens of scholars in each field and arrange them in an easily accessible format, with a comprehensive table of contents that allows the reader to locate excerpts by topic and subtopic. The articles and books from which the excerpts are drawn were written for an audience of lawyers, legal academics, and judges. Both international and U.S. intellectual property law have undergone some dramatic changes in the years since the two anthologies listed here were published; those changes, naturally, are not reflected in the anthologies, but should be kept in mind while reading them.

INTELLECTUAL PROPERTY AND THE INTERNET

- Lawrence Lessig, *Code and Other Laws of Cyberspace* (New York: Basic Books, 1999).
- Lawrence Lessig, *The Future of Ideas: The Fate of the Commons in a Connected World* (New York: Random House, 2001).
- Lawrence Lessig, *Free Culture: How Big Media Uses Technology and the Law to Lock Down Culture and Control Creativity* (New York: Penguin, 2004).
- Siva Vaidhyanathan, *Copyrights and Copywrongs: The Rise of Intellectual Property and How It Threatens Creativity* (New York: New York University Press, 2001).
- Siva Vaidhyanathan, *The Anarchist in the Library: How the Clash between Freedom and Control Is Hacking the Real World and Crashing the System* (New York: Basic Books, 2004).

Professors Lessig and Vaidhyanathan are two well-known commentators on law and the Internet, especially intellectual property law and the Internet, and most especially copyright law and the Internet. In the five books listed here they develop parallel, but not identical, arguments to the effect that the apparently ongoing increase in the scope of intellectual property protection is stifling innovation and creativity, damaging the U.S. (and world) economy and polity, and will ultimately backfire, harming even those industries it is intended to protect.

Code, Lessig's 1999 work, was a breakthrough in at least two ways: It brought awareness of the emerging field of Internet law to the wider world beyond law schools, the intellectual property profession, and a few federal regulatory agencies. And it predicted that "we will see the Net move to an architecture of control," a prediction that the past five years of evolution in digital rights management, software licensing practices, and diminishing individual privacy have shown to be prescient. In *The Future of Ideas* Lessig continues to develop this theme, warning of creativity-stifling corporate control of the Internet, and also warns of the need for public awareness of and participation in the Internet and intellectual property governance process. *Free Culture* focuses on copyright law, looking at Internet law's main battleground of the moment—file-sharing—and at Lessig's involvement in *Eldred v. Ashcroft,* an ultimately unsuccessful court battle against the Sonny Bono Copyright Term Extension Act.

Vaidhyanathan, a communications professor and former journalist, reaches similar conclusions by a somewhat different path. In *Copyrights and Copywrongs* he also warns of the stifling effect that overzealous protection of copyright will have on creativity. He points out that the effect of current trends in copyright law is to stifle all cultural expression, but that the effect is unevenly distributed and that minority cultures will be disproportionately affected. In *The Anarchist in the Library* he carries this idea further, looking at the ways in which the tension resulting from attempts to control Internet content and attempts to avoid that control lead to extremism that carries over into the larger world, feeding into the trends toward anarchy and terrorism on the one hand and totalitarianism on the other.

THE TECHNICAL SIDE OF INTERNET SECURITY

- Jeff Moss, ed., *Stealing the Network: How to Own the Box* (Rockland, MA: Syngress 2003).
- Bruce Schneier, *Secrets and Lies: Digital Security in a Networked World* (New York: John Wiley and Sons, 2000).

An understanding of the technology and business realities of Internet security is often essential to an understanding of legal problems arising from breaches of security; unfortunately, many technical books about the Internet are written in jargon at least as impenetrable as that in many legal treatises. The works listed here address the technical side of security problems. In *Stealing the Network,* Jeff Moss has put together a collection of short stories written by hackers, many of them white hat hackers working as security experts. While nominally fiction, the stories provide detailed accounts of hacker break-ins—and the ways in which they could have been avoided. In *Secrets and Lies* Bruce Schneier, also a security expert and well-known encryption researcher, provides a comprehensive survey of security threats and solu-

tions. Computer and network security are often overlooked simply because they are perceived as boring; both books manage to counter this problem by presenting material in an entertaining manner.

FREE SPEECH

- Andrea Dworkin, *Pornography: Men Possessing Women* (New York: Perigee Books, 1981).
- Mike Godwin, *Cyber Rights: Defending Free Speech in the Digital Age* (Cambridge, MA: MIT Press, 2003).
- Kathryn Kolbert and Zak Mettger, eds., *Justice Talking: Censoring the Web: Leading Advocates Debate Today's Most Controversial Issues* (New York: The New Press, 2002).
- Kevin W. Saunders, *Saving Our Children from the First Amendment* (New York: New York University Press, 2004).
- Madeleine Schachter, *Law of Internet Speech,* 2d ed. (Durham, NC: Carolina Academic Press, 2002).
- Dick Thornburgh and Herbert S. Lin, *Youth, Pornography and the Internet* (Washington, DC: National Academies Press, 2002).

Although the problem of freedom of expression online has many facets, it is the problem of pornography, and of minors' access to it, that attracts the most attention. In *Cyber Rights,* Mike Godwin of the Electronic Frontier Foundation discusses attempts to censor Internet pornography, as well as censorship issues relating to copyright, defamation, encryption, and warez trading. The book takes an anticensorship position, but it presents all sides of the various questions fairly and completely.

Andrea Dworkin's classic work *Pornography* predates the Internet, but is an essential starting point for anyone wishing to understand opposition to pornography from a feminist perspective. Kevin Saunders, in *Saving Our Children from the First Amendment,* makes the difficult case for more censorship, not only of pornography but also, and perhaps especially, of violence and racist hate speech; Saunders makes a compelling argument that exposing minors to these materials will lead to an increase in hate crimes and other acts of violence. Encryption expert Herbert Lin and former Pennsylvania governor and U.S. Attorney General Dick Thornburgh, meanwhile, take a different approach: In *Youth, Pornography and the Internet* they provide information on technical and educational methods by which parents can restrict their children's access to pornography—and, by extension, to other types of content.

Censoring the Web includes a transcript and audio disk of a debate on National Public Radio's *Justice Talking* show between two partisan advocates of different approaches to Web censorship. The two participants are Nadine Stossen, president of the American Civil Liberties Union, and Bruce Taylor, executive director of the National Law Center for Children and Families. Where *Censoring the Web* presents two diametrically contrasting views, Madeleine Schachter's book, *Law of Internet Speech,* takes a different approach to achieving balance: It presents the issues, law, and policy reasoning on a wide range of Internet free speech issues objectively and in considerable depth.

FILE-SHARING

- Stuart Biegel, *Beyond Our Control? Confronting the Limits of Our Legal System in the Age of Cyberspace* (Cambridge, MA: MIT Press, 2001).
- Joseph Menn, *All the Rave: The Rise and Fall of Shawn Fanning's Napster* (New York: Crown Business, 2003).
- Trevor Merriden, *Irresistible Forces: The Business Legacy of Napster and the Growth of the Underground Internet* (New York: John Wiley and Sons, 2002).

File-sharing is the most controversial and most heavily litigated aspect of the Internet today. A great many books have been written about it; the three listed here are only a tiny sample. *Irresistible Forces* and *All the Rave* tell the history of Napster—and *Irresistible Forces,* in particular, goes on to follow the post-Napster history of P2P. Stuart Biegel's *Beyond Our Control* also focuses on P2P, but uses the story of P2P file-sharing networks as a lens through which to view the evolution of Internet law.

THE INTERNET AS A CULTURAL PHENOMENON

- John Brunner, *The Shockwave Rider* (New York: Ballantine, 1976).
- Thomas M. Disch, *The Dreams Our Stuff Is Made Of: How Science Fiction Conquered the World* (New York: Touchstone, 1998).
- William Gibson, *Neuromancer* (New York: Ace, 1984).
- Bruce Sterling, ed., *Mirrorshades: The Cyberpunk Anthology* (New York: Arbor House, 1986).

The Internet is not, and should not be, a primarily legal phenomenon. The Internet is constantly redefining its own place in popular culture as well as in the legal system. Technological advances and their social consequences are often anticipated in fiction, and fiction in turn creates expectations that shape the evolution of technology: It is no accident that today's cell phones resemble the communicators of the original crew of the *Starship Enterprise* in a television show nearly forty years old. Thomas M. Disch, in *The Dreams Our Stuff Is Made Of,* investigates the influence of SF on the real world, and vice versa.

SF writers anticipated and wrote about information networks for decades before they became reality, but among the most accurately predictive works is *The Shockwave Rider,* by the late British author John Brunner. Writing three decades ago, Brunner anticipated aspects of the Internet ranging from worms to data havens. A decade later William Gibson wrote the novel that was to define the Internet in the popular imagination and in academia: *Neuromancer. Neuromancer* and its sequels brought cyberpunk to the world's attention and made information networks romantic and interesting. A good place for an introduction to cyberpunk as a genre is *Mirrorshades,* an anthology of short stories edited by Bruce Sterling.

❖ APPENDIX V: TABLE OF AUTHORITIES ❖

TREATIES

- Agreement between the United Nations and the World Intellectual Property Organization, Dec. 17, 1974.
- Agreement between the World Intellectual Property Organization and the World Trade Organization, Dec. 22, 1995, 35 I.L.M. 754 (1996).
- Agreement on Trade-Related Aspects of Intellectual Property Rights (TRIPS), Marrakesh Agreement Establishing the World Trade Organization, Annex 1C, Apr. 15, 1994, 33 I.L.M. 81 (1994).
- Brussels Convention Relating to the Distribution of Programme-Carrying Signals Transmitted by Satellite, May 21, 1974, 13 I.L.M. 1444.
- Budapest Treaty on the International Recognition of the Deposit of Microorganisms for the Purposes of Patent Procedure, Apr. 28, 1977, as amended on Sept. 26, 1980, 32 U.S.T. 1241, 1861 U.N.T.S. 361.
- Buenos Aires Convention, Aug. 20, 1910, 38 Stat. 1785, 155 L.N.T.S. 179.
- Convention Concerning the Creation of an International Union for the Protection of Literary and Artistic Works (Berne Convention), Sept. 9, 1886, as last revised at Paris, July 24, 1971 (amended 1979), 25 U.S.T. 1341, 828 U.N.T.S. 221.
- Convention Establishing the World Intellectual Property Organization, July 14, 1967, as amended on Sept. 28, 1979 (WIPO Convention), 21 U.S.T. 1749, 828 U.N.T.S. 3.
- Convention for the Protection of Producers of Phonograms against Unauthorized Duplication of Their Phonograms, Oct. 29, 1971, 25 U.S.T. 309.
- Convention on the Grant of European Patents, Oct. 5, 1973, 13 I.L.M. 276, text as amended through Dec. 10, 1998, available at http://www.european-patent-office.org/legal/epc/e/ma1.html.
- Convention Relating to the Distribution of Programme-Carrying Signals Transmitted by Satellite, May 21, 1974, 13 I.L.M. 1444 (1976).
- General Agreement on Trade in Services, Marrakesh Agreement Establishing the World Trade Organization, Annex 1B, Apr. 15, 1994, 33 I.L.M. 1168 (1994).
- Hague Agreement Concerning the International Deposit of Industrial Designs, Nov. 6, 1925, 74 L.N.T.S. 343.
- Lisbon Agreement for the Protection of Appellations of Origin and their International Registration, Oct. 31, 1958, as revised at Stockholm on July 14, 1967, and as amended on Sept. 28, 1979, 923 U.N.T.S. 205.
- Locarno Agreement Establishing an International Classification for Industrial Designs, Oct. 8, 1968, as amended Sept. 28, 1979, 23 U.S.T. 1389.
- Madrid Agreement Concerning the International Registration of Marks, Apr. 14, 1891, as revised at Brussels, Dec. 14, 1900, at Washington, June 2, 1911, at The Hague, Nov. 6, 1925, at London, June 2, 1934, at Nice, June 15, 1957, at Stockholm, July 14, 1967, and as amended Sept. 28, 1979, available from http://www.wipo.int/madrid/en/legal_texts/.
- Madrid Agreement for the Repression of False or Deceptive Indications of Source on Goods, Apr. 14, 1891, as revised at Washington on June 2, 1911, at The Hague on Nov. 6, 1925, at London on June 2, 1934, and at Lisbon on Oct. 31, 1958, and Additional Act, Stockholm, July 14, 1967, 828 U.N.T.S. 389.
- Nairobi Treaty on the Protection of the Olympic Symbol, Sept. 26, 1981, available at http://clea.wipo.int/PDFFILES/English/WO/WO018EN.PDF.
- Nice Agreement Concerning the International Classification of Goods and Services for the Purposes of the Registration

of Marks, June 15, 1957, as revised at Stockholm on July 14, 1967, and at Geneva on May 13, 1977, and amended on Sept. 28, 1979, 23 U.S.T. 1336, 550 U.N.T.S. 45.

- Paris Convention for the Protection of Industrial Property, Mar. 20, 1883, as revised at Brussels on Dec. 14, 1900, at Washington on June 2, 1911, at The Hague on Nov. 6, 1925, at London on June 2, 1934, at Lisbon on Oct. 31, 1958, and at Stockholm on July 14, 1967, and as amended on Sept. 28, 1979, 21 U.S.T. 1583, 828 U.N.T.S. 305.
- Patent Cooperation Treaty, Washington on June 19, 1970, as amended on Sept. 28, 1979, and as modified on February 3, 1984, and October 3, 2001, 28 U.S.T. 7645, 9 I.L.M. 978 (1970).
- Patent Law Treaty, June 1, 2000, 39 I.L.M. 1047 (2000).
- Protocol Relating to the Madrid Agreement Concerning the International Registration of Marks, June 27, 1989, available from http://www.wipo.int/madrid/en/ legal_texts/.
- Rome Convention for the Protection of Performers, Producers of Phonograms and Broadcasting Organizations, Oct. 26, 1961, 496 U.N.T.S. 43.
- Strasbourg Agreement Concerning the International Patent Classification, Mar. 24, 1971, as amended Sept. 1979, 26 U.S.T. 1793.
- Trademark Law Treaty, Oct. 27, 1994, available at http://www.wipo.int/clea/ docs/en/wo/wo027en.htm.
- Treaty on Intellectual Property in Respect of Integrated Circuits, Washington, May 26, 1989, 28 I.L.M. 1477 (1989).
- Universal Copyright Convention, Sept. 6, 1952, 6 U.S.T. 2731, revised at Paris July 24, 1971, 25 U.S.T. 1341.
- Vienna Agreement Establishing an International Classification of the Figurative Elements of Marks, June 12, 1973, as amended Oct. 1, 1985, available at http:// www.wipo.int/clea/docs/en/wo/wo031en. htm.
- WIPO Copyright Treaty, Dec. 20, 1996, 36 I.L.M. 65 (1997).
- WIPO Performances and Phonograms Treaty, Dec. 20, 1996, 36 I.L.M. 76 (1997).

STATUTES

Federal

- Anticybersquatting Consumer Protection Act, 15 U.S.C. § 1125(d).
- Audio Home Recording Act, 17 U.S.C. §§ 1001–1003, 1008.
- Bank Fraud Act, 18 U.S.C. § 1344.
- Child Online Protection Act, 47 U.S.C. § 231.
- Child Pornography Prevention Act of 1996, 18 U.S.C. §§ 2251–2260.
- Children's Internet Protection Act, 47 U.S.C. § 254(h).
- Children's Online Privacy Protection Act, 15 U.S.C. §§ 6501–6506.
- Communications Assistance for Law Enforcement Act (CALEA) of 1994, Pub. L. No. 103-414, 108 Stat. 4279.
- Communications Decency Act, Pub. L. No. 104-104.
- Computer Fraud and Abuse Act of 1986, 18 U.S.C. § 1030.
- Computer Matching and Privacy and Protection Act, 5 U.S.C. § 552a(o).
- Controlling the Assault of Non-solicited Pornography and Marketing (CAN-SPAM) Act of 2003, 15 U.S.C. §§ 7701–7713.
- Copyright Act of 1976, 17 U.S.C. §§ 101–1332.
- Credit Card Fraud Act, 18 U.S.C. § 1029.
- Digital Millennium Copyright Act, Pub. L. No. 105-304.
- Digital Performance Right in Sound Recordings Act, 17 U.S.C. 106(6).
- Economic Espionage Act of 1996, 18 U.S.C. § 1831 et seq.
- Electronic Communications Privacy Act, 18 U.S.C. § 2703.
- Electronic Signatures in Global and National Commerce Act (E-Sign), 15 U.S.C. § 7001 et seq.
- Federal Anti-Lottery Act, 18 U.S.C. §§ 1301–1304.
- Federal Trade Commission Act, 15 U.S.C. § 45.
- Federal Trademark Dilution Act of 1995, 15 U.S.C. § 1125(c).
- First Inventors Defense Act, 35 U.S.C. § 273.
- Full Faith and Credit Statute, 28 U.S.C. § 1738.
- Identity Theft and Assumption Deterrence Act, amending and codified at 18 U.S.C. § 1028.

- Internet Tax Freedom Act, P.L. 105-277, Title XI.
- Lanham Trademark Act, 15 U.S.C. § 1115(b).
- National Information Infrastructure Protection Act (NII) of 1996, codified at 18 U.S.C. 103.
- Neighborhood Children's Internet Protection Act, 47 U.S.C. § 254(l).
- No Electronic Theft Act, amending and codified at 17 U.S.C. §§ 101, 506, and 507 and 18 U.S.C. §§ 2319–2320.
- Patent Code, 35 U.S.C. §§ 1–376.
- Privacy Act, 5 U.S.C. § 552a.
- Semiconductor Chip Protection Act, 17 U.S.C. §§ 901–914.
- Sherman Antitrust Act, 15 U.S.C. § 1.
- Sonny Bono Copyright Term Extension Act, amending and codified at 17 U.S.C. §§ 101, 108, 110, 201, 301–304, 512.
- Technology, Education and Copyright Harmonization Act amendments, 17 U.S.C. §§ 110(2), 112.
- Telecommunications Act of 1996, 47 U.S.C. § 151 et seq.
- Trademark Law Treaty Act of 1998, 15 U.S.C. § 1051.
- Unfair Methods of Competition, 15 U.S.C. § 45.
- Uniting and Strengthening America by Providing Appropriate Tools Required to Intercept and Obstruct Terrorism Act (USA PATRIOT Act) of 2001, Pub. L. No. 107-56, 115 Stat. 272.
- Visual Artists Rights Act, 17 U.S.C. § 106A.
- Wire Act, 18 U.S.C. § 1084.
- Wire Fraud Act, 18 U.S.C. § 1343.

State
- Consumer Protection against Computer Software Act, S.B. 1436 (California 2004).
- Spyware Control Act, H.B. 323 (Utah 2004).
- Official Code of Georgia Annotated § 16-9-93.1.

Proposed Legislation (Federal)
- Consumer Broadband and Digital Television Promotion Act, S. 2048, 107th Cong., 2d Sess., Mar. 21, 2002, available at http://thomas.loc.gov/cgi-bin/query/z?c107:S.2048:.
- Inducing Infringement of Copyrights Act of 2004, S. 2560, 108th Cong., 2d Sess., June 22, 2004.

- Protecting Intellectual Rights against Theft and Expropriation (PIRATE) Act of 2004, S. 2237, 108th Cong., 2d Sess., Mar. 25, 2004.
- Public Domain Enhancement Act, H. R. 2601, 108th Cong., 1st Sess., June 25, 2003, available at http://thomas.loc.gov/cgi-bin/query/z?c108:H.R.2601:.
- Safeguard against Privacy Invasions Act, H.R. 2929, 108th Cong., 1st Sess. (2003), reported to and passed by House of Representatives as Securely Protect Yourself against Cyber Trespass Act ("SPY ACT").
- Security and Freedom through Encryption (SAFE) Act, H.R. 850, 106th Cong. (1999).
- Software Principles Yielding Better Levels of Consumer Knowledge ("SPY BLOCK") Act, S. 2145, 108th Cong., 2nd Sess. (2003).
- Unlawful Internet Gambling Funding Prohibition Act, H.R. 2143, 108th Cong., 1st Sess. (2003).

EUROPEAN UNION DIRECTIVES

- Council Directive 93/98/EEC of 29 October 1993 Harmonizing the Term of Protection of Copyright and Certain Related Rights, 1993 O.J. (L 290) 9.
- Directive on the Approximation of the Laws, Regulations and Administrative Provisions of the Member States relating to the Advertising and Sponsorship of Tobacco Products, 2003 O.J. (L 152) 16.
- Directive on Privacy and Electronic Communications, Council Directive 2002/58/EC, 2002 O.J. (L 201) 37.
- EU Directive 2001/29/EC on the Harmonisation of Certain Aspects of Copyright and Related Rights in the Information Society, 2001 O.J. (L 167) 10.

CASES

Supreme Court
- *Alabama Great Southern Railroad Company v. Carroll*, 97 Ala. 126, 11 So. 803 (1892).
- *Ashcroft v. American Civil Liberties Union*, 124 S. Ct. 2783 (2004).

- *Ashcroft v. Free Speech Coalition*, 535 U.S. 234 (2002).
- *Brandenburg v. Ohio*, 395 U.S. 444 (1969).
- *Brockett v. Spokane Arcades Inc.*, 472 U.S. 491 (1985).
- *Campbell v. Acuff-Rose Music, Inc.*, 510 U.S. 569 (1994).
- *Diamond v. Diehr*, 450 U.S. 175 (1981).
- *Eldred v. Ashcroft*, 123 S. Ct. 769 (2003).
- *Feist Publications v. Rural Telephone Service Co.*, 499 U.S. 340 (1991).
- *Festo Corp. v. Shoketsu Kinzoku Kogyo Kabushiki Co., Ltd.*, 535 U.S. 722 (2002).
- *Gottschalk v. Benson*, 409 U.S. 63 (1972).
- *Hamling v. United States*, 418 U.S. 87 (1974).
- *Harper & Row Pub. v. Nation Enterprises*, 471 U.S. 539 (1985).
- *Hilton v. Guyot*, 159 U.S. 113 (1895).
- *International Shoe v. Washington*, 326 U.S. 310 (1945).
- *Jacobellis v. Ohio*, 378 U.S. 184 (1964).
- *Miller v. California*, 413 U.S. 15 (1973).
- *Mishkin v. New York*, 383 U.S. 502 (1966).
- *New York v. Ferber*, 458 U.S. 747 (1982).
- *Osborne v. Ohio*, 495 U.S. 103 (1990).
- *Paris Adult Theatre v. Slaton*, 413 U.S. 49 (1973).
- *Pinkus v. United States*, 436 U.S. 293 (1978).
- *Pope v. Illinois*, 481 U.S. 497 (1987).
- *Quill Corp. v. North Dakota*, 504 U.S. 298 (1992).
- *Reno v. American Civil Liberties Union*, 521 U.S. 824 (1997).
- *Roth v. United States*, 354 U.S. 476 (1957).
- *Sony Corp. of America v. Universal City Studios, Inc.*, 464 U.S. 417 (1984).
- *Two Pesos, Inc. v. Taco Cabana, Inc.*, 505 U.S. 763 (1992).
- *United States v. American Library Association, Inc.*, 539 U.S. 194 (2003).
- *Whalen v. Roe*, 429 U.S. 589 (1977).
- *Wheaton v. Peters*, 33 U.S. (8 Pet.) 591 (1834).
- *White v. Dunbar*, 119 U.S. 47 (1886).

Federal Appellate Courts

- *A & M Records, Inc. v. Napster, Inc.*, 239 F.3d 1004 (9th Cir. 2001), on remand, 2001 WL 227083 (N.D. Cal. 2001), affirmed, 284 F.3d 1091 (9th Cir. 2002).
- *Abercrombie & Fitch Co. v. Hunting World, Inc.*, 537 F.2d 4 (2d Cir. 1976).

- *ALS Scan, Inc. v. RemarQ Communities, Inc.*, 239 F.3d 619 (4th Cir. 2001).
- *Amazon.com, Inc. v. Barnesandnoble.com, Inc.*, 239 F.3d 1343 (Fed. Cir. 2001).
- *American Civil Liberties Union v. Ashcroft*, 322 F.3d 240 (3d Cir. 2003).
- *American Civil Liberties Union v. Reno*, 217 F.3d 162 (3d Cir. 2000).
- *American Library Association v. United States*, 201 F.Supp.2d 401 (E.D. Pa. 2002).
- *Andrews v. TRW, Inc.*, 225 F.3d 1063 (9th Cir. 2000), reversed, 534 U.S. 19 (2001).
- *Apple Computer, Inc. v. Franklin Computer Corp.*, 714 F.2d 1240 (3d Cir. 1983).
- *Apple Computer, Inc. v. Microsoft Corp.*, 799 F.Supp. 1006 (N.D. Cal. 1992), affirmed, 35 F.3d 1435 (9th Cir. 1994).
- *AT&T Corp. v. City of Portland*, 216 F.3d 871 (9th Cir. 2000).
- *Atari v. JS & A*, 747 F.2d 1422 (Fed. Cir. 1984).
- *Atari Games Corp. v. Nintendo of America, Inc.*, 975 F.2d 832 (Fed. Cir. 1992).
- *Bernstein v. United States*, 176 F.3d 1132 (9th Cir. 1999); rehearing granted, opinion withdrawn, 192 F.3d 1308 (9th Cir. 1999).
- *Bonneville International Corp. v. Peters*, 153 F.Supp.2d 763 (E.D. Pa. 2001).
- *Brand X Internet Services v. FCC*, 345 F.3d 1120 (9th Cir. 2003).
- *Brooktree Corp. v. Advanced Micro Devices, Inc.*, 977 F.2d 1555 (Fed. Cir. 1992).
- *Computer Associates International v. Altai*, 126 F.3d 365 (2d Cir. 1997).
- *Cosmetically Sealed Industries, Inc. v. Chesebrough-Pond's USA Co.*, 125 F.3d 28 (2d Cir. 1997).
- *CPC International, Inc. v. Skippy, Inc.*, 214 F.3d 456 (4th Cir. 2000).
- *Cybersell, Inc. v. Cybersell, Inc.*, 130 F.3d 414 (9th Cir. 1997).
- *Dastar v. Twentieth Century Fox, Inc.*, 539 U.S. 23 (2003).
- *Data East USA v. Epyx*, 862 F.2d 204 (9th Cir. 1988).
- *Dowling v. United States*, 473 U.S. 207 (1985).
- *Eclipse Associates Ltd. v. Data General Corp.*, 894 F.2d 1114 (9th Cir. 1990).
- *Falcon Rice Mill, Inc. v. Community Rice Mill, Inc.*, 725 F.2d 336 (5th Cir. 1984).

- *Fonovisa, Inc. v. Cherry Auction, Inc.*, 76 F.3d 259 (9th Cir. 1996).
- *Frisch's Restaurants, Inc. v. Elby's Big Boy, Inc.*, 670 F.2d 642 (6th Cir.), cert. denied 459 U.S. 916 (1982).
- *Gershwin Publishing Corporation v. Columbia Artists Management, Inc.*, 443 F.2d 1159, 1162 (2d Cir. 1971).
- *Hendrickson v. Ebay, Inc.*, 165 F.Supp.2d 1082 (C.D. Cal. 2001).
- *Hoehling v. Universal City Studios, Inc.*, 618 F.2d 972 (2nd Cir. 1980).
- *Hotel Security Checking Co. v. Lorraine Co.*, 160 F. 467 (2nd Cir. 1908).
- *In re Aimster Copyright Litigation (Aimster II)*, 252 F.Supp.2d 634 (N.D. Ill. 2002); affirmed in part, 334 F.3d 643 (7th Cir. 2003); certiorari denied sub nom. *Deep v. Recording Industry Ass'n of America, Inc.*, 124 S. Ct. 1069 (2004).
- *In re Alappat*, 33 F.3d 1526 (Fed. Cir. 1994).
- *In re Crawford*, 194 F.3d 954 (9th Cir. 1999), cert. denied sub nom. *Ferm v. U.S. Trustee*, 528 U.S. 1189 (2000).
- *In re International Flavors & Fragrances, Inc.*, 183 F.3d 1361 (Fed. Cir. 1999).
- *In re Pharmatrak, Inc. Privacy Litigation*, 220 F.Supp.2d 4 (D. Mass. 2002); 329 F.3d 9 (1st Cir. 2003).
- *Interstellar Starship Services, Ltd. v. Epix, Inc.*, 304 F.3d 936 (9th Cir. 2002).
- *Keds Corp. v. Renee Int'l Trading Corp.*, 888 F.2d 215 (1st Cir. 1989).
- *Kellogg Co. v. Pack'em Enterprises, Inc.*, 951 F.2d 330 (Fed.Cir. 1991).
- *Kelly v. Arriba Soft Corp.*, 336 F.3d 811 (9th Cir. 2003).
- *L. Batlin & Son, Inc. v. Snyder*, 536 F.2d 486 (2nd Cir. 1976).
- *Lewis Galoob Toys v. Nintendo of America*, 964 F.2d 965 (9th Cir. 1992).
- *Lotus Development Corp. v. Borland International*, 140 F.3d 70 (1st Cir. 1998), affirmed, 516 U.S. 233 (1996).
- *MAI Systems v. Peak Computer*, 991 F.2d 511 (9th Cir. 1993).
- *Mainstream Marketing Service v. Federal Trade Commission*, 358 F.3d 1228 (10th Cir. 2004).
- *Massachusetts v. Microsoft Corp.*, 373 F.3d 1199 (D.C. Cir. 2004).
- *Mead Data Central, Inc. v. Toyota Motor Sales, Inc.*, 875 F.2d 1026 (2d Cir. 1989).
- *Name.Space, Inc. v. Network Solutions, Inc.*, 202 F.3d 573 (2nd Cir. 2000).
- *New Kids on the Block v. News America Publishing, Inc.*, 971 F.2d 302 (9th Cir. 1992).
- *Panavision International L.P. v. Toeppen*, 141 F.3d 1316 (9th Cir. 1998).
- *Piper Aircraft Corp. v. Wag-Aero, Inc.*, 741 F.2d 925 (7th Cir.1984).
- *Pippinger v. Rubin*, 129 F.3d 519 (10th Cir. 1997).
- *Playboy Enterprises Inc. v. Netscape Communications Corp.*, 354 F.3d 1020 (9th Cir. 2004).
- *Playboy Enterprises, Inc. v. Welles*, 279 F.3d 796 (9th Cir. 2002).
- *Polaroid Corp. v. Polarad Electronics Corp.*, 287 F.2d 492 (2d Cir. 1961).
- *Recording Industry Association of America v. Diamond Multimedia Systems, Inc.*, 180 F.3d 1072 (9th Cir. 1999).
- *Recording Industry Association of America, Inc. v. Verizon Internet Services*, 351 F.3d 1229 (D.C. Cir. 2003).
- *Red Baron-Franklin Park, Inc. v. Taito Corp.*, 883 F.2d 275 (4th Cir. 1989).
- *Sega Enterprises v. Accolade*, 977 F.2d 1510 (9th Cir. 1992).
- *Shields v. Zuccarini*, 254 F.3d 476 (3rd Cir. 2001).
- *Singer Manufacturing Co. v. June Manufacturing Co.*, 163 U.S. 169 (1896).
- *Sony Computer Entertainment, Inc. v. Connectix Corp.*, 203 F.3d 596 (9th Cir. 2000).
- *Sporty's Farm L.L.C. v. Sportsman's Market, Inc.*, 202 F.3d 489 (2nd Cir. 2000).
- *State Street Bank & Trust v. Signature Financial Group, Inc.*, 149 F.3d 1368 (Fed. Cir. 1999).
- *Steve Jackson Games v. United States Secret Service*, 36 F.3d 457 (5th Cir. 1994).
- *Texas Instruments Inc. v. U.S. International Trade Commission*, 988 F.2d 1165 (Fed. Cir. 1993).
- *Theofel v. Farey Jones*, 341 F.3d 978 (9th Cir. 2003); 359 F.3d 1066 (9th Cir. 2004).
- *United States v. Cohen*, 260 F.3d 68 (2d Cir. 2001).
- *United States v. Hsu*, 364 F.3d 192 (4th Cir. 2004).
- *United States v. Microsoft Corp.*, 980 F.Supp. 537 (D.D.C. 1997), reversed, 147 F.3d 935 (D.C. Cir. 1998).

www.efn.no/DVD-dom-20031222-en.html (visited July 27, 2004).

United Kingdom
- *Cheavin v. Walker*, 5 Ch. Div. 850 (1877).
- *Donaldson v. Beckett*, 2 Bro. P.C. 129, 1 Eng. Rep. 837 Burr. (4th ed.) 2408, 98 Eng. Rep. 257 (H.L. 1774).

World Trade Organization
- Report of the WTO Panel, United States: Section 110(5) of the U.S. Copyright Act, WT/DS160/R, June 15, 2000.